MEASUREMENT AND EVALUATION
in Education
and Psychology

FOURTH EDITION

MEASUREMENT AND EVALUATION in Education and Psychology

William A. Mehrens
MICHIGAN STATE UNIVERSITY

Irvin J. Lehmann
MICHIGAN STATE UNIVERSITY

Harcourt Brace College Publishers
Fort Worth   Philadelphia   San Diego
New York   Orlando   Austin   San Antonio
Toronto   Montreal   London   Sydney   Tokyo

Publisher   Ted Buchholz
Acquisition Editor   Jo-Anne Weaver
Project Editor   Hal Lockwood
Production Manager   Kenneth A. Dunaway
Design Supervisor   Vicki McAlindon Horton
Cover Design   Pat Sloan
Text Design   Rita Naughton

Printed in the United States of America

ISBN 0-03-030407-5

3 4   016   9 8 7 6 5 4 3

Dedicated to our four grandchildren

JENNIFER
ALEXI
TRENT
MAXWELL

Preface

Educators have always been concerned with measuring and evaluating the progress of their students. As the goals of education have become more complex, and with the increasing demand by all parts of our citizenry for accountability on the part of educators, these tasks of measurement and evaluation have become more difficult. There has been increased criticism of the quality of our educational product. There are students who are unable to read, students who are unable to write effectively, students who lack a knowledge of the fundamental arithmetic processes, and students who cannot engage in higher-order thinking processes. International studies indicate that U.S. students compare poorly to students in many other countries. All of these factors require us more than ever before to be concerned with valid and reliable measures of our educational products. Educational measurement and evaluation can, very broadly, be divided into two areas: the construction, evaluation, and use of (1) teacher-made classroom assessment procedures and (2) standardized tests. This text covers both broad areas. In addition, it covers auxiliary topics related to the informed use of measurement.

Measurement and Evaluation in Education and Psychology, Fourth Edition, can serve as the main text in the first course in measurement and evaluation at either the undergraduate or the graduate level. The major focus of the text remains unchanged from the third edition. This is so, in part, because the previous editions have been well received by our students and colleagues. Just as important, however, is the fact that the basic principles involved in the construction, selection, evaluation, interpretation, and use of tests have

not changed radically since the first edition was published. Nevertheless, we have thoroughly updated the text. (For example, we have added 278 references dated 1985 through 1990.) Further, this revision should not be construed as only an updating of the previous edition. Changes have been made both in the organization and in the relative emphases of topics. And there have been, as one would expect, changes made with respect to those selections that hindsight reveals to be deserving of expansion, modification, or deletion.

The basic rationale behind this text is that educational decisions are continually being made. These decisions should be based on information that is accurate. The responsibility of gathering, using, and imparting that information belongs to educators. The contents of this book are based on the authors' conviction that there are certain knowledges, skills, and understandings for which classroom teachers and school counselors and administrators should be held accountable in order to meet the responsibilities listed above. The selection of topics and the coverage given them have benefited from the advice of many colleagues. At all times, the needs of present and future educators have been kept foremost in mind.

No formal course work in either testing or statistics is necessary to understand the text. When we felt that the topic being presented could not be treated without some theoretical background, we attempted to present a simple but clear treatment of the theory. When we felt that the topic being discussed did not require theoretical treatment, we chose to omit the theory.

The book is divided into five major parts. The

unit and chapter organizations differ somewhat from the third edition. At the beginning of every chapter we present a set of objectives stated as general outcomes. Some teachers may prefer to develop more specific behavioral objectives to aid in instructional planning. They are, of course, free to do so. In Unit 1 we have an introductory chapter in which we briefly discuss the relationship between information gathering and educational decision making and present a classification of the purposes of measurement and evaluation as well as an introduction to some of the current issues in measurement. Chapter 2 covers norm- and criterion-referenced measurement.

Unit 2 is on teacher-constructed measurement procedures. Chapter 3 considers the role of objectives in educational evaluation. It covers the need for objectives and methods of determining and stating them. Chapter 4 is an overview of teacher-constructed tests. Chapter 5 is on essay test construction. Chapters 6 and 7 are on objective test construction. Chapter 8 discusses procedures for analyzing, evaluating, and revising teacher-constructed instruments. Chapter 9 covers other teacher-constructed devices, with increased attention to performance assessment. Topics covered include rating scales, observational techniques, anecdotal records, and peer appraisal. Numerous examples of both poor and good test items have been provided in this unit to help illustrate the various test-construction principles discussed.

Unit 3 covers the interpretation of test scores. Chapter 10 covers methods of describing educational data. Chapter 11 (previously Chapter 13) discusses norms, types of scores, and profiles. Chapter 12 covers reliability, and Chapter 13, validity. Some readers of this text may wish to skip (or only skim) several sections of Chapter 12. For example, the section "Reliability of Difference Scores" is more technical than the rest of the chapter, and understanding it is not necessary to comprehend the other material.

Unit 4 covers professionally constructed (standardized) measuring procedures. Chapter 14 presents an overview of standardized instruments.

Chapters 15 through 17 cover aptitude, achievement, and noncognitive measures, respectively. We have expanded our discussion of interest inventories and career assessment tools. That chapter, while thoroughly updated, is more similar in coverage to the second edition than the third edition. Chapter 18 (previously Chapter 21) covers assessing exceptionality. Some brief reviews and critiques of standardized tests and inventories are provided to familiarize potential test users with the diversity of tests available and the factors they must consider when selecting a test and using its results. At no time should it be considered that the tests reviewed are necessarily the best tests available—they are only exemplars. In addition, the reader is not expected to remember the many specifics discussed. Why, then, one might ask, should we discuss them? We mention them to give the reader some acquaintance with the different kinds of standardized tests available and how they should be evaluated. We have tried to evaluate the various tests critically, pointing out their strengths and weaknesses, so that users will have some general notion as to what questions should be asked when they select tests: how they should interpret the information presented in the test manual regarding the test's psychometric problems, and what one test has to offer, if anything, over other available tests. To derive maximum value from these brief test descriptions, we strongly urge the reader to have a specimen set of the test (including the manual) available. Finally, examples are provided to illustrate how test results can be used in making educational decisions.

Instructors stressing teacher-made tests might wish only to skim Unit 4. Instructors stressing standardized tests could skim Unit 2.

Unit 5 includes four chapters: Chapter 19 (previously in Unit 3) on factors influencing the measurement of individuals, Chapter 20 on marking and reporting, Chapter 21 on accountability and evaluation programs (local, state, and national), and Chapter 22 on some public concerns and future trends in educational evaluation.

Special thanks are due to seven external reviewers who provided us with many insightful suggestions. Finally, we appreciate the valuable assistance given in the production of this book by Jo-Anne Weaver, our Holt editor.

We also wish to thank Chery Moran and Marj Oyer for extensive secretarial services and pleasant demeanor over successive revisions.

We wish to thank George Denny for his library research and his many helpful suggestions.

Finally, we wish to thank our wives, Beth and Ruth, for their unceasing support.

W. A. M.
I. J. L.

Contents

Unit 1

EVALUATION IN EDUCATION

Chapter 1

Introduction to Measurement and Evaluation

- ■ **Need for Decision Making**
- ■ **Definitions: Test, Measurement, Evaluation, and Assessment**
- ■ **Information Gathering and Educational Decision Making**
- ■ **Purposes of Measurement and Evaluation**
- ■ **Issues in Measurement and Evaluation**

Educational and psychological testing represents one of the most important contributions of behavioral science to our society. It has provided fundamental and significant improvements over previous practices in industry, government, and education. It has provided a tool for broader and more equitable access to education and employment. . . . The proper use of well-constructed and validated tests provides a better basis for making some important decisions about individuals and programs than would otherwise be available. (AERA/APA/NCME, 1985, p. 1.)

NEED FOR DECISION MAKING

Decision making is a daily task. Many people make hundreds of decisions daily; and to make wise decisions, one needs information. The role of measurement is to provide decision makers with accurate and relevant information. Both ed-

ucators and behavioral scientists have been concerned with measurement as a necessary component in both research and practical decision making. The whole field of differential psychology is based on the fact that individuals differ, that these differences are important, and that we need to measure these differences and use this information in decision making. Employers, for example, are concerned with hiring, placing, and promoting the best people for the good of the organization and the welfare of the employees. Educators are concerned with measuring and evaluating the progress of their students, the value and relevance of the curriculum, and the effectiveness of instruction.

The most basic principle of this text is that *measurement and evaluation are essential to sound educational decision making.* We believe that educational decisions should be based on accurate, relevant information and that the responsibility of gathering and imparting that information belongs to the professional educators and psychologists.

In this chapter we will (1) define some terms, (2) discuss the role of information in educational decision making, (3) present a classification of purposes of measurement and evaluation, and (4) present a brief overview of some of the more exciting issues to be covered in this book.

After studying this chapter, you should be able to:

1. Define and differentiate the terms *test, measurement, evaluation,* and *assessment.*
2. Recognize that measurement and evaluation are essential to sound decision making.
3. Understand the components of a model of decision making.
4. Classify the purposes of measurement and evaluation.
5. Recognize the ways measurement and evaluation can assist in instructional, guidance, administrative, and research decisions.
6. Appreciate the variety of interesting issues in measurement and evaluation that will be covered in subsequent chapters.
7. Understand several of the controversial issues at a basic level.

DEFINITIONS: TEST, MEASUREMENT, EVALUATION, AND ASSESSMENT

The terms *test, measurement, evaluation,* and *assessment* are occasionally used interchangeably, but most users make distinctions among them. *Test* is usually considered the narrowest of the four terms; it connotes the presentation of a standard set of questions to be answered. As a result of a person's answers to such a series of questions, we obtain a measure of a characteristic of that person. *Measurement* often connotes a broader concept: We can measure characteristics in ways other than by giving tests. Using observations, rat-

ing scales, or any other device that allows us to obtain information in a quantitative form is measurement. Also, measurement can refer to both the score obtained and the process used.

Evaluation has been defined in a variety of ways. Stufflebeam et al. (1971, p. xxv) stated that evaluation is *"the process of delineating, obtaining, and providing useful information for judging decision alternatives."* Used in this way, it encompasses but goes beyond the meaning of the terms *test* and *measurement.* A second popular concept of evaluation interprets it as the determination of the congruence between performance and objectives. Other definitions simply categorize evaluation as professional judgment or as a process that allows one to make a judgment about the desirability or value of something. One can evaluate with either qualitative or quantitative data.

Thus, measurement is not the same as evaluation. Two students may obtain the same measure (test score), but we might evaluate those measures differently. Suppose, at the end of the fifth grade, we have two students who are both reading at the fifth-grade level. However, at the beginning of the year, one student was reading at the third-grade level, and one at the fourth-grade, fifth-month level. Our evaluations of those outcomes are not the same. One student progressed at an above-average rate, and the other at a below-average rate.

The term *assessment* is also used in a variety of ways. Much of the time the word is used broadly, like evaluation; or it is often used to indicate the use of both formal and informal data-gathering procedures and the combining of the data in a global fashion to reach an overall judgment. At times, *assessment* is used more particularly to refer to the clinical diagnosis of an individual's problems.

It is important to point out that *we never measure or evaluate people.* We measure or evaluate *characteristics or properties of people:* their scholastic potential, knowledge of algebra, honesty, perseverance, ability to teach, and so forth. This should not be confused with evaluating the worth of a person. Teachers, parents, and students do not always seem to keep this distinction clearly in mind.

INFORMATION GATHERING AND EDUCATIONAL DECISION MAKING

The direct involvement of everyone in education means that every person must at some time make *educational decisions*. Likewise, those who work for a living or hire others make employment decisions. Some decisions will affect many people (for example, federal decisions regarding funding of mammoth projects); other decisions may involve only a single person (Johnny's decision not to review his spelling list). There are many decisions that educators must make, and many more that they must assist individual pupils, parents, and the general public in making. Should Susan be placed in an advanced reading group? Should Johnny take algebra or general mathematics next year? Should the school continue using the mathematics textbook adopted this year, revert to the previous text, or try still another one? Is grammar being stressed at the expense of pronunciation in first-year German? Am I doing as well in chemistry as I should? Have I been studying the right material? Should I go to college? These are just a few of the types of questions and decisions facing educators, parents, and students. Whoever makes a decision, and whether the decision be great or small, it should be based on as much and as accurate information as possible. The more, and the more accurate, the information on which a decision is based, the better that decision is likely to be.

Professional educators and psychologists have the important responsibilities of (1) determining what information needs to be obtained, (2) obtaining accurate information, and (3) imparting that information in readily understood terms to the persons responsible for making the decisions—students, parents, teachers, college admissions officers, counselors, personnel officers, government officials, or judges. The philosophy, knowledge,

and skills that are covered in this book should assist the educator in fulfilling such responsibilities. This book, in general, deals with the development of information-gathering techniques and information that all those concerned with the teaching-learning process need if they are to make the soundest educational decisions possible. This brief introductory section is intended to focus the reader's attention on the basic notions that *educational decisions* must be made, that these decisions should be based on *information*, that this information should be *accurate*, and that the responsibility of gathering and imparting that information belongs to educators.

Some people argue that we should use test data to enhance learning rather than to make decisions. Such a reaction indicates a misunderstanding. Of course, the primary role of schools is to enhance learning. Tests should and can assist in this when test data are used to make decisions—decisions about what and how to teach, decisions about what and how to study, and so on. Test data will not enhance learning unless we use the data to guide us in subsequent actions—in other words, use the data for decision making.

Certainly, no single course in educational measurement can teach you how to obtain all the information needed to make all the decisions with which you will be confronted as educators, but it can be of considerable help. It can suggest principles and methods of deciding what information would be useful for various decisions and how this information should be gathered. If these principles and methods are applied, it is more likely that the information gathered will be accurate and useful. Teacher-constructed instruments as well as numerous existing tests and inventories can be used to gather important data, particularly with regard to the probabilities of alternative courses of action. However, there are limitations of measurement data that users should know about.

Occasionally the notions of measurement and decision making are misunderstood. Some people seem to feel that if a decision leads to a poor outcome, then that shows the data on which the decision relied should not have been used. For example, some argue that educators and employers should not use selection tests since selection decisions are imperfect. Such reasoning is faulty. In making decisions we are always taking risks since we cannot predict outcomes with complete certainty. A good decision is one that is based on all relevant available data. This increases the chances of a favorable outcome—it does not guarantee it. The major mistake in decision making is that decisions are too often based on incomplete and/or faulty data. In general there should be a variety of accurate data from diverse sources in order to make the best decision possible. Any moratorium on the use of certain types of data would almost invariably result in poorer decisions.

PURPOSES OF MEASUREMENT AND EVALUATION

Decisions are often classified as *institutional* or *individual* decisions. *Institutional decisions are ones where the choice confronting the decision maker will rarely or never recur.* In education, institutional decisions are typically those made by school personnel concerning students (for example, grouping and college admissions). *Individual decisions are typically those the individual makes about himself*[1] (for example, vocational choice). At times, institutional decision making will restrict individual decision making (for example, when a college does not admit a student who would like to attend).

Another way to classify educational decisions is as *instructional, guidance, administrative,* or *research/program evaluation.* These categories are, of course, somewhat arbitrary and overlapping. If a decision is made that programmed texts are to be used in all ninth-grade algebra classes, it might be

considered either an instructional or an administrative decision. Ordinarily, instructional decisions are thought of as decisions that affect activities occurring in a particular classroom, and administrative decisions are those that affect activities in the total school building(s). Table 1-1 shows some of the functions of various kinds of data.

Instructional Decisions

The major role of the school and of the individual classroom teacher is to facilitate certain types of student learning. The teacher should *encourage* activities that promote desirable student learning and *discourage* those that do not. Sometimes teachers feel that evaluation is the antithesis of instruction—that somehow the role of an evaluator is at odds with the role of a stimulator and promoter of learning. That is not true, even if evaluation is defined narrowly as judging. This view is certainly not true under the broader definition of evaluation. Evaluation incorrectly done may be at odds with the promotion of learning. Evaluation correctly done should enhance learning because it aids both the teacher in teaching and the student in learning. The Joint Committee of the American Association of School Administrators stated that "to teach without testing is unthinkable" (1962, p. 9). Parnell put it well:

> Measurement is the hand-maiden of instruction. Without measurement, there cannot be evaluation. Without evaluation, there cannot be feedback. Without feedback, there cannot be good knowledge of results. Without knowledge of results, there cannot be systematic improvement in learning (1973, p. 2698).

Measurement and evaluation can help both the teacher and the student. Let us look at both aspects more carefully.

Measurement and Evaluation Help the Teacher As stated above, the major role of the school is to facilitate learning. The kinds of changes we wish to obtain in pupils are commonly

---

[1]For clarity and economy, we use the masculine form of pronouns throughout this text when we refer to students and the feminine form when we refer to teachers, counselors, principals, and so on. We hope the reader will impute no sexist motives; none are intended.

TABLE 1-1 Purposes of Various Kinds of Data

				Kinds of Data			
	Aptitude Tests	Classroom Achievement Tests	Classroom Observations	Standardized Achievement Tests	Interest Inventories	Personality Inventories	Attitude Inventories
INSTRUCTIONAL							
Evaluation of learning outcomes	X*	X	X	X			
Evaluation of teaching	X	X	X	X	?	?	?
Evaluation of curriculum	X	?	X	X	?		
Learning diagnosis	X	X	X	X			
Differential assignments within class	X	X	X	X			
Grading	?	X	X	?	?	?	?
Motivation		X	X	?	X	X	X
GUIDANCE							
Occupational	X	X	X	X	X	X	X
Educational	X	X	X	X	?	?	X
Personal	?	?	X	?	X	X	X
ADMINISTRATIVE							
Selection	X	X	X	X	?		
Classification	X	X	X	X	X		
Placement	X	X	X	X	?		
Public relations (information)	X	?	?	X	?		
Curriculum planning and evaluation	X	X	X	X			
Evaluating teachers	?		X	?		?	
Providing information for outside agencies	X	?	?	X			
Grading	?	X	X	?			
RESEARCH AND PROGRAM EVALUATION	X	X	X	X	X	X	X

*An X indicates that the data can and should be used for that purpose.
A ? indicates that there is some debate about whether or not the data can serve that purpose.

7

referred to as *objectives*, or goals. The methods we employ to help pupils realize the objectives constitute *educational experiences* or instruction. The *evaluation procedures* are the means of determining the extent to which the instruction has been effective. There is a definite relationship among instruction, objectives, and evaluation. Schematically, we can represent this relationship as follows (Furst, 1958, p. 3):

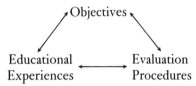

Tentative, preliminary objectives determine the instructional procedures and the methods used to evaluate both educational experiences and objectives. At the same time, evaluation and educational experiences help clarify the objectives, and the learning experiences help determine the evaluative procedure to be used. Moreover, the results of evaluation provide feedback on the effectiveness of the teaching experience and ultimately on the attainability of the objectives for each student.

There are several ways, then, in which evaluation procedures aid the teacher: (1) they help in providing knowledge concerning the students' entry behaviors; (2) they help in setting, refining, and clarifying realistic goals for each student; (3) they help in evaluating the degree to which the objectives have been achieved; and (4) they help in determining, evaluating, and refining the instructional techniques.

The importance of readiness for learning is a well-accepted principle. To teach effectively we must establish where a student is, and start there. We should have estimates of the student's capacity for learning, as well as estimates of what he currently knows. We cannot, for example, teach long division to a student who cannot subtract. To be effective teachers, we must be aware of what our students already know.

There are many ways we can obtain data about entry behavior. Aptitude tests provide general information concerning the speed and ease with which a student can be expected to learn. Achievement tests provide information as to whether a student is weak or strong in a subject-matter area. For more specific information regarding the deficiency, diagnostic instruments are needed. Knowledge obtained from parents and previous teachers also assists in determining entry behavior. These various instruments and techniques will be discussed more in later chapters. The major point we wish to make here is that effective instruction does take into account what an individual knows or does not know at the beginning of instruction. It is inefficient—and perhaps even damaging to the individual—to place him at too high or too low a step in an instructional sequence. The determination of entry skills should occur every time one is considering a new unit of instruction.

Measurement and evaluation also aid the teacher in setting, refining, and clarifying realistic goals for each student. Knowledge of the pupil's entry behaviors obviously helps in the setting of realistic goals. The very act of building a measurement-evaluation device and carefully looking at the outcomes should help in refining and clarifying these goals. Nothing is quite so helpful in forcing a teacher to think through her goals carefully as is the act of constructing or choosing measuring devices. To determine what behaviors will be observed in order to ascertain whether the derived goals have been reached requires careful consideration of those goals.

After administering an instrument following an instructional unit, one can make some judgment about how realistic the goals were and about the degree to which the instructional objectives have been achieved and the effectiveness of the instructional procedure. For example, if a third-grade teacher used the Cuisenaire method for teaching arithmetic, knowledge about the degree of student success would be necessary to evaluate the efficacy of that method. Program evaluation is a complicated topic. It relates to instructional, administrative, and research uses of measurement and evaluation. We will discuss this topic further in Chapter 21. However, we would like to point out here that teachers can use the results of evaluation to improve their classroom procedures. Such techniques as preparing an analysis of the errors on classroom tests (described in Chapter 8) and looking carefully at the results of standardized achievement tests (Chapter 16) can give good clues to the teacher regarding strengths and weaknesses in her instruction.

Measurement and Evaluation Help the Student Measurement and evaluation aid the student by (1) communicating the teacher's goals, (2) increasing motivation, (3) encouraging good study habits, and (4) providing feedback that identifies strengths and weaknesses.

The goals of instruction should be communicated to students well in advance of any evaluation. Students are much more apt to learn what we deem important if they know what it is. But if we never evaluated to find out whether our objectives were being achieved, the students might well become cynical about what our goals really were, or indeed whether we had any. Reliable and valid examinations[2] during and at the end of a course are very effective ways of convincing the students of our objectives. Occasionally, people will criticize testing because the student tries to "psych out the teacher" and learn what the teacher thinks is important. This criticism seems to assume that it is better if students do not bother trying to ascertain the teacher's objectives! Once goals are stated and understood, they become the "property" of the students, and this should serve to increase their motivation. (Of course it is possible to teach too directly toward a test. This is true because the test

covers only a sample of a broader set of objectives. It is this broader domain toward which one should ideally teach.)

Knowing that one's performance will be evaluated generally increases motivation, which facilitates learning. Some have argued that we should not have to resort to measurement techniques (such as testing) in order to motivate students. They believe that learning should be fun and that the intrinsic joy of learning is more desirable than extrinsic motivation. However, as Ebel (1972, p. 42) pointed out, "no choice need be made between extrinsic and intrinsic motivation." Learning should be fun, but this does not mean that measurement and evaluation are bad. In fact, learning is apt to be made even more fun, and intrinsic motivation (as well as extrinsic motivation) should increase, if students realize that their efforts and achievements are being recognized. Realists, though, are aware that striving toward excellence in any endeavor is not all fun. A professional baseball player does not play ball just for fun. Extrinsic factors such as money, fame, and fear of losing a job exist in real life. Without extrinsic motivation many people would not work so hard or accomplish so much. The same is true of students. This may not be an ideal picture of the world, but it is a realistic one.

One aspect of good study habits is frequent review. Frequent evaluation encourages this practice. Another important aspect of learning is that the student must be aware of his strengths and weaknesses. Evaluation and subsequent feedback can play a major role in guiding the student's future efforts. In recent years there has been an increasing awareness of the importance of giving students information as well as teaching students self-evaluation. Of course, there are always a few educators who argue that we should not evaluate—or at least not communicate the results of the evaluation—because it might harm a pupil's self-concept. This is faulty reasoning. There is no good evidence that accurate feedback damages students' self-concepts, but there is much evidence that such feedback improves subsequent performance. Going over tests constructed by the class-

---

[2]Reliability and validity are technical terms that pertain to test quality and are covered in more detail in Chapters 12 and 13. However, the terms are used throughout this text and you need a *basic* understanding of them now. Reliability means consistency. If we measure reliably, very little of the obtained score is due to random error and we are likely to obtain a similar score on remeasurement. Validity pertains to the correctness of the inferences one makes from the scores. To make correct inferences, the test must measure the same thing we *think* it measures. In Units 1 and 2 we are primarily concerned with content validity—i.e., does the content of the test adequately represent the content of the domain to which we wish to infer.

room teacher is an excellent technique for providing both feedback and a learning experience. Even the experience of taking a test itself facilitates learning. Stroud stated:

> It is probably not extravagant to say that the contribution made to a student's store of knowledge by the taking of an examination is as great, minute for minute, as any other enterprise he engages in (1946, p. 476).

This may be particularly true if a student is using an answer sheet that provides immediate feedback as to the correctness of the answer. In summary, then, students learn while studying for the test, while taking the test, and while going over the test after it is completed.

Guidance Decisions

Students may seek guidance in their vocational planning, in their educational planning, and in their personal growth. Testing can help in this guidance (see Harmon, 1989). What courses should Sharon take in the tenth grade? Should she improve her study skills? In what should she major in college? What should she do after graduation from college? Should she try to become more assertive, more orderly, more independent, or more nurturant? Students must have accurate self-concepts in order to make sound decisions. Students depend, in part, on the school to help them form those self-concepts. Tests of aptitude and achievement, and interest and personality inventories, provide students with data about significant characteristics and help them develop realistic self-concepts. The classroom teacher can help also, particularly by providing the student with information concerning his mastery of subject matter.

Administrative Decisions

Administrative decisions include *selection, classification,* and *placement* decisions. In selection decisions one decides whether to accept or reject a person for a particular program or treatment. In classification one decides the type of program or treatment (for example, enrolling in the college of education, engineering, or liberal arts), and in placement one decides the level of treatment (for example, no-credit English, the regular program, or the honors program). Administrative decisions are also involved in areas such as curriculum planning, hiring or firing teachers, and—in some schools—career ladder or merit pay decisions.

Knowledge of various characteristics of the student body is required to answer some of the questions. What should be the ratio of algebra to general math sections in ninth grade? Does the school system need another remedial reading teacher? Should the school district offer more college prep courses, or should it emphasize vocational education? Should the work-study program be expanded? Other decisions depend on knowledge concerning individual students. Should Billy be admitted to kindergarten this year, or should he wait until he is one year older? Will Susan profit from a remedial reading program? Whatever the question, the administrator often depends on the teacher to obtain the necessary data, and at times to make the actual decision.

There has been a trend to move away from the use of measurement for educational selection decisions and toward measurement for aid in the instructional decisions mentioned earlier (Bloom et al., 1981). This development reflects a general disenchantment with the notion that educators should be engaged in any selection processes. However, decisions such as who makes the traveling squad in an athletic, a music, or a dramatic activity and who represents the school in a state math contest or science fair, are more reasonably referred to as selection rather than classification or placement decisions. There will continue to be activities in educational institutions that by their very nature must restrict the number of students who participate. Although we agree with those who say that the most important role of measurement in education is to aid in decision making designed to improve the development of all individuals, we also think that selection decisions are necessary in education and that measurement should play an important role in making these decisions.

Research (and Program Evaluation) Decisions

Research and program evaluation decisions cut across the three preceding types of decisions. Instructional, guidance, and administrative decisions may all be based on research. In fact, under a broad definition of research, one could say research decisions are being made whenever information is gathered as a prelude to the decision making. Often research is not directed toward the making of one specific decision, but is intended instead to enlighten a whole range of possible future decisions.

ISSUES IN MEASUREMENT AND EVALUATION

Thus far in this chapter we have stressed the point that measurement and evaluation aid in decision making. While we hope this simple statement is unarguable we do not mean to imply, nor would we want you to infer, that the field of measurement and the materials covered in this text are dull and noncontroversial. There are many exciting and controversial issues to be discussed, of an intellectual, philosophical, political, social, legal, and psychometric nature. We believe (as do Stetz & Beck, 1981) that a thoughtful and balanced presentation of the issues is called for. We hope our discussion of these issues can be both objective and interesting. Some of the issues we will be discussing in this text are very general, others quite specific.

Probably the most important issues in educational measurement are not debatable. Those are as follows: (1) The assessment, grading, and evaluation of students is one of the teacher's six core job functions (Rosenfeld, Thornton, & Sturnik, 1986). (2) Teachers can spend a major portion of their instructional time on assessment-related activities (Stiggins & Conklin, 1988). (3) Teachers are not well trained to do these activities (Schafer & Lissitz, 1987—as well as many other references). Thus, (4) we need to train teachers better so that they can choose, develop, administer, and interpret measures (both formal and informal) of important educational outcomes. This whole textbook is written in an attempt to do just that!

More specific—and more debatable issues—are also addressed in the text. A partial listing of them follows: several include a brief discussion in order for you to get the "flavor" of these issues.

1. The General Value of Standardized Tests

While some consider standardized tests to be extremely useful (see the quote at the beginning of the chapter) others are very opposed to such tests. Consider the following quote:

> I feel emotionally toward the testing industry as I would toward any other merchant of death. I feel that way because of what they do to the kids. I'm not saying they murder every child—only 20 percent of them. Testing has distorted their ambitions, distorted their careers (Zacharias, quoted in Kohn, 1975, p. 14).

The January-February 1980 *NEA Reports* featured an article entitled "Teachers and Citizens Protest the Testing Ripoff," suggesting that both teachers and citizens are opposed to standardized tests. But that is misleading. A survey by Stetz and Beck (1981), for example, indicated that only 16 percent of teachers agreed with the National Education Association's proposed moratorium on standardized testing. In general, national polls suggest that parents overwhelmingly feel that such tests are useful (see Lerner, 1981).

We are not suggesting that the issue of the value of standardized tests can be settled by popular vote. We are only demonstrating that the issue does exist. Throughout this book, especially in Unit 4, we will be discussing the uses and misuses of standardized tests. We hope you will conclude, as we do, that proper education can minimize the misuse and that the positive functions of such tests outweigh the negative results that may follow from their misuse.

2. Testing for Accountability

Historically tests have been used as aids in the educational process. In recent years there has been an increased emphasis on holding educators accountable for student results and using state-built and/or standardized test scores as evidence of school or teacher quality. The public and legislators believe that holding teachers responsible for the achievement will result in better education. As of 1987, thirty-two states tested elementary children on a statewide basis (Cannell, 1987). The wisdom of using test scores for accountability purposes is much debated, and we will discuss this further in Chapter 21. One implication of using tests for accountability purposes is that

> raising test scores may now be the number-one un-acknowledged goal of schools in this country (Pipho, 1988, p. 278).

A specific accountability use is to base teachers' salaries (or career-ladder level) in part on student test scores. Most measurement professionals would not support this practice. It will be discussed further in Chapter 22.

3. Minimum Competency Tests for Students

A large number of states, and local districts within states, are mandating what are generally called minimum competency tests. These are tests that students must pass in order to obtain high school diplomas, competency certificates, or promotions from grade to grade. In general, the public has backed this expansion of the use of tests. For example, in a 1988 Gallup survey 73 percent of the respondents believed all high school students should pass an exam in order to receive a high school diploma (Gallup & Elam, 1988). However, there are a myriad of social, legal, philosophical, educational, and measurement issues connected to minimum competency testing that we will discuss in the last chapter. At that point, you should have the background to better understand the issues.

4. The Merits of Measurement-Driven Instruction

Tests that are used either to hold teachers accountable or that are required for high school graduation are considered "high-stakes" tests be-

cause the decision being made—at least in part—from the test score is a high-stakes decision—that is, one with important consequences. These high-stakes tests influence the nature of instructional programs. The term *measurement-driven instruction (MDI)* is used when this occurs. There is debate about whether MDI is good or bad. Popham has emphasized that "MDI can be a potent force for educational improvement" (1987, p. 680). The tests can serve as a powerful curricular magnet directing instructional efforts to important objectives. However, others worry about the effects of MDI. Bracey (1987), for example, argued that MDI lends to fragmentation and narrowing of the curriculum, discourages teaching for transfer, and leads to trivialization.

Airasian, in a thoughtful analysis of MDI, suggested that

> the nature of the content measured and the standards established for satisfactory test performance interrelate with the test stakes to determine the instructional response to an MDI program (1988, p. 10).

If the content is basic and the standards are quite low (so mastery is easily attained), the testing program will not likely have much of an impact on instructional practice. However, high standards for high-stakes tests will result in MDI.

5. Teaching (to) the Test

Measurement-driven instruction results in teaching toward the test—which, as already suggested, may be helpful or harmful. If the instruction is toward the objectives being tested—not the test items—*and* if the objectives indeed comprise a sufficiently important domain—as opposed to being a representative sample of the domain—then teaching to the objectives is quite useful. However:

> Teachers should not teach to the specific questions on a test, or indeed to the specific objectives if the test samples objectives from a broader set ... of course, teachers should never limit their instructional programs to the general content of the test (Mehrens, 1984a, p. 13).

Teaching too directly to the specific objectives or items on the test means one cannot make an inference to the broader domain that was sampled by the test. What activities constitute legitimate instruction and what activities are inappropriate teaching to the test will be discussed further in Chapter 19.

6. The Lake Wobegon Effect

Lake Wobegon was a mythical town (Garrison Keillor) where all the children were above average. According to one report, the average in every state was above the national average, 90 percent of the school districts claimed to be above average, and more than 70 percent of the students were told they are performing above the national average (Cannell, 1987). There are many possible reasons for such a finding, and they are discussed quite thoroughly by several authors in the Summer, 1988, issue of *Educational Measurement: Issues and Practice* (*EM:IP*, 1988; see also Mehrens & Kaminski, 1989). The major possible reasons are "outdated" norms and teaching too directly toward the test.

If education is improving in the United States, then it is inevitable that in 1990 (say) more than 50 percent of the students will be above the average student in (say) 1984. Historically new norms have been gathered only when a test was revised, so if a test was revised in 1984 norms gathered in that year would be used until the test was once again revised (perhaps in 1991). Currently some publishers are providing updated annual norms as well as the original normative data (see Chapter 11).

As already mentioned, if scores are used for high-stakes decisions, educators may inappropriately teach too directly toward the test (teach the test). This may well cause the scores to increase, but those scores no longer truly indicate the level of achievement (see Mehrens & Kaminski, 1989).

7. Testing Teachers

Concern with the quality of education in the United States has led to many national reports on educational reform (e.g., National Commission,

1983) and the appointment of nearly 300 task forces to study ways to improve education (Cross, 1984). One of the ways chosen to improve education was to focus on the quality of teachers (Carnegie Task Force, 1986; Holmes Group, 1986). One of the ways chosen to improve the quality of teachers was to implement testing programs for entry into and exit out of the teacher education programs and to eventually receive a license to teach. As of 1986, 46 states had mandates for some sort of teacher testing (Sandefur, 1988). Current plans are underway to implement a test as a requirement for national certification (Shulman, 1987).

Teacher testing programs are both politically based and supported by the public (see Gallup, 1984, 1986; Gallup & Elam, 1988; *Newsnotes*, 1984). However, as might be expected, the vast effort to establish teacher testing programs has not been without controversy (see Mehrens, 1987, 1989; Rebell, 1986). This issue will also be discussed further in the last chapter.

Other controversial issues discussed in this text include the following:

8. Are norm-referenced tests and criterion-referenced tests built differently? How should each be constructed and when should each be used?
9. What is the role of objectives in educational evaluation and how should the objectives be worded?
10. Do essay tests measure objectives which cannot be measured by objective tests?
11. Is performance assessment underutilized by classroom teachers?
12. Is it important and ethical to measure affect? How can it be done?
13. Are tests fair to both sexes and various ethnic groups? How should fairness be defined? What test construction procedures can make tests "fairer" without negatively impacting test validity? Is the "Golden Rule" approach psychometrically sound?
14. What is a reasonable definition of intelligence? What respective roles do genetics and

environment play in "determining" intelligence?

15. Are tests reliable enough to provide diagnostic information? Can educators wisely differentiate instructional procedures based on diagnostic information?

16. Should grades have a common meaning? If so, how can that goal become more closely approximated? Should grades be used as measures of achievement, as motivators, and/or as builders of self-concept?

17. Who should have access to test data? How can we assure appropriate privacy of data?

18. Can we fairly test children with special needs?

19. Should test data be used for selection decisions (such as college admissions and hiring decisions)?

We hope you will enjoy learning more about the issues listed (or briefly discussed) above, as well as others discussed in the text. You will not get a final, correct answer to each issue. You will receive as objective a discussion as possible from two authors who admit to one bias at the outset: In general measurement is a good thing, and educators will make better decisions using appropriate data than without it. Happy reading.

■ SUMMARY

The following statements summarize the major points of this chapter:

1. Measurement and evaluation are essential to sound educational decision making.

2. The term *test* often suggests presenting a standard set of questions to be answered.

3. The concept of measurement is broader than that of testing. We can measure characteristics in ways other than by giving tests.

4. Evaluation is the process of delineating, obtaining, and providing useful information for judging decision alternatives. Some prefer to use the term *assessment* for this process. Oth-

ers use assessment to refer to clinical diagnosis.

5. Every person must at some time make educational decisions.

6. A good decision is one that is based on relevant and accurate information. The responsibility of gathering and imparting that information belongs to the educator.

7. Educational decisions are classified as instructional, guidance, administrative, and research decisions.

8. Evaluation aids the teacher by (a) helping to provide knowledge concerning the students' entry behaviors; (b) helping to set, refine, and clarify realistic goals for each student; (c) helping to determine the degree to which objectives have been achieved; and (d) helping to determine, evaluate, and refine her instructional techniques.

9. Evaluation aids the student by (a) communicating the goals of the teacher; (b) increasing motivation; (c) encouraging good study habits; and (d) providing feedback that identifies his strengths and weaknesses.

10. Evaluation aids in the administrative decisions of selection, classification, and placement.

11. A variety of controversial issues exist in measurement. These are intellectual, philosophical, political, social, legal, educational, and psychometric in nature.

■ POINTS TO PONDER

1. What educational decisions should be made without a consideration of standardized test data? Should any educational decisions be made in the absence of data?

2. Is the decision about whether a person attends college an individual or an institutional decision? Can it be both?

3. Should public school educators be concerned with the research functions of standardized tests? Has too much class time been devoted to this function?

Chapter 2

Norm- and Criterion-Referenced Measurement

- ■ **Distinctions between Norm- and Criterion-Referenced Measurement**
- ■ **Constructing Norm- and Criterion-Referenced Achievement Tests**
- ■ **Uses for Norm-Referenced Measurement**
- ■ **Uses for Criterion-Referenced Measurement**
- ■ **Comparing the Two Measures**

One current issue in measurement concerns the distinctions between, and relative advantages and disadvantages of, norm-referenced and criterion-referenced measurement (NRM and CRM). What do those two terms mean? What are the advantages and disadvantages of each? Which is the more useful for various purposes?

Although measurement specialists disagree on the use of terms, the degree to which existing tests have appropriate properties, and how ideal our expectations should be with respect to these properties, there is little disagreement over the *ideal* properties that tests should have in order to facilitate various kinds of interpretations.

We believe a brief discussion of this topic early in the book will benefit our readers. Further elaborations of this same topic will occur at subsequent places in the book. Later you may wish to reread this chapter for further insights. After completing this chapter, you should be able to:

1. Recognize the distinctions and similarities between norm- and criterion-referenced measurement.
2. Recognize the need for both norm- and criterion-referenced measurement.
3. Determine, for a given decision, which types of data are likely to prove most useful.

DISTINCTIONS BETWEEN NORM- AND CRITERION-REFERENCED MEASUREMENT

Much confusion exists in the literature on the definitions of the concepts of NRM and CRM. Different authors mean different things when they use the term *NRM*. (For example, some authors mean standardized tests when they say norm-referenced and vice versa, although they are not synonymous terms.) Likewise, CRM gets used differently by different specialists. No wonder that educators and the public are confused. The measurement profession is confused! (Of course, no author thinks he or she is confused about the issue—only the other writers are!)

With respect to *score referencing*, the distinction is one of absolute versus relative meaning. Individuals have, at times, been inclined to interpret scores on tests as if they have absolute meaning. For example, educators often set a passing score (such as 60 percent) that is the same across different tests. Thus, if Mary scores 62 percent on a spelling test and 58 percent on a mathematics test, one would conclude that Mary did better on the spelling test than on the math test. The trouble with this inference is that it assumes absolute meaning of the scores. If one concludes she "passed" the one and "failed" the other, then two more assumptions are made: (a) that the amount needed to pass can be determined, and (b) that it is equal in both cases. All of these assumptions are open to question.

Since there are so many questionable assumptions involved in the absolute method of interpretation just described, measurement specialists developed the notion of norm-referenced (NR) interpretation—that of adding meaning to a score by comparing it to the scores of people in a reference (or norm) group. For example, Mary's score of 62 percent in spelling may place her at the 50th percentile rank in comparison to her classmates (in other words, she scores better than 50 percent of her classmates), whereas her math score of 58 percent may place her at the 80th percentile rank.

Some people have suggested the norm-referenced approach does not tell us the really important information of what and how much the students have learned. They wish to use the absolute notion of interpretation and have coined a term for it—criterion-referenced (CR) interpretation. But if one is to make this type of absolute interpretation, the test must have certain properties. Thus, there seem to be two major types of distinctions made between NRM and CRM. Some talk about the distinction between NRM and CRM in terms of the method of referencing the score. Others talk about the difference in the kinds of tests. There are many subcategories within each of these types.

It would seem that the distinction between the two types of scores should be clear enough. If we interpret a score of an individual by comparing it with those of other individuals (called a norm group), this would be norm referencing. If we interpret a person's performance by comparing it with some specified behavioral domain or criterion of proficiency, this would be criterion referencing. To polarize the distinction, we could say that the focus of a normative score is on how many of Johnny's peers perform (score) less well than he does; the focus of a criterion-referenced score is on what it is that Johnny can do. Of course, we can, and often do, interpret a single test score both ways. In norm referencing we might make a statement that "John did better than 80 percent of the students in a test on addition of whole numbers." In criterion referencing we might say that "John got 70 percent of the items correct in a test on addition of whole numbers." Usually we would add further "meaning" to this statement by stating whether or not we thought 70 percent was inadequate, minimally adequate, excellent, or whatever.

There is some debate about whether CRM carries with it any implied standard or set of standards. That is, do we reference the performance to a cutoff score (or set of cutoff scores)? It depends on what one means by "criterion" or "standard."

Glaser (1963) was one of the first to use the

term *CRM*. At one point he suggested that "criterion-referenced measures indicate the content of the behavioral repertoire, and the correspondence between what an individual does and the underlying continuum of achievement" (1963, p. 520). A bit later in the same article, however, he stated that "we need to behaviorally specify minimum levels of performance" (p. 520). In 1971, Glaser and Nitko defined a criterion-referenced test (CRT) as "one that is deliberately constructed so as to yield measurements that are directly interpretable *in terms of specified performance standards*" (Glaser & Nitko, 1971, p. 653, emphasis added). However, although often misinterpreted by subsequent CRM advocates, they apparently did not mean the standard was a cutting score. In 1980, Nitko continued to use the 1971 definition but clearly stated that one ought not to "confuse the meaning of criterion-referencing with the idea of having a *passing score or cut off score*" (Nitko, 1980, p. 50, emphasis in original).

Popham, another leading advocate of criterion-referenced measures, suggested in 1969 that "criterion" meant performance standard (Popham & Husek, 1969, p. 2). However, by 1981 he argued "that to interpret criterion as a level of examinee proficiency yields almost no dividends over traditional testing practices" (Popham, 1981, p. 28). We do not cite these quotations to suggest that the leading writers in a new field should never change their minds. The quotations, however, do indicate why there is confusion among the followers of this movement. At any rate, everyone agrees that with a criterion-referenced interpretation of the scores the focus is on "what Johnny can do," and the comparison is to a behavioral domain. Whether there should be an implied standard of proficiency or cutoff score(s) is debatable. We suspect most users think of the criterion referencing of scores in this fashion because of the close association in most people's minds between CRM and mastery or minimum competency testing.

Despite some disagreement about the proficiency aspect, measurement experts generally agree on the basic distinction between norm-referenced and criterion-referenced *score interpretation*. However, there are many disagreements about the distinctions between norm- and criterion-referenced *tests*. The definitions discussed earlier suggest that criterion-referenced tests are constructed to permit inferences from the results of test questions to the entire domain. Other definitions have varied (Ivens, 1970; Harris & Stewart, 1971; Millman, 1974).

Actually, most authors (for example, Popham, 1978, 1981; Hambleton & Eignor, 1979; Nitko, 1980) now admit that "domain-referenced" is the more accurate term. It carries no implication of a cutoff score or standard, which suits those who wish to delete this meaning from "criterion-referenced." Unfortunately (in our opinion) Popham and others have chosen to continue using the term *criterion*. Their argument for doing so is that "even though in many educators' minds there was more confusion than clarity regarding that measurement notion, it was generally conceded that in criterion-referenced measurement educators had found a new approach to assessment which, for certain purposes, offered advantages over traditional measurement strategies" (Popham, 1981, p. 30). It seems unfortunate to retain a term that educators accept in spite of (or due to) their confusion.

The existing confusion over terms and definitions is partly caused by misunderstanding content validity. (See Chapter 13 for a discussion of content validity. Basically, content validity is related to how adequately the items in a test sample the domain about which inferences are to be made.) Some proponents of CRTs have said or strongly implied that norm-referenced measurement is limited to comparing people and unable to provide any information about what an individual can do—as if the comparison was not based on any content (Samuels & Edwall, 1975; Popham, 1976). The debate often is really about the relative merits of "traditional" standardized achievement tests, which "people usually now refer to as norm-referenced tests" (Popham, 1981, p. 24) and tailor-made domain-referenced tests. Some people think that scores from traditional tests cannot be domain-referenced because the domain is not clearly defined and the items are not a random sample from the domain. Although publishers of some standardized tests do describe their content only in very general terms, others provide detailed content outlines. To be meaningful, any type of test score must be related to test content as well as to the scores of other examinees (Ebel, 1962, p. 19). Any achievement-test samples the content of some specified domain and has an implicit behavioral element. In norm-referenced measurement, in contrast to criterion-referenced measurement, "the inference is of the form—'more (or less) of trait x than the mean amount in population y'—rather than some specified amount that is meaningful in isolation" (Jackson, 1970, p. 2).

Careful reading of the content-validity section of Chapter 13 should convince you that experts in achievement-test construction have always stressed the importance of defining the specified content domain and sampling from it in some appropriate fashion. All achievement-test items, norm- or criterion-referenced, should represent a specified content domain. If they do, the test is likely to have content validity. Although all good achievement tests (those with high content validity) are objective-based, very few can truly be called domain-referenced. In constructing such tests, one defines a content domain (but generally not with *complete* specificity) and writes items measuring this domain. But if any procedure (statistical or judgmental) has been used to select items on the basis of quality, then the test user can no longer infer that a student "knows" 75 percent of the domain because he answered 75 percent of the items correctly. The inability to draw this particular inference comes from the use of nonrandom procedures in choosing items. Actually there are few situations where we need to make the pure criterion-referenced interpretation. To know that an individual can type 60 words per minute on an IBM PC using WordPerfect is a useful datum whether or not the words on the test were randomly chosen from some totally specified domain of words. To know that an individual can correctly add 80 percent of the items on paired three-digit whole numbers asked on a test is useful whether or not those items were randomly pulled from the total set of permutations possible.

Actually, the distinction many authors currently make between "norm-referenced tests" and "criterion-referenced tests" is based on the degree of precision in specifying the content domain and on the item-generating rules for sampling from that domain. Strong advocates of CRTs argue for very precise specifications of domains and item-generating rules. As they admit, most CRTs are not built with such precision and are not superior to traditional tests in content validity.

The difference between existing CRTs and NRTs is most obvious when considering the *breadth of the domain*. The typical norm-referenced achievement test is a survey instrument covering a broad domain, such as knowledge of the basic arithmetic functions of addition, subtraction, multiplication, and division, each with whole numbers, decimal fractions, and common fractions. One could think of twelve subdomains and sample from each when constructing the test. A typical criterion-referenced test would be likely to cover only one of these subdomains, or perhaps an even more specific domain (such as horizontal addition of two-digit numbers to two-digit numbers).

In our opinions, current terminology is quite misleading. We can recognize differences in *degree* as to whether or not a test represents a well-defined domain (is content valid). We can also recognize differences in degree of breadth of the domain. The terms *norm-referenced* and *criterion-referenced* should not be used to categorize tests on either of these bases. We believe the most logical distinction between NRM and CRM has to do with whether the score is compared with other individuals' scores (norm referencing) or to some specified standard or set of standards (criterion referencing). In either case we wish to infer from a test score to the domain that the test samples. Only in rare cases can we do this so precisely that we can estimate the percentage of items known for the entire domain. That would be the ideal goal with respect to content validity. What we can do is to make sure the test, whether norm- or criterion-referenced, covers an identifiable content.

CONSTRUCTING NORM- AND CRITERION-REFERENCED ACHIEVEMENT TESTS

There are times when we do wish to differentiate among individuals. At other times, however, it is not necessary, and perhaps not even advisable, to do so at all degrees of achievement. We may simply want to find out whether individuals have achieved a specific set of objectives. In other words, we reference a person's score to a criterion. Thus, there are really two different goals or objectives in achievement testing : (1) to discriminate among all individuals according to their degrees of achievement and (2) to discriminate between those who have and have not reached set standards (or to determine whether each person has achieved [at a sufficiently high level] a specific set of objectives).

Traditional test theory and techniques of test construction have been developed on the assumption that the purpose of a test is to discriminate among individuals. If the purpose of a test is to compare each individual to a standard, then it is irrelevant whether or not the individuals differ from each other. Thus, some of the criteria of a measuring instrument considered essential for a norm-referenced measure are not important for criterion-referenced measures (see Popham & Husek, 1969). What one looks for in item analysis, reliability, and some types of validity are different in a criterion-referenced measure.

For many aspects of test construction, however, such as considering the objectives, preparing test blueprints, and wording the items, there are more similarities than differences in the preparation of norm- and criterion-referenced *tests*. For example, criterion-referenced tests emphasize that items measure certain specified objectives; a norm-referenced instrument should do the same

thing. As mentioned earlier, a test intended for criterion-referenced interpretation typically samples a more limited number of objectives more thoroughly than a norm-referenced one.

Differences and similarities between the two approaches pertaining to test blueprints, item writing, item analysis, reliability, and validity will be further discussed later in the text.

USES FOR NORM-REFERENCED MEASUREMENT

Most actual testing as well as the traditional or "classical" theory of testing, have been based on a norm-referenced approach. Such an approach is useful in aptitude testing where we wish to make differential predictions. It is also often very useful to achievement testing. For many purposes the role of a measuring device is to give us as reliable a rank ordering of the pupils as possible with respect to the achievement we are measuring. Students will learn differing amounts of subject matter even under a mastery learning approach. It may happen that all students, or at least a high percentage of them, learn a significant enough portion of a teacher's objectives to be categorized as having "mastered" the essentials of the course or unit. But some of these students have learned more than others, and it seems worthwhile to employ measurement techniques that identify these pupils. In the first place, students want and deserve recognition for accomplishment that goes beyond the minimum. If we gave only a minimum-level mastery test, those students who achieve at a higher level would lose an important extrinsic reward for learning—recognition for such accomplishments.

Perhaps a more important reason for normative testing than student recognition is in its benefits for decision making. Often, for vocational or educational planning, students wish to know how they compare to others with similar plans. Norm referencing is also necessary in selection decisions. If two physicians have mastered surgery, but one has mastered it better, which one would you want to have operate on you? If two teachers have mastered the basics of teaching, but one is a much better teacher, which one do we hire? If two students have mastered first-semester algebra, but one has learned it much more thoroughly, which one should receive more encouragement to continue in mathematics? We probably all agree on the answers. If, however, we have not employed measurement techniques that allow us to differentiate between the individuals, we cannot make these types of decisions. Certainly, norm-referenced measures are the more helpful in fixed-quota selection decisions. For example, if there were a limited number of openings in a pilot training school, the school would want to select the best of the applicants—even though all may be above some "mastery level" (see Hunter & Schmidt, 1982).

Because standardized NRTs are often broader in focus than CRTs, they are more useful for providing a *broad overview* of the achievement levels in a given subject matter. They are better for monitoring the general progress of a student, classroom, or school. Although some individuals believe that general norm-referenced tests are insensitive to instruction, they do in fact show gains from grade to grade. Recall, however, that a score from any test, broad or narrow in focus, can be either norm-referenced or criterion-referenced.

Norm-referenced testing is often considered a necessary component of program evaluation. We have mentioned that CRTs are often narrower in focus than NRTs. Some view this narrow focus as advantageous in program evaluation. We can construct a CRT over the particular program objectives to see if they have been achieved. In evaluating a program, however, we would also wish to know how effective the program is in comparison to other possible programs. Without random assignment of students to programs (which is seldom possible in schools), the comparison needs to be through some norm-referenced procedure that compares the performance of the pupils in the program with a norm group. Moreover, the more

narrow focus of a CRT may not be an unmitigated blessing. At times we desire to evaluate broader outcomes (see Cronbach, 1963).

USES FOR CRITERION-REFERENCED MEASUREMENT

The support for criterion-referenced measurement originated in large part from the emphasis on behavioral objectives, the sequencing and individualization of instruction, the development of programmed materials, the learning theory that suggests that almost anybody can learn almost anything if given enough time, the increased interest in certification, and the belief that norm referencing promotes unhealthy competition and is injurious to low-scoring students' self-concepts.

The principal uses of criterion-referenced measurement have been in mastery tests within the classroom; for minimum competency tests, for example, high school graduation; and for licensure tests. A mastery test is a particular type of criterion-referenced test. Mastery, as the word is typically used, connotes an either/or situation. The person has either achieved (mastered) the objective(s) satisfactorily or has not. Criterion-referenced testing in general could also measure degrees of performance. Mastery tests are used in programs of individualized instruction, such as the Individually Prescribed Instruction (IPI) program (Lindvall & Bolvin, 1967) or the mastery learning model (Bloom, 1968). These programs are composed of units or modules, usually considered hierarchical, each based on one or more instructional objectives. Each individual is required to work on the unit until he has achieved a specified minimum level of achievement. Then he is considered to have "mastered" the unit. In such programs instructional decisions about a student are not dependent on how his performance compares to others. If he has performed adequately on the objectives, then the decision is to move on to the next unit of study. If he has not, then he is required to restudy the material (perhaps using a different procedure) covered by the test until he performs adequately, that is, "masters" the material. If instructional procedures were organized so that time is the dimension that varies and degree of mastery is held constant, then mastery tests would be used more frequently than they are now.

Mastery testing requires the tester to set a cut-off score. There should be a careful rationale and procedure for choosing that point. No very useful information can be obtained regarding degree of proficiency above or below the cutting score.

A related use of criterion-referenced testing is minimum competency testing. As mentioned in Chapter 1, we will discuss this issue in Chapter 22. Minimum competency testing is one area where cutting scores are set, and degrees of performance above the cutoff are not considered in making promotion, graduation, or certification decisions.

Licensure tests for teachers are considered criterion-referenced. The purpose of a licensure test is to ensure that the public health, safety, and welfare will be protected. Thus, licensure tests are to help determine whether individuals have *minimal* competence to practice their profession. Thus, a cutting score must be established.

Employing the individually prescribed instruction or mastery model of learning, minimum competency testing and licensure are not the only uses for criterion-referenced measures; one may also use such measures to help evaluate (make decisions about) instructional programs. In order to determine whether specific instructional treatments or procedures have been successful, it is necessary to have data about the outcomes on the specific objectives the program was designed to teach. A measure comparing students to each other (norm referencing) may not present data as effectively as a measure comparing each student's performance to the objectives.

Criterion-referenced measurements also offer certain benefits for instructional decision making within the classroom. The diagnosis of specific difficulties accompanied by a prescription of certain instructional treatments is necessary in instruction

whether or not the teacher uses a mastery approach to learning.

Because criterion-referenced tests are often narrower in scope, there may be enough items on a given objective to make inferences about an individual's general performance on that objective. This cannot typically be done on a traditional norm-referenced test because there are too few items on any specific objective.

Finally, criterion-referenced tests can be useful in broad surveys of educational accomplishments such as the National Assessment of Educational Progress or state or local assessment programs.

COMPARING THE TWO MEASURES

All measurement specialists agree that both NRM and CRM are sometimes necessary for effective decision making. When to use norm-referenced and criterion-referenced interpretations depends on the kind of decision to be made. For guidance decisions, we should employ both NR and CR interpretations. For selection decisions, an NRT is preferred. For classification decisions, one might use both. For placement and certification decisions, one might well primarily use a CRT. For instructional decisions, it depends mostly on the instructional procedures employed. If instruction is structured so that time is the variable, and a student keeps at a task until he has mastered it, then we should use mastery testing. This type of instruction is often employed in individualized instruction. If instruction is structured so that time of exposure is constant, then students will achieve at different levels, and we should attempt to detect this differential achievement with a test that discriminates, although we might well want to attach both normative and criterion-referenced meaning to the score. Which instructional procedure should be used depends on the structure and importance of the subject matter being taught.

There are some subjects so hierarchical in structure that it is futile to teach higher concepts until basic ones have been mastered. For example, students cannot do long division until they can subtract and multiply at some basic level (although precisely at what level is unknown). This is certainly not the case for all subjects, however. We do not really need to have mastered (or even have read) *A Tale of Two Cities* before reading *Catcher in the Rye,* or vice versa.

Likewise, as mentioned earlier, there may well be some skills or knowledge so important that all students should master them, regardless of how long it takes. Knowing how to spell one's name probably fits in this category. But, again, this is not true of all subjects. As Ebel stated:

> We might be willing to allow one student a week to learn what another can learn in a day. But sum these differences over the myriads of things to be learned. Does anyone, student, teacher, or society, want to see one person spend 16 or 24 years getting the same elementary education another can get in eight? Should it be those least able to learn quickly who spend the largest portion of their lives in trying to learn? Our present practice is quite the reverse. Those who are facile in learning make a career of it. Those who are not find other avenues of service, fulfillment and success (1969, p. 12).

Gronlund (1985, p. 27) made a distinction between instructional objectives that should be mastered by all students and those that provide for maximum development. For the former, one would want to employ criterion-referenced testing; for the latter, norm-referenced testing. Thus, for instructional decision making, there is a place for both mastery (criterion-referenced) and discriminative (norm-referenced) testing. Mastery testing is probably more important in the early elementary grades than later in school.

Finally, we should mention again that many tests are amenable to both norm- and criterion-referenced interpretation. Publishers of some standardized achievement tests, for example, report a norm-referenced score on each subtest and within each subtest report whether a pupil answered each item correctly, as well as the percentage of pupils in the classroom, building, dis-

trict, and national norm group who got the item correct. These item statistics are also frequently summarized over items for each objective.

■ SUMMARY

The principal ideas, conclusions, and implications of this chapter are summarized in the following statements:

1. Norm referencing is used to interpret a score of an individual by comparing it with those of other individuals.
2. Criterion referencing is used to interpret a person's performance by comparing it to some specified behavioral domain or criterion.
3. To be most meaningful, a test score should be related to both norms and criteria.
4. An achievement test should have content validity whether norm or criterion referencing is employed.
5. A pure criterion-referenced test (more accurately called a domain-referenced test) is one consisting of a sample of questions drawn from a domain in such a fashion that one may estimate the proportion of questions from the total domain a student knows, based on the proportion correct in the test. Few tests fit this narrow definition.
6. Typically, the objectives sampled in a criterion-referenced test are more narrow in focus but sampled more thoroughly than the objectives sampled in a norm-referenced test.
7. Presently, the principal uses of criterion-referenced measurement is in mastery, minimum competency, and licensure testing.
8. In mastery testing, one is concerned with making an either/or decision. The person has either achieved (mastered) the objective satisfactorily or has not.
9. Mastery tests are probably most useful for subjects at the early elementary school level.
10. There are limitations to both norm-referenced tests and criterion-referenced tests.

11. If students differ from each other in achievement levels, this normative information can often assist in decision making.
12. Norm-referenced testing is often considered a substantial component of program evaluations.
13. Whether one uses norm- or criterion-referenced measurement depends upon the kind of decision one wishes to make.
14. Norm-referenced measurement is necessary to make differential predictions.

■ POINTS TO PONDER

1. If you were going to implement a mastery-learning–mastery-testing approach to eleventh-grade English literature, how would you (a) determine the domain, (b) build a test such that the domain was sampled, and (c) determine what percentage of the domain indicated mastery?
2. Most criterion-referenced tests sample from a narrow domain whereas many norm-referenced tests sample from a broad domain. Why do you suppose this distinction exists?
3. Some people have made statements as follows: "I do not believe in norm-referenced grading because I do not believe we should fail anyone." What is wrong with the logic of that sentence?
4. In making a judgment about whether a 14-month-old child "walks adequately," would you want norm-referenced or criterion-referenced data?

Unit 2

TEACHER-MADE EVALUATION TOOLS

Chapter 3

The Role of Objectives in Educational Evaluation

- ■ **Definition of Terms**
- ■ **Why Have Goals or Objectives?**
- ■ **Approaches to Determining (Selecting) Objectives**
- ■ **Approaches to Stating (Communicating) Goals**
- ■ **Making Objectives Amenable to Measurement and Evaluation**
- ■ **Objectives for Criterion Referenced Tests**
- ■ **Unanticipated and/or Unmeasurable Outcomes**
- ■ **An Example of Stating Objectives for Instruction and Evaluation**

"Would you tell me, please, which way I ought to go from here?"

"That depends a good deal on where you want to get to," said the Cat.

"I don't much care where—" said Alice.

"Then it doesn't matter which way you go," said the Cat.

"—so long as I get somewhere," Alice added as an explanation.

"Oh, you're sure to do that," said the Cat, "if you only walk long enough" (Carroll, 1916, p. 60).

Teaching consists of five steps: (a) defining goals or instructional objectives, or outcomes, (b) choosing content, (c) selecting the appropriate instructional strategy(ies), (d) teaching, and (e) measuring the results. In this chapter, we are concerned with the first of these—instructional objectives.

The role of objectives in education has been a controversial topic. Some of you may wonder why you just can't go to the next chapter and learn how to write test items. Writing instructional objectives is not an easy task and is time-consuming. But we strongly believe that the time spent in writing good instructional objectives (what we mean by "good" will be discussed later in the chapter) will reap bountiful rewards in making you a more effective teacher and a better test-maker. In this chapter we define some terms, discuss the importance of objectives, cover approaches to determining and communicating educational objectives, explain how objectives can be made amenable to evaluation, discuss objectives for criterion-referenced tests, cover the topic of unanticipated and/or unmeasurable outcomes, and present an example of how to state objectives for instruction and evaluation.

After studying this chapter, you should be able[1] to:

1. Understand the basic terms used in discussing objectives.
2. Recognize several purposes of objectives.
3. Recognize some factors that must be considered in determining objectives.
4. Know some sources of information about objectives.
5. Appreciate the necessity for communicating objectives to different groups of people.
6. Comprehend that objectives are stated differently, depending on the purpose of the communication.
7. Recognize the advantages and disadvantages of different ways of stating objectives.
8. Judge whether an objective has been written in behavioral terms.
9. Appreciate the value (and potential dangers) of making objectives behavioral.
10. Effectively determine, communicate, and evaluate objectives in your own areas of teaching.

---

[1]We recognize that the objectives stated here and at the beginning of each chapter are *not* behavioral. They are similar in format to Gronlund and Linn's (1990) general "instructional objectives." Behavioral objectives are *essential* in evaluation and may well be useful in planning instructional strategies. It may not *always* be best to *communicate* specific behavioral objectives to the student. You will understand why as you read this chapter.

DEFINITION OF TERMS

Part of the controversy concerning objectives is due to semantic problems. Terms such as *needs, goals, behavioral goals, aims, outcomes, objectives, instructional objectives,* and *behavioral* or *performance objectives* have been used almost synonymously by some writers but with sharply different meanings by others. We do not wish to suggest that each of these terms must be defined by everyone in the same fashion—but it would be beneficial to the readers trying to formulate their own opinions as to, say, the importance of behavioral objectives if they could be certain as to how writers were using the term. When and if objectives are either poorly defined, or not defined, we won't know what we should be measuring, and unless we can measure, it will be very difficult, if not impossible, to tell whether or not, and to what degree, our objectives have been realized by the students. The definitions we are using are stated below:

Outcome:	What occurs as a result of an educational experience.
Goal:	A general aim or purpose. A broad outcome.
Objective:	(Also called *Instructional Objective*) A stated desirable outcome of education. More specific than a goal but may be broad enough to contain several outcomes.
Need:	The discrepancy between an objective and the present level of performance.
Behavioral (or Performance) objective:[2]	A statement that specifies what observable performance the learner should be engaged in when we evaluate achievement

---

[2]The phrase "behavioral objectives" should not be confused with behaviorist psychology. Cognitive psychologists also infer learning from behavior or performance. The potential confusion has resulted in increased use of the term *performance* in lieu of behavior.

of the objective. Behavioral objectives require action verbs
such as discuss, write, and read.
Verbs such as understand or appreciate are *not* considered behavioral because one cannot observe a person "understanding"
or "appreciating."

WHY HAVE GOALS OR OBJECTIVES?

A fanatic has been defined as one who, having lost
sight of his goals, redoubles his efforts. The occasionally heard statement that there are too many
fanatics in education is not without some truth. It
is absolutely necessary to establish goals in education, for without them we would have no way
of knowing in which direction to head.

Educational goals are many and varied. They
are not easy to specify or agree upon. Indeed, educators have long been faced with choosing between competing, if not conflicting, goals. Not all
worthwhile goals will be attained, nor should they
all be striven for with equal fervor.

Priorities must be established. What and how
much should students learn? Should schools strive
for excellence or equality, diversity or conform-
ity? Should schools be more concerned with
teaching the three R's, developing character, or
instilling good self-concepts? Ordering, or attach-
ing values to goals or objectives, precedes many
other educational decisions, such as which instructional strategies should be employed.

Traditionally, educational measurement has
been more helpful in determining the degree to
which certain outcomes have been achieved than
in determining the goals of education and in setting priorities. But, as we pointed out in Chapter
1, there is a circular relationship among objectives, instruction, and evaluation, and thus measurement has played some part in the determination of objectives. The importance of stating
educational objectives and determining their priorities has been stressed by those responsible for
measurement, and this emphasis has provided the
impetus for others to consider objectives.

Why state objectives? As we have already suggested, objectives give direction to education:
They tell us which way to head, a decision necessary before taking the first step on an educational journey. Specifically, objectives help a
teacher plan instruction, guide student learning,
and provide criteria for evaluating student outcomes. Furthermore, once stated, they provide a
public record of intent and therefore facilitate
open discussion of their appropriateness and adequacy.

Not only do objectives aid in suggesting a particular instructional strategy(ies), and in evaluation, but evaluation assists in examining objectives
and the teaching strategy(ies) as well. Measurement specialists have pointed out that the measurement of what education *has* achieved may be
useful for determining what education *should*
achieve (Dyer, 1967). Thus, the specification and
measurement of objectives are cyclical. One needs
to set tentative objectives, employ a strategy to
reach those objectives, measure the degree of attainment, and then reevaluate both objectives and
strategy.

In addition to stressing the importance of objectives and the cyclical nature of objective specification and evaluation, educational psychologists
have suggested certain approaches to choosing objectives and methods of wording them.

APPROACHES TO DETERMINING (SELECTING) OBJECTIVES

Two considerations in setting objectives are the
relevance and *feasibility* of the goals. We will also
discuss assigning priorities to goals and some
sources of information about them, giving particular attention to various existing taxonomies. Finally, in this section we will discuss two types of
objectives (minimum and developmental) and provide a checklist for consideration in selecting or
developing objectives.

Relevance of Goals

Goal relevance is dependent upon both the needs of society and the needs of the learner (Tyler, 1950). In the satirical story of *The Saber-Tooth Curriculum* (Peddiwell, 1939), a society was described in which the major tasks necessary for survival were catching fish to eat, clubbing horses, and scaring away the saber-tooth tigers. The school in this society set up a curriculum ideal for the society's needs, that is, teaching a course in each of those three areas. But the environment changed; the stream dried up, and the horses and tigers went away. The new society was faced with different tasks necessary for survival, but strangely enough the school curriculum did not change!

Teachers, school districts, and the entire "educational establishment" must continually reexamine the goals of education in view of society's needs. What kinds of marketable skills do present-day students need to be taught? Should education be job-oriented or more general in nature? Do we need to teach individuals what to do with their leisure time? Should we be stressing achievement or affiliation? Questions such as these can be answered on both philosophical and empirical bases (Flanagan & Russ-Eft, 1975).

The psychological needs of the learner must also be considered when specifying relevant goals. The need to achieve, for example, is related to the probability of success. Students' aspirations vary, depending upon how they perceive their chances of success and whether they were successful on a previous task. (A series of successes or failures will have a cumulative effect on level of aspiration.) Needs such as affiliation, self-worth, and nurturance may help determine the goals of education.

Realism of Goals

As Dyer (1967, p. 20) suggested, knowledge of present outcomes should help in setting realistic objectives. Realism can relate to either the age of the children or to the time available for teaching. For instance, the objective, "Will sit quietly for ten minutes," is *unrealistic* for five-year-old kindergarten children. Setting unrealistic goals is a sure way to discourage *both* students and teachers. The psychological and developmental nature of individuals delimits to a large extent what teachers should and should not expect.

Other delimiting factors in goal attainment include the facilities of the school. Given a set of teachers with certain qualifications, a certain number of hours available to devote to a given objective, certain constraints due to lack of equipment, and so forth, certain goals may be quite unrealistic. In short, we should strive for goals that are in harmony with what educational psychologists know about how children develop, how they learn, and how they differ from one another, as well as the availability of resources necessary to reach those goals successfully.

Priorities of Goals

The term *needs assessment* is popular among those who advocate the systems approach to education. It is based on the notion that the relevance of education must be empirically determined and should identify the discrepancy between "what is" and "what should be" (Kaufman, 1971). Klein (1971) suggested that needs assessments should include four basic activities:

1. Listing the full range of possible goals (or objectives) that might be involved in the needs assessment;
2. Determining the relative importance of the goals (or objectives);
3. Assessing the degree to which the important goals (or objectives) are being achieved by the program (i.e., identifying discrepancies between desired and actual performance);
4. Determining which of the discrepancies between present and desired performance are the ones most important to correct.

In preparing sets of goals we should, of course, consult with teachers, students, parents, and the general public. If such groups are included from the very beginning, however, the process of building goals can be very frustrating. Klein (1971) suggested that it is most efficient to first have a team of experts construct a *full set* of objectives that might be included in a needs assessment. These experts should not, at this stage, be concerned with what should be accomplished but rather with what might be. After a full set of potential objectives is drawn up, this total list could be presented to teachers, students, parents, and others for the process of selecting and ordering a subset of the objectives most relevant for that particular school district.

Sources of Information About Goals

Although establishing objectives for a school, a class, or even a single student is certainly not an easy task, one does not have to start from scratch. Many published statements of educational goals can serve as guidelines. Some of these, such as *The Seven Cardinal Principles of Secondary Education* (Commission, 1918) and a classical eight-year study (Aikin, 1942), while helpful in spelling out why schools exist in a very general or philosophical sense, are somewhat too vague to be of much help for the specific purpose of guiding instruction. For example, one of the general objectives of the former is "to offer civic education." The principle of "good citizenship" does not really present an adequate guideline for classroom instructional practices.

A source of objectives that presents more detailed statements is the National Assessment of Educational Progress (NAEP), which in 1969 began testing students at ages 9, 13, and 17 (in 1983–1984, the project began sampling students in grades 4, 8, and 12 as well as by age). Originally, NAEP published separate booklets of objectives for ten subject-matter areas[3]: art, occupational de-

velopment, citizenship, literature, mathematics, music, reading, science, social studies, and writing. The objectives in each of these areas had to meet three criteria: They had to be ones that (a) the schools were currently seeking to attain, (b) scholars in the field considered authentic to their discipline, and (c) thoughtful lay persons considered important. Initially, this third criterion was the unique aspect of the National Assessment approach. Today, however, with state competency-testing programs, more of these published lists of objectives meet the first two criteria and are being scrutinized by members of the public before publication.

Two other major sources for specific objectives include the Instructional Objectives Exchange and the Westinghouse collection. At the time of this writing, the Instructional Objectives Exchange had thousands of instructional objectives and test items. There are different collections of behavioral objectives covering a range of subject matter. Most objectives are accompanied by six test items, which may be used to assess whether the objective has been achieved.[4] The Westinghouse collection contains more than 4,000 behavioral objectives covering language arts, social sciences, mathematics, and sciences for grades 1–12. In addition, Westinghouse has published four volumes containing over 5,000 learning objectives for individualized instruction in the same four areas for basic college and precollege courses (Westinghouse Learning Press, 1975a, 1975b, 1975c, 1975d).

Some other sources of instructional objectives are state curriculum guidelines (which often include objectives), the Greater Phoenix Curriculum Council, the University of Massachusetts Objectives and Items Co-Op, and the Northwest Regional Educational Laboratory Clearinghouse for Applied Performance Testing (CAPT). (We believe that the CAPT is the *most* comprehensive source for performance testing.) In addition, the special reports issued by various professional or-

---

[3]Today, only instructional booklets in math, reading, science, and writing are published regularly every five years. Objectives booklets in other areas such as basic life science, computer competency, career and occupational development are published infrequently since these areas are not on a regular assessment schedule.

---

[4]A current description of available objectives can be obtained from the Instructional Objectives Exchange, Box 24095, Los Angeles, Calif. 90025.

ganizations, such as the National Council of Teachers of Mathematics, the National Science Teachers Association, and the National Council of Teachers of English, are good sources. Still another source is selected yearbooks of the National Society for the Study of Education. Obviously, a variety of sources are available for lists of instructional objectives. There are, however, some problems in using these lists.

One of the limitations of many national sources of objectives is that they do not provide for local options. Obviously, there are objectives not listed in these sources toward which school districts, classrooms, and individual pupils should strive. We wish to stress that this limitation is not an argument for ignoring the aforementioned publications. But local educators should not accept them as definitive guides; educators still have the obligation of stating, teaching toward, and evaluating objectives that may be unique to their communities. Another limitation is the variability in how the objectives are stated, whether as very specific or very general. Some will be stated in terms of what pupils are to do, while others are stated in terms of teacher activities. Some are stated in behavioral terms, while others are written in nonbehavioral terms. This suggests that teachers may first wish to develop their own preliminary lists of instructional objectives and only use outside sources for support.

Major textbooks can be quite useful in determining objectives for specific courses. It is possible, however, to be too dependent upon a textbook when developing objectives. Such a source is often an inadequate guide for developing affective objectives (those related to the development of attitudes and appreciations). Other specific aids would be publications of the local curriculum and previously developed course syllabi, classroom experiences and observations, and previously used tests.

Although the teacher has access to a variety of sources for help in identifying appropriate objectives, the ultimate responsibility for selecting and implementing these objectives rests with the teacher.

Taxonomies of Educational Objectives

Educational psychologists have assisted in specifying (as well as communicating and evaluating) goals by constructing taxonomies of educational objectives. These taxonomies classified the goals of education and are useful as a means both of communicating goals and of understanding some relationships among them. Original plans for one classification system called for the development of taxonomies in three domains—cognitive, affective, and psychomotor. *The Cognitive Domain, Handbook I*, was published in 1956 (Bloom, 1956) and *Handbook II, The Affective Domain*, in 1964 (Krathwohl et al., 1964). Simpson (1966), Kibler et al. (1970), and Harrow (1972) among others, have published taxonomies in the psychomotor domain. Derr (1973) published a taxonomy of social purposes of public schools. He felt that such a taxonomy would serve the purpose of identifying various options and pointing out their possible advantages and disadvantages, in order to facilitate efforts in judging the social role of the schools.

The *cognitive domain* "includes those objectives which deal with the recall or recognition of knowledge and the development of intellectual abilities and skills" (Bloom, 1956, p. 7). The cognitive taxonomy contains six major classes of objectives arranged in hierarchical order on the basis of the complexity of the task (knowledge, comprehension, application, analysis, synthesis, and evaluation). *Knowledge* (the simplest) is defined as the remembering of previously learned material. *Comprehension* is defined as the ability to understand the meaning of material. *Application* is defined as the ability to use learned material in new situations. *Analysis* refers to the ability to break material down into specific parts so that the overall organizational structure may be comprehended. *Synthesis* is the ability to put parts together to form a whole. *Evaluation* (the most complex) refers to the ability to judge the worth of material for a given purpose. Each of these six classes is subdivided further (see Table 3-1).

The *affective domain* (developed by Krathwohl et al., 1964) describes objectives related to emo-

TABLE 3-1 Instrumentation of the Taxonomy of Educational Objectives: Cognitive Domain

Taxonomy Classification	Key Words	
	Examples of Infinitives	Examples of Direct Objects
1.00 Knowledge		
1.10 Knowledge of specifics		
1.11 Knowledge of terminology	To define, to distinguish, to acquire, to identify, to recall, to recognize	Vocabulary, terms, terminology, meaning(s), definitions, referents, elements
1.12 Knowledge of specific facts	To recall, to recognize, to acquire, to identify	Facts, factual information, (sources), (names), (dates), (events), (persons), (places), (time periods), properties, examples, phenomena
1.20 Knowledge of ways and means of dealing with specifics		
1.21 Knowledge of conventions	To recall, to identify, to recognize, to acquire	Forms(s), conventions, uses, usage, rules, ways, devices, symbols, representations, style(s), format(s)
1.22 Knowledge of trends, sequences	To recall, to recognize, to acquire, to identify	Action(s), processes, movement(s), continuity, development(s), trend(s), sequence(s), causes, relationship(s), forces, influences
1.23 Knowledge of classifications and categories	To recall, to recognize, to acquire, to identify	Area(s), type(s), feature(s), class(es), set(s), division(s), arrangement(s), classification(s), category/categories
1.24 Knowledge of criteria	To recall, to recognize, to acquire, to identify	Criteria, basics, elements
1.25 Knowledge of methodology	To recall, to recognize, to acquire, to identify	Methods, techniques, approaches, uses, procedures, treatments
1.30 Knowledge of universals and abstractions in a field		
1.31 Knowledge of principles, generalizations	To recall, to recognize, to acquire, to identify	Principle(s), generalization(s), proposition(s), fundamentals, laws, principal elements, implication(s)
1.32 Knowledge of theories and structures	To recall, to recognize, to acquire, to identify	Theories, bases, interrelations, structure(s), organization(s), formulation(s)
2.00 Comprehension		
2.10 Translation	To translate, to transform, to give in words, to illustrate, to prepare, to read, to represent, to change, to rephrase, to restate	Meaning(s), sample(s), definitions, abstractions, representations, words, phrases
2.20 Interpretation	To interpret, to reorder, to rearrange, to differentiate, to distinguish, to make, to draw, to explain, to demonstrate	Relevancies, relationships, essentials, aspects, new view(s), qualifications, conclusions, methods, theories, abstractions

(Continued)

TABLE 3-1 (*Continued*)

| Taxonomy Classification | Key Words | |
	Examples of Infinitives	Examples of Direct Objects
2.30 Extrapolation	To estimate, to infer, to conclude, to predict, to differentiate, to determine, to extend, to interpolate, to extrapolate, to fill in, to draw	Consequences, implications, conclusions, factors, ramifications, meanings, corollaries, effects, probabilities
3.00 Application	To apply, to generalize, to relate, to choose, to develop, to organize, to use, to employ, to transfer, to restructure, to classify	Principles, laws, conclusions, effects, methods, theories, abstractions, situations, generalizations, processes, phenomena, procedures
4.00 Analysis		
4.10 Analysis of elements	To distinguish, to detect, to identify, to classify, to discriminate, to recognize, to categorize, to deduce	Elements, hypothesis/hypotheses, conclusions, assumptions, statements (of fact), statements (of intent), arguments, particulars
4.20 Analysis of relationships	To analyze, to contrast, to compare, to distinguish, to deduce	Relationships, interrelations, relevance/relevancies, themes, evidence, fallacies, arguments, cause-effect(s), consistency/consistencies, parts, ideas, assumptions
4.30 Analysis of organizational principles	To analyze, to distinguish, to detect, to deduce	Form(s), pattern(s), purpose(s), point(s) of view(s), techniques, bias(es), structure(s), theme(s), arrangement(s), organization(s)
5.00 Synthesis		
5.10 Production of a unique communication	To write, to tell, to relate, to produce, to constitute, to transmit, to originate, to modify, to document	Structure(s), pattern(s), product(s), performance(s), design(s), work(s), communications, effort(s), specifics, composition(s)
5.20 Production of a plan, or proposed set of operations	To propose, to plan, to produce, to design, to modify, to specify	Plan(s), objectives, specification(s), schematic(s), operations, way(s), solution(s), means
5.30 Derivation of a set of abstract relations	To produce, to derive, to develop, to combine, to organize, to synthesize, to classify, to deduce, to develop, to formulate, to modify	Phenomena, taxonomies, concept(s), scheme(s), theories, relationships, abstractions, generalizations, hypothesis/hypotheses, perceptions, ways, discoveries
6.00 Evaluation		
6.10 Judgments in terms of internal evidence	To judge, to argue, to validate, to assess, to decide	Accuracy/accuracies, consistency/consistencies, fallacies, reliability, flaws, errors, precision, exactness
6.20 Judgments in terms of external criteria	To judge, to argue, to consider, to compare, to contrast, to standardize, to appraise	Ends, means, efficiency, economy/economies, utility, alternatives, courses of action, standards, theories, generalizations

SOURCE: Reprinted from N. Metfessel, W. B. Michael, and D. A. Kirsner, "Instrumentation of Bloom's and Krathwohl's Taxonomies for the Writing of Behavioral Objectives," *Psychology in the Schools*, 1969, 6, 227–231. With permission of the publisher.

tions, feelings, values, or attitudes and is concerned with changes in interest, attitudes, and values and the development of appreciations and adjustment. It is divided into five major classes arranged in hierarchical order on the basis of level of involvement (receiving, responding, valuing, organization, and characterization by a value). *Receiving* is the ability of the student to be attentive to particular stimuli. *Responding* refers to the student being an active participant. *Valuing,* like evaluation in the cognitive domain, concerns the worth the student attaches to some entity. *Organization* is concerned with bringing together things into a whole. *Value* refers to an individual's life style that has been built on his/her value system and that controls his/her behavior.

The *psychomotor domain* includes objectives related to muscular or motor skill, manipulation of material and objects, and neuromuscular coordination. It has been found the most difficult to categorize since all but the simplest reflex actions involve cognitive and affective components.

The psychomotor domain's taxonomy developed by Harrow (1972) is especially useful for elementary school teachers and for teachers of dance or physical education and those courses that involve considerable movement. The categories vary depending on which taxonomy is used. Harrow (1972) has the following categories: reflex movements, basic–fundamental movements, perceptual abilities, physical abilities, skilled movements, and nondiscursive communication. Simpson (1972) on the other hand has the following classification scheme: perception, set, guided response, mechanism, complex overt response, adaptation, and origination.

The taxonomies have provided a common basis or "jargon" for communicating about objectives and have been of assistance in helping educators think about goals for their students, the relationships among these goals, and how different assessment procedures need to be established to evaluate these various goals. Educators have a tendency to spend an inordinate amount of time teaching and testing for the lower-level objectives in the cognitive domain, such as knowledge, comprehen-

sion, and application. The taxonomies call attention to the higher-level cognitive and affective objectives and thereby assist teachers in reaching a better balance of objectives.

We have not discussed any of the taxonomies in so great detail as to obviate the need for a serious student to turn to them directly. To condense and incorporate in this book all the useful material in those sources would be impossible. In the last few pages we have tried to alert the reader to general sources of information useful in formulating objectives and also to several taxonomies useful in formulating and communicating objectives as well as helpful in determining instructional and diagnostic procedures. In Chapter 4 we will discuss some uses of the taxonomies in test-construction procedures.

Minimum (Mastery) versus Developmental Objectives

Generally, objectives can be divided into those that all students should master (minimum objectives) and those that provide for maximum individual development (Gronlund & Linn, 1990). In determining or selecting objectives, one must determine which should be minimum objectives to be achieved by everyone and which should be classified as maximum development objectives (those that are unlikely to be fully achieved). If one considers only minimum objectives, the teaching/learning tasks will tend to focus on fairly low-level objectives that typically are concerned with relatively simple knowledge and skill outcomes such as "adds two-digit numbers with carrying." Unfortunately, the better students will not be challenged. This is why some people worry about minimum objectives and fear that "the minimums will become maximums." We should not allow the *total* set of educational objectives to be set so low that *all* students will master them. Likewise, there is a danger of ignoring minimum-level objectives and stressing only higher-level developmental objectives. This may cause teachers to neglect those students who have not learned the minimum, prerequisite objectives.

In general, when an objective is essential to the learning of subsequent important objectives or considered an important skill to have as an adult, it should be considered a minimum objective. Examples might be knowing the alphabet, telling time, and knowing the rank order of the numerals. When objectives are not prerequisites to learning subsequent important objectives or essential in their own right, they need not be mastered by everyone. Examples would include knowledge of the "soul" struggles in Browning's plays, ability to differentiate functions, and understanding French history prior to WWI. Of course, it is probably reasonable to expect everyone who does take calculus to be able to differentiate some basic functions. But some individuals will probably learn to differentiate more complex functions than others. Thus, even within specific classes and specific units within classes, it may well be appropriate to have both minimum and developmental objectives.

While we cannot be specific in helping you decide which of your objectives should be minimal and which should be developmental, we urge you to think seriously about it. The decision will affect your teaching and therefore your testing.

A Checklist for Selecting or Developing Objectives

1. Are the objectives relevant?
2. Are the objectives feasible given student and teacher characteristics and school facilities?
3. Are all relevant objectives included?
4. Are the objectives divided into minimal and developmental levels?
5. Are the objectives stated in terms of student behavior (the product or outcome of instruction) rather than the teacher's learning or teaching activities?

APPROACHES TO STATING (COMMUNICATING) GOALS

Not all ways of wording goals aid communication. For example, in 1947 the report of the President's Commission on Higher Education contained the following paragraph:

> The first goal in education for democracy is full, rounded, and continuing development of the person. The discovery, training, and utilization of individual talents is of fundamental importance in a free society. To liberate and perfect the intrinsic powers of every citizen is the central purpose of democracy, and its furtherance of individual self-realization is its greatest glory (1947, p. 9).

As Dyer (1967) pointed out, this is an example of word magic—an ideal that many Americans would enthusiastically support without knowing what the words are saying. Educational goals—no matter how appropriate—that do not communicate clearly are relatively worthless. Many such goal statements serve more as political documents designed to placate the public rather than as guides in directing and guiding the work of the schools.

To Whom Must Educators Communicate Goals?

Many individuals and groups need to be told the goals of education in words they can understand. Consider the goals that Mr. Howe, a ninth-grade social studies teacher, has for his students. Students, other teachers, the principal, the school board, parents, and indeed the whole taxpaying public have both a need and a right to know what goals Mr. Howe has set for his students. If he cannot articulate them, we may have doubt if he even has any!

Logic and research studies (e.g., Dallis, 1970; Huck & Long, 1972; Morse & Tillman, 1972) tell us that students are more apt to learn what the teacher expects them to learn if they are told just what those things are. Other teachers should know what Mr. Howe expects the students to learn so they will not duplicate that material in their classes or skip some important complementary material; in turn, Mr. Howe needs to be aware of their objectives. If curricula are to be coordinated, it is obvious that the tenth-grade history teacher needs to know the goals of the ninth-grade and eleventh-grade social studies teachers. The principal and school board members need to know goals so that they can evaluate both the goals and the degree to which they are being reached. They also have responsibility for curriculum coordination and need to know goals for that reason. Parents, and the public in general, also have a right to know what the schools are attempting to accomplish so that they can understand and evaluate the objectives and judge how well they are being accomplished.

While it may seem ridiculous to say so, Mr. Howe also needs to communicate his goals to himself. Most teachers believe that they know what their goals are. But only if they can *articulate* them clearly will they find them useful in planning curriculum and instructional strategies.

How Should Goals Be Communicated?

There is no single best way to state goals; it depends on whom you are communicating with and the purpose of the communication. For example, goals should be stated one way for helping plan instructional strategies and another for informing taxpayers. The format for evaluation purposes differs from that used to explain the school's goals at a PTA meeting. In this book, we are *not* interested in stating instructional objectives in terms of teaching strategies. Rather, we are primarily interested in discussing how objectives should be stated for evaluation purposes. Stating objectives in a form functional for evaluation, however, is not necessarily the best procedure to follow for the purposes of communicating objectives.

In this section we will discuss some general considerations in stating objectives for communication purposes. In the next section we will discuss specifically how one states objectives so that they serve as adjuncts to the evaluation process.

Teacher- or Learner-Focused   Goals can be stated either in terms of what teachers are going to do or in terms of the outcomes they expect from their students. Most educational psychologists feel it is more fruitful to state the goals in

terms of expected student outcomes of the instruction rather than the teaching activity or process. This is in keeping with the generally accepted definition of teaching as an activity for which the goal is to induce learning or change behavior.

Eisner was one of the leading spokesmen for those who do not think *all* goals need to be stated in terms of student outcomes. He distinguished between establishing a direction and formulating an objective and said "much in school practice which is educational is a consequence of establishing directions rather than formulating objectives" (Eisner, 1969, p. 13). Eisner thus argued for two kinds of objectives. He agreed that some objectives should be stated as student outcomes. (He labeled these *instructional objectives*.) He also believed there is a place in education for what he called *expressive* objectives. These are objectives that describe educational encounters.

Eisner contended that "instructional objectives emphasize the acquisition of the known; while expressive objectives, its elaboration, modification, and, at times, the production of the utterly new" (Eisner, 1969, p. 17). He used the following as an example of appropriate expressive objectives: A teacher may want her suburban class to visit a slum, but may be either unable or unwilling to formulate specific outcomes for the multiplicity of potential learning experiences the students will undergo. Strong believers in the value of stating all objectives in terms of student outcomes might argue that the teacher should not provide the students with the experience unless she is willing to specify anticipated, desirable behavioral changes in the students.

We believe that teachers should strive to express as many goals as possible in terms of student outcomes, but that, on occasion, the wish to expose students to an experience may in and of itself constitute an objective even though specific outcomes of the exposure may not be identifiable. Thus, we are, in general, arguing *against* wording objectives like the following:

The teacher will lead a discussion on ecology.

A better wording would be:

> The students will be able to accurately describe the U.S. conditions with respect to air and water pollution.

Immediate versus Ultimate Goals   The welfare of our nation depends upon what people are able and willing to do. Everything we teach in school is intended to have a permanent effect on the learner. Granted, testing for immediate objectives is easier than testing for ultimate ones. For example, in a science course, it is much easier to measure students' knowledge of valence than it is to measure their appreciation for science. We, as educators, however, are interested in the ultimate behavior of our students. In our society, they should be—among other things—informed voters, able to handle their own finances, and capable of holding jobs.

It is certainly appropriate to communicate these ultimate goals, but a generalized statement is insufficient for several reasons. Generalizations of ultimate goals are not adaptable to the processes of meaningful evaluation. Certainly, education of the past can be evaluated in a very general sense by looking at today's society, and we will be able to evaluate today's education some time in the future. But this evaluation is far too broad—it cannot be applied to a particular teacher's instructional procedure or even to a general curriculum. Ultimate goals are not sufficient guidelines for the administrator, teacher, or student.

In communicating goals, then, we should also talk about immediate goals. When setting these *immediate* goals, we should consider how their achievement will relate to the ultimate goals, and we should communicate this relationship.

As Lindquist pointed out, "Unfortunately this ideal relationship among ultimate objectives, immediate objectives, and the content and methods of instruction has only rarely been approximated in actual practice" (1951, p. 121). The same unfortunate circumstance exists today, but educators should continue to emphasize such relationships. Although the empirical support for such relationships is admittedly difficult to build, the logical relationships should at least be clear. For example, we could probably successfully argue that some basic knowledge of our governmental structure is necessary (although not sufficient) for a person to be an informed voter. Also, some basic knowledge about arithmetic processes is necessary for a person to make purchases, to balance a checkbook and, generally, to function as a consumer in our society.

General or Specific   Educational goals and objectives can be written at very general or very specific levels. The earlier quote by the President's Commission would be an example of an extremely general goal, one so general as to be vague and therefore meaningless. Also, words like *understands* and *appreciates* may be too general and ambiguous to permit evaluation. A goal (behavioral objective) that Johnny will answer "two" when asked "What is one plus one?" is a very specific goal. That goal is certainly not vague, but the degree of meaning is limited. Certainly, it would be inefficient to *communicate* goals to anyone—student, parent, or other teacher—at that level of specificity. It would be much better to state that Johnny should be able to add all combinations of single-digit numbers, or two-digit numbers, or whatever. Popham (1981, 1984), an early advocate of using very specific objectives in the same way as Mager (1962), has recognized the *inappropriateness* of communicating *very* specific objectives.

Of course, when *evaluating* Johnny's ability to add, we will ask him to add several specific combinations. The tasks we ask Johnny to perform in a test are objectives stated in a highly specific fashion, so we are not denying that specific objectives are relevant. But we wish to generalize from observing Johnny's addition performance on a limited number of combinations to his ability to add other combinations. If we had *communicated* to Johnny *which* specific combinations we were going to test, we would be unable to infer or generalize about his ability to add other combinations.

This is not always a well-understood point by educators. The philosophy of stating goals, teaching toward them, and then assessing their attainment has confused some people. They argue as follows: "If we really want students to know certain things, we should tell them which specific things we wish them to learn, teach those things, and then test over those same things." This way of looking at the teaching-learning process and communicating objectives is accurate only if the objectives communicated are all-inclusive. Otherwise, students will concentrate on those objectives communicated and ignore those that are not. In such a situation we cannot *generalize* from the achievement of those specifics to what the students know about the subject matter as a whole.

Very specific objectives (e.g., test questions) should not be communicated in advance of assessment unless those specifics are indeed absolutely essential or when we have such a small set of goals that all specifics can be defined. Communicating specific objectives may be appropriate for almost any training program of limited duration. The goals are probably essential and few enough so that they can all be specified. However, when education—as opposed to training—is taking place, the number of specific goals that may be appropriate is too large. *All specific objectives cannot be communicated.* In courses like ninth-grade social studies or college sophomore educational psychology, one has to communicate at a more general level. Giving examples of specific goals is appropriate, but the students should be told that these objectives are only sample ones and that their learning should not be restricted to those specifics.

A further difficulty with very detailed objectives is that they may actually complicate the measurement process. Often it is the *wording* of the objective, and *not* the *intent* of the objective that dictates the form of the test items. This type of objective wording is counterproductive.

Of course, it is easy to be too general in the communication of goals. To say that a student should "understand mathematics" or "understand music" is not adequate. Many measurement specialists prepare different levels of objectives. For example, Krathwohl and Payne (1971) advocate

three levels of objectives. The first level contains very broad objectives, the second level more specific, and the third level quite specific objectives. A fourth level would be the test items themselves: very specific objectives usually *not* communicated in advance of instruction. One could communicate all the objectives at the first or second level. At times, *samples* of third-level objectives and test questions would be useful for communication purposes.

Single-Course versus Multiple-Course Objectives   Some educational objectives, such as those dealing with knowledge of subject matter (e.g., what is the valence of iron, or what is the meaning of strabismus), are unique to only a single course and any other educational experiences will have little or no effect on their realization.

On the other hand, there are some instructional objectives, such as problem-solving skills, that are shared by many teachers and many courses. Teachers must therefore be cognizant in their evaluation process of the fact that objectives may be specific to a single course or shared by two or more courses.

Behavioral (Performance) versus Nonbehavioral Objectives   Perhaps one of the more heated controversies with respect to the communication of goals is whether or not they must be stated in behavioral terms. A behavioral goal (usually called an objective) specifies what the learner will be *doing* when we evaluate whether or not he has attained the goal. (Thus, a behavioral objective would read "the student will add" instead of "the student will understand how to add.") Behavioral objectives use action verbs, whereas nonbehavioral objectives do not. There is no disagreement that when we evaluate whether students have met certain goals, we must also evaluate their behaviors. There is some disagreement, however, about whether we should, before the evaluation, specify our goals in behavioral terms or, indeed, whether all goals are required to be adaptable to evaluation processes.

Some of the controversy in this area cuts across

two other dimensions we have discussed: degree of specificity and whether the goals focus on the teacher or the learner. Behavioral objectives focus on learner outcomes; nonbehavioral objectives may focus on learner outcomes or teacher activities. Behavioral objectives in the past have tended to be more specific than nonbehavioral objectives. This last point has contributed to the controversy about behavioral objectives. Advocates of behavioral objectives originally preferred to state the objectives very precisely, even to the point of detailing what *conditions* must exist while the behavior is being performed and of specifying the *criteria* that must be met in order to conclude that the objective has been attained satisfactorily. For example, a nonbehaviorally worded objective might be the following:

1. The students will understand how to take the square root of 69.

The behavioral counterpart would be the following:

2. The students will compute the square root of 69.

Many advocates of behavioral objectives might have argued that this statement is still not specific enough. They would prefer even more detail such as,

3. The students will compute the square root of 69 without the use of tables, slide rules, or any mechanical device. They will use paper and pencil, show all work, finish within 60 seconds, and be accurate to the nearest hundredth.

Again, conditions and criteria must be specified for evaluation, but currently most educators do not feel it necessary to communicate specific behavioral objectives prior to instruction. Few would specify as much detail as is presented in the third statement for planning instruction. We should keep in mind, however, that the debate about using behavioral terms is often intertwined with the debate about how specific our communication of goals needs to be.

Advocates of behavioral objectives state that they are clearer and less ambiguous than nonbehaviorally stated objectives. Behavioral objectives are supposedly a better aid in curriculum planning, promoting student achievement, and improving evaluation (Dallis, 1970; Huck & Long, 1972). Supposedly, teachers better "understand" behaviorally stated objectives and therefore "know" more about how to teach.

It is certainly true that the following statements of objectives are ambiguous: a student will *understand* how to add, subtract, multiply, and divide; or *appreciate* classical music; or *enjoy* physical activity; or *comprehend* the workings of an internal combustion engine; or *relish* literature. What do we mean by understand, appreciate, enjoy, comprehend, or relish? It is difficult, if not impossible, to tell when a child is relishing great literature. One way we can explain what we mean by "understand" is to describe how a person who understands behaves differently from one who does not understand. If a person who "appreciates" classical music does not behave any differently from one who does not appreciate classical music, then the goal of classical music appreciation is not worth working for.

Thus, we argue that every worthwhile goal of education is, in *principle*, capable of being stated in behavioral terms. But it does not necessarily follow that behavioral statements are the best way to communicate goals to all people. We in education often do have what Waks (1969) called mentalistic aims. We actually do want students to appreciate, comprehend, understand, and think creatively. The fact that we can evaluate these goals only through the observation of behaviors does not mean that the behaviors, per se, are our goals.

As a matter of fact, if we tell our students what behaviors we are going to observe to infer "appreciation," the inference may no longer be correct. (This seems to be more of a problem if our goal is affective rather than cognitive.)

We could specify, for example, that a person who appreciates classical music, in contrast to one who does not appreciate such music, will (1) spend more time listening to classical music than,

say, to "rock" on the radio, (2) be more attentive while listening, and (3) buy more classical than "pop" records. We could make a long, but not exhaustive, list of such behaviors. These would be the behaviors from which we would infer appreciation. But if we *told* our students that our goals were the behaviors listed, they might engage in those behaviors only during the time period in which the teacher was doing the evaluation without ever appreciating classical music at all! The students would not be performing the behaviors under natural conditions.

Stating objectives in behavioral terms is necessary to *evaluate* objectives. Behavioral objectives may also be desirable in planning instructional strategies. Stating objectives in behavioral terms forces teachers to think clearly, and in some detail, about just what they are trying to accomplish. Thus, behavioral objectives serve valuable functions. But we are suggesting that there are potential problems of communication in using behavioral objectives. One of these problems is to mistake the product or behavior as an end in itself rather than as evidence that the end has been

achieved. A related problem is that one may mistake a set of stated behavioral objectives as exhaustive when, in fact, they are only a sample of the behaviors we wish the student to be able to exhibit.

By suggesting that there are problems in communicating via behavioral objectives, we are not suggesting that adequate communication can always take place without them. If your instructor tells you that you are to "understand" the concept of reliability in measurement, what does she mean? Does she want you to be able to define it, compute it, or list factors that affect reliability? If she wants you to understand correlation, does she wish you to be able to compute a correlation coefficient, interpret one, determine its statistical significance, derive the formula, or list common errors of interpretation? If the teacher means all of these by "understand," she should say so. If she means only certain ones, she should so state. Students have a right to know, in general, what types of behaviors the teacher expects them to exhibit when they are being evaluated. But if we expect a student to derive an equation, it is not likely that the derivation, per se, is our goal. Rather, we wish to infer some mental process such as understanding from that act. If we teach a particular derivation and the student memorizes it, we may end up making an incorrect inference of understanding rather than memory.

The problems that result from confusion as to whether a behavioral objective is really our main objective or only an indicant of it can usually be minimized by employing the levels approach discussed in the previous section. If we *start* with the broader goal statements and develop our behavioral objectives (usually third-level objectives) from them, it will typically be clear whether they are main intents or only indicants. Further, we wish to emphasize that it is preferable to *start* with the broader goals. Although it occasionally may help clarify goals by first attempting to list all the possible specific behaviors, it is likely to be more beneficial to work the other way around (McAshan, 1974, pp. 47–48). And thinking of behaviors first does put the cart before the horse. As important as evaluation is, it should *not determine* the goals of education.[5]

A General Approach to Goal Communication: A Summary

Ordinarily, goals or objectives should be stated in terms of learner outcomes, not teacher processes. We should communicate both immediate and ultimate goals. Goals should be specific enough that they are not vague, yet general enough to communicate efficiently. Very specific goals are almost always only samples of what we want students to have learned. When listing specific goals, we should make clear that these are samples only. Neither teachers nor students should concentrate on these specifics to the exclusion of other material. We can infer the accomplishment of goals only through observing behavior. Specifying the type of behavior we will accept as evidence that

the student has reached the goal is helpful. Sometimes the behavior itself is the goal. At other times it is only an indicant of the goal. This is an important distinction. Behavior is an indicant of the accomplishment of a mentalistic aim only when performed under natural conditions. If a teacher or student concentrates on the specific behavior as the goal, it can no longer be interpreted as an indicant that the desired goal has been attained. By listing objectives in levels and by listing only samples of third-level objectives and fourth-level test items, it should be clear when specific behaviors are our objectives and when they are only indicants.

An Anecdote

By way of summarizing the importance of communicating goals, we present the following anecdote:

At a parent-teachers conference the teacher complained to Mr. Bird about the foul language of his children. Mr. Bird decided to correct this behavior. At breakfast he asked his older son, "What will you have for breakfast?" The boy replied, "Gimme some of those damn cornflakes." Immediately Mr. Bird smashed the boy on the mouth. The boy's chair tumbled over and the boy rolled up against the wall. The father then turned to his second son and politely inquired, "What would you like for breakfast?" The boy hesitated, then said, "I don't know, but I sure as hell don't want any of those damn cornflakes!" *Moral:* If you want someone to change his behavior, tell him your goals.

MAKING OBJECTIVES AMENABLE TO MEASUREMENT AND EVALUATION

1. *Objectives should begin with an action verb.* The key to making an objective behavioral and therefore subject to measurement lies in the verb used. General objectives such as to "become cognizant of," "familiar with," "knowledgeable about," "mature," or "self-confident" are *not* be-

---

[5]There is somewhat of a heated discussion about whether testing (and hence evaluation) is (or should be) driving the curriculum or vice versa.

havioral. They do not tell us what the learner will be *doing* when *demonstrating* his achievement of the objective. For behavioral objectives, action verbs are needed. Claus (1968) suggested that one use only imperative sentences in stating educational objectives. These sentences begin with a verb and are a call to action. Claus compiled a list of 445 "permissible" verbs and placed them in various categories. Examples from the list are presented in Table 3-2. These may assist teachers who are trying to decide what student behaviors are required for one to infer understanding, cognizance, or maturity. Table 3-1 presents some examples of infinitives that relate to Bloom's taxonomic classification of cognitive objectives.

2. *Objectives should be stated in terms of observable changes in behavior.* For example, an objective written as, "Always considers the views/opinions of others" is *not* stated in behavioral terms. Why? Can't we observe this over time and see if there's a change? Yes. However, one can't "always" observe anything. Another poor objective is, "Practices good citizenship." Why is this poor? Because many of the types of behavior that exemplify realization of this behavior occur outside of school and hence the teacher can't observe them.

Although there are certain techniques of wording objectives in order to make them behavioral, the major problem in writing them is in thinking through what behaviors are reasonable indicants of their nonbehaviorally stated objectives. Writing objectives that are amenable to measurement requires considerable knowledge about the subject matter being taught and about the changes in behavior likely to result.

Certainly, it is more difficult to word objectives behaviorally in some areas than in others. Affective objectives are particularly hard to specify behaviorally. As we stated before, this is because the behaviors themselves are often not our objectives, but are the indicants of the particular affect that we are trying to instill.

Besides specifying the *performance* or behavior of the learner, it is often helpful to specify the *conditions* that will be imposed upon the learner while demonstrating ability to perform the objective. It is one thing to compute a square root on an electronic calculator and quite another to do it by hand. Computing the volume of a sphere requires different knowledge if one needs to know the formula from that needed if the formula is available.

Some advocates of behavioral objectives also suggest specifying the *criterion*, or *standard*, by which the behavior is evaluated. This is clearly necessary if by "standard" one means the criterion that will be used in evaluating, for example, the goodness of a bead in welding or the quality of a vocal solo. One cannot evaluate unless there are criteria that can be used to differentiate quality of behavior. However, if by "standard" one means setting an arbitrary cutoff determination of whether one can weld or sing, the advisability of setting a criterion becomes more debatable. Usually, there are *degrees* of performance. It is not particularly wise to think of an objective as being either met or not met. More often the degree to which the objective has been achieved is the information desired.

3. *Objectives should be stated in unambiguous terms.* The previous example, "Practices good citizenship," is *poor* because the word "good" can mean different things to different people. To one teacher, it may mean that the students are willing to serve on the student council. To another teacher, it may mean that the students vote in school elections.

4. *Objectives should be stated so that they are content-free.*

Poor: Can divide fractions in arithmetic.
Better: Can divide fractions.

By keeping objectives content-free, we are able to use them as models for different specifics. For example, in our "better" division objective, we could use it in arithmetic or science. And, in arithmetic, we could use it for decimals, fractions, whole numbers, mixed numbers, and so forth.

5. *Objectives should be unitary; that is, each statement should relate to only a single process.* For instance, the objective "understands the digestive process and is willing to accept dieting when nec-

TABLE 3-2 Index Verborum Permissorum*

"CREATIVE" BEHAVIORS

Alter	Paraphrase	Rephrase
Change	Question	Restructure
Design	Reconstruct	Synthesize
Generalize	Reorganize	Vary

GENERAL DISCRIMINATIVE BEHAVIORS

Collect	Discriminate	Match
Define	Identify	Order
Describe	Isolate	Select
Differentiate	List	Separate

LANGUAGE BEHAVIORS

Abbreviate	Outline	Spell
Alphabetize	Punctuate	Syllabicate
Capitalize	Recite	Translate
Edit	Speak	Write

MUSIC BEHAVIORS

Blow	Harmonize	Practice
Clap	Hum	Sing
Compose	Play	Strum
Finger	Plunk	Whistle

ART BEHAVIORS

Assemble	Draw	Paint
Brush	Form	Sculpt
Carve	Illustrate	Sketch
Cut	Mold	Varnish

MATHEMATICAL BEHAVIORS

Bisect	Extract	Plot
Calculate	Graph	Solve
Derive	Interpolate	Tabulate
Estimate	Measure	Verify

COMPLEX, LOGICAL, JUDGMENTAL BEHAVIORS

Analyze	Criticize	Formulate
Combine	Deduce	Generate
Conclude	Defend	Infer
Contrast	Evaluate	Plan

SOCIAL BEHAVIORS

Agree	Discuss	Participate
Aid	Forgive	Praise
Contribute	Interact	React
Cooperate	Invite	Volunteer

"STUDY" BEHAVIORS

Arrange	Diagram	Organize
Categorize	Itemize	Quote
Compile	Mark	Reproduce
Copy	Name	Underline

PHYSICAL BEHAVIORS

Arch	Hit	Ski
Bat	Hop	Skip
Climb	March	Swim
Face	Run	Swing

DRAMA BEHAVIORS

Act	Enter	Respond
Direct	Express	Show
Display	Pantomime	Start
Emit	Perform	Turn

LABORATORY SCIENCE BEHAVIORS

Apply	Dissect	Reset
Calibrate	Manipulate	Set
Convert	Operate	Transfer
Demonstrate	Report	Weight

GENERAL APPEARANCE, HEALTH, AND SAFETY BEHAVIORS

Button	Dress	Tie
Clean	Empty	Wash
Comb	Fasten	Wear
Cover	Lace	Zip

SOURCE: C. K. Claus, "Verbs and Imperative Sentences as a Basis for Stating Educational Objectives." Paper given at a meeting of the National Council on Measurement in Education, Chicago, 1968.

*In contrast, Sullivan (1969) states that most, if not all, cognitive learning outcomes in the school are encompassed by only *six* action verbs: *identify, name, describe, order, construct,* and *demonstrate.*

essary," contains two processes—a cognitive process of the recall and understanding of digestion and an affective process of the acceptance of dieting.

One more point should be mentioned. Writing behavioral objectives is a difficult task. Most educators do not do this task nearly so well as the theorists suggest (see Ammons, 1964). As a partial help for teachers who recognize the need for behavioral objectives, but who have neither the time nor desire to develop a comprehensive list of their own, the sources listed earlier (e.g., Popham, 1970; Flanagan et al., 1971; NAEP, 1969) may be helpful. Also, several small books have been written by educational psychologists to teach educators how to write objectives (see Mager, 1962; Yelon & Scott, 1970; Burns, 1972; Vargas, 1972; McAshan, 1974; Gronlund, 1978; Kibler et al., 1981).

OBJECTIVES FOR CRITERION-REFERENCED TESTS

As mentioned in Chapter 2, the advocates of criterion-referenced testing emphasize the importance of operationally defining the domain of content or behavior the test is to measure. (We hope you also recall that whenever one wishes to generalize from a sample of items to a broader domain, the domain has to be defined. This is true in either a norm-referenced or a criterion-referenced test. Criterion-referenced testing advocates stress this idea more but, on occasion, inappropriately claim it as a concern unique to their kind of test.) Historically, a domain has been defined through content outlines and statements of behavioral objectives. Often, tables of specifications or test blueprints are used to assist in communicating the domain. We will discuss these more in Chapter 4. Some proponents of criterion-referenced testing, however, argue that this type of approach is too subjective and leads to an ambiguous definition, allowing item writers too much freedom. Different writers could well develop items of quite different

levels of difficulty covering the same ill-defined domain, thus making any inference from the percentage of items answered correctly to the percentage of domain the person knows suspect. What is needed, they claim, is an unambiguous definition of a domain and a set of item-writing rules for generating the items so that different test-makers could construct equivalent sets of items.

Popham (1980, 1984) has described four different strategies the Instructional Objectives Exchange has tried since 1968. First, the staff tried *behavioral objectives*, but decided they were too terse and left too many decisions to the writers. Next, they tried *item forms*, which were very specific and detailed rules for creating test items. Popham reports, however, that they ended up with too many item forms and too few writers willing to pay attention to the details. Next they tried *amplified objectives*, more elaborate behavioral objectives that compromised between behavioral objectives and item forms. They found that these also allowed item writers too much latitude. Their current approach is to use what they call *test specifications*. Separate test specifications are written for each set of items that measure the same class of student performance. Generally, this involves a delimited and clearly defined achievement domain and a set of test specification components. These test specification components consist of: a general description, that is, a one- or two-sentence summary of what the test measures, a sample item, a set of response attributes, and, at times, a set of specification supplements (see Popham 1980, 1984, for details).

Although such detailed test specifications may be time-consuming to prepare, if carefully prepared, the specifications will indicate what student performance is being measured and the characteristics of items to be prepared. Such a procedure is invaluable in developing item pools where one wishes to have test items that are measuring the same skills, knowledge, and the like. Additionally, such detailed specifications can be of great value to the test *user* because they indicate what the test scores represent, that is, what the test measured.

Berk (1979) reviewed these and three other approaches: item transformations, algorithms, and mapping sentences. He suggested, and we would agree, that the rigor and precision of these strategies are inversely related to their practicability. While research should continue to be done on these approaches, and while some large test-builders can use them with some success, the typical educator should feel no shame for preferring to develop items from the third level of performance objectives described earlier. Since this allows for some flexibility in item writing, we cannot make any absolute statements with respect to the percentage of a domain one knows. Such is the state of our art.

UNANTICIPATED AND/OR UNMEASURABLE OUTCOMES

Most educators will admit that stating objectives is not a panacea for existing weaknesses and limitations of educational evaluation. Lists of objectives will always be incomplete. There will be unanticipated outcomes, and these too should be evaluated. Also, while in principle every objective is measurable, we must admit that in practice it is not so.[6] Eisner's example of a teacher taking her suburban children to visit a slum is a good illustration of an educational procedure with both unanticipated and unmeasurable outcomes. The same holds true of *any encounter* with students; there will always be unanticipated and unmeasurable outcomes. Educators should be alert in seeking clues to unanticipated outcomes and attempting to evaluate them. These clues may be obtained in many ways, such as by interviewing students or parents and by carefully observing classroom, lunchroom, and recess situations. There are probably not so many "unmeasurable outcomes" as many educators suppose. By employing a variety of measurement techniques, many of the outcomes considered unmeasurable can be measured. Certainly, a fair number of outcomes cannot be measured via the traditional paper-pencil achievement test, but such procedures as observations, anecdotal records, sociometric devices, and attitude inventories can be used to obtain evidence for many of these outcomes.

AN EXAMPLE OF STATING OBJECTIVES FOR INSTRUCTION AND EVALUATION

In writing instructional objectives, one begins by stating a general learning outcome. For this statement such nonaction verbs as "applies," "comprehends," "knows," and "understands" are permissible. (These may be first- and/or second-level objectives.) Examples of objectives for this chapter, stated as general learning outcomes, would be as follows:

1. Knows some sources of information about objectives;
2. Comprehends that objectives are stated differently, depending on the purpose of the communication;
3. Appreciates the value of making objectives behavioral.

Once all general outcomes are stated, the next task is to make a representative list of explicit student behaviors that can be used as evidence that the general objective has been achieved. Since making affective objectives behavioral is the most challenging, let us try to specify some behavioral objectives for the general statement 3 listed above.

a. Completes a nonrequired assignment on writing behavioral objectives;
b. Gives a report on one of the texts mentioned on behavioral objectives;
c. Enrolls in a one-hour seminar devoted solely to writing behavioral objectives;
d. Proselytizes the need for behavioral objectives with other students;

---

[6]This can be seen if learning is defined as the predisposition to respond in a certain way under certain environmental conditions. The evaluator may simply not have the environmental conditions sufficiently under control to make an evaluation of whether learning has occurred.

e. Completes favorably a confidential rating scale on the importance of behavioral objectives;
f. Asks for further information about affective behavioral objectives.

This sample of specific learning outcomes could be made much more complete. Only time, divergent thinking, an understanding of the word *appreciates*, and an awareness of the multiple ways to measure them are necessary. These behaviors, if performed under natural conditions, are ones from which we can reasonably infer positive affect. Of course, it is always possible to *fake* affect. This is one reason we advance for not considering a student's affect in a course when reporting his level of achievement. (See Chapter 20, "Marking and Reporting the Results of Measurement," for a fuller discussion of this issue.)

■ SUMMARY

The principal ideas, conclusions, and implications of this chapter are summarized in the following statements:

1. One of the important tasks of educators is to determine the goals of education.
2. Goals (objectives) help an instructor to plan instruction, guide student learning, and provide a criterion for evaluating student outcomes.
3. Two considerations in selecting goals are their relevance and their feasibility. After they are selected, their priorities must be determined.
4. Many published statements can serve as guidelines for the teacher involved in determining goals.
5. The cognitive, affective, and psychomotor taxonomies have been of assistance in helping educators determine and communicate about goals. They are also helpful in preparing assessment devices.
6. Once goals are selected, they need to be communicated to a variety of people. There is no one best way to communicate educational goals; it depends upon the intended audience and the purpose of the communication.

7. It is generally better to state goals in terms of student outcomes than in terms of teaching processes.
8. We should communicate both immediate and ultimate goals and the relationships between them.
9. Most educational goals can be more efficiently communicated in somewhat general terms. At times, however (e.g., in specific training programs within an educational setting), it is appropriate and expedient to communicate very specific objectives.
10. Some instructional objectives are the shared responsibility of several teachers (courses).
11. Where feasible, objectives should be stated so they are content-free.
12. A behavioral objective is one that specifies what the learner will be doing when we evaluate whether or not he has attained the goal. Hence, statements of behavioral objectives make use of action verbs.
13. Stating objectives in behavioral terms is necessary if we are to evaluate those objectives. Such behavioral statements are also typically helpful in planning instructional strategies.
14. One potential problem of behavioral objectives is confusion of the behavior with the objective. At times, the behavior is the objective. At other times, it is only an indicant of an objective.
15. Various new approaches to defining domains and building tests have been tried by advocates of criterion-referenced tests. These are generally difficult techniques for the classroom teacher to use.
16. Stating objectives through a levels approach has much to recommend it. First, one states general learning outcomes, often in nonbehavioral terms. Then one lists under each of those outcomes a representative sample of the specific types of behavior that indicates attainment of the objective.
17. Objectives should begin with an action verb, be stated clearly in terms of observable changes, be unitary, and represent intended outcomes of the teaching-learning process.
18. Unanticipated and/or unmeasurable out-

comes do occur as a result of education. If there are too many of these, it may well indicate that insufficient thought went into specifying the original objectives and planning the instruction and evaluation procedures.

■ POINTS TO PONDER

1. Suppose you are given the task of conducting a needs assessment in a school district. How would you proceed?

2. What proportion of a teacher's efforts should be directed toward students' achievements of minimum versus developmental objectives? Support your answer.

3. Is it reasonable to expect a relationship between all immediate objectives and ultimate goals? Why or why not?

4. Why would a teacher wish to keep striving toward some goals even if they were not measurable?

5. What instructional objectives are the shared responsibility of several teachers (courses)?

Chapter 4

Classroom Testing: The Planning Stage

■ **Why Teacher-Made Tests?**
■ **Deficiencies in Teacher-Made Tests**
■ **Classification of Teacher-Made Tests**
■ **Planning the Teacher-Made Test**
■ **Differences between the Essay and Objective Test**

- **Factors to Consider When Selecting an Item Format**
- **Additional Details in Test Planning**
- **General Considerations in Writing Test Items**
- **What Does It Take to Be a Good Item Writer?**
- **Constructing Criterion-Referenced Tests**

Despite the ever increasing use of portfolios, samples, and performance tests to assess student progress, teacher-made achievement tests are frequently the major basis for evaluating students' progress in school (Herman & Dorr-Bremme, 1984; Stiggins & Bridgeford, 1985). One would have great difficulty in conceptualizing an educational system where the child is not exposed to teacher-made tests. Although the specific purposes of the tests and the intended use of the results may vary from one school to another or from one teacher to another, it is essential that we recognize the part that test results can play in the life of the student, parent, teacher, counselor, and other educators.

Classroom evaluation instruments are *not* restricted to conventional pencil-and-paper achievement tests. Stiggins and Bridgeford (1985) reported that while elementary teachers preferred observations, secondary teachers preferred testing. This of course, is to be expected, especially for primary teachers, who seldom (if ever) use pencil-and-paper tests because some of their more important instructional objectives cannot be evaluated by a pencil-and-paper test. Rather, they must use rating scales, checklists, and other observational techniques. Rogers (1985), Stiggins and Bridgeford (1985), and Anderson (1987) reported that teachers believe observations of student performance and product rating are desirable supplements to pencil-and-paper tests. Herman and Dorr-Bremme (1984) reported that nonformal test procedures were the teachers' *most* important source of information for making decisions about graduation, initial placement, and moving students from one instructional group to another. The discussion in this and the next four chapters is concerned with teacher-constructed achievement tests. Other teacher-made evaluation instruments will be considered in more detail in Chapter 9.

After studying this chapter, you should be able to:

1. Discuss the advantages of teacher-made tests over commercially published tests.
2. Understand the major problems associated with teacher-made tests.
3. Classify teacher-made achievement tests according to item format, nature of stimulus, and purpose.
4. Explain how purposes, content, method, timing, test length, item difficulty, and test blueprints relate to the planning of an evaluation procedure.
5. Construct a test blueprint.
6. Understand the importance of, and be able to construct, an item that matches an instructional objective.
7. Understand the differences between essay and objective tests.
8. Evaluate the strengths and weaknesses of essay and objective items.
9. Understand the factors to be considered in selecting a particular item format.
10. Understand the factors to be considered when deciding upon a test's length.
11. Define and discuss item difficulty.
12. Follow the guidelines offered for preparing test items.
13. Discuss the six characteristics (abilities) a person needs to write good test items.
14. Specify the sources of ideas upon which to base test items.
15. List the criteria to be met when selecting ideas for test items.

WHY TEACHER-MADE TESTS?

Teachers have an obligation to provide their students with the best instruction possible. This implies that they must have some procedure(s) whereby they can reliably and validly evaluate how effectively their students have learned what has been taught. The classroom achievement test is one such tool. But if there are commercially available achievement tests, why is it so important that classroom teachers know how to construct their own tests? Why not use the commercial tests?

Commercially prepared achievement tests are seldom administered more than once a year. Teacher-made tests can be and generally are given with much greater frequency. In addition, teacher-made tests can be more closely related to a teacher's particular objectives and pupils. Who knows better than the classroom teachers the needs, backgrounds, strengths, and weaknesses of their pupils? The classroom teacher, of course, is in the best position to provide answers to questions such as, "Does Ilene know how to add a single column of numbers well enough to proceed to the next instructional unit?" or "What relative emphasis has been placed on the Civil War in contrast to the Declaration of Independence?" Not only is the classroom teacher able to "tailor" the test to fit her particular objectives, but she can also make it "fit" the class and, if she wishes, "fit" the individual pupils. Commercially prepared tests, because they are prepared for use in many different school systems with many different curricular and instructional emphases, are unable to do these things as well as the teacher-made test.

Also, the content of commercially prepared tests tends to lag behind, by a few years at least, recent curricular developments. Teacher-made tests are more likely to reflect *today's* curriculum. This is especially true in subject-matter areas such as science and social studies, which may change rather rapidly.

Classroom test results may also be used by the teacher to help her develop more efficient teaching strategies. For example, Ms. Atom may feel that her pupils must understand valence before they can be introduced to balancing chemical equations. She could develop her own tests, administer them to her students as pretests, and then proceed on the basis of the test results to (a) reteach some of the information she falsely assumed the students

already knew, (b) omit some of the material planned to be taught because the students already know it, and (c) provide some of the students with remedial instruction while giving other students some enrichening experiences. She could have obtained this information with a commercial test only *if* that test reflected her particular objectives. Many times such tests do not.

There are many instances when a teacher wants to sample thoroughly in a particular area. That is, she is interested in obtaining as much information as possible from a test in a specific content area such as refraction, reflection, or valence. Normally, the commercial test will sample a variety of skills and knowledge rather than focus on any single aspect of the course content. Hence, teachers who want to sample thoroughly in a particular area can do this best by preparing their own tests. Even if a teacher can find a commercial test that sampled a particular concept to her liking, what would she do with the remainder of the test? It would be rather uneconomical to buy the total test for such a limited purpose. Yet the limited purpose should be evaluated. It is best evaluated by a well-constructed teacher-made test.

Classroom tests, because they can be tailored to fit a teacher's particular instructional objectives, are essential if we wish to provide for optimal learning on the part of the pupil and optimal teaching on the part of the teacher (see Bejar, 1984). Without classroom tests, those objectives that are unique to a particular school or teacher might never be evaluated. Our emphasis on the desirability and importance of the classroom teachers being able to construct their own personal, unique, and relevant tests should *not* be construed as a de-emphasis or an implied lack of value of commercial tests. On the contrary! Both serve a common function—the assessment of a pupil's skills and knowledge. But because they differ in scope, content, and use, we should capitalize on how they complement each other rather than argue that one is better than the other.

A survey by Stiggins and Bridgeford (1985) on the uses of various types of tests—teacher-made objective; standardized objective; and structured (planned and systematically designed to include prespecified purposes, exercises, observations, and scoring procedures) and spontaneous (arises naturally in the classroom upon which the teacher makes a judgment of the student's level of development) performance assessment—reported that:

1. *For assigning grades and evaluating the effectiveness of an instructional treatment*, teachers said they give most weight to their own objective tests. It's interesting to note that with respect to grading, the weight given to teacher-made objective tests and structured performance assessment increases while that given to published tests and spontaneous performance assessment decreases as the grade level increases.

2. *For diagnosis*, teachers give *most* weight to teacher-developed objective tests, followed closely by performance assessments in assisting them to diagnose pupil strengths and weaknesses. The former are most often used in science and math. Structured and spontaneous performance assessments are given most weight in speaking diagnosis and writing assessment, respectively.

3. *For reporting achievement to parents*, the teachers surveyed said they relied most heavily on their own objective tests and structured performance assessment.

To this point we have attempted to explain why teacher-made tests are necessary, even though there are good commercially prepared achievement tests available. However, in recent years there has been an attempt to build up item banks that can be used by the classroom teacher to prepare her test. Does this imply that teacher-made tests will be gradually discarded? We think not. At present these item banks—such as the Instructional Objectives Exchange, the Clearinghouse for Applied Performance Testing, the Objectives and Items Co-Op, and the School Curriculum Objectives-Referenced Evaluation—are *not* geared to provide the kind of service that would be required if large numbers of teachers were to avail themselves of the service. More important, however, is that such agencies would *not* encourage dispensing with teacher-made tests. With few exceptions,

they provide only the raw materials, *not* the finished test. Teachers would still have to know how to build, plan, score, and analyze the test. There is still a preponderance of schools having local, unique objectives that would not be measured by materials contained in these item banks, and teachers would have to write some items. Item banks can be of value to the classroom teacher. We do not think, however, that they will replace the need for the teacher's having knowledge of the processes involved in building a good achievement test.

DEFICIENCIES IN TEACHER-MADE TESTS

Students sometimes complain that they are fed up with tests that are ambiguous, unclear, and irrelevant. Student comments such as "I didn't know what the teacher was looking for" and "I studied the major details of the course but was only examined on trivia and footnotes" are not uncommon. Nor are they necessarily unjustified (see Planisek & Planisek, 1972; Haertel, 1986; Stiggins, 1988; Cohen & Reynolds, 1988). By and large, teacher-made achievement tests are quite poor. But that shouldn't be surprising or unexpected. In their pre-service education programs our teachers are trained to teach and *not* to assess (test) their students (Gullickson, 1986; Gullickson & Ellwein, 1985; and Marso & Pigge, 1989).

Let us look briefly at some of the major deficiencies commonly associated with teacher-made achievement tests. The deficiencies discussed below can be minimized by careful planning, by meticulous editing and review, and by following some simple rules of test-item construction.[1]

---

[1]Carter (1986) showed that test-wise students are able to use secondary clues to deduce the correct answer for faulty multiple-choice items. Possibly more shocking was her finding that teachers were unaware that they provided any clues such as the longest foil being the correct answer. Gullikson (1984) and Stiggins and Bridgeford (1985) reported that teachers felt deficient and needed more training in test construction.

1. *Ambiguous questions.* When a statement or word can be interpreted in two or more ways, we have ambiguity. In the essay test, words such as "discuss" and "explain" may be ambiguous in that different pupils interpret these words differently. In a true–false test, the item[2] "It is very hot in Phoenix in August" might be true or false depending upon the student's referent. In comparison to Siberia, the statement is true. But in comparison to Death Valley, the statement may be false. In other words, how "hot" is "hot"? Students should *not* be required to guess at an answer because the question is ambiguous. The question should be worded in such a way that it is interpreted in the *same* way by *all* students. Differential performance should be the result of differences in knowledge of the subject matter, *not* of differences in the interpretation of the item. After writing a test item, ask yourself "Can I make this item any more direct and clear?" Editing and some independent review of the test items by another teacher should help minimize ambiguity.

2. *Excessive wording.* Too often teachers think that the more wording there is in a question, the clearer it will be to the student. This is not always so. In fact, the more precise and clear-cut the wording, the greater the probability that the student will not be confused.

3. *Lack of appropriate emphasis.* More often than not, teacher-made tests do not cover the objectives stressed and taught by the teacher and do not reflect proportionately the teacher's judgment as to the importance of those objectives. Frequently, teacher-made achievement tests are heavily loaded with items that only test the student's ability to recall specific facts and information, such as "In what year was the Magna Carta signed?" Fleming and Chambers (1983) after reviewing about 9,000 items written by Cleveland, Ohio, classroom teachers (we believe they are typical of classroom teachers) found that nearly 80 percent of the items dealt with facts and knowledge. Only a minimal number of the items required students to *apply* their knowledge.

We do not negate the value of knowing certain specific facts and details, such as the multiplication tables. We feel that knowledge of such information should be tested. But this is markedly different from having the student quote the first five lines from "To be or not to be . . . ." Why are so few of the test items constructed by classroom teachers devoted to measuring the higher mental processes of understanding and application? Primarily because it is so much easier to prepare items that measure factual recall than it is to write test items that measure comprehension, synthesis, and evaluation. Also, students don't like items that measure higher-order thinking skills; they believe they are more difficult (S. B. Green et al., 1989).

4. *Use of inappropriate item formats.* Some teachers use different item formats (such as true–false or essay) solely because they feel that change or diversity is desirable. But the need for diversity should *not* govern the type of item to be used. There are, as will be discussed in later chapters, advantages and limitations associated with each type of item format. Teachers should be selective and choose the format that is most effective for measuring a particular objective.

CLASSIFICATION OF TEACHER-MADE TESTS

There are a variety of ways in which teacher-made tests (or, for that matter, commercially published tests) can be classified. One type of classification is based upon the type of item format used—*essay* versus *objective.* Another classification is based upon the type of stimulus material used to present the problems to the student—*verbal* or *nonverbal.* Still other classifications may be based upon the purposes of the test and the use of the test results—*criterion-referenced* versus *norm-referenced*; *achievement* versus *performance*; and *formative* versus *summative* evaluation. We will now con-

---

[2]Item and question are used interchangeably. Item format refers to the type of item, such as true–false or multiple-choice.

sider the various classification schemes in greater detail.

It should be recognized at the outset that these classification schemes are not mutually exclusive. For example, a test may be of the essay type, but the student may be required to react to a picture he sees or music he hears, and the results may be designed to assist the teacher in correctly placing him at an appropriate step in the learning (instructional) sequence.

Classification by Item Format

There are several ways in which items have been classified by format—supply and selection type; free answer and structured answer; essay and objective. (See Lien, 1976; Thorndike & Hagen, 1977, Ebel & Frisbie, 1986; Gronlund & Linn, 1990.) Some prefer to make the distinction in format as free response (supply) versus choice response (select), and scoring is dichotomized as objective versus subjective. Accordingly, questions can be classifed as follows:

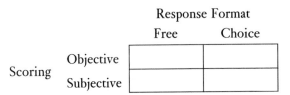

We will classify item types into two major categories—*essay* and *objective*—and place the short-answer form under objective rather than essay primarily because short-answer items can generally be scored more objectively than essay questions.[3]

It is not possible to classify tests solely on the basis of whether or not subjectivity is involved. Subjectivity is involved when *any* test is constructed—deciding upon the purpose(s) of the test, deciding upon the kinds of questions to ask, deciding upon the difficulty level of the test, deciding upon whether or not a correction formula

should be used—and hence one *cannot* say that an objective test does not involve some degree of subjectivity on the part of the test-maker. Also, even though some educators argue that essay tests are more susceptible to subjectivity in scoring than are objective tests, techniques are available (see Chapter 5) to make essay scoring more objective. At any rate, objective and essay[4] tests do differ quite markedly in the degree to which they are amenable to objective scoring. It is primarily for this reason that we favor the classification of teacher-made achievement tests shown below:[5]

A. Essay type:
  1. Short-answer or restricted response (about one-half of an 8½ × 11-inch page);
  2. Discussion or extended response (about 2 to 3 pages);
  3. Oral.
B. Objective type:
  1. Short-answer;
    a. Single word, symbol, formula;
    b. Multiple words or phrase;
    c. One to three complete sentences;
  2. True–false (right-wrong, yes-no);
  3. Multiple-choice;
  4. Matching.

Classification by Stimulus Material

We generally think of tests in terms of a series of verbal problems that require some sort of verbal response. There are many instances, however, where the stimulus material used to present the problem to the student need not be verbal. In a humanities or art course, the stimulus materials can be pictorial. In a music course, it could be a recording. In a woodworking course, the stimulus material might be the tools. In a pathology course,

---

[3]Objectivity of scoring refers to the extent to which the personal judgment of the scorer affects the score credited to a particular response.

[4]The oral examination, which is less popular today, could be classified as being of the essay type.
[5]We recognize that if we adopted a supply vs. select type classification for the essay and objective type, respectively, short-answer items would be found under what we presently call "essay."

it could be the specimen viewed through the microscope. Nevertheless, the student is still being tested to see what abilities, skills, and knowledge he possesses. Although nonverbal stimulus material items are infrequently used in the classroom, this does not mean that they are not a good medium to use.

Classification by Purpose

Teacher-made, or for that matter, standardized achievement tests can also be classified in terms of their purpose or use.

Criterion versus Norm-Referenced Interpretation
As discussed in Chapter 2, the test score in a criterion-referenced interpretation is used to describe the status of the individual. Does Maxwell know how to add a single column of figures? Does Allan know how to balance an equation? A norm-referenced interpretation of the test score permits the teacher to make meaningful comparisons among students in terms of their achievement. Hence, if the teacher wants to compare Maxwell's performance in arithmetic to that of his peers, she would use norm-referenced interpretation.

Achievement versus Performance
The educational process is *not* restricted to achievement in such areas as reading, science, social studies, or mathematics. There are many instances where teachers are just as, if not more, concerned with what the pupil can *do*. For example, an art teacher might be as interested in seeing how well students can draw or paint as she is in whether they know the distinction between form and symmetry. And a woodworking teacher might be more concerned with ascertaining whether her students can operate a lathe than she is in knowing whether they know the parts of a lathe. Education is concerned with both what we know in an academic sense and how well we are able to apply our knowledge. For this reason, teachers could use achievement tests, performance tests, or a combination of the two, depending upon the subject matter. In Chapters 5

through 7, we will concern ourselves with teacher-made achievement tests. In Chapter 9, we will discuss other teacher-made evaluation procedures.

Formative versus Summative Evaluation
The way test results are used determines whether we are engaging in formative or summative evaluation. If tests are given frequently during the course of instruction and the data are used to modify and direct learning and instruction, we are engaged in *formative* evaluation. If the test is given at the end of the unit, chapter, or course to determine how well the students have mastered the content, we have engaged in *summative* evaluation. Summative evaluation is often used as a basis for assigning final course grades.

The item format used and the types of items written generally do not differ for tests used for formative and summative evaluation. What differ are the frequency of testing and the table of specifications (see p. 58). Since formative evaluation is designed to provide the teacher with continuous and immediate feedback so that she can govern her instructional strategy, such evaluation is more frequent. With respect to the table of specifications, for formative evaluation as in the case of criterion-referenced and diagnostic tests, there will be a very thorough sampling of a limited content area. In summative evaluation, there will be a more restricted sampling across a larger content area.

PLANNING THE TEACHER-MADE TEST

Although more elaborate and detailed planning goes into the development of a large-scale standardized test than we would expect in a teacher-made test, this does *not* imply that teacher-made tests should be or are hastily constructed without any kind of planning.

Good tests do not just happen! They require adequate and extensive planning so that the instructional objectives, the teaching strategy to be employed, the textual material, and the evaluative procedure are all related in some meaningful fashion. Most teachers recognize the importance of having some systematic procedure for ascertaining the extent to which their instructional objectives have been realized by their pupils. And yet, one of the major errors committed by teachers when preparing classroom tests is *inadequate planning.* Too often, teachers feel that they can begin thinking about the preparation of their test one or two weeks before it is to be administered. More often than not, they leave it until the last possible moment and rush like mad to prepare something. This is indeed unfortunate, for the test produced may contain items that are faulty, for example, the items are ambiguous, not scorable, or too difficult. Professional item writers are seldom able to write more then ten good items per day. It would therefore seem unrealistic to expect the ordinary classroom teacher to be able to prepare a 50-item test if she begins thinking about her test only a few days before it is scheduled. The solution to the problem lies in adequate planning and in spreading out the item-writing phase over a long period of time.

Ideally, every test should be reviewed critically by other teachers to minimize the deficiencies noted earlier. All the deficiencies discussed earlier are related in one way or another to inadequate planning. This is not to imply that careful planning will *ipso facto* remove these deficiencies; rather, without adequate and careful planning, one can be fairly certain that one's test will not be very good. We agree with Tinkelman (1971, p. 46) who wrote, "At the very least, inattention to planning can lead to waste and to delay due to failure to coordinate properly the various phases of test construction."

Developing the Test Specifications

Before the classroom teacher (or, for that matter, the professional item writer) sits down to write her test items, she must develop a set of *test specifications.* (NOTE: The test specifications differ from the table of specifications/test blueprint/2-way grid to be discussed in the next section.) The *sine qua non* of initial test planning is developing the test specifications. They should be so complete and explicit that two classroom teachers operating independently but using these specifications would produce equivalent tests differing only in the sampling of questions from the content domain. In some sense, the test specifications consist of a series of questions. The two most general questions the classroom teacher must consider are (a) What do I want to do? and (b) What is the best way in which I can accomplish my goal? Table 4-1 sets forth the kind of questions that should be asked by the classroom teacher in the test-planning stage. In subsequent sections of this chapter we will consider the first nine questions contained in the checklist. In the succeeding chapters we will concentrate on answers to the remaining questions—the techniques of writing essay and objective test items, assembling, reproducing, administering, scoring, and analyzing the test.

Purpose of the Test   The most crucial decision the test constructor has to make is *"Why am I testing?"* You will recall that in Chapter 1 we discussed the many ways in which evaluation can aid both the pupil and the teacher. To be helpful, classroom tests must be related to the teacher's instructional objectives, which in turn must be related to the teacher's instructional procedures, and eventually to the use of the test result. But what are the purposes of the test? Why is the test being administered? How will the test results be used by the pupil, teacher, counselor, administrator, and parents?

Classroom achievement tests serve a variety of purposes, such as (a) judging the pupils' mastery of certain essential skills and knowledge, (b) measuring growth over time, (c) ranking pupils in terms of their achievement of particular instructional objectives, (d) diagnosing pupil difficulties, (e) evaluating the teacher's instructional method, (f) ascertaining the effectiveness of the curriculum, (g) encouraging good study habits, and (h) motivating students. These purposes are not mutually exclusive. A single test can and should be

TABLE 4-1   Checklist for the Planning Stage in Preparing Classroom Tests

1. What is the purpose of the test? Why am I giving it?
2. What skills, knowledge, attitudes, and so on, do I want to measure?
3. Have I clearly defined my instructional objectives in terms of student behavior?
4. Have I prepared a table of specifications?
5. Do the test items match the objectives?
6. What kind of test (item format) do I want to use? Why?
7. How long should the test be?
8. How difficult should the test be?
9. What should be the discrimination level of my test items?
10. How will I arrange the various item formats?
11. How will I arrange the items within each item format?
12. What do I need to do to prepare students for taking the test?
13. How are the pupils to record their answers to objective items? On separate answer sheets? On the test booklet?
14. How is the objective portion to be scored? Hand or machine?
15. How is the essay portion to be graded? Global or analytical?
16. For objective items, should guessing instructions be given? Should a correction for guessing be applied?
17. How are the test scores to be tabulated?
18. How are scores (grades, or level of competency) to be assigned?
19. How are the test results to be reported?

---

used to serve as many purposes as possible. For example, a classroom achievement test in fifth-grade arithmetic can be used to diagnose student strengths and weaknesses, to rank pupils, and to evaluate a particular instructional strategy. This, however, should *not* be construed as de-emphasizing the need for every classroom teacher to specify in advance the purposes to which her test results will be put. The classroom teacher should not hope that because a test can serve many masters, it will automatically serve her intended purpose(s). The teacher must *plan* for this in advance.

A test can serve many purposes, but it cannot do so with equal effectiveness. It is essential that teachers know the major use of the test results. Otherwise, we fear that they will not be able to prepare a test that will be most useful to them or their pupils.

What Is to Be Tested?   The second major question that the classroom teacher, now turned test-constructor, must ask herself is "*What is it that I wish to measure?*" What knowledge, skills, and attitudes do I want to measure? Should I test for factual knowledge or should I test the extent to which my students are able to *apply* their factual knowledge? The answer to this depends upon the teacher's instructional objectives and what has been stressed in class. If the teacher emphasized the recall of names, places, and dates, she should test for this. On the other hand, if in twelfth-grade chemistry she has stressed the interpretation of data, then her test, in order to be a valid measure of her teaching, should emphasize the measurement of this higher mental process. In this stage of thinking about the test, the teacher must consider the relationships among her objectives, teaching, and testing. The following checklist should assist the teacher in her role as test-constructor:

1. Specify the course or unit content.
2. List the major course or unit objectives.
3. Define each objective in terms of student behavior.
4. Discard unrealistic objectives.

TABLE 4-2   Two-Way Table of Specifications for a Final Examination in Natural Science

Course Content	Knowledge	Comprehension (Translation, Interpretation, Extrapolation)	Application	Analysis	Total
		Objectives*			
1. Methods of science; hypotheses concerning the origin of the solar system	5	2		3	10
2. Minerals and rocks	5	5			10
3. Changes in land features	4	4	2		10
4. Interpretation of land features	2	2	6		10
5. Animal classifications	2	4	4		10
6. Plants of the earth	4	4	2		10
7. Populations and the mechanisms of evolution	3	3		4	10
8. Variation and selection		1	5	4	10
9. Facts of evolution and the theory that explains them		2	2	6	10
10. Evolution, genetics, and the races of man		3	4	3	10
Total	25	30	25	20	100

*Objectives are based on Bloom's taxonomy.
SOURCE: C. H. Nelson, 1958, *Let's Build Quality into Our Science Tests*. Washington, D.C.: National Science Teachers Association.

5. Prepare a table of specifications.
6. Prepare test items that match the instructional objectives.
7. Decide on the type of item format to be used.[6]

Then, in order to further relate testing to teaching, the teacher should:

8. Evaluate the degree to which the objectives have been learned by the pupils.
9. Revise the objectives and/or teaching material and/or test on the basis of the test results.

---

[6]We recognize that only the first five points are directly related to the *"what is to be tested?"*. Because the *"what"* helps determine the *"how"* and because testing should be related to teaching, we have chosen to include the additional points at this time.

Specifying the Course Content   An important first step for the teacher in determining what is to be tested is to specify or outline the content of the course or unit. Tables 4-2 and 4-3 present in general terms the outline for a college freshman course in natural science and a third-grade test on subtraction of fractions, respectively.

Specifying the Major Course Objectives   The second, and for teachers, undoubtedly the *most* difficult step in determining what to test is to define and delineate the objectives of instruction. Yet this is essential, for without objectives the teacher is at a loss to know *both* what is to be taught and hence what is to be measured. It is vital that the teacher, individually but preferably in consultation with other teachers (using a variety of sources such as those discussed in Chapter 3), specify in advance the *major* course objectives for her pupils. Then the teacher can develop appropriate measurement tools to determine the extent to which her pupils have achieved her objectives. For example, one of the objectives in seventh-grade science might be "to understand the operating principles of a four-cycle internal combustion engine." The teacher who accepts this objective must not only teach this material but also must test her pupils for their understanding of the principles involved in the operation of the four-cycle engine. We realize that it may be difficult to delineate all major course objectives. We also are aware that circumstances beyond the teacher's control might result in some of her instructional objectives not being taught. However, *those objectives for which learning experiences are provided must be subjected to some form of testing and evaluation.*

Defining Behavioral Objectives One of the major deficiencies in teacher-made tests results from inadequate attention being paid to the expression of instructional objectives in terms of student behavior. Too often, objectives are expressed as vague generalities, such as effective citizenship, critical thinking ability, or writing ability. Vague, general goals often do not offer adequate direction to the teacher. As pointed out in Chapter 3, objectives should provide direction

to the teacher so she can prepare and organize appropriate learning experiences for her pupils. A good rule of thumb in writing objectives is to ask yourself, "Can my students do these things?" For example, can they

1. change Fahrenheit temperatures to Celsius?
2. explain how an internal combustion engine works?
3. divide with carrying?
4. describe the three major branches of the federal government, and explain their duties and powers?
5. quote the Declaration of Independence from memory?
6. read a wet-bulb thermometer?

It matters little whether goal 6 involves a skill, goal 5 concerns memory, or goal 2 measures understanding. What does matter is that each of these goals is very precise, observable, and measurable. Each of these very fine or specific subdivisions of some larger whole pertains to some aspect of human behavior. With goals phrased or expressed in this matter, the teacher knows *both* what to teach and what to test for.

To help in developing a test that has adequate content validity, the teacher should develop some scheme whereby instructional objectives are related to course content and eventually to the kinds of test questions she proposes to use for measuring the degree of student mastery of these objec-

TABLE 4-3 Table of Specifications for a Chemistry Unit on Hydrogen

Content, Percent	Recall of Information	Understanding Concepts	Application in New Situations	Total, Percent
Physical properties	8	6	6	20
Chemical properties	12	9	9	30
Preparation	4	3	3	10
Uses	16	12	12	40
Total	40	30	30	100

tives. Such a scheme is referred to as a table of specifications.

Table of Specifications[7]

One of the major complaints that students make of teacher-made tests is that they are often invalid. Students may not use the technical term *validity*, but their comments—"We were tested on minute, mundane facts," "The material we were tested on wasn't covered in class"—all point out that the test lacked content validity. We recognize that there may be some instances where students are only displaying a "sour grapes" attitude and complaining for the sake of complaining. But we know from looking at a plethora of teacher-made achievement tests that there is some justification for the complaints made. Although a table of specifications is no guarantee that the errors will be corrected, such a blueprint should help improve the content validity of teacher-made tests.

How often have you seen a plumber or electrician work without referring to some type of blueprint? How often have you seen a tailor make a suit without a pattern? Very seldom, we bet! But we have seen some tests constructed by teachers and college professors who did not use any type of plan or guide or blueprint, and their tests reflected it.

The purpose of the table of specifications is to define as clearly as possible the scope and emphasis of the test, to relate the objectives to the content, and to construct a *balanced* test.

When to Prepare Specifications Ideally, to be of most benefit, the table of specifications should be prepared *before* beginning instruction. Why? Because these "specs" may help the teacher be a more effective teacher. They should assist the teacher in organizing her teaching material, her outside readings, her laboratory experiences (if necessary)—all the resources she plans on using in teaching the course. In this way, the specs can help provide for optimal learning on the part of the pupils and optimal teaching efficiency on the part of the instructor. In a way, then, the specs serve as a monitoring device and can help keep the teacher from straying off her instructional track.

Preparing the Table of Specifications Once the course content and instructional objectives have been specified, the teacher is ready to integrate them in some meaningful fashion so that the test, when completed, will be an accurate measure of the students' knowledge. Table 4-2 contains the course content in natural science that simultaneously relates to the course content to Bloom's (1956) taxonomy.

One could, of course, delineate the course content into finer subdivisions. Whether this needs to be done depends upon the nature of the content and the manner in which the course content has been outlined and taught by the teacher. A good rule of thumb to follow in determining how detailed the content area should be is to *have a sufficient number of subdivisions to ensure adequate and detailed coverage*. The more detailed the blueprint, the easier it is to get ideas for test items.

You will notice in Table 4-2 that there are numbers in certain cells and blanks in other cells. Now, what do all these numbers mean? The number 100 in the bottom right-hand corner is the total percentage (it can be, however, related to the number of items on the test) or point value of the test. The numbers at the bottom of each column indicate the percentage of the test devoted to a particular objective. Hence, in this hypothetical test, 25 percent of the test items measured knowledge, 30 percent of the items measured comprehension, and so forth. The numbers in the last column signify the percentage of test items that were allocated to each content area. The boldface number 5 in the first column and first row tells you that 5 percent of the total test was devoted to the measurement of "knowledge" in methods of science. At this point you might ask, "Who determines the weights?"—that is, who determines the propor-

---

[7]The table of specifications is sometimes called the test blueprint, test grid, or content-validity chart.

tion of items that are designed for each content area and for each objective?

Determination of Weights You will recall that one of the major advantages of the teacher-made versus commercially published test is that the teacher-made test can be tailor-made to fit the teacher's unique and/or particular objectives. In this way, Ms. Molecule, who stresses the gas laws in eleventh-grade physics, can do so while Ms. Element, who stresses heat and mechanics, is also at liberty to do so. Each teacher can prepare a test that is valid for her students. Because the classroom teacher—more so than any other person—knows the relative emphasis placed upon the various instructional objectives, it naturally follows that she should have the major responsibility in assigning the various weights to the cells in Table 4-2. There is no hard-and-fast rule that can be prescribed for the teacher to use in determining the weights to be assigned to the various cells in the table of specifications. The weights assigned should reflect the relative emphasis used by the teacher when she taught the course.

As an example, we give a very simplified illustration of how a classroom teacher can *initially* determine the weights to be assigned to a particular cell in the table of specifications. Assume that Ms. Atom will spend five class periods on a unit in hydrogen, and she wants to prepare a test on this unit. Ms. Atom plans to spend one period (20 percent of the time) discussing the physical properties of hydrogen; one and one-half periods (30 percent) on the chemical properties of hydrogen; one-half period (10 percent) on the preparation of hydrogen; and two periods (40 percent) discussing the uses of hydrogen. These values are represented as the *row* totals in Table 4-3. In teaching this unit, Ms. Atom will be concerned with three instructional objectives: the pupils' ability to (a) recall information; (b) apply information, concepts, and principles in new situations; and (c) understand basic concepts and principles. The relative emphasis placed on each of these instructional (behavioral or performance) objectives will be 40,

30, and 30 percent, respectively. These values are represented as the *column* totals. Ms. Atom must now assign values to each of the 12 cells. This could be done by multiplying the row totals by the column totals. For example, the cell involving recall of information in physical properties would have a weight of .20 × 40 = 8 percent; the cell incorporating application and uses would have a weight of .40 × 30 = 12 percent. This procedure is repeated for each cell and is illustrated in Table 4-3. Ms. Atom now has a blueprint (table of specifications) to guide her both in teaching this unit and in constructing a test on this unit.

Table 4-4 illustrates a table of specifications for a 35-item test dealing with subtraction of fractions.

How firm should the assignment of weights in each cell be? We believe that the initial weights in each cell of the table of specifications should be considered as *tentative.* It is only after the course has been taught that the weights can be considered definite. And, because conditions may vary from one class to another, the final weights may be somewhat different for different classes taught by the same teacher. This, however, does not mean that the teacher should depart from her original "specs" because she finds it difficult to write items designed to measure the higher mental processes. As Tinkelman (1971, p. 56) wrote: "If a test blueprint rests upon a sound judgmental basis, the test constructor has the professional obligation to obtain items of satisfactory quality and in sufficient numbers to satisfy blueprint specifications." Without a well-thought-out and prepared table of specifications, there is a great possibility that the test, when finally constructed, will lack content validity.

Tables of Specifications for Criterion-Referenced Tests

As mentioned in Chapter 2, the major difference between criterion- and norm-referenced tests is in terms of score interpretation—whether we interpret a person's score by comparing it with a spec-

TABLE 4-4 Table of Specifications for a Test on Subtraction of Fractions

| | Instructional Objectives | | | |
Content	Subtracts Fractions	Subtracts Fractions and Mixed Numbers	Subtracts Mixed Numbers	Total Items
Denominators are unlike with common factor	3	3	4	10
Denominators are unlike with uncommon denominator	3	4	3	10
Denominators are alike	5	5	5	15
Total items	11	12	12	35

ified behavioral criterion of proficiency (90 percent of the items answered correctly) or by comparing it with the scores of other people (Allan did better than Ilene). However, *both* norm- and criterion-referenced test scores are related to *content*; therefore, in building an achievement test whose scores will be norm-referenced, we must be as concerned with *content* validity as when building a test whose scores will be criterion-referenced. In *both* cases, there is a domain of relevant tasks or behaviors from which we wish to sample. In both cases, we should use a table of specifications to ensure that our sample of test items is representative of the domain of behaviors. The major difference is that for the specific types of instructional decisions where one usually finds criterion referencing to be of more value, the content domain is quite limited in focus. For those educational decisions where one is likely to make a normative interpretation of the score, the domain of tasks is usually more broad. Thus, when building a test whose scores will be interpreted by comparison with some specified criterion, we may well have only one cell in the table of specifications. The domain is so narrow that it need not be subdivided. For example, we might build a criterion-referenced test on the task of adding two single-digit whole numbers. A table of specifications

for such a test would not need to be subdivided. If a test had a broader focus—that is, was designed to measure addition of whole numbers, fractions, and decimals—then one would build a table of specifications so that each subtype of addition problem was represented. This would be true whether one wished to interpret the scores in an absolute or relative fashion.

Distributing the Table of Specifications The table of specifications *should be given to the students* (especially those in the upper elementary grades and above) at the beginning of the instruction and should be discussed thoroughly with them. This can help minimize, if not eliminate, future misconceptions, misunderstandings, and problems. This would also allow students to voice their opinions concerning the course content and the relative emphasis. If changes are made as a result of this interaction, the pupils should be given a revised set of "specs."

Using the Table of Specifications We have already discussed how the table of specifications can assist the teacher. Especially since the "age of accountability," there has been some concern voiced by educators that teachers will be prone to "teach for the test." As we said in Chapter 3, if the teacher has an appropriate set of instructional objectives, she should teach her pupils to realize these objectives. It is *not* wrong to "teach for the test" in this sense. In fact, we would be most pleased if teachers would take the time to develop appropriate instructional objectives, teach them, and then test to see the extent to which they were realized by their pupils. This is markedly different from teaching the test items *per se*. Also, teaching to a teacher-made test is different than teaching to a standardized test because of the different domains and different inferences drawn (Mehrens, 1984a; Mehrens & Kaminski, 1989).

In summary, the use of a test blueprint or table of specifications will help ensure that (1) only those objectives actually involved in the instructional process will be assessed, (2) each objective will receive a proportional emphasis on the test in relation to the emphasis placed on that objective by the teacher, and (3) no important objective or content area will be inadvertently omitted. Much time and effort are (or can be) expended in preparing a table of specifications, but in the long run, the time and effort expended will be worthwhile. The table of specifications can aid immensely in the preparation of test items, in the production of a valid and well-balanced test, in the clarification of objectives to both teacher and students, and in assisting the teacher to select the most appropriate teaching strategy. Remember: The "table" is only a guide; it is *not* designed to be adhered to strictly.

Relating the Test Items to the Instructional Objectives

Obtaining a "match" between a test's items and the test's instructional objectives is *not* guaranteed by a test blueprint or table of specifications. The test blueprint only indicates the number or proportion of test items to be allocated to each of the instructional objectives specified. Following are some examples of learning outcomes expressed in terms of specific behavioral objectives, with accompanying test items designed to measure the learning outcome.

Example 1
Learning outcome (L.O.): The student will be able to define (in one or two sentences) the following terms: dividend, divisor, product, quotient, sum.

Test item (T.I.): In one or two sentences, define the following terms:

1. Dividend
2. Divisor
3. Product
4. Quotient
5. Sum

Do we have a "match" between the learning outcome and test item?

Example 2
Learning outcome (L.O.): The student will be able to identify living and nonliving things.

Test item (T.I.): Which *one* of the following is a nonliving thing?

1. Bear
2. Ice Cube
3. Rose
4. Yeast

Do we have a "match"?

Example 3
Learning outcome (L.O.): The student can identify the path in an electrical circuit.

Test item (T.I.): Design a circuit for a light with two switches at different locations.

Do we have a "match"?

Example 4
Learning outcome (L.O.): The student can perform mouth-to-mouth resuscitation on a drowning victim.

Test item (T.I.): Describe the correct procedure for administering mouth-to-mouth resuscitation on a drowning victim.

Do we have a "match"?

Of the four examples given, only the *first and second* examples display a "match" between the learning outcome (L.O.) and the test item (T.I.) The third is *not* a "match" because the student could perform the L.O. but yet be unable to perform the T.I. In the fourth example there is *no* match because describing something is not valid evidence that the person can *do* something. On the surface, one might say that those examples illustrating the lack of a "match" between the test item and learning outcome illustrate minor, insignificant, semantic differences between the L.O. and the T.I. However, even the smallest difference is *unacceptable* if one wishes to be a "stickler" and say that to have a valid measure of a L.O., there must be a *perfect* match.

Wherever *possible*, there must be a "match." Where would we be willing to deviate? Example 4 illustrates a situation where one could *not* match the T.I. to the L.O. How can one demonstrate whether he is able to correctly apply mouth-to-mouth resuscitation on a drowning victim unless he happens to come upon a drowning victim? It is readily evident that you can't go out and drown someone. But you could have a simulated situation and ascertain whether the student can demonstrate his knowledge. In any event, where it is impossible to obtain a "match" because of situations beyond the examiner's control, it is important that the student perform the main intent despite the artificiality of the situation.

The major step, then, in preparing relevant test items is to *carefully analyze the behavior called for in the learning outcome.* Is the learning outcome to have the student demonstrate his knowledge of or ability to *name, identify, compute?* Is it to reflect knowledge at a lower mental process level (recall or recognition or application) or at a higher level of mental process such as synthesis or evaluation? In the examples given above, the learning outcomes were very specific. One can, if she wishes, have a more general learning outcome—one that is not specifically related to course content—a content-free learning outcome, an example of which is:

> The student will be able to identify (recognize) the function of a given tool.

The "shell" of such an item would be, "The student will be able to *(insert L.O. verb)* the function of *(insert name of tool or apparatus)*."

The virtue of having content-free learning outcomes is that they can serve as models upon which content-specific learning outcomes can be written. In other words, they are a frame or shell upon which the item is then built. A major limitation of the content-free learning outcome is that it may result in the item writer losing sight of the fact that before a test item can be written, the learning outcome(s) must be made very specific; otherwise the item may not "match" the instructional objective. [For a more detailed discussion of matching items with objectives, see Mager (1962) and Gronlund (1985, 1988).]

Selecting the Appropriate Item Format

Now that the teacher has decided on the purpose of the test and *what* she is interested in measuring—both in terms of the objectives and the content—she must decide on the best *way* of measuring her instructional objectives. This, of course, does not preclude "mixing" different, but *appropriate*, item types on a test. In fact, Ackerman and Smith (1988) and Murchan (1989), among others, recommend a combination of essay and objective items because different skills and abilities are measured by each.

As will be evident in our discussions of the various item formats, some are less appropriate than others for measuring certain objectives. For example, if the objective to be measured is stated as "the student will be able to organize his ideas and write them in a logical and coherent fashion," it would be inappropriate to have him select his answer from a series of possible answers. And, if the objective is to obtain evidence of the pupil's factual recall of names, places, dates, and events, it would not be efficient to use a lengthy essay question. For true–false and short-answer questions, one can use either an oral or a written medium, but the oral approach is definitely *not* recommended for the multiple-choice or matching format. In those instances where the instructional objective can be measured by different item formats, the teacher should select the least complicated one and the one with which she feels most comfortable and adept.

The discussion of the advantages and limitations of the various item formats as well as the actual preparation of essay and objective test items will be found in Chapters 5 through 7. Inasmuch as it is important for the classroom teacher to give some thought to whether she should use an essay or objective test before she actually sits down to write test items (i.e., she must engage in some sort of item-format planning), we will at this time discuss some of the more general factors the classroom teacher should consider when deciding upon the type of test to use. But before doing so, let us look at the differences between an essay and objective test.

DIFFERENCES BETWEEN THE ESSAY AND OBJECTIVE TEST

Ebel and Frisbie (1986, pp. 130–131) noted the following differences between the two major types of teacher-made tests—essay and objective.

1. Essay tests require an individual to organize and express his answers in his own words. In the essay or "free response" item, the student is not restricted to a list of responses from which he is to select the answer. Objective tests, on the other hand, require that the individual either supply a brief answer (one or two words) or choose the correct answer from among several alternatives. Many people seem to think that admitting this difference implies the superiority of essay exams, but this is not necessarily so. Nevertheless, we do occasionally wish to measure ability to organize and to write cogently, and essay tests are superior for that purpose.

2. An essay test consists of fewer questions but calls for more lengthy answers. An objective test has more questions but ones taking less time to answer. Sampling adequacy, efficiency, and reliability are therefore likely to be superior in objective tests.

3. Different skills and processes are involved in taking the tests (see Ward et al., 1980). In the essay test, the student spends most of his time thinking and writing. In the objective test (especially the multiple-choice), most of the student's time is spent on reading and thinking.

4. The quality of the essay test is dependent largely on the skill of the reader (the person grading the answer); that of an objective test, on the skill of the test constructor.

5. Essay tests are relatively easy to prepare but more difficult to grade accurately since they are graded by humans (who may be subjective) rather than by impersonal machines. Some teachers believe that essay questions can be prepared while they are on their way to school and may then be written on the blackboard. Although this may be possible, it does not lead to the preparation of good questions.

6. Essay tests afford both the student and grader the opportunity to be individualistic. Objective tests afford this freedom of expression (item writing) only to the test-maker.

7. On objective tests the examinees' tasks and the scorers' criteria tend to be more explicit. Although the task for the examinee and the criteria for grading may be made more explicit in essay tests, they seldom are.

8. Objective tests are more susceptible to guessing; essay tests are more susceptible to bluffing. The seriousness of both problems, however, has been grossly overestimated.

9. The score distribution in the essay test may vary from one reader (scorer) to another; on the objective test, the distribution is determined almost completely by the test.

Two popular misconceptions *not* supported by the empirical evidence are that (a) essay tests assess certain skills such as analysis and critical thinking better than objective tests and (b) essay tests contribute to better pupil study and work habits.

Misconceptions of the different types of item formats have resulted in much debate about the relative merits of one type of examination over another. Look at the following example that illustrates that higher-order thinking skills can be measured by a multiple-choice item.

Ruth bought 6 balloons. She bought at least 1 green, 1 red, and 1 yellow balloon. She bought 3 more yellow than red balloons. How many yellow balloons did she buy?

1. One
2. Two

3. Three
4. Four

Rather than argue whether essay tests are better than objective tests, or vice versa, we should understand the strengths and weaknesses associated with each type (essay and objective) and capitalize on their strengths.

FACTORS TO CONSIDER WHEN SELECTING AN ITEM FORMAT

If a classroom teacher were to ask us, "Which item format would you recommend?" we would say, "It depends on many things." Although we are unable to provide you with a definite set of rules, we are able to give some suggestions for your consideration in deciding which item format to use. Factors to consider include the following: (a) the purpose of the test, (b) the time available to prepare and score the test, (c) the number of pupils to be tested, (d) skill tested, (e) difficulty desired, (f) the physical facilities available for reproducing the test, (g) the age of the pupils, and (h) your skill in writing the different types of items.

1. *Purpose of the test.* The most important factor to be considered is what you want the test to measure. To measure written self-expression, you would use the essay; for spoken self-expression, the oral. To measure the extent of the pupil's factual knowledge, his understanding of principles, or his ability to interpret, we prefer the objective test because it is more economical and tends to possess higher score reliability and content validity. If your purpose is to use the test results to make binding decisions for grading purposes or admission to college, we recommend the objective test because of greater sampling of content and more objective scoring. To see whether the pupils can produce rather than recognize the correct answer, you would use the completion or short-answer *supply* type rather than the matching, or true–false, or multiple-choice *recall* type objective test.

2. *Time.* It will take less time to prepare 5 extended-response essay questions for a two-hour twelfth-grade history test than it would to prepare 75 multiple-choice items for that same test. However, the time saved in preparing the essay test may be used up in reading and grading the responses. The time element becomes of concern in relation to *when* the teacher has the time. If she is rushed before the test is to be administered but will have sufficient time after it has been given, she might choose to use an essay examination. But, if she must process the results within two or three days and has no additional readers, she should use the objective test, *provided* she has sufficient time to write good objective items. We should also consider the long-term vs. short-term time investment. Over an extended period of time, one would have to write many essay items because of loss of security but could, in that same time, have built up an extensive item bank of objective-type items.

3. *Numbers tested.* If there are only a few pupils to be tested and if the test is not to be reused, then the essay or oral test is practical. However, if a large number of pupils are to be tested and/or if the test is to be reused at a later time with another group, we recommend the objective test. It's much harder to remember 75 objective items than it is to remember 5 or 6 essay topics.

4. *Skill tested.* Hanson et al. (1986) showed that certain item formats worked better for one skill than for another. They also provided a design that could be used to determine the specific combination and number of items that should be included in a CRT for each skill to be tested.

5. *Difficulty desired.* Early research consistently indicated that use of different formats had little effect on pupils' ranking but did have a differential effect on item-difficulty levels (Heim & Watts, 1967; Traub & Fisher, n.d.). Multiple-choice formats were consistently found easier to answer than constructed formats.

6. *Physical facilities.* If stenographic and reproduction facilities are limited, the teacher is forced to use either the essay test, with the questions written on the board, or the oral test; or she can

use the true–false or short-answer item by reading the questions aloud. However, multiple-choice items must (because of their complexity and/or amount of material to be remembered) be mimeographed or reproduced mechanically. We believe that all tests should be mechanically reproduced if possible.

7. *Age of pupils.* Unfortunately, there are still some teachers who believe that a good test is characterized by many different item formats. They no doubt feel that this introduces an element of novelty or that a change of pace will result in keeping the pupils' motivation high. This *may* be true for older pupils, but is definitely *not* so for younger pupils. In fact, we believe that changing item formats with accompanying changes in directions to be followed will, for younger children especially, result in confusion in adapting to new instructions, and whatever novelty might be introduced will be at the expense of valid and reliable test results.

8. *Teacher's skill.* Teachers may be prone initially to more frustration and disappointment when writing test items of one item format than another. As will be seen in later sections, some item formats are easier to write than others, and teachers do a better job with one type than another. In fact, Ebel (1975a) found that teachers are able to write more discriminating multiple-choice items than true–false items.

Because of the differences in teachers' skills in writing different types of items, we urge you to try your hand at writing all item formats. Item writing is a skill that can be improved with practice. However, to write good items requires careful construction, but, even more important, it also requires careful planning.

The various item formats are compared in Table 4-5. The (+) indicates a slight advantage; the (+ +) a marked advantage; the (− −) a marked disadvantage; and the (−) a slight disadvantage of that item type for that factor.

TABLE 4-5   Evaluation of Various Item Types

Factor	Essay or Oral	Short-Answer	True–False, Matching, Multiple-Choice
Measures pupil's ability to select, organize, and synthesize his ideas and express himself coherently.	+ +	+	−
Discourages bluffing.	− −	−	+ +
Potential diagnostic value.	− −	−	+ +
Answer cannot be deduced by process of elimination.	+ +	+ +	−
Can be rapidly scored.	− −	+	+ +
Can be scored by machine or untrained person.	− −	−	+ +
Scoring is reliable.	− −	−	+ +
Independent of verbal articulation (fluency).	− −	+	+ +
Provides for good item pool.	− −	+	+ +
Takes relatively little time to prepare.	+	+	−
Measures higher mental processes.	+ +	−	+ +
Provides for broad content sampling.	− −	+	+ +
Measures application in novel situations.	+ +	+	+ +
Provides for adequate sampling of objectives.	− −	+	+ +
Measures originality.	+ +	+	− −

SOURCE: Adapted with permission from R. L. Thorndike and E. Hagen, *Measurement and Evaluation in Psychology and Education* (3d ed.). New York: Wiley, 1969, p. 71. By permission of John Wiley & Sons, Inc.

ADDITIONAL DETAILS IN TEST PLANNING

Once we have decided on the purpose of the test and have at least tentatively decided on the item format(s) to be used, we still must answer five questions before we are able to sit down and begin writing test items and administer the test. They are (a) How long should the test be? (b) How difficult should the test be? (c) When and how often should tests be given? (d) Should the nature of the stimulus (the item) be pictorial, verbal, or of some other type? (e) Should the test (exam) be open- or closed-book?

Test Length

There is no readymade formula to tell the teacher how many items should be used. Suffice to say that the total number of items should be large enough to provide for an adequate sample of student behavior across objectives and content areas. Although the teacher's intent, especially on CRTs is to allow each student sufficient time to demonstrate his knowledge of the subject, there must be, for practical reasons, a time limit imposed on all classroom tests. The length of the test will vary according to its purpose, the kinds of items used, the reliability desired, the age and ability of the pupils tested, the time available for testing, the length and complexity of the item, the amount of computation required, and the instructional objective tested.

1. *Purpose.* If the test is only for a unit or chapter of work rather than for the total term's or year's work, it will require fewer items. For diagnostic (rather than prognostic) purposes, there will generally be a need for more items, inasmuch as the teacher is concerned with a more thorough and intensive coverage in a diagnostic test than she would be in a survey achievement test. The length of a test will also be dictated by whether the test is to be used for formative evaluation (where there is frequent testing) or for summative evaluation.

2. *Kinds of items used.* The essay question will require more time than the objective item. Short-answer items will require more time than true–false items. True–false items will require less time than multiple-choice items (Frisbie, 1971). Some general guidelines that we can offer about test length in relation to the kind of item format used are as follows:

A. For the four- or five-response multiple-choice item used in the higher elementary and senior high grades, the majority of students should be able to respond to the item in about 75 seconds. Hence, if the testing period is 50 minutes, the teacher can plan on using 35 five-response multiple-choice items. Although only about 44 minutes are used for actual testing, the remaining time is needed to distribute and collect the test, give directions, and answer any questions that the students might have. Naturally, the complexity of the subject matter and objectives being measured, the fineness of the discrimination needed, and the number of alternatives will affect the time needed for the pupil to respond to the item (Frisbie, 1971).[8]

B. For a short-essay response (about a half-page), most students can answer about six questions in a one-hour testing period. These estimates, of course, would vary according to the nature of the questions, the content area, and the students' age.

C. For the longer essay (two or three pages), most junior and senior high pupils can answer about three questions in one hour. For students in the fourth or fifth grade, one might only be able to ask two "long"

---

[8]Some research has shown that the three-response MC item is frequently about as good as the four- or five-response MC item (Ebel & Frisbie, 1986; Haladyna & Downing, 1989a). Hence, teachers using the three-response format should find that students take only about 60 seconds to answer the item and in a 50-minute testing period about 40 such items could be asked (the additional time is used to distribute and collect the materials).

essay questions in a one-hour testing period. If the teacher feels that she must use a longer essay test and if the ability and/or age of her pupils dictate a shorter testing time, she should divide the test and administer it on successive days.

D. For the short-answer, matching, or true–false item, a rough guideline is that it will take the pupil about 50 seconds to respond to each item.

E. For every pair of four-response multiple-choice questions answered, the student is able to answer three true–false items (Frisbie, 1971).

We strongly recommend that the teacher consider these times as *suggestive* only, and early in the term she should administer a test to her pupils, record the actual time required for the majority of her pupils to complete the test, and govern herself accordingly for future tests with these pupils. Remember—you do not want to hurry the student, but you must impose some arbitrary time limits.

3. *Reliability desired.* In Chapter 12 we point out that (other things being equal) the longer the test, the more reliable it tends to be, since random errors cancel each other out. Hence, the degree of reliability desired will influence test length.

4. *Pupil's age.* By and large, young children tend to read, write, and maybe even think slower than older children. Also, young children tend to become restless and tire more readily than older children. Hence, tests for primary grade pupils cannot be as long as tests for junior and senior high pupils. A general rule of thumb is that for pupils in the primary grades, we try to limit testing time to 30 minutes; for those in the intermediate elementary grades, we should make our testing time about 40 minutes; for junior and senior high school students, tests can take 90 minutes.

5. *Ability level of pupils.* Just as young children

need more time to respond to a test item than do older children, slow-learning children also require more time than average or gifted children. The teacher must know her pupils and be governed not only by the item format used, but also by the students' characteristics insofar as the length of the test is concerned.

6. *Time available for testing.* Most achievement tests, especially cognitive rather than skill tests, should be *power* rather than speed tests. Accordingly, nearly all of the students taking the test should be able to attempt every test item in the time allotted. We can think of few, if any, situations where speed is a relevant aspect of achievement. Remember: In an achievement test we are typically trying to learn *how much* students know and *not* how fast they can work.

7. *Length and complexity of the item.* The greater the amount of stimulus material (e.g., map or graph, tabular material, report of an experiment), the more reading time will be required and hence the fewer the number of items that can be asked in a given time. For example, the instructional objective is "Interpretation of Data Presented Graphically or in Tables," and the test item is as follows:

Cost of	1970	1975	1980	1990
Gas/gal.	$ 0.35	$ 0.32	$ 0.76	$ 1.10
Eggs/doz.	$ 0.70	$ 0.70	$ 0.60	$ 0.70
Shoes/pair	$40.00	$42.00	$50.00	$95.00

According to the chart, the article that has had the greatest percentage change in price from 1970 to 1990 is _____. More time will be needed for the student to respond than if the test item were:

"Write the formula for the mean _____."

8. *Amount of computation required.* Somewhat similar to our previous discussion of the type of item format used is the fact that if the items require a great deal of computation time, fewer items could be asked in a given time in contrast to items that are only verbal.

9. *Instructional objective tested.* Items that only require recall of factual material can be answered more quickly than those requiring understanding or the higher-order thinking skills.

It should be readily evident now why we said that there is no formula the classroom teacher can use to determine the length of her test. We have offered some suggestions regarding the time needed by pupils to read and respond to different item formats. But these are *suggestions* only and must be interpreted in the light of a variety of factors and conditions. Although more items may improve a test's reliability, we must realize that fatigue can distort a pupil's score appreciably. Use common sense, however. If pupils become restless, unruly, or disinterested, stop for a little break. Gauging the amount of time needed to complete a test is something that develops with experience. Much depends on the nature of the content and the skill of the teacher in writing clear, concise, unambiguous items. Each teacher must, through experience, determine time limits that are practical for her students and her test. When in doubt, be overgenerous in setting time limits. For a more extended discussion on the test length and setting of passing scores for criterion-referenced tests, see Millman (1972, 1973), Hambleton et al. (1978), and Hambleton (1984).

Item Difficulty[9]

Classroom teachers can make their tests very easy, very difficult, or in between.[10] Some teachers feel that they can purchase the respect of their students by giving them easy tests. They are wrong! Some other teachers feel that the more difficult the test, the better; that a difficult test will command respect from pupils and parents. They are also wrong. About the only positive thing that we know about difficult tests is that they tend to make pupils study harder (Sax & Reade, 1964; Marso, 1969). (Actually, it is the pupil's *anticipation* of a hard test that may do this since the pupils have to study *before* taking the test.) The concept of difficulty or the decision of how difficult the test should be depends on a variety of factors: notably, (a) the purpose of the test, (b) the ability level of the students, and (c) the age or grade level of the students. (These are the same factors that must be considered in planning the number of items as well as the item format to be used.) We do not think that it is bad to give a very easy test occasionally if for no other reason than to instill some feelings of confidence and self-respect in the slow-learning student. On the other hand, we recommend the use of an occasional hard test to challenge the brighter students. There is a time and a place for the more difficult test—it is especially valuable for the good students so that they will be prepared for such exams as the College Boards. But be careful not to make the difficult test so excessively difficult that you really frighten the students.

The concept of difficulty has more meaning for the objective type of test than it does for the essay or oral examination. In the former, the answer is either right or wrong; in the latter, there can be varying degrees of correctness. Item difficulty is also of more concern when we want the test to discriminate among pupils in terms of their achievement than if the test is designed to be used as a *diagnostic* or *mastery* test. In a diagnostic arithmetic test given in an average class, we might reasonably expect the majority of pupils to do well and have only a few relatively low scores (an "easy" test). In a diagnostic test we are *not* interested in comparing the relative standing of Ilene and Lori; rather, we want to know the strengths and weaknesses of *both* girls so that we can recommend appropriate remedial instruction if and

---

[9]Item difficulty is expressed in terms of the number of examinees who answer an item correctly. This will be discussed more fully in Chapter 8.

[10]Regretfully, most classroom achievement tests are on the easy side and focus primarily on testing for knowledge via factual recall (or recognition) items. It is also disappointing to see that students tend to judge novel, application-type problems as more difficult than knowledge items despite the fact that they are of similar difficulty (S. B. Green et al., 1989). If this is so, we might expect that items measuring higher-order thinking skills would be judged even more harshly.

when it is warranted. In a mastery test we would also expect the test to be relatively easy because, presumably, the teacher taught in such a way that certain minimal essentials (skills and/or knowledge) were learned or mastered by all or by a great majority of her pupils. If the test is being used as a pretest (i.e., given to the students before a particular unit or concept is introduced) to help develop effective teaching materials and/or strategies, we would expect most students to do poorly because they have not as yet been *taught* the material. Hence, for *mastery, diagnostic,* and *most pretests,* we are less concerned with difficulty because it is *not* our intent to differentiate or spread out people according to their achievement level. But there are many instances where our intent is to discriminate among pupils. For *selection* and *classification* purposes, we ordinarily want a test that produces a spread of scores.

To obtain information that will enable the teacher to differentiate (discriminate)[11] among her pupils in terms of their relative achievement, the teacher should prepare questions that, if no guessing occurs, about one-half of the pupils would be expected to answer the items incorrectly (the test is then said to be of average difficulty).

We believe that even a test used for discrimination purposes should contain a few very easy and a few very difficult items. If this policy were adopted, the poorer students could be motivated to continue, especially if the easy items were at the beginning of the test, while the brighter students could be challenged. *But, by far, the majority of the items should be of average difficulty.*

A very effective way to obtain item-difficulty estimates is to pilot the items on a group of students similar to those for whom the test is designed. Item-analysis techniques (see p. 161) can then be used to obtain difficulty and discrimination indices. Because pilot testing is generally impossible for the ordinary classroom teacher, sub-

jective judgment must often be relied on. We recommend that teachers only categorize their items as "difficult, average, or easy."

In summary, how difficult a test should be depends to a large extent upon its purpose. If the test results are to be used to describe the status of the individual pupils (criterion-referenced), item difficulty will not be a factor in the selection of the test items. However, if the test results are to be used to differentiate among pupils in terms of their achievement, the concept of test and item difficulty has meaning. This is still another reason that teachers must know what use will be made of the test results.

When to Test

Teachers often ask, "Should I test every week? Once or twice a semester?" Some teachers prefer to test on small segments of the course at frequent intervals. Other teachers prefer testing less frequently and on large units of the course. The majority of teachers usually govern themselves by the marking and reporting schedules of their schools. As of now, there is no evidence to show that a test based on a small segment of the course is better than a test that samples a larger unit of the work. We prefer frequent testing because it can provide a more thorough basis for keeping both teachers and students better informed of student (and teacher) progress.

Once again, the *uses* of the test results will determine the frequency of testing. In most objective-based instructional programs where formative evaluation procedures are appropriate, pupils are (or should be) given short, criterion-referenced tests frequently to inform the teacher of the pupils' performance and identify those in need of additional or remedial instruction.

The nature of the pupils may also affect the frequency of testing. Teachers dealing with the slow learner, the child in need of remedial instruction, and the very bright child may test at frequent intervals. Our opinion is that the teacher should determine the frequency of testing, for she is in the best position to make this decision. In general, we

---

[11]The extent to which we know how well the students are being differentiated by the items is referred to as item discrimination. Item discrimination will be discussed in greater detail in Chapter 8.

recommend that tests be administered at least twice a semester and, where feasible, more often since more frequent evaluation is superior to less frequent evaluation (Martin & Srikameswaran, 1974; Gallagher & Gay, 1976; Gaynor & Millman, 1976). We realize that too frequent testing might impinge on instructional time. However, we disagree with those critics of testing who contend that testing time detracts from teaching time. This may be so if poor tests are used or if the teacher does not use the results of the tests to obtain information on the pupils' strengths and weaknesses. But if valid tests are used, and if teachers take the time to analyze the nature of both the correct and incorrect responses, and if the test is discussed in class, test results can be an effective and valuable source of information for both teachers and learners.

Nature of the Stimulus: Verbal, Pictorial, or Other?

The nature of the test-item stimulus is highly dependent on the nature of the content being tested (e.g., a performance test in woodworking lends itself better to use of nonverbal stimuli) and the age of the pupils tested (very young children cannot read). For young children we recommend using lots of pictures, a minimum of verbal material (unless one is measuring reading or reading readiness), and a simple vocabulary appropriate to the students' age and ability, lest the test become a reading or general aptitude test.

Somewhat related are the questions of "How should the test items be presented? Should they be printed in a test booklet or should the items be administered by means of a filmstrip, slides, or other audio-visual methods?" Research has shown that examinees can be paced in their response rate to answer more rapidly if the test were administered by some audiovisual aid than they would working by themselves in a test booklet. And they could work faster without any loss in accuracy. A few years back, audio-visual test administration would have been unheard of. Today, however, computer-assisted testing is becoming more and more prev-

alent. (See the special issue of *Educational Measurement: Issues and Practice*, Vol. 3, No. 2, 1984, for a comprehensive look at computer testing.)

Open-Book versus Closed-Book Examinations

Most teachers want to maximize the opportunity for their students to do their best on classroom achievement tests. There is some disagreement, however, as to the best method for achieving this. There are some teachers who contend that students should be able to use any and all external aids such as notes, their text(s), and other references when taking an exam. Teachers preferring open-book exams say that (a) they eliminate cheating; (b) they do not substitute for studying because the time required to look through one's notes or references for answers will dissuade pupils from relying on these sources; (c) there are not too many instances in life where one cannot look up a formula, or equation, or piece of factual information; and (d) they make students study for the application and comprehension of knowledge rather than for sheer recall of facts. There are other teachers who disagree and say that the disadvantages far outweigh the value of open-book exams and contend that *no* aids should be permitted when taking an exam. Who is right?

The empirical evidence, although sparse, does indicate the following: (a) Students prefer open-book exams, possibly because they are less anxiety-producing. (b) There is very little difference in performance between students who take open-book exams and and those who take closed-book exams. (c) Different abilities are tested by the two methods. (For example, open-book exams test the higher mental processes of reasoning and judgment to a greater extent than do closed-book exams. We do *not* wish to imply that closed-book exams do *not* test higher-order thinking skills. They do! Our better standardized achievement and aptitude tests attest to this.) (d) Students prepare differently for the two types. (e) It is more difficult to discriminate between the better and average student in an open-book exam. What then?

It would appear that one's decision whether to use an open- or a closed-book exam is heavily dependent on one's instructional objectives. If the teacher's goals are to ascertain whether her students have mastered certain factual material (and there are many instances where it is important for students to memorize certain facts and details), then it is appropriate for her to use a closed-book exam. On the other hand, if the teacher's goals are to evaluate the students' grasp of, understanding of, and application of concepts; the students' ability to retrieve and synthesize information; and the students' ability to write a cogent report, then either an open- or closed-book exam would be appropriate.

GENERAL CONSIDERATIONS IN WRITING TEST ITEMS

Regardless of the item format used, the two essential ingredients of a good test item are that it must measure what it is designed to measure (validity) and must do so consistently (reliability). Validity and reliability of the individual items as well as the test as a whole can be achieved only when (a) each test item is expressed in clear, unambiguous language; (b) the students are not given any clues to the correct answer; (c) the scoring is objective; and (d) a table of specifications has been prepared and followed.

The different item formats are susceptible to different types of errors. These specifics will be dealt with when we consider the preparation of the essay question and the different types of objective items in the chapters to follow. However, there are some general factors that should be discussed at this time. Some have already been mentioned, and some will be elaborated on in Chapters 6 and 7, but we feel that they bear repetition because of their importance in writing good test items.

At the outset, we want to caution the reader that the writing of test items *cannot* be reduced to a set of rules that will guarantee that the test is reliable and has content validity. However, there are some guidelines and specific suggestions that should be considered by the classroom teacher when she changes into an item writer.

Preparing the Test Item[12]

1. *Carefully define your instructional objectives.* Without well-defined, specific, and clear instructional objectives, it will be very difficult to provide for optimal learning on the part of the student and optimal instruction on the part of the teacher. And, since a teacher-made test—regardless of the item format—is prepared specifically to measure the extent to which the instructional objectives have been realized, one cannot begin the preparation of a valid test without carefully defined instructional objectives.

2. *Prepare a table of specifications, keep it before you, and continually refer to it as you write the test item.* You will recall that the test blueprint or table of specifications relates the course objectives to the subject-matter content. The test item is an outgrowth of one or more cells of the table of specifications. Continually refer to your test blueprint to help ensure that you will have a test with adequate content validity.

3. *Formulate well-defined questions.* Some of the criticisms leveled against tests are the result of questions that are vague, ambiguous, and too global. Not only may such questions cause the student difficulty in that he is unsure of what the teacher is looking for, but they may also cause the teacher problems in reliably scoring the answer (especially the essay and short answer). In addition, the test items should be grammatically correct and free from spelling and typing errors.

4. *Avoid excess verbiage.* Verbal overload must be controlled lest the test become one of reading ability or general intelligence. Teachers, in their attempt to clarify, too often confuse rather than

---

[12]See Chambers (1984) for the development of an in-service training package to help teachers improve the quality of their pencil-and-paper tests.

elucidate by excessive wording. Avoid needlessly complex sentences.

5. *The test item should be based on information that the examinee should know (or be able to deduce from the context) without having to consult a reference source.* The best test contains only a sample of the possible questions that can be asked. And we are all aware that no one student can commit all the course content to memory. We should therefore not expect the student to have an encyclopedic mind. The course objectives upon which the test is based should not test minutiae unless those minute details are vital to meeting the course objectives. For example, in a course in pharmacology we should not expect students to memorize the dosages or limits of normal values of toxicity of every drug that is on the market. There are, of course, certain drugs that are frequently used or dispensed, and we might expect the student to know the characteristics of them. We should only test on information that is within the daily working knowledge of the examinee. Naturally, if certain formulae, for example, are needed to solve a problem, and a course objective was not to commit formulae to memory, they should be provided to the examinee. The crux of this issue, of course, is getting agreement as to what are the basic objectives.

6. *Use the most appropriate stimulus.* Although the actual test item may be verbal, if the test is based on some external stimulus, the stimulus need not be verbal. There are many instances in achievement testing where equipment configurations can only be presented pictorially or where the material in, say, economics might be clearer if presented in graphic or tabular form than by means of a verbal description. When this is the case, the nature of the stimulus is nonverbal. But the test-constructor must think about the most effective method of presenting the stimuli before the item is written. Schwartz (1955) compared illustrated items with written items and found, as might be expected, that illustrations were better in the lower grades than the upper grades. Accordingly, we recommend that at least for the lower elementary grades and for some specialized tech-

nical content areas, serious consideration be given to using an illustrated stimulus, a minimum of verbal material (unless one is measuring reading or reading readiness), and a vocabulary that is appropriate to the students' age and ability, lest the test become a general aptitude or reading test.

7. *Try to avoid race and sex bias.* Many persons, both within and outside the education profession, have criticized tests (primarily standardized tests), claiming that they exhibit a race and sex bias. We will discuss this issue more thoroughly in later chapters when we consider standardized tests and inventories. Even though bias is seldom a problem in teacher-made achievement tests, we believe that teachers should be aware of, and concerned with, these issues so that they will strive to develop tests that are as free as possible from race and sex bias.

Not directly related to achievement tests in general, or teacher-made tests in particular, are Scheuneman's (1987) findings. In studying the Graduate Record Examination, she recommended that to more favorably reflect the abilities of black examinees, item writers should (a) use quantitative language, diagrams, figures, or anything that will reduce verbiage; (b) try to avoid superlatives like *most* or *best* in the stem unless a definite distinction must be made between two potentially correct responses; and (c) avoid items that ask for the one *false* response.

We favor taking all possible precautions in using words or vocabulary that are free from racial or sexual bias or stereotyping. Teachers must correctly select words that are not differentially understood by different ethnic groups or by males and females. If all the story problems on a teacher-made mathematics test involved males engaged in athletic events or females engaged in homemaking activities, this would be an example of sex stereotyping. If one used the vocabulary of black inner-city youth and if these words were not understood by other students unfamiliar with this vocabulary, this would be an example of inappropriate, biased vocabulary unless one was specifically testing for the pupils' knowledge of these words. This last point needs to be emphasized! If vocabulary knowledge or understanding of a concept is the learning objective being tested and it is seen that one ethnic or racial or sex group does better on the test because they really know more or understand better, we would *not* call the test biased. But, if one group did better on a test because of the language used, the test *may* be biased. Actually, if teachers follow the guidelines offered in this and succeeding chapters for writing test items, there should be little bias in their tests.

8. *Write each test item on a separate card.* This will permit you to record any item-analysis data (see Chapter 8) directly with the item and will be the beginning of a test file that can be used for future tests. To assist in checking the test items against the blueprint so as to obtain content validity, we suggest that the item be keyed to the objective and content area measured, the key being placed in either the card's upper right- or left-hand corner. Finally, with each item on a separate card, it is easy to sort the cards so that all item formats are together.

9. *Prepare more items than you will actually need.* Every teacher should prepare extra test items to replace those discarded in the review process. For an essay test, we suggest that you prepare about 25 percent overage of items. For an objective test, we suggest about 25 percent extra items be written for each cell in the test blueprint. For example, assume that you wanted a 100-item objective science test. If 5 percent of the test is devoted to knowledge of methods of science, you should prepare 6 items. We are quite certain that some of your original items will have to be replaced. But even if you are fortunate and have to replace only 2 or 3 items, the remainder can be used as the base for a later test.

10. *Write and key the test item as soon as possible after the material has been taught.* The best time to write and key an item dealing with a particular behavioral objective (outcome) is immediately after covering the material in class. At this time the item appears in its complete context and the relationship of the item to a particular objective is most clear. Even if the teacher only sketches out two or three items when the material is presented in class,

over a period of time she will have a sizable pool of tentative items that can be refined later and incorporated into her test. By writing the items over a long period, the teacher avoids some of the problems discussed earlier.

11. *Prepare the items well in advance to permit review and editing.* Very seldom is an item writer fortunate enough to prepare a test item that does not require at least some slight revision or modification. Ideally, the review phase and subsequent editing should occur some days after the item has been written. This will allow the item writer to look at her items with a fresh perspective so that hopefully she will be able to see any errors she may have originally missed. One of the major faults of poor items is that they often do not communicate effectively the item writer's intent. The item writer knows implicitly what she is trying to measure—the pupil must be told explicitly. The best approach is to have a fellow teacher (one who teaches the same subject matter) review the test items and directions.

12. *Avoid specific determiners.* Don't give the test-wise student any undue advantage over the naive but equally knowledgeable student.

13. *Be careful when rewording a faulty item.* The item writer must be very careful in rewording an item that has been found faulty lest she alter the "match" between the item and the particular objective the item was originally written to measure. Subtle changes in the behavior measured are likely to occur when we rewrite some of the distractors in the multiple-choice item (Gronlund & Linn, 1990) and when we change a completion item to a multiple-choice item, or vice versa (Knapp, 1968).

14. *Insert some novelty into your test.* In a study of eighth graders, incorporating humor in test items had no effect on the test score nor did it lower test anxiety. However, the students favored inclusion of humor in tests and thought that the humorous items were easier (they weren't). We agree with McMorris et al. (1985, p. 154) who said that "if humor helps create a positive affect, reduces negative affect, and does not depress

scores, its use is warranted. . . . With the inclusion of humor, the whole testing industry could be somewhat more humane." This latter point is significant considering the public's as well as students' views of testing.

15. *Avoid textbook or stereotyped language.*

16. *Obtaining the correct answer to one test item should not be based on having correctly answered a prior item.*

For those interested in another approach to item development, Willson (1989) presents an excellent, although somewhat theoretical, discussion of the various components to be considered in the development of aptitude- and achievement-test items. With respect to the latter, he says that item writers should pay attention to (a) prior knowledge needed by the test-taker to answer the item, (b) item features (such as the use of different test stimuli) perceptible to the test-taker but independent of prior knowledge, (c) learner processes involved in the solution of the problem, and (d) response qualities to be assessed (e.g., in a multiple-choice item one could look at the correct answer only, the distracters selected, or both).

Computer-Assisted Item Writing

Computers are being used to construct tests (Millman & Arter, 1984), to develop test items (Oosterhof, 1990; Cronbach, 1990), to administer and score tests and interpret the results (Millman & Arter, 1984), to provide feedback (Oosterhof, 1990), and for record-keeping purposes (Hsu & Nitko, 1983). However, the actual writing of test items by computer is now only beginning to appear, with greater frequency on the horizon.

Millman and Westman (1989) present five approaches (actually there are only four) to computer-assisted item writing that rely heavily on artificial intelligence. Using a hierarchy of computer involvement in the actual test-item writing, the approaches are (a) the author-supplied approach, (b) the replacement-set procedures, (c) the computer-supplied prototype items, (d) subject-matter

mapping, and (e) discourse analysis. In the first approach, the author-supplied approach, the item is written completely by the author, and the computer acts only as a typewriter to print the items and then store them for later retrieval. Hence, this is not really an approach or technique as are the others. In the replacement-set procedures approach, the items are produced according to algorithms, and the computer acts more as a processor of the information programmed than an actual item writer. In the computer-supplied prototype items, the item writer and computer interact to write the text for the item. In the subject-matter mapping approach, the item writer and computer work interactively to build a frame—a network of nodes and relations—and using instructions supplied by the item writer, the computer generates "rough" items for the item writer to review. In the fifth stage—discourse analysis—algorithms are used for the analysis and transformation of text into test questions.

According to Millman and Westman, the most viable approach is the computer-supplied prototype items approach, and they present a detailed description of how one can use this approach. We agree with them that this technology will no doubt be used primarily by commercial test publishers. However, with more and more school systems having access to computer facilities, developing and maintaining their own test files, and becoming involved in student-competency testing, we envisage that computer-assisted item writing will filter down to classroom teachers in the next decade.[13]

WHAT DOES IT TAKE TO BE A GOOD ITEM WRITER?

The process of writing good test items is not simple—it requires time and effort. It also requires certain skills and proficiencies on the part of the

---

[13]A variety of software programs are available today to assist the classroom teacher. IBM, for example, has the Teacher's Quiz Designer, which creates, edits, and administers tests to students and keeps track of student scores and averages.

item writer, some of which can be improved by formal course work; others require considerable practice. Rules, suggestions, guidelines, and text-books may be useful, but they are *not* magic wands for producing high-quality test items. Just as a surgery course in third-year medical school does not prepare the student to be a certified surgeon, no single course in tests and measurements (nor, for that matter, reading a textbook) will prepare a student to be an innovative item writer. There is no doubt, however, that all the following aids will be of some assistance, *provided* the item writer is willing to devote the necessary time and energy to the preparation of test items. In the long run, practice of the rules of item writing will help one achieve proficiency.

To be a good item writer, one should be proficient in six areas.

1. *Know the subject matter thoroughly.* The greater the item writer's knowledge of the subject matter, the greater the likelihood that she will know and understand *both* facts and principles as well as some of the popular misconceptions. This latter point is of considerable importance when writing the selection type of item in general, and the multiple-choice item in particular (because the item writer must supply plausible although incorrect answers).

2. *Know and understand the pupils being tested.* The kinds of pupils the teacher deals with will determine in part the kind of item format, vocabulary level, and level of difficulty of the teacher-made test. For example, primary school teachers seldom use multiple-choice items because young children are better able to respond to the short-answer type. The vocabulary level used for a class of gifted children will probably be very different from that used with a class of educable mentally retarded children. The classroom teacher who knows and understands her pupils will generally establish more realistic objectives and develop a more valid measurement device than will the teacher who fails to consider the characteristics of her students.

3. *Be skilled in verbal expression.* Some of the major deficiencies of teacher-made achievement tests are related to problems of communication—ambiguous wording, poor choice of words, and awkward sentence structure. The item writer must be scrupulously careful when expressing herself verbally. It is essential that the item writer clearly convey to the examinee the intent of the question.

4. *Be thoroughly familiar with various item formats.* The item writer must be knowledgeable of the various item formats—their strengths and weaknesses, the errors commonly made in writing this or that type of item—and the guidelines that can assist her in preparing better test items.

5. *Be persevering.* Writing good test items, regardless of their format, is both an art and a skill that generally improves with practice. There are very few, if any, professional item writers who are so gifted, able, and blessed that they can write an item that requires absolutely no editing or rewriting. Classroom teachers who are trained as teachers rather than as item writers should be persevering and not give up hope, even though the task seems overwhelming.

6. *Be creative.* The abundance of sterile, pedantic items normally found on teacher-made achievement tests results from the reluctance of teachers to be creative. Tests need not be somber and imposing. Items can be novel! Occasionally, in the item stem or descriptive material (or pictorial) upon which some items are based, the writer can inject some humor. For example, in an arithmetic test, why not in a word problem on addition say "Mr. Adder," instead of Mr. Jones? At the same time that we urge you to be creative, we must caution you not to become too creative, since your enthusiasm might lead to the preparation of items that no longer test for, or are related to, the instructional objective for which they have been written. Also, be careful that in your attempt to become creative you do not become overly verbose.

Ideas for the Test Items

While the table of specifications lists the content areas to be covered and the relative emphasis to be placed on each area and instructional objective, it does *not* directly give the item writer ideas that she can develop into test items. These the item writer must supply on her own. Where, then, does the classroom teacher get ideas? Primarily from the textbook or syllabus, other tests, journal articles, and questions raised by her pupils in class. It is not too difficult to develop ideas for measuring factual recall of information. It becomes progressively more difficult as one climbs the hierarchy in the taxonomy (Bloom et al., 1956) and as one tries to invent appropriate novel situations. The final selection of ideas to be developed into test items is dependent on (a) the purpose of the test, (b) the test blueprint, (c) the importance of specific material covered in class, and (d) the items' ability to discriminate between those students who do and do not know the material. Each of these factors must be considered.

CONSTRUCTING CRITERION-REFERENCED TESTS

Criterion-referenced tests (CRTs) appeal to classroom teachers because they can be tailored to match what is actually being taught, they provide diagnostic information that is valuable to both teacher and student, and they may suggest strategies for program and instructional improvement.

The procedures (and principles to be followed) for writing criterion-referenced test items do not differ appreciably from those to be considered when writing norm-referenced test items. In fact, one cannot distinguish between a criterion-referenced and norm-referenced item merely by inspection. *Both* CRTs and NRTs should be developed with a table of specifications; *both* should be concerned with validity and reliability, and *both* should help users make decisions about the individual, differing only in the context within which these decisions are made. Generally speaking, we do not expect CRTs to have norms, but it is not unusual to find them having some normative data (Popham, 1978). The major differences between a well-constructed CRT and NRT is that the CRT has a more limited focus (fewer objectives but they are more thoroughly measured by having more test items per objective) and the CRT has a well-defined, precise test domain.

The major difficulty but perhaps the most important steps in constructing CRTs are defining the test domain and then developing test tasks that are clearly members of the domain. Two general approaches frequently used to construct CRTs are (a) the empirical approach and (b) the universe-defined approach.[14] In the empirical approach, items are selected on the basis of their ability to differentiate between pupils who *have* been taught the material and those who have *not* been taught the material (this will be discussed in greater detail in Chapter 8). In the universe-defined approach, a universe or domain is specified and a "pool" of items is developed. The goal of the universe-defined method is to define the universe of all possible items in a given domain so that one may be able to generalize from an individual's test score on a representative sample of items to a statement about his proficiency in the total domain. Associated with this is developing the set(s) of rules needed to generate the test items (see Hively et al. 1968; Osburn, 1968.) The Osburn and Hively methods are similar in that both use the item-form approach, that is, they generate a population of items that directly mirror the logical structure of the subject-matter content in some domain rather than the learning outcomes of the sort usually embodied in instructional objectives. Hively's model differs from Osburn's in that instructional objectives are clearly transformed into item forms without going through the subject-matter structure. Thus, for each skill, a series of domains is specified, and within each domain the skills to be tested

---

[14]See Jackson (1970), Millman (1973), Hambleton et al. (1978), Martuza (1979), Popham (1981), Roid (1984), and Berk (1984) for reviews of literature on constructing criterion-referenced tests.

are listed. For each skill, an item form consisting of a "general form" and a series of "generation" rules is developed (see Popham, 1984 for a more detailed discussion). Unfortunately, there are few domains other than computational problems in science and mathematics and possibly certain facets of reading (such as comprehension) where it would be possible to specify item-generation rules of the type Hively proposed. In addition, our technology, to date, restricts us to measuring the lower-level mental processes such as recall or computation. It would appear then that a combination of the Osburn and Hively models would be best. Then, the test-constructor will have her domain (collection of item forms) from which test items can be selected, and the teacher will have her domain that clearly specifies what is to be taught. Even though there have been tremendous advances, much work remains to be done before this becomes feasible for classroom teachers.

In constructing a CRT, one does *not* want to have a large spread of scores (variability). In fact, after the pupils have been taught, we would hope that nearly all of them answered all the items correctly.

Most NRTs use multiple-choice or true–false items. In CRTs where we expect students to "do"—for example, to balance an equation, to label a diagram—it has been suggested (Hills, 1981) that items be of the supply-type (short-answer or essay).

Two additional factors that must be considered when developing CRTs are (a) the number of items needed to measure reliably each of the instructional objectives being tested and (b) the criterion or cutoff score to reliably indicate mastery. Generally speaking, between 5 and 20 test items per behavior is sufficient (Popham, 1978). However, if significant decisions are to be made on the basis of the test results, we recommend between 10 and 20 items per instructional objective tested.

■ SUMMARY

The principal ideas, conclusions, and recommendations presented in this chapter are summarized in the following statements:

1. Teacher-made test results are often the major basis for evaluating student progress.
2. All teachers have an obligation to assess the efficacy of their instructional procedures. The teacher-made test is one procedure for accomplishing this.
3. Although paper-and-pencil tests are the most frequently used formal evaluation procedure, some important instructional objectives can be evaluated only by observational techniques.
4. Classroom tests, despite some of their limitations, will never be replaced because they (a) tend to be more relevant, (b) can be tailored to fit a teacher's particular instructional objectives, and (c) can be adapted better to fit the needs and abilities of the students than can commercially published tests.
5. A major deficiency of teacher-made tests is that they suffer from inadequate planning.
6. Teacher-made tests may be classified on the basis of item format, nature of stimulus material, and purpose.
7. Classroom tests may be classified as either essay or objective. Objective tests may be classified as supply or select type.
8. In the test-planning stage, one must consider two general questions: (a) What is the purpose of the test? (b) What is the best means whereby the purpose can be achieved?
9. In developing a specific measuring instrument, the first task is to review the instructional objectives. Following this, the objectives are expressed in terms of student behavior. Then, a table of specifications should be constructed.
10. The table of specifications ideally should relate the content to the instructional objectives.
11. There should be a match between every item and every instructional objective.
12. The essay test is especially appropriate for measuring the pupil's ability to synthesize his ideas and express them logically and coherently in written form. Its major limitations are that it has limited content sampling and low scorer reliability.

13. The objective test permits the teacher to obtain a broader sampling of content in a given time, has higher scorer reliability, and is less susceptible to bluffing than is the essay test.
14. Both the objective and essay test have important roles to play in evaluating pupil achievement.
15. In the planning stage, before a test item is written, a variety of factors—such as the test's purpose, type of item format, length, difficulty, and nature of the stimulus material—must be considered.
16. The determination of appropriate item difficulty depends on the purpose of the test. In general, achievement tests should be of average difficulty. A test that is either too difficult or too easy provides the teacher with little meaningful information.
17. The two major considerations that item writers must consider relate to (a) clarity of communication from the item writer to the examinee and (b) writing the item so that the answer is not given away.
18. Skilled item writers know their subject matter thoroughly, understand their pupils, are skilled in verbal expression, and are familiar with the various item formats.
19. Criterion-referenced item writers employ procedures and principles essentially similar to those used by norm-referenced item writers.
20. The two most commonly used approaches for constructing criterion-referenced tests are the empirical approach and the universe-defined approach. In the former, items are selected on the basis of their ability to discriminate between pupils who have been taught the material and those who have not. In the latter, items are generated on the basis of item-generation rules.

■ POINTS TO PONDER

1. Discuss the four major deficiencies of teacher-made tests. Point out what step(s) can be taken to help overcome each of the deficiencies.
2. Prepare a table of specifications for a 20-item test on Chapter 4 of this text.
3. What are the major factors that one must consider in the planning stage of the test?
4. If a teacher wishes to determine whether her pupils can synthesize, should she use an objective-type test? Why?
5. Under what circumstances should item difficulty and item discrimination be a consideration when planning a test?
6. Discuss the empirical and universe-defined approaches in the construction of a criterion-referenced test.
7. Do you believe that the time will come when teacher-made achievement tests will be replaced? Defend your answer.
8. Should achievement tests in a school system be developed by the individual teacher or by a committee? Discuss the pros and cons of each approach.
9. How would you defend your use of objective-type tests to a group of parents who were opposed to these tests?

Chapter 5

The Essay Test: Preparing the Questions and Grading the Responses

© 1970 United Feature Syndicate, Inc.

■ **Classification of the Essay Question**
■ **Advantages and Limitations of the Essay Test**
■ **Why Are Essay Tests Still Popular?**
■ **Suggestions for Preparing Good Essay Tests**
■ **An Example of the Development of a Good Essay Question**
■ **Grading Essays**
■ **The Oral Question**

In Chapter 4, our activities in the development of a high-quality, accurate test of pupil achievement focused on what might be referred to as the "get ready" or planning stage. It is in this planning stage that the purposes of the test are set forth, the table of specifications (which relates the course content to the instructional objectives) is prepared, thought is given to the kind of item format to be used, and decisions are made about the length and difficulty of the test. The next step is to write test items. We must now translate our behavioral objectives into test questions that will elicit the types of behavior we are interested in measuring. One type of test item is the essay question.

With the exception of the oral test, the essay is the oldest test format in use today. The distinctive features of the essay question are: (1) the examinee is permitted freedom of response, and (2) the answers vary in degree of quality of correctness (Stalnaker, 1951).

Because for many teachers the essay examination is the one used most frequently (whether appropriately or inappropriately), it seems advisable to try to develop procedures that will maximize the advantages and at the same time minimize the limitations of essay examinations. In this chapter we consider (1) the two major types of essay questions, (2) the advantages and limitations of the essay question, (3) the reasons that essay tests are still so popular with teachers despite the many criticisms leveled at them, (4) some suggestions on how to prepare and grade the essay question, and (5) the oral question.

After studying this chapter, you should be able to:

1. Understand the differences between the restricted- and extended-response essay question.
2. List the two most serious limitations of essay questions and discuss methods of combating these limitations.
3. Discuss the reasons that essay tests are so popular, pointing out which reasons are supported by empirical research and which are mainly hearsay.
4. Follow the guidelines offered when constructing essay questions.
5. Differentiate between global and analytical scoring.
6. Follow the guidelines offered when grading essay questions.
7. Discuss the similarities between the essay and oral question.
8. Appreciate the value of, and need for, the essay question in classroom tests.
9. Do a better job in constructing and grading the essay question.

CLASSIFICATION OF THE ESSAY QUESTION

Essay questions are subdivided into two major types—*extended* and *restricted* response—depending on the amount of latitude or freedom given the student to organize his ideas and write his answer.

Extended Response

In the *extended*-response type of essay question virtually no bounds are placed on the student as to the point(s) he will discuss and the type of organization he will use. This advantage, unfortunately, is counterbalanced by the fact that *flexibility* and *freedom of choice* contribute to (1) the essay being an inefficient format for measuring specific instructional objectives and (2) scorer unreliability (this will be discussed later in the chapter). An example of an extended-response essay question for students in a measurement course would be:

> Describe what you think should be included in a school testing program. Illustrate with specific tests, giving reasons for your test selection. Your essay should be about 300 to 400 words in length (2 to 3 pages).

An example for students in twelfth-grade literature is:

> Do you believe that the portrayal of Shylock supports the claim made by some that Shakespeare was anti-Semitic? Support your answer. Your essay should be about 2 to 3 pages long (300 to 400 words).

An example for fifth-grade students is:

> What keeps a hot-air balloon from falling to the ground?

In answering the first question, the student may select those aspects of the school testing program that he *thinks* are most important, pertinent, and relevant to his argument; and he may organize the material in whichever way he wishes. In short, the extended-response type of essay question permits the student to demonstrate his ability to (1) call on factual knowledge, (2) evaluate his factual knowledge, (3) organize his ideas, and (4) present his ideas in a logical, coherent written fashion. It is at the levels of synthesis and evaluation of writing skills (style, quality) that the extended-response essay question makes the greatest contribution.

Restricted Response

In the *restricted*-response essay question, the student is more limited in the form and scope of his answer because he is told specifically the context that his answer is to take. An example of the restricted-response essay question for high school or college students is:

> Pavlov found that sometimes dogs he had previously conditioned to salivate when a bell rang failed to do so later on. How do you account for this? Your answer should be about one-half page in length.

An example for the upper elementary or middle school is:

> Tell how plants make food. Your answer should be about one-half page long.

These questions are *more* restrictive than the example given for the extended-response essay in that the student must only address himself to one specific area rather than discuss a variety of alternatives.

By aiming the student at the desired response we minimize somewhat the problems of unreliable scoring, and we may possibly make scoring easier. But by restricting the student's response we give up one of the major advantages of the essay question—a measure of the student's ability to synthesize his ideas and express them in a logical, coherent fashion. Because of this, the restricted-response type of essay is of greatest value for measuring learning outcomes at the comprehension, application, and analysis level, and its use is best reserved for these purposes.

Examples of Different Types of Essay Questions

One can make a more elaborate classification of essay questions on the basis of the types of mental activities required of the pupil. Weidemann (1933, p. 82) classified the essay examination into 11 major categories. Arranged from the simple to higher mental processes, these categories are as follows: (1) *what, who, when, which,* and *where;* (2) *list;* (3) *outline;* (4) *describe;* (5) *contrast;* (6) *compare;* (7) *explain;* (8) *discuss;* (9) *develop;* (10) *summarize;* and (11) *evaluate.* In Monroe and Carter's (1923) 20-category scheme, the question itself describes specifically the nature of information to be recalled by the student in answering the question. However, it is very difficult to classify each of Monroe and Carter's 20 categories as either restricted or extended, since the nature of the question posed will, in many instances, determine whether it calls for a restricted or an extended response. What is more important, however, are the kinds of questions that can be posed.

It will be readily evident when you read the examples given below that some of the classifications are related more to the *restricted* response; others, to the *extended* response.

1. Comparison of two things:
   Compare norm- and criterion-referenced measurement.
2. Causes or effects:
   Why did fascism develop in Italy and Germany but not in the United States or England?
3. Analysis:
   Does the Gulf of Tonkin resolution suffice as an explanation of U.S. involvement in Indochina? Support your answer with reasons.
4. Discussion:
   Discuss Canadian Confederation under the following headings:
   a. The important reasons for a union
   b. The Confederation Conference
   c. The reasons for a choice of a federal union
   d. The important terms of the B.N.A. Act
   e. The division of powers between the Dominion and Provincial governments
5. Reorganization of facts:
   Trace the development of the industrial (in contrast to the laboratory) preparation of nitric acid.
6. Formulation of new question (problems and questions raised):
   Assuming that (1) the East and West will continue in their arms buildup, (2) more of the smaller nations will develop nuclear arms, and (3) minor skirmishes will be on the increase, what are some of the problems that people will have to face in the next decade? Discuss at least three such problems.
7. Criticism (as to the adequacy, correctness, or relevance of a printed statement):
   Criticize or defend the statement: "The central conflict in Barometer Rising is between Geoffrey Wain and Neil Macrae."

ADVANTAGES AND LIMITATIONS OF THE ESSAY TEST

The advantages of the essay examination most frequently cited are that (1) it is easier to prepare an essay test than to prepare a multiple-choice test; (2) it is the only means that we have to assess an examinee's ability to compose an answer and present it in effective prose (Ebel & Damrin, 1960); (3) it tests the pupil's ability to *supply* rather than select the correct answer; (4) it helps induce a "good" effect on student learning; (5) many students prefer essay over multiple-choice tests; (6) open-ended and free-response items would "... allow ... inferences about the thought-processes contributing to an answer" (Alexander & James, 1987); and (7) they possess ecological validity or present a realistic situation (How many real-life problems present themselves in a multiple-choice format? Do we not generally work out the solution to a problem in a supply-type atmosphere?).

The two most serious limitations of essay tests are (1) their poor (limited) content sampling, especially in the extended-response type of essay, and (2) their low reader reliability. Regardless of the thoroughness with which an essay test is constructed, you cannot sample the course content as well with 6 lengthy essay questions as you could with 90 multiple-choice questions. Not surprisingly, some students do better on some questions while others do better on others (Godshalk et al., 1966; Gosling, 1966). Thus, a student's raw score (and relative score) will depend to some extent on the particular questions asked. The more questions, the less likely a student's score will suffer because of inadequate sampling of content and the greater the likelihood that the test will be reliable. Therefore, essay tests that contain several questions requiring short answers are preferable to a test that asks only one or two questions requiring a lengthy answer.

The second major problem, that of reader reliability, can be minimized by careful construction of the questions and by setting up specified scoring procedures. To give you some idea as to the magnitude of the problem of reader reliability, let us relate the study of Falls (1928), which, though a study of reader reliability of an actual essay response, gave results highly similar to results of essay tests. In 1928, Falls had 100 English teachers grade copies of an essay written by a high school senior. The teachers were required to assign both a numerical grade to the essay as well as to indicate what grade level they thought the writer was in. The grades varied from 60 to 98 percent and the grade level varied from fifth grade to a junior in college! With this type of variation across readers, it is no wonder that measurement specialists are concerned about the adequacy of essays (or essay tests) as evaluation procedures. If a score is so dependent on who reads the paper rather than on the quality of the written exposition, it is probably not a very accurate reflection of the student's achievement.[1]

A third problem or limitation of essay tests is that the student does not always understand the questions and therefore is not sure how to respond. (This problem also occurs in objective items but to a much less degree.)

A fourth limitation of the essay examination relates to the amount of time needed to read and grade the essay. Reading essays is very time-consuming and laborious. Unlike objective items, essays can be read only by the teacher and/or competent professionals. This is still the case, even though there was earlier research conducted to study the feasibility of grading essays by computer (Page, 1966, 1967, 1972; Whalen, 1971).

We do not deny that some valid criticisms can be leveled at essay tests. True, the questions may be ambiguous, the students may be able to bluff their way through an essay test, and the grading may be dependent as much on the idiosyncracies of the reader as on the quality of the response. This does *not* mean that the essay test question should be removed from either teacher-made or commercially published tests. The fault lies in the construction and scoring of the essay examination and is *not* inherent in the essay item, per se. It would indeed be unfortunate if essay questions were abolished from achievement tests, because they perform an important function in measuring one of our more important educational objectives—the ability to select and synthesize ideas and express oneself in writing.

French stated the point well when he said:

> So, if we psychometricians can encourage testing and further clarification of those aspects of writing that objective tests cannot measure, encourage the use of readers who favor grading the particular qualities that are desirable to grade, and see to it that the students are aware of what they are being graded on, we can enlighten rather than merely disparage the polemic art of essay testing (1965, p. 596).

WHY ARE ESSAY TESTS STILL POPULAR?

As Coffman (1971) pointed out, "Essay examinations are still widely used in spite of more than a half century of criticism by specialists in educational measurement." Reintroduction of an essay question into the 1977 College Board English Composition Test, after a six-year lapse, and its inclusion in the new ETS Basic Skills Assessment Program and in some state testing programs should be interpreted cautiously. However, this does *not* indicate that an expanded use of essay questions in general is underway, because in these programs, essays are actually being used as *writing* tests rather than as a testing format for a content area.

Given the potential disadvantages of essay tests—limited content sampling, scorer unreliability, and scoring costs—why are they still in use, especially since there is a fairly high relationship (correlation) between direct (essay) and indirect (objective) measures of writing skill? Many reasons have been advanced for their popularity and importance in classroom testing. Perhaps one rea-

---

[1]See also Eells (1930), who showed that teachers scoring the same set of papers on a several month interval between readings did not agree with their original judgments of the papers' quality. See also Starch and Elliott (1912), Marshall (1967), and Coffman and Kurfman (1968).

son is that teachers are unaware of their limitations. However, there are other reasons—some with which we agree and others with which we disagree.

Acceptable Claims-Supporting Evidence

1. *Essay tests can indirectly measure attitudes, values, and opinions.* The student may be more likely to reveal his true feelings in an extended-response essay than if he responded on an attitude scale because, in the latter, he might consciously provide a socially acceptable answer. There is some evidence that the extended-response essay serves as a projective technique (Sims, 1931).

2. *Good essay tests are more easily prepared than are good objective tests.* It is easier, per unit of testing time, to prepare a good essay examination because only a few essay questions are needed for an essay test, in comparison to the number of objective items needed for an objective test.

No doubt the factors of cost, time, and difficulty in writing multiple-choice test items to measure the higher mental processes make and keep the essay test popular.

3. *Essay tests provide good learning experiences.* Developing one's ability to select ideas, organize them, synthesize them, and express them in written form is an important educational objective. By writing essays, students are given practice in organizing their ideas, expressing their thoughts, and thinking through solutions to problems. Essay tests are a good learning experience for students (Vallance, 1947), especially when teachers take time to write comments on the papers. However, we do not feel that this is a very good or efficient way to teach writing skills because of artificial time constraints. Rather, we encourage teachers to use take-home projects, term papers, and the like. We believe they are a superior measure of writing skill.

4. *The use of essay tests may serve as an incentive for teachers to engage in more thorough and effective*

instruction in good writing skills. That is, the *type* of test, as well as the content, drive instruction.

Rejected Claims—Justifying Evidence

1. *The essay test and only the essay test can be used to measure the higher mental processes of analysis and evaluation.* Although different skills are measured by essay and objective items, we can cite no evidence to substantiate proponents' claims that the essay test is superior to the objective test for measuring learning outcomes involving the higher mental processes. Ackerman and Smith (1988) found, for example, that procedural type writing skills are better measured by the direct methods while indirect methods were better for testing declarative-type writing skills.

This does not mean that essay tests are useless and should be abolished from our classroom testing programs. Essay tests are probably the *best* procedure for measuring some characteristics, such as writing ability, and the ability to create, synthesize, and evaluate ideas. But some objectives such as analysis and comprehension can perhaps be better (more objectively) measured by using a type of free-response (see Ackerman & Smith, 1988) or the objective-type item. As an example, we use two questions cast in different formats but measuring the same skills with each item format.

The Setting or Background Information
A little mining town in Pennsylvania gets all of its water from a clear mountain stream. In a cabin on the bank of the stream above the town one of two campers was sick with typhoid fever during the winter. His waste materials were thrown on the snow. In the spring the melting snow and other water ran into the stream. Several days after the snow melted, typhoid fever and death struck the town. Many of the people became sick and 144 people died.[2]

---

[2]Louis M. Heil et al., "The Measurement of Understanding in Science," in *The Measurement of Understanding*, 45th Yearbook of the National Society for the Study of Education, Part I. Nelson B. Henry, ed. (Chicago: University of Chicago Press, 1946), pp. 129–130.

Essay Question

Does the incident described above show how the illness of one person caused the illness and death of many people? Support your answer using scientific facts or principles. (Your answer should be about 300 to 400 words in length [2 to 3 pages].)

Objective Question[3]

Part A. Directions: Below is a list of statements about the story. If you were to say that the man's sickness caused the sickness and death in the town, you may believe some or all of the statements. If a statement says something that an intelligent person should believe, then mark it as true.

Part B. Directions: If you were to decide that the man's sickness caused the sickness and death in the town, you would want to be sure about several things before you made that decision. Read the statements below again and check (√) the three which you believe are the most important to be sure about before you decide that the man's sickness caused the sickness and death in the town. Do not check more than three.

Part A I believe the statement is true.		Statements	Part B
Yes	No		
————	————	A. Water in mountain streams usually becomes pure as it runs over rocks.	—— a
————	————	B. Typhoid fever germs in drinking water may cause typhoid fever.	—— b
————	————	C. All of the drinking water of a small town like this one came from the mountain stream.	—— c
————	————	D. In a small town like this one there would not be nearly so many people sick at the same time with typhoid as the story tells.	—— d
————	————	E. Typhoid germs were the only kind of germs in the water.	—— e
————	————	F. There was no other possible way of getting typhoid—such as an impure milk supply in the town.	—— f
————	————	G. Typhoid fever germs did not get into the stream from some source other than the sick man.	—— g
————	————	H. A person by himself, like the camper, can get typhoid.	—— h

2. *Essay tests promote more effective study habits than do objective tests.* As of now, there is *no* proof that essay tests are superior to objective tests insofar as motivation and study habits are concerned. Earlier research showed only that different skills are involved when the student *supplies* rather than selects the answer and that the study habits differ depending on whether one is writing an essay or objective exam.

---

[3]Heil et al. (1946), p. 130

SUGGESTIONS FOR PREPARING GOOD ESSAY TESTS

You will recall that the essay test places a premium on the student's ability to produce, integrate, and express his ideas and allows the student to be original and creative. These are the major distinguishing factors between the essay and objective item insofar as the purpose(s) of the test is concerned. A well-prepared essay question should give the student the opportunity to reveal those skills and abilities that you are interested in measuring. Merely writing a question in the essay format does *not* guarantee that these skills will be tapped. For example, the question "Compare the extended- and restricted-response essay item" will require very little on the examinee's part other than the regurgitation of factual material.

Although we cannot give any "pat" answers to the question "In a given amount of testing time, how can the essay test yield the most accurate sample of an examinee's achievement?" we can offer some suggestions that, if followed, may help make this goal attainable.

1. *The essay question should be used only to assess those instructional objectives that cannot be satisfactorily measured by objective items.* There are many instances where an essay test is used to measure factual recall or simple understanding of a concept or principle. No doubt you are all familiar with items such as "Define valence." "What are mutations?" "What is a pronoun?" and so forth. This is a poor use of the essay examination. It is not appropriate to use the essay examination for the "who, where, when" situation (the objective test is vastly superior from the standpoint of adequate content sampling and reliable scoring). The major advantage of the essay examination is that it gives the student the opportunity to decide for himself *what* he wants to say (select ideas that he feels are most relevant to his discourse), *how* he wants to say it (organization of ideas), and then present his thoughts in his own words. If one of our instructional objectives is "the student will be able to select, integrate, and write effectively," the only way that we are able to measure the student's achievement is to have him write on a number of different topics and then grade his performance. For this objective, the essay is the most appropriate and valid medium. It boils down to this: If you want to see how well a student is able to express himself (be it on a writing sample in English composition or a discourse on the inevitability of the Civil War), by all means use the essay test. If you are concerned with his thoughts or feeling about an issue and how he defends them, to explain methods and procedures, by all means use the essay test. If you are interested in measuring the stu-

dent's ability to criticize, to state cause-and-effect relationships, to apply principles in a novel situation, you could use *either* the essay or objective test. *But do not use the essay test to measure rote memory of facts or definitions.*

2. *Give adequate time and thought to the preparation of essay questions.* In a given testing time one can ask fewer essay than objective items. Hence, "goofs" made in preparing essay questions loom greater than those committed in an objective test. (One or two ambiguous questions in a 100-item objective test will have significantly less effect on the pupil's score than would one poor essay question worth 20 points.) Faults, such as failure to delimit the problem, ambiguity of wording, and the global nature of the question, are all directly related to inadequate thought being given to the preparation of essay questions. Although the idea for an essay question and the preliminary wording may come more quickly than for a true–false or multiple-choice item, the teacher should allow herself sufficient time to edit each question so that she is satisfied that (1) it is measuring the intended objective, (2) the wording is simple and clear to the students, and (3) it is reasonable and can be answered by the students. Unless adequate time has elapsed from the preliminary planning to the final writing of the essay question, it is very doubtful that the teacher can prepare a valid essay examination.

3. *The question should be written so that it will elicit the type of behavior you want to measure.* On the surface, this statement appears to be both obvious and easy to do. It is not. If a teacher is interested in learning the extent to which her history class students understand the difference between the League of Nations and the United Nations, she should not frame a question such as "What do you think of the United Nations in comparison to the League of Nations?" Framed this way, she will elicit the students' *opinions* rather than their understanding of the two organizations. If she is interested in measuring understanding, she should not ask a question that will elicit an opinion.

4. *A well-constructed essay question should establish a framework within which the student operates.* We recognize that there must be a "tradeoff" of some sort in making questions sufficiently specific and detailed to remove any possible sources of ambiguity[4] and yet give the student sufficient latitude to demonstrate his abilities. Latitude of response should not be interpreted as complete freedom of response. The teacher preparing essay tests must carefully tread the path between highly specific essay questions and too-general questions that confuse the student and for which no answer can be adequately given in the allotted time. We recognize that in our attempts to "aim" the student, we might remove one of the virtues of the essay examination—to measure the student's ability to select, integrate, and express his ideas. We take the position that we would rather remove some of the uniqueness of the essay test if by doing so we would be able to prepare essay questions that tell the student what direction his answer should take.

Quite often, it is this lack of a framework that gives rise to the difficulty encountered by the student in knowing exactly what it is the teacher expects him to do. And absence of a framework makes it more difficult for the teacher to grade the response fairly, since she may get a variety of answers to the same question, depending upon how the students interpreted it. This lack of a framework is primarily responsible for the common belief that you can bluff your way through an essay exam.

Among the many ways in which a framework to guide the student may be established are (a) delimiting the area covered by the question, (b) using words that themselves give directions, (c) giving specific directions, or "aiming" the student to the desired response, and (d) indicating clearly the value of the question and the time suggested for answering it.

a. *Delimit the area covered by the question.* A high school chemistry teacher could ask an essay item such as "Describe the operation of a fire extinguisher." If she did, she might receive answers describing the operation of a soda-acid extinguisher or a foam type of extinguisher. The answers might be based on the chemical changes that take place, on the physical manipulations involved, or a combination of these and other factors. Some students might illustrate their answer with chemical equations, some might prepare a labeled diagram of the fire extinguisher, some might do both, and some students might do neither. The students should know exactly what they are to do. If, for example, the chemistry teacher is interested in learning the extent to which her pupils understand and can explain the operation of the soda-action type of fire extinguisher, she should rephrase her question as follows:

> With the aid of a diagram, explain the operation of the soda-acid type of fire extinguisher. Label the diagram. Write the equation(s) showing the reaction that takes place when the extinguisher is put into operation.

b. *Use clear, descriptive words.* Words such as "define," "outline," "select," "illustrate," "classify," and "summarize" are reasonably clear in their meaning. On the other hand, "discuss" can be ambiguous. If "discuss" is used, there should be specific instructions as to what points should be discussed. Otherwise, differences in response to an essay question may reflect differences in semantic interpretation rather than differences in knowledge of the material among the pupils tested.

The vocabulary used should be as clear and as simple as possible so that the task required of the examinee will be as clear as possible. Although some students may not know the answer, all students taking the test should have a clear idea of what it is they are being asked to do.

c. *"Aim" the student to the desired response.* For the restricted-response essay, the teacher should write the question so that the student's task is defined as completely and specifically as possible.

---

[4]To measure attitudes and values, we might want some ambiguity, but *not* to measure achievement.

That is, the student is "aimed" at the response. He knows the specific factors the teacher wishes him to consider and discuss in his answer. Some might interpret this as being contradictory to the point raised earlier that "the essay question gives the student freedom of response" (see p. 82). We do not think so. The student must still select, integrate, and express his ideas, even though his range may be more restricted. All we are really doing when we aim the student to the desired response is to say, in effect, "we would like you to do your thinking and organization along these lines." We feel that the student is still permitted latitude even though he has been "aimed." An example of a question that does not "aim" the student is discussed in an interesting fashion by Calandra (1964).[5] We quote in part:

> Some time ago, I received a call from a colleague who asked if I would be the referee on the grading of an examination question.

[5]Special permission granted by *Current Science*, published by Xerox Education Publication, © 1964, Xerox Corp.

It seemed that he was about to give a student a zero for his answer to a physics question, while the student claimed he should receive a perfect score and would do so if the system were not set up against the student. The instructor and the student agreed to submit this to an impartial arbiter, and I was selected.

I went to my colleague's office and read the examination question which was, "Show how it is possible to determine the height of a tall building with the aid of a barometer."

The student's answer was, "Take the barometer to the top of the building, attach a long rope to it, lower the barometer to the street, and then bring it up, measuring the length of the rope. The length of the rope is the height of the building."

Now, this is a very interesting answer, but should the student get credit for it?

I pointed out that the student really had a strong case for full credit, since he had answered the question completely and correctly.

On the other hand, if full credit were given, it could well contribute to a high grade for the student in his physics course. A high grade is supposed to certify that the student knows some physics, but the answer to the question did not confirm this.

With this in mind, I suggested that the student have another try at answering the question. . . .

Acting in terms of the agreement, I gave the student six minutes to answer the question, with the warning that the answer should show some knowledge of physics. At the end of five minutes, he had not written anything.

I asked if he wished to give up, since I had another class to take care of, but he said no, he was not giving up. He had many answers to this problem; he was just thinking of the best one. I excused myself for interrupting him, and asked him to please go on.

In the next minute, he dashed off his answer which was:

"Take the barometer to the top of the building and lean over the edge of the roof. Drop the barometer, timing its fall with a stopwatch. Then using the formula, $S = \frac{1}{2} \cdot AT$ squared, calculate the height of the building."

At this point, I asked my colleague if he would give up. He conceded.

In leaving my colleague's office, I recalled that the student had said he had other answers to the problem, so I asked him what they were.

"Oh, yes," said the student. "There are many ways of getting the height of a tall building with the aid of a barometer. For example, you could take the barometer out on a sunny day and measure the height of the barometer, the length of its shadow, and the length of the shadow of the building, and by the use of simple proportion, determine the height of the building."

"Fine," I said, "And the others?"

"Yes," said the student. "There is a very basic measurement method that you will like. In this method, you take the barometer and begin to walk up the stairs. As you climb the stairs, you mark off the length of the barometer along the wall. You then count the number of marks, and this will give you the height of the building in barometer units. A very direct method.

"Of course, if you want a more sophisticated method, you can tie the barometer to the end of a string, swing it as a pendulum, and determine the value of g at the street level and at the top of the building.

"From the difference between the two values of g the height of the building can, in principle, be calculated."

Finally he concluded, "If you don't limit me to physics solutions to this problem, there are many other answers, such as taking the barometer to the basement and knocking on the superintendent's door. When the superintendent answers, you speak to him as follows: 'Dear Mr. Superintendent, here I have a very fine barometer. If you will tell me the height of this building I will give you this barometer.'"

The intent of this humorous parable was to convey the message, "Ask a stupid question (one so ambiguous and nondirective that nearly any type of answer would be acceptable), and you get a stupid answer."

Assume that a twelfth-grade teacher of Canadian history is interested in measuring the extent to which her pupils know and understand the terms of the Quebec Act, how it was received by various groups, and the permanent effect of the act. We seriously doubt that she would elicit this response were she to frame the question as, "Discuss the Quebec Act of 1774," even though most of her students might know the answer. The question as written is so ambiguous that almost any answer could be given, including "it was one of the most important acts in Canadian history." On the other hand, one student might concentrate on the terms of the act; another might discuss the reactions of the clergy or habitants to the act; and still another might discuss the permanent effects of the act. Each treatment might be well done and appropriate, but how are the answers to be graded?

The "better" example given below illustrates how this same essay question could be written so that it aims the student and still permits him some freedom of response and an opportunity to evaluate his ideas.

> *Better:* Discuss the statement "The Quebec act of 1774 has been described as one of the most important measures in Canadian history." In your answer, refer to (1) the terms of the act; (2) how the act was received by a) the French clergy, b) the seignors, c) the habitants, d) the Thirteen Colonies, and e) the British; and (3) the long-range effects of the act. Your answer should be about 300 to 400 words in length (2 to 3 pages).

Note: Don't be afraid to use long instructions or even give hints if this might help "aim" the student to the desired response. For the extended-response essay, the amount of structuring will vary from item to item, depending upon the objective being measured. The student should be given as much latitude as possible to demonstrate his synthesis and evaluation skills, *but the item should give enough direction* so that it is evident to the student that the question elicits these skills.

d. *Indicate the value of the question and the time to be spent in answering it.* The student should be given an approximate time limit for answering each question, as well as the value of the question in relation to the total test score. The student can then govern himself accordingly in deciding where he should place his emphasis in responding to the various essay questions.

5. *Decide in advance what factors will be considered in evaluating an essay response.* At this time we are not concerned with the substantive material desired in an essay response. This will be discussed in "Grading Essays." What we are concerned with here is whether or not spelling, punctuation, composition, grammar, quality of handwriting, and clarity of expression are to be considered in evaluating a pupil's response and, hence, in the score assigned to that response. If they are, this should be made very clear to the students before they begin their examination. An example of such directions is as follows:

> These questions are a test of your judgment, knowledge, and ability to present such knowledge in an appropriate manner. Give specific facts to substantiate your generalizations. Be as specific as possible in illustrating your answers. Do not neglect to give dates where they are necessary for a fuller understanding of your response. Clearness of organization as well as the quality of your English will be factors considered in scoring your answers (Solomon, 1965, p. 149).

Our contention is that the "ground rules" of the test, especially the weighting of the questions and the subparts of the question(s), as well as information on the general criteria to be used in grading the test response, should be made known to the student *beforehand* with sufficient time so that he can organize and plan his study habits more effectively.

We feel strongly that, with the exception of an English or composition test, a student should *not* be marked down for misspelled words, faulty grammar, and poor handwriting. Similarly, he should *not* be given extra marks for displaying proficiency in these factors. This does *not* mean that teachers should not correct spelling, grammar, and punctuation errors and comment on the quality of handwriting. They should! What it does mean is that unless that is an explicit course objective, it should not be considered in grading the pupil's answer.

6. *Do not provide optional questions on an essay test.* Students like optional questions because it gives them an opportunity to select those questions they know most about. However, three major reasons can be given why optional questions should *not* be given on an essay test: (a) it is difficult to construct questions of equal difficulty; (b) students do not have the ability to select those questions upon which they will be able to do best; and (c) the good student may be penalized because he is challenged by the more difficult and complex questions. Unless all pupils "run the same race" by answering the same questions, it will not be possible to make valid comparisons of achievement among them (Swineford, 1956; DuCette & Wolk, 1972; Futcher, 1973).

Should the teacher be more lenient in grading those students who have selected the more difficult questions? Should she rate more severely the students who have answered the easy questions? It is not possible to compare students who have taken different tests.[6] Another reason against permitting a choice of questions is that if the students know this, they will be less motivated to study *all* the material, reasoning (whether correctly or in-

---

[6] Only if the items are scaled through a process such as item-response theory can students be compared to each other on different items.

correctly depends upon what they studied and the questions asked) that if they have a choice of questions, they should be able to find *some* questions that they will be able to answer moderately well.

With some possible exceptions (discussed in the next paragraph), we find no compelling reasons or arguments to support the claim that permitting students a choice of questions will be fairer because it will permit each student equal opportunity to do well. All factors considered, it is *not* beneficial to the student to give him options. Remember—the purpose of a test is not to show how well a student can do if allowed to select his own questions; rather, it is to ascertain his proficiency when responding to a representative set of questions.

There are, of course, circumstances where a partial choice of questions is justified. Although Ms. Molecule might be teaching Chemistry I to four classes, there may be some classes where the students are not presented with or taught common materials. For example, a high school chemistry class where the method of instruction was independent study might contain some students who spent the whole year working on the gas laws, some who worked on organic derivatives, and some who studied the toxicological effects of DDT. Or there may be five chemistry classes taught by team-teaching wherein there are deviations from the common syllabus. Depending on the nature of the course content, there may be a set of common questions for all students to answer, but there may also be a choice of questions to accommodate inter- and intraclass variations.

7. *Use a relatively large number of questions requiring short answers (about one-half page) rather than just a few questions involving long answers (2 to 3 pages).* We prefer having many short, restricted-response essay questions, for a variety of reasons: (a) They will provide for a broader sampling of content, thereby reducing the error associated with limited sampling. (b) They tend to discourage bias on the part of the teacher who grades for quantity, rather than quality. (c) The teacher will be able to read the answers more rapidly and

more reliably because she has a mental set of what she should be looking for. (d) It is easier to "aim" the student to the desired response.

8. *Don't start essay questions with such words as "list," "who," "what," "whether."* These words tend to elicit responses that require only a regurgitation of factual information. If this is the only way that you can begin the question, it is likely to be a short-answer (one or two lines) recall question and not an essay question as we have defined it.

9. *Adapt the length of the response and the complexity of the question and answer to the maturity level of the student.* A common fault of teachers using essay questions is that they expect too much from their students. The depth and breadth of discussion anticipated for sixth- and tenth-graders should be markedly different for the two groups. We might give a doctoral candidate a six-hour examination on only one item, such as "Discuss the Civil War." But you would surely agree that this topic is too complex for undergraduate history majors (even if they were also given six hours to answer the question).

10. *Use the novel type of question wherever feasible.* To answer a question discussed in the textbook or in class requires little more than a good memory. But, to apply that same principle or thought process to a new situation requires a higher level of learning. Too many teachers think that they are measuring understanding and application when, in reality, they are only measuring factual recall.

Summary

We have suggested that it is essential to control all elements in the structure of the essay test that have no relevance to the pupil's performance if we hope to obtain a fair measure of his competence. To accomplish this, we should restrict the use of the extended-response essay and "aim" the student in the direction that we wish him to take in answering the question. Three major factors

TABLE 5-1 Checklist for Writing Essay Questions

Factor	Yes
1. Is the question restricted to measuring objectives that would not be assessed more efficiently by other item formats?	X
2. Does each question relate to some instructional objective?	X
3. Does the question establish a framework to guide the student to the expected answer?	X
a. Is the problem delimited?	X
b. Are descriptive words such as "compare," "contrast," and "define" used rather than words such as "discuss" or "explain"?	X
c. For the restricted-response essay in particular, is the student "aimed" to the answer by appropriate subdivisons of the main question?	X
4. Are the questions novel? Do they challenge the student? Do they require the student to demonstrate originality of thought and expression?*	X
5. Are the questions realistic in terms of—	
a. difficulty?	X
b. time allowed the student to respond?	X
c. complexity of the task?	X
6. Are all students expected to answer the *same* questions?	X
7. Is there a preponderance of short-answer (restricted-response) questions?	X
8. Has a model answer been prepared for each question?	X

*Originality need not be an objective for every essay question.

should be considered in constructing essay tests: (1) the wording of the questions, (2) the use of many questions requiring relatively short answers, and (3) requiring all students to answer the same questions.

Table 5–1 lists the major factors to be considered when writing essay questions. It should be used *both* as a preliminary and final checklist rather than as a compilation of *the* rules to be followed in writing good essay questions.

AN EXAMPLE OF THE DEVELOPMENT OF A GOOD ESSAY QUESTION

Ms. Social Studies, *before* teaching the unit on the Civil War to her twelfth-grade American history class, began to give some thought to the kinds of essay questions that she would use on her unit test. After looking through the textbook and her teaching notes and materials, she prepared the following question:

> List the events immediately preceding Lincoln's call to arms on April 12, 1861.[7]

When she first looked at this question it appeared acceptable. But her table of specifications indicated a question that involved the higher mental processes of synthesis and evaluation. (Had she referred to her test blueprint before writing the item, she could have saved herself some time. But better late than never.)

_____

[7]Adapted with permission of Frank F. Gorow (1966).

Ms. Social Studies then prepared the following question:

> What were the main issues that caused Americans to be divided and that eventually led to the Civil War?

On further reflection, Ms. Social Studies saw an undue emphasis upon the recall of factual material ("what"), and she decided that such an item would be better measured by a series of multiple-choice items. Ms. Social Studies was not dismayed. She went back to her desk and formulated this question:

> There has been much debate and controversy among historians as to whether or not the Civil War was unavoidable. Some historians go so far as to say that it was a stupid war. Do you agree that the Civil War was inevitable? Why? Why not? Support your reasons with facts.

Ms. Social Studies felt that it still didn't "tap" the students' analytical skills. She reworked the question as follows:

> Although historians have argued about the inevitability of the Civil War, let us assume that there never was a Civil War in the United States. How do you think this would have affected the development of the United States subsequent to 1865? In your answer consider the slavery issue, the development of the West after 1865, economic factors, and our relations with European nations after 1865.

Ms. Social Studies now has a "good" essay item. It is specific, related to the course objective, and is sufficiently delimited to give some direction to the student in preparing his response. But Ms. Social Studies could make the item even more interesting by setting in a novel situation as follows:

> It is the morning of April 14, 1861. President Lincoln has called his cabinet into an emergency session to discuss the recent events. YOU have been invited to the cabinet meeting. As the meeting progresses, telegrams begin arriving, telling of the defeat of the northern troops by the experienced southern troops. Each cabinet member is asked his opinion on what to do. President Lincoln listens to all his cabinet and then turns and faces you. He asks YOU two questions: (1) What, if any, are the alternatives to war? and (2) What might happen if we don't go to war?

> Your response should consider the development of the West after 1865, the social and economic factors, and U.S. relationships with European nations.

Before she is able to "put the question to bed," Ms. Social Studies still has to prepare an adequate set of instructions. It should be recognized that this is only an example of the steps that the teacher goes through to prepare a valid essay question. As written, the question is very complex and would take a great deal of time to answer. In fact, we seriously doubt whether more than two or three such questions can be asked in a two-hour testing period. We also recognize that by attempting to cast the item in a novel situation, we may be accused of excessive "window dressing." There is no doubt that the same abilities could have been tapped by asking just two questions and giving the directions the student is to take. Our intent here is only to provide an illustration. However, we would not discourage having one such "window-dressed" question occasionally.

GRADING ESSAYS

In the essay test, the measurement of a student's ability does *not* end with his answer, but depends to a large extent on the person who reads his answer and assigns a grade to that answer, as well as on the grading method used. The effectiveness of an essay examination depends to a large degree on how well it is graded. An ill-conceived, poorly prepared essay test cannot be salvaged by even the most refined grading method. *But* the most careful planning and construction can be ruined by improper grading procedures and standards. We cannot overemphasize the importance of reliably grading essay tests.[8] Unreliable grading has been

---

[8]See Van Der Kamp and Mellenbergh (1976) for a somewhat technical discussion of how to obtain reliable teacher ratings; Mullis (1976) for scoring writing tasks; Martin (1976) for scoring free-response mathematics items; Harris (1977) and Freedman (1979) on how the characteristics of the answer affect the reader and hence the grade.

one of the major and most valid criticisms leveled against their use.

In grading essay responses, one must (1) use appropriate methods to minimize biases,[9] (2) pay attention only to the significant and relevant aspects of the answer, (3) be careful not to let personal idiosyncrasies affect grading, and (4) apply uniform standards to all the papers. Undoubtedly, the uniformity of grading standards is a crucial aspect of essay grading. For without uniformity there is no fair way of comparing students. Moreover, without uniformity one cannot be certain that the score represents a valid measure of the student's achievement.

Two commonly used methods have been developed for grading essay examinations—the *analytical* method and the *global* method. (For a more thorough discussion, see Spandel, 1981, and Spandel & Stiggins, 1988). Which one should be used will depend to a large extent on the use and/or purpose of the test, the time and facilities available for reading the papers, and whether the essay is of the restricted- or extended-response type. Presently, some states use the global or holistic method to grade essays, and, if the student fails, the paper is reread with the analytical method.

Analytical and Global Methods of Grading Essays

In both the analytical and global methods, the ideal answer to a question should preferably be prepared when the question is written.

Analytical Method   In the *analytical* method (sometimes called the "point-score" method), the ideal or model answer is broken down into specific points. The student's score is based upon the number of points contained in his answer. Com-

ponent parts such as "effectiveness of expression," "logical organization," and "support of statements" are specified and assigned points or values. We then end up with a checklist that can be used quite objectively.

The following example is a scoring guide that was employed in the 1964 College Entrance Examination Board Advanced Placement Examination in American History[10] but was subsequently replaced by the global scoring method discussed on pages 98–100.

> *Question:* The Civil War left the South with a heritage of intense regional self-consciousness. In what respects and to what extent was this feeling weakened during the next half-century, and in what respects and to what extent was it intensified?

Grading Standards:

General Criteria:

1. Does the student state clearly the forces a) weakening southern regional self-consciousness and b) intensifying southern regional self-consciousness? (See Checklist below.)
2. Does he develop his statement by showing how these forces actually operated to weaken or strengthen southern self-consciousness?
3. Does he draw an over-all conclusion as to the condition of southern self-consciousness at the turn of the century?

High Honors: Summarizes clearly the forces weakening and strengthening southern self-consciousness and develops them fully by showing explicitly how they operated. Draws an explicit over-all conclusion.

Honors: Summarizes the forces clearly, but develops them less effectively, OR treats one side of the question well and the other less well. Draws an over-all

---

[9]Huck and Bounds (1972) reported a significant interaction between the graders' handwriting neatness and the neatness of the essay answer they were grading. To minimize this, they recommend analytical scoring (this is discussed in the next section). See also Chase (1979, 1983, 1986) and Hughes et al. (1983).

[10]Advanced Placement scoring guidelines selected from *The Advanced Placement Examination in American History*, College Entrance Examinations Board (1966, 1988). Reprinted by permission of Educational Testing Service, the copyright owner of the test questions.

Disclaimer: Permission to reprint the above material does not constitute review or endorsement by Educational Testing Service or the College Board of this publication as a whole or of any other questions or testing information it may contain.

conclusion, but does so more implicitly or more generally.

Satisfactory: Discusses the forces weakening or strengthening southern self-consciousness, but develops them rather thinly, OR shows noticeable imbalance in treating the two sides of the question. May draw an over-all conclusion in a few general remarks.

Passing: Discusses only one side of the question, but does so with some thoroughness, OR discusses, with some development, a few forces on each side, OR merely catalogues forces on both sides without developing them.

Fail: Merely talks about the South in general.

Checklist:

Forces weakening southern regional self-consciousness:

Growth of railroads and desire for federal subsidies

Old Whigs join northern businessmen in Compromise of 1877

Desire for northern capital to industrialize the South

Efforts of magazines and writers to interpret the South

The vision of the New South

Aid to Negro education by northern philanthropists

New state constitutions stressing public education

Supreme Court decisions affecting Negro rights

Tom Watson's early Populist efforts

Booker T. Washington's "submissiveness"

The Spanish-American War. The white man's burden

After 1890, new issues did not conform to a North-South political alignment

First World War

Forces strengthening southern regional self-consciousness:

Destruction caused by the war and its long-range effects

Reconstruction policy of Congress

One crop economy, crop-lien system, and share-cropping

Carpetbaggers, Ku Klux Klan, Red Shirts

Waving the bloody shirt

Memories of the lost cause

Glorify the prewar tradition

Continuing weakness of southern education compared with rest of Union

Populism

Jim Crow laws after 1890

Solid South

The checklist consists of the major points that should be discussed in the pupils' answer to the question. You will note that there are 13 points listed for forces weakening southern regional self-consciousness and 11 points listed for forces strengthening regional self-consciousness. Should the teacher assign numerical values to each point, and should there be different values for different points? For example, to the question on the Civil War, should a student who mentions "growth of railroads and desire for federal subsidies" receive 2 points, and the student who mentions "the Spanish-American War" receive 1 point?

We recommend that the teacher *not* be concerned with the weighting of the various points within the essay question inasmuch as research has shown it to be of negligible value (Stalnaker, 1938). This does *not* mean that essay questions per se should all be assigned the same point values in the test. Factors to be considered in assigning point values to the respective essay questions include (1) the time needed to respond, (2) the complexity of the question, and (3) the emphasis placed on that content area in the instructional phase. As the teacher (reader) reads the responses to a particular question, she gives points for those component parts contained in the answer.

For many years the analytical method was considered by measurement experts to be more reliable than global scoring because it was believed that the key provided a better basis for maintaining standards (uniformity) from reader to reader and from paper to paper. However, Gosling's (1966) studies did not show consistent results.

Ideally, the analytical method minimizes the influence of extraneous material. In actual practice, however, controlling for human variability is difficult to achieve, even though a detailed scoring guide is employed, because of the fallibility of the human reader. The major advantages of the analytical method of grading are as follows:

1. It can yield very reliable scores when used by a conscientious reader.
2. The very process of preparing the detailed answer may frequently bring to the teacher's attention such errors as faulty wording, extreme difficulty and/or complexity of the question, and unrealistic time limits. Hence, if the model answer had been prepared before the test was administered, the question could have been reworded or the time extended.
3. The fine subdivision of the model answer can make it easier to discuss the grade given to the student.

Two major limitations of analytical scoring are:

1. It is very laborious and time consuming.
2. In attempting to identify the elements, undue attention may be given to superficial aspects of the answer (Diederich, 1967, pp. 582–583).

Although the analytical method may be used for both extended- and restricted-response types, it is recommended primarily for the latter inasmuch as responses will tend to be very specific and not too lengthy. It is also more reliable for the latter for the same reasons.

Global Scoring In *global* scoring (sometimes referred to as the *holistic* or *rating* method), the ideal answer is *not* subdivided into specific points and component parts; it simply serves as a standard. Papers that are less than ideal and vary across the quality continuum should be selected as other standards or anchor points. The rater is then instructed to read the response rapidly, form a general impression, and, using some standard, assign a rating to the response. The scorer makes a single overall judgment of the quality of the writing sample. No single factor is given undue weight. Rather, *all* factors are taken into account in forming the judgment about the adequacy of the response. The crux of this method is to select papers that vary in quality, to serve as anchor points, and to train readers to go rapidly through a response and give some general or global impression of the quality of the response.

Establishing Standards or Anchor Points. Regardless of the scale values employed (e.g., "good," "average," and "poor"), the procedure employed to establish the scale values is the same. The teacher could prepare a variety of answers corresponding to the various scale points, or she could select papers from those already written and let the actual responses establish the various anchor points. (See National Assessment of Educational Progress, 1970b. See also Cross et al. (1985) for using blind and informed review to establish minimum standards for essays.)

Reading the Responses. Depending upon the degree of discrimination required, papers may be read on a 2-point "acceptable-unacceptable" scale up to a 5-point "superior-inferior" scale. Four or five rating categories are probably sufficient for most purposes, although Coffman's (1971) review of research performed at ETS suggested that *with trained readers* as many as 15 categories can be used without slowing the reading rate or decreasing reliability.

Although the training period should make readers consistent in applying the prescribed standards, it is suggested that occasional checks be made.

Let us assume that one wishes to employ a 5-point scale such as

1. Superior quality
2. Above-average quality
3. Average quality
4. Below-average quality
5. Inferior quality

On a rapid reading of the response, the reader would assign it to one of five piles, depending on the quality of the answer in relation to the different samples. For example, a student whose paper was judged to be "average" would be placed in pile 3. It would then be a simple clerical task to assign score values to the papers in the various piles.

With global reading, each set of responses should be read and classified at least twice—preferably by a different reader the second time, who would assign an independent rating. This is not an undue hardship, nor is it overly time-consuming—global rating is considerably faster than analytical rating once the standards have been established.

The global approach is very effective when large numbers of essays are to be read. It also can be used by the classroom teacher who has as few as 30 papers to read. However, it might be more difficult to select papers for anchor points when only a limited number of papers are available to begin with (this would be especially true if the class were quite homogeneous). We suggest that when only a few papers are to be read, the teacher make a preliminary reading and assign each paper (actually each question being read) to one of the piles. Then, each question should be reread one or two times, and those found to have been misclassified should be reclassified.

Following is an example of the scoring guide used in the 1988 College Entrance Examination Board Advanced Placement Examination in American History[11]:

Question:
"American reform movements between 1820 and 1860 reflected both optimistic and pessimistic views of human nature and society."

Assess the validity of this statement in reference to reform movements in THREE of the following areas.

Education
Temperance
Women's rights
Utopian experiments
Penal institutions

Scoring Guide: Five categories of scoring standards are developed to "identify qualities that sep-

---

[11]Advanced Placement scoring guidelines selected from *The Advanced Placement Examination in American History,* College Entrance Examinations Board (1966, 1988). Reprinted by permission of Educational Testing Service, the copyright owner of the test questions.

Disclaimer: Permission to reprint the above material does not constitute review or endorsement by Educational Testing Service or the College Board of this publication as a whole or of any other questions or testing information it may contain.

arate each response category" (College Entrance Examinations Board, 1989, p. 31). Five categories are developed, as follows:

13–15   Coherent essay, logically structured, and well written; assesses the validity of the statement, discussing the tension between optimism/pessimism in views of human nature and/or society; informed, reasonably balanced discussion of three reform movements chosen from the list provided by the question; accurate and detailed information that places discussion of each movement within the chronological period 1820–1860. May take discussion outside of the period (bring up to date, or find historical roots of a movement) so long as there is no confusion about chronological focus of question.

10–12   Coherent, well-written essay; makes *attempt* to assess the validity of the statement, but may not fully develop the question of optimism/pessimism regarding human nature and/or society, OR interprets the optimism/pessimism issue as pertaining to the movements themselves; demonstrates an understanding of reform movements, including in the essay a discussion of three reforms, chosen from the list provided; must understand time period, and focus discussion of reforms in 1820–1860; may contain minor errors of fact and chronology; includes some specific details, used effectively in support of an argument.

7–9   Adequately organized essay; some treatment of the central question of pessimism/optimism about society and/or human nature, but may be confused, or apply question to other issues; poor understanding of what it means to "assess the validity" of the statement given; must discuss three reforms, but may be imbalanced; some specific information given, but may have factual and chronological errors.

4–6 Poorly organized general essay; may have illogical or contradictory use of evidence or arguments; little or no discussion of optimism/pessimism issue; vague discussion of reform movements; may discuss only two movements, or include a reform movement not listed; general discussion with little or no specific detail; factual errors.

1–3 Has hardly a clue to the focus of the question!; incoherent and inept essay; does not address the question and shows no understanding of optimism/pessimism issue; superficial, or discusses only one reform; major errors of fact, or not specific information; incorrect chronology.

Suggestions for Grading Essay Tests

As mentioned earlier, one of the major limitations of essay examinations pertained to their reliability. The guidelines offered below should help increase the reliability of the grading.

1. *Check your scoring key against actual responses.* If a teacher prepares a model answer when the essay question is prepared, it is conceivable that she may be overly optimistic about the clarity of the question and/or the nature of the responses to be elicited by the question. Before actually beginning the grading process, it is suggested that a few papers be selected at random to ascertain the appropriateness of the scoring guide. If it is seen that most students are giving responses different from those established *a priori*, this may be due to the students' misinterpretation of the intent of the question. For example, if the question was intended to measure "interpretation," but the responses indicate that the answers are at a lower level of understanding, the scoring criteria can be revised. *Once the grading has begun, however, the standards should not be changed, nor should they vary from paper to paper or reader to reader.*

2. *Be consistent in your grading.* It is one thing to say that all questions should be graded uni-

formly and another thing to actually achieve uniformity. Graders are human and therefore fallible. They may be influenced by the first few papers they read and thereby grade either too leniently or too harshly, depending on their initial mind set (Hales & Tokar, 1975). For this reason, once the scoring criteria have been checked out against actual responses and once the grading has begun, teachers should occasionally refer to the first few papers graded to satisfy themselves that the standards are being applied consistently. Otherwise, the grade a student receives is dependent on the chance appearance of his paper in the order in which the papers are read. This will be especially true for those papers read near the end of the day when the reader might be physically and mentally weary.

3. *Randomly shuffle the papers before grading them.* Research shows that a student's essay grade will be influenced by the position of his paper, especially if the preceding answers were either very good or very poor (Hales & Tokar, 1975). For example, an essay answer that is worth a B might receive only a C if many of the previous papers were very good and received B's. On the other hand, this same answer could receive an A if many of the preceding papers were of only average quality (Hughes et al., 1980; Daly & Dickson-Markham, 1982). Accordingly, we suggest that the reader randomly shuffle essay exam papers prior to grading to minimize the bias introduced. This random shuffling of papers is especially significant when teachers are working with high- and low-level classes and read the best papers first or last.

4. *Grade only one question at a time for all papers.* To reduce the "halo" effect (the quality of the response to one question influences the reader's evaluation of the quality of the response to subsequent questions), we strongly recommend that teachers grade one question at a time rather than one paper (containing several responses) at a time, shuffle the papers, read the answers to the next question, and so on, until all the papers have been graded. In addition to minimizing the halo effect, such a procedure will make it possible for the

reader to concentrate and become thoroughly familiar with just one set of scoring criteria and not be distracted by moving from one question to another. Also, by recording the grades to each question on a separate sheet, the halo effect may be minimized.

5. Try to grade all responses to a particular question without interruption. One source of unreliability is that the grader's standards may vary markedly from one day to the next and even from morning to afternoon of the same day. We would be very unfair to our students if we allowed a personal argument with one's spouse, a migraine headache, or an upset stomach to influence the grade we give a student for his answer. Our grading is valid only to the degree that it is based upon the *quality* of the student's answer and *not* on the reader's disposition at a particular moment. Of course, there should be short breaks during the reading period. There must be some short diversionary periods so that the reader will not become fatigued. But, in order to keep the standards clearly in mind, the set of papers should be graded without excessive interruption and delay. If a lengthy break is taken, the reader should reread some of the first few papers to refamiliarize herself with her grading standards so that she will not change them in midstream. This is especially important in global reading.

6. Grade the responses without knowing the pupil's identity. Regardless of the reason, it is only natural that the teacher might favor the response of one student over that of another even though the answers are of equal quality (Sullivan et al., 1989). We recognize that this is a natural tendency, but a student's grade should *not* be influenced by his teacher's bias. Even though a scoring guide is employed, to protect the student from reader bias, we advise teachers to do whatever is needed so that they *not* know whose paper is being graded.

Another reason for preserving anonymity of the pupil is that it can promote and/or maintain a healthy classroom atmosphere. There are, no doubt, some students who feel that they are subjected to prejudice of one form or another, and these students would argue that the grades they receive are a reflection of their teacher's biases toward them. But if, say, the pupils' names were removed or hidden from the reader, not only would this protect the teacher, but it would also indicate to the students that their teacher is treating them fairly.

Anonymity of the pupil can be obtained in a variety of ways. One way would be to have the student write his name on the back page of the test booklet rather than on the front page. We assume, of course, that if this procedure is adopted, the teacher will not look at the name before she grades the paper. Another way would be to have students select a card with a number on it, write their name on the card and only their number on the paper. The teacher would then match the numbers and names when she records the grades. We recognize, of course, that even though the teacher might take pains to have student anonymity when she grades the papers, it may be that she will recognize a student's handwriting. In such cases, we can only hope that the teacher will strive to be as objective as possible in her grading.

7. The mechanics of expression should be judged separately from the content. For those teachers who feel that the mechanics of expression are very important and should be reflected in the grade, given the answer, we strongly suggest that they assign a proportion of the question's value to such factors as legibility, spelling, handwriting, quality, punctuation, and grammar. The proportion assigned to these factors should be spelled out in the grading criteria, and the students should be so informed in advance. In any event, the teacher must be careful not to let such factors influence her evaluation of the answer's subject-matter content.

For those teachers who contend that they are not influenced by how a person writes, but only by what he writes, we can only say be careful! It has been shown that when teachers are told to *disregard* spelling, punctuation, and grammatical errors, they still assign lower grades to papers containing such errors (Scannell & Marshall, 1966; Chase, 1979).

Chase (1983) and Hughes et al. (1983) reported that essay test answers that were more difficult to read were given lower grades than responses that were less difficult to read even though each type was correct in spelling and grammar. Chase (1979) reported that untidy writers have an advantage if the reader has high expectations. But in a later study, Chase (1986) studied the effects of students' gender and race, reader expectation, and handwriting on essay grading and reported that, although each of these variables has an effect on the score given, the effect is *not* attributable to the variables singly but to their interactions. As Chase pointed out, whether these findings would hold if essays of varying quality were read is a matter of conjecture. Nevertheless, we should be cognizant of the interaction. On the other hand, Hughes et al. reported *no* interaction between quality of handwriting and scorer expectations and its influence on the essay grade. And Murchan (1989) said there was insufficient evidence to prove that handwriting quality affects scores given to essay responses.

8. *If possible, have two independent readings of the test and use the average as the final score.* A double reading by two independent readers will make the scores more reliable. If independent readings are done, the scores should be written on separate sheets.

When it is not possible to have two different readers, but it is possible to have the same teacher grade the papers twice (to check on the consistency of grading), this should be done with an interval of several days elapsing between the two readings so that the teacher begins her second reading with a new perspective. Once again, the scores should *not* be recorded on the test booklet.

We recognize that it is difficult for the ordinary classroom teacher to find the time to do one reading of a set of essay papers, let alone find the time to read the papers twice. Also, we realize that it is difficult to get two independent readers to grade the essay responses. This does not preclude us from recommending it when it is feasible. We strongly recommend that two independent ratings by competent readers be obtained when the results

of the examination are to be used to make important decisions such as the awarding of a scholarship or admittance to graduate school.

9. *Provide comments and correct errors.* You will recall that some of the purposes of testing are to provide the student with information regarding his progress, to motivate him, and indirectly to teach him. Although it is time-consuming to write comments and correct errors, it should be done if we are to help the student become a better student. Also, the teacher may become a more effective teacher if she makes a tally of the kinds of errors committed and then attempts to analyze the reasons for these errors. Isn't it possible that the students did not do well because they were not taught well? However, unless the teacher has made some sort of tally of the types of errors made by her students, it will be very difficult to analyze the errors and initiate any called-for remediation.

Another value of providing comments and noting errors is that it will be much easier for the teacher to explain her method of assigning a particular grade. There are some instances when the student does not understand why he received the grade he obtained. But, with a detailed scoring guide as well as with appropriate comments, it should be much easier for the teacher and student to communicate.

Regardless of the type of test used, a test that is used *only* to assign grades is of little value for developing an effective teaching-learning environment. The test, per se, will be of little help to either the teacher or the student. That is why we feel strongly that the teacher should make comments, correct errors, and analyze the errors made.

10. *Set realistic standards.* Unfortunately, some teachers use tests as punitive devices rather than as instructional and evaluation tools. Such teachers contend that unless one grades a test exceedingly stringently, the pupils will not work hard. On the other hand, there are some teachers who will bend over backwards to grade the test as leniently as possible, believing they will be able to buy the students' respect and affection. Being overly lenient, in our opinion, is just as bad as being a "hard-

nose." Both types of teachers may, in the long run, do more damage than good. Such teachers hold a very distorted view of the evaluation process. A teacher whose grades are significantly higher or lower than those of her colleagues teaching the same subject matter to the same kinds of students should reflect for a moment to see whether or not she is at fault. And if she is, she should correct the problem. The only bit of practical advice that we can offer at this time to avoid being caught in the "generosity/hard-nose trap," is that essay readers should use all the scale points when they grade the pupils' responses. Although this may not completely prevent the problem, it should help reduce it.

Somewhat related is Busch's (1988) study where three different grading approaches were studied (1) providing judges with information about the score assigned to an essay, (2) providing no information, and (3) having the judges discuss each essay thoroughly. He reported that giving more information and discussion resulted in changes in the standards. He also found that following discussion, the recommendations of the public school teachers were more variable than those of college faculty but that there was no significant difference in the average recommended standards.

In summary, the evidence on grading essay tests suggests that, with special precautions, the papers can be scored reliably. But most of the time, these precautions are either not known to the teacher, or they are ignored, with the end result that reader reliability is low. If a teacher uses essays as an evaluation tool, we believe that she has the professional obligation to spend the necessary time to grade the answers as reliably as is humanly possible.

THE ORAL QUESTION

The oral approach, rather than the oral exam, is frequently used by the classroom teacher. Every day, pupils are questioned by their teachers. Although the results of these questions may not be used by the teacher to help assign a final course grade, both teachers and pupils can, if they wish, profitably use the results obtained to improve the teaching-learning situation. Oral questioning provides immediate feedback to both pupil and teacher.

The oral question is a variation of the essay question. Although not so popular in American schools as in foreign schools, and although more frequently used in final examinations of graduate students or in the senior comprehensives of college students than as a measurement device for schoolchildren, it deserves brief mention because of its utility in the classroom, especially in the primary grades.

Both oral and essay examinations have certain limitations and advantages that they share in common.

Limitations in common
1. Both provide for a very limited sampling of content.
2. Both have low rater reliability.

Advantages in common
1. Both permit the examiner to determine how well the pupil can synthesize and organize his ideas and express himself (be it in written or spoken form).
2. Both are not so dependent as the multiple-choice form on the ability of the pupil to *recognize* the correct answer; rather, both require that the pupil know and be able to *supply* the correct answer.
3. Both permit free response by the pupil.

Oral tests are very costly and time-consuming (only one student can be tested at a time); may not be equally fair to all pupils; often encourage lack of teacher planning; and do not permit or provide for any record of the examinee's response to be used for future action by the teacher and pupil *unless* the examination process is recorded. Even so, listening to a "playback" can be time-consuming. Finally, the oral examination may be advantageous to the highly articulate students who may know very little but can express their limited knowledge so eloquently that they make a good impression and are often given a grade higher than warranted.

The major advantage of the oral test is that it permits detailed probing by the examiner and hence may be very useful in the diagnostic sense. In fact, a very qualified examiner can elicit responses that may be indicative of a student's thinking process. Oral exams are also useful in the sense that the pupil can ask for clarification. As noted earlier, one of the major disadvantages of the essay and objective types of questions is that they are very susceptible to ambiguity in wording. Many times, incorrect responses are given *not* because of the pupil's lack of knowledge but because of ambiguous wording or misinterpretation of what was asked for. In the oral examination, ambiguity also may be present, but the pupil can ask to have the question rephrased. The oral approach may be traumatic for some pupils. However, it may also be very settling and reassuring, depending upon the examiner. Unfortunately, the examiner is unable to calm a student in a written examination, but an alert oral examiner often can do this by either rephrasing the question or by reassuring the nervous pupil. Oral examinations are also valuable for testing physically handicapped students who are unable to take written tests or in those situations where the objective is to see how the pupil will conduct himself before a group of people (e.g., a course in public speaking).

■ SUMMARY

The principal ideas, suggestions, and recommendations made in this chapter are summarized in the following statements:

1. The essay is the only test procedure that the teacher can use if she wants to see whether her students can express themselves effectively in written form.
2. The two major types of essay questions are the extended- and restricted-response types.
3. A variety of different mental processes and skills can be measured by the essay.
4. Many of the "claimed" advantages of the essay over the objective test are not substantiated by research. The major advantages are that they (a) permit the teacher to assess the extent to which the student is able to compose an answer and present it in effective prose, (b) are easier to prepare, and (c) make teachers emphasize certain pupil skills.
5. The two most serious limitations of essay questions are their poor content sampling and their low reader reliability.
6. Adequate planning and conscientious scoring minimize most of the faults of essay tests.
7. Essay tests should be restricted to measuring the higher mental processes. They should not be used to measure factual recall.
8. A well-constructed essay question should provide a framework to guide the student in preparing his answer. The problem should be delimited, worded so that the student knows exactly what is expected of him, and realistic with respect to the complexity of the question and the time allowed the student to answer it.
9. All students should be required to answer the same questions.
10. Content sampling may be improved by having many relatively short essay questions.
11. Avoid starting essay questions with "who," when," "where," and "what."
12. Adapt the complexity of the question and the length of response to the maturity level of the students.
13. Use a novel type of situation wherever possible.
14. The two most commonly used methods to grade essays are the analytical and the global approaches.
15. Both global and analytical methods require the preparation of a model answer. Preferably, this should be done early, to check on the realism of time allotted, the complexity of the question, and the clarity of wording.
16. The analytical method is recommended for the classroom teacher when only a few papers are to be graded.
17. The global method is recommended when large numbers of papers have to be graded.
18. If possible, try to have two independent ratings for each question.

19. Grade essays without knowing the identity of the students.
20. Grade one question at a time. This will tend to reduce the "halo" effect.
21. If more than one factor is being judged, such as legibility of handwriting and spelling, judge these other factors independently from what the student wrote.
22. Try to score all the responses to a single question without interruption.
23. The teacher should make comments and correct errors so that the test may be used as a learning device.
24. Teachers should avoid the penalty and generosity errors. That is, they should not be overly strict or overly lenient in their grading standards.
25. The oral question is a variation of the essay. It is well suited for testing students who are unable to write because of physical handicaps.
26. There is a place in our schools for essay tests that are carefully structured and reliably graded. Rather than argue whether essay tests are superior or inferior to objective tests, we should focus our attention on how both can be used most effectively.

■ POINTS TO PONDER

1. What are the two most serious limitations of the essay test question? How would you control or try to minimize them?
2. Is it true that the essay test, and only the essay test, can be used to measure the higher mental processes? Defend your answer with an example.
3. If essay tests are so full of problems, why are they still popular?
4. Under what circumstances, if any, should a student's answer to an essay question be lowered because of poor handwriting, grammar, and punctuation?
5. What is wrong with this essay topic: "Discuss the British North America Act." What would you do to make it a better essay question?
6. What is the difference between global and analytical scoring? Which type would you use and under what circumstances?
7. Give three examples of essay questions that you could prepare for this chapter. For one of the examples, prepare a scoring guide that you would use for both the global and analytical scoring methods.
8. Under what circumstances, if any, should essay tests contain optional questions? Defend your answer.
9. Some say that a student should be "aimed at the desired response," while some say that this detracts from the basic value of the essay question. What position do you hold? Why do you feel this way?
10. When would you use an essay test rather than an objective-type test?

Chapter 6

Writing the Objective Test Item: Short-Answer, Matching, and True–False

■ **Objective-Type Tests**
■ **Suggestions for Writing Objective Items**
■ **Writing Short-Answer Items**
■ **Writing the Matching Exercise**
■ **Writing True–False Items**

The planning stage discussed in Chapter 4 provided us with some guidelines to follow in our attempt to obtain a valid measure of pupil achievement. In Chapter 5 we discussed the essay as a testing medium. We are now at the stage where we consider the various types of objective formats that can be used. As will be evident after studying this chapter and Chapter 7, there are advantages and limitations associated with each item format.

Because clarity of wording is so vital in writing good test items, we will elaborate further on our previous discussion. In addition, we will discuss in this chapter some of the factors to be considered when writing the objective-type item, regardless of format. We will then present some guidelines to follow when preparing the short-answer,

matching, and true–false item. In Chapter 7, we will discuss the preparation of the multiple-choice item. Writing test items (regardless of format used) that are unclear, inappropriate, and containing technical defects will make the best planning go for naught.

After studying this chapter, you should be able to:

1. Understand the steps to be considered when writing the objective-type item.
2. Understand why clarity of expression is so important in test items.
3. Recognize how irrelevant clues to the correct answer can easily creep into objective items.
4. Define and discuss the following objective-

type formats: short-answer, matching, and true–false.

5. Differentiate between the various types of short-answer items.

6. Apply the guidelines offered for constructing short-answer items.

7. Apply the guidelines offered for constructing the matching exercise.

8. Apply the guidelines offered for constructing true–false items.

9. Write better short-answer, matching, and true–false items.

OBJECTIVE-TYPE TESTS

The objective-type item was developed in response to the criticisms leveled against the essay question—poor content sampling, unreliable scoring, time-consuming to grade, and encouragement of bluffing—discussed in Chapter 5. All objective-item formats may be subdivided into two classes: *supply* type (short-answer) and *select* type (true–false, matching, and multiple-choice). The *supply* and *select* types of objective-item formats are sometimes called *recall* and *recognition*, respectively. And, they are sometimes called *free-response* and *choice-response*, respectively. All objective tests have the students working in a completely structured situation and responding to a large number of items. All can be objectively scored, and with the exception of the short-answer/completion, by machine or untrained personnel.

One of the virtues of the objective item is that it is an economical way of obtaining information from a pupil because, in general, it takes less time to answer an objective item than an essay question. Because of the lessened amount of time needed for pupils to respond to objective items, many questions can be asked in a prescribed examination period and more adequate content sampling can be obtained, resulting in higher reliability and better content validity. In addition, objective items can be scored more easily and more accurately. Finally, objective items *may* create an incentive for

pupils to build up a broad base of knowledge, skills, and abilities.

Some very vocal critics of the objective-type item contend that it does *not* measure the higher mental processes, but rather encourages rote memory, encourages guessing, and neglects the measurement of writing ability. Yes, objective items often are used to measure rote recall of facts, dates, names, and places. But, as will be evident after you have studied this and the next chapter, objective items *can* be written so that they measure the higher mental processes of understanding, application, analysis, and interpretation.

Look at the following examples of objective-type items that measure higher-order thinking skills.

1. Mayors are to cities as governors are to the
   1. Congress
   2. House
   3. Senate
   4. States

2. T <u>F</u> If Billy had 10 feet of fencing material, he would have enough fence to make a rabbit pen 5 feet long and 4 feet wide.

3. At $0.30 a square yard, how much will it cost to tile a floor 12 feet by 15 feet? <u>$6.00</u>

Yes, the objective test item may encourage guessing, but as seen in Chapter 5, the essay question encourages bluffing. And yes, the objective item neglects writing ability, per se, but it was *never* designed to measure it.

SUGGESTIONS FOR WRITING OBJECTIVE ITEMS

Teacher-made achievement tests are generally deficient in several ways. The most common fault is related to *ineffective communication*. We will now offer some general guidelines for writing objective items. These will be followed by guidelines for each particular item format.

1. *Test for important learning outcomes.* Some teacher-made objective tests consist of items testing for material contained in a footnote or asking questions on other trivia. It is no wonder, then, that pupils taking such tests memorize details and specific facts rather than concentrate on developing an understanding of the material.

We recognize that the knowledge of many specific facts is both important and necessary—such as knowing the alphabet, addition facts, the multiplication table, and the like. However, teachers who teach and test for the students' ability to recall or supply trivial details are practicing pedagogically unsound methods.

2. *Tailor the questions to fit the examinees' age and ability levels as well as the purpose of the test.* The vocabulary used should be commensurate with the age and ability of the examinees. Similarly, the type of objective-item format to be used (as well as the manner in which answers are to be recorded) is, in part, dependent on the age and ability level of the pupils. For example, the slow learner might not be able to comprehend the tasks involved in a matching exercise, but would have less difficulty with the short-answer format. Primary school children should be able to handle items that involve simple matching, but might have difficulty with the multiple-choice format. Elementary school children might be better able to handle "knowledge of facts" and "simple applications and understanding" than interpretation of a complex reading passage. We do not mean to imply that achievement tests for younger children should test only for the factual recall of knowledge. They should not! However, the abilities taught and tested should be realistic for the pupils.

The beauty of the teacher-made test in contrast to the commercially prepared achievement test is that the teacher-made test can be "tailored" to *fit* the needs of the pupils and the teacher's instructional objectives.

3. *Write the items as clearly as possible. Ambiguity is one of the chief weaknesses of objective test items.* Lack of clarity may arise from a variety of sources, such as the inappropriate choice of words used, the awkward arrangement of words, and excessive verbiage. What is clear to the item writer is often vague and ambiguous to the examinee reading the question. A good rule of thumb to follow is to ask yourself: "Does the question as written ensure that the examinee will understand the task he is to perform? Can I make this item any more direct and clear?"

Poor: Columbus discovered America in _____.

As written, the question is ambiguous because the examinee does not know whether the teacher wants to know the year, the date, or the name of the ship he was on. If interested in seeing whether the pupils know the year in which Columbus discovered America, the question should be rewritten as follows:

Better: In what year did Columbus discover America? (1492)

Ambiguity can often occur when *qualitative* rather than quantitative language is used. Words such as *hot, few, many,* and *low* can mean different things to different people. Wherever possible, we advocate the use of *quantitative* language.

Clarity can also be improved by using good grammar and sentence structure. Selecting words that have a precise, exact meaning will help achieve clarity by removing ambiguity. However, in their attempt to achieve clarity, teachers too often resort to using sentences that contain many qualifying statements, parenthetical statements, repetition of words, and the like. Sentence structure, like test directions, should be clear and simple. Long sentences should be broken up into smaller sentences. Vocabulary should be as simple as possible. Again, what may be implicit to the examiner must be made explicit to the examinee. The following example—written by a twelfth-grade civics teacher to ascertain whether her students know that, in the United States, all cases of impeachment are tried by the Senate—is poor because it is ambiguous.

Poor: Impeachment cases are tried by the _____.

Better: According to the U.S. Constitution, all cases of impeachment are tried by the (Senate).

If the students had studied various governments, they would not know to which country the question applied. Also, because of its ambiguity, there would be more than one correct answer. In rewording such an item, the teacher must be careful not to introduce qualifiers that will make the sentence awkward.

4. *If the purpose of a test item is to measure understanding of a principle rather than computational skill, use simple numbers and have the answer come out as a whole number.* A fifth-grade teacher who wants to learn whether her students understand the meaning of *discount* could either have her students supply or select the definition, or she could present them with a verbal problem. In any event, her test item should be presented clearly and concisely.

5. *Avoid lifting statements verbatim from the text.* Lifting statements verbatim from the text and omitting one or two words to make a short-answer item, or inserting a negative to get a true–false item that is false, is poor testing. Statements lifted out of context may lose most of their intended meaning and may result in ambiguous items. This is especially so for true–false items. Also, such an item-writing procedure might result in poor study habits on the part of the pupils. The use of textbook language in a test encourages the pupils to memorize rather than to understand the subject matter and can enable them to answer items correctly without a clear understanding of what their answer means.

6. *Avoid using interrelated items.* Some tests consist of a series of items in which the correct answer to one item is necessary for the pupil to get the correct answer to another item. Teachers should avoid writing items that have this type of dependency.

Interdependent items are grossly unfair, since they may penalize the student who knows how to compute the correct answer to one question but gets an incorrect answer because of an incorrect answer to another question. Let us assume that Allan knows that the formula for the area of a circle is $A = \pi r^2$. However, if Allan computed the value of r incorrectly in an earlier item, he would obtain the wrong answer to the item dealing with the area of a circle even though he had the necessary knowledge and skills. If the teacher wants to learn whether her students know how to compute the area of a circle, she should give them hypothetical values to substitute into the formula. Or if the teacher's intent is to see whether the students know the formula for the area of a circle, she can test for this without reference to the answer of a preceding item.

We are not advocating the removal of computational problems from teacher-made tests. On the contrary, in science and mathematics courses it is important that the student be able to engage in certain arithmetic processes. Nor are we advocating that teachers should not ask a series of questions on a set of common materials. (It is more economical when a series of items can be asked on a common set of materials.) What we are saying is that a pupil should get only *one* item wrong and not two or more because of an error in his arithmetic on a previous item. The use of interrelated or interdependent items should be avoided.

7. *There should be only one correct (or best) answer.* Having more than one correct answer encourages students to quibble, argue, and challenge the "correctness" of their wrong answers. We are *not* opposed to students questioning the appropriateness of the answer keyed as correct. In fact, we encourage it. Done in a constructive and positive fashion, it can be a meaningful learning experience for both pupil and teacher. However, teachers who frequently change their answers contribute little to establishing and maintaining harmonious classroom relationships. And, if many "double-keyed" (two answers are correct) items are deleted, it may affect the test's content validity.

Somewhat related to this point is the case where there is some disagreement among experts in the field as to *the* correct answer. For example, some cardiologists may believe that cholesterol is a major cause of heart attacks but other cardiologists may disagree. Generally, we prefer that teachers not write items where there is no single correct or best answer. However, when different opinions are held, the item should cite the authority(ies) holding a particular view.

> *Poor:*   T   F   A major cause of heart attacks is cholesterol.
>
> *Better:*   T   <u>F</u>   According to White, a major cause of heart attacks is cholesterol.

8. *Avoid negative questions whenever possible.* This is especially true for choice-response (select) items. Indiscriminate use of the negative should be avoided. Since the pupil has to change his normal thought processes, he may overlook the negative aspect and answer the item incorrectly even though he knows the correct answer. Also, it takes the examinee longer to answer a negative item than a comparable one stated positively, and more errors are introduced (Wason, 1961; Zern, 1967). It should also be noted that inserting the word *not* into an otherwise true statement generally results in a low-quality item. Whenever a pupil overlooks the negative because of carelessness, the validity and reliability of the test are lowered. If negative questions are to be used, the negative should be made explicit (by underlining or using all capital letters) so that the examinee does not overlook the negative statement. Double negatives are grammatically incorrect, confuse the student, and contribute nothing to valid evaluation. In fact, we can think of no instance where the double-negative item should be used.

> *Poor:*   T   <u>F</u>   A United States congressman is not elected for a two-year term.
>
> *Better:*   <u>T</u>   F   A United States congressman is elected for a two-year term.
>
> *or*
>
> T   <u>F</u>   A United States congressman is elected for a six-year term.

For the multiple-choice item, avoid using such words as *not*, *never*, and *least*. If such words must be used, attention should be drawn to them.

9. *Do not give the answer away.* A pupil should get the correct answer to a test question only because he has learned the material. Unfortunately, there are many instances where test-wise (but not necessarily content knowledgeable) students obtain the correct answer because of some irrelevant clue(s). Look at the following item:

> *Poor:*   Among the causes of the League of Nations becoming ineffective were the
>
> A. Western-bloc nations distrusted the Eastern nations.
> B. Eastern-bloc nations distrusted the Western nations.
> C. European nations opposed the appeasement tactics of England.
> <u>D.</u> differing views on punishing belligerent nations and protecting internal rights.

To answer this item correctly, the student need only look for a response (answer) that contains two or more reasons, since the stem calls for a plural (*were*) response. To prevent such a clue, all responses should contain two or more reasons, or the stem should be reworded as "The League of Nations became ineffective because . . . ."

Some other irrelevant clues are grammatical clues such as an *a* or *an* preceding a blank in the short answer or at the end of the stem in the multiple-choice; and using words like *always*, *never*, *sometimes*, *all*, and *normally* in true–false items.

10. *Avoid having a position pattern for the correct answer.* A test assembled in haste may give irrelevant clues if a particular pattern to the position of the correct answer is established (Jones & Kaufman, 1975). For example, the correct answer may follow a pattern in true–false tests such as T, F, T, F, . . . T, F; or, in multiple-choice tests, it may be A, D, C, B, A, D, C, B. Randomly positioning the correct response as well as having approximately an equal number of true–false statements or having approximately an equal number of correct answers for each response position (A, B, C, D, E) in the multiple-choice item will minimize pattern clues.

11. *Get an independent review of your test items.* Many of the flaws found in teacher-made tests can be spotted by having an independent review made of the items. Preferably, this review should be made by a teacher who teaches the same subject matter. Such a review will permit the item writer to obtain another opinion about the difficulty of the items, the adequacy of content sampling, the plausibility of the distracters (in a multiple-choice item), the adequacy of the scoring key, and the technical quality of the items. Of course, unless the test has been planned and the items written well in advance of the time the test is scheduled, such a review is not possible.

A Checklist for Writing Objective Test Items

Just as no commercial pilot should take off from a runway before he or she has completed a detailed pre-flight checklist, so should no teacher administer a test before she has thoroughly checked out the items she has written.

Table 6-1 is a summary of the points discussed above. It presents a list of the more important factors to be considered when writing objective test items, regardless of their format. If any of your objective items "fail" this checklist, you should go back to the actual textual discussion. Now that we have considered some general issues to be considered in developing good objective test items, we will focus on writing good short-answer, matching, and true–false items. Multiple-choice, inter-linear, and context-dependent items will be considered in Chapter 7.

WRITING SHORT-ANSWER ITEMS

The short-answer (sometimes called *completion*) item is classified as a supply-type objective item. It is easily recognized by the presence of one or more blanks in which the student writes his answer to the question with a word, phrase, short sentence, mathematical symbol, formula, and so on. The three common varieties of the short-answer form are (1) the *question* variety, in which the item is presented as a direct question; (2) the

TABLE 6-1   Checklist for Writing Objective Test Items

Factor	Yes
1. Are the instructional objectives clearly defined?	X
2. Did you prepare a test blueprint? Did you follow it?	X
3. Did you formulate well-defined, clear test items?	X
4. Did you employ "correct" English in writing the items?	X
5. Did you specifically state all necessary qualifications?	X
6. Did you avoid giving clues to the correct answer? For example, grammatical clues, length of correct response clues?	X
7. Did you test for the important ideas rather than the trivial?	X
8. Did you adapt the test's difficulty to your students?	X
9. Did you avoid using textbook jargon?	X
10. Did you cast the items in positive form?	X
11. If negative items were used, did you draw the students' attention to them?	X
12. Did you prepare a scoring key? Does each and every item have a single correct answer?	X
13. Did you review your items? Yourself? Another teacher?	X

completion variety, in which an incomplete statement is used; and (3) the *association* variety. Examples of each variety follow.

1. *Question variety:*
   In what city was the first experimental psychology laboratory located? (<u>Leipzig</u>)

2. *Completion variety:*
   The first experimental psychology laboratory was located in the city of (<u>Leipzig</u>).

3. *Association variety:*
   After each city, write in the name of the state in which the city is located.

   Detroit (<u>Michigan</u>)
   Chicago (<u>Illinois</u>)
   Boston (<u>Massachusetts</u>)

Short-answer items are somewhat of a cross between the essay and other objective items. On the one hand, like essay items, they require recall rather than recognition. On the other hand, they can be objectively scored.

Advantages and Limitations of the Short-Answer Item

Short-answer items are useful in areas such as spelling and foreign language evaluations, where specific bits of information are usually tested. Short-answer items are particularly useful in mathematics and the sciences, where a computational answer is required or where a formula or equation is to be written. In fact, Forsyth and Spratt (1980) found that short-answer items that required computation were more discriminating than true–false or multiple-choice items that required only recognition. And Oosterhof and Coats (1984) found that for quantitative word problems, providing examinees with alternative answers resulted in about 20 to 30 percent higher scores than when a completion format was used. They also found that more multiple-choice items would be needed to obtain comparable reliability estimates as that for the short-answer format. Accordingly, notwithstanding the inefficiency of scoring responses of large numbers of students, Oosterhof

and Coats (1984) recommend that serious consideration be given the short-answer format.

To test for the students' knowledge of definitions and technical terms, use the short-answer item. Generally, when testing for the student's knowledge of definitions or technical terms, we feel more confident that we are getting a valid measure when the student *supplies* rather than selects the answer.

Illustrated below are examples of different skills that can be measured with the short-answer item.

1. *Knowledge of a procedure.*
   What instrument is used to measure the resistance in an electrical circuit? <u>ohmmeter</u>

2. *Knowledge of specific facts.*
   The president of the United States is elected for <u>4</u> years.

3. *Interpretation of data.*
   In the triangle below, how many degrees are in angle BAC? <u>45</u>

4. *Higher-order thinking.*
   The sum of twice a number and 5 is 39. What is the number? (<u>17</u>)

To solve this problem, the student would first have to introduce an unknown to stand for the number he is looking for. He would then have to translate the verbal problem into an equation such that $2x + 5 = 39$. Then he would solve for x.

First-grade teachers preferred the constructed-response test over the multiple-choice test despite the fact that constructed-response tests are more time-consuming and difficult to score. The teachers felt that they (1) were easier to administer, (2) eliminated copying, (3) motivated the children, and (4) provided more diagnostic information than recognition-type tests (Niedermeyer & Sullivan, 1972).

Finally, because students must *supply* an answer, they will seldom obtain the correct answer by guessing.

The major *limitations* of the short-answer item are:

1. Because short-answer items are best for measuring highly specific facts (dates, names, places, vocabulary), excessive use may encourage rote memory and poor study habits.
2. Scoring may not be quick, easy, routine, and accurate because of the variety of acceptable answers. Frequently the scorer must decide whether a given answer is right, wrong, or partially right. (For example, do you give credit to "ohmeter" even though it is incorrectly spelled?) This can lead to bias in scoring. Also, because of the multiplicity of plausible answers, clerks generally cannot be used as scorers.
3. They are limited to questions that can be answered by a word, phrase, symbol, or number. There are very few instances when an abstraction, generalization, or interpretation can be adequately presented by the examinee in one or two words. This, no doubt, accounts for the fact that the preponderance of short-answer items measures little more than factual recall. However, as seen earlier, short-answer items *can* measure understanding and application.
4. It is almost impossible to write good short-answer items that require the student to exhibit synthesis and interpretation so that one and only one answer will be correct.

Suggestions for Writing Short-Answer Items

1. *For computational problems, the teacher should specify the degree of precision and the units of expression expected in the answer.*

> *Poor:*   The value of π is (3.1? 3.14? 3.142?).
> *Better:* The value of π (to two decimals) is (3.14).

In science and mathematics it may be just as important for the student to know and use the correct unit of expression as the procedure involved in arriving at the answer.

Following is a set of directions that specifies the manner in which answers are to be expressed:

> *Directions:*   This science test consists of 60 questions, some of which require computations to be made. For those questions involving computations, you must (1) carry out your answer to two decimals, and (2) express the answer in proper units such as pounds, grams, or volts.

2. *Omit important words only.* A short-answer item involves more than just having one or more blanks in a sentence. The words that are to be omitted when writing the exercise must be important or key words. The student should be asked to supply an important fact. If verbs, pronouns, or adverbs are omitted, a variety of plausible answers will be received, and the item may no longer assess the instructional objective. Look at the following "poor" example. As written, answers such as "left," "sailed to," "discovered," "came to" would all have to be considered correct:

> *Poor:*   Columbus (discovered) America in 1492.

Needless to say, if there were good instructional objectives, for example, "student will furnish the year when Columbus discovered America," the "poor item" might not have been written.

3. *Avoid excessive blanks in a single item.* Excessive omission of key words may result in the item losing its specific meaning. Omitting too many key words may turn an achievement test into an intelligence test or a guessing game. Overmutilation can only result in the item being ambiguous and confusing. An item writer may have the tangent-ratio concept in her mind when she prepares the following item: *The ratio of the _____ to the _____ is called the _____.* But how is the examinee to know this? Might he not answer "opposite side," hypotenuse," and "sine" for the three respective blanks? If the teacher wishes to learn whether her students know the formula for the tangent, she should test for this.

4. *Have the blanks occur near the end of the sentence.* When the blank is at the beginning or middle of the sentence, the essential point of the question may be overlooked or forgotten by the time the student reads the item. This is especially true when dealing with complex material and/or testing young children who have a limited attention and retention span.

> *Poor:* The _____ is authorized by the U.S. Constitution to try all cases of impeachment.
>
> *Better:* The U.S. Constitution states that all cases of impeachment will be tried by the Senate.

The essential point of this question—who is responsible for trying impeachment cases—should come as close to the end of the item as possible so that students can immediately focus their attention on the problem.

5. *Generally speaking, it is advantageous to use the direct question rather than the incomplete statement.* The direct question is preferred because (a) it may be easier to phrase the question so that it is less ambiguous and does not provide irrelevant clues and (b) it is more natural to pupils who are used to answering the teacher's questions in class rather than answering the teacher's incomplete statement. When the item writer uses the direct-question approach, she will tend to write the item more clearly because she has to clarify in her own mind exactly what it is she intends to measure.

> *Poor:* Neil Armstrong walked on the moon in 1969 _____.
>
> *Better:* (But still poor) When did Neil Armstrong walk on the moon? ____1969____
>
> *Best:* In what year did Neil Armstrong walk on the moon? ____1969____

The first two examples above are poor (even though we have a "better") because the statements could be completed with "in the morning."

6. *To test for the knowledge of definitions and/or the comprehension of technical terms, use a direct question in which the term is given and a definition is asked for.* Quite often when writing the definition, the item writer will provide the student with a clue to the correct answer.

> *Poor:* What is the technical term that describes the synthesis of chemical compounds in plants with the aid of light? _____
>
> *Better:* What is photosynthesis? _____

The latter is to be preferred because the word *synthesis* in the poor example may provide the student with a clue to the correct answer.

7. *Don't skimp on the answer space provided.* If the student is asked to fill in a blank or to give a short answer to a question, the teacher should provide sufficient space for the pupil to record his answer. But be careful—an irrelevant clue to the correct answer might be given by the length of the blank provided. To minimize this, we suggest that *all* blanks be of uniform length, regardless of the length of the answer. And, to make scoring easier, we suggest that for those tests that require only a single word, number, formula, or symbol, all blanks be in a single column, either at the right- or left-hand side of the page. Where the item may have more than one blank to be filled in, such as, "The tangent is the ratio of the ____(1)____ to the ____(2)____," the blanks can be numbered and the pupil instructed to write his answer in the corresponding numbered blank at the side of the page. (We will discuss test layout in greater detail in Chapter 8.)

8. *Avoid giving irrelevant clues.* Check the grammar of the sentence carefully so that no clue is given by the wording to indicate that the correct answer is a singular or plural word. Also, don't have an *a* or *an* before a blank since it would indicate that the answer begins with a consonant or a vowel, respectively. Use either a(n) _____ or *the* _____.

9. *Write the item so that there is only one correct answer.*

> *Poor:* Who was president of the United States in World War II? _____

This is a poor item because *both* Roosevelt and Truman were president at that time.

If the instructional objective was to know that Roosevelt served as president during *most of* World War II, one should use:

Better: What was the name of the U.S. president for most of World War II?

_____

10. *Don't take statements directly from the text, omit a word, and use the statement as a test item.* More often than not, if this is done, a statement taken out of context is ambiguous. It also places too much emphasis on rote memory.

11. *Word the item so that the required answer is brief and specific.* As stated earlier, the answer should consist of a word, phrase, symbol, number, or short sentence.

12. *Check the "Suggestions for Writing Objective Items" on pages 107–111.*

A Checklist for Writing Short-Answer Items

The material previously discussed is summarized in Table 6–2. We strongly urge you to refer to it (and the discussion) when writing short-answer items.

WRITING THE MATCHING EXERCISE

In the traditional format, the matching exercise consists of two columns—one column consists of the questions or problems to be answered (premises); the other column contains the answers (responses). The examinee is presented with the two lists and is required to make some sort of association between each premise and each response. He pairs the corresponding elements and records his answers. Because it's like a game, this item format is perceived as a "fun game" by young children.

Directions: In the blank to the left of each discovery or invention described in column A, write the letter of the discoverer or inventor listed in column B. You may use a letter in column B once, more than once, or not at all.

Column A	Column B
_C_ 1. Discovered penicillin	A. Curie
_F_ 2. Discovered x-rays	B. DeBakey

TABLE 6-2 Checklist for Writing Short-Answer (Supply-Type) Items

Factor	Yes
1. Can each item be answered in a word, a phrase, with a symbol, formula, or short sentence?	X
2. Do the items avoid the use of verbatim textbook language?	X
3. Is each item specific, clear, and unambiguous?	X
4. Are all irrelevant clues avoided? Grammatical? Length of blank? Other?	X
5. Do computational problems indicate the degree of precision required? Whether or not the unit of measurement is to be included in the answer?	X
6. Do the blanks occur near the end of the sentence?	X
7. Have only key words been omitted?	X
8. Was excessive mutilation kept to a minimum?	X
9. Have direct questions been used where feasible?	X
10. Are the items technically correct?	X
11. Is there one correct or agreed-upon correct answer?	X
12. Has a scoring key been prepared?	X
13. Has the test been reviewed independently?	X
14. Is this format most efficient for testing the instructional objectives?	X

<u> A </u> 3. Discovered radium   C. Fleming
<u> G </u> 4. Discovered polio vaccine   D. Harvey
<u> B </u> 5. Invented an artificial   E. Pasteur
        heart   F. Roentgen
<u> D </u> 6. Discovered blood   G. Salk
        circulation

Note that the list of responses is homogeneous, that is, all the persons are scientists. Second, there are more entries in one list than the other, which prevents some students from getting the correct answer by the process of elimination. Finally, the list of premises deals with only discoveries or inventions. We'll elaborate on these points later on.

There are many modifications of the matching exercise that can be used. (Gerberich, 1956, lists 38 versions of the matching exercise.) For example, the student may be given a map on which certain locations are assigned letters or numbers. These letters or numbers are then to be matched with the names of cities, lakes, rivers, continents, or other entities. Or the student may be given a diagram of a piece of electrical equipment such as a voltmeter with the various parts assigned numbers. His task would then be to match the name of the part with the number on the diagram.

A variation of the traditional or simple matching exercise is the classification variety. (It is sometimes classified as a key type of multiple-choice exercise.) Here, a classification scheme (parts of speech, types of rocks) is presented, and the examinee classifies each according to the scheme. This variation is well suited to topics dealing with criticism, explanation, and understanding. Following are two examples of classification exercises.

Directions: Items 1–7 each contain a complete sentence. Determine whether the sentence is simple, compound, complex, or compound-complex. Using the key below, write the letter of the type of sentence it is in the blank to the left of the sentence. You may use each sentence type, once, more than once, or not at all.

Key: A. Simple sentence
       B. Compound sentence

      C. Complex sentence
      D. Compound-complex sentence

<u> C </u> 1. The teacher said that his answer was correct.
<u> A </u> 2. They made him chairman.
<u> D </u> 3. After I had gathered the information, I turned it over to him, and he started the report.
.
.
.
<u> B </u> 7. I warned her, but she was persistent.

Items 8–12: For each definition below, select the most appropriate term from the set of terms at the right. Mark your answer in the blank before each definition. Each term may be used once, more than once, or not at all.

Definitions	Terms
<u>3</u> 8. A professional judgment of the adequacy of test scores.	1. Behavioral objective 2. Criterion-referenced test 3. Evaluation 4. Measurement 5. Norm-referenced
<u>4</u> 9. Determination of the amount of some skill test or trait.	6. Test
<u>1</u> 10. Specification of what a child must do to indicate mastery of a skill.	
<u>6</u> 11. A series of tasks or problems.	
<u>5</u> 12. Tests used to compare individuals.	

Budescu (1988) described a new test format—the *multiple-matching test.* Under this format, responses from a multiple-choice format are pooled into a single-response list. Examinees are asked to match one correct answer to each of the test items.

Although there are problems associated with this item format, it appears to be feasible, and the tests developed are valid and reliable. Also, it appears that random guessing is reduced. Budescu cautioned us that his study used vocabulary items that are amenable to the generation of large numbers of response lists and that the multiple-matching format might not be feasible with other subjects.

Advantages and Limitations of the Matching Exercise

The matching exercise is well suited to those situations where one is interested in testing the knowledge of terms, definitions, dates, events, and other matters involving simple relationships. It is well suited to the "who," "what," "when," "where" types of learning. Dates may be matched with events, authors with book titles, and tools with their uses. In many learning situations, we try to stress the association between various ideas; for example, Columbus discovered America in 1492; Fleming discovered penicillin; Bell invented the telephone. Here, the matching exercise, when properly constructed, is a very valuable measurement tool.

The two major advantages of matching exercises are as follows:

1. Because they require relatively little reading time, many questions can be asked in a limited amount of testing time. This then affords the opportunity to have a larger sampling of content and, other things being equal, a resultant reliability that is higher than if fewer questions were asked.
2. Like true–false or multiple-choice items, matching exercises are amenable to machine scoring. Even if they are hand-scored, they can be scored more easily than the essay or short-answer and can be scored by clerks, paraprofessionals, and even the students, since there should be just one correct answer.

The three major deficiencies associated with simple matching exercises are as follows:

1. If sufficient care is not taken in their preparation, the matching lists may encourage serial memorization rather than association.
2. It is sometimes difficult to get clusters of questions that are sufficiently alike so that a common set of responses can be used. This makes this item format highly susceptible to irrelevant clues.
3. It is generally restricted to the measurement of factual material based on rote learning.

As in all achievement tests, clarity of the items is to be maximized; irrelevant clues and confusion should be minimized. Some of the more common faults of teacher-made matching exercises are (1) the directions are vague, (2) the sets to be matched are excessively long, (3) the list of responses lacks homogeneity, (4) the material is set up so that it is not simple for the student to respond, and (5) the premises are vaguely stated. Following are some suggestions to guide the item writer in her efforts to write a valid matching exercise.

Suggestions for Constructing the Matching Exercise

1. *If at all possible, have the response list consist of short phrases, single words, or numbers.* Putting the lengthier questions in the premise column at the left-hand side of the page will make for easier reading by the pupil, who normally reads from left to right. He would read the lengthier premise list first and then just scan the short responses to find the correct answers.

2. *Each matching exercise should consist of homogeneous items.* A single-matching exercise, to be most valid, should consist of items that deal with only a single concept, classification, or area. For example, in a single-matching exercise do not include items that involve book authors, titles, and inventors. Have separate homogeneous lists. Lists lacking in homogeneity are likely to measure verbal association, which can be readily answered by students who have only a superficial knowledge of the subject matter.

Following is an example of a *poor* matching exercise, because we have a heterogeneous list of scientists, explorers, authors, artists, and inventors.

Directions: On the line to the left of each achievement in column A, write the letter of the man's name in column B who is noted for that achievement. Each name in column B may be used once, more than once, or not at all.

Column A	Column B
__H__ 1. Invented the cotton gin	A. da Vinci
__C__ 2. First man to orbit the earth	B. Fleming
	C. Glenn
	D. Hitler
__A__ 3. Painted the *Mona Lisa*	E. Mozart
__G__ 4. Composed the 1812 Overture	F. Rembrandt
	G. Tchaikovsky
__B__ 5. Discovered penicillin	H. Whitney
__D__ 6. Wrote *Mein Kampf*	

Obtaining homogeneity in the lists may be easier to say than to accomplish. In fact, violation of this prescription is one of the more frequent ones committed by those using the matching exercise.

3. *Keep each list relatively short.* Long lists require that the students spend too much time reading and looking for the answer. Excessively long lists also lend themselves to concentration or emphasis on one or two objectives, which can adversely affect the validity of the test. The number of premises and responses in each list for a single-matching exercise should ordinarily range from 5 to 12, the optimum size being 5 to 8 items per matching exercise (Shannon, 1975). An exercise that consists of 20 premises and 20 responses requires the student to choose 400 different combinations, which makes for a rather lengthy and tedious task. And the economy to be achieved by using a matching exercise is no longer realized.

Short lists are also preferred because lists that are long make it more difficult to maintain the homogeneity of the material. Finally, short lists are to be preferred because, in an excessively long list, the pupil may inadvertently miss the correct answer.

4. *Avoid having an equal number of premises and responses.* If the student is required only to make a one-to-one match, it is conceivable that for an eight-item exercise, the student who knows seven of the eight answers can get the eighth answer correct solely on the basis of elimination. A good rule of thumb to follow is to have two or three more responses than premises.

Somewhat related to this point is the practice of writing matching exercises in which the student can use any one response once, more than once, or not at all. We encourage this to help minimize guessing.

5. *Arrange the answers in some systematic fashion.* For the convenience of the student, words should be listed in alphabetical order; dates and numbers, in either ascending or descending order. The simpler we can make the task for the examinee, the more effective the item is likely to be.

6. *Avoid giving extraneous irrelevant clues.* Do not have the name of one woman among ten men and ask for the name of the actress who won an Academy Award in 1963. Mixing the lists may provide irrelevant clues.

7. *Explain clearly the basis on which the match is to be made.* Although it would appear self-evident that the student matches something with something, how he is to match is not always clear. For example, if a list of authors and a list of book titles are presented to the examinee, is he to match title with author, or vice versa? Although it does not make any difference how the match is accomplished when a single statement in one list is matched with a single answer in the other list (the one-to-one match), confusion can result when any single response may be used once, more than once, or not at all. It is therefore essential that the student be given explicit instructions so that he will know what he is to do and how he is to do it.

Here is a set of directions that convey the essence of the examinee's task:

Directions: In the blank at the left of each author in column A, write the letter of the book title in column B that he/she wrote. You may use a letter in column B once, more than once, or not at all. The first item is answered as an example.

	Column A		Column B
A	X. Arthur Hailey	A.	*Wheels*
J	1. Pearl Buck	B.	*Main Street*
I	2. Ken Follett	C.	*Winds of War*
K	3. Alex Haley	D.	*Love Story*
L	4. John Jakes	E.	*Seven Minutes*
D	5. Eric Segal	F.	*QB VII*
F	6. Leon Uris	G.	*The Winding Staircase*
E	7. Irving Wallace	H.	*The New Centurions*
H	8. Joseph Wambaugh	I.	*Pillars of the Earth*
C	9. Herman Wouk	J.	*Good Earth*
		K.	*Roots*
		L.	*California Gold*

Ordinarily, a separate set of instructions will be needed for each matching exercise, to ensure that the student understands exactly what he is to do.[1]

_____

[1]Because of space limitations, we do not always have a separate set of directions for the various examples discussed in this chapter.

8. *Maintain grammatical consistency.* Use all proper names or all common nouns; all singular or all plurals; all men or all women.

9. *Every response in one column should be a plausible answer to every premise in the other column.*

10. *Check "Suggestions for Writing Objective Items" on pages 107–111.*

A Checklist for Writing the Matching Exercise

Table 6-3 presents the checklist to be used when preparing the matching exercise. In addition, the suggestions previously given for writing the objective item should be considered.

WRITING TRUE–FALSE ITEMS

The true–false (also called the alternate-response) item is essentially a two-response multiple-choice item in which only one of the propositions (answers) is presented and the student judges the truth or falsity of the statement. Two erroneous, but serious misconceptions, are that (1) T–F items are easy to construct—they aren't; to write unambiguous and unequivocally true or false statements is very difficult—and (2) because many

TABLE 6-3   Checklist for Writing Matching Exercises

Factor	Yes
1. Have you given the student clear, explicit instructions?	X
2. Are the response and premise lists both homogeneous?	X
3. Is one list shorter than the other?	X
4. Are both lists between 5 and 12 entries?	X
5. Are the premises longer and more complex? The responses simple and short?	X
6. Did you arrange the responses in some systematic order?	X
7. Do both lists of a matching exercise appear on the same page?	X
8. Are your lists relatively free of clues?	X
9. Did you have your materials reviewed independently?	X

© 1968 United Feature Syndicate, Inc.

items can be answered in a short period of time, you have good content sampling—you may not! Some of the more common variations of the true–false item are (1) yes–no, (2) right–wrong, (3) cluster variety (sometimes called multiple true–false), and (4) correction variety. The right–wrong and yes–no varieties (the yes–no format is often used to measure attitudes, values, beliefs, and interests) are essentially similar to the traditional true–false format except that the nature of indicating the answer is different. The right–wrong or yes–no varieties are more useful for testing young children, who are better able to comprehend the concept of right–wrong than true–false. Following are some illustrations of the true–false item and the cluster and correction variations.

True–False Variety

The student is presented with a declarative statement that is true or false.

    T <u>F</u>   The cube root of 27 is 9.

<u>R</u> W   The square root of 25 is 5.
Y <u>N</u>   The sum of 4 and 6 is 9.

Cluster (Multiple True–False) Variety

In the cluster variety (sometimes called the multiple true–false format), which is frequently found in health science examinations, there is a cluster that resembles a multiple-choice item. The cluster has a stem that is an incomplete statement with several suggested answers that independently complete the stem. Each of the suggested answers is to be judged as true or false.

    We can help keep our teeth in good condition

    T F   by brushing in the morning and night.
    T F   by visiting the dentist regularly.
    T F   by eating both hard and soft foods.

The cluster variety permits the item writer to ask many questions, using a single stem and thereby conserving on space and reading time. Sometimes the cluster of statements will refer to a drawing, graph, or photograph.

There is some disagreement as to the relative merits of the multiple true–false format. Frisbie and Sweeney (1982) compared multiple true–false (MTF) and multiple-choice (MC) items and found that (1) in a given testing time, examinees can attempt 3.5 times more MTF than MC items, (2) reliability was not sacrificed by using MTF items, (3) both MTF and MC items were measuring the same thing, (4) students thought the MTF items were easier, and (5) students preferred the MTF format. (See also Frisbie, 1990.)

Correction Variety

In the correction variety, the subject is required to make every false statement true by crossing out the incorrect portion (it may be a word or phrase) and replacing it with the correct word or phrase. We recommend that the portion of the statement to be judged true or false be underlined. Otherwise, there may be instances when the student will judge the accuracy of the statement in a different light and will make a correction that was not an instructional goal for the teacher. For example, assume that Ms. Adder wanted to discern whether

her students knew that the square root of 64 is 8. If she prepared her item as

T F̲   The square root of 64 is 9.

one student might cross out the "64" and substitute "81"; another might cross out the "9" and substitute "8." Since Ms. Adder's intent was to measure knowledge of the square root of 64, she should rewrite her item as

T F̲   The square root of 64 is 9̲.

Then the student knows that he is to determine whether or not 9 is the square root of 64. If it isn't, he is to write in the correct value.

Another variation of the correction variety is frequently used in the language arts. Here a single sentence is presented and broken up into segments. For each of the designated segments, the student must determine whether it is right or wrong. He then can be asked to correct the error(s). Like the simple correction type, this variation is economical from the standpoint of space needed and time required to read and respond on the part of the pupil. However, it is quite difficult to write sentences that contain errors but that still seem sensible before they have been corrected.

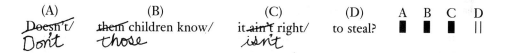

In the preceding example, sections A, B, and C are incorrect. The subject indicates this by blackening in the spaces A, B, and C. (Of course there could be a true–false under each of A, B, C, D, but this method consumes more space.) As noted earlier, the pupil could also be instructed to correct the incorrect parts of speech.

True–false items, while very popular in the early days of testing, have lost much of their popularity. They are seldom used in standardized tests, and most authors of measurement texts speak disparagingly of them (see Stanley, 1964; Wesman, 1971; Gronlund & Linn, 1990; Ahmann

& Glock, 1981). Ebel (1970), one of the few who favors the true–false item, suggested that many of the weaknesses of this item format (ambiguity, measures triviality) are not inherent in the form of the item; rather, the weaknesses are due to misuse and lack of skill on the part of the item writer. He presents a cogent argument and concludes there is "no necessary reason why true–false items should be more trivial, irrelevant, or badly written than other forms of test items" (Ebel, 1970, p. 288). Furthermore, he contends that if true–false items do about the same job and discriminate about as well in tests of equal length (in minutes), why should they not be used? He disagrees with the recommendations that classroom teachers should give preference to writing multiple-choice over true–false items (Ebel, 1975a).

Versatility of the True–False Item

Many of the so-called faults of true–false items— such as "they are most susceptible to guessing," "they encourage students to memorize rather than understand," and "they do not measure the higher mental processes" —are more the fault of the item *writer* than the item format, per se (Ebel, 1975a). True–false items need not encourage and reward verbal *memory*. They *can* be written (as seen below) so that they measure comprehension, un- derstanding, application, deduction, and problem solving (Jenkins & Deno, 1971). And true–false tests can be highly reliable (Frisbie, 1974; Ebel, 1979). But special talents are needed to write valid true–false items (Storey, 1966; Wesman, 1971). More importantly, avoiding their use sacrifices many of their advantages. Following are some ex- amples to illustrate the versatility of the true–false item.

Testing for Factual Knowledge

   <u>T</u> F Hodgkin's disease is characterized by an in- crease in the size of lymph nodes.

To answer this question correctly, the student need only recall one of the symptoms of Hodg- kin's disease. He does not have to know how to test for it, nor be able to recognize it in a patient in order to answer the item correctly, nor know what *are* the characteristics of Hodgkin's disease.

Testing for Comprehension or Understanding[2]

   T <u>F</u> Kinetic energy is found in a wound spring.

Here, the student would have to know more than the textbook definition of kinetic energy. He

---

[2]Our examples of items to measure understanding, application, deduction, and problem solving would be little more than fac- tual recall of information if the student had studied these same or comparable items in class or read them in the textbook.

would have to understand what kinetic energy is and relate the concept of kinetic energy to the type of energy found in a wound spring.

Testing for Application

   T <u>F</u> If heat is supplied at a constant rate to va- porize a substance, the temperature of the substance will also increase at a constant rate.

Testing for Deductive Skill

   <u>T</u> F If the ceiling height of an organ chamber is 20 feet, one can install an organ with a 30- foot stop.

Here the student must know something about the physics of sound and the relationship between pitch and open-ended pipes; that is, that an open pipe will produce twice the pitch of a closed pipe.

Testing for Problem-Solving Ability

   T <u>F</u> Given the general gas law, where $PV/T = k$, where $k = 2$, $P = 5$, and $T = 50°C$, then $V = 20$.

Advantages and Limitations of True–False Items

The major *advantages* of true–false items are that they—

1. Are good for young children and/or pupils who are poor readers.
2. Can cover a larger amount of subject matter in a given testing period than can any other ob- jective item, that is, more questions can be asked. A student can answer about three T–F items for every two multiple-choice items (Frisbie, 1971; Oosterhof & Glassnapp, 1974; and Green, 1979, reported ratios of 1.5, 1.7, and 2.4, respectively). With the MTF format, the ratio to multiple-choice items is 3.5:1. But the time ratio depends on the content, as well as the difficulty/comprehension factor of the item. Measuring factual information will gen- erally show less time-to-respond variability than measuring comprehension (Frisbie, 1971).

3. Generally provide high reliability per unit of testing time. This should be interpreted very carefully. It does not mean that T–F tests have the highest reliability. Oosterhof and Glassnapp (1974) said that one needs 2½ to 4½ times as many T–F as multiple-choice items to get equivalent reliability. However, more T–F than multiple-choice items can be asked and answered per unit of testing time.

4. Can be scored quickly, reliably, and objectively by clerks.

5. Are particularly suitable for testing beliefs in popular misconceptions and superstitions.

6. Are adaptable to most content areas.

7. May provide a salvage pool for multiple-choice items that should be discarded because only two of the responses provided are selected by the majority of students. The true–false item needs only one good response to a stem.

8. Can, if carefully constructed, measure the higher mental processes of understanding, application, and interpretation.

9. Are as valid as multiple-choice items.

The major *disadvantages* of the true–false item are that—

1. Pupils' scores on *short* true–false tests may be unduly influenced by good or poor luck in guessing.

2. True–false items are more susceptible to ambiguity and misinterpretation than any other selection-type objective item.

3. They lend themselves most easily to cheating. If a student knows that he is to take a T–F test, it doesn't require much effort to work out a system in which one of the better students signals a T versus F answer.

4. They tend to be less discriminating, item for item, than multiple-choice tests.

5. They are susceptible to an acquiescence response set; that is, subjects tend to develop a pattern of responding (true) in a somewhat automatic form without really giving thought to the item.

6. There are many instances when statements are *not* unequivocally true or false; rather, there are degrees of correctness. For example, the boiling point of water depends upon the pressure. Hence, "water boils at 212°F" as written, would *not* be a good T–F item since the statement is true only at sea level. Many true–false items require qualifiers, which in themselves may provide an irrelevant clue. Because of the phenomenon of degree of correctness, good true–false items are difficult to write.

7. Specific determiners (a type of irrelevant clue) are more prevalent in true–false items than in any other objective-item format. Specific determiners generally appear because the item writer wishes to have a completely true or false statement.

In conclusion: When very young children and/or persons with limited vocabulary and reading speed are to be tested; if one desires broad content sampling in a relatively short testing time; if one wants a test that can be scored accurately, quickly, and objectively by clerks, the true–false item is recommended. Although writing true–false items to measure the higher mental processes can be both difficult and time-consuming, it is less difficult to write a good true–false item than to write a good three- or four-response multiple-choice item.

Suggestions for Writing True–False Items

1. *Avoid ambiguous words and statements.* Ambiguous statements resulting from loose or faulty wording are a frequent cause of faulty true–false items.

Poor: T F All men are created equal.

As a proposition, the Declaration of Independence stated by the writers, the item is true. But a student could interpret the item in terms of mental ability, pain threshold, physical strength, or other characteristics and mark the item false. If the teacher wants to know whether her pupils understand "equality" as stated in the Declaration of Independence, she should write the item as follows:

Better: T̲ F The Declaration of Independence *states* that all men are created equal.

Ambiguity is often present when an item deals with qualitative terms such as "more," "few," "lighter," and the like. Since these words are somewhat vague, they may be interpreted differently by different people. It is suggested that, wherever possible, *quantitative* rather than qualitative terminology be employed.

Poor: T F Dukakis received a large number of votes in the.1988 presidential election.

How much is "large?" Is it 30 or 40 or 46 percent? A student could answer a test item incorrectly because of his interpretation of the qualitative terms used.

Better: T F Humphrey received more than 40 percent of the votes in the 1968 presidential election.

2. *True–false items must be based on statements that are clearly true or clearly false.* It is not uncommon to find T–F items consisting of two statements, one part correct, the other part wrong. In the following example:

```
            (1)                    (2)
```
Poor: /Whales are mammals, /and/ with the exception of humans, they are the most intelligent mammals/.

Statement (1) is correct, but statement (2) is false.

Better: T F Whales are the most intelligent mammals.

When a true–false item does not satisfy the condition of being completely true or clearly false, we inject an element of ambiguity or trickiness into the item. Whenever the knowledgeable student is confused by the wording and answers incorrectly because he reads too deeply into the question and recognizes that there are possible exceptions, we have a faulty item. Trying to doctor up a true–false item that is not unequivocally true or false by inserting a series of qualifiers or exceptions will likely result in a more confusing item.

We recognize that there are some statements, especially generalizations, that need not be wholly true or false. When this is the case, we recommend a variation of the true–false item—true, false, sometimes—be used. For example, we would want to have stability in an intelligence test. But in a personality test we might not want to have stability. Therefore, to write an item regarding the stability of test scores, we recommend the following item format.

T F S Stability of test scores is essential.

3. *Avoid trick questions.* One of the easiest and surest ways of disenchanting and "souring" students toward tests and teachers is to have a test full of trick questions, such as

T F O. Henry was William Sidney Porter.

The "trick" here is that Porter's middle name is spelled Sydney.

We must remember that students are under pressure when they take tests. They tend to read very rapidly and pay little attention to "tricky" wording. More important, one of our objectives in giving tests is to see what the student has learned, *not* whether he can be tricked. In addition to jeopardizing the affective relations between student and teacher, "trick" questions affect the test's validity.

4. *When the true–false item is used to test for cause-and-effect relationships, we strongly recommend that the first proposition in the statement always be true, with the subordinate clause (reason or explanation) being written as either false or true.* The student could be told that the first part of the statement is true and that he is only to judge the truth or falsity of the subordinate clause.

T F Marble rarely, if ever, contains fossils
(true)
because it is a metamorphosed igneous rock.
(true or false)

5. *Word the item so that superficial knowledge suggests a wrong answer.* This does not mean that the wording should be ambiguous or overly complex. Rather, it means that the wording should be

such that the student who has only superficial knowledge may answer incorrectly. For example,

T <u>F</u>   In a storm, a ship is safer near the shore than it is far from shore.

Wave action is greater closer to the shore. However, it would seem logical that the closer the ship is to the shore (and supposed safety), the safer it would be.

<u>T</u> F   More sugar can be dissolved in a glass of warm water than in a glass of cold water.

On the surface, the student who doesn't know the answer would respond false; thinking that the volume of water is more important than its temperature, vis-à-vis the amount of a substance that can be dissolved in it.

6. *False items should be written so that they sound plausible to someone who doesn't know the answer.* Popular misconceptions provide good bases for false items. But don't insert the word *not* in a true statement to accomplish this.

7. *Avoid specific determiners.* Specific determiners are more prevalent in true–false items than in other objective-item formats. In the true–false test, the teacher, in her attempt to write an item that is clearly true, may use such qualifiers as *usually, some, generally, should, sometimes, often, most, several, as a rule,* and *may* to make the statement true. On the other hand, the teacher who wishes to ensure falsity in an item may use qualifiers such as *always, never, only, completely, none,* and *all.* Pupils learn very quickly that the odds are in their favor to mark test items as true or false, depending upon the qualifiers used. If the true–false item cannot be rewritten to avoid the use of specific determiners, we recommend that a different item format be used. Occasionally, to thwart the test-wise student, write an item with *never* that is true. For example,

<u>T</u> F   In a matching exercise, never have an equal number of premises and responses.

8. *Avoid lifting statements verbatim from the text.* All textual material should be rephrased or put in a new context to discourage rote memory.

9. *Avoid making true statements consistently longer than false statements.* Teachers, in their attempt to ensure absolute truth in a statement will employ qualifying statements that make the item longer. Pupils readily learn to recognize this irrelevant clue. To minimize this effect, the item writer should vary the length of both true and false statements.

10. *For the correction type of true–false item, underline the word(s) to be corrected.*

11. *Avoid a disproportionate number of either true or false items.* Approximately half the statements should be false. Since true statements are generally easier to construct, they tend to predominate. Some students have a tendency (response set) to mark items that they are unsure of as "true" while other students mark "unsure" items "false." By having approximately an equal number of true and false statements in the test, we limit the influence of response set on the validity of the test score. But having exactly the same number of true–false statements or a pattern of *always* having more T than F or vice versa could be a clue to the test-wise student. Ebel (1979) and Frisbie (1974) suggest having more false than true statements since there is evidence that false statements tend to be more discriminating. Gronlund and Linn (1990) recommend varying the percentage of true statements somewhere between 40 and 60 percent.

12. *Write true–false statements positively.* If a negative must be used, underline, italicize, or capitalize the negative. And under *no* circumstances should you use a double-negative.

13. *Check "Suggestions for Writing Objective Items" on pages 107–111.*

A Checklist for Writing True–False Items

Table 6-4 presents a checklist for preparing true-false items. We urge you to review the material

TABLE 6-4 Checklist for Writing True–False Items

Factor	Yes
1. Is each item expressed in clear, simple language?	X
2. Did you avoid lifting statements verbatim from the text?	X
3. Have negative statements been avoided where possible?	X
4. Have specific determiners such as "all," "may," "sometimes," been avoided?	X
5. Have double-barreled items (part true, part false) been avoided?	X
6. Have trick questions been removed?	X
7. In the correction-type true–false, is the word(s) to be corrected clearly indicated?	X
8. Is each item clearly true or false?	X
9. Are there approximately the same number of true and false items?	X
10. Have the items been edited?	X
11. Have the items been independently reviewed?	X

previously discussed for writing objective-type items.

■ SUMMARY

The principal ideas, conclusions, and recommendations presented in this chapter are summarized in the following statements:

1. Objective-type items can be written to measure higher-order thinking skills.
2. Objective test items must be written as simply and clearly as possible so that all examinees will be able to make the same interpretation of the items' intent.
3. Test items should be tailored to fit the age and ability level of the examinees.
4. Textbook language, technical jargon, and excessively difficult vocabulary should be avoided wherever possible. Otherwise, we have a test of verbal fluency or general intelligence.
5. Irrelevant clues should be avoided. The test-wise student should not have any undue advantage over the comparably knowledgeable but non-test-wise student.
6. There should be only one correct or best answer. We prefer the correct answer variety

inasmuch as it is difficult to obtain agreement, even among experts, on what is the "best" answer.

7. Test items should be reviewed, preferably by a fellow teacher.
8. Important ideas rather than trivial details should be stressed. Otherwise, we encourage rote memory.
9. Short-answer items are well suited to those objectives and content areas where the answer can be provided by a word, phrase, symbol, number, or formula. They can measure interpretation of data as well as memory of facts and dates.
10. For short-answer items (a) omit only key words, (b) avoid over-mutilated sentences, (c) use the direct-question format where feasible, (d) don't lift statements directly from the text, (e) avoid giving irrelevant clues, (f) use it for items that have a brief answer, and (g) for numerical problems, tell the student the degree of precision desired and indicate whether the unit of expression is expected in his answer.
11. For matching exercises (a) keep the lists relatively short (5 to 12 entries in each list), (b) keep each list homogeneous, (c) arrange each list in some systematic fashion (e.g., order by length of response, alphabetical order, or in

ascending or descending order for dates and numbers), (d) have both lists appear on the same page, (e) have one list shorter than the other, and (f) have very clear directions. The multiple-matching test is a promising format.

12. For true–false items (a) avoid double-barreled items (part true, part false), (b) avoid negative questions where possible, (c) avoid double-negatives, (d) have an approximately equal number of true and false statements to counteract the effects of the examinee's response set, (e) restrict their use to items for which the answer is clearly true or false, and (f) avoid trick questions.

13. There is disagreement on the merits of the cluster variety.

■ POINTS TO PONDER

1. What steps should be followed when writing an objective-type item?

2. What are the different types of objective-type items? Under what circumstance is one type to be preferred over the other?

3. A major criticism of objective-type tests is that they only measure trivia. How would you answer a pupil or parent who challenged you with this statement?

4. Objective-type tests can use either the "one correct answer" or the "best-answer" format. Which one would you use? Why would you use this type over the other?

5. What advantages and limitations are there in selecting an objective-type over an essay format? Could you use an objective-type format to measure critical thinking? Give an example of such an item.

6. What are some of the clues that examiners unwittingly give when using a matching or true–false format? Give some examples of poor items and better items.

7. If you were preparing a true–false test would you have more true than false items? Why? Why not?

8. Teachers have a tendency to lift statements verbatim from the text when preparing an objective-type item. Some critics claim that this encourages rote memory. But aren't there some instances when factual details should be committed to memory? Regardless of whether you agree or disagree, support your stand.

9. How much truth is there to the claim that students can guess their way through an objective-type test and bluff their way through an essay?

Chapter 7

Writing the Objective Test Item: Multiple-Choice and Context-Dependent

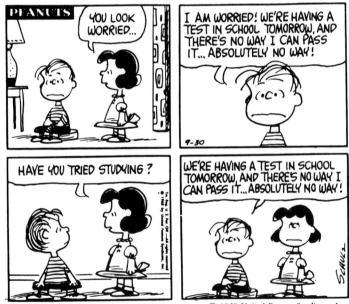

© 1968 United Feature Syndicate, Inc.

- ■ **The Multiple-Choice Item**
- ■ **Advantages and Limitations of Multiple-Choice Items**
- ■ **Item Shells**
- ■ **Suggestions for Writing Multiple-Choice Items**
- ■ **Writing Context-Dependent Items**

Multiple-choice (MC) items are presently the most frequently used and, among measurement specialists, the most highly regarded objective test item (Ebel & Frisbie, 1986; Gronlund, 1985; Nitko, 1983). They are the most popular and versatile of the selection-type objective item (Fleming & Chambers, 1983; Marso & Pigge, 1988, Ellsworth et al., 1989). They are widely adaptable to different content areas and objectives and can be used to measure rote memory as well as complex skills (see Mosier et al., 1945). No doubt, such adaptability and versatility are responsible for these items being the workhorse of many commercially prepared achievement and aptitude tests. They are also the preferred format for college selection tests, licensure examinations, and student and teacher competency tests.

There are, however, some measurement experts who contend that MC tests do *not* measure higher-order thinking skills (e.g., Jones, 1988). In fact, Jones (1988) stated that MC tests are ill-suited for assessing productive thinking and problem-solving skills. Norris (1988) cautions us to be aware of some potential dangers in using multiple-choice items with only *one* correct answer. He also claims that for many multiple-choice critical thinking tests, score variance may be due more to differences in background beliefs than differences in examinees' critical thinking ability.

Contrary to the opinion of some critics, the measurement of the higher mental processes *can* be attained objectively. Our discussion in Chapter 6 and some of our discussion in this chapter concerns the use of single, independent test items to measure complex achievement. There are, however, some cases in which items based on an external source (such as a graph, diagram, table, chart, or verbal passage) are more suitable for measuring complex achievement. Items based on such external sources are called *context-dependent* and are considered in this chapter.

After studying this chapter, you should be able to:

1. Define and discuss the multiple-choice format and some of its more frequently used variations.
2. Understand why the multiple-choice format is so popular.
3. Discuss the advantages and limitations of the multiple-choice format.
4. Understand and apply the guidelines offered when writing multiple-choice items.
5. Define and discuss the following context-dependent item formats: pictorial, interlinear, and interpretive exercises.
6. Understand and apply the guidelines offered when writing items based upon pictorial materials.
7. List the two most serious limitations of the interpretive exercise as a measure of complex learning.
8. Understand and apply the guidelines offered for writing interpretive exercises.
9. Write better multiple-choice items.

THE MULTIPLE-CHOICE ITEM

The multiple-choice item consists of two parts: (1) the stem, which contains the problem; and (2) a list of suggested answers (responses or options). The incorrect responses are often called *foils* or *distracters* (*distracters* is sometimes spelled with an "o": *distractors*; we prefer the first spelling, which is usual in measurement texts). The correct response is called the *key*. The stem may be stated as a direct question or an incomplete statement.

From the list of responses provided, the student selects the one that is correct (or best).

Haladyna and Downing, (1989b) recommend that the question variety be used. The direct question format has several advantages: (1) it forces the item writer to state the problem clearly in the stem; (2) it reduces the possibility of giving the examinee grammatical clues; and (3) it may be more easily handled by the younger and less able students because less demand is placed on good reading skills. One disadvantage of the direct question form is that it may require lengthier responses.

However, there is some disagreement regarding the relative superiority of the question variety over the incomplete statement variety (Dunn & Goldstein, 1959; Crehan & Haladyna, n.d.; Schrock & Mueller, 1982; Board & Whitney, 1972; Haladyna & Downing, 1989b). Regardless of the empirical research, one thing is clear: if the incomplete statement form is used, the stem must be clear and meaningful in and of itself and *not* lead into a series of unrelated true–false statements.

Variations of the Multiple-Choice Format

The five most frequently used variations of the multiple-choice item are (1) one correct answer, (2) best answer, (3) analogy type, (4) reverse type and (5) alternate-choice. A sixth but infrequently used approach is the subset-selection technique suggested by Dressel and Schmidt (1953). Some other variations are *association, substitution, incomplete-alternatives, combined-response*, and *multiple-response*. Excellent descriptions and illustrations of these variations can be found in Gerberich (1956) and Thorndike (1971c).

What might more properly be referred to as a procedure, rather than a format, per se, is the answer-until-correct (A-U-C) variety. Although this procedure may result in higher test reliability, it consumes more time per item and may lower the test's validity (Gilman & Ferry, 1972; Hanna, 1975). Because of the paucity of research, we do not recommend the A-U-C procedure at this time.

One Correct Answer   This is the simplest type of multiple-choice item. The student is told to select the *one* correct answer listed among several plausible, but incorrect, options.

Incomplete Statement	*Direct Question*
If $R^3 = 27$, then R is	If $R^3 = 27$, what is R?
A. 3	or
B. 9	What is R in $R^3 = 27$?
C. 11	A. 3
D. 30	B. 9
	C. 11
	D. 30

Best Answer   There are times where it is difficult, if not impossible, to express one unequivocal right answer within the limits of the multiple-choice format. For example, "the purpose of the United Nations," does not lend itself to the single-correct-answer format. And yet there still may be one answer that is "best." When this is the case, the best-answer variation is useful. The directions are similar to those of the single correct answer except that the student is told to select the best answer.

Analogy Type   In this format, the student is required to deduce the relationship that exists between the first two parts of the item and then apply it to the third and fourth parts. Normally, the third part is given and the missing fourth part is selected from the list of options on the basis of the relationship existing between the first two parts.

Irregular curvature of the lens: astigmatism::deficiency in thyroid secretion:
A. cretinism
B. hybridism
C. hydrocephaly
D. mongolism

Reverse Multiple-Choice Type   This format is the opposite of the single correct answer in that all but one of the answers are correct. It is sometimes called the negative variety of multiple-choice item. As will be discussed in a later section (pp. 136–137), one of the most difficult tasks in writing multiple-choice items is to provide wrong answers (distracters) that are plausible and homogeneous. In some cases it is easier to construct three or four options that are true about a given fact than it is to prepare an adequate number of plausible distracters. If this format is used, the students' attention should be drawn to the fact that they are to select the *incorrect* answer.

Alternate-Choice Items   Once can write a multiple-choice item as a simple declarative statement where one of two alternative words, terms, or phrases could be used to complete the sentence. The examinee is asked to select the revision that most nearly makes the sentence *true*.

In writing an alternate-response item, one first thinks of items in pairs: one statement in the pair is true; the other statement of the pair is false. For example,

A criterion-referenced test should be used when one wishes to describe pupils.   (T)

A criterion-referenced test should be used when one wishes to compare pupils.   (F)

The alternate-response item is then written as

Criterion-referenced tests should be used to (1) describe (2) compare pupils.

Another example is,

The sum of 64 and 17 is more than 80. (T)
The sum of 64 and 17 is less than 80. (F)

Written as an alternate-response item, we have

The sum of 64 and 17 is (1) more (2) less than 80.

On the surface, alternate-response items resemble true–false items, and in a sense, they are. They differ, however, in the sense that in the true–false item, the examinee looks for a counterexample to make the comparisons, but in the alternate-choice item the comparison is built into the item. What then, are the advantages of this type of item in comparison with the traditional multiple-choice or true–false item? According to Ebel and Frisbie (1986) there are three: (1) they are easier and more efficient to write than traditional multiple-choice items because they are based on simple relationships; (2) because of their brevity, examinees can respond to more alternate-choice than traditional multiple-choice items in a given testing period, thereby improving the content sampling and test reliability; and (3) because the comparison to be made is built into the item, they tend to be less ambiguous than true–false items. Also, we believe they obviate the need for having absolute judgments of truth or falsity—something essential (but often difficult to achieve) for true–false items.

Subset-Selection Technique   In this approach, examinees are informed that there is only one correct answer for each item. They are told to select the correct alternative or any number of alternatives that they think includes the correct one. Their score is based on the number of item alternatives less the number of alternatives selected *provided* that the correct answer is included in the chosen set. If the correct answer is not circled, the examinees' score is minus the number of alternatives selected. When Jaradat and Sawaged (1986) studied the effects of the subset-selection technique (SST), the number-right method (NR), and the correction-for-guessing technique (CFG) on the psychometric properties of the test and on the performance of examinees' with different levels of risk-taking and achievement, they found that the SST method yielded *higher* validity and reliability coefficients *without* favoring high risk-takers. The researchers stress the importance of instructions to the examinees regardless of the technique used. This latter point supports Lord's (1975) contention that much of the conflicting research concerning the correction-for-guessing format is due to poor test instructions. Jaradat and Sawaged concluded that SST possesses two desirable properties for testing: (1) control of examinees' random guessing and (2) provision for examinees to use partial knowledge and obtain some credit for it.

ADVANTAGES AND LIMITATIONS OF MULTIPLE-CHOICE ITEMS

There are several major advantages of multiple-choice items:

1. Possibly the outstanding advantage is their versatility. Multiple-choice questions can not only measure factual recall, but they can also measure the student's ability to reason, to exercise judgment, and to express himself correctly and effectively. One should interpret the last statement carefully. We did *not* say that the MC test could measure writing ability. Rather, we said that the MC test could measure certain factors involved in writing, for example, organizational skills. Benton and Kierwa (1986) studied 105 undergraduate students to ascertain the relationship among holistic writing ability, the Test of Standard Written English (TSWE), and four tests of organizational ability—anagram solving, word reordering, sentence reordering, and paragraph assembly. They found that holistically scored writing was significantly correlated with performance on the four organizational ability tests and the TSWE.

2. They afford excellent content sampling, which generally leads to more content-valid score interpretations.

3. They can be scored quickly and accurately by machines, clerks, teacher aides, and even students themselves.

4. They are relatively efficient. True–false and matching items are slightly more efficient (in terms of the number of questions that can be asked in a prescribed time and the space needed to present the questions), whereas the essay question is far less efficient.

5. The degree of difficulty of the test can be controlled by changing the degree of homogeneity of the responses. If, for example, one

is giving a test to discriminate among pupils in terms of their achievement, then one should use items that are neither too difficult nor too easy. Knapp (1968) conducted a study that compared three versions of multiple-choice items and found that the choice of responses often drastically affected the item difficulty.

6. Compared to true–false items, multiple-choice questions have a relatively small susceptibility to score variations due to guessing because the probability of guessing a correct answer depends on the number of options. For a three-option item, the chances are 1 in 3; for a five-option item, the chances of guessing the correct answer are 1 in 5.

7. They can provide the teacher with valuable diagnostic information, especially if all the responses vary only in their degree of correctness.

8. They usually provide greater test reliability per item than do true–false items. Increasing the number of alternatives not only reduces the opportunity of guessing the correct answer, but in effect it is similar to increasing the test reliability (see p. 258) by increasing the test length (Ebel, 1969a).

9. Multiple-choice items are easier to respond to and are better liked by students than true–false items. Students feel they are less ambiguous than true–false items.

10. Of all the selection-type objective items, the multiple-choice item is most free from response sets (the tendency for an individual to give a different answer when the *same* content is presented in a different form).

11. They may be less prone to ambiguity than the short-answer item.

12. In contrast to matching and true–false tests, MC tests don't require homogeneous items (similar to the list of responses in the matching item) or qualifications to make the answer unequivocally true or false (as in T–F items).

In spite of their popularity, multiple-choice tests are *not* without their critics. Some individuals have voiced their concern about the validity of multiple-choice tests. Barzun (1947), Getzels (1960), and Hoffmann (1962) contend that the multiple-choice item punishes the more-able student and rewards the less-able student. One reason given by these critics for the multiple-choice item discriminating against the more-able student is because of the ambiguity in multiple-choice items. We contend that an item is ambiguous because of the item writer and not because of the item format, per se. Another criticism is that in testing (or for that matter, teaching) for incorrect spelling, using a multiple-choice format with distracters may in the long run be detrimental (Brown, 1988).

Two important facts, however, detract from the critics' credibility: (1) the critics supply no empirical evidence supporting their contentions; and (2) they offer no alternative methods of assessment and appear unaware of the serious limitations of essay testing. We agree, however, that there are deficiencies or limitations associated with multiple-choice items. Some of the more serious limitations of the multiple-choice item are as follows:

1. They are very difficult to construct. Teachers cannot always think of plausible sounding distracters (incorrect alternatives), and if only one good distracter is listed, they wind up with a multiple-choice item with as large a guessing factor as for a true–false item.
2. There is a tendency for teachers to write multiple-choice items demanding only factual recall. This tendency is probably less for multiple-choice items than for other objective-type items, but it still persists.
3. Of all the selection-type objective items, the multiple-choice item requires the *most* time for the student to respond, especially when very fine discriminations have to be made.
4. Research has shown that test-wise students perform better on multiple-choice items than do non-test-wise students and that multiple-choice tests favor the high risk-taking student (Rowley, 1974). Also, students who are skillful in recognizing ambiguity do better than stu-

dents who do not (Alker, Carlson, & Hermann, 1967).

5. Some examinees are able to *recognize* the correct answer that ordinarily they would not be able to produce (Popham, 1981). On the other hand, a pupil *must know the correct answer*; he just can't get credit for knowing that a statement is incorrect.

The reproductive organ of a flower is called the *stamen*.

The reproductive organ of the flower is the
   A. antler.
   B. filament.
   C. pistil.
   D. stamen.

ITEM SHELLS

Before beginning our discussion on some of the guidelines or suggestions to be considered in writing the multiple-choice item, we would like to discuss, briefly, an approach—*item shells*—that appears promising insofar as the development of multiple-choice items is concerned.

In the conventional approach, multiple-choice item writers have a great deal of freedom and latitude. And this freedom may result in problems since different item writers develop different tests. Is there some way a more standardized approach could be developed and still be feasible? We know that the traditional approach affords latitude. But the restriction of latitude by the newer technologies is compensated for in providing for greater objectivity. The compromise is the "item shell."

"An item shell is a 'hollow' item that contains the syntactic structure and context of an item without specifying content . . . empirically developed from successfully used items" (Haladyna et al., 1987, p. 4).

Haladyna et al. (1987, p. 7) provide an example of how one develops an "item shell."

A six-year-old child is brought to the hospital with contusions over the abdomen and chest as a result of an automobile accident. Initial treatment should consist of:

   A.
   B.
   C.
   D.

This item, written as an "item shell" would be as follows:

> A (age, pre-existing condition, sex of patient) is brought to the hospital (complaining of, with injuries showing symptoms of) (as a result of). Initial (treatment, intervention, diagnosis, laboratory studies) should consist of:
>   A.
>   B.
>   C.
>   D.

It should be readily obvious that the open feature of the "item shell" affords the item writer a variety of options based on the information that "someone is brought to the hospital, complaining of, and requiring some sort of action."

This newer approach, appears to be promising but requires additional study.

SUGGESTIONS FOR WRITING MULTIPLE-CHOICE ITEMS

A test item is good or bad depending upon its clarity of expression. The multiple-choice item is no exception. The multiple-choice item must have, in addition to a stem that is clear and free from ambiguity, a correct (or best) answer and a set of plausible responses (distracters). The "goodness" of a multiple-choice item depends to a large degree on the skill with which the various distracters are written. It will be evident when reading these guidelines that a common theme pervades the writing of all test items, regardless of the format used. Two basic questions that an item writer must continually ask herself are: (1) did I communicate well? and (2) did I provide any clues to the correct answer? Because it is so important that the item writer communicate effectively and not

give the answer away, we will repeat some of the suggestions discussed in the previous chapters. (See Board & Whitney, 1972, for a discussion of the effects of item-writing flaws on a test's difficulty, reliability, and validity. See also Haladyna & Downing, 1989a, for a discussion of a taxonomy of MC item-writing rules.) It is interesting to note that of the theoretical and empirical studies reviewed by Haladyna and Downing, the two item rules studied most frequently dealt with the number of options and key-balancing, that is, having an equal number of each response as the correct answer. Also, see Carter (1986) and Ellsworth et al. (1989).

It should be noted, that some of these "rules" (we prefer "suggestions") are not testable (Haladyna & Downing, 1989a).

1. *The essence of the problem should be in the stem.* The stem should contain the central problem so that the student will have some idea as to what is expected of him and some tentative answer in mind before he begins to read the options. There are some exceptions, such as in a literature test.

If the objective is to ascertain the pupil's understanding of the main theme in a story or poem, the stem may be short and the options long. An easy way to ascertain whether or not the stem is meaningful in and of itself is to cover up the responses and just read the stem. If the stem is well written, it could easily become a short-answer item by drawing a line after the last word. If it would not be a good short-answer item, something is wrong with the stem. The stem must consist of a statement that contains a verb.

Poor Stem: A criterion-referenced test is

This example is poor because it does *not* contain a problem in the stem. That is, the stem does *not* ask a question or set a task. The student is unable to obtain a glimmer of what is asked without reading *all* the answers. It is essential that the *intent* of the item be stated clearly in the stem.

2. *Avoid repetition of words in the options.* The stem should be written so that key words are incorporated in the stem and will not have to be re-

peated in each option. This will save reading time on the part of the student as well as help focus the student's attention on the problem. It will also conserve space.

Poor: According to Engel's law,
      A. family expenditures for food increase in accordance with the size of the family.
      B. family expenditures for food decrease as income increases.
      C. family expenditures for food require a smaller percentage of an increasing income.
      D. family expenditures for food rise in proportion to income.
      E. family expenditures for food vary with the family's tastes.

Better: According to Engel's law, family expenditures for food
      A. increase in accordance with the size of the family.
      B. decrease as income increases.
      C. require a smaller percentage of an increasing income.
      D. rise in proportion to income.
      E. vary with the tastes of families.

3. *Avoid superfluous wording.* The stem should be concise, clear, and free of "window dressing." Verbal overload should be avoided, since it demands extra reading time on the examinee's part and thereby reduces the number of items that can be asked in a given testing time. This, of course, affects the test's content sampling and reliability.

Poor: Billy's mother wants to bake an apple pie for his birthday. When she went to the fruit basket, she noticed that she had no apples. Her recipe called for 6 medium-sized apples. She phoned her grocer and learned that there was a sale going on and apples were selling for 2 for 25 cents. If Billy goes to the store and buys 6 apples, how much change should he get from $5.00?
      A. $3.00
      B. $3.50
      C. $4.25
      D. $4.75

Better: If you buy 6 apples selling for 2 for 25 cents, how much change will you get from $5.00?
      A. $3.00
      B. $3.50
      C. $4.25
      D. $4.75

4. *When the incomplete statement format is used, the options should come at the end of the statement.* All test items should present the problem to the student as *early* and clearly as possible. The following two items measure the student's knowledge of the concept of the probable causes of cardiovascular disease.

Poor: According to DeBakey, (1) cholesterol, (2) overweight, (3) smoking, (4) stress, (5) none of these is the leading cause of cardiovascular disease.

Better: According to DeBakey, the leading cause of cardiovascular disease is
      A. cholesterol.
      B. overweight.
      C. smoking.
      D. stress.
      E. none of the above.

In the "poor" example, the students' continuity of reading is impaired, and this may result in confusion. In the "better" example, the essence of the problem is presented early and clearly. Also, the examinees need not engage in extensive rereading of the item to see what they are expected to do.

5. *Arrange the alternatives as simply as possible.* Although the responses could be placed after the stem in run-on fashion (as in the "poor" example above), it is preferable to list them in some order below the stem (alphabetical if a single word, in ascending or descending order if numerals or dates, or by length of response). This makes it easier for the examinee to read the material. Also, in the incomplete statement format, where each response completes the sentence, listed alternatives are easier to consider separately than if placed in paragraph fashion, as in the preceding "poor" example.

6. *Avoid Type K multiple-choice items.* This item-type format was very popular in medical and allied health testing and is sometimes called a "Key-type" item format. An example of such an item is as follows:

The major deficiencies of teacher-made tests are
1. Ambiguous questions.
2. multiple correct answers.
3. poor intructional objectives.
4. use of inappropriate item formats.

A. 1, 2, and 3.
B. 1 and 4.
C. 2 and 3.
D. 2 and 4.
E. All of the above.

Plake and Huntley (1984) and Tripp and Tollefson (1983) among others found that K-type items, in contrast to comparable multiple-choice items, tend to be more difficult, less efficient to construct, and more laborious to read.

Other researchers (Hughes & Trimble, 1965; Mueller, 1975; Williamson & Hopkins 1967) reported contradictory findings regarding the K-type items' difficulty index and discrimination power. Currently, it is seldom used.

7. *Avoid highly technical distracters.*[1] Occasionally, teachers will attempt to make a test item more difficult by using unfamiliar or difficult vocabulary either in the stem or in the distracters. Look at the following example:

Insulin is often used in the treatment of
A. diabetes.
B. gout.
C. paralysis.
D. tachycardia.

This, of course, should be avoided for many reasons, one of them being that nontechnical, familiar options are chosen as the correct answer more often than technical options regardless of the students' familiarity with the technical options (Strang, 1977). As we have said throughout Chapters 5 and 6, the difficulty of an item should be related to the content and instructional objectives, not to the vocabulary used.

8. *All distracters should be plausible and homogeneous.* One of the advantages of the multiple-choice over the true–false item is that the examinee is required to select the correct or best answer from among the many answers provided, thereby reducing the probability of guessing the correct answer. The student should be forced to read and consider all options. No distracter should be automatically eliminated by the student because it is irrelevant or a stupid answer.

Poor: Which of the following men invented the telephone?
A. Bell
B. Marconi
C. Morse
D. Pasteur
E. Salk

This question is concerned with an inventor in the field of communications. Therefore, for the distracters to be plausible, all should deal with inventors in the field of communications who lived at about the same time. It is true that all five persons listed in the example invented or discovered something, but their discoveries differ markedly. Only Bell, Marconi, and Morse were inventors in the field of communications. Salk is in virology, and Pasteur was a bacteriologist. Only Bell, Morse, and Pasteur lived at about the same time. The distracters provided in the "poor" item are definitely *not* plausible, nor do they offer a realistic challenge to the student's knowledge.

Better: A. Bell
B. Edison
C. Marconi
D. Morse

We have emphasized that all distracters should be plausible and appealing to the student. Unless each distracter attracts some pupils who have certain misconceptions, the item is not functioning

---

[1]With reference to distracters, it is interesting to note that Haladyna and Downing (1984) reported that in a survey of 25 textbooks, the most extensive advice (26 of the 50 rules) dealt with the construction of distracters.

effectively. But how does the item writer get such distracters? This is, without a doubt, one of the most difficult aspects of preparing good multiple-choice items. And yet, it is important since good distracters are the crux of the multiple-choice item.

Teachers, in their attempts to write plausible distracters, could (1) guess at the plausibility of the distracters on the basis of their experience and knowledge of how pupils behave, (2) administer a completion test and use the most frequently occurring errors as plausible distracters, or (3) administer a completion-type test and select as distracters those errors that best discriminate among the high- and low-scoring students. Currently, cognitive psychologists would use *theory* to determine distracters, that is, each distracter is due to some cognition. It makes little difference which of these approaches one uses to obtain plausible distracters, inasmuch as there is no significant effect on the test's validity (Owens et al., 1970; Frisbie, 1971). We have found it useful to use the completion type of format because a large number of incorrect yet plausible responses are obtained. When a teacher is trying to conjure up typical errors in, say, mathematics—be they computational or because of misunderstanding—what is a better source than *actual* errors most often made by the students? We cannot think of a better pool of errors that represents genuine misunderstanding and/or confusion among pupils.

9. *Avoid making the correct answer consistently longer than the incorrect ones.* Strang (1977), among others, found that long options were selected more often than short ones. Jones and Kaufman (1975) found that a "guessing" response set resulted from a *position* and *length* response set, the frequency of guessing varying according to the number of items answered correctly by the student as well as the frequency of the position and length of the distracters. Board and Whitney (1972) reported that this item-writing flaw benefited the poor student more than the good student and reduced the test's validity and internal consistency. We recognize that *occasionally*, because of the need for qualifying words, the correct answer

is longer than the incorrect distracters (Chase, 1964). If this is the case, lengthen the distracters with qualifiers so that they will also look plausible.

10. *Avoid giving irrelevant clues to the correct answer.* We have already said that the length of the response can be a clue to the correct answer. Other clues may be of a grammatical nature, such as the use of an "a" or "an" at the end of the statement; lack of parallelism between stem and responses; asking for the name of a male, but having all but one of the distracters with female names; and using a singular or plural subject and/or verb in the stem, with just one or two singular or plural options. At times, a key word in the stem repeated in the correct option will provide a clue. Any clues that assist the examinee in making the correct association on some basis other than knowledge are to be avoided. Following is just one example of an unintentional clue provided the student. Can you find the clue?

Which of the following diseases is caused by a virus?
A. Gallstones
B. Scarlet fever
C. Typhus fever
D. Typhoid fever
E. Viral pneumonia

The clue is "virus" in the stem and "viral" in response E. The item is also defective in that gallstones is not a disease.

The item writer should also be on her guard to make sure that there are no overlapping items such that the information presented in one item may provide a valuable clue for answering another item. Look at the following two items:

Item 8: The "halo" effect is most pronounced in essay examinations. The best way to minimize its effects is to
A. provide optional questions.
B. "aim" the student to the desired response.
C. read all the responses for one question before reading the responses to the other questions.
D. permit students to write their essay tests at home where they will be more at ease.

Item 37: In what type of test is the "halo" effect more operative?
A. Essay
B. Matching
C. True–false
D. Short-answer
E. Multiple-choice

The student could obtain the correct answer to item 37 because the answer is in the stem of item 8.

Absurd options should also be avoided. For example,

Poor: The capital city of Mexico is
A. Acapulco.
B. Merida.
C. Mexico City.
D. Washington, D.C.

Washington is *not* in Mexico.

Still another clue is provided when the correct answers assume some definite pattern or position. Some teachers like to place the correct answer in the first or second position, others prefer the third or fourth position, while still others prefer the middle postion in a 5-choice item. All positions should be used with approximately equal frequency and be randomly assigned throughout the test lest students become test-wise. Again, we must admit that there are no definitive research findings related to having a random distribution of correct responses. Some researchers have shown that a "pattern effect" does not alter the item's difficulty (Hopkins & Hopkins, 1964; Wilbur, 1965), while others have shown that a guessing response set might be induced (Jones & Kaufman, 1975), thereby affecting the item's psychometric properties. Fagley (1987), on the other hand, found *no* positional response bias.

What is more disconcerting than the errors made is Carter's (1986) finding that teachers were *unaware* of specific item-writing principles related to item-writing faults.

11. *Consider providing an "I don't know" option.* Strong arguments can be advanced against the use of this option—low-ability students tend to avoid it, the average or higher-ability students use it more frequently than lower-ability children (Finley & Berdie, 1970). Also, use of this option may be a reflection of the pupil's personality (Sherman, 1976). Why, then, even consider this option?

If the test results are to be used in a judgmental or summative evaluation sense, this option will probably be ineffective. However, if the test results are to be used in a formative evaluation sense to assist in instructional guidance of the pupil, and the test score is *not* going to affect a student's grade, then it is to the pupil's advantage to be honest and mark "I don't know" rather than to guess at the answer. To guess correctly could result in a student being placed in an instructional sequence at too high a level. In tests used, then, for instructional guidance as opposed to final evaluation, including an "I don't know" option may be beneficial to both pupils and teachers. Of course, pupils have to be taught that it is to their advantage to use this option rather than guess blindly at an answer.

Are we contradicting ourselves here, since in Chapter 19 we will encourage students to attempt all the items? Not really. We still claim that if an "I don't know" option is not provided, it is to the student's benefit to guess at answers he is unsure of. However, if such an option is provided and the test results are used for formative evaluation, it would be to the student's benefit to use it.

12. *There should be only one correct or best answer to every item.* We have seen, and occasionally even we ourselves have prepared, test items where "experts" would fail to agree on the single correct answer. Quite often, the disagreement about a correct or best answer occurs because of ambiguity in the stem, which results in different pupils making different interpretations of the intent or meaning of the question. For example, look at the following item.

Choose the man who doesn't belong in the group.
A. Bell
B. Pasteur
C. Sabin
D. Salk

The pupil who is thinking about virologists would select item A because Bell was not a virologist.

Another pupil could reason that the item calls for the identification of scientists, and hence he would also select A, but for a different reason. Still another pupil could select B if his classification scheme was United States citizens. How could the teacher score the different responses? She really couldn't.

Somewhat related to the point discussed above is the situation where we have identical options. For example, in the item,

The square root of 16 is
   A. 2
   B. 4
   C. 8/4
   D. 8

options (A) and (C) are identical.

We prefer writing the multiple-choice item—any test item, in fact—so that there is one and only one correct response rather than a "best" answer. In those cases—such as controversial issues—where the "best" answer is to be selected, this should be made clear to the students in the test directions as well as in the item itself.

13. *Avoid using "all of the above" as an option.* This option is seldom justified as a viable option on the typical multiple-choice test. Items using this option were found to be easiest, especially when this alternative was keyed as the correct response (Mueller, 1975). If a student is able to recognize that just one answer is incorrect, he can automatically disregard this option. And, if on the typical four-option one-correct answer multiple-choice item the student is able to recognize that at least two of the responses are correct, he can automatically select this option and get credit for having complete information, even though this may not be the case.

14. *Use the "none of the above" option sparingly, if at all.* Crehan and Haladyna (n.d.) caution against the use of this option. Haladyna and Downing's (1989b) survey indicated no clear support for this rule. In fact, one can say that some controversy exists. Of 34 references, 19 were in favor of using "none-of-the-above" as an option, while 15 were against this option. Research has

also shown that when this option is used, the items were more difficult.

Some teachers use this option to "cure" multiple-choice item susceptibility to guessing and/or emphasis on measuring recall. Using this option will *not remove* the guessing factor. Rather, it can only *lower* its effect. The process of obtaining the correct answer may still involve recognition rather than recall. For example, the pupil could look at each of the options, and if he didn't "recognize" the correct answer, he could select the "none of the above" options as the correct answer. This option helps the teacher who wants to reduce the effects of guessing but does not change the item's emphasis on recognition.

This does not mean that the "none of the above" option is useless. In some areas, such as spelling or punctuation or arithmetic, where there is an absolute standard of correctness, the "none of the above" option could be used either as a useful distracter or the correct answer. We can only say that this option should be used very infrequently, and, when it is used, it should be the correct answer some of the time. For the "none of the above" option to be most useful, pupils must be convinced that it is a viable response. We suggest that it be used early in the test as a correct answer for some of the easier items. Then the student will see that he cannot automatically ignore it as a correct answer. If it is never the correct answer, the test-wise student is given an irrelevant clue. Also, its use should be limited to those items where there is a single correct answer rather than a "best" answer.

What is the value of π?
   A. 0
   B. 1
   C. 2.17
   D. 3.14
   E. None of the above.

What do we do with the pupil who selects E as the answer to the question? Is the student right or wrong? It depends. As written, the student could argue that the "keyed" answer of 3.14 is *not* the absolute value of π. If "none of the above" were not an option in this question, there could be no argument about the best or even the one correct answer.

15. *Use three to five options.* The number of options to use is another area of disagreement. There are some (Costin, 1970, 1972; Grier, 1975; Lord, 1977; Ebel & Frisbie, 1986; Haladyna & Downing, 1989a) who say that a three-option test is just as reliable, difficult, and discriminating as a four-option test; that it requires less time to construct because it's easier to come up with two plausible distracters than with three or four; that it requires less reading time on the examinee's part, thereby permitting more questions to be asked per unit of testing time and thus permitting greater content sampling to be achieved. In fact, Costin (1972) found the three-choice *superior* to the four-choice. Lord (1977) says that it depends on the pupils' ability level. Using item-information curves, Lord (1977) showed that the two-option test works best at the upper range of the score scale and that the three-option test item provides the most information at the midrange of the score scale. Four- and five-option items seem to work best at the lower range where guessing is more frequent and plausible distracters more likely to be effective. On the other hand, there are some (Sax, 1980; Ahmann & Glock, 1981; Gronlund & Linn, 1990; Hopkins & Antes, 1990; Budescu & Nevo, 1985) who recommend using four or five options.

There is no set formula that one can employ to determine the number of options to use. The number of distracters to be used should be governed by such factors as (a) the age of the children tested and (b) the nature of the material being tested.

a. *Age of children.* The multiple-choice item places somewhat of a premium on the examinee's powers of retention and reading comprehension. Not only must the examinee be able to read the stem and options, but he must also remember the central problem so that he will not need to reread the stem with each option. Therefore, younger children should be given multiple-choice items with fewer options than older children because the comprehension span of younger children is

more limited. On the basis of our experience working with younger children, second-graders appear able to handle two- or three-choice items without too much trouble; third- and fourth-graders should be able to handle the three- or four-choice item; students in the middle school (sixth grade) and above should have little difficulty handling the four- or five-choice item.

b. *Nature of the material.* There are some subjects such as spelling or mechanical arts for which two or three distracters may be the maximum that can be written and still be plausible. Why, then, waste your time trying to conjure up distracters that are not plausible and that just take more space and reading time? You shouldn't! Two plausible distracters are to be preferred over four or five implausible ones. When no pupils choose some of the distracters, they contribute nothing to the test and only take up valuable time and space that could be better used by including more items.

There is no empirical evidence to suggest that every item in a multiple-choice test should contain the same number of options. As stated earlier, the *effectiveness* of the distracters is *more* important than their number. In fact, it has been shown that when the number is reduced, there is little effect upon test reliability (Williams & Ebel, 1957).

In conclusion, it would appear that the evidence, albeit sometimes contradictory, suggests that three options are preferred. This suggestion should *not* be misinterpreted. There is nothing wrong with a *well-written* four-option item. In fact, most standardized tests, as are most items in the Instructor's Manuals accompanying textbooks (and as written in this text), are of the four-option variety. Again, we say it is the *quality* rather than the number of options that is important.

16. *Avoid overlapping options.* Sometimes the teacher, in her haste to prepare distracters, may heed the caution to make them plausible but may commit the error of overlapping options (if one option is correct, another option also has to be correct, since one may incorporate the other). The following example is really a three-option rather than a five-option item.

The average weight of the adult United States female is

   A. less than 104 pounds.
   B. less than 110 pounds.
   C. between 110 and 117 pounds.
   D. more than 117 pounds.
   E. more than 120 pounds.

If A is correct, then B must also be correct. And, similarly, if E is correct, then D must be correct also. To prevent such overlapping in options, the item should be rewritten as:

The average weight of the adult United States female is

   A. less than 104 pounds.
   B. between 104 and 109 pounds.
   C. between 110 and 116 pounds.
   D. between 117 and 119 pounds.
   E. more than 119 pounds.

17. *To measure the higher mental processes, cast the item in a novel situation.* Many teachers do not realize that if they have used a particular example in class they cannot use this same item on a test to measure understanding or interpretation. If they do, they are only measuring recall.

18. *Use the multiple-choice item where more appropriate.* Although the multiple-choice item has many valuable features, there are some subjects for which it is less suitable than other item formats. For computational problems in mathematics and science, we recommend the short-answer format. Where fact and/or opinion are to be measured, the true–false item should be used. When it is difficult to write plausible distracters, but there are many homogeneous items, the matching exercise is superior. The multiple-choice format has wide applicability, but it is not always the best choice. We reiterate one of the basic tenets of test construction—use the item format that measures the objective most directly and efficiently.

A Checklist for Writing Multiple-Choice Items

Table 7–1 presents the essential elements to be considered in writing multiple-choice items. Of course, the general considerations for writing any test item, discussed on pp. 73–76, should be consulted.

In summary, then, even though the research dealing with the effect of poor item-writing practices on item difficulty and discrimination and the test's validity and reliability is inconclusive and sometimes contradictory, we still recommend that teachers be cognizant of the various types of errors as well as of some techniques whereby such errors can be minimized or prevented. Why, if there is no demonstrable harmful effect? Because we feel that poor item-writing practices serve to obscure (or attenuate) differences between good and poor students chiefly by making the latter look more like the former than their performances (scores) on "error-free" tests would suggest. We also believe that even though there may not be a statistically significant effect on the psychometric properties of a test or a test item, we should not feed our critics with ammunition (sloppy test construction) to support their contention that tests and testing are invalid and therefore should be removed from the classroom. Finally, although some item-writing errors may not have an effect upon pupil performance or the psychometric properties of a test or test item, some do. And if teachers become sloppy in some areas, it won't take too much to have them become sloppy or unconcerned in those areas that are more important.

WRITING CONTEXT-DEPENDENT ITEMS

Up to this point, our discussion of the various item formats dealt primarily with independent units; that is, the mode previously illustrated has been the conventional verbal approach. Occasionally, however, the essential elements of the problem need not be verbal for a pencil-and-paper test. Many different kinds of stimuli—pictures, graphs, tables, diagrams, film strips, tape recordings, and the like—can be used, even though the examinee's response mode is marking an answer on a piece of paper. Items based upon an external source—be it

TABLE 7-1   Checklist for Writing Multiple-Choice Items

Factor	Yes
1. Has the item been clearly presented? Is the main problem in the stem? Has excess verbiage been eliminated?	X
2. Has the item been cast so that there is no repetition of key words or phrases for each option?	X
3. Do the options come at the end of the stem?	X
4. Have the responses been arranged in some systematic fashion, such as alphabetical or length of response?	X
5. Are all distracters plausible? Are the number of distracters related to the examinees' age level? To the subject matter? To the time available for testing?	X
6. Have all irrelevant clues been avoided (grammatical, rote verbal association, length of correct answer, and so on)?	X
7. Are the correct answers randomly assigned throughout the test with approximately equal frequency?	X
8. Has an "I don't know" option been considered?	X
9. Is there only one correct (or best) answer?	X
10. Has "all of the above" been avoided?	X
11. Has the "none of these" option been used sparingly? Only when appropriate?	X
12. Have overlapping options been avoided?	X
13. Have negative statements been avoided? If used, has the negative been underlined or written in capital letters?	X
14. Have the items been reviewed independently? By you?	X

pictorial or verbal—are called *context-dependent.* A teacher interested in learning whether her pupils can read and interpret a graph or table, interpret a poem or short story, identify a painting, read the dials on a piece of electrical equipment, and the like would provide this material to the student. The student would then use it as his frame of reference to answer items based on this external material.

In the next section, we will discuss the *pictorial* form (the medium used to present the problem to the examinee). It is *not* an item format. We discuss context-dependent items in this chapter, however, since the multiple-choice format is the one most frequently used with such items. We recognize that true–false items, or some variation thereof, could also be used. We will also consider two types of context-dependent items—the *interlinear* exercise and the *interpretive* exercise—which can be, but need not be, based upon only pictorial materials. Objective test items can be based upon pictorial materials, verbal materials, or a combination of the two.

Objective Test Items Based Upon Pictorial Materials

The *pictorial* form is very useful for younger children and those with reading difficulties. Kindergarten children can be shown different colored pictures and asked to identify various colors. First-graders can be shown a picture having various lengths of string and asked to select the longest string (or shortest or in-between length). For measuring a young child's ability to count, to measure, and to discriminate, pictorial material is an excellent medium. To measure some of the more complex skills such as reading a graph, using an income tax table, and using an index, pictorial materials are ideally suited.

In some instances the item writer would have to include a great deal of information in the stem or introductory material to remove possible ambiguity. In some cases, a picture would have been worth many hundreds of words and the problem would have been clearer to the examinee had a pictorial medium been employed to present the problem. Is it not easier to classify rocks from pictures of rock samples than it is to classify them on the basis of verbal descriptions of their properties? Would it not be easier for the examinee to classify a tissue sample in pathology with a slide or picture of that tissue specimen than it would be if a verbal description were used?

In addition, pictorial materials lend a degree of realism to the test situation and introduce an element of novelty and interest. These, however, should *not* be the underlying reason for using this medium. Pictorial materials, or for that matter any medium, should be used only when they are the most appropriate and effective method of presenting the problem.

Test constructors using pictures must be careful that they only use materials that are common to the experiential background of the children being tested. Following are some examples of test items based upon pictorial materials.

*   *   *

True–False Test Items

The following items are designed for first-grade children who have just completed a unit on telling time.

Directions: In the picture below, there are four clocks. I am going to tell you some things about these clocks. If they are right, draw a line through the letter Y. If they are wrong, draw a line through the letter N.

1. You have lunch at the time shown in clock 2.   Y   N̶
2. The time shown in clock 1 is 5 o'clock.   Y̶   N

*   *   *

Short-Answer Test Items

Based on the pictures of the clocks, the following short-answer questions could be written for a group of second- or third-graders.

1. What time is it on clock 2? (3 o'clock)
2. What clock shows the time that is closest to 12 o'clock? (4)

*   *   *

Multiple-Choice Items

You would have lunch at the time shown in clock
  A. 1.
  B. 2.
  C. 3.
  D. 4.
  E. None of the above.

*   *   *

The Interlinear Exercise

The *interlinear* exercise is analogous to the correction true–false item discussed on page 121. It is somewhat of a cross between the essay question (the student is given some latitude of free expression in that he decides what is to be corrected and how it is to be corrected) and the objective item (the answer can be objectively scored). It is a semi-objective test of writing ability developed to overcome the unreliability of scoring the essay

test. In the interlinear exercise, the student is given a piece of prose that may contain spelling, grammatical, and punctuation errors. He must read the material, recognize the errors, and then correct the errors so that the material will be a better piece of prose. An example of an interlinear exercise with the changes made by the student is presented below.

Billy ~~ain't~~ a good boy. When he ~~has went~~ to the store, he ~~don't~~ look out for cars. One
     isn't   goes   doesn't

of these days, ~~him~~ going to get hurt ~~bad~~. He not only ignores his parents, but he also
           he is   badly

laughs at ~~him~~.
      them

In scoring this exercise, only those elements (errors) introduced in the material by the item writer are considered. Other revisions or editing are disregarded. Although we have an element of objective scoring, there is still some subjectivity, since we are still dealing with free-response materials. However, if a detailed scoring key is followed, scorer reliability can be quite high.

The Interpretive Exercise

The *interpretive* exercise consists of either an introductory statement, pictorial material, or a combination of the two, followed by a series of questions that measure in part the student's ability to *interpret* the material. All test items are based on a set of materials that is *identical* for all pupils.

In the past, the interpretive exercise was seldom used by classroom teachers. It was used most frequently in commercially published reading comprehension and ability tests. No doubt one of the reasons that it was seldom used in teacher-made tests was that it is rather difficult and time-consuming to prepare. However, such exercises should find their way into teacher-made tests in greater numbers because of their many distinct advantages over the traditional items.

1. The structuring of the problem assists both examiner and examinee. *Both* approach the problem with the *same* frame of reference, which should help reduce ambiguity.

2. They lend themselves to, and place more emphasis on, the measurement of understanding, interpretation, and evaluation.
3. Complex material can be measured with a series of different items based upon a single introductory passage, graph, chart, or diagram.
4. They minimize the amount of irrelevant factual material.
5. They lend themselves to a variety of item formats and modes of presentation.
6. In contrast to the essay, complex achievement is measured in a more structured situation, but objective scoring is employed.

Although the interpretive exercise has wide applications, such exercises are not free of problems and/or deficiencies. A major limitation of interpretive exercises is that they are difficult to find and/or construct. Relevant but novel material (new to the student) is difficult and time-consuming to locate. And if and when it is found, it invariably requires considerable editing so that it is relevant to the instructional objectives. If the exercises are based on a paragraph, they make a heavy demand on reading skill, and therefore they are not too suitable for very young children and for those students who have reading problems. (In the primary grades, or in classes with poor readers, the interpretive exercises should be based on pictorial materials.) And, if they can't be found and edited, they are very difficult to prepare, especially those dealing with complex topics. Because of the time needed to administer them, one is restricted somewhat in the number of items that can be asked in a given time, and hence the reliability of the test per unit of time is reduced. For that reason alone, the interpretive exercise should not be used to measure factual knowledge.

In comparison with the essay questions, the interpretive exercise has two limitations as a measure of complex learning (Gronlund, 1985). First, the results indicate to the teacher only that the student is or is not able to function at higher levels—*not* whether the pupil has the ability to integrate these skills in a different situation. Second, the interpretive exercise indicates only whether the pupil can *recognize* the answer—*not* whether he can supply evidence to demonstrate his problem-solving skills and his organizational ability. "To measure the ability to define problems, to formulate hypotheses, to organize data, and to draw conclusions, supply procedures such as the essay test must be used" (Gronlund, 1985, p. 206).

Following is an example of an interpretive exercise based on a map that measures the students' ability to read and interpret the map. The actual item and ensuing discussion is taken from the pamphlet, *Multiple-Choice Questions: A Close Look* (1963).[2] Although the items are written in the multiple-choice format, the item writer is free to use whichever formats she wishes.

> In the following question you are asked to make inferences from the data that are given on the map of the imaginary country, Serendip. *The answers in most instances must be probabilities rather than certainties.* The relative size of towns and cities is not shown. To assist you in the location of the places mentioned in the questions, the map is divided into squares lettered vertically from A to E and numbered horizontally from 1 to 5.

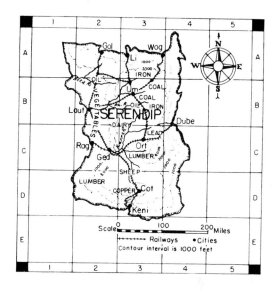

(B) Which of the following cities would be the best location for a steel mill?
  (A) Li (3A)
  (B) Um (3B)
  (C) Cot (3D)
  (D) Dube (4B)

A map of an imaginary country, such as that shown above, offers numerous possibilities for questions which measure important understandings. One could ask several questions requiring an understanding of the symbols used on the map. To measure student comprehension of contour lines, for example, one might ask which railroad has the steepest grades to climb. Questions can be developed which require knowledge of the factors influencing population distribution, economic activities, and so on.

The test item below the map requires knowledge of the natural resources used in producing steel and an awareness of the importance of transportation facilities in bringing these resources together.

The student who knows that iron is the basic raw material of steel and that coal commonly provides the necessary source of heat would proceed to locate deposits of these resources in relation to the cities in the question. He would be able to eliminate Cot immediately, since there is no iron or coal in its vicinity, although Cot might be an attractive choice to students who mistakenly think that copper is a basic ingredient of steel. Both Li and Dube are located reasonably near supplies of iron, and therefore might be attractive choices. Um, however, is the more clearly "correct" response, because not only are deposits of iron and coal nearby, but they are more readily transportable by direct railroad routes.

Suggestions for Writing Interpretive Exercises

In order to have a valid and reliable interpretive exercise, the item writer, of course, must follow the basic tenets of good test construction, such as clearly communicating to the student the intent of the question and making certain that no irrelevant clues are provided the student. However, two additional tasks are required: (1) the selection and/or preparation of the introductory material and (2) writing test items that are dependent on the introductory material and call on the higher mental processes to answer the questions. The suggestions that follow are restricted to the interpretive exercise. Depending on the item format used, the material previously discussed is also pertinent, but it will not be repeated here.

1. *Carefully select the material to be interpreted so that the interpretations to be made will be significant and representative of course content and objectives.* This stage is analogous to selecting the topics for which independent items will be written. For the interpretive exercise, the introductory material (be it verbal or pictorial) is the topic. There are a variety of excellent sources for introductory verbal materials, such as digests, summaries, and abstracts of articles. Although these sources may not be completely appropriate as they stand (one will seldom find introductory material that is completely relevant to the instructional goals without at least some minor revision), they do provide good raw material for the item writer to use in developing materials that will be most appropriate and meaningful. If the material selected is adapted, it must be within the experiential background of the pupils; it must be within their reading ability; it must be brief and yet say something; and it must measure specifically what it is the teacher wants

the student to interpret. In many instances, the preparation of the introductory material and the writing of the test items go hand in hand.

The essence of the interpretive exercise lies in the adequacy of the introductory material (be it prose or pictorial) presented to all examinees. It is therefore vital that the material be selected and/or prepared very carefully. The item writer has *control* of what she wishes to present and how much information she wishes to give the student. Hence, she is able to measure the degree of proficiency possessed by the examinee.

2. *Keep the introductory material brief.* Other things being equal, for younger children and for children who have difficulty in reading we prefer the interpretive exercise based on pictorial materials. For children in the higher grades, one could use either written material or pictorial material, or a combination of the two. Although reading ability is required in any test except the oral examination, the teacher must be very careful that she does not make the interpretive exercise primarily a test of reading ability or general intelligence. Although brevity is desirable, if the introductory material is verbal it must contain all information needed to measure the pupils' interpretive skills.

3. *Be novel and creative in preparing introductory materials.* In the interpretive exercise, creativity is very important. But teachers must be careful that they do not become too creative or too novel. They must reach a happy compromise of instilling something new and different but not being so novel that they fail to measure instructional objectives that are relevant.

4. *Base the items on the introductory material.*[3] This does *not* mean that the teacher should con-

---

[3]Pyrczak (1974, 1976) and Tuinman (1974), among others, showed that supposedly context-dependent reading tests were, in fact, not so because specific clues were present that enabled the examinee to answer the item correctly without reading the associated material on which the item was supposedly based. They developed formulas for determining the degree to which test items based on a particular reading passage are, in fact, dependent on that passage.

struct items that are answered *directly* in the introductory material. Such items measure only reading ability and/or memory. At the same time, she should *not* write items that are irrelevant to the introductory material. Such items may be a measure of general intelligence. The items prepared should be based on the introductory material. It does not matter whether the pupil must call forth basic knowledge not purposely presented in the material, as long as the interpretive skill measured has some foundation in the introductory material.

5. *Write true–false or multiple-choice items to measure interpretive skills.* Again, we say that the short-answer item is not designed to measure complex achievement efficiently. The essay item could be used, but would be inefficient. Either the true–false or multiple-choice format could be used. In general, we prefer the multiple-choice format because of its greater versatility. However, there are times when the true–false item is preferred because of its simplicity.

6. *Regardless of the item format used, the guidelines previously discussed should be followed.* The use of verbal or pictorial introductory materials, no matter how good, is no substitute for well-constructed test items.

7. *If pictorial materials are used, they should be relevant and of high quality.* Any diagrams, charts, graphs, maps, and the like should be well drawn, clear, and easily recognized (read) by the examinee. Sloppy materials may confuse the student, thereby affecting test validity.

8. *If the interpretive exercise items use key-type, make sure that the categories are homogeneous and mutually exclusive.* You will recall that the key-type item is a cross between the multiple-choice and matching item. It is similar to the matching exercise in that it uses a common set of responses to classify each of the statements or items. Because the student makes some sort of classification of the statement, it is vital that the key contain distinctly separate categories so that there is no possibility of having two correct answers because one category overlaps another category. The following

example[4] illustrates the use of mutually exclusive and homogeneous categories.

Directions: Items 12–14 are based on the following preliminary information and experiment:

Preliminary information. In the presence of gaseous oxygen, Solution X is purple. When gaseous oxygen is absent, Solution X is a colorless liquid. Yeast is a plant.

Experiment. Five drops of Solution X were placed in each of four (4) small tubes. A brass screw was dropped into each tube to serve as a platform. Four pieces of filter paper were rolled; one was dipped into glucose solution; one was dipped into a yeast suspension; one was dipped into a yeast suspension to which glucose had been added; and one was dipped into water. Each of the pieces of rolled filter paper was placed into one of the tubes. A cork was then inserted into each tube. The tubes were placed in a drawer and were left there for an hour. At the end of the hour the tubes were examined. The color of Solution X at the end of the hour is recorded in the table below for each tube.

Tube	Filter paper dipped into:	Color of Solution X
1	Glucose solution	Purple
2	Yeast solution	Pale purple
3	Yeast suspension + glucose	Colorless
4	Water	Purple

For items 12–14 select your response from the list below, numbered 1 through 8.

1. Statement of an observational fact.
2. An experimental assumption, that is, something which must be assumed about the experiment or experimental materials, in order to interpret the experiment.
3. An immediate conclusion.
4. A conclusion, interpretation, or generalization that can be formulated on the basis of the data.
5. A statement that can be contradicted on the basis of the data.
6. A prediction, a deduction, or an expectation.

---

[4]We are grateful to Dr. Clarence Nelson, for permitting us to adapt this example from his test file. Many more items were written, but we have reproduced only a few.

7. A statement that is probably false but that cannot be contradicted on the basis of these data.
8. The statement may be true, but the truth of the statement cannot be established on the basis of these data.

* * *

12. *Carbon dioxide is produced by yeast.*
    A. 1 B. 2 C. 4 D. 7 E. 8
13. *The amount of oxygen utilized by yeast per unit time is related to the available food supply.*
    A. 1 B. 2 C. 4 D. 7 E. 8
14. *If the gases in Tube 3 were collected and run through a phenol red solution, the phenol red would change from red to orange or yellow.*
    A. 2 B. 3 C. 4 D. 6 E. 7

9. *Get the most mileage out of the interpretive exercise.* It would be ridiculous to spend countless hours looking for and preparing the introductory material and then ask just one question on the material. And it would be ludicrous from the examinee's point of view to read the introductory material and then be asked only one question. Such a procedure would be a very inefficient use of testing time, both for the examiner and the examinee. We cannot provide a formula that relates the number of items to the length of the introductory material. Other things being equal, we favor short introductory materials with a relatively large number of test items based on the material. This will provide for more adequate content sampling in a limited amount of testing time, recognizing that the interpretive exercise requires more time than the conventional objective item. Be careful though! Do not overload the test with interpretive exercises. Writing a large number of interpretive exercises can severely upset the balance of the test and result in a test that lacks content validity.

Some Suggestions for Writing the Introductory Material The following steps for the preparation of the introductory material should be of assistance.

1. Look through materials that contain a reading passage, to see whether they might be appropriate for having interpretive exercises prepared from them.

2. Make certain that the material used is completely *new* to all students. Otherwise, you are measuring prior knowledge and/or mental ability.
3. Write some items based on the selected material.
4. See whether there are some instructional objectives that you would like to measure but are unable to do so because the material does not lend itself to such items. Rewrite the material so that you can develop certain kinds of items. In the rewrite stage, remove any irrelevant material that is not related to the items written and can be removed without destroying the continuity of the passage.
5. Ask yourself whether you could prepare some additional good items by rewriting the passage further.
6. Revise the passage until you are satisfied that it is brief but still clear; that it has continuity; that it is interesting; that it is appropriate to the reading level of the pupils; that the pupils have been exposed to the tasks called for by the items; and that you have been able to get full mileage from the selection. You may be very surprised to find that the final selection bears little resemblance to the original passage.

■ SUMMARY

The principal ideas, conclusions, and recommendations presented in this chapter are summarized in the following statements:

1. Multiple-choice items are the most popular and flexible of the objective-type *selection* items.
2. The criticism that the multiple-choice test rewards the poorer student and penalizes the more able student is not supported by empirical evidence.
3. Ambiguity in multiple-choice items can be avoided by carefully preparing the test item.
4. Five commonly used variations of the multiple-choice format are the one-correct answer, the best answer, the analogy type, the reverse

type, and the alternate-choice type. The sub-set-selection technique is seldom used. The item shell is a promising approach.

5. Of all the selection-type objective items, the multiple-choice item requires the most time for the student to respond.

6. The multiple-choice item is the least efficient objective item for measuring factual recall. The multiple-choice item is ideally suited for measuring the higher mental processes.

7. Two of the major deficiencies in teacher-made multiple-choice items are ambiguity and imprecise (or superfluous) wording.

8. Multiple-choice questions can be presented as either direct questions or as incomplete statements. Regardless of the form used, the options should come below the stem.

9. The options should be arranged as simply as possible. If numbers, they should be in ascending or descending order; if single words, alphabetically; if phrases, in order of length.

10. Highly technical distracters, negative statements, and textbook jargon should be avoided.

11. All responses should be plausible and homogeneous. One way to increase the difficulty of the test is to increase the homogeneity of the distracters.

12. Avoid giving the student clues to the correct answer by (a) making the correct answer longer than the incorrect ones, (b) having overlapping items, and (c) giving grammatical clues.

13. There should be only one correct or best answer for every item.

14. Avoid "all of the above" as an option.

15. Use "none of the above" sparingly. To avoid irrelevant clues, this option should be the correct answer only some of the time. We suggest that this option be used only with the correct-answer variety of multiple-choice questions.

16. In general, we recommend that three options be used. The distracters must all be plausible. In addition, the age of the pupils tested, the nature of the material, and the time available

for testing will influence the number of distracters.

17. Independent review of the items will generally improve their quality.

18. Items that depend upon information presented in pictorial material or in a reading passage are called context-dependent items. Interlinear and interpretive exercises are examples of context-dependent items.

19. Pictorial materials are very well suited to younger children and those with reading difficulties.

20. If pictorial materials are used, they should be familiar to children coming from different backgrounds.

21. Pictorial materials are often the only testing medium possible for measuring certain skills, such as ability to read a chart, table, or graph.

22. If pictorial materials are used, they should be of high quality and related to the content and objectives being measured.

23. The true–false and multiple-choice formats are best suited for interpretive exercises.

24. A major problem with the interpretive exercise is the selection and subsequent revision of the introductory material on which the items are based.

25. The introductory material for the interpretive exercise should be brief, yet meaningful.

26. The number of items to be written for a particular interpretive exercise will depend to some extent on the length of the introductory material. It would be foolish to have a one-page article and then ask just one or two questions on it. Get the most mileage out of the material, but not at the expense of content validity.

■ POINTS TO PONDER

1. What are some of the advantages and limitations of the multiple-choice item? Do you feel that one or the other supports the continued use or discontinuance of this item format?

2. Proponents of the multiple-choice item claim that it can be used successfully to measure the

higher mental processes. Give an example of an essay item and a multiple-choice item, both of which measure analysis.

3. Discuss some of the errors committed in writing multiple-choice items that provide irrelevant clues to the test-wise student. How can these be avoided?

4. How many distracters should there be? What factor(s) influence one's choice?

5. What are the major difficulties involved in writing good multiple-choice items? How might they be minimized?

6. There are some who claim that one should not use an "all of the above" or "none of the above" option. Do you agree? Why?

7. What is meant by a context-dependent item?

8. Is it true that the multiple-choice item is the most versatile of the objective-type item formats? Give a few examples to support your answer.

9. It is said that "a picture is worth one thousand words." Do you agree? When might pictorial materials not be suitable as a testing medium?

10. Do you think that the interpretive exercise has any merit? Support your answer.

Chapter 8

Assembling, Reproducing, Administering, Scoring, and Analyzing Classroom Achievement Tests

- ■ Getting the Test Ready
- ■ Reproducing the Test
- ■ Administering the Test
- ■ Recording and Scoring the Answers
- ■ Testing the Test: Item Analysis

In Chapter 4 we discussed the "get-ready" or planning stage in preparing classroom tests. In Chapters 5 through 7 we discussed the preparation of essay and objective-type items. We are now at the "get-set" and "go" stages where we begin assembling our ingredients (test items) into the final product (the test). All the planning and preparation for the test that has taken place will be in vain if we "goof" in these next stages. The care, time, and effort expended in this mixing or blending stage will be positively related to the goodness of the final product. Extreme care must be exercised in planning the test—delineating the course objectives and expressing them in terms of pupil behavior, preparing the table of specifications or test blueprint—and writing the test items if a teacher is desirous of obtaining valid measurement of her pupils' achievement. However, there are other aspects that must be considered in teacher-made tests besides those mentioned under planning and the techniques of item writing.

In the "get-set" and "go" stages of teacher-made achievement tests, the teacher must consider such questions as

1. How should the various item formats be organized in the test?
2. How should the various items within a particular format be organized?
3. How should the test be reproduced?
4. Should pupils be encouraged to answer all test items, even those they are unsure of?
5. What kinds of directions should the student be given?
6. Should the students record their answers directly in the test booklet or should a separate answer sheet be used for objective-type tests?

In addition, the teacher must also pay some attention to the analysis of the test items and to the interpretation of the test results. Unless the teacher has some evidence that her test is valid and reliable, it would indeed be ludicrous to use the test results to make decisions—be they group or individual, instructional, administrative, or counseling.

This chapter is devoted to a consideration of the major questions posed above. After studying this chapter, you should be able to:

1. Appreciate the importance of paying careful attention to the assembly, reproduction, administration, and scoring aspects of classroom tests.
2. Follow the guidelines offered when assembling the various item formats into a test.
3. Appreciate the importance of having clear, concise directions for the student.
4. Follow the guidelines offered when writing test directions.
5. Appreciate the importance of encouraging all students to attempt all test items, even though they may be unsure of the correctness of their answers.
6. Follow the guidelines offered when laying out and reproducing the test.
7. Recognize the importance of physical and psychological conditions in test taking.
8. Understand why cheating must be discouraged and know how to minimize it.

9. List the four major points to consider in scoring the test.
10. Understand the instructional and learning value of feedback.
11. Understand the importance of analyzing a test.
12. Understand the difference between item difficulty and item discrimination.
13. Compute and evaluate a difficulty index.
14. Compute and evaluate a discrimination index.
15. Understand the relationship between difficulty and discrimination.
16. Understand the major uses of item-analysis data.
17. Recognize the limitations of item-analysis data.
18. Be acquainted with the opinions about, and methods of, computing item-analysis data for criterion-referenced tests.

GETTING THE TEST READY

Objective tests, especially multiple-choice tests and some variants of the true–false items, *cannot* be administered orally. Neither can the items be written on the blackboard a few minutes before the examination is scheduled to begin. The test must be reproduced. The reproduction process used is not important. The material need only be legible. What is important, however, is to have similar item formats grouped together, to have clear and concise directions, and to decide upon the manner in which the pupils are to record their answers. The test-taking conditions should be such that every pupil is given maximum opportunity to perform at his highest level. The steps to be discussed below may appear obvious. However, you would be surprised at the large number of errors teachers make, errors that do not enhance their opportunity to obtain valid and reliable measurement of the pupils' achievement.

Arranging the Test Items

Throughout our discussion on the writing of the various item formats, we have emphasized and reemphasized that the task given the student must be as clear as humanly possible. One way to achieve this is to group all items of the same format together rather than to intersperse them throughout the test. There is no empirical evidence to suggest that grouping items of similar content will lead to more valid and reliable measurement, or that it will help ensure positive pupil motivation. Nevertheless, we feel such a grouping is advantageous for a variety of reasons: (1) younger children may not realize that the first set of directions is applicable to all items of a particular format and may become confused; (2) it makes it easier for the examinee to maintain a particular mental set instead of having to change from one to another; and (3) it makes it easier for the teacher to score the test, especially if hand scoring is done.

We recommend that the various item formats be presented in such a way that the complexity of mental activity required by the student will progress from the simple to the complex. For example, simple recall measured by the completion item should precede the interpretive exercise. Hambleton and Traub (1974) indicated that ordering items in ascending order of difficulty leads to better performance than either a random or hard-to-easy ordering. Lafitte (1984) and Plake et al. (1980, 1982), on the other hand, reported inconclusive data. Gronlund (1985, p. 233) suggested the following scheme, which roughly approximates the complexity of the instructional objectives measured—from simple to complex.

1. True–false or alternative-response items
2. Matching items
3. Short-answer items
4. Multiple-choice items
5. Interpretive exercises
6. Essay questions

Within each item format, the exercises should, wherever feasible, be grouped so that those dealing with the same instructional objective (such as "knowledge of terms," "application of principles," and "synthesis") are grouped together. Such a grouping can help the teacher ascertain which learning activities appear to be most readily understood by her pupils—those that are least understood and those that are in between. Although the empirical evidence is inconclusive about using statistical item difficulty as a means of ordering items (Newman et al., 1988), we recommend, as do others (Sax & Cromack, 1966; Towle & Merrill, 1975), that for lengthy tests and/or timed tests, items should progress from the easy to the difficult—if for no other reason than to instill confidence in the examinee—at least at the beginning. If the test were to begin with two or three easy items that almost everyone could answer correctly, even the less able students might be encouraged to do their best on the remaining items.

The test items should be arranged so that they are easily read by the examinees. This means that the reproduction should be legible and that the items not be crowded together.

If diagrams or drawings are used, they should be placed above the stem. If placed below the stem, there will be a break in the examinee's reading continuity between the stem and the options. As noted earlier, if the illustrative material is considered to be part of the problem, the problem should be placed early in the stem. Finally, arrange the items in such a way that the correct answers follow a random pattern. An easy way to do this is to use a die. The die is rolled, and the number appearing face-up becomes the option for the correct response.

In summary: the organization of the various test items in the final test should:

1. Have separate sections for each item format.
2. Be arranged so that these sections progress from the easy (true–false) to the difficult (interpretive exercise and essay).
3. Group the items within each section so that the very easy ones are at the beginning and the items progress in difficulty.
4. Space the items so that they are not crowded and can be easily read.
5. Keep all stems and options together on the same page; if possible, diagrams and questions should be kept together.
6. If a diagram is used for a multiple-choice exercise, have the diagram come above the stem.

7. Avoid a definite response pattern to the correct answer.

Writing Test Directions

The directions provided should be clear and concise and should tell the students what they are to do, how they are to do it, and where they are to record their answers. They should tell the students (1) the time to be allotted to the various sections, (2) the value of the items, and (3) whether or not students should guess at any answers they may be unsure of. Except for young children, the written test directions should be so explicit that the student can begin the test without any additional oral instructions. If this criterion is not met, the directions are not sufficiently clear and should be revised.

1. *Each item format should have a specific set of directions.* In addition to a general set of instructions, there must be a specific set of instructions that are applicable to a particular item format. For computational problems, the students should be told the degree of precision required; whether they are to express their answers in the proper units (such as volts, ohms, square feet); whether they should show their work; and, if so, where.

2. *For objective tests at the elementary level, give the students examples and/or practice exercises so that they will see exactly what and how they are to perform their tasks.*

3. *Students should be told how the test will be scored.* They should be told, for example, if on an essay examination whether such factors as spelling, punctuation, and grammar will be considered and, if so, what proportion of the question's value will be assigned to these factors. For responses that require a short answer (1 to 2 sentences), pupils should be told whether or not their answers are to be in complete sentences. Or, on an arithmetic test, they should be told whether they will receive part scores for showing a correct procedure even though they may have obtained an in-

correct answer. When pupils know the "ground rules" they can operate accordingly. For example, they can be more careful in their computations if they know there are no "part" scores. Or, if a guessing correction is being applied, they might be less prone to guess and have more omits. (Traub & Hambleton, 1972, found that the way a test is scored had a significant effect on the number of items omitted.)

Somewhat related is the factor of informing pupils about the test's difficulty. Huck (1978) reported that students earned higher scores on classroom achievement tests (regardless of the item format) when they were told about the difficulty of the test items. This information did *not* affect the test's reliability.

4. *Above the second grade, all directions should be written out.* For some groups, especially younger children, slow learners, or pupils with reading problems, the directions may be read aloud *in addition* to being printed and available to each examinee.

Although we could give the specific directions to be employed with the various item formats, we have chosen to give a set of directions (see Table 8–1) for just one type of examination—a final examination for high school seniors consisting of four-option multiple-choice items—where the responses are to be recorded on a separate sheet and no guessing correction will be made. Different formats, wording, and methods of recording the answers would entail slight modifications of these instructions.

Instructions for Guessing Guessing is recognized as a persistent source of error in cognitive tests of achievement and aptitude (faking rather than guessing is a problem in affective tests and will be discussed in Chapter 17), and a variety of procedures have been devised—applying a correction formula, giving explicit instructions, employing confidence-weighting scoring schemes—to combat this problem. We contend that, on the basis of the research evidence, *students should be instructed to answer every item and that no correc-*

TABLE 8-1   General Directions for a Multiple-Choice Test

General Directions: DO NOT open your test booklet until you have read, understood, and carried out the directions below. SINCE YOUR ANSWER SHEET WILL BE SCORED BY MACHINE, IT IS ABSOLUTELY NECESSARY THAT YOU MARK YOUR ANSWER CORRECTLY TO AVOID ERRORS IN THE GRADE YOU RECEIVE.

Specific Directions: This final course examination consists of 75 multiple-choice items, each worth 1 point. You will have 2 hours to complete the test. Read each question carefully and decide which of the alternatives (answers) given best completes the statement or answers the question.

1. On your answer sheet, print in the appropriate spaces your name, the name of the examination, and the date.
2. Be extremely careful to mark your answer to each item in the appropriate space on the answer sheet by darkening the letter corresponding to the answer you select.
3. Do any necessary figuring or scribbling in the test booklet. Answers are to be marked on the answer sheet only.
4. **Keep the marked part of your answer sheet covered at all times.**
5. Mark only one response per item. If you mark more than one answer per item, if you make stray dots on the answer sheet, or if you fail to erase completely an answer you wish changed, **your response to that item will not be counted.**
6. Note that the items have only FOUR responses. Be careful not to use the fifth-response position on your answer sheet.
7. Your score on this examination will be the number of answers you have marked correctly. Try to answer every item, but do not spend too much time on any one item.
8. Are there any questions about what you are to do and how you are to do it? You may now begin. Good luck!

THIS EXAMINATION CONSISTS OF 75 ITEMS ON 8 PAGES.
BE SURE YOU DO NOT OVERLOOK ANY ITEMS.

---

tion for guessing be applied. Guessing will be discussed in Chapter 19.

Should Students Change Their Answers on Objective Tests?   Although this point is not directly related to the written instructions the teacher prepares for her classroom test, this question is frequently asked by pupils before, during, or after the test. We feel that it deserves some mention, albeit briefly.

A myth that has persisted for some time is that students taking an objective test should not change their answers when they review the test before handing it in, the reason being that the first answer is usually the correct answer. Empirical evidence does not substantiate this myth. In fact, most studies have shown that, by and large, students—be they elementary, secondary, college, or adult—profit from changing an answer (Mueller & Wasser, 1977; Smith et al., 1979; Crocker & Benson,

1980; Cummings, 1981; McMorris et al., 1987; McMorris & Weideman, 1986; Vaas & Nungester, 1982).

No one really knows why students may or may not change answers. Whether it is due to their personality or to their obtaining more insight or some other factor(s) on rereading the item is not clear. McMorris et al. (1987) reported that the most frequently mentioned reasons given by college students were: "Rethinking the item and conceptualizing a better answer"; followed by "Rereading the item and better understanding of the question"; followed by "rereading/rethinking" combined and "making a clerical error." The majority of changes for each frequently mentioned reason was from wrong-to-right. McMorris et al.'s findings corroborated those of others that stated answer changing was productive for *all* students, regardless of their test score—the middle group gained the most totally; the top third, although making the fewest number of changes, gained more per change; and the bottom third made more wrong–right changes than wrong–wrong and right–wrong combined.

We strongly urge teachers to de-emphasize the conventional caution that "the first answer is invariably the best answer." Pupils should be encouraged to review their answers, and they should be told that if on further consideration they obtain a better understanding of the item and/or are able to recall additional information the second time through, or if they feel that they answered incorrectly the first time, then by all means they should change their original answer. A change will tend to raise, rather than lower, the pupil's score.

Somewhat related to this is the question of whether changing answers will affect the test's quality. Crocker and Benson (1980) reported that there was no effect on the test's reliability or item difficulty and discrimination indices.

REPRODUCING THE TEST

Careful attention to the reproduction phase will not only make it easier for the examinee, but may also make hand scoring much easier. To assist both examinee and examiner, we suggest the following practices (recognizing that some points have been previously discussed):

1. *Space the items so that they are not crowded.* In multiple-choice items, reading the stem becomes very difficult when items are tightly crammed together with options. For multiple-choice tests, the options should be placed in a vertical column below the test item rather than in paragraph fashion.

2. *For the alternate-response test, have a column of T's and F's at either the right- or left-hand side of the items.* Then the student need only circle, underline, or cross out the correct response. This is better than having the student write T or F. When writing rapidly, examinees, especially young chil-

dren, often make the letters T and F look alike. As mentioned earlier, for very young children we recommend the use of "yes–no" rather than true-false.

3. *For matching exercises, have the two lists on the same page.*

4. *For the multiple-choice item that uses a key list, try to keep all item using a particular key on the same page.* If this is not possible, the key should be repeated on the new page.

5. *For the interpretive exercise, the introductory material—be it a graph, chart, diagram, or piece of prose—and the items based on it should be on the same page.* If the material used is too long, facing pages should be used, if possible.

6. *All items should be numbered consecutively.* For the matching and multiple-choice item, the material in the list to be matched and/or the options to be used should be lettered.

7. *For the short-answer items (1 to 2 words), the blanks should be numbered and the responses recorded in blanks (vertically arranged and numbered to correspond to the number of the blank) on one side of the answer sheet used.* For example:

1. The product of 10 and 7 is <u>(1)</u> times as large as the sum of 8 and 6.

It is essential, of course, that adequate space be provided the student to write his answer. Young children especially vary in the size of their handwriting, so it is difficult to accurately say that 1, or 1½, or 2 inches of space should be provided. When in doubt, err on having a little more space.

8. *If the responses are recorded directly on the test booklet, it will make scoring easier if all responses to objective items are recorded on one side (left or right) of the page, regardless of the item format used.*

9. *In the elementary grades, if work space is needed to solve numerical problems, provide this space in the test booklet rather than having exam-*

inees use scratch paper. Majors and Michael (1975) found that seventh-graders did better when they did their computations in the test booklet's work space than when scratch paper was used. There are too many opportunities for making recording-type errors when an answer from one place must be transferred to another place.

10. *All illustrative material used should be clear, legible, and accurate.*

11. *Proof the test carefully before it is reproduced.* If possible, try to have the test reviewed independently, preferably by a teacher who teaches the same subject. If errors are found after the test has been reproduced, they should be called to the students' attention *before* the actual test is begun.

12. *Even for essay tests, every pupil should have a copy of the test.* Teachers should *not* write the questions on the blackboard.

ADMINISTERING THE TEST

According to the *Standards for Educational and Psychological Testing* (AERA/APA/NCME, 1985) the test administrator must establish conditions so that each examinee can do his best.

The physical conditions should be as comfortable as possible, and the examinees should be as relaxed as possible, even though the evidence is inconclusive regarding the effects of physical and environmental conditions on test performance. Whereas distractions during testing have little effect on the scores of high school and college students, young children *may* be affected (see Trentham, 1975; Thorndike & Hagen, 1977; Anastasi, 1981; Gronlund & Linn, 1990). If we know that conditions are not what we would like them to be, the interpretation of the pupils' scores must be made accordingly.

Finally, do not give tests when the examinees would normally be doing pleasant things, such as lunch, recess, gym. Also, do not give tests immediately before or after long vacations or a holiday, or the day before or after a championship game or the "BIG" dance.

Psychological Aspects

Individuals usually perform better at any endeavor, including test taking, if they approach the experience with a positive attitude. Yet teachers frequently fail to establish a positive mental attitude in the pupils tested. People cannot do their best when they are excessively tense and nervous, and tests do induce tenseness, more so in some pupils than in others. At present, the research on the general mental attitude and motivation of individuals and the correlation of these traits with test performance is inconclusive. We do know, however, that test anxiety affects optimum performance (Sarason et al., 1964; Culler & Hollohan, 1980; Clawson et al., 1981). The psychological traits of the examinee, such as test-taking style, propensity to guess, and the like will be discussed in Chapter 19.

Some Additional Considerations

When administering the test, the teacher should make sure that the students understand the directions and that answer sheets, if they are being used with the younger pupils, are being used correctly. In addition, the teacher should keep the students informed of time remaining (e.g., writing the time left on the blackboard at 15-minute intervals). Careful proctoring should take place so that cheating is eliminated, discouraged, and/or detected. We have seen many teachers in public schools, as well as in college, who define proctoring as "being present in the room." They are physically present but spend their time reading a novel, writing a letter, or grading papers.

The *single most effective* method to minimize cheating is careful proctoring. Considering the prevalence of cheating on exams, it is obvious that many teachers do not take their proctoring responsibilities seriously enough. We agree with Frary (1981) and Roberts (1987) that the best way to detect cheating is to observe students during the examination—not by being preoccupied at one's desk.

Some educators have suggested the honor system as a deterrent to cheating. However, as most educators now realize, the honor system really does not work very well.

In the final analysis, we believe that cheating is more likely to occur on a poorly planned test in which the test items do not cover what was taught or focuses on straight memorization of trivia rather than upon reasoning skills.

RECORDING AND SCORING THE ANSWERS

In Chapter 5 we discussed the scoring of the essay test in a fairly detailed fashion. Our ensuing discussion will therefore be restricted to the recording and scoring of answers to objective-type tests.

Should a pupil record his answers directly on the test paper or should he use a separate sheet?[1] It depends upon the item format used, the age and ability level of the pupils, and the nature of the content. Generally speaking, separate answer sheets will provide more accurate and reliable scores, especially if they are machine-scored. Although, as mentioned earlier, for tests involving computation, it might be better to have pupils record their answers directly in the test booklet, rather than use a separate answer sheet.

There are essentially two types of scoring processes: (1) hand scoring, either in the booklets themselves or on separate answer sheets, and (2) machine scoring. This means, therefore, that there are also two methods by which the pupil can record his answers. The manner in which the answers are to be recorded, and hence scored, will be governed (in part at least) by the availability of special scoring equipment, the speed with which test results are needed, and the monetary resources available to have the answer sheets scored by an independent scoring service.

Hand Scoring

For the completion-type item, the teacher may prepare a scoring key by writing out the answers on a test paper, or she may make a separate strip key that corresponds to the column of blanks provided the student. With either of these methods, the teacher or aide can place the scoring key next to the pupils' responses and score the papers rather quickly.

Pupils, of course, may use a separate answer sheet which is hand-scored. A punched key, which is nothing more than the regular answer sheet with the correct responses punched out, can be placed over the pupil's answer sheet and the teacher or pupil can count the number of blackened spaces to determine the number of items answered correctly. The teacher must check to see that no paper contains more than one mark per item.

Another technique that may be used to record and score responses is the silver-overlay answer sheet. Here, the correct answers are previously placed in the appropriate squares, and the total answer sheet is covered by a silver overlay that conceals the correct answers. Students erase the square they feel corresponds to the correct answers. This procedure is used quite effectively in classroom testing because it provides immediate feedback. Research has also shown that such a self-scoring procedure results in a higher reliability than the conventional right–wrong method (Gilman & Ferry, 1972).

Two other variations are the carbon booklet and pinprick methods. They will not be discussed here because of their limited use in the classroom.

Machine Scoring

The simplest way to score select-type objective-test items is to have the students record their an-

---

[1]For a discussion on the effect of type of answer sheet used on test performance, see Hayward (1967).

swers on a separate answer sheet and then have the answer sheets machine-scored. Although separate answer sheets make scoring easier and generally more reliable, they are not recommended for young and for slow-learning children because of the inconclusive evidence regarding their use with these children (McKee, 1967; Cashen & Ramseyer, 1969; Gaffney & Maguire, 1971; Ramseyer & Cashen, 1971; Beck, 1974). When a separate answer sheet is used, the pupil must remember the question that he is answering (especially if he skips one), the answer selected, and then transfer this accurately to the answer sheet. Such a task may be too demanding for very young children (kindergarten and first-graders definitely). If separate answer sheets are used, students have to be taught how to use an answer sheet, should be given practice with it, and should be given examples on the test booklet. It would be helpful for the teacher to also give examples on the use of the answer sheet before the test begins, using the blackboard. Then, any questions or problems that exist can be dealt with before the test begins.

When feasible, we recommend the use of a separate machine-scorable answer sheet for efficiency and accuracy. Although small schools would not be in a position to justify the expenditure of funds to purchase or lease elaborate, sophisticated test-scoring equipment, simpler versions are available to them. In the past few years, small, relatively inexpensive scoring machines have appeared. Information on these machines can be obtained by writing directly to the manufacturers.

For volume users, commercial firms will provide test-scoring services for a very nominal charge. It is also possible to have the papers scored by some state universities or large school districts for a small charge. Those persons considering the processing of separate answer sheets by machine should compare the costs and services offered so that they will be able to process their answer sheets most economically. (Most agencies will, in addition to scoring the answer sheets, provide printouts of the pupils' scores and provide a variety of statistical reports.)

Some General Considerations for Scoring Objective-Type Tests

Regardless of whether the pupil records his answer directly in the test booklet, or on a separate answer sheet, or whether the responses are scored by hand or machine, there are still certain precautions that the teacher can take to ensure that her scoring key is properly prepared. Some of the points have been discussed earlier but deserve repetition here because, if adopted, they may avoid needless quibbling between teacher and student.

1. The scoring key should be prepared and checked well in advance. One way to check on the correctness of the scoring key is to have another teacher either check your key or prepare her own and compare the two keys. Another way to check on the adequacy of the scoring key, especially for completion items, is to select the papers of a few of the more able students and compare their responses with the key. This "dry run" may indicate some discrepancies in the scoring key that are the result of an ambiguous item and/or an answer that is correct but was not anticipated. Naturally, any time a correct but unanticipated answer is received, the key should be corrected accordingly. If an error is found after the papers are scored, they should be rescored.
2. If factors other than the correctness of the answer (such as spelling, grammar, or legibility of handwriting) are to be considered, they should be given a separate score.
3. Generally speaking, all objective items should have equal weight.[2] Needless problems will be avoided if each objective-test item is assigned

---

[2]For a comprehensive survey of research on weighting, see Stanley and Wang (1970). See also Patnaik and Traub (1973), Kansup and Hakstian (1975), Raffeld (1975), and Echternacht (1976).

the *same* point value. Trying to justify that one item is worth 2 points, another 1 point, and still another ½ point is very difficult. With differential weighting, the teacher is really saying that knowledge of one concept is more important than knowledge of another concept. If the teacher believes that this is so, she should sample more heavily in these areas rather than use differential weights.

4. Whether students should receive credit for partial knowledge is another perplexing problem that deserves some consideration.[3] On a computational problem, should the student who demonstrates knowledge of the process and concepts, but makes a simple arithmetic error, be given partial credit?

To overcome the criticism that dichotomous scoring of multiple-choice tests restricts the examinee from showing his knowledge (Bock, 1972; Claudy, 1978; Waters, 1976), a variety of approaches have been devised, for example, answer-until-correct, degree of confidence weighting, response weighting, and the like. (See, e.g., Echternacht, 1976, and Raffeld, 1975.) Smith (1982), however, pointed out several methodological problems associated with response-weighting techniques.

We believe that for some tests (such as essay or problem-solving), students should receive partial credit for partial knowledge. For objective tests, however, weighting is too complex and is not warranted. (See Frary, 1989, for a fairly comprehensive review of studies dealing with partial-credit scoring.)

TESTING THE TEST: ITEM ANALYSIS[4]

It is important that tests give information that is as accurate as possible. If they do not provide ac-

curate data, teachers should want to know this so that they could (1) place less emphasis on the data in decision making and (2) improve their measuring instruments for use in future evaluations and decision making. More often than not, teachers prepare, administer, and score a test; sometimes return the papers to their students; possibly discuss the test; and then either file or discard the test. One of the more common mistakes teachers make is that they do not check on the effectiveness of their tests. This is probably because teachers (1) do not always understand the importance of accurate evaluation, (2) are not aware of the methods of analyzing tests, or (3) feel that test analysis is too time-consuming. We certainly hope that by now *you* realize that important decisions are often based on classroom achievement tests and that accuracy is, therefore, important.

Evaluate with Respect to Measurement Criteria

There are certain psychometric criteria that evaluation instruments should possess. Teachers do not have the time to check all aspects of these characteristics for all evaluative instruments, but many of them can be checked for most instruments without consuming a great deal of teacher time. For example, reliability can and should be checked for major evaluative instruments such as the end-of-semester exams. The scorer reliability of essay exams can and should be checked by correlating the values given by two or more readers. (See Chapter 12 for methods of estimating reliability.) The difficulty and discrimination indices of the test items used should be checked every time a test is administered.

For achievement tests, educators are most concerned with *content* validity. As was mentioned

---

[3]See Volume 1 (4) of *Applied Measurement in Education* (1988) for a collection of articles dealing with the application of Item Response Theory (IRT) to partial-credit scoring.

[4]Less relevant to classroom teachers and their achievement

tests is the use of a form of item analysis concerned with detecting item bias. For those interested in the use of distracter analysis to detect differences in test performance among ethnic, racial, and religious groups, see Green et al. (1989), Dorans and Kulick (1986), and Schmitt and Dorans (1987).

under the section on planning (see pp. 56–63), a blueprint should be constructed for every test so that the test content will be appropriate to the course objectives. Teacher-constructed instruments such as rating scales, sociograms, or observational techniques (see Chapter 9) are in a sense checked for content validity when the teacher rethinks whether the behavior observed is really relevant to her educational objectives and decision making. Other teachers and students, and at times even parents, can be valuable resource people in examining the validity of any measuring instrument.

Objectivity and efficiency can be examined for any instrument. Discrimination and item difficulty, a related variable, can be checked by a procedure known as item analysis. While something analogous to item analysis can be performed on any instrument, it is most useful for objective tests. Although we will discuss item analysis of essay and criterion-referenced tests, we will concentrate on the item analysis of multiple-choice items. Many of the principles discussed, however, are applicable to true–false and matching items.

Item Analysis

Item analysis is like a handmaiden to the builder of tests. It is the process of examining the students' responses to each test item, to judge the quality of the item. Specifically, what one looks for is the difficulty and discriminating ability of the item as well as the effectiveness of each alternative. We agree with Thissen et al., who say, "... when the quality of a multiple-choice item must be judged, a thorough analysis of the item's alternatives should be an important part of any item analysis" (1989, p.101).

When item writers prepare test items, they must make some judgments regarding the difficulty level, discrimination power, and content validity of their items. Normally, item writers make some "gut level" decisions (they may incorporate the views of others) about content relevance, but difficulty and discrimination indices will require

some quantitative evidence. Such quantitative estimates can be obtained from item analysis.

Still another value accrues from performing an item analysis. Many teachers fail to reuse test items. Often those teachers who do reuse test items use *both* the better and poorer items. It is indeed unfortunate when a teacher fails to reuse her better test items and possibly more unfortunate (at least to the students) when she reuses poor items on subsequent tests. The time, effort, and energy expended in the planning and writing of test items is wasted if the good items are discarded. If the better items—those that possess content validity and that discriminate between high and low achievers—were only filed, they could at some future date be reused. It is ridiculous for teachers to have to write new items every time they prepare a test. Over time, they should have built up a test file of the better items to be reused. However, in order to build this test file, it is necessary to know how the items behave.

There are more than 50 different item-analysis procedures ranging from the less technical to the more technical (see, e.g., Davis, 1964; Engelhart, 1965; Henryssen, 1971; Oosterhof, 1976; Baker, 1977; Weiss & Davison, 1981; Schittjer & Cartledge, 1976). In general, the simpler procedures as described in an Educational Testing Service bulletin (1960) are as effective as the more statistically complicated ones for purposes of analyzing classroom tests (Henryssen, 1971, p. 145).

In conducting an item analysis of a classroom test, one should follow the steps listed below (see Educational Testing Service, 1960).

1. Arrange the test papers from the highest score to the lowest score.

2. From the ordered set of papers, make two groups: Put those with the highest scores in one group (the top half) and those with the lowest scores in the other group (the bottom half). There are some statistical reasons why one should place the best 27 percent of the papers in one group and the poorest 27 percent in the other group. But for classroom tests it really is not too important what percentage is used (D'Agostino & Cureton, 1975).

If the class is small (say 40 or fewer students), there would be too few papers in the top and bottom 27 percent to obtain very reliable item-analysis indices. In the typical classroom situations it is quite appropriate to simply divide the total group into the top and bottom halves.

3. For each item, count the number of students in each group who choose each alternative (in the completion or true–false item, it would be the number who answered the item correctly).

4. Record the count as follows for each item (assume a total of 30 papers, 15 in each group, for this example), in which the asterisk indicates the correct answer.

			Alternatives			
	A	B	C*	D	E	Omits
Upper group	0	0	15	0	0	0
Lower group	4	2	8	1	0	0

5. For each item, compute the percentage of students who get the item correct. This is called the *item-difficulty index* (P),[5] which can range from .00 to 1.00. The formula for item difficulty is

$$\text{Item Difficulty} = P = \frac{R}{T} \times 100$$

where R = number of pupils who answered the item correctly and
T = total number of pupils tested.

---

[5]Difficulty can be expressed as either average *test* difficulty or *item* difficulty. Average test difficulty is defined as the ratio between the average score and the total test score. For example, on a test where the maximum score was 100 and the average score was 70, we would say that the average test difficulty is 70/100 = .70. If all pupils who took the test received a perfect score, the average test difficulty would be 100/100 = 1.00; if no pupil answered any item correctly, the average test difficulty is 0/100 = .00.

On the surface, the term *item difficulty* appears to be a misnomer since the larger the value of P, the *easier* the item. But because this terminology is common, we don't use "item ease."

In the example in step 4, $R = 23$ (this is the total number of students who answered C, the correct answer) and $T = 30$ (the number of students tested). Applying the formula,

$$P = \frac{23}{28} \times 100 = 77\%$$

(For those who like to express difficulty as decimals rather than percentages, compute only R/T.)

If one did not divide the total group into two halves but put the top 27 percent in the upper and the bottom 27 percent in the lower group, one could obtain an *estimate* of item difficulty by dividing the number of persons in the two groups who answered the item correctly by the total number of people in those two groups. (Be careful! *Not* the total number of students tested!)

One must be cautious when interpreting a P value. Eignor and Cook (1983) and Kingston and Dorans (1982, 1984), among others, found differences in item difficulty depending on the location of the item in the test. Hence, computing P for an item when it was pretested at the beginning of the test can be, and often is, different (sometimes markedly) when that item is located elsewhere.

6. Compute the *item-discrimination index*[6] for each item by subtracting the number of students in the lower group who answered the item correctly from the number in the upper group who got the item right and dividing by the number of students in either group (e.g., half the total number of students when we divide the group into upper and lower halves). In our example,

$$\text{Discrimination} = \frac{R_U - R_l}{\frac{1}{2}T} = \frac{15 - 8}{15} = .47$$

This value is usually expressed as a decimal and can range from -1.00 to $+1.00$. If it has a positive value, the item has positive discrimination. This means that a larger proportion of the more knowledgeable students than poor students (as de-

---

[6]Item discrimination is the difference between the difficulty in the high group and the difficulty in the low group.

termined by the total test score) got the item right. If the value is zero, the item has zero discrimination. This can occur (1) because the item is too easy or too hard (if everybody got the item right or everybody missed the item, there would be zero discrimination) or (2) because the item is ambiguous. If more poorer than better students get the item right, one would obtain a negative discrimination. With a small number of students, this could be a chance result. But it *may* indicate that the item is ambiguous or miskeyed. In general, the higher the discrimination index, the better, recognizing that there are situations where low discrimination is to be expected. For classroom tests, where one divides the class into upper and lower halves as we have done, one would hope that most of the items would have discrimination indices above .20. (If one uses the upper and lower 27 percent, one should expect higher values, since there is more of a difference between the groups.)

7. Look at how the distracters (incorrect options or alternatives) worked by using the same process specified above. For the distracters, we hope to get *negative* values. That is, more poor students than good students should choose incorrect answers.

Quite often, a visual inspection is all that is needed to evaluate the effectiveness of the distracters. Look at the following example, which is taken from an actual test and measurement examination.

It is readily evident in the example (even if the discrimination indices were not provided) that the item discriminates in a positive direction, (i.e., a larger percentage of the higher-scoring than lower-scoring students answered the item correctly). Alternatives A and C are effective in the sense that they attracted more students from the lower group than from the upper group. Alternative D is a poor distracter because it attracted no one and may need to be replaced or revised. Alternative E is also poor because it attracted a higher proportion of the better than poorer students. The item writer must ask herself, "Why were the brighter students attracted to E?" Was it

Topic	Objective
Table of Specifications	Understanding

12. In planning a test, the table of content and process objectives is least useful in

A. relating content to behavioral objectives.
B. deciding whether to use essay or objective items.
C. judging relative emphases to be given to different objectives.
D. judging relative emphases to be given to different content areas.
E. gearing the test to the instruction it follows.

	A[a]	B*	C	D	E	OMIT		
U	0	83	0	0	17	0	DIFF	.67
L	42	50	8	0	0	0	DISC	.33

[a]Numbers are percentages.
*Correct answer.

because of ambiguity? Was it because there were two equally correct answers? Was it because of carelessness on the part of the examinees? It would appear that the better students misread the question that asked for the least useful aspect of the table of specifications. Without a doubt, "E" is a very useful aspect of the table of specifications. Generally, if any one of the distracters is *over*selected by students in the upper group (such as E in this example), it should be revised to make it less attractive.

In the item analysis below, where the asterisk indicates the correct answer, the item is discriminating in a negative direction.

	A	B	C	D	E*	Omits
			Alternatives			
Upper 20 students	0	1	7	2	4	6
Lower 20 students	0	1	5	3	6	5
TOTAL:	0	2	12	5	10	11

What is the "ideal" discrimination index? Generally, for a norm-referenced test, the higher the discrimination index, the better. *What is the "ideal" difficulty index?* Teachers should try to have their classroom achievement tests be of appropriate difficulty because test difficulty is related to *discrimination power*. If an item is so easy that everyone answers it correctly, or so hard that no one can answer it correctly, it cannot discriminate at all and adds nothing to test reliability or validity. So, then, what is the "ideal" index of difficulty that the teacher should strive to obtain? The designation of the "ideal" difficulty level is dependent upon many factors, the most important ones being the purpose of the test and the type of objective items used.

If the purpose of the test is to determine the extent to which fourth-grade students have *mastered* the multiplication tables, the teacher (after completing this unit) might expect all her test items to have a difficulty value approaching 1.00. That is, she would expect most, if not all, of her students to answer each multiplication item correctly. But, if the purpose of the test was to achieve maximum discrimination among her pupils in terms of a final examination on the year's work, she should not expect all her students to obtain perfect or near-perfect scores. Rather, she would want a spread of scores and would want items having a medium level of difficulty. If chance didn't operate, such as in completion items, we would expect an examinee of average ability to answer about one-half the items correctly with the range of difficulty across items being rather restricted.[7]

Although a general rule of thumb is to prepare a test for which the mean is halfway between a chance and perfect score, Lord (1952) showed that for tests where guessing can occur, more reliable results can be obtained if the test as a whole is just a bit easier. This reduces the effect of

chance guessing and increases test reliability. Lord gave the following guide for preparing tests with different item formats:

Item Format	Ideal Average Difficulty for a Maximally Discriminating Test
Completion and short-answer	50
Five-response multiple-choice	70
Four-response multiple-choice	74
Three-response multiple-choice	77
True–false (two-response multiple-choice)	85

If we had a 60-item completion test, we would want the average score for the class to be 30 (60 × .50). If the 60 items were four-response multiple-choice, we would want the average score for the class to be 44–45 (60 × .74). And if our test consisted of true–false items, we would want the average score for the class to be 51 (60 × .85). You should remember that the chart values are "ideal" values if the purpose is to get a test that is *maximally* differentiating among pupils.

In the long run, what is more important than the level of difficulty is to have a test that possesses adequate content validity. In addition, we want a test in which, for each item, a larger proportion of the better able than less able students can answer the item correctly.

The above suggestions have *nothing* to do with passing or failing. Assigning grades is discussed in Chapter 20.

A word of caution—or how not to make a test more difficult. For motivational purposes, we should have both some very easy and some very difficult items. But, if the teacher is preparing a test to select one scholarship winner to Michigan State University, she might want to have a test that is quite difficult. However, in attempting to write

---

[7]For a more intensive treatment of the effect of population homogeneity and item heterogeneity on item difficulty, see Cronbach and Warrington (1952), Lord (1952), and Tinkelman (1971).

more difficult items, we must be very careful not to resort to (1) ambiguity, (2) emphasis on trivial details, and (3) outright trickery. Emphasis on the trivial aspects of the course content will invariably lead students to memorize details at the expense of the more important learning outcomes, such as comprehension or analysis. Therefore, by emphasizing the trivial, we are not only contributing to undesirable learning outcomes, but we are also lowering the test's content validity.

Other things being equal, the more positive and usually more profitable approach to use to increase test difficulty is to have more items calling for the application of the higher mental processes, such as application of principles and understanding of concepts, analysis, synthesis, and the like.

Using Item-Analysis Results[8]

Item-analysis data have several values: (1) They help one judge the worth or quality of a test; (2) they can be of aid in subsequent test revisions; (3) they can be used to build a test file for future tests; (4) they lead to increased skill in test construction; (5) they provide diagnostic value and help in planning future learning activities; (6) they provide a basis for discussing test results; and (7) they can be a learning experience for students, if students assist in or are told the item-analysis results.

Although item difficulty, item discrimination, and the response frequency of the distracters are useful in judging the adequacy of the test already given, they are probably more useful in helping revise the test (or the items) for future occasions. Very poor items should be discarded or, better yet, rewritten. Lange, Lehmann, and Mehrens (1967) showed that items can be improved, without too much effort, through using item-analysis data. Revising poor test items is probably more economical than simply discarding them and attempt-

ing to write new ones. (We realize, of course, that some items are so poor that it would be better to prepare new ones than to try to patch them up.) By keeping a record of item-analysis data (one of the reasons we suggested that each item be written as a separate card), one can refer to it on subsequent revisions and determine the effectiveness of the changes. This continual revision and rechecking process leads to increased skill in test construction in that a teacher gradually learns what methods of wording and what type of distracters will work best. It is important to recognize that *careful inspection of the item itself is needed before making any changes.*

Item-analysis data can also be used to choose the most discriminating items for selection and placement purposes. For example, if Ms. Divider wants to develop a test that will be used to select ninth-graders for Algebra I, she can use item-analysis data for that purpose. Also, if Ms. Helper wants to prepare a test to place poor readers into special reading groups, she would want to have relatively easy items.

It should be noted that if the purpose of a test is for selection or placement purposes, each item should not only be positively discriminating (i.e., contribute to the total score), but also correlate with some external criterion. You will recall that our discrimination index is based upon an *internal* criterion (the total test score), which tells us how well each item contributes to the test as a whole. It does *not* tell us how valid a predictor the test is of some *external* criterion. Ideally, we would want a test with high, positive discriminating items and which also has high criterion-related validity.

Another use of item-analysis data relates to its impact on instructional procedures. If students all do poorly on some items, it may be due to poor teaching of that content. By carefully looking at the content of the hard items, a teacher can identify those areas in which students are not learning, so that in future classes she can do a more effective job by emphasizing the relevant material. Also, wrong answers do give valuable information not provided by just looking at correct answers. For

---

[8]For interesting discussions on the future of item analysis, see Wainer (1989) and Tucker (1987).

example, look at the following response to the multiplication item

$$730 \times 12 =$$

	Upper Group	Lower Group
A. 1190	0	8
B. 2190	4	3
C. 8760	11	2
D. 9560	0	2

Note that most of the errors are in response to options A and B. In both of these, the students did *not* move the place value to the left in the second stage, for example,

$$
\begin{array}{cc}
\text{A.} \quad 730 & \text{B.} \quad 730 \\
\underline{12} & \underline{12} \\
1460 & 1460 \\
\underline{730} & \underline{730} \\
\overline{1190} & \overline{2190}
\end{array}
$$

and in option A, the student also did not carry in the addition. With this information, the teacher should be better able to teach or reteach this multiplication fact. *Each* distracter must be *plausible*, that is, be obtainable from a reasonable type of student error/misunderstanding (see Brown & Burton, 1978; Tatsuoka, 1981; Gronlund & Linn, 1990).

Providing Feedback to Students

It is our firm conviction that every classroom teacher should incorporate the discussion of the individual test items as part of her instructional strategy for a variety of reasons:[9]

1. To correct students' errors in thinking and to clear up possible misconceptions and misunderstandings (some of these errors being the result of poor study habits or sloppy test-taking skills). Birenbaum and Tatsuoka (1987) found that feedback for *incorrect* responses is more important than for correct responses and that the more informative the feedback mode, the better the performance. However, we must interpret their findings cautiously since only a six-item posttest was used; and only arithmetic was studied for eighth-graders.

2. To motivate pupils to do better on subsequent tests.

3. To demonstrate to pupils those instructional objectives that are being stressed and tested so that they can organize their study habits accordingly.

Feedback is extremely useful in the teaching-learning process (Kulhavy, 1977). Although it might be considered by both teachers and pupils as time-consuming and detracting from the time available for learning new material, we are firmly convinced that it is important to learn the material covered well before moving on to new areas. As of now, there appears to be some disagreement as to the time when feedback should be given. Some feel that it is more effective if done as soon as possible after the test has been given so as to correct errors immediately, before they have a chance to solidify in the pupils' minds. Others say that feedback can be delayed for up to one week without serious dilatory effects. Still others feel that delayed feedback is best and that it enhances retention (Kippel, 1975; Surber & Anderson, 1975). The evidence bearing on the question of feedback time is inconclusive. What is conclusive, however, is the research that demonstrates that pupils given feedback, regardless of the delay, perform significantly better on similar type items at a later date (Wexley & Thornton, 1972).

---

[9]We realize that for test security purposes some teachers, especially college faculty, might disagree with our position. We can readily envision students madly taking notes while the items are being discussed, thereby destroying the security of items that have been carefully written or selected and which will be reused. However, both of us have routinely discussed our tests with the students, and the test means have not increased—so test security has evidently been maintained. Test security concerns should *not* preclude teachers from distributing and discussing practice items.

Feedback will be dealt with more fully in Chapter 20 where we will discuss reporting to parents, pupils, and teachers.

Interpreting Item-Analysis Data

Item-analysis data should be interpreted with caution for a variety of reasons (Furst, 1958; Helmstadter, 1974; Gronlund, 1985):

1. *Item-analysis data are not analogous to item validity.* In order to judge accurately the validity of a test, one should use some external criterion. You will recall from our discussion of the item-analysis procedure that no external criterion was used. In reality, we used an internal criterion. The total test score was used to select the better and poorer groups. In other words, a form of circular reasoning was employed. Therefore, it would appear that we were studying the internal consistency of the items rather than their validity.

2. *The discrimination index is not always a measure of item quality.* Generally speaking, the index of discrimination tells us about the quality of an item. In general, a discrimination index of .20 is regarded as satisfactory. However, one should not automatically conclude that because an item has a low discrimination index it is a poor item and should be discarded. Items with low or negative discriminating indices should be identified for more careful examination. Those with low, but positive, discrimination indices should be kept (especially for mastery tests). As long as an item discriminates in a positive fashion, it is making a contribution to measurement of the students' competencies. And we need some easy items to instill proper motivation in the examinees.

There are a variety of reasons why an item may have low discriminating power: (a) The more difficult or easy the item, the lower its discriminating power—but we often need such items to have adequate and representative sampling of the course content and objectives; and (b) the purpose of the item in relation to the total test will influence the magnitude of its discriminating power. Remember that we are dealing with the total test score as our internal criterion. Hence, if on an eleventh-grade physics test Ms. Magnet wants to measure various objectives and different content areas such as heat, light, magnetism, and electricity, she would need a variety of different items. If only 5 percent of her course deals with "the ability to apply principles," and this is spread over the various content areas, these "application" items might have low discriminating power because the major portion of the test may be measuring, for example, "knowledge and understanding." Removing these low discriminating items could seriously impair test validity. As long as Ms. Magnet teaches for "application," she is obliged to test for application. In this case, since the typical classroom test measures a variety of instructional objectives, we might expect to find that "low positive indices of discrimination are the rule rather than the exception" (Gronlund, 1985, p. 253).

3. *Item-analysis data are tentative.* Some teachers assume that difficulty and discrimination indices are fixed. This is *not* true. Item-analysis data are influenced by the nature of the group being tested, the number of pupils tested, the instructional procedures employed by the teacher, chance errors, and the position of the item in the test. Our judgment of the quality of an item should be predicated more by whether or not it measures an important instructional objective rather than by the magnitude of its difficulty and discrimination indices. As long as the item discriminates positively, is clear and unambiguous, and is free from technical defects, it should be retained at least for possible future use. Naturally, if a better item is developed, it should be used.

4. *Avoid selecting test items purely on the basis of their statistical properties.* One of the better ways to select test items is to choose those that have appropriate difficulty and discriminating power for the intended purpose of the test. Statistical efficiency is *not* the *sine qua non*, especially in teacher-made achievement tests in the elementary grades where item statistics are computed on only about 25 to 30 pupils, and hence are not too reliable. Another reason for not selecting test items

solely on the basis of their statistical properties—even if a sufficiently large sample was used—is that item difficulty can be affected by guessing, the location of the correct answer among the alternatives, and the serial location of the item in the test (Huck & Bowers, 1972). Still another reason for being cautious is that in some cases the statistical selection of test items results in a test that is unrepresentative and *biased*. Cox (1964) found that a test composed of items selected *purely* on their statistical properties may be biased in that it may not evaluate the instructional objectives in the same proportion as would the original item pool; that is, the content validity is actually lowered. Cox recommended that the most discriminating items *within* each taxonomical category be selected, rather than selecting the most discriminating items from the entire pool of items where the taxonomical structure is ignored. Unless this were done, the teacher would never be certain that her final form of the test would validly measure the instructional objectives specified in the test blueprint in the planning stage.

Item-analysis data provide a valuable service in selecting good test items. But they should be used as a "flag" to identify items that may require more careful examination rather than as a shovel to bury the suspect item. We must temper our predilection to select only items bearing certain statistical properties. A good rule of thumb is to use rational procedures as a basis for initial selection of test items, and then use statistical techniques to check on your judgment. However, we believe that even after item analysis, items must be carefully reviewed to ensure adequate content sampling.

Item Analysis for Essay Tests

Most people think of item analysis only in terms of objective tests. But it is just as important, if not more important, for essay tests to have good questions, considering that they have so few questions (thereby making each question carry a great deal of weight). Whitney and Sabers (1970) proposed the following approach to compute the difficulty and discrimination indices of essay tests.

1. Identify the upper and lower 25 percent of the group tested.
2. Compute the sum of scores for the "highs" and "lows" for each item.
3. Apply the formula.

$$\text{Disc.} = \frac{\Sigma_\mu - \Sigma_L}{N(\text{Score}_{max})}$$

where Σ_μ = sum of scores for upper 25%
Σ_L = sum of scores for lower 25%
N = 25% of number tested
Score_{max} = highest possible score on the question

$$\text{Diff.} = \frac{H + L}{2N(\text{Score}_{max})}$$

Example The following score distribution was obtained for a question on a tenth-grade essay in literature.

Item Score(s)	High Group* f	High Group* fs	Low Group f	Low Group fs
5	8	40	3	15
4	5	20	7	28
3	6	18	8	24
2	4	8	6	12
1	7	7	2	2
0	0	0	4	0
	30	93	30	81

$$\text{Disc.} = \frac{93 - 81}{30(5)} = \frac{12}{150} = .08$$

$$\text{Diff.} = -\frac{93 + 81}{60(5)} = .58$$

*f = frequency (number) obtaining the score.

Item Analysis for Criterion-Referenced Tests

In criterion-referenced tests, especially mastery tests, the concepts of difficulty and discrimination are antithetical to the philosophy underlying the mastery concept—that all, or nearly all, students should pass the item. Therefore, should we be concerned with identifying the nondiscriminating items when ideally there should be no discriminating items? Yes! We still should be concerned with identifying those items that may be in need of revision.

There are those who contend that the conventional item-analysis procedure for NRTs is inappropriate for CRTs because in CRTs there need not be any variability and conventional techniques depend on variability. There are some (Harris & Subkoviak, 1986; Harwell, 1983; Lord, 1980) who believe that item-response theory can be used to determine the discrimination index for CRTs. There are some, such as Popham and Husek (1969), who contend that for criterion-referenced tests, less attention should be paid to discrimination and difficulty. There are some who say that conventional procedures can be used because pre- and posttest scores can be used to obtain variability and hence enable one to compute reliability. And, there are some, such as Harris and Stewart (1971, p. 3), who contend that "item difficulty techniques cannot be properly used in constructing tests to assess skill in mastery when the population of performance (content) is specifically defined." Cox and Vargas (1966) concluded that selection based on the difference in percentages passing the item on the pre- and posttest yielded good items. Hopkins and Antes (1978) selected CRT items using the difference between the proportion of persons answering each item correctly who (1) met the criterion and (2) did not meet the criterion. Brennan and Stolurow (1971) presented a variety of decision rules that can be applied to either pretest data only, posttest data only, or pre- and posttest data.

We feel that more research is needed before any conclusive answer can be obtained with regard to the usefulness of conventional item-analysis procedures for criterion-referenced tests. It may well be that conventional item analysis is appropriate but that we will have to interpret the data in a slightly different manner.

Even if we dispense with the traditional item analysis for CRTs, we must still be concerned with ascertaining whether the items in a CRT be-

have similarly, inasmuch as they are supposed to measure a well-defined domain. How, then, does one go about selecting appropriate items for a CRT? Popham (1972) proposed using an index of homogeneity based upon a chi-square technique, but this requires the administration of a pre- and posttest—a procedure that is neither economically efficient nor possible in many cases. Pettie and Oosterhof (1976) proposed an adaptation of Popham's method to compute item difficulty that did not require an index of variability and only required a single test administration. Further research is needed, however, before the validity of this procedure can be established. Hambleton et al. (1978) recommended making a logical (content analysis) as well as an empirical (difficulty and discrimination indices) review of items used in CRTs. Haladyna and Roid (1981, p. 40) recommended using item sensitivity ("the tendency for an item to vary in difficulty as a function of instruction") as another criterion in selecting CRT items. They reviewed numerous item-sensitivity indices and concluded that the most useful one for constructing item domains was the one that considered the difference between pretest and posttest item difficulty.

Following is an example of the behavior of four items *before* (B, pretest) and *after* (A, posttest) instruction:

	1		2		3		4	
	B	A	B	A	B	A	B	A
Alexi	−	+	−	−	+	−	−	+
Garrett	−	+	−	−	+	−	−	+
Jennifer	−	+	−	−	+	−	+	+
Maxwell	−	+	−	−	+	−	+	+
Nathan	−	+	−	−	+	−	−	−

B = Pretest; A = Posttest.
+ means item *correctly* answered.
− means item *incorrectly* answered.

From this matrix, the following conclusions could be drawn:

Item 1. This is what would be expected in an "ideal" CRT. No one answered the item correctly *before* instruction; everybody after. This *suggests* that the instruction was effective.

Item 2. We would *not* want these results in a CRT. No pupil answered the item correctly *either* before or after instruction. This may be indicative of a poor item, poor teaching, or both; or it may simply indicate a very hard item.

Item 3. We would *not* want these results in any test—be it CRT or NRT. Why should pupils who answered correctly *before* instruction answer incorrectly *after* instruction? Were these five students lucky in their guessing? Maybe, but it would be highly unlikely for all of them to guess correctly. Was it due to a very poor item? Maybe, but if it was a very poor item to begin with, why wasn't it still a very poor item later on? Was it due to poor instruction? Quite likely.

Item 4. This is how we would expect good test items to behave. We would expect some pupils to know the correct answer *before* instruction but a larger number to answer the item correctly *after* "effective" instruction.

To compute the sensitivity index *(S)* Haladyna and Roid (1981) proposed the following formula to obtain a measure of *sensitivity to instructional effects (S)*

$$S = \frac{R_A - R_B}{T}$$

where R_A = number of pupils who got the item right *after* instruction

R_B = number of pupils who answered the item correctly *before* instruction

T = total number of pupils who attempted the item *both* times

Using this approach, *S* ranges from 0.00 to 1.00, where the higher the positive value, the more sensitive the item to instruction and vice versa. Naturally, for a CRT one would want *high positive values.*

Item 1, for example, has

$$S = \frac{5 - 0}{5} = 1.00$$

Item 2, for example, has

$$S = \frac{0 - 0}{5} = 0.00$$

It is readily obvious that *S* resembles *D* (index of discrimination), insofar as the range of values (−1.00 to +1.00) is concerned. However, other than that, there is *no* similarity, and caution must be exercised *not* to confuse the two indices. *S* indicates the degree to which an item reflects the intended effects of instruction. *D*, however, pertains to how well an item discriminates between *high* and *low* achievers. *S* requires two test administrations; *D* requires only one administration.

We believe that, regardless of whether a test is criterion- or norm-referenced, we should *not* automatically discard a negatively discriminating item if it reflects an important attribute of the criterion. Rather, the item should be looked at carefully. In criterion-referenced tests as well as in norm-referenced tests, a negative discriminator may be due to a faulty item, ineffective instruction, inefficient learning on the part of the pupil, or chance.

■ SUMMARY

The principal ideas, conclusions, and recommendations presented in this chapter are summarized in the following statements:

1. All test items should be prepared early enough to have a thorough critical review and editing, preferably by another teacher.
2. Test items should be grouped according to

item format and ordered according to difficulty within each format.

3. All test directions must be simple, clear, and concise. If diagrams or illustrative materials are used, they should be of good quality and be accurate.

4. Students should be told how the test will be scored.

5. Test directions should be written out. They may also be given orally, but they should be available for student reference when needed.

6. Every student should have his own copy of the test.

7. Any general questions that students have should be clarified before the test begins. Naturally, if a student reports a misprint, all students should be informed.

8. Teachers should proctor the test diligently and conscientiously. Otherwise, cheating may occur, and the results will be invalid.

9. Pupils should be taught how to take tests, especially essay tests.

10. Students should be encouraged to answer every test item.

11. Pupils should be encouraged to review the test and change answers.

12. Responses may be made either directly on the test or on a separate answer sheet. Separate answer sheets should not be used for children below third grade unless special instructions and practice have been given.

13. Teachers should attempt to provide optimal physical conditions. Also, they should consider the pupils' psychological reactions to test taking.

14. Each item in an objective test should be given equal weight. Differential weighting should be avoided. (Essay tests, however, are a different matter.)

15. For some tests and for some purposes, students should receive partial credit for partial information.

16. Test results should be discussed with the class as a whole and/or with individual pupils.

17. Pupils should be motivated to do their best on tests.

18. Teachers should use basic item-analysis procedures to check the quality of their tests. The results of item analysis should be interpreted with caution.

19. Some measurement people feel that conventional item-analysis procedures are not applicable to criterion-referenced tests. More research is needed in this area.

■ POINTS TO PONDER

1. There are some who say that tests should be organized so that they begin with the easy items and progress in difficulty. And there are some who contend that a test should begin with simple recall items and end with essay items or interpretive exercises. Do you think it matters how the test is organized?

2. What are the advantages of grouping items by type? What are the disadvantages?

3. Assume that your test instructions suggested that students should change their answers when they review their test answers. Assume further that three or four students in your class claim that as a result of changing their answers, they obtained a lower score. What should you say to these students to defend your position?

4. How important is it to pay attention to the physical arrangement and reproduction of the test? Would a poorly organized, sloppy test result in less valid and reliable measurement?

5. Assume that you prepared a scoring key and recognized that there were two answers that were acceptable. You could either give credit for each of the two answers or you could omit the two items. What might be the consequence of each of the two decisions made?

6. How might you use item-analysis data to improve your test?

7. Is there such a thing as "too hard/easy" a test? When would it be legitimate to have a very

difficult/easy test and when would it be improper?

8. What factors should be considered when evaluating a test item for difficulty and discrimination?

9. Is there a difference in computing item-analysis data for criterion-referenced tests and for norm-referenced tests? How?

10. Does item-analysis data have any value for students? How?

11. Why is it valuable to discuss the test answers with students?

Chapter 9

Other Teacher-Made Evaluation Procedures

- ■ **Performance Assessment: Evaluating Procedures and Products**
- ■ **Observational Tools and Techniques**
- ■ **Types of Observational Tools**
- ■ **Evaluating Personal-Social Adjustments Sociometrically**
- ■ **Measurement in the Affective Domain**
- ■ **Measuring Attitudes**

The primary way that teachers obtain data concerning their pupils' achievements and attainments is by their daily contacts with students. Teacher observations of daily behavior and the tests they give constitute the major impact upon teacher evaluations of student achievement (Stiggins & Bridgeford, 1985; Herman & Dorr-Bremme, 1983; Salmon-Cox, 1981; Kellaghan et al., 1982; Airasian, 1979b). In fact, research has shown that observing overt classroom behavior (at least for second-graders) is not only useful in predicting school progress at the end of the school year but also leads to a better understanding of the child's progress (McKinney et al., 1975).

Part of effective teaching is knowing what kind of assessment will give teachers meaningful data as well as knowing how to go about getting the information. In Chapters 5 through 8 we considered evaluating student behavior through teacher-made

cognitive tests. However, there are certain elements of practical work that cannot be tested by the conventional paper-and-pencil test but can be measured only with observational tools and techniques. For example, how can you assess whether a student can operate a lathe, type a letter, weld and bead, and so on with the conventional pencil-and-paper test? You can't! In addition, education is, or at least should be, concerned with more than cognitive objectives or work samples of products. We concur with Klausmeier and Goodwin (1975, p. 382), who wrote "attitudes and values are among the most vital outcomes learned in schools for they are important in determining how individuals react to situations, and also what they seek in life." Our schools should be concerned with producing independent, competent thinkers who possess both cognitive and affective skills (Bloom, 1978). Our future society depends as much on the affective behavior of its citizenry as it does on its intellectual prowess.

We, as educators, must therefore recognize that pencil-and-paper achievement tests are only *one* of the methods of evaluation available to teachers. Tests must be supplemented with other procedures if we are desirous of measuring or describing the multifacets of human behavior. Tests periodically measure certain outcomes of instruction (primarily those in the cognitive domain) under contrived conditions. A little over 20 years ago, Stake and Denny (1969, p. 380) said, "needed, but not available, are reliable classroom observation techniques and instruments . . . the affective component of instruction is almost neglected in the current instructional-assessment schedules." These noncognitive instructional objectives should be measured continuously in more natural settings. Direct observation of performance is the appropriate technique in a variety of learning situations from kindergarten to college, where the instructional objective is "to do . . . ." In the past decade, and particularly within the past five years, researchers like Stiggins (1984, 1988), and his colleagues (Stiggins & Bridgeford, 1985; Stiggins et al., 1988; Stiggins & Conklin, 1988) have made tremendous advances in noncognitive assessment techniques. However, the affective component in assessment is still lagging.

This chapter covers methods of measurement other than paper-and-pencil testing. Many of these methods depend upon the observation of pupils' behavior. In general, the methods to be discussed here are less adaptable than achievement tests to the criteria of measurement procedures discussed in previous chapters. However, as observation becomes more systematized and less like everyday perception, such evaluation can and has become quite accurate. The topics to be discussed in this chapter are (1) evaluating procedures and products, (2) observational tools and techniques, (3) advantages of observation, (4) participation charts, (5) checklists, (6) rating scales, (7) anecdotal records, (8) evaluating personal-social adjustment by sociometric methods, (9) measurement in the affective domain, and (10) attitude scales. These topics are related both to methods of

observing and methods of *recording* behavior. In many of the procedures the student does not record any response and/or is unaware that data are being collected, and even when the student does record a response, there is no "right" or "wrong" answer. For these reasons, the procedures are sometimes referred to as *nontest* procedures. Nevertheless, these nontest procedures must still enable us to *quantify* our observations so that they are valid, reliable, and free from bias.

After studying this chapter, you should be able to:

1. Know the functions and value of performance assessment.
2. Recognize the difference between procedures and products.
3. Discuss the two major concerns in evaluating products and processes.
4. Know how to evaluate procedures and products.
5. Know the steps in developing a performance test.
6. Understand the advantages and major limitations of observations.
7. Follow the suggestions offered for improving observations.
8. Differentiate between an observational tool and an observational technique.
9. List, define, and discuss the uses of six nontesting methods of evaluation: participation charts, checklists, rating scales, anecdotal records, sociometric methods, and attitude scales.
10. Develop and use effectively participation charts and checklists.
11. Discuss the five major types of rating scales.
12. List the major sources of error in rating scales and understand their effects.
13. Follow the suggestions offered for improving rating scales.
14. Follow the suggestions for improving raters.
15. Follow the suggestions for improving ratings.
16. Understand the advantages and limitations of anecdotal records.
17. Follow points offered for effectively constructing and using anecdotal records.

18. Understand the myriad of issues related to, and the need for resolving, the storage of anecdotal record data controversy.
19. Discuss the different sociometric devices used to evaluate personal-social adjustment.
20. Use sociometric data.
21. List six limitations of sociometric data.
22. Follow the guidelines provided and be able to construct a good attitude scale.
23. Know the three major approaches for constructing attitude scales.
24. Know how to construct a Likert scale.
25. Know how teachers can use information about students' attitudes.

PERFORMANCE ASSESSMENT: EVALUATING PROCEDURES AND PRODUCTS

The *primary* function of education is to effect some change on the part of the learner. This change may be in the cognitive, affective, or psychomotor domain. Up to this point in this unit, we focused our attention on the measurement of behavioral changes in the cognitive domain with conventional teacher-made pencil-and-paper achievement tests. There are, however, many times when we want to evaluate not only what a person knows but what a person can or will do. We are interested in performance because, so often, what a person knows is not a good predictor of what a person can or will do. And measuring what a person can or will do requires both an instrument (performance test) and a procedure.

The past decade, however, has shown increased attention being paid to alternative modes of assessment to supplement conventional objective measures. One such alternative mode is *performance assessment*. "Performance assessment is a 'systematic' attempt to observe and rate a person's ability to use skills and knowledge to achieve specified goals ... described in terms of four major attributes: assessment context, stimulus conditions or the test exercise, response mode, and scoring procedures" (Stiggins & Anderson, 1981, p. 1).

Performance assessment can play a valuable role in classroom testing. It can provide data that can be of invaluable assistance in the diagnosis of pupil strength and weaknesses, for course placement, reporting student progress to parents, and guidance. Also, it can provide data for educational program evaluation. (See Wolf, 1989; Hiebert & Calfee, 1989; Calfee et al., 1988.)

Performance tests are techniques that try to establish what a person can do (the examinee makes some type of motor or manual response, e.g., adjusting a microscope) as distinct from what he knows (e.g., Who was the fifth U.S. President?)[1]. Performance testing is not new. If we go back to the time of the Greeks, we read about athletic contests such as the marathon and other endurance sports. If we look in the Bible, we see evidence of different types of performance and performance testing. Musical, artistic, and literary accomplishments have been measured and rated for many years. Although the procedures used in the past might have lacked refinement and psychometric elegance, they nevertheless were examples of performance testing. Why then, the surge in interest in performance assessment?[2] Why is California using a writing assessment and studying portfolio assessments in their state assessment program? Why is Connecticut using real world performance tasks? Why are some states engaged in student assessment paying attention to performance assessment, which includes direct observations of behavior, logs and journals, videotapes of student performance, and the like? We agree with Stiggins and Anderson (1981) that there are several reasons:

1. Test validity is maximized by sampling behavior using real life exercises to elicit real behavior.
2. Sampling a variety of behaviors permits more

---

[1] We recognize that achievement can be measured using *either* written or performance modes.
[2] See Costa (1989) for a brief but thought-provoking and insightful view of why we need to reassess assessment. Also see Lewis and Lindaman (1989) for one school district's approach to evaluating student writing.

appropriate generalizations of student development. Conventional tests generally sample only *one* type of behavior.

3. Observing and rating the performance of handicapped and learning disabled students (many of whom can't be tested with conventional tests) offers a viable assessment alternative.

4. Potential bias toward minority students may be reduced if the performance test is carefully developed.

Stiggins and Anderson (1981) offered various design alternatives, pointing out the advantages and limitations of each as well as considering issues of validity, reliability, and cost.

Performance tests generally fall into one of three categories: (1) *Tests under simulated condition.* The training of pilots in a Link trainer would be an example of such a test. A limitation of this method is that the behavior in a simulated situation might be markedly different than in the real situation, thereby resulting in a less valid assessment of the examinee's performance. (2) *Work sample tests.* This is the most valid type. It is realistic because the examinee actually produces or performs something. For example, stenographers would be required to take shorthand and transcribe their notes; a music student would be required to perform and would be judged. (3) *Recognition tests.* As the name implies, the test measures whether the examinee can recognize the essential characteristics of a product or performance or can identify certain botanical specimens. Although these tests are easy to prepare, they do *not* directly measure an examinee's skill, procedure, or technique. Work samples are major procedures, but we may also be interested in those tasks involved in generating (making or producing or creating) the product so that we will be able to diagnose weaknesses in either the instructional system, the learning process, or both.

Procedure refers to the steps followed in doing some task and generally is described by *verbs* such as *drawing, adjusting, taking,* and *making.* In typing, procedure refers to one's posture, finger placement on the keys, looking at the material to be typed rather than at the keyboard, strike, and so forth. The *product* refers to the end result and generally involves *nouns* such as *cake, letter, poem, story, picture,* and *dress.* In typing, the product would be the typed letter. In language arts, it could be the theme written, the speech delivered, or the poem read aloud to the class. In many instances, it is very difficult to separate the procedure from the product. For example, in basketball, is dribbling a procedure or a product? Is singing a procedure (process) or a product? There is no definite answer. Many times it depends upon whether the instructional objective involves the *performance* of a set of tasks (typically in a prescribed order such as adjusting a microscope) or *making* something, such as a cake or a dress. The pupils' ability to *do* or *make* something is an important instructional objective, especially in such courses as home economics, industrial arts, the physical and biological sciences, and public speaking. The student in chemistry and physics should be able to work with laboratory equipment, just as the student in woodworking must work with a hammer and saw. The student taking a laboratory course in the biological sciences should be facile in operating a microscope, just as he should be able to list the steps to be followed in preparing a tissue specimen.

Products and processes are *not* relegated solely to the nonacademic areas, although they are generally of more concern to technical and vocational teachers. Yet most of our commercially prepared achievement tests and the majority of teacher-made achievement tests pay little attention to products and processes. Why? Primarily for two reasons: (1) Measuring pupil performance tends to be more subjective than measuring pupil achievement; and (2) because of the complexity of measuring one's performance, such tests tend to be more difficult to administer, score, and interpret (Ahmann & Glock, 1981). This, however, should not deter us from measuring performance and product, since they are important instructional objectives. As you read this chapter, it will be evident that there have been successful attempts to develop valid and reliable measures of performance skills. (Stiggins, 1984, provides detailed information for developing formal and informal observations.)

Although procedures and products are interrelated (a particular procedure must be followed to bake a cake, weld a bead, antique a piece of furniture), they are generally separate entities that can be observed, measured, and evaluated independently. As Gronlund (1985, p. 393) pointed out: "In some areas . . . it might be more desirable to rate *procedures* during the early phases of learning, and *products* later, after the basic skills have been mastered."

Highland (1955), on the other hand, offers the following guidelines for deciding on whether to evaluate the process or the product. He believes that process evaluation is warranted when (1) performance requires sequential steps, (2) deviations from accepted procedures can be detected accurately, and (3) no product results from the performance. Product evaluation is in order when (1) a product results from the performance (e.g., a cake or a dress) and (2) there are many ways to produce the product.

The importance of process evaluation can be illustrated by using typing as an example. A student who has "played around" on the typewriter prior to his first formal typing course may, by the end of the second study week, outperform all his peers in terms of a product—typing a letter faster and more accurately. However, he may be using such an inefficient process (e.g., hunt and peck) that his chances of any further product improvement are severely limited. Music, art, home economics, physical education, shop, and science all require correct processes in order for the products to achieve real excellence.

Process evaluation is also very important in the affective domain. Observation of a student while he is performing a particular task can provide useful information concerning his attitudes toward the task. Observational techniques are particularly valuable in assessing processes.

All evaluation—be it of knowledge, procedures, or products—requires that some criterion of correctness be established a priori by the evaluator. For procedural evaluation, we are generally concerned with both efficiency and accuracy. For example, to ascertain whether her students are able to operate a microscope, Ms. Pathology would first have to delineate the steps involved and then observe each and every student to see how well these steps were followed. For accuracy, she might use as a criterion the precision with which the slide is focused. (This could be a sole criterion or one of many.) However, there are some skills, because of their complexity, that preclude the establishment of a set of rigid procedural steps that must be followed in a prescribed order. In such instances, the teacher must establish her own criteria and then subjectively compare the pupil's performance against them. This, in a sense, is what a music, book, or drama critic does in writing a review.

The evaluation of *both* products and processes can be either *subjective* or *objective*, or a *combination of the two* (Stiggins et al., 1988). It depends upon what is being evaluated. For example, in art, Ms. Easel is exercising a certain degree of subjectivity when she says that the shading is too weak. On the other hand, she is being objective when she says that the lines are crooked. Whenever a product or process can be broken down into separate, specific categories, it generally lends itself to more objective measurement. This is so because a global interpretation of the value or goodness of a product may vary from time to time, depending upon the mood of the evaluator.

Teachers developing and using performance tests in the classroom must adhere to the *same* psychometric standards demanded of other tests. Despite the fact that it may be, and often is, more difficult to satisfy these standards with observations and performance tests, the sine qua non of observational tools and techniques are objectivity, reliability, and relevance.

Concerns in Evaluating Procedures and Products

The two major concerns encountered in evaluating procedures and products are obtaining data that are reliable and valid. In order to have valid measurement, the teacher must know specifically what qualities of the product or process are to be evaluated. Teachers are too often prone to rate a speech, debate, or some product on just general impressions. In other words, it is an evaluation predicated upon *affect*. Such visceral or "gut level" decisions are *not* appropriate when valid and reliable measurement is desired. Why? The teacher's feelings toward a student at a particular moment in time may markedly influence her evaluation of the procedure or product. If she likes the student, she may be overly generous; if she does not like the student, she may be overly severe in her rating. This not only affects the quality of measurement, but also has a marked influence on the student's motivation to learn. The best way to overcome this is to make a listing of all *significant* qualities of the product before evaluating the product or process, and then to follow this listing religiously. (This is analogous to the test blueprint stage in cognitive tests.)

In any free-response exercise—art, music, writing—the essential ingredient needed to obtain valid measurement is to develop a thorough scoring system and to use it with well-trained scorers. Knight (n.d.) feels that with simple scoring dimensions defined with a minimum of esoteric language, persons without specific training in art can make relatively complex judgments about art works.

Developing a Performance Test

The steps involved in developing a performance test[3] are as follows:

1. *Conduct a job (task) analysis to determine what abilities are to be tested.* One of the best ways of determining the essential characteristics of a job or task is to have the examiner learn the job

---

[3] A good annotated bibliography on performance testing is *Annotated Bibliography on Applied Performance Testing* published by the Center for the Advancement of Performance Testing. See also Stiggins (1984).

and actually go through the training stage. This would give the test constructor a better picture of what is actually involved than would be obtained only by observing the workers.

2. *Select the significant tasks, skills, and abilities involved in the job.* On the basis of the job analysis, certain operations or skills should have been identified. Wherever possible, a wide variety of tasks should be used to represent those skills. Then, after deciding what abilities are to be tested, one must determine whether the performance of the task, per se, or the product of the performance, or a combination of the two are to be tested.

3. *Develop an observation/rating form.* This form should contain the types of observations to be made and the manner in which they are to be recorded. For example, is quality of a product important? Is speed in performance important? Whatever skills or abilities are deemed important should, where feasible, be evaluated.

4. *Develop some type of task-sampling plan.* We recognize that no single test can contain everything one wishes to measure. This is true for any test. Hence, for a performance test, the test constructor, on the basis of the job analysis, should select the most significant aspects of the task.

5. *Develop an administration format.* Prepare the instructions, time limits, materials—if any are needed—scoring instructions, and so on.

6. *Try out the test items before developing a final form.*

7. *Decide upon the weight to be assigned to each criterion after specifying the evaluative criteria to be used* (the teacher must be satisfied that the criteria are related to the instructional objectives). The weight assigned to each step or characteristic should reflect the instructional emphasis placed on each criterion. For example, the presentation of any report generally involves three major factors: (1) content; (2) organization; and (3) presentation. Each of these can be further subdivided into smaller units. For example, presentation can be subdivided into five units:

1. Stereotyped diction
2. Clear, concise diction
3. Diction at the appropriate level
4. Too soft-spoken
5. Emphasis on significant points

The teacher may think that content is the most important part and assign one-half of the total score to that feature. She may think that organization and presentation are equally important and assign one-fourth of the grade to each of these. Each component and each subcomponent are then assigned some numerical value that has been predetermined by the teacher.

Evaluating a process or product can range from the very subjective to the highly objective. Wherever possible, the objective (and preferably quantitative) approach should be used. There are times, when on the surface at least, it appears that subjective ratings are the only ones possible to make, but steps can sometimes be taken to increase their objectivity. These steps will be discussed in a later section.

OBSERVATIONAL TOOLS AND TECHNIQUES

Systematically observing students in natural or simulated settings (the former is preferable) is a very useful technique for gathering data about students' performance and about their affective behavior. Systematic, direct observation is perhaps the most common assessment technique that teachers use, despite the methodological problems associated with observational tools and techniques. For example, what pupils should be studied? All the pupils? Those who are continually causing problems? When should pupils be observed? Who should make the observations? What inferences can one draw from a limited sample of behavior? These are just some of the problems that must be faced by the user of the observational method.

Classroom teachers continually observe their students. The observations, however, are typically informal and unsystematic, and carried on without benefit of specific planned procedures.[4] Since so much of what teachers "know" about and do for children is based on their observations, it is important that these observations be as accurate, reliable, systematic, selective, and carefully recorded as possible.[5] Scientists are rigorously trained in observation. They are taught the value derived from accurate observations and are willing to have their observations (actually recordings or findings) checked by other scientists. Teachers should be taught to appreciate the value of systematic observations and should receive training similar to that given scientists (Noll et al., 1979).

In those situations in education where no tangible product is produced, such as participating in class discussion, but where an important instructional objective needs to be evaluated, teachers must depend on their observation of the pupils' behavior and then make valid inferences as to whether the goal or instructional objective was achieved. Because the evaluation of a pupil's performance may, depending upon the nature of the task, involve a great deal of subjectivity and immediate judgment of its worth, obtaining valid and reliable evaluation is extremely difficult. There are so many instances where these types of judgments must be made and where formal pencil-and-paper testing procedures are not appropriate that it behooves us to consider the use of observational tools and techniques and to look at some ways of making them as valid and reliable as humanly possible—recognizing that we will not achieve the same degree of success as we would in measuring cognitive skills.[6]

---

[4]It should be noted that there are numerous classroom observation schedules available for research. (See Borich & Malitz, 1975, for their discussion of the validity of these measures.) Brophy et al. (1975) feel that classroom observation scales are a convenient and reliable way to obtain descriptive measures of classroom processes.

[5]See McGaw et al. (1972) and Medley and Mitzel (1963) for discussions of sources of error in making observations.

[6]See Herbert and Attridge (1975) for an excellent review and synthesis of the literature. They identified 33 criteria that observational systems should satisfy.

The terms *observation tools* and *techniques* are *not* synonymous, although they are used interchangeably by many persons. An observational technique generally implies the use of a particular observational tool such as a checklist, rating scale, participation chart, or anecdotal record. The process of observing and recording an individual's behavior is what is meant by the term *observational technique*. The observational technique has certain limitations associated with it. Because it requires the observation of some form of behavior, it may be subject to the idiosyncracies of the observer. The observer should be completely objective and come as close as possible to being a mechanical recording device—recording the actual behavior (e.g., Maxwell laughed when Alexi told a joke) without attempting to synthesize or interpret the behavior.

Advantages of Observations

There are several advantages of observational data:

1. Frequent observation of a student's work (and work habits) can provide a continuous check on his progress. The teacher can detect errors or problems as they arise and take corrective action quickly.
2. Observational techniques are not so time-consuming or threatening for the pupil as are achievement tests.
3. Observational data provide teachers with valuable supplemental information, much of which could not be obtained in any other way.

Some Suggestions to Help Make Valid Observations

If you have ever been in a courtroom and heard two witnesses describe an accident they saw, you no doubt are aware of the unreliability of observations. It has been said that people engage in selective perception, that is, they see what they want to see and disregard other, sometimes more relevant behaviors. Generally, observers fail to agree on what has been observed for a variety of reasons—the most significant one being that they have *not* been trained to observe objectively.

It is not easy to learn to see objectively and in depth, to record one's observations, and finally to organize and interpret them. In spite of the difficulty in obtaining accurate and significant data from observations, teachers continually do observe and make decisions based on these observations. Therefore, it is essential that the observations made (which involve *both* the tools and the techniques) attempt to satisfy the same criteria expected of a written, cognitive test—validity, reliability, objectivity, and practicality of construction, administration, and scoring. Specifying what behavior(s) to observe and specifying a time schedule for such observation will improve the data considerably. Also, training the observer with the necessary skills needed to make systematic and objective observations cannot be overemphasized. To help make observations more valid, we offer the following suggestions:[7]

1. *Plan in advance what is to be observed and prepare an observational list, guide, or form to make the observation objective and systematic.* One of the major difficulties in obtaining useful data from observations is to determine or specify in advance a meaningful and productive set of behaviors to be observed. This determination, like deciding what content to put in an achievement test, must be dependent upon the objectives one wishes to evaluate and the decisions one hopes the data will help determine. However, it is often somewhat more difficult to specify what observed behaviors are relevant than it is to specify what questions should be asked on a test or what characteristics should be judged on a rating scale. Just watching children every day without any systematic plan will be like looking for a needle in a haystack without knowing what a needle looks like.

---

[7]For a thorough discussion of observational tools and techniques, see Tuckman (1979) and Irwin and Bushnell (1980).

What we observe and the significance of the observed behavior are two different aspects. For the former, we must delineate our course objectives and ask ourselves two basic questions: (1) What is the purpose of the observation? (2) What behaviors should be observed? One way to avoid determining what to observe is *not* to specify in advance what categories of behavior to observe. This, however, takes us back to an unsystematic procedure and could lead to a teacher saying something like: "The students were using class time for independent study, so there was no behavior for me to observe!" Of course, the students were behaving. It is just that the teacher had no idea what to look for. Behaviors that could be observed (but which weren't) would be such things as chewing fingernails, looking out the window, talking out of place, doodling, and pushing a fellow student.

What the behavior signifies is also important and is related to what we observe. This may be easy enough to determine in a psychomotor skill area (the significance of a person watching the typewriter keys or looking at the basketball while dribbling is obvious enough), but the significance of isolated bits of behavior in the affective domain is more difficult to determine.

Even though observational tools are not tests in the conventional sense, they are still used to attain the same overall objectives—(1) to tell us *how* people behave (analogous to criterion-referenced behavior) or *whether* people differ (analogous to norm-referenced behavior); (2) to permit us to make valid predictions about future behavior; and (3) to provide the user with information that will permit her to undertake appropriate action to correct or modify undesirable behavior. Therefore, it is essential that we know in advance what will be observed and why we are observing this or that behavior.

We also recommend that all observation forms contain the following information:

1. Name of pupil(s) being observed (if confidentiality is being preserved, some type of code should be used)

2. Name of observer(s)
3. Date, time, and situation relevant to the observation
4. Name of teacher, classroom, and school

2. *The teacher should concentrate on only one or two behaviors.* With a class of 30 students it is impossible to observe all the different kinds of behavior occurring at a given time. More reliable data will be forthcoming if the teacher observes or concentrates on just one or two behaviors at a time. For example, in a football game the teacher may limit her observations to just perseverance and sportsmanship, although she may also be interested in cooperation and aggressiveness. She cannot concentrate on all four traits at any one time. For those who contend that she may miss something significant by concentrating on only one or two behavioral incidents, we maintain that if a behavior pattern is typical, it will recur. If it does not, we can assume that it is insignificant. Naturally, the teacher should be on the alert for unanticipated incidents that may be important in obtaining a better understanding of the pupil. Generally, however, we favor the concentration on just one or two aspects at a time.

3. *Use clear, unambiguous terminology in the observational tool(s).* Unless the terminology used is clearly defined and accompanied by a description of the type of behavior attendant to or associated with that behavior, reliable observations will be difficult to obtain.

4. *Each trait (item) should be mutually exclusive.* When this criterion is not met, the observer will encounter difficulty in classifying and/or appropriately coding the observation made.

5. *The observer must be cognizant of time-sampling errors.* If we observe Alexi at 9:20 A.M., we cannot necessarily infer from her behavior at that time how she would behave at other times. To minimize errors that may occur due to sampling, a technique called time sampling is often employed. In time sampling, a teacher develops either systematically or randomly a schedule for observa-

tions to ensure that each pupil is observed at many different times during a day, week, or semester. Thus, Alexi's observation schedule may call for an observation at 9:15–9:20 A.M. on Monday; 10:20–10:25 A.M. on Tuesday; 2:30–2:35 P.M. on Wednesday, and so forth. Maxwell's observational schedule would be on a different but comparable schedule.

We recommend that there be frequent, short observations distributed over a period of several weeks and at different times of the day. This should provide for a more representative sample of the pupil's behavior.

The accuracy of teacher reports, although not too valid in and of themselves, may be improved by increasing the number of observations (Hook & Rosenshine, 1979). Somewhat related to this are Rowley's (1978) data, which showed that the reliability of observations is increased by increasing either the number or the length of the observation periods. He also showed that if observation time is held constant, the reliability is greater for a larger number of shorter observation periods.

6. *Coordinate the observations with your teaching.* Systematic observation requires that observation and teaching be coordinated. When the teacher is planning her instructional strategy, she should also plan her observations so that the two will be related. Otherwise there is great danger that invalid observations will result.

7. *Extensive observations should be selective.* We recommend that extensive observations be confined to only those few selected students (the slow learner, the hyperactive child, the autistic child, the "loner") who are in need of special help.

8. *Carefully record and summarize the observation immediately after it has occurred.* If this is *not* done, one runs the risk of forgetting not only the incident but, if anecdotal records are used, the conditions under which it occurred. Ideally, using tape recorders or videotaping apparatus is desirable. However, be aware that use of such recording tools *might* border on the *unethical* and/or *illegal.* If such equipment is used to record observations,

precautions must be taken so that only authorized personnel can access the tape(s).

9. *Make no interpretations concerning the behavior until later on.* Too often, trying to interpret a pupil's behavior when a particular behavior is observed will interfere with the objectivity of gathering the observational data.

10. *Have categories and coding schemes that are simple to use, that call for behaviors easily observed, and that deal with behaviors that can be conveniently recorded.* When an observer must infer a particular behavior from a series of different (and sometimes unrelated) behaviors, we run the risk of invalid inferences being drawn. We are well aware of the fact that any observation requires the observer to make some type of judgment. What we imply by this caution is that the degree of observer inference be reduced as much as possible during the actual observational period. Inferences, in an ideal setting, should typically occur only after the data have been gathered and coded.[8]

11. *Wherever possible, observers and observations should be unobtrusive.* When people know they are being observed, they tend not to exhibit normal behavior. Some children will avoid certain behaviors while others will overemphasize them in order to gain attention.

TYPES OF OBSERVATIONAL TOOLS

Recording observations is not difficult, but it does require thought and planning. The four most commonly used and effective observational tools are participation charts, checklists, rating scales, and anecdotal records. All are relatively easy to construct. All can be used to record any type of be-

---

[8] Popham (1987) has a somewhat opposite view as it relates to teacher evaluations. He believes that professionals should be able to draw inferences "on the spot" (so to speak) using a *gestalt* approach. We concur with Popham in part, recognizing that his "gestalt, on-the-spot" inferences may not hold in all cases.

havior, be it cognitive, affective, social, or psycho-motor.

Participation Charts

How well does Lori participate in a group discussion? Does Machell tend to participate more in larger groups than in smaller groups? Does Ilene tend to engage in athletic activities more than in social activities? Is Allan a leader or a follower? By means of a participation chart, the teacher can plot a pupil's behavior throughout the year and then make some evaluative judgment about it.

It should be noted that the participation chart per se does *not* indicate *why* some pupils do not participate in group activities and/or *why* they participate in one type of activity but not in another. Nor will the data collected by means of a participation chart help explain why some pupils use group participation to gain attention from their peers. Nevertheless, because group participation is needed to participate effectively in our society, teachers should be concerned with its measurement. If it is found that some students are isolates or "loners," it may be possible for the teacher to help them. Figure 9.1 is an example of a participation chart that measures pupil involvement in discussion. The example contains a tally

of the participation by four students in a group discussion. In the course of the discussion, the teacher would check off each point (statement) made by each pupil. In Figure 9.1 the tally indicates that Lois dominated the discussion in that she raised or introduced six points. Of these six points, the teacher judged that two made a significant contribution to the discussion, three made a secondary contribution, and one point was irrelevant. Each of the other three members of the group introduced five points to the discussion. But note that of Peter's five points, two were irrelevant.

Whether or not the behavior of any of the students in this particular group is good, bad, or indifferent should not be the issue. What is important is that if the teacher is interested in learning the extent of pupil contribution in small discussion groups without relying on her memory, she must use some type of participation chart to give her the desired information. And, as we noted earlier, she should use a time-sampling plan to gather this information. It would also be advantageous to use event (topic or issue discussed) sampling to obtain a fuller picture of the individual pupil's behavior.

The teacher engaged in evaluating pupil participation will be very occupied in her task. This

---

Objective: Discussion of the importance of the U.N.

	Group Members			
Extent of contribution	Lois	Peter	Dave	Jeanette
Significant*	/ /	/	/ / /	/ / /
Secondary	/ / /	/ /	/	/
Doubtful				/
Irrelevant	/	/ /	/	

*Significant: introduces new ideas in the discussion;
Secondary: introduces important but minor idea;
Doubtful: insufficient evidence to evaluate contribution—need more information;
Irrelevant: introduces irrelevant ideas and contribution detracts from discussion.

FIGURE 9.1   Measuring Participation in a Small Group.

leads us to making the following recommendations for teachers using participation charts:

1. Try to rate participation in small group settings rather than in large class discussions. It is just too difficult to concentrate when there are many pupils involved.
2. The teacher should only observe and not partake in the discussion. Noting and recording the behavior of the participants is a full-time task. By entering into the discussion, the teacher may overlook something significant.
3. The behavior noted should be recorded immediately after it has happened. Delaying notation until the end of the discussion lends itself to bias and selective perception on the part of the observer.

Checklists

A checklist consists of a listing of steps, activities, or behaviors that the observer records when the incident occurs. It is similar in appearance and use to rating scales (which will be discussed next) and is classified by some as a type of rating scale. It should be emphasized that a checklist enables the observer to note—albeit very quickly and very effectively—only whether or not a behavior occurred. It does *not* permit the observer to rate the quality of, degree to which, or frequency of occurrence of a particular behavior. When such information is desired, the checklist is definitely *inappropriate*, and a rating scale or anecdotal record is recommended.

Checklists are adaptable to most subject-matter areas. They are useful in evaluating those learning activities that involve a product, process, and some aspects of personal-social adjustment. They are especially useful at the primary level where observation, rather than formal testing, is used for evaluation. They are most useful, however, for evaluating those processes that can be subdivided into a series of clear, distinct, separate actions, such as welding a bead, making a mortise joint, or operating a microscope.

The values to be derived from checklists (actually, from any observational tool) depend on the skill and care with which the checklist is constructed. When properly prepared, checklists (1) force the observer to direct her attention to clearly specified traits or characteristics, (2) allow interindividual comparisons to be made on a common set of traits or characteristics, and (3) provide a simple method to record observations.

An example of a checklist to measure personal and social adjustment is presented in Figure 9.2. The Tyler microscope checklist illustrated in Figure 9.3 is a good example of a performance checklist. The student's goal is to find a specimen present in a culture. The teacher's goal is to see whether the student is able to operate a microscope so that the specimen is located. The student is provided with all the necessary materials, and the teacher observes his actions, numbering them in the order of their occurrence. In addition, you will note that there are sections devoted to (1) areas that require further training, (2) the student's behavior, and (3) the mount.

Some Suggestions to Consider When Using Checklists

1. Use checklists only when you are interested in learning whether a particular trait or characteristic is present or absent.
2. Clearly specify the behaviors to be observed.
3. Observe only one child at a time, and confine your observations to the points specified on the checklist.
4. Have a separate checklist for each child. If you want an overall impression of the class, the individual observations can be recorded on a master checklist.
5. The teacher must be trained how to observe, what to observe, and how to record the observed behavior. The directions given the observer must be very specific and clear. Raters should be told to *omit* recording those behav-

Pupil _____ School and Grade _____

Setting _____ Date _____

Observer _____

Directions: Listed below are a series of characteristics related to "concern for others." For the pupil listed above, check those characteristics that are applicable.

_____ Sensitive to the needs and problems of others
_____ Prefers to play with younger children
_____ Respects the views and opinions of his peers
_____ Helps other students when they have problems
_____ Respects the property of other children
_____ Willingly accepts suggestions
_____ Works cooperatively with other children
_____ Is a "loner"
_____ Resents criticism

FIGURE 9.2   A Checklist Recording Concern for Others.

NOTICEABLE CHARACTERISTICS OF STUDENT'S BEHAVIOR	Sequence of Actions			Sequence of Actions
a. Awkward in movements		g. Obviously angry		
b. Obviously dexterous in movements		h. Does not take work seriously		
c. Slow and deliberate	✓	i. Unable to work without specific directions		✓
d. Very rapid		j. Obviously satisfied with his unsuccessful efforts		✓
e. Fingers tremble				
f. Obviously perturbed				

SKILLS IN WHICH STUDENT NEEDS FURTHER TRAINING	Sequence of Actions		CHARACTERIZATION OF THE STUDENT'S MOUNT	Sequence of Actions
a. In cleaning objective	✓		a. Poor light	✓
b. In cleaning eyepiece	✓		b. Poor focus	
c. In focusing low power	✓		c. Excellent mount	
d. In focusing high power	✓		d. Good mount	
e. In adjusting mirror	✓		e. Fair mount	
f. In using diaphragm	✓		f. Poor mount	
g. In keeping both eyes open	✓		g. Very poor mount	
h. In protecting slide and objective from breaking by careless focusing	✓		h. Nothing in view but a thread in his eyepiece	
			i. Something on objective	✓
			j. Smeared lens	✓
			k. Unable to find object	

FIGURE 9.3   Checklist for Evaluating Skill in the Use of the Microscope. (From Ralph W. Tyler, "A Test of Skill in Using A Microscope," *Educational Research Bulletin,* 9:493–496. Bureau of Educational Research and Service, Ohio State University. Used by permission.)

iors for which they have insufficient information to make a valid judgment.

Rating Scales

Rating scales provide systematic procedures for obtaining, recording, and reporting the observer's judgments. Rating scales resemble checklists in that both can be completed on the spot or after the fact, but rating scales are used when finer discriminations are needed. Instead of merely indicating the presence or absence of a characacteristic, a rating scale enables the user to indicate the status or quality of what is being rated. Both rating scales and checklists can be used for single observations or over long periods of time.

The major practical advantage of rating scales over other observational techniques is that rating scales take little time for the teacher to complete and can therefore be used with a large number of students. In addition, they tend to be very adaptable and flexible.

Although there are a variety of rating scales (see Guilford, 1954, pp. 263–301), we will consider the following: numerical, graphic, comparative (sometimes referred to as product scales), and paired comparisons. Ranking procedures are also often considered as a type of rating scale and will be considered here.

Numerical Rating Scales　This is one of the simplest types of scales. The rater simply marks, circles, or checks a number that indicates the degree to which a characteristic (or trait) is present. The trait is presented as a statement and values from 1 to 5 are assigned to each trait being rated. (The range is arbitrary,[9] but we strongly recommend that it be a maximum of 10, since finer discriminations are too difficult to make.) We believe

that generally, 5- to 7-point scales serve adequately (see p. 189). Typically, a common key is used throughout, the key providing a verbal description. For example, a key might be as follows:

1 = outstanding	or	1 = very active
2 = above average		2 = quite active
3 = average		3 = average activity
4 = below average		4 = somewhat inactive
5 = unsatisfactory		5 = very inactive

A numerical rating scale might be as follows:

Activity: Participation in School Activities

1. How active is the student in class projects? $\begin{bmatrix} 1 = \text{very active} \\ 5 = \text{very inactive} \end{bmatrix}$
   1　2　3　4　5
2. How well does the student relate to his peers? $\begin{bmatrix} 1 = \text{very well} \\ 5 = \text{very poor} \end{bmatrix}$
   1　2　3　4　5
3. To what extent does the student participate in discussions? $\begin{bmatrix} 1 = \text{very much} \\ 5 = \text{very little} \end{bmatrix}$
   1　2　3　4　5

Graphic Rating Scale　The graphic display is similar to the numerical rating scale in that the rater is required to assign some value to a specific trait. This time, however, instead of using predetermined scale values, the ratings are made in graphic form (a position *anywhere* along a continuum is checked). The rater is not restricted to any particular point, but can record anywhere between points. An example of a graphic rating scale is presented in Figure 9.4. (The example shown is in the "horizontal" format. One could also use a "vertical" format.)

Graphic rating shares the disadvantages associated with numerical rating. For classroom use, neither of the two scales has any particular advantages over the other, although the numerical scale

---

[9]Guilford (1954) recommended an 11-point scale (0 to 10), arguing that even though the extreme positions are rarely used (raters tend to avoid using extremes), their presence will more than likely force raters to use the 1 to 9 points. Another reason why he feels an 11-point scale is better than a 4- or 5-point

scale is because, other things being equal, the "larger" scale will be more reliable than the "smaller" scale. Gronlund and Linn (1990) and Cronbach (1990) recommend 5- to 7- and 5-point scales, respectively. Oosterhof (1990) recommends a 4- to 7-point scale.

Directions: Following is a list of characteristics that are descriptive of your instructor. Please rate your instructor for each characteristic listed below along the continuum from 1 to 5. You are encouraged to use points between the scale values. Mark an "X" at the appropriate place along the continuum.

How enthusiastic was your instructor in presenting the course material?

Very unenthusiastic				Very enthusiastic
1	2	3	4	5
	unenthusiastic		enthusiastic	

How much material did your instructor attempt to cover?

Too little		Adequate		Too much
1	2	3	4	5
	Little		Much	

Generally, how attentive were you in class?

Very inattentive				Very attentive
1	2	3	4	5
	Inattentive		Attentive	

FIGURE 9.4   An Example of a Graphic Rating Scale to Rate Instructors.

may be somewhat easier to construct. The important point for either is that the numbers or periodic points on the lines must be described sufficiently so that every rater has the same understanding of their meaning. For example, "extremely active" may be defined as "always jumps out of seat" while "extremely inactive" may be defined as "nearly always sits quietly in seat."

Comparative Rating Scale   This type of scale provides the rater with several standard samples of different degrees of quality with which to compare the sample being rated. The scale is used chiefly for products and is often called a *product* scale. An example of such a scale is presented in Figure 9.5. The rater compares the pupil's product (in this case, handwriting) to a carefully selected series of samples of the product. The pupil's product is then assigned the scale value of the sample product

it most closely resembles. (As you will recognize, this procedure is similar to the global procedure in scoring essays.)

There are very few commercially published product scales such as the one illustrated in Figure 9.5. This means, therefore, that in the majority of instances the teacher will have to prepare her own product scale. The procedure discussed in selecting samples for scoring essays by the global method (see pp. 98–100) is appropriate for developing such scales.

Ranking   In this procedure the rater, rather than assigning a numerical value to each student with regard to the characteristic being rated, ranks a given set of individuals from high to low. (Or one can rank *intra*individual characteristics.) A useful procedure to help ensure that pupils are validly ranked is to rank from both extremes toward the

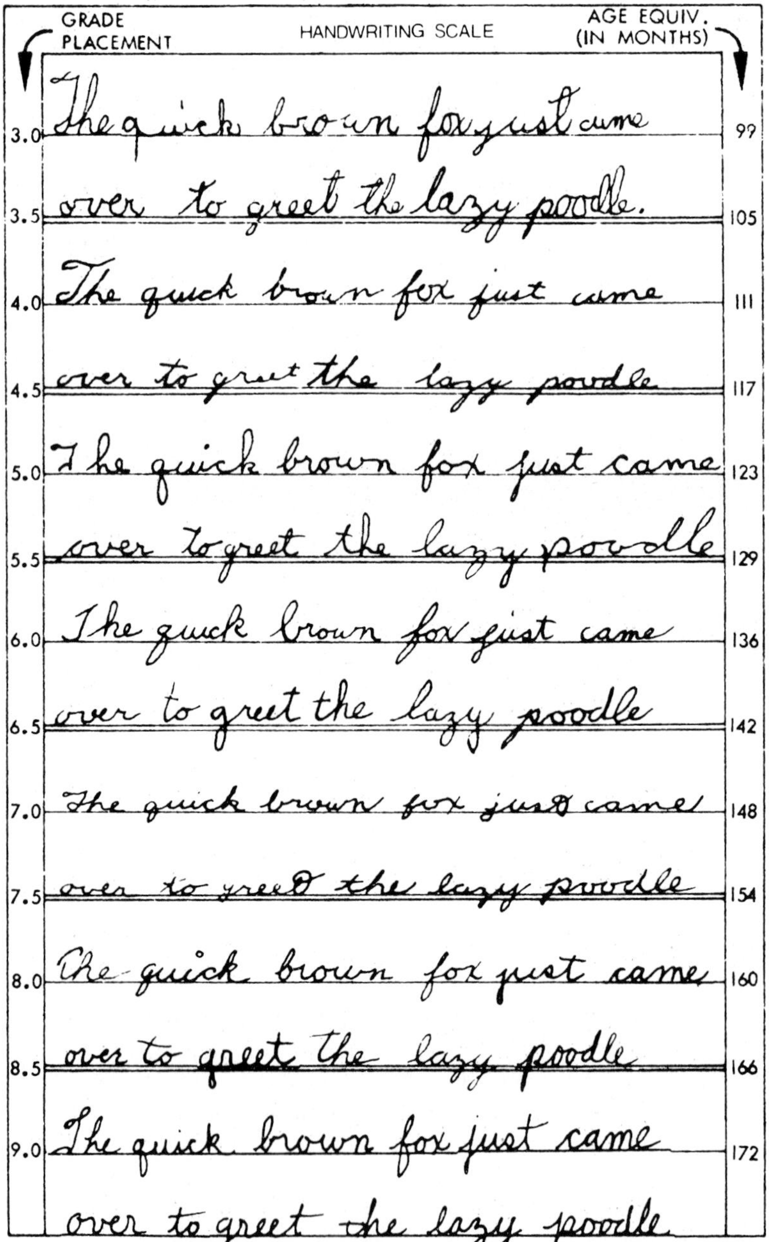

GRADE PLACEMENT	HANDWRITING SCALE	AGE EQUIV. (IN MONTHS)
3.0	*The quick brown fox just came*	99
3.5	*over to greet the lazy poodle.*	105
4.0	*The quick brown fox just came*	111
4.5	*over to greet the lazy poodle*	117
5.0	*The quick brown fox just came*	123
5.5	*over to greet the lazy poodle*	129
6.0	*The quick brown fox just came*	136
6.5	*over to greet the lazy poodle*	142
7.0	*The quick brown fox just came*	148
7.5	*over to greet the lazy poodle*	154
8.0	*The quick brown fox just came*	160
8.5	*over to greet the lazy poodle*	166
9.0	*The quick brown fox just came*	172
	over to greet the lazy poodle	

FIGURE 9.5 Handwriting Scale Used in the California Achievement Tests. (Copyright © 1957 by McGraw-Hill, Inc. Used by permission of the publisher, CTB/McGraw-Hill, Del Monte Research Park, Monterey, CA 93940.)

middle. Here, the subjects ranked first and last are identified; then the student ranked second best and the one second from the bottom, and so forth. Although this simplifies the task for the teacher, the ranking method becomes very cumbersome when large numbers of students and/or characteristics are to be ranked. Also, the serial position of the trait(s), the characteristic(s), or behavior(s) to be ranked (i.e., where it appears on the scale) may affect the ranking.

We recommend that the number of traits on which students are to be ranked be limited to a maximum of seven. Also, the number of persons to be ranked should be limited. Trying to rank too many traits and/or persons will make the task so cumbersome that the validity and reliability of the measure will be affected (Wagner & Hoover, 1974).

There can be a marked difference between the rating and ranking methods. The difference in results can be shown by the following example. Suppose two different fourth-grade teachers were to judge their students on their "ability to get along with others." If a rating procedure were used, one set of students might come out with much higher ratings due to a generosity characteristic of one teacher. If each teacher were forced to rank her students from high to low, this generosity effect (or, conversely, a severity effect) could be avoided. However, another source of error becomes possible. The student ranked fifth in one class may actually be superior with respect to the characteristic to the person ranked fifth in the other class because the two classes differ. In addition to this problem, ranking is very hard to do (students at the extremes may cause no problem; students near the middle are very hard to rank because they are so very similar), and teachers resent having to make such discriminations. Also, if teachers perceive all their students as very superior (or inferior), they would like to have the opportunity to say so rather than rank them. In general, rating scales are preferred to ranking for evaluating social-personal adjustment and development and when dealing with large numbers of students. Rankings, when used, are probably most appropriate for evaluating students' products. We prefer, however, classifying the product as superior, average, and inferior, rather than using the ranking method.

Paired Comparisons The *paired-comparison* method, although more precise than the ranking method, is more time-consuming. In this method each student is paired with every other student, and the rater indicates which of the two students is superior on the trait being rated. The rater then has only to make a tally of the number of times each pupil is rated superior to make her ranking. This procedure tends to produce more reliable results and should be used whenever high reliability is of concern.

Sources of Error in Rating Scales

There are several common sources of error in rating scales. Errors may be due to the scale itself (ambiguity), the personality of the rater, the nature of the trait(s) being rated, and the opportunity afforded the rater for adequate observation. By "ambiguity" we refer to wording and meaning of the traits being measured—such that the rater may be uncertain as to what it is she is really being asked to rate. Two teachers rating students on "aggressiveness" may be making ratings on quite different characteristics. To one teacher, "aggressiveness" may be a positive trait, suggesting that the student is appropriately self-assertive. To the other teacher, aggressiveness may connote hostility. This suggests that such terms as "honesty," "effective citizenship," and "personality" must be clarified for the rater. Unless all pupils are being rated based on a common understanding of the attributes, the ratings will be invalid and unreliable.

Ambiguity of the frame of reference is another problem of rating scales. When criteria such as "superior," "good," and "inferior" are used, what do these words really mean? What is "good"? Is doing the 100-yard dash in 20 seconds "good"? It depends. For a 60-year-old man it is good. For a 70-year-old with arthritis, it is outstanding. For a 16-year-old boy it may be poor. Quality must be interpreted in terms of the nature of the trait being rated and the age and ability of the ratee.

As mentioned earlier, the problem of "trait" ambiguity may be reduced quite extensively by breaking up the trait to be measured into a series of specific, observable, and measurable behaviors; by describing fully what the trait represents; and by giving examples of the different kinds of behavior associated with differing levels of the trait.

Sources of Error in Raters

In addition to the sources of error associated with the rating scale, there are also constant sources of error associated with the *raters*. Some of these are *the halo effect, generosity error, the severity effect, central tendency error, bias, logical error,* and *the rater's attitude*.

If we were asked, "What are the characteristics of an ideal rater?", we would respond that she must be competent, objective, and well trained in the use of the scale. Personal bias must be controlled if we wish to obtain valid ratings.

The *halo effect* occurs when the rater's general impressions of a person influences how she rates him on individual characteristics. If we like a student and think that he is handsome, studious, neat, punctual, and does his homework, we may be apt to rank him high on arithmetic skills because of traits that may be quite unrelated to arithmetic skills. Or if we have a generally unfavorable attitude toward a person, we may rank him low on all traits. In one study where college students rated well-known personalities, it was found that about 20 percent of the variance was due to the halo effect (Blumberg et al., 1966). In another study it was found that the degree of composite halo exhibited by teachers when rating pupils was affected by the race and sex of *both* rater and ratee (Jaeger & Freijo, 1975). One way to minimize the halo effect is to reverse the "high and low" or "desirable and undesirable" positions on the continuum. Another is to define traits in terms of concrete behavior. Still another is to rate *all* persons

on one trait before moving on to rate persons on the next trait. This, however, may confuse the naive rater (Guilford, 1954). A better way is to be alert to the dangers of the halo effect and act accordingly. As of now, no method has been devised to effectively eliminate it, although research is going on (see Feldman, 1986; Murphy & Blazer, 1986; Kozlowski et al., 1986).

Raters who continually favor the desirable end of the continuum are committing the *generosity error*. Less frequent in occurrence, but a response set with some people, is the tendency to favor the low end of the continuum—that is, to be overly harsh. This is called the *severity error*. Still another type of response set is when a person avoids using the extremes and favors the middle positions—that is, she rates everybody about "average." This is called the *central tendency error*. The *generosity*, *severity*, and *central tendency* errors all arise when raters do not use uniform standards. One way to eliminate these errors is to use some type of ranking procedure.

Bias is the tendency to rate high or low because of factors other than the trait(s) being rated. Research has shown that bias in rating or grading is quite common. As discussed earlier, we know that many teachers assign a higher grade to a typed essay than to a handwritten one, especially if the latter is not too neat. Bias is usually subconscious and therefore hard too prove. Nevertheless, it is very common and steps should be taken to eliminate it.

Another type of rater error, which is not related to response set, is called *logical error*. Logical error is closely related to the halo effect, but is not due to personal bias. Rather, it occurs when two traits such as intelligence and socioeconomic status or achievement and aptitude are closely related, and the rater is influenced in the rating of one by the presence (or absence) of the other. When a rater bases her ratings for an individual on a general relationship she *thinks* exists in the population, she has committed a logical error (Gronlund & Linn, 1990).

There are still two other factors that can affect the validity of a rating: (1) the rater's attitude and

(2) the rater's opportunity for adequately observing the person (and traits) being rated.

Attitude of Raters Accurate observation is very time-consuming, especially if large numbers of students are involved. Unless teachers truly believe that there is some value to be derived from ratings, they may consider them only as another administrative chore and not do a conscientious job.

Extensive Opportunity for Observation
Possibly more serious than any of the errors previously discussed are the errors a rater makes because she does not know the person she is rating well enough. In the elementary grades, the teacher gets to know her students fairly well, even if her knowledge is confined to the classroom setting. In junior and senior high school, the teachers see their students less frequently. As would be expected, teachers are more familiar with those students who are at the extremes (very gregarious, very withdrawn, very uncooperative, very bright, very lazy). However, they may be asked to rate a student who is not at the extremes and/or one they do not know very well. We have had requests from prospective employers to fill out rating sheets for students we hardly know. The only reasonable thing to do is to refuse to rate the person on those characteristics about which you have little or no knowledge.

Ways to Improve Data from Rating Scales

Although data from rating scales are often not very valid or reliable, error can be reduced by improving the rating scale, improving the raters, improving the rating method, or some combination of these. The following suggestions should be helpful.

Improving the Scale

1. *Identify the domain of particular behaviors (traits)—be it a psychomotor skill or some performance task—that you wish to rate.* Make sure they are educationally significant. Also make sure that they occur in the school setting so that the teacher can observe them.

Some traits are more amenable to reliable rating than others. In general, when traits can be expressed as simple, unitary aspects of behavior and can be operationally defined, they will be amenable to reliable rating. The more complex the trait, the more difficult it is to obtain high agreement among the raters (inter-rater reliability).

2. *Clearly define the traits to be rated and the scale points to be used.* Many of the problems and errors associated with rating scales are due to undefined trait characteristics and poorly designated scale points. One way of avoiding some of these problems is to avoid the use of labels and technical jargon such as "hostility," "reticence," and "aggressiveness." If slang will help convey the intent, by all means use it. A simple rule of thumb is: Break down the trait into several smaller components, each of which is quite limited and specific. For example, "good adjustment" can be broken down into emotional adjustment, social adjustment, wholesomeness, and similar attributes. Social adjustment can then be subdivided into many specific components, such as "playing with other children," "sharing with other children," respecting other children's property," and "working cooperatively with other children." Ratings can then be made on each of the specific components, but it may be necessary to break the subcomponents into still finer divisions. For example, "works with children" could be further delineated as "help others," "accepts suggestions," "provides ideas," and "accepts majority rule." The more specific the behavior to be rated, and the more descriptive the response options (points along the scale or continuum), the greater the likelihood that raters will be on the same "wavelengths" and will exercise uniformity. Also, they will have a clearer idea as to what observations are to be made and considered in their rating.

Somewhat related is the influence of labels and positions in rating scales. Klockars and Yamagishi

(1988) investigated whether a verbal label (e.g., Very Poor, Excellent) and the position it was assigned on the scale defines the meaning of the labels. For example, is there a difference between the meanings of Excellent and Very Good, when used in different positions? They also investigated the relative importance of the label and the position. They found that the meaning of the scale points is systematically altered by movement of the verbal labels associated with these points.

3. *Sample carefully from the behaviors in the trait domain to permit generalizability.*

4. *Express the traits to be rated as questions rather than as declarative statements.*

5. *For the graphic and descriptive graphic rating scales, the continuous line should follow immediately after the question (trait to be rated) or be placed below the question.*

6. *Determine how discriminating you want the ratings and divide the continuum accordingly.* As mentioned earlier, we recommend that the continuum be subdivided into 5- to 7-point intervals. Raters should also be encouraged to mark at intermediate points.

Improving the Rater

1. *Conduct a thorough training session.* Lack of training or poor training of observers accounts for most of the problems in using ratings. In the training session, point out the value of accurate and honest ratings. Point out the kinds of errors commonly committed by raters and how they might be avoided, or at least minimized. Discussing such things as halo effects can reduce their effects. Have some "dry runs" to give the raters practice. Research has shown that training increases the ratings' validity and reliability by reducing common judgment errors (McIntyre et al., 1984; Pulakos, 1984).

2. *Motivate the raters to do as accurate a job as possible.*

3. *Select persons who can provide objective, unbiased ratings.* Avoid persons who are either overly critical or solicitous. Avoid people who have an "axe to grind."

Improving the Rating Method The validity of ratings will be improved if care is taken in the construction of the scale, in the selection and training of the raters, and by using more than one rater where feasible. In addition, there are several factors that can help improve the validity of the rating but that are not necessarily related to the improvement of the scale or the raters per se.

1. *Encourage raters* not *to rate those traits or persons for which they have insufficient knowledge to make a valid rating.* Two ways in which this can be done are (1) provide an "insufficient information" point on the scale (this will then suggest to the rater that she need not rate every trait) and (2) require the rater to provide evidence for her ratings, especially those at the extremes.

2. *Combine (or average) judges' ratings.*[10] In general, the larger the number of independent ratings and raters, the higher the reliability. Why? Because individual errors and personal biases should cancel out each other. Also, multiple observations should provide for a more representative sample of the ratees' behavior. This is especially true in junior and senior high school, where an individual teacher has only limited contact with her students.

3. *Rate only one trait or characteristic at a time.* For example, if a rating scale consists of 15 traits and 30 pupils are to be rated, all 30 pupils should be rated on Trait 1 before proceeding to Trait 2. This will permit the rater to give her undivided attention to the trait and should provide for more reliable measurement.

4. *The numerical rating scale should be used to rate only those characteristics that can be categorized into a small number of subdivisions and where there*

---

[10]See Werts et al. (1976) for a description of a model to analyze rating data on multiple dimensions by multiple raters. See Van den Burgh and Eiting (1989) for a method of assessing interrater reliability when *all* raters cannot rate *all* products.

is good agreement among raters on what kind of behavior is represented by "outstanding" or "average" or other descriptions assigned to the numbers on the scale. More often than not, there is considerable variation in the interpretation of scale values, and hence the scale is often less valid than anticipated.

5. *To reduce the influence of the halo effect, define the traits in terms of concrete, observable behaviors.*

6. *Avoid making the extremes so atypical of behavior that few raters will use these points.*

7. *Control the effect of extraneous variables.* Be on guard to confine the rating to—and *only* to—the attributes being measured. Do *not* be influenced by a pretty binder or a professional typing job when rating an essay or term paper. "Don't judge a book by its cover" is very apropos, since too often we are unduly influenced by extraneous factors, the result being invalid data.

8. *Make ratings as soon as possible after observations.* Delayed ratings may result in rating perceptions rather than actual behavior(s).

Uses of Rating Scales Rating scales are most helpful in evaluating procedures, products, and personal-social development (see Gronlund, 1985, pp. 393–396). Such procedures as those necessary in typing, working with laboratory equipment, shopwork, or athletic skills cannot be easily measured via pencil-and-paper tests. Many instructional objectives involve the completion of a product, which in itself should be evaluated. In home economics, it may be making a dress. In music, it may be playing an instrument. In English, it may be writing a theme or giving a speech.

Probably the most common use of rating scales in education is in the evaluation of personal-social adjustment. It is not uncommon for teachers on the students' report cards to rate them on various characteristics such as punctuality, enthusiasm, cheerfulness, consideration for others, and the like. One of the problems of such evaluations is that the observations have been spread over a long period of time. Such ratings are often broad impressions of perceived behavior rather than of actual behavior. That is, they are likely to reflect the teacher's biases concerning the student rather than the student's actual behavior. The suggestions previously offered about effective use of checklists and cautions to be applied are appropriate here also.

At the college level, there has been increased use of rating scales for evaluating teacher effectiveness and course content. As might be expected, some faculty have tended to denigrate the value of these data, especially the use of teacher rating scales, claiming that the scales are invalid and unreliable. (For an excellent review of this controversial issue, see Doyle, 1975. See also Menges, 1973; Trent & Cohen, 1973; Lehmann, 1974; Sockloff & Papacostas, 1975.)

Anecdotal Records

Anecdotal records are the *least* structured observational tool. They depict actual behavior in natural situations. They are records of specific incidents of student behavior. Over a period of time, anecdotal records can provide the teacher with a longitudinal picture of the changes that have taken place in a particular pupil.

While normally restricted to the area of social adjustment, anecdotal records may be used in many other contexts. For example, Maxwell, who has appeared to be uninterested in arithmetic, might come to school one day and tell the class a new way of working with multiplication facts. Or Allan, who has been very careless in the science lab, may suddenly become very careful for a few days and then reverts to his former behavioral traits. These examples suggest that anecdotal records possess certain characteristics:

1. They should contain a factual description of what happened, when it happened, and under what circumstances the behavior occurred.
2. The interpretation and recommended action should be noted separately from the description.

3. Each anecdotal record should contain a record of a single incident.

4. The incident recorded should be one that is considered to be significant to the pupil's growth and development

Anecdotal records are typically less formal and systematic than the data obtained through other observational techniques. Time sampling is not employed. Rather, incidents are noted as they occur. For this reason, the data from anecdotal records are ordinarily not so reliable as those obtained from other observational tools.

Advantages of Anecdotal Records The major advantage of the anecdotal record is that, if properly used, it can provide a factual record of an observation of a single, significant incident in the pupil's behavior that may be of assistance to the teacher in developing a better understanding of the growth and development of that pupil. Other advantages of anecdotal records are that they—

1. Record critical incidents of spontaneous behavior (in a natural setting), many of which do not lend themselves to systematic measurement.

2. Provide the teacher with objective descriptions rather than make her rely on vague generalizations.

3. Direct the teacher's attention to a single pupil.

4. Provide for a cumulative record of growth and development, if collected over time.

5. Can be used by the counselor as a source of information upon which to base her discussions with the pupil.

6. Can be used as a supplement to quantitative data obtained from other sources so that the teacher will better understand the behavior of her pupils.

7. Provide for a more thorough description of the pupil's behavior than will checklists, rating scales, or sociograms, because they contain the

setting in which the behavior was observed. Many teachers consider these more complete descriptions of behavior better suited to understanding and guiding pupils than the other observational tools available.

Limitations of Anecdotal Records We have already mentioned that one of the more serious limitations of anecdotal records is that they tend to be less reliable than other observational techniques because they typically tend to be less formal and systematic and ordinarily do not employ time sampling. Some other limitations of anecdotal records follow:

1. They are time-consuming to write.

2. If collected over a period of time for many students, they can create a storage problem.

3. It is difficult for the observer to maintain objectivity when she records the incident observed. Observers are human and are prone to include interpretive words or phrases in their descriptions. This can be minimized by thoroughly training teachers in the manner of recording and reporting incidents.

4. Too often, the incident is described without including the situation in which the behavior was observed. When incidents are read out of context, they may lose their meaning.

5. The major problem in using anecdotal records is being selective in deciding what incident(s), action(s), or event(s) should be recorded and which one(s) should or could be ignored. Teachers tend to use anecdotal records as a method of recording only undesirable incidents. They *neglect* the positive incidents.

6. Anecdotes present only a verbal description of the incident. They *do not reveal causes*.

Preparing Anecdotal Records: Some Suggestions

1. *Records should be complete.* There are several different styles of anecdotal records. All, however,

contain the following parts: (a) identifying information—pupil's name, grade, school, and class; (b) date of the observation; (c) the setting; (d) the incident; and (e) the signature of the observer. Some contain a section for the interpretation and recommendation for action.

2. *The behavioral incident or action should be recorded as soon as possible after it has happened.* Any lapse of time places heavy reliance on the teacher's memory, which may become blurred if too much time elapses.

3. *Keep the anecdote specific, brief, and limited to a single incident.* Just as too little information does not help much in having a better understanding of a pupil's behavior, too much information can cloud the real issue.

4. *Keep the recording process simple.*

5. *Keep the anecdote objective.*

6. *Although anecdotal records could be compiled on slips of paper, cards or any material readily handy, we do* not *recommend using slips of paper, since they can be easily lost or misplaced.* A large sheet of paper is preferred because it permits the teacher to write her interpretation on the same sheet as the description of the setting and incident. We recommend that some standard form be used for filing.

7. *Anecdotal records should not be confined to recording negative behavior patterns.* In fact, the anecdotal record should record significant behaviors regardless of their direction. Only in this way, can the teacher obtain a valid composite picture of the student.

8. *As in writing good test items, the teacher should have practice and training in making observations and writing anecdotal records.*

Figure 9.6 is an example of an anecdotal record.

Using Anecotal Records Effectively

1. *Teachers should restrict their use of anecdotal records to those behaviors that cannot be evaluated by other means.* Anecdotal records should be restricted to those situations from which we wish to obtain data on how the pupil behaves in a natural situation.

2. *Anecdotal records should be kept by all teachers and not be restricted to only the pupil's homeroom teacher.* The validity of the anecdotal record will be enhanced with a variety of common information gathered from different sources.

3. *Anecdotes should have interpretive value.* A jumbled collection of anecdotes is of little value. They must be collated, summarized, and interpreted. If, for example, Ilene has only one record of aggressiveness, this is inconsequential. On the other hand, if Ilene has been observed to display aggressive behavior on 9/6, 9/14, 10/12, 10/13, and 11/21, in a variety of different settings, this behavioral pattern does become significant.

Grade _____5_____   Pupil _____Alexi Pollet_____
Date _____4/9/90_____   Observer _____Mr. Mehrens_____
                            Place _____School Playground_____

Event
During morning recess, the class was playing baseball. Since there were no umpires, the children were told that they would be responsible for calling "outs" on the base path as well as calling "outs" in the outfield. Alexi came to bat and hit a ball into left field which she believed was a "fair" ball. Machell called it a "foul," stating that it was out of bounds. Although Alexi had only two strikes at that time, she threw her bat and walked off the playground.

Interpretation
Alexi has always been calm and collected both in the classroom and on the playground insofar as being able to handle disagreements. In fact, this is the *first* time that she has exhibited this type of behavior. Accordingly, I would ignore this outburst but be aware of any others.

FIGURE 9.6   An Example of an Anecdotal Record Form.

4. Anecdotal records must be available to specified school personnel. We feel strongly that the anecdotal record should be shared with other teachers and especially with the school counselor if there is one. Also, this material should be incorporated in the student's folder with other test information. We also believe that a general summary should be shared with the parents, and with the pupil, if he is old enough to understand it. Other than for school personnel, parents, and the students, the anecdotal record should be considered as confidential information.

5. Anecdotal records as an educational resource should be emphasized. Because anecdotal records depend so heavily on the willingness of teachers to do a good job, it is essential that teachers develop an appreciation for the value of anecdotal records to help them obtain a better understanding of their pupils. (Indirectly, this should result in the development of better-adjusted students.)

Storing Anecdotal Records What information should be kept in, or recorded in, the anecdotal record? How long should information about a student be kept? Where should the anecdotal records be stored? Who should have access to the information? Let us consider each of these questions briefly.

Information is, or should be, gathered for the purpose of making decisions that will be of benefit to the pupil. We believe that only those data that have a direct bearing and relevance to the students' growth and development be kept. We see no use for information concerning how Clarence dresses unless how one dresses has some predictive validity in the educational domain.

How long one should, or can, keep anecdotal information is analogous to asking "How hot is hot?" Who can say how long information on a rebellious, hostile third-grader should be kept? We would surmise that it should be retained until this behavior problem no longer manifests itself. But how long is that? We are cognizant of the fact that records cannot be kept *ad infinitum*. Therefore,

we believe that, if possible, records should be stored at least while the student is enrolled in a particular school.

Where the information should be stored is simply answered. All data pertaining to a student's behavior should be kept under lock and key. We are cognizant of the fact that much pupil data is now being stored on computer discs. This suggests that only authorized personnel have access to these data.

EVALUATING PERSONAL-SOCIAL ADJUSTMENTS SOCIOMETRICALLY

A variety of instruments and approaches are available for evaluating personal-social adjustment. Some of these include teacher observations and the use of checklists, rating scales, and anecdotal records previously discussed. Others involve peer ratings, self-report sociometric techniques, and projective tests. Some of the tools required can be developed and used by the ordinary classroom teacher without additional training. Others, such as projective tests, should be administered and interpreted only by skilled clinicians. Because of the limited training of teachers in clinical procedures, we will focus our attention on various teacher-made sociometric techniques such as the *guess who* and *nominating techniques*. In Chapter 18 we will consider other methods of assessing personal-social development, such as interest and personality inventories.

Sociometry is concerned with how an individual is seen and accepted by his peers. Sociometric techniques have been and are constantly being used by students. When they choose up sides for a game of baseball or a spelling bee, they are using sociometry. When they elect class officers, select the yearbook editor, the high school beauty queen, and the ugliest senior, they are employing sociometry.

The sociometric approach to studying personal-social adjustment is quite economical in time and money. The essential ingredient is to devise a series of questions that will elicit a student's *true* feeling about other members in his class. Following are some suggestions to help you prepare the questions.

1. Decide in advance what use will be made of the results, as this will determine the kinds of questions to be asked. For example, if a teacher wants to know what would be the most harmonious group to work on a social committee, she would not ask the question, "Whom would you like to sit next to in class?"
2. Write questions in clear, unambiguous language adapted to the age level of the student. Avoid technical jargon.
3. Write questions that will elicit *true* feeling about a student's peers. Some examples of "good" questions are: "Whom would you like to sit next to in class?" "Who is your best friend?" "Whom would you like to have work with you on the social committee?" "Whom would you like to have on your baseball team?"

Peer Appraisal Methods

A teacher's observation of pupil behavior is of limited value. She observes the pupil in a special setting where he may be behaving somewhat differently than he would in other situations. For example, Jim may be very cooperative in the formal classroom setting but very independent on the unsupervised playing field. Also, the teacher is necessarily observing from a certain frame of reference. Peer appraisal can be a very good supplement in the evaluation program. In evaluating such characteristics as popularity, leadership ability, power, and concern for others, fellow students are often better judges than teachers.

Peer appraisal could be obtained by using any of the rating scale methods previously discussed. If each student filled out a rating form for every other student, considerable data would be available. However, in obtaining peer appraisal, it is usually desirable to simplify the task, since stu-

dents are doing the actual work. (If one is dealing with younger students, it is *absolutely* necessary to make the task as simple as possible.) Students are untrained and generally unmotivated raters. To expect a student to fill out 30 different rating sheets without becoming quite careless or bored is asking a lot! Typically, then, the task is simplified to a *guess who* or *nominating technique*.

Whenever peer ratings are desired, two major principles must be adhered to: (1) The traits to be rated should be within the student's experiential background. Asking "Who is the most popular student?" is markedly different from asking "Who will be the most successful student?" The language used should also be simple. (2) Complete anonymity (or, at the least, confidentiality) must be maintained so that students who receive "poor" ratings will be protected from further embarrassment and possible harassment—as well as to ensure that we will obtain true responses from the students. In addition, a sociometric test should be administered as informally as possible.

Guess Who Technique In the guess who technique, each pupil is given a list of descriptions and asked to name the pupil(s) who best fits each description. The descriptions used are dependent upon the traits one wishes to measure. If one wishes to assess cheerfulness, the description might be as follows:

This person is always happy.

If one wishes to assess leadership qualities, a possible description would be:

This person is an effective leader.

In the guess who technique, one simply tallies the number of times each person was named for each description. When the tally is completed, the teacher can readily see which pupils are mentioned most frequently, seldom, or not at all for each trait or characteristic. Data regarding who names who are also available but are seldom used in the guess who technique. This method's main advantages are (1) simplicity of scoring and (2) suitability at all age levels. The major disadvantage is it provides little, if any, information of *why* some pupils are *not* named.

Nominating Technique The nominating technique is very similar to the "guess who" method except that the questions are slightly different. Instead of choosing a name to fit a description, the student is asked to nominate the person(s) with whom he would like to work, sit by, study, or play.[11] Again, what one wants to measure determines what kinds of questions are asked. We could, for example, measure perceived competence, power, or social acceptance. Occasionally, students are asked to nominate whom they would least like to sit by, play with, and so on. This is generally *not* recommended; it could hurt group morale. The nominating technique provides data relevant to the existing social relationships in the class. With this technique we are interested in who made the nomination, as well as *who was nominated*. Reciprocal relationships are looked for.

Suppose we have asked fourth-graders to list their first and second choices of fellow students with whom they would most like to play. The results can be tabulated in a matrix as shown in Figure 9.7. (We have assumed a small class for convenience of illustration.) The pupils' names are listed both on the side and on the top. The names along the side represent the person doing the nominating. The two people chosen are indicated by placing a 1 under the name of the first choice and a 2 under the name of the second choice. The totals along the bottom of Figure 9.7 indicate the number of times each person was nominated. Mutual choices are circled, ignoring the distinction between first and second choices. Notice that mutual choices are always an equal number of cells from the main diagonal (the straight line running from upper left to lower right, which divides the

figure). Although the choices could be weighted so that the first choice will count more than the second choice, we prefer to use a simple count rather than a weighting procedure since different weighting systems have shown that no one scheme is superior to another (Gronlund, 1959).

The number of choices that an individual pupil receives on a sociometric question is used as an indication of his social acceptance by his peers. From the data presented in Figure 9.7, we can identify the students who are most popular (referred to as *stars*); those who receive no choices (called *isolates*); and those who receive only a single choice (called *neglectees*). Ruth is a *star*. She received the most nominations. (Three of the four were first choices.) Bill, Irv, Ilene, Lori, and Machell all received three nominations—one more than the average. Susan is a *neglectee*. Diana, Fred, and Jake are *isolates*. Notice that of the 24 nominations made, there were 12 mutual choices. There were 6 opposite-sex choices (this is normal for fourth-graders). By using similar matrices for other nominations, such as choices for seating, working, or playing companions, the teacher can obtain some valuable insights into the group relationships present in her class.

Using Sociometric Data

As we stressed before, one gathers evaluative data to aid in decision making. Obtaining sociometric data is no exception. Although the reasons behind the nominations are unknown, teachers can use the results for organizing classroom groups and to improve the social climate in the classroom. The results can also be used to improve the social structure of the group by breaking up cliques and/ or helping the isolates become more acceptable to their peers. Further study may be needed to determine why some students are isolates. Often, teachers can assist isolates into becoming integrated into the group and thus improving their social skills. Although sociometric techniques differ from the observational techniques discussed ear-

[11]Children in the elementary grades might be limited to two or three choices; those in the upper grades, to four or five.

Chooser \ Chosen	Allan	Bill	Beth	Diana	Fred	Irv	Jake	Ilene	Lori	Machell	Ruth	Susan
Allan		2				1						
Bill			①			②						
Beth		①							2			
Diana	1									2		
Fred											2	1
Irv		②									①	
Jake	2										1	
Ilene									②		①	
Lori								②		①		
Machell			1					②				
Ruth						①		②				
Susan								2		1		
1st choice	1	1	2	0	0	2	0	0	0	2	3	1
2d choice	1	2	0	0	0	1	0	3	3	1	1	0
Total	2	3	2	0	0	3	0	3	3	3	4	1
Mutual choices	0	2	1	0	0	2	0	2	2	1	2	0

Date: April 17, 1990.

FIGURE 9.7   Matrix Showing Students' Choices of Play Companions.

lier (in sociometric tests, the data are gathered about individuals from their peers rather than from teachers or observers), all provide data necessary to obtain a better understanding of pupil behavior.

To be most effective, decisions based on sociometric data should be implemented as soon as possible. For example, if the teacher wants to establish a social committee to work on a Halloween party, she should, after asking for the information, (1) form the groups as quickly as possible and (2) form groups reflecting the students' choices. Un-

less individual preferences are honored, students will quickly lose interest, and subsequent data may be invalid. Of course, there are some instances where individual preferences cannot be honored, such as occurs when one pupil is chosen first by every other pupil.

Some other ways in which sociometric data can be used by teachers and researchers are as follows:

1. To study the effects of certain experiences on group structure.
2. To study the relationship between group struc-

ture (acceptance) and such factors as sex, religion, color, and age.

3. To study the stability (or lack of it) of group structure.

Limitations of Sociometric Data

Several points need to be considered when interpreting sociometric data.

1. The data are only as valid as the rapport that exists between the student and teacher and the student's willingness to be honest.

2. The data only reveal relationships. They do *not* establish causal relationships. In fact, more often than not, sociometric data raise more questions than they give answers to. Why did no one choose Diana as a playmate? Is she too aggressive and domineering? What can I, as a teacher, do for Diana so that she will be accepted by the other students? How can I break up a clique?

3. The group relationships depicted are dependent upon the kinds of questions asked. For example, Bill may wish to play with some peers but work on a class project with other peers.

4. The relationships are not necessarily stable, especially in younger children. They may, and often do, vary during the school year. (Maybe Jake has just moved into the school. In another three months he could be a star.) In fact, the picture obtained from sociometric data tends to be specific to a given day, and the choices made may be to a specific activity. This is important to remember, since social situations change rapidly. We therefore suggest that sociometric data be collected at frequent intervals and that the matrix be labelled for the date collected and the activity sampled.

5. It should *not* be assumed that the "star" is the most well-adjusted pupil. It indicates only that he or she is acceptable to the majority of his or her peers.

6. Sociometric data should be interpreted in the light of what we know about child development. For example, we would expect boy–girl choices in the primary grades, but not in the intermediate grades. Isolates and cliques should be interpreted with reference to such things as their cultural, social, racial, and religious backgrounds.

MEASUREMENT IN THE AFFECTIVE DOMAIN

Traditionally, public education has been primarily concerned with cognitive learning. And evaluation of our schools and educational products has generally used, as the major criterion, the degree of success that students had in learning the cognitive skills and content taught. In fact, most accountability programs—be they at the local, state, or national level —use some type of achievement test(s) as their major evaluative instrument. There are, however, other skills and behaviors—affective and psychomotor—that should be of concern to every classroom teacher, administrator, school board member, parent, pupil, and to any others associated with education. We feel that *both* parents and educators should be as concerned with affective behavior as they are with teaching students to read, write, and compute.

Because the affective disposition of the student has direct relevance to his ability to learn, his interest in learning, and his attitudes toward the value of an education, educators in general, and classroom teachers in particular, should know something about affective measurement, especially attitudes.

Quite often, learning difficulties are related to a student's attitudes. How often have you heard:

Johnny is a bright enough boy, but he just isn't interested in school. I wonder what's wrong with Ruth? She is above average in ability, and though she performs poorly in science and mathematics, she does very well in French. Allan is very interested in science but despises literature.

Some students may have learning difficulties in, say, spelling or reading or mathematics because they believe that they can't learn the material. If teachers had a better understanding of a student's affective behavior (as well as a good understanding of the student's cognitive and psychomotor behavior), some learning difficulties could be alleviated or at least ameliorated by correcting the student's inferiority complex. As long ago as 1916, Binet and Simon wrote that a person's feelings had much to do with his ability to learn and that "... attention, will, regularity, continuity, docility, and courage . . . play so important a part in school life . . . life is not so much a conflict of intelligence as a combat of characters" (Binet & Simon, 1916, p. 266).

Information derived from attitude scales can be very valuable to classroom teachers who believe that development of attitudes may be an important instructional objective (e.g., scientific attitude, civic responsiblity). In addition, teachers may wish to obtain a measure of students' attitudes toward such things as the textbook used, the relevance and value of assignments, the instructional stragegy used, and the like, in order to undertake needed corrections.

MEASURING ATTITUDES

Attitudes are descriptions of how people feel or typically behave rather than descriptions of what they know or can do. Attitudes are predispositions to respond overtly to social objects. This statement is alluded to, in part at least, by the numerous definitions of attitudes posited by psychologists.

Attitudes, per se, are *not* directly observable but are inferred from a person's overt behavior, both verbal and nonverbal.[12] You cannot see prejudice but you can observe the behavior of one who is prejudiced. Thus, on the basis of observations of a person's consistent behavior pattern to a stimulus, we would conclude that he displays this or that attitude (Shaw, 1973). Finally, attitudes are relatively stable, especially in adults.

---

[12]See Shaw and Wright (1967), Miller (1983), Anastasi (1988), and Dawes and Smith (1985) for a more thorough coverage and updating of attitude measurement.

The two major approaches to, or methods of, measuring attitudes are by *observation* of subjects in a normal (or simulated situation) and by *self-report* inventories and scales. Self-report techniques are most often used to measure attitudes even though users are cognizant of the fact that there are a multitude of problems associated with attitude measurement (Reckase, 1984a; Young, 1984).

The remainder of this chapter will consider (1) the general guidelines for constructing attitude scales, (2) the major types of self-report attitude scales, and (3) the Likert method of attitude scale construction.

General Guidelines for Constructing Attitudes Scales

Any test, scale, or inventory is no better than the items used. Previously, we provided suggestions for writing cognitive-type items. Some of these principles or suggestions also pertain to the writing of items for attitude scales. Following, however, are some suggestions that pertain particularly to writing items for attitude scales (see Edwards, 1957).

1. Write direct statements in clear, simple language. Use simple rather than complex sentences.
2. Avoid factual statements or those that may be interpreted as factual.
3. Avoid using *universal* words such as *always, never, all,* or *none.*
4. Restrict the use of words such as *only, just,* or *merely,* as much as possible.
5. Make each statement brief, preferably less than 20 words.
6. Avoid statements that are ambiguous and may be interpreted in a variety of ways.
7. Avoid suggesting a particular answer (such as, "Do you agree that welfare encourages laziness?").
8. Each statement should be unidimensional, that is, it should be related to only a single concept. Avoid double-barreled statements.

For example, "I don't like to go to parties because I'm nervous in crowds." If the subject responds in an affirmative manner you don't know whether (1) he dislikes parties, (2) he is nervous, or (3) both apply.

9. Avoid statements that are likely to receive universal endorsement or rejection.

10. It was once believed that there should be an equal number of positively and negatively worded items in order to minimize the occurrence of a response or acquiescence set. This is not so! (Block, 1972; Samelson, 1972). In fact, negatively phrased items tend to reduce the validity of a questionnaire (Benson & Hocevar, 1985), especially for elementary school children. Also, research suggests that negative phrasing *may* change the construct an item is designed to measure.

11. Randomly distribute the statements in the scale, making certain that you do not have more than four or five positive or negative items in sequence.

12. Sensitive questions should be placed around the middle of the scale.

13. Intersperse sensitive and nonsensitive questions where possible.

14. Use a 3- to 7-point continuum.

15. Follow the general guidelines for preparing any test, such as writing more items than needed, editing, pretesting, ordering, and so forth.

Types of Self-Report Attitude Scales

Attitude scales, like interest and personality inventories (these latter two types will be discussed in Chapter 17), are classified in terms of their method of construction. There are three major techniques for constructing attitude scales: (a) *summated rating scales*, such as the Minnesota Scale for the Survey of Public Opinion (Likert type); (b) *equal-appearing interval scales*, such as the Thurstone and Remmers scales (Thurstone type); and (c) *cumulative scales* (Guttman type). In addition, the Semantic Differential Technique, though not a type of scale construction, per se, is a technique used to measure attitudes (Maguire, 1972).

These techniques differ primarily in their *format*, in the *positioning* of the statements or adjectives along a continuum versus only at the extremes, and whether or not the statement "values" are *cumulative*. There are advantages and disadvantages associated with each of these techniques. For example, the Thurstone method places a premium on logic and empiricism in its construction, but unfortunately it is somewhat laborious to develop such an instrument.

In the Likert, Thurstone, and Guttman methods, statements are written and assembled in a scale, and the subject responds to each statement. On the basis of the subject's responses, an *inference* is made about the respondent's attitude toward some object(s). In the Semantic Differential, the subject rates a particular attitude object(s) on a series of bipolar semantic scales such as good-bad, sweet-sour, strong-weak. Each of the techniques makes different assumptions about the kind of test items used and the information provided, even though there are some assumptions that are basic and common regardless of the method used. For example, each method assumes that subjective attitudes can be measured quantitatively, thereby permitting a numerical representation (score) of a person's attitude. Each method assumes that a particular test item has the *same* meaning for all respondents, and therefore a given score to a particular item will connote the *same* attitude. "Such assumptions may not always be justified but as yet, no measurement technique has been developed which does include them" (Zimbardo & Ebbesen, 1970, p. 123). Since the Guttman method is too complex and beyond the scope of this book, and the Thurstone method too laborious (Thurstone & Chave, 1929), we will consider only the Likert method. (See Figure 9.8.)

The Likert Method of Attitude Scale Construction The Likert method appears to be the most popular method of attitude scale construction. Likert scales are easier to construct and

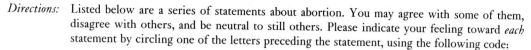

Directions: Listed below are a series of statements about abortion. You may agree with some of them, disagree with others, and be neutral to still others. Please indicate your feeling toward *each* statement by circling one of the letters preceding the statement, using the following code:

Code: SA = Strong Agree
       A = Agree
       ? = Uncertain
       D = Disagree
      SD = Strongly Disagree

SA   A   ?   D   SD   Abortion is immoral.

SA   A   ?   D   SD   Abortion should be legalized.

SA   A   ?   D   SD   Federal funds should be made available to indigent women who wish an abortion.

(a)

For young children, a series of "happy-unhappy" faces can be used for the continuum, and the children can be instructed to make a ✓ below the face they feel represents their feelings. Following is an example of a scale to measure second-graders' attitudes toward school.

I like reading.

I like spelling.

I like school.

I like my teacher.

(b)

FIGURE 9.8   (a) An Example of a Likert Scale: Attitude Toward Abortion. (b) An Example of a Likert Scale: Attitude Toward School.

score than either the Thurstone or Guttman scales. Other advantages of the Likert scale are that it (1) produces more homogeneous scales, (2) allows the subject to indicate the degree or intensity of his feeling, and (3) permits a greater spread of scores (variance).

In the Likert method, the researcher or test constructor collects or writes a large number of statements (varying in degree of positive and negative feelings) about an object, class of persons, or institution. (A good pool of items can be obtained by having your students write a number of positive and negative statements about some issue(s).) For example, in constructing a scale to measure "Attitudes Toward Chemistry," a number of items like the following may be written:

> Chemistry is interesting.
> Chemistry is boring.
> Chemistry is challenging.
> Chemistry is a waste of time.

The preliminary scale should have few neutral items, and it should have few items at either end of the continuum. The positive and negative items should be mixed. The preliminary scale is then given to a large number of subjects who respond to teach item by means of a 5-point[13] scale ranging from "strongly agree" to "neutral" to "strongly disagree." The items are then each weighted from 1 to 5 and a total score obtained. Correlations are then computed between each item and the total score. Only those items that demonstrate a high correlation with the total score are retained. This method of selecting the final items to be used in the scale attempts to produce a scale that is internally consistent. The Likert method helps assure unidimensionality (making sure that all the items measure the same thing) and often yields reliabilities that are higher than those obtained using an interval scale (Thurstone type).

The Likert method considered in this chapter is well within the capabilities of the classroom teacher and requires no formal course work. For other approaches to measuring attitudes one might wish to refer to other textbooks on measuring attitudes such as Shaw and Wright (1967), Edwards (1970), Zimbardo and Ebbesen (1970), and Bills (1975). For published tests, see Johnson (1976)

and the various *Mental Measurements Yearbooks*.

■ SUMMARY

The principal ideas, conclusions, and recommendations presented in this chapter are summarized in the following statements:

1. Tests should not be the only means of measurement. They need to be supplemented by other procedures such as rating scales, anecdotal records, and sociometric methods. In fact, data on some characteristics cannot be gathered by conventional paper-and-pencil tests.
2. Observational techniques are particularly useful in evaluating performance skills and products and some aspects of personal-social adjustment.
3. All observational techniques are limited because (1) the observer may be biased; (2) the scale used might be poorly constructed; (3) they are time-consuming; and (4) the subjects might behave in an abnormal fashion if they know they are being observed.
4. A checklist is a type of rating scale that is useful in rating those behaviors where the only information desired is the presence or absence of a particular characteristic.
5. Rating scales are most helpful in evaluating procedures and products.
6. Rating methods provide a systematic method for recording the observer's judgments.
7. Rating scales can be classified into numerical, graphic, comparative, ranking, and paired-comparisons ratings scales.
8. There are several sources of error in rating scales. Some of the most common errors are due to ambiguity, halo effect, leniency or severity effects, errors of central tendency, logical error, and error due to raters' attitudes.
9. Control of rating scale errors is a major consideration in constructing and using these scales. Errors can be minimized by (1) select-

---

[13]The number of categories is variable. Masters (1974) found that when opinions are widely divided on an issue, increasing the number of categories had little effect on internal consistency. However, when opinion is not widely divided, a small number of categories can result in low reliability.

ing only educationally significant characteristics; (2) limiting ratings to observable behavior; (3) clearly defining the characteristics and scale points; (4) limiting the number of scale points; (5) encouraging raters to omit the rating of those characteristics for which they have insufficient information; (6) thoroughly training raters in how to observe; and (7) pooling, wherever possible, the ratings from several raters.

10. The least structured observational technique is the anecdotal record. Anecdotal records are recorded incidents of specific student behavior. Good records describe events rather than evaluate them.

11. Anecdotal records provide for a description of behavior in a natural setting.

12. Limitations of anecdotal records are that (1) they are time-consuming to write; (2) they may not present a representative sampling of the pupil's behavior; and (3) it is sometimes difficult to prepare objective descriptions of the behaviors thought to be important and those that are irrelevant to the student's growth.

13. Anecdotal records can be improved when (1) the setting in which the observation was noted is fully described; (2) the record is made as soon as possible after the observation; (3) each anecdote is restricted to a single, educationally relevant incident; (4) both positive and negative aspects of a student's behavior are noted; (5) the anecdote reports rather than interprets (interpretation should be done separately); (6) a variety of incidents occurring under different conditions is collected before making an inference; and (7) observers are trained on what and how to observe.

14. Peer appraisal can be a very good supplement in an evaluation program. In evaluating such characteristics as popularity, sportsmanship, leadership ability, and concern for others, fellow students are often better judges than teachers.

15. Peer appraisal methods include the guess who technique, the nominating technique, and the sociogram.

16. The guess who technique requires pupils to name those classmates who best fit each of a series of descriptive behaviors. The number of nominations received by each pupil on each characteristic indicates his popularity or reputation with his peers.

17. The nominating technique is very similar to the guess who except that the questions asked are slightly different. Also, nominees and nominator are identified and therefore it is possible to see reciprocal relations. The data can be expressed in tabular form or pictorially (sociogram). The number of choices a pupil receives is an indicant of his social acceptance.

18. Sociometric techniques are most helpful in obtaining a better understanding of personal-social adjustment.

19. Sociometric data can be used to arrange (or rearrange) groups, to improve the pupils' personal-social adjustment, and to evaluate the effect of various experiences on pupils' social relations.

20. When sociometric techniques are used, it is important that the pupil understand what he is to do and know that anonymity will be preserved.

21. Sociometric data are *specific* rather than general. They apply to the kinds of questions asked and the number of choices made. Sociometric choices for young children tend to be less stable than for older children.

22. Sociometric data do *not* provide for causal explanations.

23. Social distance scales indicate the "degree" of acceptance.

24. Classroom teachers need to know about their pupils' affective behavior in general, and attitudes in particular, so that they will have a better understanding of their pupils.

25. Affective measurement is sorely lacking in our schools, despite the fact that there has

been some interest evidenced in the past few years.

26. A variety of teacher-related and technical factors have inhibited appropriate emphasis on affective measurement.

27. Attitudes are a predisposition to respond overtly to social objects in terms of some favorable or liking continuum.

28. The two major approaches to studying or measuring attitudes are by observation and self-report.

29. Three self-report approaches used to construct attitude scales are the Thurstone, Likert, and Guttman methods. The Semantic Differential is a *way* of measuring attitudes rather than a type of scale construction. The simplest, both in terms of construction and scoring, is the Likert method.

30. Most attitude scales are "homemade" rather than commercially published and, although primarily used for research purposes, can provide classroom teachers with invaluable information.

■ POINTS TO PONDER

1. What is the difference between procedure and product? Are there any instances where they may be interrelated. If so, give some examples.

2. What are the two major problems in evaluating procedures and products and how might they be minimized?

3. What is the difference between an observational tool and an observational technique?

4. What factors should govern a teacher's decision of (1) what to observe, (2) whom to observe, and (3) when to observe?

5. The four major types of observational tools are participation charts, checklists, rating scales, and anecdotal records. Give an example where it would be *most* appropriate to use each of these tools.

6. Five major types of rating scales are numerical, graphic, comparative, ranking, and paired-comparison. Which type should be used to gather what type of pupil information?

7. Would the checklist in Figure 9.2 be improved by having a "Yes, No, Sometimes" method of responding? Why?

8. Four sources of error in rating scales are the halo effect, severity effect, central tendency error, and logical error. How serious are these errors to valid measurement? How might these errors be controlled?

9. It has been suggested that in order to obtain a valid measure of a pupil's behavior, an ongoing anecdotal record should be maintained. Do you think that this would improve the reliability to any substantial degree?

10. Some contend that in order for behavioral information to be of most value, it should be gathered over a period of time. And yet, we face the dilemma of the legality of storing information and the invasion of privacy issue. How would you attempt to resolve this dilemma?

11. Do you think that peer appraisal methods are of any value? Why?

12. What stance would you take to support the statement "Affective measurement should be encouraged in our public schools?" What stance would you take to refute the statement?

Unit 3

INTERPRETING TEST SCORES

Chapter 10

Describing Educational Data

- ■ **Kinds of Scores**
- ■ **Presenting Data Succinctly: Tabulating and Graphing**
- ■ **Shapes of Data Distributions**
- ■ **Measures of Central Tendency**
- ■ **Measures of Variability**
- ■ **Measures of Relationship**

When an educator receives a set of students' test scores she may have some difficulty in determining the meaning of the scores—unless she has some understanding about the nature of information that can be inferred from numbers. If people are going to use data successfully in decision making, they must have some knowledge of how to describe, synthesize, and interpret data. This knowledge is also important if one is presenting data to others—such as parents at a PTA meeting or in an individual parent-teacher conference—to assist in their decision making. In this chapter, the following topics are presented: (a) a discussion of four different kinds of score; (b) some suggested methods for tabulating and graphing data; (c) a look at various kinds of data distributions; and (d) a review of some very basic concepts of descriptive statistics, such as measures of central tendency, variability, and relationship.

While some individuals seem to dread "statistics," we assure the reader that only a very basic mathematics knowledge is required to fully master this chapter. Knowing the basic functions of addition, subtraction, multiplication, and division—or using a basic calculator—is all the mathematics skill required.

After completing this chapter, you should be able to:

1. Comprehend the differences between nominal, ordinal, interval, and ratio data.
2. Interpret correctly data presented in a tabular or graphic format.
3. Arrange data in tables and graphs in a correct fashion.
4. Recognize the relationship between the shape of the data distribution and the relative positions of measures of central tendency.

5. Determine the mean and median of a set of test scores.
6. Understand how the measures of central tendency differ and the significance of those differences.
7. Determine the variance and standard deviation of a set of test scores.
8. Know the relationship between standard deviation units and the area under a normal curve.
9. Interpret the Pearson r as a measure of relationship.
10. Appreciate the value of the information presented in this chapter to educators, psychologists, and others who wish to describe or interpret data.

KINDS OF SCORES

Data differ in terms of what properties of the real number series (order, distance, or origin) we can attribute to the scores. The most common—though not the most refined—classification of scores is one suggested by Stevens (1946), who classified scales as *nominal, ordinal, interval,* and *ratio* scales.

Nominal Scales

A nominal scale is the simplest scale of measurement. It involves the assignment of different numerals to categories that are qualitatively different. For example, for purposes of storing data on computer cards, we might use the symbol 0 to represent a female and the symbol 1 to represent a male. These symbols (or numerals) do not have any of the three characteristics (order, distance, or origin) we attribute to the real number series. The 1 does not indicate more of something than the 0. Some psychologists do not wish to consider the nominal scale as a scale of measurement, but others do. It depends on how one defines measurement. If measurement is defined as "the assignment of numerals to objects or events according to rules" (Stevens, 1946), then nominal data indi-

cate measurement. If, on the other hand, measurement implies a *quantitative* difference, then nominal data do not indicate measurement.

Regardless of how we define measurement, nominal data have some uses. Whether or not categories (such as sex) are ordered, it is often helpful to know to which category an individual belongs.

Ordinal Scales

An ordinal scale has the order property of a real number series and gives an indication of rank order. Thus, magnitude is indicated, if only in a very gross fashion. Rankings in a music contest or in an athletic event would be examples of ordinal data. We know who is best, second best, third best, and so on, but the ranks provide no information with regard to the differences between the scores. Ranking is obviously sufficient if our decision involves selecting the top pupils for some task. It is insufficient if we wish to obtain any idea of the magnitude of differences or to use the process to perform certain kinds of statistical manipulations.

Interval Scales

With interval data we can interpret the distances between scores. If, on a test with interval data, Shelly has a score of 60, Susan a score of 50, and Sally a score of 30, we could say that the distance between Susan's and Sally's scores (50 to 30) is twice the distance between Shelly's and Susan's scores (60 to 50). This additional information is obviously of potentially greater use than just knowing the rank order of the three students. It has been hotly debated whether or not most psychological data really have the properties of an interval scale (see, e.g., Coombs, 1964.) In general, however, educators and psychologists have treated (interpreted) most test data as being interval measurement.

Ratio Scales

If one measures with a ratio scale, the ratio of the scores has meaning. Thus, a person who is 86″ is twice as tall as a person who is 43″. We can make this statement because a measurement of 0 actually indicates no height. That is, there is a meaningful zero point. Very few (if any) psychological measures provide ratio data. (Occasionally, a psychologist will suggest that something like attitude can be measured on a ratio scale, since a neutral attitude could be considered a meaningful zero.) Note that in the interval-data example of Shelly's, Susan's, and Sally's scores, we could not say that Shelly had twice as much of the characteristic being measured as Sally. To make such a statement would require that one assume a score of 0 to actually represent *no amount* of the characteristic. In general, if a person received a score of 0 on a spelling test, we would not interpret the score to mean that the person had *no* spelling ability. The same is true of any other test.

Educators, then, usually interpret (treat) test data as representing interval but not ratio scales, although when using some scores (such as percentiles—see Chapter 11) only ordinality need be assumed. Assuming we obtain a set of scores having properties of interval data, what can we do to aid us in interpreting these scores?

PRESENTING DATA SUCCINCTLY: TABULATING AND GRAPHING

Suppose a teacher has just given a final examination to a group of 50 pupils and has obtained the results shown in the first two columns of Table 10-1. How can the data be arranged to make them easier to interpret? One way, of course, is to *order the test scores*, as shown in Table 10-2. By looking at this table one can immediately see that the scores ranged from a high of 95 for Student 39 to a low of 17 for Student 7. Note that several students had identical scores. For these students, it does not matter which one is listed first. For example, Student 28 could have been listed before Student 42.

At times, teachers will want to present these data in other tabular or graphic forms. Table 10-2 presents a fairly clear picture of how the students

performed; but a frequency distribution, a histogram, or a frequency polygon would make the data even more interpretable. Even if teachers think it is unnecessary to prepare one of these graphic forms for their own ease of interpretation, they may well want to prepare such an aid for their students, or for occasional presentation at a teachers' meeting, or to the PTA. A frequency distribution, histogram, or frequency polygon would be particularly beneficial if there were many more scores (as might be the case if teachers gave the same exam to five different sections of the same course.) Whether or not a teacher ever tabulates data by any of the methods to be discussed, every teacher will read literature where such tabulation is presented, and it is vital that teachers be able to interpret data when presented in such formats.

Frequency Distributions

One way to reduce the size of Table 10-2 (and thereby make it easier to interpret and/or graph) would be to list every different score and then, to the right of each score, list the number (or frequency) of times that score occurred in the distribution. Since there are 40 *different* math scores in Table 10-2, that would reduce the number of entries in the test score column from 50 to 40. To reduce the number in the column still further, one could *group* the data or combine different scores into class *intervals*. Table 10-3 shows a frequency distribution using a class interval of five. There are some general guidelines for preparing class intervals:

1. The size of the class interval should be selected so that between 10 and 18 such intervals will cover the total range of observed scores.
2. The size of the class interval should be an odd number so that the midpoint of the interval is a whole number (see Table 10-3, column 2). This makes some types of computation easier and facilitates graphing.
3. It is generally considered good style to start the class interval at a value that is a multiple of that interval. For example, the interval in

TABLE 10-1 Scores of 50 Students on a Classroom Mathematics Exam and Their Previous Grade Point Average (GPA) and IQ Scores

Student	Math Scores (X)	GPA (Y)	IQ Score (Z)	Student	Math Scores (X)	GPA (Y)	IQ Score (Z)
1	83	3.6	120	26	71	2.6	111
2	72	3.5	121	27	29	2.7	109
3	53	2.5	105	28	93	3.5	118
4	35	2.4	104	29	45	3.1	120
5	39	2.9	106	30	88	3.0	115
6	53	2.8	110	31	82	2.9	113
7	17	1.9	85	32	75	2.9	112
8	19	2.1	93	33	40	2.1	103
9	64	2.4	112	34	31	2.0	100
10	24	2.5	107	35	59	2.6	111
11	42	2.5	111	36	61	2.7	110
12	31	2.5	108	37	34	2.8	103
13	45	2.8	109	38	66	2.8	109
14	77	2.7	106	39	95	3.7	119
15	76	3.3	115	40	49	2.2	105
16	80	3.1	114	41	54	3.1	113
17	70	3.0	117	42	93	3.3	111
18	58	2.9	116	43	36	2.6	103
19	68	3.2	118	44	55	2.3	103
20	86	3.2	117	45	49	2.9	112
21	50	2.6	113	46	63	3.0	115
22	34	2.2	110	47	83	3.4	118
23	64	3.4	111	48	55	3.3	110
24	42	2.7	109	49	47	2.4	100
25	21	2.3	100	50	92	3.1	118
				Totals	2848	140.0	5498

Table 10-3 is 5, so the lowest class interval started with a value (15) that is a multiple of 5.

Of course, it should be recognized that when grouping occurs, some information is lost. For example, the scores of 61, 63, 64, and 64 have all been put in the interval 60–64. When one computes certain statistics or prepares graphs from frequency distributions, it is necessary to make an assumption regarding the values within the intervals. One typically assumes that either (1) the observations are uniformly distributed over the theoretical limits of the interval or (2) all scores fall on the midpoint of the interval. The degree to which such assumptions affect the accuracy of the graphs and statistics computed from the class intervals depends upon the accuracy of the assumptions, the size and number of class intervals, and the total frequency of scores.

Histograms

The data displayed in Table 10-3 may also be graphed. Graphic representation helps greatly in enabling us to understand the data of frequency distributions and in comparing different frequency distributions to each other. A histogram (sometimes referred to as a bar graph) is a graph in

TABLE 10-2 Mathematics Test Scores in Table 10-1 Ordered from Highest to Lowest

Student	Test Score	Student	Test Score	Student	Test Score
39	95	38	66	13	45
42	93	23	64	24	42
28	93	9	64	11	42
50	92	46	63	33	40
30	88	36	61	5	39
20	86	35	59	43	36
47	83	18	58	4	35
1	83	48	55	37	34
31	82	44	55	22	34
16	80	41	54	34	31
14	77	6	53	12	31
15	76	3	53	27	29
32	75	21	50	10	24
2	72	45	49	25	21
26	71	40	49	8	19
17	70	49	47	7	17
19	68	29	45		

TABLE 10-3 Frequency Distribution of the Mathematics Test Score of Table 10-1

Class Interval	Midpoints	Frequency f
95–99	97	1
90–94	92	3
85–89	87	2
80–84	82	4
75–79	77	3
70–74	72	3
65–69	67	2
60–64	62	4
55–59	57	4
50–54	52	4
45–49	47	5
40–44	42	3
35–39	37	3
30–34	32	4
25–29	27	1
20–24	22	2
15–19	17	2

which the frequencies are represented by bars. Figure 10.1 displays the data of Table 10-3 in the form of a histogram. Notice that frequencies are along the vertical axis, and the scores are along the horizontal axis. This arrangement is not mandatory, but it is, by far, the most usual procedure. In making a histogram from grouped data, one assumes that the scores are evenly distributed within the class interval, thus giving rectangular bars. It is difficult to superimpose more than one histogram on the same figure. Thus, comparisons of several frequency distributions cannot readily be made via histograms. Frequency polygons are much better suited to that purpose.

Frequency Polygons

A frequency polygon (or graphed frequency distribution) is shown in Figure 10.2. As with the histogram, one could construct such a polygon either from original data or from grouped data. Figure 10.2 was constructed from the grouped data of Table 10-3. In constructing a frequency polygon for grouped data, one assumes that all scores

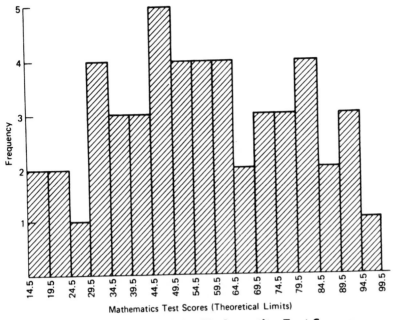

FIGURE 10.1 **Histogram of the Mathematics Test Scores.**

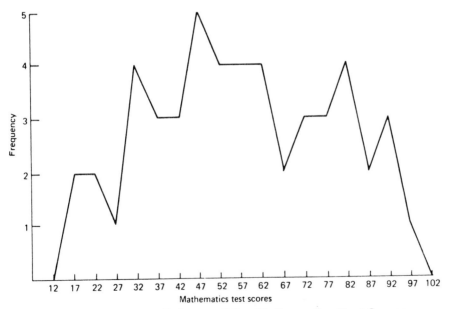

FIGURE 10.2 **Frequency Polygon of the Mathematics Test Scores.**

within a class interval fall at the midpoint of that interval. Notice that the midpoint of the class intervals just above and below the highest and lowest intervals that contain actual scores are also marked on the horizontal axis and given a frequency of zero. This is typically done. For example, in Table 10-3 the midpoints of the lowest and highest class intervals with actual scores are 17 (15 to 19) and 97 (95 to 99), respectively. The next lower and highest interval midpoints (12 and 102, respectively) are plotted as having a frequency of zero. If a teacher had frequency distributions for other classes that she wished to compare with this one, she could plot them on the same graph by using colored lines, broken lines, dotted lines, or some other differentiating procedure and by labeling the lines appropriately. Of course, if class sizes differed, it would be better to change all frequencies to percentages and plot percentile polygons.

SHAPES OF DATA DISTRIBUTIONS

Distributions of scores such as that shown in Figure 10.2 could assume many different shapes. When only a small number of scores are plotted, the shape of the curve will be very uneven or irregular. With a large number of scores, the curve will ordinarily be expected to take on a more smoothed or regular appearance. The shape of this smooth curve will depend both upon the properties of the measuring instrument and the distribution of the underlying characteristic we are attempting to measure. Four types of distributions most frequently discussed in educational and psychological measurement are *normal distributions, positively skewed distributions, negatively skewed distributions,* and *rectangular distributions.*

A *normal distribution* is a bell-shaped curve, as shown in Figure 10.3. There has been considerable discussion in the past about whether human characteristics are normally distributed. Evidence from physical characteristics such as height and weight lend some support to those who take the position that these characteristics are normally distributed. Whether one can infer anything about the distribution of psychological characteristics from this observation is debatable. The distributions obtained from tests cannot be used as evidence of the distribution of the characteristic itself because the test-score distributions may be influenced greatly by the characteristics of a test. For example, tests that are difficult will result in positively skewed distributions of scores (see explanation below). Whatever the truth about the underlying distribution of a characteristic for humans in general, classes of 20 to 50 students are not likely to be distributed normally with respect

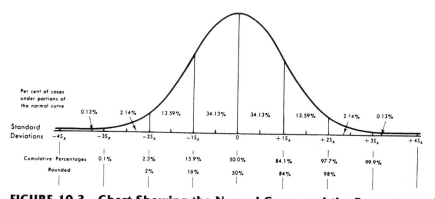

FIGURE 10.3   Chart Showing the Normal Curve and the Percentage of Cases Under Various Portions of the Normal Curve. (Reproduced by permission. All rights reserved. Copyright 1953, © 1964, 1967 by The Psychological Corporation.)

to any characteristic. The test results from the large norm groups used for standardized tests are likely to be more normal in appearance. (We will not concern ourselves about whether this is due to the normal distribution of the characteristic we are measuring or is an artifact of the properties of the measuring instrument.) We will discuss further some properties of the normal curve when discussing measures of central tendency and variability and types of scores.

In a *positively skewed distribution* (see Figure 10.4) most of the scores pile up at the low end of the distribution. This might occur, for example, if we gave a test that was extremely difficult for the students. Or, if we were plotting teachers' salaries and most of the teachers had very little experience (thus having relatively low salaries), we might obtain a positively skewed distribution.

A *negatively skewed distribution* is shown in Figure 10.5. In this case, the majority of scores are toward the high end of the distribution. This could occur if we gave a test that was easy for most of the students, such as a minimum competency test. Or, if we were plotting teachers' salaries in a school district where most of the teachers were experienced and were close to the maximum on the salary schedule, we would expect such a distribution.

A *rectangular distribution* will result if the same number of people obtain each of the possible scores (see Figure 10.6). This would occur, for example, if one were plotting percentiles (see Chapter 11).

In the next session we will relate measures of central tendency to score distributions.

MEASURES OF CENTRAL TENDENCY

It is often valuable to summarize characteristics of a distribution of test scores. One characteristic of particular interest is a measure of central tendency, which gives some idea of the average or typical score in the distribution. For example, you might wish to know the typical temperature in Miami, Florida, during the month of January.

If you took an examination in measurement, surely you, as a student, would wish to know not only how you performed on the examination but also how well, in general, the other students performed. You would want some measure of central tendency to help interpret your own score. When you teach, of course, your students may desire the same information. We discuss two measures of central tendency—the *mean* and the *median*—that present this type of information.[1]

Mean

The mean ($\overline{X}$) is the arithmetic average of a set of scores. (Sometimes M is used as the symbol for the mean.) It is found by adding all the scores in

---

[1]The mode is occasionally used as measure of central tendency. It is the most frequently occurring score in the distribution. Because it can be greatly influenced by chance fluctuations, it is not recommended.

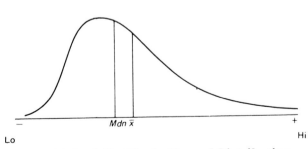

FIGURE 10.4   A Positively Skewed Distribution.

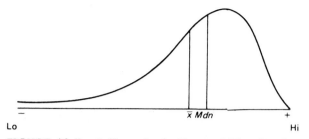

FIGURE 10.5   A Negatively Skewed Distribution.

the distribution and dividing by the total number of scores (*N*). The formula is

$$\overline{X} = \frac{\Sigma X}{N} \qquad (10\text{-}1)$$

where $\overline{X}$ = mean
X = raw score for a person
N = number of scores
Σ = summation sign indicating that all X's in the distribution are added (sigma)

The mean for the test scores (*X*) given in Table 10-1 is

$$\overline{X} = \frac{\Sigma X}{N} = \frac{2848}{50} = 56.96$$

which would, for most practical purposes, be rounded off to 57.0.

Median

The median (Mdn) is the point below which 50 percent of the scores lie. An approximation to that point is obtained from ordered data by simply finding the score in the middle of the distribution. For an odd number of scores, such as 25, the approximation to the median would be the middle-most score, or the score below which and above which 12 scores lie (actually, 12½ if one splits the middle score and considers half of it to be above the midpoint and half below). That is, the median is considered to be the thirteenth score. For an even number of scores, the median would be the point that lies halfway between the two middle-most scores. For the data in Table 10-2, the median would be 55, since both the 25th and 26th scores are 55.

Comparisons of Mean and Median

Statisticians generally prefer the mean as the measure of central tendency. The mean takes into account the actual numerical value of every score in the distribution. The median is preferred if one desires a measure of central tendency that is not affected by a few very high or very low scores. The median is also sometimes preferred by class-

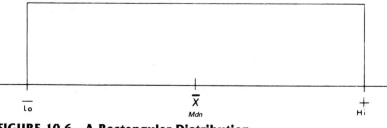

FIGURE 10.6   A Rectangular Distribution.

room teachers because it is easier to determine. The mean sometimes can be a misleading figure, since it is greatly influenced by students with very high or very low scores.

If you will reexamine the distributions presented in Figures 10.3 through 10.6, you will note that there is a relationship between the shape of the distribution and the relative placement of the mean and the median. For normal and rectangular distributions (or for any distribution that is symmetrically shaped), the mean and the median coincide. In a positively skewed distribution, the mean will give the higher measure of central tendency. In a negatively skewed distribution, just the opposite occurs. Thus, for classroom tests or teacher salary distributions, one could present a different image by presenting a median instead of a mean. But for standardized test results with fairly normal distributions, it would matter little which measure of central tendency was used. The mean is most often used, however, because it can be used in the calculation of other statistics, such as the standard deviation and correlation coefficients discussed below.

MEASURES OF VARIABILITY

To know only a person's raw score is of little value. To know that a person's score is so much above or below the mean is of some value. If one has an indication of the variability of a distribution of scores as well, much more information is obtained. (To go back to the example of the temperature in Miami, knowing only the average temperature is not nearly so useful as also knowing something about the variability of the temperature.)

The measures of variability most often used in testing are the standard deviation (S) and the variance (S^2).[2] These two have a precise mathematical

relation to each other: The standard deviation is the square root of the variance. This relation is indicated in the symbols by use of the exponent 2 when indicating variance. The variance can be computed by

$$S_x^2 = \frac{\Sigma(X - \overline{X})^2}{N} \qquad (10\text{-}2)$$

where all symbols on the right-hand side have been previously defined and the subscript x identifies the score distribution (here the X scores) whose variance is being computed.[3]

Equation 10-2 is sometimes called a *definitional formula*. Expressed in words, it states that the variance is the arithmetic average (notice that we are summing several values and dividing by the number we sum, just as when computing the mean) of the squares of the deviation scores from their mean. The $(X - \overline{X})$, then, is known as a *deviation* value showing the distance between a person's score (X) and the mean ($\overline{X}$). (Computational formulas are available in most basic statistical texts. There are many inexpensive calculators that have built-in variance and standard deviation programs, and a user need only push the appropriate buttons.)

The standard deviation (S_x) is obtained by taking the square root of the variance. The standard deviation, then, is

$$S_x = \sqrt{\frac{\Sigma(X - \overline{X})^2}{N}} \qquad (10\text{-}3)$$

Two examples of computing the variance and the standard deviation are illustrated in Table 10-4.

To carry out the computation using the equations given, the following steps are completed.

---

[2]Occasionally the range (high score–low score + 1) is used. But this measure, like the mode, is very unstable.

[3]When *estimating* the variance of a population from a sample, one uses $N - 1$ instead of N in the denominator to get an unbiased estimator. Typically, in using the test data for *descriptive* purposes, we do not estimate the population variance but rather present the variance for the given scores. Thus, N is the appropriate denominator.

TABLE 10-4 Two Distributions of IQ Scores with Equal Means but Unequal Variances

	Example A			Example B	
X	$(X - \bar{X})$	$(X - \bar{X})^2$	X	$(X - \bar{X})$	$(X - \bar{X})^2$
109	9	81	185	85	7225
108	8	64	147	47	2209
107	7	49	121	21	441
105	5	25	108	8	64
105	5	25	106	6	36
103	3	9	104	4	16
102	2	4	103	3	9
101	1	1	103	3	9
101	1	1	102	2	4
101	1	1	101	1	1
99	−1	1	99	−1	1
99	−1	1	96	−4	16
97	−3	9	91	−9	81
97	−3	9	83	−17	289
96	−4	16	82	−18	324
95	−5	25	80	−20	400
95	−5	25	74	−26	676
94	−6	36	74	−26	676
93	−7	49	71	−29	841
93	−7	49	70	−30	900

$\Sigma X = 2000 \qquad \Sigma(X - \bar{X})^2 = 480$

$N = 20 \quad \bar{X} = \dfrac{\Sigma X}{N} = \dfrac{2000}{20} = 100$

$S_x^2 = \dfrac{480}{20} = 24$

$S_x = \sqrt{24} = 4.9$

$\Sigma X = 2000 \qquad \Sigma(X - \bar{X})^2 = 14,218$

$N = 20 \quad \bar{X} = \dfrac{\Sigma X}{N} = \dfrac{2000}{20} = 100$

$S_x^2 = \dfrac{14,218}{20} = 710.9$

$S_x = \sqrt{710.9} = 26.66$

1. Compute the mean by adding all the X scores and dividing by the total number of scores. $\Sigma X = 2000$, $N = 20$, so $\bar{X} = 100$.
2. Subtract $\bar{X}$ from each individual's X score $(X - \bar{X})$ (e.g., for the first individual in Example A, $X = 109$, so $X - \bar{X} = 109 - 100 = 9$).
3. Square these $(X - \bar{X})$ numbers to get an $(X - \bar{X})^2$ for each individual (e.g., $9^2 = 81$).
4. Add the column of $(X - \bar{X})^2$ scores. This value, $\Sigma(X - \bar{X})^2 = 480$, is the numerator of Equation 10-2.

5. Divide $\Sigma(X - \bar{X})^2$ by $N(480/20)$ to get the variance ($S_x^2 = 24$).
6. Take the square root of the variance to obtain the standard deviation ($S_x = \sqrt{24} = 4.9$).

If a new student with an IQ score of 120 (assume all IQ scores were obtained from the same test) joins a class of pupils with IQ scores as shown in Example A in Table 10-4, he will be 20 points above the mean and 11 points above the second pupil in his class in measured aptitude. If he joins a class with scores as shown in Example

B, he will still be 20 points above the mean, but three pupils in the class will have higher measured academic aptitude. The pupils depicted in Example B will require more individualized attention than the pupils depicted in Example A because of the extreme variability in academic aptitude of the students.

The standard deviation is used to describe the amount of variability in a distribution. Although the standard deviation can be computed for a distribution of any size, it is particularly useful for reporting the variability of large sets of scores (such as the norms on standardized tests) because of the relationship between the standard deviation and a normal distribution. In a normal distribution, a specified percentage of scores fall within each standard deviation from the mean. As can be seen from Figure 10.3, about 68 percent of the area under a normal curve (or 68 percent of the scores if the normal curve depicts a distribution of scores) falls between $\pm 1 S_x$ (i.e., plus or minus one standard deviation from the mean); 95 percent between $\pm 2 S_x$ (the 95 percent interval is actually $\pm 1.96 S_x$ but for practical work it is often computed as $\pm 2 S_x$); and 99.7 percent between $\pm 3 S_x$. More is said about this relationship between a normal curve and the standard deviation in the discussions of types of scores, reliability, and validity in Chapters 11, 12, and 13.

MEASURES OF RELATIONSHIP

If we have two sets of scores from the same group of people, it is often desirable to know the degree to which the scores are related. For example, we may be interested in the relationship between the mathematics test scores and GPA for the individuals whose scores are given in Table 10-1. (Do people who do well in mathematics also, in general, do well in other areas in school?) Or we may be interested in both, or either, of the other relationships: test score and IQ score or GPA and IQ score. We are also interested in relationships between two sets of scores when we are studying the

reliability or validity of a test (see Chapters 12 and 13 for a discussion on reliability and validity). The Pearson product moment correlation coefficient (r) is the statistic most often used to give us an indication of this relationship. It can be calculated from the formula:

$$r = \frac{\Sigma[(X - \overline{X})(Y - \overline{Y})]}{N S_x S_y} \qquad (10\text{-}4)$$

where X = score of person on one variable
Y = score of same person on the other variable
$\overline{X}$ = mean of the X distribution
$\overline{Y}$ = mean of the Y distribution
S_x = standard deviation of the X scores
S_y = standard deviation of the Y scores
N = number of pairs of scores

The value of r may range from $+1.00$ to -1.00. When an increase in one variable tends to be accompanied by an increase in the other variable (such as aptitude and achievement), the correlation is positive. When an increase in either one tends to be accompanied by a decrease in the other (such as age and value of a car), then the correlation is negative. A perfect positive correlation (1.00) or a perfect negative correlation (-1.00) occurs when a change in the one variable is always accompanied by a commensurate change in the other variable. A zero (.00) correlation occurs when there is no linear relationship between the two variables. Table 10-5 illustrates the computation of r using Equation (10-4). Again, many calculators have built-in correlation programs.

How close to 1 (positively or negatively) an r must be, in order to indicate that an important relationship exists, is difficult to specify. The scattergrams in Figure 10.7 depict the amount of relationship for various correlation coefficients. (A scattergram is a plot showing each individual's scores on both X and Y.)

Obviously, we do not expect all different sets of variables to have equal degrees of relationship. Correlations vary considerably in size, and the value of a given correlation must be interpreted,

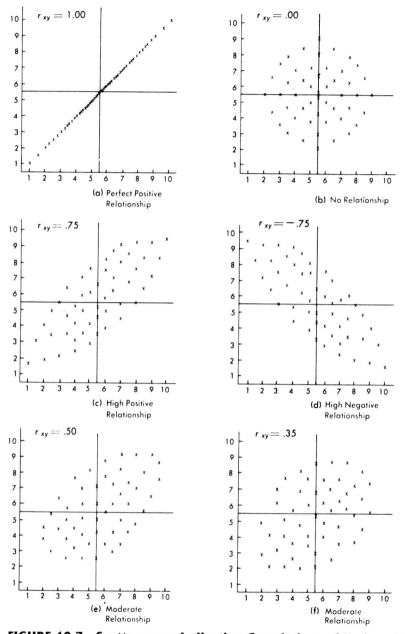

FIGURE 10.7   Scattergrams Indicating Correlations of Various Sizes (N = 50).

TABLE 10-5 The Calculation of r Using Equation 10–4

X	Y	$X - \bar{X}$	$(X - \bar{X})^2$	$Y - \bar{Y}$	$(Y - \bar{Y})^2$	$(X - \bar{X})(Y - \bar{Y})$
50	45	20	400	16	256	320
49	50	19	361	21	441	399
30	25	0	0	−4	16	0
11	10	−19	361	−19	361	361
10	15	−20	400	−14	196	280
			1522		1270	1360

$$\Sigma X = 150 \qquad\qquad \Sigma Y = 145$$

$$\bar{X} = 30 \qquad\qquad \bar{Y} = 29$$

$$\Sigma(X - \bar{X})^2 = 1522 \qquad\qquad \Sigma(Y - \bar{Y})^2 = 1270$$

$$S_x = \sqrt{\frac{\Sigma(X - \bar{X})^2}{N}} = \sqrt{\frac{1522}{5}} = \sqrt{304.4}$$

$$S_y = \sqrt{\frac{1270}{5}} = \sqrt{254}$$

$$r = \frac{\Sigma(X - \bar{X})(Y - \bar{Y})}{NS_xS_y} = \frac{1360}{5\sqrt{304.4}\,\sqrt{254}} = .98$$

in part, by comparing it to other correlations obtained from similar variables. For example, a correlation of .85 would be considered somewhat low if one were correlating two equivalent forms of an aptitude test. However, a correlation of .70 between Scholastic Aptitude Test scores and college grade point averages would be interpreted as quite high. Table 10-6 gives some typical correlation coefficients for selected variables. The more experience you obtain, the more you will know what degree of relationship can be expected between different variables.

Two cautions should be mentioned concerning the interpretation of correlation coefficients:

1. They are *not* an indication of cause and effect. One can find all sorts of variables that are related but have no causal relationship. For example, for children, the size of the big toe is slightly correlated with mental age—yet one does not cause the other. They are correlated simply because they are both related to a third variable: chronological age.

2. The Pearson product moment correlation is a measure of linear relationship. If one suspects that two variables have a relationship other

TABLE 10-6 Typical Correlation Coefficients for Selected Variables

Variables	r
Two equivalent forms of a test	.95
Intelligence of identical twins	.90
Height and weight of adults	.60
High school and college GPA	.50
Intelligence of pairs of siblings	.50
Height and intelligence	.05

than. linear, a different index of correlation should be computed.[4]

■ SUMMARY

The following statements summarize the major points of this chapter.

1. Data can be classified as nominal, ordinal, interval, and ratio data.
2. Tabulating and/or graphing data aids in ease of interpretation.
3. The shape of a distribution of scores will depend both upon the properties of the measuring instrument and the distribution of the underlying characteristic we are attempting to measure.
4. The mean and median are measures of central tendency. They give an idea of the average or typical score in the distribution.
5. The mean is generally preferred by statisticians as the measure of central tendency, but the median is easier to compute and therefore is sometimes preferred by classroom teachers.
6. For distributions that are fairly normal (such as those obtained from most standardized test results), it matters little which measure of central tendency is used.
7. The variance and standard deviation are measures of variability. They give an indication of the spread of scores in a distribution.
8. The standard deviation is the square root of the variance.
9. The Pearson product moment correlation coefficient is the statistic most often used to provide a measure of relationship. The values

of the coefficient may range between -1.00 and $+1.00$, indicating perfect negative and perfect positive relationships, respectively. A value of .00 (zero) indicates no linear relationship.

10. There are two major cautions in interpreting correlation coefficients:
    a. They are not an indication of cause and effect.
    b. The ones we have studied in this chapter are only measures of linear relationship.

■ POINTS TO PONDER

1. Assume that you are the teachers' representative at a salary-negotiating session with your school board. If you wish to show the low salaries of teachers in the system, would you use the mean or the median salary? Why?
2. If a negatively skewed distribution of test scores is obtained, what, if anything, can be inferred about the "true" distribution of the characteristic being measured?
3. Which of the scattergrams shown in Figure 10.7 would you expect to obtain if you were studying the relationship between:
    a. chronological age and intelligence?
    b. car age and car value?
    c. height and weight?
    d. aptitude test scores and college grade point average?
4. What does a correlation of .11 mean to you? Would it (or could it) be significant to a cancer researcher? How?

[4]An explanation of curvilinear relationships is found in many statistics texts, for example, William A. Hays, *Statistics for Psychologists*, 4th ed. New York: Holt, Rinehart and Winston, 1988.

Chapter 11

Norms, Scores, and Profiles

- ■ **Norms**
- ■ **Types of Norm-Referenced Scores**
- ■ **Types of Criterion-Referenced Scores**
- ■ **Expectancy Scores**
- ■ **Profiles**

In Chapter 10 we discussed some basic descriptive statistics, measures of central tendency, variability, and relationship. In this chapter we will discuss the interpretations of various types of scores. Most readers will realize that a raw score (number correct) on a test provides very little information. For that reason, the interpretation of the score is almost always facilitated by some type of transformation of the raw score that provides a frame of reference. Two such frames of reference are *norm*- and *criterion*-referenced, which were discussed briefly in Chapter 2. Recall that in the former, our frame of reference is the scores of an identifiable norm group. In the latter, the frame of reference is some performance standard. It is not necessary to review here the debates about nonstandard terminology and the relative values of the two types of referencing. The two types of referencing are used by classroom teachers in their own assessment procedures and by most publish-

ers of tests. Professionals need to be familiar with both. Thus, we will present some specific types of norm- and criterion-referenced scores that you may wish to compute for your own tests, that you may come across as a user of standardized tests, and that you should understand and be able to explain to others.

After studying this chapter, you should be able to do the following:

1. Know the definitions of the terms presented.
2. Appreciate the value of a norm group as an aid in interpreting test scores.
3. Evaluate the adequacy of a set of norms in terms of recency and representativeness.
4. Judge what would constitute a relevant norm group for a specified purpose of testing.
5. Recognize when different norm groups should be used.

6. Judge the adequacy of the norms description in a test manual.
7. Distinguish between norm-referenced and criterion-referenced scores.
8. Convert raw scores to percentiles and linear z and T scores.
9. Interpret various types of derived scores.
10. Recognize the limitations of various types of derived scores.
11. Interpret various profiles.

NORMS

The terms *norm, norm group,* and *norms* are often used in educational measurement. *Norm* is sometimes used as a synonym for average and is the mean (or median) score for some specified group of people. This specified group is called the *norm group,* or *reference group.* There may be more than one such specified norm group for any test. A table showing the performance of the norm group(s) is called a *norms table,* or (more commonly) *norms.* Norms tables typically show the relationship or correspondence between raw scores (the number correct on the test) and some type of derived scores. We will now consider the need for norms, how to obtain an appropriate norms group, some various types of norm groups, what test manuals should report about norms, and how to use norms.

Need for Norms

In Chapter 2 we discussed the differences between norm- and criterion-referenced score interpretation. Criterion referencing has a place in specific types of instructional training programs, but, in general, normative referencing is of more value. Outside of certification decisions there are very few educational situations in which criterion referencing alone is sufficient. Even in the situation where the test itself is composed of all behaviors to which we wish to infer, we usually desire normative data.

Suppose we have a 100-item test composed of all possible permutations of multiplying two one-digit numbers. If Johnny took this test and got 75 answers correct, we could clearly make a criterion-referenced statement: Johnny knows 75 percent of the material. But to know how others performed on the test would certainly help us to interpret his score. If others of his age and education can typically receive 100 percent, and have been able to do so for two years, his score would take on quite a different meaning than if he is the only one in his age group who can score higher than 50 percent on the test. Norms, then, are important in that they tell us how others have performed on the test.

An Appropriate Norm Group

An appropriate norm group must be *recent, representative,* and *relevant.*

Recency If one gives a test in a classroom and norm references the scores to that class, the norms are obviously very recent. Referencing a student's score against the total of the previous two years students' scores gives a less recent norm group. Comparing current students' scores to those of ten years ago may not really be appropriate.

Such rapid changes are occurring in education that test norms can quickly become outdated. This is particularly true in the area of achievement tests (either classroom or standardized). If we do a better job of instructing, or if we change our curricular emphasis, the achievement of ninth-grade students in a social studies test three years from now might be quite different from the achievement of present ninth-graders. Of course, as the content of a curriculum changes, not only the norms but the test itself becomes outdated. This is usually obvious to a test user who is competent in her subject matter.

A less likely detected obsolescence of norms occurs when the content of the test is still relevant but the characteristics of the reference group have changed. This may be true, for example, in a college that changes from a restricted to an open admissions policy. A prospective freshman may have quite a low test score in comparison with that of freshmen admitted under a restrictive policy; on the other hand, his score may be quite high relative to that of freshmen admitted under an open policy. Many other less obvious changes in society could also make an older reference group no longer appropriate.

One caution to be mentioned here is that the recency of the norms group on a published test cannot be judged by the copyright date of the test manual. Any change in the test manual allows the publisher to revise the copyright date of the manual, although the later date may not be an indication of the recency of the norms.

As mentioned in Chapter 1, a report by Cannell (1987) suggested that more than 50 percent of the elementary school students in the nation were above the national average on many standardized achievement tests. This has become known as the "Lake Wobegon" effect. One possible reason for the finding has to do with the recency of the norms. Tests have traditionally been normed at the time of publication. Suppose we are using a test normed in 1980. If the education of the nation's school children has improved between 1980 and 1987, then more than 50 percent of the 1987 students will score above the 1980 norm group. The norms are "time-bound" (Williams, 1988), and this needs to be kept in mind during any norm-referenced interpretation of the scores. For example, a norm-referenced report to the public should state the year the norms data were gathered.

Because of the time-bound nature of the original norms, some publishers now also offer schools annual norms. For example, CTB/McGraw-Hill offers customers of the Comprehensive Test of Basic Skills (CTBS) and the California Achievement Test (CAT) "Annual National Normative Trend Data" (NTD). Score reports are available annually for the original standardization year as well as for the most recent norming—which each year is based on the results from the previous spring. The advantage of such reports is that one can obtain a *recent* normative comparison as well

as determine whether the schools in the nation have improved across time. This improvement would not be detected readily without the stable norms from the original sample.

Representativeness There are two sources of error in any normative statement about a person's score. One, the error of measurement, is due to the imprecision or unreliability of the test or testing process and will be discussed in Chapter 12. The second, the sampling error, is the discrepancy between the scores in the sample and the population and is due to the limitations of the sample. A *population* refers to a specified group of individuals (e.g., all fifth-graders in the United States). A *sample* is a smaller number of people selected from the population and actually tested. In this section we are concerned with the adequacy of the sample. In the following section we consider the relevance of the population sampled.

One consideration of some importance in sampling is the size of the sample. Any sample should be large enough to provide stable values. By "stable" we mean that if another sample had been drawn in a similar fashion, we would obtain similar results. Most of the more popular published tests have samples of adequate size. For norming classroom tests, a single classroom would not likely provide a large enough sample for stable norms. A person could conceivably be at the 75th percentile in one class but be at the 50th percentile in another class. Teachers should accumulate data across similar classes or across several years to provide a larger normative sample.

Another important factor is the kind of sampling. (This is of more concern in standardized tests than classroom tests.) A large sample alone is not sufficient. If a sample is biased, making it larger does not solve the problem. The sampling procedure must be correct. Space does not permit us to delve into sampling techniques extensively. In general, however, stratified random sampling is the best procedure where the stratification is done on the most relevant independent variables. The relevant independent variables (such as age, sex, socioeconomic status, race, size of community, and geographic location of the subject) would vary from one kind of test to another. Perhaps the most troublesome problem in sampling is that one is dependent on the cooperation of the sample chosen. If cooperation is poor, so that the proportion of the original sample for which scores are obtained is too low, then the obtained scores may be from a biased sample. Unfortunately, the agencies do not always tell us what proportion of the originally chosen sample did cooperate and how they differed from the noncooperators. A study by Baglin (1981) suggests that there is a considerable proportion of schools who decline to participate. Those who participate are more apt to be using the publisher's tests or instructional materials than those that decline. Thus, the national norm may be biased in favor of schools having a curriculum related to the test content. This would likely result in a more difficult set of norms than a truly national norm. That is, those who participate in the norming sample should, as a group, do *better* than nonparticipants would have done. Thus, pupils would receive a lower norm-referenced score than they would have in a truly national sample. (On the other hand, motivation may be less for pupils in the normative sample than in a regular test-taking setting, thus causing the normative sample to produce a less difficult set of norms—i.e., the sample in the norm group does poorer than the national population would do.)

A poor sampling procedure would be to sample by convenience rather than by a particular sampling procedure. For example, schools in which one has professional contacts or those that have previously cooperated could be chosen because these procedures are convenient. Such a chosen sample may not be biased, particularly if the data in the sample are appropriately weighted. Nevertheless, the likelihood that such a sampling procedure will produce biased results is great enough for us to be wary of norms built in such a fashion.

As mentioned, differential cooperation and sampling by convenience are likely to produce too difficult a set of norms (i.e., the sample in the norm group does *better* than the national population would do). This would tend to produce lower norm-referenced scores. However, less motivation would produce too easy a set of norms. The Cannell report suggests that norms are too easy. Certainly test publishers could attempt to develop norms that are too easy by using a norm group that is *less* capable than a truly representative sample. Given the differential cooperation of schools, this would not be likely to occur by accident. We do *not* impugn the publishers' integrity. In fact, we doubt that most publishers' norms are too easy for the year they are gathered. We suspect the Lake Wobegon effect has more to do with the time-bound nature of the norms than it does inadequate representativeness. (Teaching too closely to the test is probably the major reason for the Lake Wobegon effect.)

Relevance   The relevance of the norm group depends upon the degree to which the population sampled is comparable to the group with which users of the test wish to compare their students. For classroom tests, other classes receiving the same instruction are likely a relevant norm group. For standardized tests, the issue is more complicated. If, for example, a tester wishes to compare a student's ability with that of students who intend to go to college, then the norm group should be a sample of students who intend to go to college and not a sample from a general population. Because a test may be used for several different purposes, it is usually necessary to have more than one norm group. Some of the more common types of norms are discussed briefly below.

Types of Norms

National Norms   The types of norms most commonly reported by test publishers and used by educators are *national norms*. These norms are almost always reported separately by the different age or educational levels for which the test is constructed. Occasionally, they are reported separately by sex. National norms can be used with all types of tests but are probably most useful for general scholastic aptitude and achievement tests. They assist in keeping one from forming too parochial a view. Suppose Mary attends a school district where the students all come from professional homes. The school, Mary's parents, and Mary herself may get quite an unrealistic picture of Mary if she is compared only to others in that district. She may be in the bottom fourth of that district but in the top 10 percent nationally.

Most major test publishers who report national norms have employed reasonably satisfactory sampling procedures. Nevertheless, there is still the obvious limitation of school cooperation, some tendency to choose samples for convenience, and the always present sampling error. Thus, national norms are not completely comparable to each other, and it is not really possible to compare a pupil's scores on two different tests unless the data were gathered on the same sample. Many testing companies do use the same sample for norming both an aptitude and an achievement battery, thus allowing intertest comparisons.

One other point should be mentioned. National norms for educational tests are most often gathered in school settings. Since 100 percent of the population is not in school, we do not have a truly national sample. The higher the grade level, the lower the proportion of children that are in school and the more biased the sample. This is not really a handicap in making educational decisions, but it is a point we need to remember if we wish to interpret the data as literally representative of the nation. Related to this point, we must remember that in any international comparisons of achievement the samples are drawn from schools, and the United States has a greater proportion of youth attending school than do other countries. In such studies, we are often comparing the top 75–85 percent of our youth to the top 20–30 percent of the youth in some other country.

Thus, as useful as national norms may be, they certainly do have some limitations. The most serious one is that often they simply do not provide the comparison data or permit us to make the interpretation we need. If a student plans to take automobile mechanics at Dunwoody Technical Institute, we would be much better able to counsel him if we knew how his aptitude in auto mechanics compares with students presently in Dunwoody.

Special Group Norms For many decision-making purposes, highly specific norms are the most desirable. Norms such as "first-year education students at state colleges," "high school juniors," or "students who have taken two years of French" may be the comparisons in which we are most interested. We are likely to want such special norm groups for specific aptitude tests, such as mechanical, clerical, and musical, and for specific subject-matter tests such as first-year Spanish, music appreciation, chemistry, and the College Board Scholastic Aptitude Test (SAT). Such special norm groups are also useful for tests designed for the physically or mentally handicapped. Intelligence tests designed for the blind or the deaf obviously need to have special group norms.

Local or State Norms Individual classroom tests will necessarily have only a local classroom norm group. District-administered tests could have district or classroom norms—although district norms seem preferable for most uses.

Standardized tests can have national, district, building, or individual classroom norms. If some intraschool comparisons or intracity comparisons are desired, many people prefer local norms for standardized tests. Although such comparisons could be made by using national norms, the users might find it more difficult to make the comparison with the data in that form. If test scoring is done by machine—whether by a test company or locally—local norms can be constructed easily. In general, it is worth the slight extra charge to have these local norms prepared. This facilitates test score interpretation to the teacher, the parent, the student, and the community.

In the past few years more states have developed their own tests. Although many of these test results are reported in a criterion-referenced fashion, there typically are also state norms published. For *required* tests, these norms are obviously accurate because the sample equals the population. However, for some optional state-built tests the norms may be "user" norms and not necessarily representative of the total state.

School Mean Norms   If we are interested in comparing the mean performance of a school (or total school district) to other schools, we must use school (or total district) mean norms. *It is not appropriate to compute a mean for a school district and interpret it as indicating the norm-referenced position of the school by using the norm tables based on individual pupil performance.* The variability of school means is far less than the variability of individual scores, and the individual norm tables would, therefore, give an *underestimate* of relative school performance for above-average schools and an *overestimate* of relative school performance for below-average schools. Not all test publishers provide school mean norms for those who wish to make such comparisons. If not provided, such comparisons cannot be made. (Of course, the local district can compute the school means for the schools in that district and build local school mean norms for those specific schools. Also, one can compare the average student in a school to the students in the nation. However, this does *not* give the *school's* norm-referenced score.)

What Test Manuals Should Report

The users of test information must be very cautious in their interpretation of the norms provided by the test publisher. Questions such as the following must be considered: How representative are the norms? What were the characteristics of the standardization and norming sample? How old are the norms? Are the norms useful for the kinds of comparisons to be made? These questions must be satisfactorily answered before one can correctly and meaningfully use the norm data—but test manuals do not always provide the data necessary to answer them. If the information is not available in a manual, it may be found in a technical supplement. At any rate, the quality of the

norms should not be accepted on faith. (This is obviously true for local and state-built tests as well as national tests.)

A manual for a standardized test may state that it has a national sample without providing the data necessary for the users to judge for themselves the adequacy of the sample (norms). The norm group must necessarily consist of those who are willing to be tested, and the test manual should state the refusal rate. The users must then decide how this information will affect their interpretations. Older tests were often normed so that the norm data really represented, for example, only the Midwest, or only the East Coast, or only the Far West. Generally, the newer tests, particularly those published by the larger reputable companies, have adequate norm data. Highly sophisticated sampling procedures exist and a representative sample can be obtained if the publishers are willing to go to the effort to achieve such an end.

Using Norms

Normative data aid greatly in the interpretation of test scores, but there are also dangers of *misinterpretation* or *misuse* of norms. It would be a misuse, for example, to interpret national norms as special group norms, or vice versa. Perhaps the greatest mistake is to interpret norms as standards. *Norms are not standards.* Norm information tells us how people actually perform, *not how they should perform.* Comparing a person's score with a norm group does not automatically tell us whether his score was above or below the level at which it should be. It tells us only how the person performed in comparison to others. A description in relative terms is not an evaluation.

One of the most ridiculous but frustrating criticisms of the schools is the complaint that there are so many students "below norms"! For example, half the sixth-graders read "below grade level"! Terrible? Of course not. If "norm" is used as a synonym for "median," half the students must be below a current, accurate norm. There is no way the schools can do such a good job that less than half the students will be below average when compared to a *current, representative* norm group. (As mentioned earlier, it is possible for more than half the current students to score better than a norm obtained in a *previous* year.)

Also, when evaluating output—such as scores on an achievement test—input must be considered. Input includes things such as previous instruction on the variable being measured, as well as family, community, and school characteristics. We talk more about the relationship between input and output in the section on accountability in Chapter 21. But output should always be interpreted in relation to input. As mentioned in Chapter 1, we would evaluate two fifth-graders' scores quite differently if, in the preceding year, one scored at the third-grade level and the other at the fourth-grade, fifth-month level.

One final point: The output on standardized achievement tests should be interpreted in view of the local curricular and instructional objectives. If the local objectives differ from the ones followed by the test-maker, any interpretation of the result must be made in light of this fact. More is said about this in Chapter 16.

TYPES OF NORM-REFERENCED SCORES

To know a person's observed score (raw score) on a measuring instrument gives us very little information about his performance. To know how that person's score compares with the mean score of an identifiable group (norm group) is of more value. If one has an indication of the variability of the distribution of scores in the norm group as well, much more information is obtained. If a person's raw score is changed into a score that *by itself* gives normative or relative information, we can present the information more efficiently, since the mean and standard deviation need not also be reported. Such expressions as *kinds of scales, kinds of norms, types of scores,* and *derived scores* all refer to those various transformations of raw scores

into scores that have normative or relative meanings.

Derived scores are useful, then, in comparing a person's score to those of others, that is, in making *interindividual* comparisons. A second use is in making *intraindividual* (within-individual) comparisons. It is not possible, for example, to compare directly a person's test score, GPA, and IQ measures. It is first necessary to transform all data into comparable units. (Of course, comparability of the norm groups is also necessary.)

The following example illustrates the importance of derived scores in interpreting data. Assume Irwin, an eleventh-grade boy, has received the following *raw scores* on the Differential Aptitude Test (DAT).

Verbal Reasoning (32)	Numerical Ability (29)	Abstract Reasoning (32)	Clerical S and A (42)
Mechanical Reasoning (42)	Space Relations (36)	Spelling (64)	Language Usage (30)

These data, in and of themselves, tell us nothing about how Irwin compares to others of his age, since we have no idea how other children score. But do they even tell us anything about whether Irwin is better in one subtest area than in another? Do we know if Irwin is better in spelling than in language usage? No, because we do not know the total number of questions on each subtest, nor whether some subtests have easier questions than the others. Some type of derived score is necessary for both inter- and intraindividual interpretations.

Another use of derived scores is to assist in a meaningful combination of data. Sometimes the teacher wishes to combine various pieces of information to make a single decision about an individual. An example would be to combine results of term papers, quizzes, and examinations to arrive at a final grade. The question is: How does the teacher weight the various pieces of data? By converting all scores to derived scores, a weighting scheme can be carried out (see Chapter 20 for a further discussion of this).

Because score reports serve a variety of audiences and purposes, it is common for them to contain a variety of derived scores. The types of norm-referenced scores that are most likely to be used by psychologists and educators can be divided into two basic types: relative position status scores and developmental level scores. The relative position status scores discussed below include percentile ranks, linear z and T scores, normalized z and T scores, normal curve equivalent scores, deviation IQ scores, and stanines. The developmental level scores we will discuss are grade equivalents, mental age scores (and the related ratio "IQ" scores), and scaled scores. We will also discuss expectancy scores, which, depending on the metric used, could be either status or developmental level scores.

Relative Position Status Scores

Percentiles and Percentile Ranks A *percentile* is defined as a point on the distribution below which a certain percentage of the scores fall. A *percentile rank* gives a person's relative position or the percentage of students' scores falling below his obtained score.[1] For example, let us assume that John has a raw score of 76 on an English test

composed of 100 items. If 98 percent of the scores in the distribution fall below a score of 76, the percentile rank of the score of 76 is 98 and the 98th percentile is a score of 76. Thus, 76 is the point below which 98 percent of the scores in the distribution fall. This does not mean that the student who scores at the 98th percentile answered 98 percent of the items correctly. If this score is equivalent to the 98th percentile, it means that 98 percent of the students who took the test received a score below 76.

Percentile ranks have the advantage of being easy to compute and fairly easy to interpret. (Occasionally, people will confuse percentile ranks with percentage correct, but this distinction can be easily explained to most people.) In explaining a national norm percentile rank to a student, the teacher will say, for example, "your percentile rank of 85 means that you obtained a score higher than 85 out of every 100 students in a representative sample of eighth-graders in the nation who took this test."

As with other derived scores, both intra- and interindividual comparisons can be made from percentiles. For example, referring to a percentile norm table for the DAT values given earlier for Irwin, we find the percentiles listed below.

We can now see how Irwin's scores in each subtest compare with those of other eleventh-graders (interindividual comparison) as well as see how his scores in the different subtests compare with each other (intraindividual comparison). As

---

[1] Statisticians differ somewhat in the precise definitions of these terms, but their differences are minor and need not concern us. Some use the terms percentile and percentile rank interchangeably.

	Verbal Reasoning	Numerical Ability	Abstract Reasoning	Clerical S and A
Raw Score	32	29	32	42
Percentile	65	70	45	40
	Mechanical Reasoning	Space Relations	Spelling	Language Usage
Raw Score	42	36	64	30
Percentile	20	55	55	65

can be seen, the *order* of Irwin's raw scores was meaningless information.

Percentile ranks have a disadvantage in that the size of the percentile units is not constant in terms of raw-score units.[2] For example, if the distribution is normal, the raw-score difference between the 90th and 99th percentiles is much greater than the raw-score difference between the 50th and 59th percentiles (see Figure 11.1). Thus, a percentile difference does not really represent the same amount of raw-score difference in the middle of the distribution as it does at the extremes. Any interpretation of percentiles must take this fact into account. We can be more confident that differences in percentiles represent true differences at

the extremes than at the middle of a normal distribution. This problem can be alleviated somewhat by presenting the information on a graph, called a *normal percentile chart*, that "accounts for" the unequal units. Some publishers do use this type of visual reporting scheme (see Figure 11.3). Of course, the ordinal nature of the percentile rank units means that one cannot treat them further statistically. But this is not a relevant limitation with respect to interpreting the scores to others. In general, the percentile rank is one of the best types of relative position status scores to use in interpreting test scores to others. Derived scores that do not have the limitation of unequal units are the *linear standard scores*, discussed below.

Linear z and T Scores   *Linear scores* (frequently called *standard scores*) are transformed scores for

---

[2]Except in the unusual case where the raw-score distribution is rectangular.

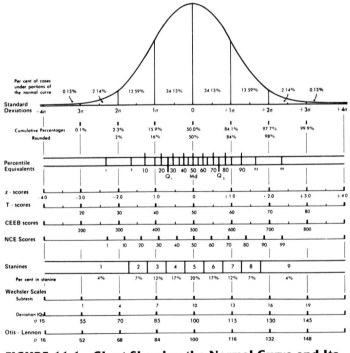

FIGURE 11.1   Chart Showing the Normal Curve and Its Relationship to Various Derived Scores. (Reproduced from *Test Service Notebook* No. 148 of The Psychological Corporation.)

which the resulting set of values has a distribution shape identical to the original raw-score distribution. In other words, if the original raw scores are plotted on one axis and the transformed scores on another, a straight line will connect the plotted points. The linear z score is the basic standard score. The formula for a linear z score is

$$z = \frac{\text{raw score} - \text{mean}}{\text{standard deviation}} = \frac{X - \overline{X}}{S_x} \quad (11\text{-}1)$$

As can be seen from the formula, a person whose raw score is equal to the mean will have a z score of zero. If a person has a raw score that is one standard deviation above the mean, his z score will be $+1.0$. Thus, z scores are standard scores with a mean of zero and a standard deviation of 1.

Linear T scores are derived scores with a mean of 50 (the T score if $z = 0$) and a standard deviation of 10. The formula for a linear T score is

$$T = 10z + 50 = 10\left(\frac{X - \overline{X}}{S_x}\right) + 50 \quad (11\text{-}2)$$

Theoretically, the T score has no advantage over the z score, or vice versa. One is simply a linear transformation of the other. Practitioners, as well as measurement experts, often prefer T scores, because then negative numbers and decimals can generally be avoided (e.g., see Cronbach, 1990).

Table 11-1 shows the computation of the linear z and T scores for an individual with a raw score of 85 on a test that has a mean of 100 and a standard deviation of 15.

TABLE 11-1 Computation of Linear z and T Scores

$$X = 85 \quad \overline{X} = 100 \quad S_x = 15$$

$$z = \frac{X - \overline{X}}{S_x} = \frac{85 - 100}{15} = \frac{-15}{15} = -1$$

$$T = 10z + 50 = 10(-1) + 50 = -10 + 50 = 40$$

When scores are *normally* distributed, there is a precise mathematical relationship between z and T scores and other derived scores. Recall that in a normal distribution, approximately 68 percent of the scores fall between $\pm 1S_x$, 95 percent between $\pm 2S_x$, and 99.7 percent between $\pm 3S_x$. Since a z score has a standard deviation of 1, approximately 68 percent of the z scores will be between ± 1, 95 percent between ± 2, and 99.7 percent between ± 3 in a normal distribution. As Figure 11.1 illustrates, a person who scores one standard deviation above the mean has a z score of 1, a T of 60, and is about the 84th percentile.

Most norm groups for standardized tests are quite large, and the distribution of their scores often approaches normality. Thus, linear z and T scores for most standardized tests can be interpreted as if they relate to percentiles, as shown in Figure 11.1. Classrooms of 50 or fewer pupils, however, do not typically present normal distributions, and the relationship depicted in Figure 11.1 would not be accurate.

Normalized z and T Scores When raw scores are *normalized*, the shape of the distribution of the transformed (normalized) scores is normal, regardless of the shape of the original distribution.[3] Test publishers often provide normalized scores, and the wise test user should be able to discern the difference between these and linear-transformed scores. If normalized z and T values are given, the relationship between those values and percentiles (as shown in Figure 11.1) is accurate, regardless of the shape of the raw-score distribution. Thus, knowing that a person had a normalized z of 1, we would know that he was at about the 84th percentile. This interpretation could not be made with a linear z of 1 unless the original raw-score distribution was normal. (It should be emphasized that

[3]It is not an objective of ours that readers of this text be able to normalize raw scores. However, for those who wish to do so, proceed as follows: Rank the raw scores, convert them to percentiles (percentile ranks), and look up the corresponding z score in a conversion table (found in almost any basic statistics or test theory text). A normalized z can be converted to a normalized T by using Equation 11-2.

the relationships shown in Figure 11.1 hold only for a normal distribution of raw scores, not for all raw-score distributions.)

Deviation IQs   The intelligence quotient (IQ) is one of the most misunderstood concepts in measurement. Much of this confusion exists because of a misunderstanding of intelligence tests. (In Chapter 15 we consider what an aptitude or intelligence test supposedly measures and how the scores can be interpreted usefully.) Part of the confusion, however, exists because people do not understand the type of score typically used to report the results of intelligence tests, that is, the IQ. Originally, the IQ was actually a quotient (a ratio). It was found by dividing a person's mental age by his chronological age and then multiplying by 100 (IQ = MA/CA × 100). (See the section "Mental Age Scores" below.)

The ratio IQ has many inadequacies. Because of these, most test constructors now report deviation IQs or some other derived scores. Deviation IQs are computed separately for each age group within the norm sample. These are not literal intelligence quotients. They are transformations much like the z or T values (usually normalized) discussed earlier. Typically, these deviation IQs have a mean of 100 and a standard deviation of 15 or 16, although some tests have standard deviations as low as 12—others, as high as 20. The fact that standard deviations may vary from test to test is just one of the reasons that we cannot compare two individuals' IQ scores unless they have taken the same test.

Normal Curve Equivalents (NCEs)   *Normal curve equivalents* (NCEs) are normalized standard scores with a mean of 50 and a standard deviation of 21.06. Only integers from 1 to 99 are assigned. Normal curve equivalents are like normalized T scores in that they have a mean of 50. However, NCEs are constructed to have a standard deviation of 21.06 instead of 10. This value was selected so that percentiles of 1 and 99 are equivalent to NCEs of 1 and 99. NCEs are related to stanines (discussed below) in that there are approximately

11 NCE units to each stanine. The formula for NCEs is

$$NCE = 21.06 \text{ (normalized } z) + 50 \quad (11\text{-}3)$$

NCEs have been used in Chapter I Evaluation reports of federally funded programs. They may be confused with percentiles if they are communicated to nonmeasurement-trained persons.

Stanines   *Stanines* are normalized derived scores with a mean of 5 and a standard deviation of 2. Only the integers 1 to 9 occur. In a normal distribution, stanines are related to other scores, as shown in Figure 11.1. As can be seen, the percentages of scores at each stanine are 4, 7, 12, 17, 20, 17, 12, 7, and 4, respectively. Whether or not the original distribution is normal, stanine scores are typically assigned so that the resultant stanine distribution is the 4, 7, 12, 17, 20 . . . 4 distribution. Thus, a plot (histogram) of the stanines would approach a normal distribution, and we can think of stanines as normalized scores. (Some authors round the percentages slightly differently and present the percentages as 4, 8, 12, 16, 20 . . . 4. This is slightly less accurate but easier to remember since one can use the "rule of four." That is, one starts with 4 percent for stanine 1 and adds 4 percent for each subsequent stanine up to stanine 5 (20 percent) and then subtracts 4 percent for each subsequent stanine.)

Stanines have no particular technical advantage over other types of derived scores. They are less precise than others because so many different raw-score values may be grouped into the same stanine score. For example, individuals at the 41st and 59th percentile rank would receive the same stanine. A supposed advantage of stanines is that if two scores are *not* interpreted as being reliably different unless there is at least one stanine score between them, there is less of a tendency to incorrectly infer a difference between two scores when no true difference exists. We believe it preferable to use confidence bands (see Chapter 12) rather than stanines in this fashion. Stanines do represent the finest discrimination that can be made on one column of an IBM card, but this is a minor point.

The major reason we present them is that they are frequently used in reporting the results on standardized tests, and a competent professional should be able to interpret such scores.

Summary of Relative Position Status Scores

While all the scores we discussed in this section have properties that make them the preferred score in certain situations, experts generally agree that in interpreting the *meaning* of a score to a lay person, the *percentile rank* is the best score to use. If data from a test that reports one of the other types of scores are being presented, the professional should convert the score to a percentile rank and relay it to the individual. Most publishers will report percentile ranks, so the professional can obtain them easily from the test manual. In *combining* scores (e.g., for the purpose of assigning a grade), most experts would advocate using z or T scores.

Developmental Level Scores

For *developmental level scores*, a normative comparison of an individual's score is made against the average scores obtained by individuals at different points (for instance, age or grade) in their developmental progress. Such scores, which are sometimes used for those characteristics that develop systematically across age or years of schooling, are quite different from the relative position status scores discussed earlier. Developmental scores should *not* be used if one is interested in comparing a pupil's performance with that of others in a particular reference group such as a specific grade. Developmental scores *must* be used if the purpose is to compare a pupil's performance with a series of reference groups that differ developmentally in the characteristic being measured.

As indicated earlier, the major types of developmental scores are (1) grade equivalents, (2) mental age scores, and (3) scaled scores.

Grade Equivalents *Grade equivalents* (GEs) can be explained best by an example. If a student

obtains a score on a test that is equal to the median score for all the beginning sixth-graders (September testing) in the norm group, then that student is given a grade equivalent of 6.0. A student who obtains a score equal to the median score of all beginning fifth-graders is given a grade equivalent of 5.0. If a student should score between these two points, linear interpolation would be used to determine his grade equivalent. Because most school years run for ten months, successive months are expressed as decimals. Thus, 5.1 would refer to the average performance of fifth-graders in October, 5.2 in November, and so on to 5.9 in June. (See Peterson, Kolen, & Hoover, 1989, for more details on methods of obtaining grade equivalent scales.)

Grade equivalents suffer from at least four major limitations. One of those limitations is the problem of extrapolation. When a test is standardized normally, one does not use students of all grade levels in the normative sample. Suppose a particular test is designed to be used in grades 4, 5, and 6. At times, the norming would be done on only these grades.[4] Now, if the median sixth-grader receives a grade equivalent of 6.0, half the sixth-graders must have a grade equivalent higher than this. How much higher—7.0, 7.8, 9.0, 12.0? We do not know. Because the test was not given to students beyond the sixth grade, there is no way of knowing how well they would have done. However, we can estimate—and that is just what is done. A curve can be constructed to show the relationship between raw scores and grade equivalents as is shown in Figure 11.2. The actual data (i.e., the median raw scores for each grade) are available only for grades 4, 5, and 6. However, the curve can be extrapolated so that one can guess at what the median raw scores would be for other grade levels. The extrapolation procedure is based on the assumption that there would be no points of inflection (i.e., no change in the direction) in

---

[4]Some publishers would norm on a wider range—perhaps grades 3 through 8. The problem of extrapolation still exists, but to a lesser degree.

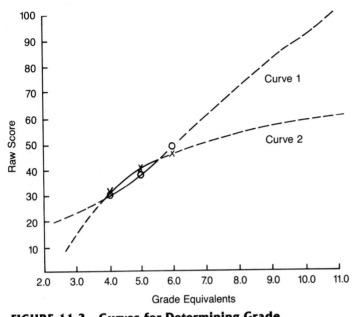

FIGURE 11.2 Curves for Determining Grade Equivalents from Raw Scores. (*O* = population median raw scores for grades 4 to 6; *X* = sample raw scores for grades 4 to 6.)

the curve if real data were available. This is a very unrealistic assumption.

Another problem in extrapolation relates to sampling error. Study the two curves in Figure 11.2. Let us assume that curve 1 is accurate for grades 4 through 6. That is, given the whole population of students in these grades, the median raw scores would fall as indicated by the circles on curve 1. However, because of a specific sampling error (i.e., not having a group with the same median as the population) within grades 5 and 6, we may obtain the medians shown by the *X*s on curve 2. The differences between the medians of the two curves are well within the range of sampling error we might expect. Now, when these two curves are extrapolated, we get completely different estimated grade equivalents. For example, a raw score of 60 is given a grade equivalent of 7.0, using curve 1 (the one we assumed accurate), whereas it would get a grade equivalent of about 10.3 if curve

2 is used. Thus, small sampling errors can make extrapolated grade equivalents very misleading.

A second limitation of grade equivalents is that they give us little information about the percentile standing of a person within his class. A fifth-grade student may, for example, because of the differences in the grade equivalent distributions for various subject matter, have a grade equivalent of 6.2 in English and 5.8 in mathematics and yet have a higher fifth-grade percentile rank in mathematics.

The third limitation of grade equivalents is that (contrary to what the numbers indicate) a fourth-grader with a grade equivalent of 7.0 does not necessarily know the same amount or the same kinds of things as a ninth-grader with a grade equivalent of 7.0. For example, a bright fourth-grader who can do very well on an arithmetic test requiring speed and accuracy may perform as well as the average seventh-grader. A weak ninth-grader may be poor in speed and accuracy and may perform at the seventh-grade level on a test demanding those skills. Yet, those two respective students receiving equal scores on an arithmetic test do not know the same things about mathematics in a more general sense.

A fourth limitation of grade equivalents is that they are a type of norm-referenced measure particularly prone to misinterpretation by the critics of education. As we have mentioned, norms are *not* standards, and even the irrational critics of education do not suggest that everyone should be above the 50th percentile. Yet, people talk continually as if all sixth-graders should be reading at or above the sixth-grade equivalent!

Finally, grade equivalents have no interpretive value beyond the eighth or ninth grade. They are appropriate only for those subjects that are common to a particular grade level.

Of the characteristics of GEs discussed above that make them subject to misinterpretation, the one that has received the most attention is the fact that a GE of, for example, 9.0 obtained by a sixth-grader does not tell us that the student can perform at a level equal to the average ninth-grader on ninth-grade content. But because the scale so "obviously" seems to say that, GEs are frequently misconstrued. A scale somewhat similar to the GE—a Grade Development Scale (GDS)—has been developed by Cole (1982) for *The 3R's Test*. It has been developed using a different empirical procedure from what publishers typically use. Cole suggests that the interpretation that a fourth-grader with a GDS of 9.0 has the same kinds of mathematical skills as the typical GE. It should be noted, however, that the GDS has all the other limitations of GE scores: It will likely have shrinking units; it is not very appropriate beyond ninth grade; it will not be comparable across school subjects; and it may well be misinterpreted as a standard.

Grade equivalents remain popular in spite of their inadequacies. Teachers are under the impression that such scores are easily and correctly understood by both children and parents—an unfortunate impression. It is probably not too dogmatic to suggest that grade equivalents, although

useful if used in conjunction with other kinds of scores such as percentile ranks, should never be used alone in reporting scores to students or parents. And, as noted, they are not at all useful for the high school level where different students study different subjects.

Mental Age Scores To obtain mental age scores, publishers give the test to representative samples of individuals at different ages and plot the results. The mean (or median) raw score for individuals in a given age group is then assigned that mental age. For example, if on a test, the average score for 4½-year-olds is 26, then the score of 26 is assigned a mental age of 4 years, 6 months. The same process is used for other specific age groups. Interpolation and extrapolation are used to determine the mental age equivalents for all the other raw scores.

Mathematical and conceptual problems with using mental age scores are the same as for grade equivalent scores. First of all, difficulties may occur in the interpolation and extrapolation of the data points. Second, the size of the mental age unit does not remain constant with age. Rather, it tends to shrink with advancing years. Thus, the distance between the mental ages of 3 and 4 represents a larger developmental difference than between the ages of 12 and 13. Also, there is some disagreement as to when one's mental age quits growing. Some psychologists may use 16 as a maximum mental age, whereas others may prefer 18. Because of the drawbacks in mental age scores and their interpretations, they should be used with great caution.

Nevertheless, there are circumstances when a careful explanation of a person's mental age may be useful. For example, to enable a parent to understand the degree of retardation of a 10-year-old child, it may be helpful to use a developmental level scale. That is, it may be better to tell a parent that the child functions mentally like an average 7-year-old than to say that the child performs better than 3 percent of a sample of 10-year-olds. Or it may be preferable to communicate to a parent of a gifted 4-year-old that the child functions mentally like an average 8-year-old than to say that the child functions mentally better than 99.9 percent of a representative sample of 4-year-olds. Both of these samples assume, of course, that the psychometric methods of obtaining the mental ages were good enough to make the scaled mental ages of 7 and 8 reasonably accurate. In deciding whether to use mental age scores, one must consider both the drawbacks and the alternatives.

A type of score that has been derived from the mental age is the IQ, or intelligence quotient. As mentioned in a previous section, the IQ was originally a quotient that was found by dividing mental age by chronological age and then multiplying by 100. One of the weaknesses of the quotient approach was that the standard deviations of the IQs were not constant for different ages, so that an IQ score of, for example, 112 would be equal to different percentiles at different ages. A second problem was that opinions varied about what the maximum value of the denominator should be. As mentioned, *when* a person's mental age quits growing is controversial. Thus, ratio IQ scores are seldom reported at the current time. The deviation IQ scores discussed earlier are much more popular.

Scaled Scores Scaled scores could be considered either developmental scores or criterion-referenced scores, depending both upon how they are constructed and how they are used. The scaled scores that most publishers report are most commonly used for developmental comparison purposes. Constructors of these scores frequently claim that they have "equal units" and are free of many of the problems associated with GE scores. While there is considerable debate about the psychometric properties of these scales (see Hoover, 1984), it is probably true that because the scales are based on some arbitrary numbering system, the scores are less likely than GE scores to be misunderstood as *standards*. However, the arbitrary numbering system makes it likely that they will not be understood at all.

The scaled scores, like GE scores, are particularly useful when one wishes to equate the raw scores from various *levels* of the same subtest. They would be useful, for example, if we wished to equate the score of Sarah, who took an out-of-level test, to the score we think she should have achieved had she taken the appropriate level test. This equating across levels and the resultant common scale are potentially useful for researchers who wish the scores to have certain mathematical properties.

As mentioned, the supposed advantage of the scaled scores over GE scores is that they have equal units because of the mathematical techniques used for constructing the scales. These techniques require certain assumptions to be made, however, and there is *considerable* debate about the reasonableness of these assumptions (see Burket, 1984; Hoover, 1984, 1988; Phillips & Clarizio, 1988a, 1988b; and Yen, 1988). The techniques most frequently used are one of the scaling models developed by Thurstone or Thorndike—or, more recently—an item-response theory model (see the next section). For example, the Stanford Achievement Test uses the one-parameter (Rasch) item-response theory model. The Comprehensive Test of Basic Skills and the California Achievement Test use the three-parameter item-response theory model. You would need to study the technical manual of the test you are using to understand just how the publisher calculated the scaled scores and what they mean. Unless you are doing research, you probably will not be using these scores. Grade equivalents are preferable for most *developmental level* test interpretations.

Item-Response Theory While the basics of item-response theory (sometimes called latent trait theory or item-characteristic curve theory) have been around for a long time, there has recently been a sharp increase in the advancement and use of the theory. One basic advantage of the theory is that if the mathematical model being used holds, the difficulty values of the scaled items do not depend on the particular sample of pupils in the standardization group and the ability estimates of the pupils are independent of the sample of items they were administered. The scaled scores of both items and people are considered to be "sample-free." Thus, once the items are scaled, one can compare the scores of people on some characteristics even though all the people did not take the same items.

There are different mathematical models used to do the estimation. The two most common ones are the one-parameter (Rasch) model and the three-parameter model mentioned in the previous section. The mathematics will not be dealt with here. However, you should note that when items are scaled with the one-parameter model, the pupils' scaled scores will be in exactly the same rank order as the raw scores. However, in the three-parameter model the particular questions answered will influence the scaled score, and two individuals could get the same number of questions correct yet obtain different scaled scores. While this may seem disconcerting, you might note that more traditional scoring has, on occasion, been criticized just because two individuals who each got 15 items correct—but *different* items—received the same score!

Arguments about using the one-parameter (Rasch) model versus the three-parameter model can get quite heated. They need not concern you. The three-parameter model is more mathematically sophisticated but requires more computer time and a larger sample size than the one-parameter model. As mentioned, the Comprehensive Test of Basic Skills and the California Achievement Test use the three-parameter model, so pupils can get the same number of items right yet obtain different scores.

Summary of Developmental Level Scores

Mental ages, grade equivalents, and scaled scores all suffer from some major weaknesses in their psychometric properties and ease of misinterpretation. Nevertheless, there are times when it is necessary to communicate a developmental level to others. If a developmental level score is chosen, one must explain the score very carefully, including a discussion of common misinterpretations. In general, you will probably choose a developmental

level score over a relative position status score fairly infrequently.

TYPES OF CRITERION-REFERENCED SCORES

The preceding discussion has focused on norm-referenced score interpretation—that is, how an examinee's score compares with the scores of other people in an identified norm group. There are instances, though, in which a criterion-referenced interpretation may be preferred. It should be emphasized that the method of referencing is *not* an either/or dichotomy. Often, it may be desirable to make *both* a norm- and a criterion-referenced interpretation of the score. As mentioned earlier, in criterion-referenced interpretation the score focuses on what the individual can (does) do rather than on the relative position of the person with respect to others. For this reason, many measurement specialists (including us) would prefer to use the term *domain-referenced* or *content-referenced*, but, unfortunately, *criterion-referenced* appears to be the most popular term.

In what situations, or with which tests, one should use norm-referenced interpretation and/or criterion-referenced interpretation is a subject of considerable debate. However, most educators and psychologists would agree that to communicate levels of performance on aptitude tests and most personality and interest inventories, one should use norm referencing. It is the relative degree of these constructs that is of interest. Furthermore, the behavioral domain of such constructs as intelligence, compulsivity, and hypochondriasis is simply not defined with enough precision to use criterion-referenced interpretations. For achievement tests, one might wish to use either a norm- or a criterion-referenced interpretation of the scores, depending on the particular decision one is trying to make.

In criterion referencing, the definition of the domain is very important. Without a clearly defined domain of material to be tested, criterion (or domain) referencing of the score is not possible.

The domain (or content) is likely to be most clearly defined on achievement tests of basic skills at the elementary grade levels. Once the domain is defined, it is necessary to establish some procedure that will meaningfully report the level at which the individual has achieved on the domain. The most commonly used methods are (1) percent correct and (2) "mastery" or "nonmastery" scores.

Percent Correct Scores

The easiest scale to compute and understand is the percentage of items that an individual got correct. If items are not all worth the same number of points, the scale can be modified to allow for a calculation of the ratio of total points earned to maximum points possible. If one has devised a test that is truly domain-referenced, it would be theoretically possible to infer from the percentage that an individual got correct on a test to the percentage of the total domain that the individual knows. Of course, most domains cannot be defined with such precision that the test literally represents a random sample of items from that domain. But the more thoroughly the domain is defined and the better the sampling is from that domain, the closer we can come to making that type of inference. (That is, if the test has good content validity [see Chapter 13], a domain-referenced interpretation makes some sense.)

However, even with a good domain definition and sampling of items from that domain, it is possible that the items in the test are more or less difficult than the average of the items in the domain. Ordinarily, we cannot check this out because the total domain of items does not actually exist; it exists only as a hypothetical construct. Further, most constructors of criterion-referenced tests use some sort of item-analysis procedure in selecting items for their test, thus guaranteeing that the selected items indeed do not represent the domain of possible items.

Although percent correct scores are still used with some frequency, they have all the problems that caused measurement experts to advocate abandoning them years ago.

Mastery/Nonmastery (Certification) Scores

One of the most common uses of criterion-referenced test scores in education is to make mastery (certification) decisions. In mastery learning, the basic notion is that students do not advance to new material until they have mastered the prerequisite material. In certification (or licensure) people do not receive a certificate (e.g., high school diploma) or license (e.g., to teach) until they have "passed" the test. The problem of defining what is meant by mastery on a test can be handled by setting a cut score in some fashion. The operational definitions of acceptable performance for certification or licensure are also handled by setting a cut score. Nitko (1983) correctly points out that any test can have a cut score. That does not necessarily mean one can make a criterion-, domain-, or content-referenced inference from the score, but if a test adequately represents a domain, and if a cut score can be set on some defensible basis, then one can say that those above the cut score have "mastered" the material, and those below the cut score have not "mastered" the material at a sufficiently high level.

This whole approach dismays many measurement experts for two important reasons. First, mastery is not really an either/or dichotomy. In most situations, there are clearly degrees of mastery. Second, the methods used to set cut scores are arbitrary. There are two counterarguments to these concerns. (1) Although degree of mastery is on a continuum, we are often forced to make dichotomous decisions. For example, we do need to decide what a passing score is on a driver's license examination. We do need to decide whether an individual has enough knowledge of a current unit of material to begin studying the next higher unit. We do need to decide who knows enough to graduate from high school. Even if everyone graduates, there has still been a categorical decision as long as the philosophical or practical possibility of failure exists. If one can conceptualize performance so poor that the performer should not graduate, then theoretically a cutoff score exists. (2) Although setting a cutting score may be arbitrary, it need not be capricious. Setting cut scores on tests is usually less capricious a choice than many other categorical decisions that are made in life.

In a basic text on standardized tests, we cannot explicate in any great detail all the methods that have been proposed to set cut scores. Summaries of these procedures can be found in Berk, 1986a; Livingston and Zieky, 1982; Mehrens, 1981b; or Shepard, 1980. These techniques can be categorized in a variety of ways. One fairly common approach to categorization is as follows:

1. *Standards based on absolute judgments of test content.* Qualified judges inspect the test content and decide what percentage of correct answers indicates mastery. Several specific methods use this general approach. However, the techniques used can lead to quite different results.
2. *Standards based on judgments about groups.* The standard is set by looking at the performance of individuals in an identified group or groups. If one can identify two contrasting groups—one composed of masters and one composed of nonmasters—they can be given the test, and the cut score can be set based on the intersection point of the two distributions. If one can identify a group of "borderline" masters, they can be given the test and the standard set at the median, thus passing 50 percent of the borderline group. (Of course, one could choose to pass some other percentage of minimally competent individuals.)
3. *Standards based on norms.* The cut score is based on the percentage of students who would be considered nonmasters. To some, setting a cutoff score by a normative approach seems to be contradictory to the purpose of criterion-referenced testing. However, as Shepard points out, "qualitative judgments about the

excellence or adequacy of performance depend implicitly on how others did on the test" (1980, p. 456).

Currently, most standard-setting approaches use some combination of procedures from categories 1 and 3. If you are using tests for which a cut score has been established by the publisher, you will want to look closely at the method the publisher used in arriving at the cut score. It may not be the most appropriate cut score for your specific situation. If you become involved in setting a cut score on a test, we urge you to check the references above prior to attempting such a process—and perhaps hire a consultant who has experience in standard setting!

Summary of Criterion-Referenced Scores

To make inferences from a score to a domain (content-validity inferences), the domain should be well defined, and the test should be an adequate sample from that domain (see Chapter 13). If that is true, one can employ both normative and criterion referencing. They are not mutually exclusive or contradictory to each other. Recently, there has been an increase in the use of mastery, certification, or minimum competency tests. The interpretation of either percent correct or mastery/nonmastery scores seems straightforward. However, remember that both types of scores have limitations. Percent correct scores obviously depend on the difficulty of the items in the test. Mastery scores obviously depend on the method employed to determine what the cutoff score should be.

EXPECTANCY SCORES

In Chapter 1 we discussed the difference between measurement and evaluation. A test score (such as, Richard's percentile is 75) represents measurement. When an interpretation or a judgment is made about the score (e.g., that it is good), that is

DIFFERENTIAL APTITUDE TESTS

G. K. Bennett, H. G. Seashore, and A. G. Wesman

School NORTH PORT HS   Counselor HERMAN DAVIS

System NORTH PORT PUBLIC

YOUR PROFILE OF DAT SCORES

The numbers that tell you how you did on each test are in the columns marked "Same-Sex Percentile" and "Opposite-Sex Percentile." The higher the number for any test, the better you did in that area as compared to students in your grade across the country. The column of percentiles on the left tells where you rank on each test in comparison with students of your own sex. The column on the right shows how you rank on each test as compared to students of the opposite sex.

If your percentile on one test is 80, you are at the top of 80 percent of the group—only 20 percent made higher scores than yours. If you scored in the 25th percentile, this means about 75 percent of the group did better than you on the test. These percentiles do NOT tell you how many questions (or what percent of them) you answered correctly.

On your profile, a bar of X's has been printed in the row for each test you took. The percentile you earned is at the middle of the bar, except in the case of extremely high or low percentiles, where the bar has been shortened so as not to run off the chart. The reason for the bar instead of a single X is that a test is not a perfect measure of your ability. You can be reasonably sure that you stand somewhere within the area covered by the bar.

HOW BIG A DIFFERENCE IS IMPORTANT?

Since tests cannot be perfectly accurate, you should not place too much importance on small differences between the percentiles for any pair of tests. The bars of X's help show the more important differences.

Look at the bars for any two tests to see whether their ends overlap. If they do not, chances are that you really are better in the kind of ability in which you scored higher. If the bars overlap, but not by more than half their length, the difference may or may not be important. To help you decide, consider whether other things you know about yourself agree with this indication. If they overlap by more than half their length, the difference between the scores can probably be ignored; your ability is really about the same in both areas. You can use this method of looking at the overlap of the bars to compare any two abilities, whether they are listed next to each other or not.

Continued on back

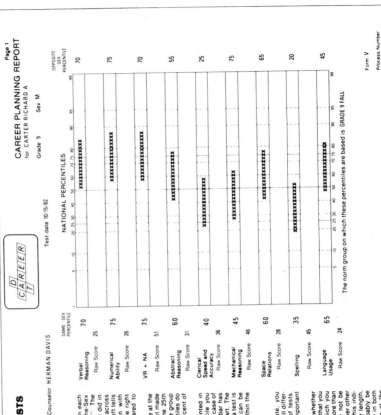

CAREER PLANNING REPORT   Page 1
for CARTER RICHARD A

Grade 9   Sex M

Test date 10/15/82

NATIONAL PERCENTILES

	SAME-SEX PERCENTILE	OPPOSITE SEX PERCENTILE
Verbal Reasoning	70	70
Raw Score	25	
Numerical Ability	75	75
Raw Score	26	
VR + NA	75	70
Raw Score	51	
Abstract Reasoning	60	55
Raw Score	31	
Clerical Speed and Accuracy	40	25
Raw Score	36	
Mechanical Reasoning	45	75
Raw Score	46	
Space Relations	60	65
Raw Score	28	
Spelling	35	20
Raw Score	45	
Language Usage	65	45
Raw Score	24	

The norm group on which these percentiles are based is GRADE 9 FALL

Form V

Process Number 001 0012 001

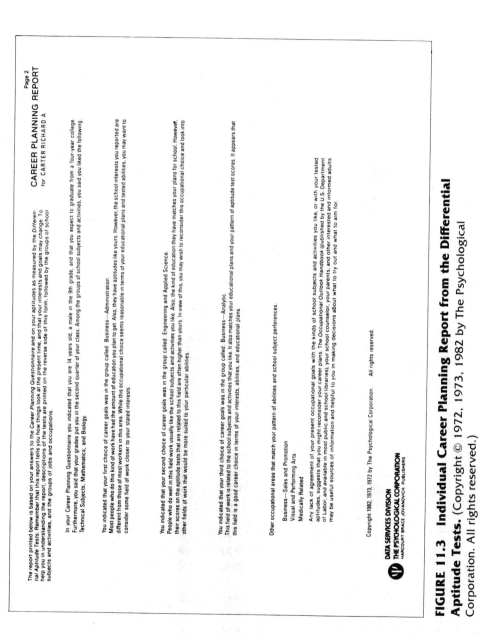

The report printed below is based on your answers to the *Career Planning Questionnaire* and on your aptitudes as measured by the *Differential Aptitude Tests.* Remember that this report tells you how things look at the present time, and that your interests and goals may change. To help you in understanding the report, descriptions of the tests are printed on the reverse side of this form, followed by the groups of school subjects and activities, and the groups of jobs and occupations.

In your Career Planning Questionnaire you indicated that you are 14 years old, a male in the 9th grade, and that you expect to graduate from a four-year college. Furthermore, you said that your grades put you in the second quarter of your class. Among the groups of school subjects and activities, you said you liked the following Technical Subjects, Mathematics, and Biology.

You indicated that your first choice of career goals was in the group called Business—Administration. Most people who do this kind of work have had the amount of education you plan to get. Also, they have aptitudes like yours. However, the school interests you reported are different from those of most workers in this area. While this occupational choice seems reasonable in terms of your educational plans and tested abilities, you may want to consider some field of work closer to your stated interests.

You indicated that your second choice of career goals was in the group called Engineering and Applied Science. People who do well in this field work usually like the school subjects and activities you like. Also, the kind of education they have matches your plans for school. However, their scores on the aptitude tests that are related to this field are often higher than yours. In view of this, you may wish to reconsider this occupational choice and look into other fields of work that would be more suited to your particular abilities.

You indicated that your third choice of career goals was in the group called Business—Analytic. This field of work is related to the school subjects and activities that you like. It also matches your educational plans and your pattern of aptitude test scores. It appears that this field is a good career choice in terms of your interests, abilities, and educational plans.

Other occupational areas that match your pattern of abilities and school subject perferences:

   Business—Sales and Promotion
   Visual and Performing Arts
   Medically Related

Any lack of agreement of your present occupational goals with the kinds of school subjects and activities you like, or with your tested aptitudes, suggests that you might reconsider your career plans. The *Occupational Outlook Handbook* (published by the U.S. Department of Labor, and available in most public and school libraries), your school counselor, your parents, and other interested and informed adults may be useful sources of information and helpful to you in making decisions about what to try out and what to aim for.

Copyright 1982, 1973, 1972 by The Psychological Corporation.   All rights reserved.

DATA SERVICES DIVISION
THE PSYCHOLOGICAL CORPORATION
HARCOURT BRACE JOVANOVICH, PUBLISHERS

Page 2
CAREER PLANNING REPORT
for CARTER RICHARD A

FIGURE 11.3 Individual Career Planning Report from the Differential Aptitude Tests. (Copyright © 1972, 1973, 1982 by The Psychological Corporation. All rights reserved.)

evaluation. The tester could, and often should, make different evaluations of the same test score made by different students. To interpret a test score, the tester should have information about other relevant variables. For an achievement test, one such relevant variable is scholastic aptitude. Many test publishers norm their scholastic aptitude and achievement tests on the same sample. They can then provide a derived set of scores that indicate the *expected* score on an achievement test based on a scholastic aptitude score. (Some publishers base the expectancy score on other variables as well, such as race and sex. The mathematical techniques also differ with publishers. We do not discuss these differences here.)

These expectancy scores help answer the question of whether a child's achievement is as high as could be reasonably expected. Discrepancy scores may be provided showing the difference between an individual's actual achievement and his expected achievement.

Discrepancy scores can be useful in dealing with an individual child. Such scores for groups of children can help in making curricular or instructional decisions about a class, building, or school district. However, such scores need to be interpreted with caution. In the first place, there is considerable debate about whether aptitude tests are really much different from achievement tests. (We discuss this further in Chapters 15 and 16.) They most assuredly are *not* pure measures of *innate* ability. They are, in part, measures of developed ability, and some of the same environmental factors that influence the scores on achievement tests also influence scores on aptitude tests. Thus, we should not form fatalistic expectations and conclude that children with low scholastic aptitude scores are innately stupid, and we should not therefore give up trying to teach them. (Actually, expectancy scores may keep us from doing this, because many students indeed do achieve higher scores than expected, thus showing it is possible.) Nevertheless, because schools do not have control over many of the factors that affect both scholastic aptitude and achievement scores, educators should not unduly chastise themselves for low achieve-

ment scores if the expectancy scores are low; nor should they feel particularly virtuous about high achievement scores if the expectancy scores are high. The discrepancy between expected achievement and actual achievement is a better measure of school impact (or absence of impact) than achievement data alone.

A second caution regarding discrepancy scores is that, since achievement scores and expectancy scores are highly correlated, the difference scores are extremely unreliable. This is particularly important to remember when interpreting an individual pupil's discrepancy score. The difference has to be quite large before we should interpret it as being due to more than chance variation. Publishers usually only encourage you to interpret these scores as significantly different from achievement scores if the differences are larger than one standard error of measurement.

PROFILES

When we wish to present two or more scores for the same person (or groups of people), we do so by means of a *profile*. Of course any such comparison is meaningless unless the raw scores have all been converted to the same type of derived score based on the same norm group. When a test is composed of several subtests (such as multifactor aptitude tests, achievement batteries, or many personality and interest inventories), these subtests will have been normed on the same sample, and meaningful profiles can be constructed. Some test companies norm different tests on the same sample, and derived scores from these tests can also be meaningfully compared.

In addition to a common norm group and a common type of derived score, some index of error should be portrayed on the profile. This has been done in different ways (and sometimes not done at all), as we shall see in the following examples.

Profile sheets should also contain complete information about the test, such as the title, form, and level; the name of the person tested; the date of the test; and the raw scores from which the scaled scores were derived.

Figure 11.3 shows a profile on the Differential Aptitude Test (DAT). The scale used is a percentile scale, but it is plotted on a normal percentile chart. These are profiles for which the scores reported are in percentiles, but the dimensions are such that equal linear distances on this chart represent equal differences between scores. (Note: Both same sex and opposite-sex percentiles are reported.) The distances between the percentiles correspond to those portrayed in Figure 11.1. The significance of differences is discussed in the text accompanying the profile in Figure 11.3. Although this discussion is for the student and is in nontechnical language, it is related to the discussion of the reliability and standard error of difference scores to be discussed in Chapter 12.

Figure 11.4 shows a profile for the Iowa Test of Basic Skills (ITBS). This profile permits the

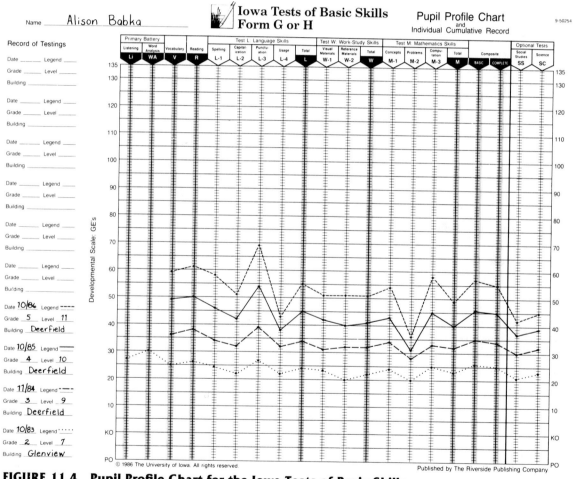

FIGURE 11.4   Pupil Profile Chart for the Iowa Tests of Basic Skills.
(Copyright © 1986 by the University of Iowa. Reprinted by permission of the publisher, The Riverside Publishing Company, 8420 Bryn Mawr Avenue, Chicago, IL 60631.)

charting of growth on the ITBS for an individual across ten different administrations of the test. The scaled scores are really grade equivalents, so a value of 65, for example, means the fifth month of the sixth grade—usually expressed as 6.5. Although this type of profile has the obvious advantage of showing growth, it also has several disadvantages:

1. The scaled scores are spaced close together so that the profile is flattened in appearance.
2. Grade equivalents are used; although these are useful for considering growth across time within a subtest, they can be misleading if one wishes to compare a student's subtest scores at one point in time. (See the discussion under "Grade Equivalents.")
3. No provision has been made on the profile for displaying error of measurement.
4. There is no place to record the raw scores.

Increasingly, publishers of standardized tests will provide computer-printed narrative test result reports to accompany the derived scores and profiles. For example, publishers of the Iowa Test of Basic Skills have prepared such reports for pupils, parents, and teachers. The reports offer information in a form easily understood by pupils and parents and are a useful supplement.

Profile Analysis

In addition to using profiles for making intraindividual comparisons, the tester may wish to compare the total profiles of two or more persons or to compare a single individual's profile against various criterion groups. The topic of such profile analyses is beyond the scope of this book. In general, multiple regression procedures could be used to weight and combine the separate scores so that a best prediction can be made of a single criterion. This approach is simply a mathematical extension of the regression procedure to be discussed in Chapter 13. Discriminant analysis procedures and similarity scores can be used if the tester wishes to determine in which criterion group the individual's profile best fits. Interested readers should

consult such references as Budescu (1980), Cooley (1971), Huba (1986), Prediger (1971), and Rulon, Tiedeman, Tatsuoka, and Langmuir (1967). Discriminant analysis procedures are most likely to be used with interest and personality inventories and are especially helpful in counseling based on the test data.

■ SUMMARY

The following statements summarize the major points of this chapter.

1. Normative data are an important aid in interpreting scores.
2. Norms should be recent.
3. Norms should be based on samples from a larger population such that the sample is representative of the population.
4. The population sampled should be relevant.
5. The type of norm most commonly used by test publishers is the national norm.
6. Special group norms or local norms are often more meaningful than national norms.
7. School mean norms must be used if one is interested in comparing one school district's performance to those of other school districts.
8. Norms are not standards.
9. Norm-referenced scores can be divided into relative position status scores and developmental level scores. Both types are potentially useful and serve somewhat different purposes. Relative status scores are more frequently used and less subject to misunderstanding.
10. A percentile rank for a person indicates the percentage of students' scores falling below his obtained score.
11. Percentiles ranks are easy to interpret, but have the disadvantage of unequal units.
12. z and T scores are derived scores with means of 0 and 50 and standard deviations of 1 and 10, respectively.
13. NCEs are derived scores with a mean of 50 and a standard deviation of 21.06.

14. Deviation IQs are standard scores with means of 100 and, depending on the test, with standard deviations usually (but not always) of 15 or 16.

15. Stanines are normalized derived scores with a mean of 5 and a standard deviation of 2.

16. When scores are normally distributed percentiles, z, T, and stanine scores have the relationship depicted in Figure 11.1.

17. Grade equivalents have several major limitations. The technical limitations are due to extrapolation and absence of any information regarding the shape or variance of the grade equivalent distribution. Practically, grade equivalents are likely to be misinterpreted as indicating the actual grade level at which a person is performing and/or as standards of performance.

18. Mental age scores are subject to most of the same limitations as grade equivalents.

19. Scaled scores are supposed to have equal units, but this claim is disputed by some. Scaled scores are useful for research, but not for reporting scores to others.

20. The criterion-referenced scores used most frequently are percent correct or a mastery/nonmastery classification.

21. Expectancy scores are derived scores usually based on the regression of scholastic aptitude test scores on achievement test scores. Such scores are useful in helping answer the question of whether a child's (or school mean) score is about at the level that could be reasonably expected. Such scores need to be interpreted with caution.

22. Profiles are useful aids in interpretation when we have several scores for the same individual.

23. In order to use profiles, scores must all be converted to the same type of derived score and must be based on the same norm group. In addition, some index of error should be portrayed on the profile.

■ POINTS TO PONDER

1. Can norms be recent and representative without being relevant? Explain your answer.

2. Do the following numbers look reasonable? Explain.

Lori's national percentile	95
Lori's local percentile	85
The school mean percentile of Lori's school	35

3. What additional information might you need to compare your score on the midterm (43) and your score on the final (62)?

4. Given a normal distribution of raw scores, which of the following standard scores is farthest from the mean?

$$T = 65$$
$$z = -2.0$$
$$\text{Percentile rank} = 90$$
$$\text{Stanine} = 7$$

5. Figure 11.3 shows that a clerical speed and accuracy raw score of 36 is equivalent to a percentile of 40. However, a space relations raw score of 28 is equivalent to a percentile of 60. How do you account for this wide discrepancy in percentiles? How would you explain this to Jane and her parents?

Chapter 12

Reliability

- ■ **Definition of Reliability**
- ■ **Classical Theory of Reliability**
- ■ **Standard Error of Measurement**
- ■ **Estimates of Reliability**
- ■ **Factors Influencing Reliability**
- ■ **Reliability of Difference Scores**
- ■ **Reliability of Criterion-Referenced Tests**
- ■ **Reliability and Instrument Construction and Administration**
- ■ **Reliability and Test Use**

As we have mentioned before, we base decisions on data. These data may come from both classroom and standardized test scores, classroom observations, parental reports, student lunchroom behavior, or many other sources. In using the data for decision making, we should know something about the *quality* of the data. High-quality data should be weighted more heavily in our decision than poor-quality data. Technically speaking, data should be reliable, and the inferences we draw from the data should be valid. These concepts of reliability and validity are presented in this chapter and the next one. Although validity is the more important concept, reliability is discussed first, because validity encompasses reliability to some extent and, therefore, the structure of the subject matter makes that order of presentation a little more straightforward.

Most experts in educational or psychological measurement (including us) feel it is not necessary for practitioners to understand reliability in any great depth. In fact, this chapter does not present a very theoretical approach. Nevertheless, the typical reader may find this chapter somewhat more difficult than other chapters in this text. Reliability is, after all, a technical subject, and any discussion of the topic beyond the most superficial will necessarily be somewhat technical.

One of the most important points about reliability for practitioners is that builders of assessment procedures (e.g., classroom tests) understand what steps can be taken to increase the reliability of a set of scores. A second major point is that choosers of assessment instruments (e.g., standardized achievement tests) need to understand enough about the topic of reliability to choose tests wisely. A third major point is that users must constantly remember that test quality should impact the confidence one places on the results, that reliability is an important aspect of test quality, and that no measure is perfectly reliable.

We have, of course, addressed the topic of constructing good instruments in the previous unit of this book. Following the construction procedures discussed there should result in a reasonably reliable test. However, in this chapter we will specifically mention some additional factors that are likely to contribute to reliable measures.

But we have gone beyond that in this chapter. We believe that professionals should be able, for example, to estimate the reliability of their own instruments, to interpret score bands, and to know when difference scores are reliable enough to warrant diagnostic assessment. Those teachers who do not feel that such skills are useful to the professional educator may choose to skip several sections of this chapter. For example, the section on "Reliability of Difference Scores" is more technical than the rest of the chapter, and understanding it is not necessary to understanding the other material.

A thorough understanding of this chapter does *not* require any mathematical ability beyond what was required for Chapters 10 and 11 or more statistics than was presented in Chapter 10. For those readers who have the necessary statistical background and prefer a more sophisticated treatment of the topics, we highly recommend Cronbach (1971); Cronbach et al. (1972); Feldt and Brennan (1989); and Stanley (1971b).

After studying this chapter, you should be able to:

1. Recognize some sources of error variance in educational and psychological measurement.
2. Understand the theoretical concept of reliability as the ratio of true to observed score variance.
3. Recognize that the standard error of measurement can be derived from the theoretical reliability formula.

4. Understand the meaning of the standard error of measurement and interpret score bands.
5. Obtain various estimates of reliability and understand how these estimates differ.
6. Recognize several factors that influence reliability estimates and understand the nature of the influence.
7. Understand and interpret the reliability of difference scores.
8. Understand that estimating the reliability of decisions made from criterion-referenced tests requires different approaches than does the traditional estimations of the reliability of norm-referenced tests.
9. Appreciate the importance of reliability in data used for decision making.

DEFINITION OF RELIABILITY

Reliability can be defined as the degree of consistency between two measures of the same thing. This is more of a conceptual (or lay person's) definition than it is a theoretical or operational definition. What we hope is that a person's scores would be similar under slightly different measurement conditions. For example, if we measure a person's weight twice, we hope that we would obtain almost the same measure if we use a different scale or weigh the individual one day later. If we measure a person's level of achievement, we hope that the scores will be similar under different administrators, using different scorers, with similar but not identical items, or during different times in a day. In other words, we wish to generalize from the particular score obtained to the score we might have received if conditions had been slightly different.

In physical measurement we can ordinarily obtain very reliable measures. This is true primarily for three basic reasons:

1. Physical characteristics can usually be measured directly rather than indirectly.
2. The instruments used to obtain the measures are quite precise.

3. The traits or characteristics being measured are relatively stable.

Even in physical measurement, however, there is some unreliability or inconsistency. If we are interested in determining the reliability with which we can measure a person's weight, we may proceed in a variety of ways. We may, for example, have a person get on and off a scale several times, and we may record his weight each time. These recorded weights may differ. The person may stand somewhat differently on the scale from one time to the next—a factor that would influence the reading—or the person doing the measuring may not read or record the numbers correctly.

Another method of checking the consistency with which we can measure weight is to record the weight of a person as obtained on ten different scales and to compare these values. The values may vary for the reasons just given. They may also vary because of whatever differences exist in the scales. Thus, one would expect to obtain a somewhat more variable (less consistent) set of values.

Still different methods of checking the consistency of weight measures would be to weigh a person on ten successive Saturday mornings (1) on the same scale each time or (2) on ten different scales. With these two procedures one would have an additional source of variance from those already mentioned: the stability of the person's weight from one week to the next.

In all methods mentioned so far, we would be obtaining information about consistency by determining how much variation exists in a specific individual's score (intraindividual variability). This variability is commonly expressed as a *standard error of measurement* and is explained in a later section.

Another approach to studying consistency would be to have a group of people weigh themselves twice (changing scales and/or times and/or the reader and recorder of the measure) and determine whether the relative weights of the persons remain about the same. This would give us an estimate of the *reliability* (or interindividual vari-

ability) of the measure. In educational or psychological measurement, it is often unrealistic, or indeed impossible, to measure a single person repeatedly, so ordinarily no direct measure of intraindividual variability is obtained. Reliability theory, however, gives us ways to estimate this intraindividual variability through interindividual variability data, as we will see in the subsequent two sections. Thus, there are many different procedures for estimating the consistency or reliability of measurement. Each procedure allows a slightly different set of sources of variation to affect the values obtained.

A pupil's test score may vary for many reasons.[1] The amount of the characteristic we are measuring may change across time (trait instability); the particular questions we ask in order to infer a person's knowledge could affect the score (sampling error); any change in directions, timing, or rapport with the test administrator could cause score variability (administrator error); inaccuracies in scoring a test paper will affect the scores (scoring error); and finally such things as health, motivation, concentration, degree of fatigue of the person, and good or bad luck in guessing could cause score variability.

The variation in a person's scores is typically called *error variance*, and the sources of the variation (such as trait instability or sampling error) are known as *sources of error*. The fewer and smaller the errors, the more consistent (reliable) the measurement. With this general background, let us turn to a brief discussion of the classical theory of reliability.

CLASSICAL THEORY OF RELIABILITY

The classical theory of reliability can best be explained by starting with observed scores (Xs).

---

[1]For ease of our writing and your reading, we use the word test, but you should recognize everything said in these chapters about reliability and validity pertains to any method of measuring—including observations, rating scales, and so forth.

These are simply the scores individuals obtain on the measuring instrument. These observed scores may be conceptualized as containing various component parts. In the simplest case, we think of each observed score as being made up of a "true score" (T) and an "error score" (E) such that

$$X = T + E \qquad (12\text{-}1)$$

where X = observed score
T = true score
E = error score

The true score is similar to what some psychologists refer to as the "universe score" (see Cronbach et al., 1972). The true score is unobservable, and the term can be a bit misleading. The true score is that portion of the observed score not affected by *random* error. Any *systematic* error (such as a scale always weighing everyone two pounds too heavy) does not affect reliability or consistency, and so in reliability theory, it is considered part of the "true," stable, or unchanging part of a person's observed score. The assumption that a true score of a person is constant or unchanging may not, in fact, be accurate. Nevertheless, in classical theory, *changes* in a person's observed score are considered to be due to error.

People, of course, differ from one another with regard to both their true scores and their observed scores. Because the errors are assumed to be random, theoretically the positive and the negative errors will cancel each other, and the mean error will be zero. If the errors are random, they will not correlate with the true scores or with each other. By making these assumptions, we can write the variance of a test (or any other measurement) as

$$S_x^2 = S_t^2 + S_e^2 \qquad (12\text{-}2)$$

where S_x^2 = variance of a group of individuals' observed scores
S_t^2 = variance of a group of individuals' true scores
S_e^2 = error variance of a group of individuals' scores

Theoretically, reliability (r_{xx}) is defined as the ratio of the true score and observed score variances

$$r_{xx} = \frac{S_t^2}{S_x^2} \qquad (12\text{-}3)$$

Reliability, then, tells us to what extent the observed variance is due to true score variance. The symbol r_{xx} is used for reliability, because so many of the reliability estimates are computed by the Pearson product moment correlation coefficient (r) procedure. The double x subscript is used to indicate measurement of the same trait. Equations (12-2) and (12-3) are basic formulas from which most of the commonly written expressions concerning reliability and the standard error of measurement (see the following section) are derived. Rewriting Equation (12-2) as $S_t^2 = S_x^2 - S_e^2$ and substituting into Equation (12-3), we get

$$r_{xx} = 1 - \frac{S_e^2}{S_x^2} \qquad (12\text{-}4)$$

Reliability is often expressed in this fashion.

STANDARD ERROR OF MEASUREMENT

Solving Equation (12-4) for S_e, we get

$$S_e = S_x \sqrt{1 - r_{xx}} \qquad (12\text{-}5)$$

which is called a *standard error of measurement.*[2] This is an estimate of the measure of *intraindividual variability* mentioned earlier. Because we often cannot test a person repeatedly, this statistic is typically estimated from group data, using Equation (12-5). It is frequently conceptualized, however, as the standard deviation of a single person's observed scores (from many administrations of the same test) about that person's true score on that test. By definition, the true score (T) of an individual does not vary. If we retested the same per-

---

[2] Other methods for computing the standard error of measurement exist but we do not cover them in this basic introduction.

son many times, there would be some inconsistency (error), and, therefore, the observed scores (X) of this single person would vary, sometimes being greater than T and sometimes less. Making the assumption that the errors within a person's scores—across testing sessions—are random, the positive and negative errors will cancel each other, and the mean error will be zero. Thus, the mean of the observed scores over repeated testings is the individual's true score ($\overline{X}_i = T_i$), where the subscript i refers to the individual.

It is assumed that the observed scores for an individual will fall in a normal distribution about his true score. The standard deviation of the observed scores across repeated testings should become clear if we examine Equation (12-2):

$$S_x^2 = S_t^2 + S_e^2$$

If we think of these values as being obtained from the data for a *single individual* over many testings, then, by definition the true score does not change and hence $S_t^2 = 0$. Changing the notation of S_x^2 to S_{xi}^2 to indicate the variance of a single person's observed scores over repeated testings, we get

$$S_{xi}^2 = 0 + S_e^2$$

$$S_{xi} = S_e$$

Note that this holds only for the case where S_{xi} represents the standard deviation of a person's observed scores over repeated testing. If a test has any reliability at all, S_e will be smaller than S_x for a group of individuals, each tested once, because as a group their true scores will vary, even though for each *individual* $S_t^2 = 0$.

To repeat: The standard error of measurement is conceptualized as providing information about the variability of a person's scores on repeated testings. Ordinarily, we do not give a person the same test many times, because it is uneconomical and because these repeated testings could result in changes in the individual (fatigue, learning effects). Thus, the standard error of measurement is usually estimated from group data. Using group

data and Equation (12-5), we obtain only one standard error and interpret every individual's score using this same standard error. This interpretation could lead to slight misinterpretations, particularly if the group is fairly heterogeneous. The better commercially published tests report different standard errors of measurement for different homogeneous subgroups along the continuum of the trait being measured.

The standard error of measurement has an interpretive advantage over the reliability coefficient in that it allows us to state how much we think an individual's score might vary. The standard error of measurement is often used for what is called "band interpretation." Band interpretation helps convey the idea of imprecision of measurement. (We can think of the band as the score's erroneous zone!) If we assume that the errors are random, an individual's observed scores will be normally distributed about his true score over repeated testing. Thus, one can say that a person's observed scores will lie between $\pm 1 S_e$ of his true score approximately 68 percent of the time, or $\pm 2 S_e$ of his true score about 95 percent of the time (see Figure 10.3). Of course, we do not know the true score, but one can infer with about 68 percent (or 95 percent) certainty that a person's true score is within $\pm 1 S_e$ (or $\pm 2 S_e$) of his observed score. (Note that this is not the same as saying a person's true score is within those limits 68 [or 95] percent of the time. The true score is fixed and either is or is not within the given interval. But we can talk about how confident we are that the true score is within a given interval.) The interval $X \pm 1 S_e$ is ordinarily the band used when interpreting scores to others.

Suppose, for example, that a scholastic aptitude test has an r_{xx} of .91 and an S_x of 15. Thus, using Equation (12-5),

$$S_e = S_x \sqrt{1 - r_{xx}}$$

$$= 15\sqrt{1 - .91} = 15\sqrt{.09} = 15(.3) = 4.5$$

The band interpretation of the above computed standard error of measurement of the observed score would be as follows: If Jeffrey obtains a score of 112, we could be about 68 percent confident that his true score lies between 112 ± 4.5, or 107.5 to 116.5. We would be about 95 percent confident that his true score lies between 112 ± 2(4.5), or between 103 and 121.

ESTIMATES OF RELIABILITY

Now that reliability has been defined and discussed conceptually and theoretically, let us consider the operational definitions of reliability. How do we obtain estimates of the theoretically defined reliability? Given one set of observed scores for a group of people, we can obtain S_x^2. From Equation (12-4) we can see that one must get an estimate of either r_{xx} or S_e^2 in order to solve the equation. Ordinarily, one estimates r_{xx} first and then uses Equation (12-5) to estimate S_e.

The methods used to estimate reliability differ in that they consider different sources of error. Many different approaches can be used to estimate reliability, but the more common ones used by teachers for their own tests or reported in test manuals are listed below:

1. Measures of stability
2. Measures of equivalence
3. Measures of equivalence and stability
4. Measures of internal consistency
   a. Split-half
   b. Kuder-Richardson estimates
   c. Coefficient alpha
   d. Hoyt's analysis of variance procedure
5. Scorer (judge) reliability

Methods 1, 2, 3, and 4(a) all use the Pearson product moment correlation coefficient. It is not obvious why this should be a reasonable estimate of reliability as defined in Equation (12-3). Space does not allow us to present all algebraic derivations. However, given the assumption that the error is random and that the two distributions have equal means and variances, it can be shown that Equation (12-3) is equal to Equation (10-4) for the Pearson product moment coefficient. Thus, a correlation coefficient is a good estimate of reliability to the extent that the assumptions are met.

Measures of Stability

A measure of stability, often called a test-retest estimate of reliability, is obtained by administering a test to a group of persons, readministering the same test to the same group at a later date, and correlating the two sets of scores. This approach is seldom used by classroom teachers but may be used by commercial test publishers in certain circumstances.

With this type of reliability estimate, we can determine how confidently we can generalize from the score a person receives at one time to what he would receive if the same test had been given at a different time. There are various possible time intervals. The estimate of reliability will vary with the length of the interval, and thus this interval length must be considered in interpreting reliability coefficients. Therefore, when stability reliability is reported in a test manual, the time interval between testings should always be specified, as well as some indication of the relevant intervening experiences. Any change in score from one setting to the other is treated as error (it is assumed that the trait measured is stable). This is analogous to weighing a person at two different times on the same scale and ascribing to error the difference in the two recorded measures. The difference may be due to the person's standing on the scale somewhat differently; it may be due to the scale's breaking (becoming inaccurate) between measures; it may be due to a mistake in reading or recording the numbers; or it may be due to an actual weight change (trait instability) over time. In this type of estimate, we cannot isolate which of the sources of error contribute to the difference in performance (weight). What is really being measured is the consistency over time of the examinees' performances on the test.

The stability estimate is often difficult to obtain and interpret in psychological measurement. Many psychological tests are reactive measures (Webb et al., 1981). That is, the very act of measurement causes the person to change on the variable being measured. The practice effects from the first testing, for example, will probably be different across students, thus lowering the reliability estimate. On the other hand, if the interval is short, there may be a strong recall or memory effect. That is, students may mark a question the same as before, not because they decide again that is the correct answer but just because they remember marking it that way previously. This memory effect would tend to make the retest reliability estimate spuriously high. Problems such as memory are usually of less concern for tests in the psychomotor domain, but could be troublesome in tests in the cognitive and affective domains.

Measures of Equivalence

In contrast to the test-retest procedure, the equivalent-forms estimate of reliability is obtained by giving two forms (with equal content, means, and variances) of a test to the same group on the same day and correlating these results. As with stability estimates, this procedure is typically not used by classroom teachers, but rather by commercial publishers. With this procedure, we are determining how confidently we can generalize a person's score to what he would receive if he took a test composed of similar but different questions. Here, also, any change in performance is considered error; but instead of measuring changes from one time to another, we measure changes due to the specificity of knowledge. That is, a person may know the answer to a question on form A and not know the answer to the equivalent question on form B. The difference in the scores would be treated as error. This procedure is somewhat analogous to weighing a person on two different scales on the same day. Here, we are unlikely to have much of a difference score (if any) due to weight change, but a difference could exist because two different scales are being used.

In constructing equivalent tests, care must be taken that the two measures are equivalent in a statistical sense with equal means, variances, and item intercorrelations. But the equality of content is also important. (Sometimes the term *parallel* is used instead of *equivalent* to connote the similarity of content.) The same table of specifications in building the test (see Chapter 4) should be followed for both forms. The items should be of similar difficulty and of the same format (e.g., multiple choice), and administrative instructions should be the same for both tests.

Equivalent forms of a test are, of course, useful for reasons other than estimating reliability. For curriculum and/or student evaluation, the teacher might want to administer a posttest covering the same type of material presented in a pretest. Using an equivalent form, instead of repeating the same test, helps reduce teaching for the test (in a specific pejorative sense), as well as reducing the memory effects noted earlier.

The stability and equivalent-forms methods of estimating reliability are quite different and may give different results. Which, then, should be used? The method chosen depends on the purposes for which the test is administered. If we wish to use the test results for long-range predictions, then we wish to know the coefficient of stability. For example, in order for a scholastic aptitude test in the ninth grade to predict college GPA (grade-point average), scholastic aptitude must be fairly stable. If not, we would fail in long-term predictions. Thus, we desire a reliability estimate to reflect any trait change as error so that our confidence in any prediction would be appropriately tempered by a lower reliability coefficient.

If the purpose of giving a test is not for long-range prediction, but rather for the purpose of making inferences about the knowledge one has in a subject-matter area, then the tester would be primarily interested in a coefficient of equivalence. In this case we are less interested in how stable the knowledge is over time and more interested in whether we can infer or generalize to a larger domain of knowledge from a sample. If there was a marked change in score from one equivalent form to another, then the score on either or both forms is due, in large part, to specificity of knowledge. Inferences to the domain of knowledge from a score so influenced by the properties of a specific sample are hazardous. This fact would be reflected by a low equivalent-forms reliability estimate.

Measures of Equivalence and Stability

People are sometimes concerned with both long-range prediction and inferences to a domain of knowledge. Actually, they are more likely to be concerned about these than about only stability. For example, the measurement of constructs,[3] such as intelligence, creativity, aggressiveness, or musical interest, is probably not dependent upon a specific set of questions. If it is, the construct is not of very much interest. We would like to know whether a different but similar set of questions asked at a different point in time would give similar results. In that case, a coefficient of equivalence and stability could be obtained by giving one form of the test and, after some time, administering the other form and correlating the results. This procedure allows for changes both in scores due to trait instability and in scores due to item specificity. This estimate of reliability is thus usually lower than either of the other two procedures.

Measures of Internal Consistency

The three estimates of reliability previously discussed require data from two testing sessions. Sometimes it is not feasible to obtain these kinds of data. Teachers would hardly ever estimate reliability by those methods. However, it is possible to obtain reliability estimates from only one set of test data, and teachers could well use these approaches. With the exception of the split-half method, these estimates are really indices of the homogeneity of the items in the test, or the degree to which the item responses correlate with the total test score. If there is a high degree of internal consistency, then it is reasonable to assume that had another set of similar questions been asked, the results would have been comparable.

Split-Half Estimates The split-half method of estimating reliability is theoretically the same as the equivalent-forms method. Nevertheless, the split-half method is ordinarily considered as a measure of internal consistency, because the two equivalent forms are contained within a single test. That is, instead of administering an alternate form of the test, only one test is administered; in estimating reliability, a subscore for each of two halves is obtained, and these two subscores are correlated. In most cases the Pearson product moment correlation coefficient (described in Chapter 10) is used. This correlation coefficient ($r_{1/2\ 1/2}$) is an estimate of the reliability of a test only half as long as the original. To estimate what the reliability of the whole test would be, a correction factor needs to be applied. The appropriate formula is a special case of the Spearman-Brown prophecy formula.

$$r_{xx} = \frac{2r_{1/2\ 1/2}}{1 + r_{1/2\ 1/2}} \qquad (12\text{-}6)$$

where r_{xx} = estimated reliability of the whole test
$r_{1/2\ 1/2}$ = reliability of the half-test

Thus, if two halves of a test correlated .60 ($r_{1/2\ 1/2}$ = .60), the estimated reliability of the whole test would be

$$r_{xx} = \frac{2(.60)}{1 + .60} = \frac{1.20}{1.60} = .75$$

The advantage of the split-half method is that only one form of the test need be administered only once.

The Spearman-Brown prophecy formula assumes that the variances of the two halves are equal. If they are not, the estimated reliability of the whole test will be greater than that obtained by other methods of internal consistency. Thus, one of the problems that exists in the split-half method is how to make the split. This problem can

---

[3]Constructs are unobservable phenomena, both inferred from and used to help explain an individual's behavior.

be approached in a variety of ways. But if one really attempts to make the two halves equivalent (and parallel), it requires all the efforts necessary to construct two equivalent forms (except that only half as many items are needed). Ordinarily, the test is split into two parts by a preconceived plan to make the two parts equivalent.[4]

Kuder-Richardson Estimates If items are scored dichotomously (right or wrong), one way to avoid the problems of how to split the test is to use one of the Kuder-Richardson formulas. The formulas may be considered as representative of the average correlation obtained from all possible split-half reliability estimates. K-R 20 and K-R 21 are two formulas used extensively. They are as follows:

$$\text{K-R 20: } r_{XX} = \frac{n}{n-1}\left(1 - \frac{\Sigma pq}{S_x^2}\right) \quad (12\text{-}7)$$

$$\text{K-R 21: } r_{xx} = \frac{n}{n-1}\left(1 - \frac{\overline{X}(n-\overline{X})}{nS_x^2}\right) \quad (12\text{-}8)$$

where n = number of items in test

p = proportion of people who answered item correctly (item difficulty) (If, for example, on Item 1, 6 of 30 people answered the item correctly, p for this item would be $6/30 = .20$.)

q = proportion of people who answered item incorrectly ($q = 1 - p$; if $p = .20$, $q = .80$)

pq = variance of a single item scored dichotomously (right or wrong)

Σ = summation sign indicating that pq is summed over all items

S_x^2 = variance of the total test

$\overline{X}$ = mean of the total test

The distinction between K-R 20 and K-R 21 is that the latter assumes all items to be of equal difficulty; that is, p is constant for all items. If this assumption is not met, K-R 21 will give a slightly lower estimate of reliability. Both formulas are frequently used by test publishers.

K-R 21 is a particularly useful formula for teachers. It requires less computation than K-R 20. Given the number of items in the test, one needs only to compute the mean and variance of the test, substitute these three values into Equation (12-8), and do the arithmetic. Using this formula teachers can, with very little effort, obtain estimates of the reliability of their classroom tests. However, since both give lower bounds to reliabilities, the higher estimate (K-R 20) is always better and should be used wherever possible. Most of the extra labor involved for the teacher is in the calculation of item difficulties, but the information contained in item difficulties is so valuable that we would hope teachers would always want to calculate them anyway.

Coefficient Alpha (α) Developed by Cronbach (1951), the coefficient alpha method is a generalization of the K-R 20 formula when the items are not scored dichotomously. The formula for coefficient alpha is the same as the K-R 20 formula except that the Σpq is replaced by ΣS_i^2, where S_i^2 is the variance of a single item. It is a useful formula to use for a test composed of essay questions where a student's score on each question could take on a range of values. The formula is

$$\alpha = \frac{n}{n-1}\left(1 - \frac{\Sigma S_i^2}{S_x^2}\right) \quad (12\text{-}9)$$

where S_i^2 is the variance of a single item. All other terms have been defined previously.

Hoyt's Analysis of Variance Procedure The important point to remember about Hoyt's (1941) procedure is that it yields exactly the same results as K-R 20 or coefficient alpha. This method has been mentioned here only because you will probably see references made to it in the literature.

---

[4]In consulting other materials, such as test manuals for standardized tests, the reader may see references made to Rulon's, Guttman's, or Flanagan's split-half procedures. If the two halves of the test have equal variances, the results will be the same by using their methods as by using the procedure discussed here. If not, they will give slightly lower reliability estimates.

Stanley (1971b) and Feldt and Brennan (1989) discuss both coefficient alpha and the analysis-of-variance procedures in more detail.

Scorer (Judge) Reliability

In the introduction to this section, we mentioned various sources of random error. We have just studied some methods of estimating reliability that have allowed or prevented various sources of error to occur. Thus, trait instability can occur and is counted as random error if we use stability estimates; sampling error can occur if we use equivalent (or split-half) estimates; and administrator error can occur if two different administrations of the same test, or equivalent tests, are given.

For most objective tests, we need not concern ourselves with scorer reliability. However, for such measures as essay tests of achievement, projective personality tests, and various rating scales, one should attempt to determine how much error may occur in a score due to the person(s) who did the scoring or rating.

If a sample of papers has been scored independently by two different readers, the traditional Pearson product moment correlation coefficient (r) can be used to estimate the reliability of a single reader's scores. If one wished to know the reliability of the sum (or average) of the two readers' scores, she could use the Spearman-Brown prophecy formula given in Equation (12-6). In this case, the $r_{1/2 \ 1/2}$ would be the correlation between the two sets of scores, and r_{xx} would be the estimated reliability of the summed (or averaged) scores. At times, one or even two judges will not provide data that are reliable enough. If more than two judges are used, there are various intraclass correlation formulas that one can use to obtain estimates of the scorer reliability of the summed scores. Since these require analysis-of-variance procedures, we will not discuss them here but will refer interested readers to Cronbach et al. (1972). An estimate of what the reliability would be for the summed (or average) score using three or more judges could be obtained by substituting the obtained correlation for scores of two judges into the general expression of the Spearman-Brown prophecy formula given in Equation (12-10) and letting K equal the total number of judges who will be used to determine the summed score.

Comparison of Methods

Table 12-1 presents a comparison of the different methods of estimating reliability. As can be seen, more sources of error can occur with the coefficient of equivalence and stability procedure than with any other method. Thus, reliability estimated by this procedure is likely to be lower. In choosing a standardized test or in interpreting its results, it is not sufficient to merely look at the nu-

TABLE 12-1 Sources of Error Represented in Different Methods of Estimating Reliability

	Method of Estimating Reliability				
Source of Error	Stability	Equivalence	Equiv. and Stab.	Internal Consistency	Scorer Reliability
Trait instability	X		X		
Sampling error		X	X	X	
Administrator error	X	X	X		
Random error within the test	X	X	X	X	X
Scoring error					X

merical value of a reliability estimate. One must also take into account which estimate is being reported.

FACTORS INFLUENCING RELIABILITY

As has been pointed out, the specific procedure (equivalent forms, test-retest, and so on) used will affect the reliability estimate obtained. Other factors will also affect the reliability estimates. Five of these are now discussed: test length, speed, group homogeneity, difficulty of items, and objectivity.

Test Length

In general, longer tests give more reliable scores. This is true because the random positive and negative errors within the test have a better chance of cancelling each other out, thus making the observed score (X) closer to the true score (T). One must keep this general fact in mind when constructing tests and interpreting test scores. Very short tests or subtests simply give less reliable scores than they would if they were composed of more items. (The same point, of course, holds for all measurement—for example, rating scales, classroom observations, and so forth.)

To estimate what the reliability of a test would be if it were made longer or shorter, use the general Spearman-Brown prophecy formula. In the discussion of the split-half method of estimating reliability, a specific case of the Spearman-Brown prophecy Equation (12-6) was illustrated. The more general expression of this equation is

$$r_{xx} = \frac{Kr}{1 + (K-1)r} \qquad (12\text{-}10)$$

where r_{xx} = predicted reliability of a test k times as long as original test

r = reliability of original test

K = ratio of number of items in new test to number of items in original one

Thus, if a test has an original reliability of 0.60 and if the test was made three times as long ($K = 3$) (e.g., going from a 20-item test to a 60-item test), we would predict the reliability of the lengthened test to be

$$r_{xx} = \frac{3(.60)}{1 + 2(.60)} = .818$$

As previously stated, when $K = 2$ (as in the case of split-half reliability) the Spearman-Brown prophecy formula makes the assumption that the two subtests are equivalent. A more general way of stating this assumption is that the items added to a test must be equivalent to the items already in the test and that the additional items do not cause other factors such as fatigue to become important.

Just as adding equivalent items makes a test score more reliable, so deleting equivalent items makes a test less reliable. A test may have very high reliability but may be too long to be usable. Equation (12–10) can also be used to estimate the reliability of a test shorter than the original. For example, if one wishes to know what the estimated reliability of a test half as long as the original would be, $K = 1/2$ could be used in the equation.

Speed

A test is considered a pure speed test if everyone who reaches an item gets it right but no one has time to finish all the items. Thus, score differences depend upon the number of items attempted. The opposite of a speed test is a power test. A pure power test is one in which everyone has time to try all items but, because of the difficulty level, ordinarily no one obtains a perfect score. (Items in a power test are usually arranged in order of difficulty.) Few tests are either pure speed or pure power tests. However, to the extent that a test is speeded, it is inappropriate to estimate reliability through the methods of internal consistency, and the measures of stability or equivalence should be used.

It is easy to see that in a pure speed test, if the items were split into odd and even, then a person who got n odd items right would get either n or $n - 1$ even items right. (For example, if a person answered the first 30 items correctly, he would get 15 odd and 15 even items right. If he answered the first 31 items correctly, he would get 16 odd and 15 even items right.) If all examinees answered an even number of items correctly, the correlation between the two split-halves would be 1. It would be slightly less than 1 if some examinees answered an odd number of items. Thus, odd-even reliabilities of speeded tests are spuriously high. Typically, other internal consistency estimates also are too high, since some items are reached by some pupils but not by others, a factor that tends to increase the mean interitem correlation. If a test is speeded, reliability should be computed by one of the methods that requires two administrations of the test (or tests).

Group Homogeneity

A third factor influencing the estimated reliability of a test is group homogeneity. Other things being equal, the more heterogeneous the group, the higher the reliability. The reason for this can be best explained by referring to Equation (12-4).

$$r_{xx} = 1 - \frac{S_e^2}{S_x^2}$$

There is no reason to expect the precision of a person's observed score to vary as a result of group characteristics. Because S_e^2 is conceptually thought of as the variance of a person's observed score about his true score, S_e^2 should remain constant with changes in group heterogeneity. But S_x^2 increases with group heterogeneity. If S_e^2 remains constant and S_x^2 increases, r_{xx} increases. Thus, it is important to note the heterogeneity of the group from which the reliability was estimated. If the reported reliability was estimated on a group of sixth- through ninth-graders, and if the test was then administered to only seventh-graders, it

would be safe to conclude that because the students in the seventh grade are more homogeneous, the reliability of the test for those seventh-graders would be lower than the reported reliability.

Difficulty of Items

The difficulty of the test, and of the individual items, also affects the reliability of the scores. Since traditional reliability estimates are dependent upon score variability, tests in which there is little variability among the scores give lower reliability estimates than tests in which the variability is large. Tests that are so easy that almost everyone gets all the items right or, conversely, so hard that almost everyone gets all the items wrong (or a chance score if guessing is involved) will tend to have lower reliability. Items that are so easy that virtually everybody answers them correctly will have little or no influence on reliability. The effect is just the same as if a mark was added to everybody's score. But items that are so difficult that almost nobody can answer them correctly decrease the reliability if they result in large amounts of random guessing.

Objectivity

As already discussed under score reliability, the more subjectively a measure is scored, the lower the reliability of the measure.

RELIABILITY OF DIFFERENCE SCORES

Is Juan really better in numerical ability or in verbal ability? Did Kim gain significantly in reading ability this year? Whose arithmetic skill is better, Jane's or Bill's? To answer each of these questions, we need to consider whether there are reliable differences between two observed scores. We wish to know how appropriate it is to generalize from an observed difference to a "true" difference.

Unfortunately, difference scores are much less reliable than single scores. The errors of measurement on each test contributes to error variance in the difference scores, and the true variance that the two tests measure in common reduces the variability of the difference scores (see Thorndike & Hagen, 1977, pp. 98–100). If two tests have equal variances,[5] the reliability of a difference score can be computed as follows:

$$r_{\text{diff}} = \frac{\dfrac{r_{xx} + r_{yy}}{2} - r_{xy}}{1 - r_{xy}} \quad (12\text{-}11)$$

where r_{diff} = reliability of the difference scores
r_{xx} = reliability of one measure
r_{yy} = reliability of the other measure
r_{xy} = correlation between the two measures

From this equation it can be seen that three variables affect the reliability of the difference scores: the reliability of each of the two measures and their intercorrelation. To obtain reliable difference scores, we need tests that have high initial reliabilities and low intercorrelation. For example, if the two tests had reliabilities of .90 and .86 (r_{xx} = .90, r_{yy} = .86) and if they had an intercorrelation of .20 (r_{xy} = .20), the reliability of the difference score would be

$$r_{\text{diff}} = \frac{\dfrac{.90 + .86}{2} - .20}{1 - .20} = \frac{.68}{.80} = .85$$

However, if the reliabilities of the tests were the same but the intercorrelation was .80, the reliability of the difference score would be

$$r_{\text{diff}} = \frac{\dfrac{.90 + .86}{2} - .80}{1 - .80} = \frac{.08}{.20} = .40$$

As can be seen, the intercorrelation of the two tests can have quite an impact on the reliability of the difference scores. A similar drop in the reliability of the difference scores would occur if the reliabilities of the tests were lower.

Significance of Difference Scores

A commonly suggested caution in standardized test manuals is that a difference between two scores should not be interpreted as significant unless the lower score plus one standard error of measurement of that score is less than the higher score minus one standard error of measurement of that score. In other words, if one uses the band interpretation of scores discussed in the section "Standard Error of Measurement," it is only when the two bands do not overlap that one assumes a significant difference exists between the scores[6] (see Figure 11.3).

In interpreting difference scores, two types of errors can be made: (1) interpreting an observed difference as a true one when in fact it was due to random error (type I error) or (2) interpreting an observed difference as due to chance when in fact a true difference exists (type II error).

A type I error may be considered one of overinterpretation; a type II error, one of underinterpretation (Feldt, 1967). If one follows the commonly suggested procedure of interpreting the scores as not different if the $X \pm 1S_e$ bands of the two scores overlap, then the chance of a type I error is quite small (around .16 if the S_es of the two tests are equal). This kind of interpretive guideline, if followed, increases the chances of making a type II error. Publishers and educators evidently feel that a type I error is more costly, and so risks of making it should be minimized.

---

[5]The assumption of equal variance is somewhat restrictive. A formula that does not make that assumption can be used, but the points made in this section can be better understood using the simple formula given here.

[6]Formulas for computing the standard error of difference scores can be found in the first edition of this text as well as most textbooks on measurement theory.

(See Feldt, 1967, for a further discussion of this point.)

Gain Scores

A special type of difference score that has received considerable attention from many of the advocates of accountability and program evaluation is a gain (or change) score. In education, we often wish to know how much our students have learned (gained) from a particular instructional process.

Statistically, we can estimate the reliability of a gain score by using Equation (12-11). In measuring gain, the r_{xx} would be the pretest, r_{yy} the posttest (which may be the same test or an equivalent form), and r_{xy} the correlation between the pretest and the posttest. One particular problem with gain scores, however, is that r_{xy} is usually reasonably high, thus reducing the reliability of the gain scores. We could, of course, attempt to construct intentionally a posttest so that r_{xy} would be low and r_{diff} high, but then we are faced with the logical dilemma of whether the difference score is really a change in whatever characteristics were being measured on the pretest. If r_{xy} is low, maybe the pretest and posttest are not really measuring the same thing; therefore, the difference is not a gain. Bereiter (1963) refers to this as the unreliability-invalidity dilemma. There are many other troublesome aspects of measuring gain. Refer to Harris (1963), Cronbach and Furby (1970), Stanley (1971b), and Overall and Woodward (1975) for more technical treatments of this topic. In spite of the very real problems in obtaining reliable gain scores, there are professionals who argue that, at least under certain conditions, gain scores may well be reliable enough for certain types of decision making (Rogosa, Brandt, & Zimowski, 1982; Rogosa & Willett, 1983; Willett, 1988; Zimmerman & Williams, 1982).

The major points to be kept in mind are that (1) difference scores are less reliable than single scores; (2) gain scores are in general the least reliable of all difference scores; (3) although difference or gain scores may be too unreliable for use with individuals, they may be reliable enough for making decisions about groups (group means are always more reliable than individual scores because the random errors of the individual scores tend to cancel themselves out, thus making the mean reasonably accurate); and (4) anyone who intends to use difference (or gain) scores for important educational decisions is well advised to study the references given in the preceding paragraph.

RELIABILITY OF CRITERION-REFERENCED TESTS

As mentioned in Chapter 2, the purpose of a norm-referenced test is to discriminate among individuals or compare them to one another. The purpose of a criterion-referenced test is to compare each individual to some standard. For a criterion-referenced interpretation of test scores, student variability is not essential. In fact, if all students received a perfect score on a mastery test, we would be happy. Yet, since classical reliability depends upon the existence of differences among students' observed scores, the reliability of such a mastery test would be undefined.

Let us rewrite slightly the basic definitional formula Equation (12-3) for reliability.

$$r_{xx} = \frac{S_t^2}{S_x^2} = \frac{S_t^2}{S_t^2 + S_e^2}$$

If the variability in true scores is reduced, the ratio is reduced and classical reliability goes down. At the point where S_t^2 (true–score variance) is reduced to zero, reliability is zero, except for the situation where S_e^2 (error-score variance) is also zero, so that everyone receives the same observed score. Then the denominator would be zero, and the ratio would be undefined.

It has, therefore, been argued that classical estimates of reliability are not completely appropriate for criterion-referenced measures, particularly for that subset of criterion-referenced measures called mastery tests. Yet, the concept of a precise measure—one that has a small standard error of measurement—is still important. We do wish to measure with as much precision as possible, and we should have estimates to tell us what precision we have obtained.

Whereas in classical test theory we are interested in the precision of the score, in criterion-referenced interpretation we are sometimes interested in the precision of the score, but at other times only in the precision of the decision. This depends partly on the definition of criterion-referenced tests. Those who intend that the score should be referenced to a domain ought to be interested in the precision of the score. Those who intend that the score should be referenced to a cutting score (standard of proficiency) are interested in the precision of the categorization decision. For example, in mastery or minimum competency testing, our decision is to categorize individuals as masters or nonmasters. We are really more interested in the precision of the decision than in how precise a score is. Different mathematical formulations are needed to estimate the reliability of a decision and the reliability of a score.

As is pointed out in the AERA/APA/NCME *Standards for Educational and Psychological Testing*:

> Estimates of the consistency of decisions are needed whenever decision rules assign people to categories according to specified test score intervals. An estimate of the standard error of measurement at the cut score is helpful (AERA/APA/NCME, 1985, p. 20).

More work still needs to be done in the conceptual and operational definitions of reliability where norm referencing is not used. For both criterion-referenced and gain-score measurements, where we may not be interested in maximizing the differences between individuals, classical reliability estimates may yield values that present too pessimistic a picture of the precision of the scores or categorization decisions. Excessive emphasis

should not be placed on them in judging the technical adequacy of such scores.[7]

RELIABILITY AND INSTRUMENT CONSTRUCTION AND ADMINISTRATION

One of the most important points mentioned in this chapter is that if we are to use data to make decisions, we want those data to be of as high a quality as possible. The reliability of the data—or conversely, the amount of random error in the data—is certainly an important factor in test quality. As previously noted, if the reader follows the suggestions for instrument construction given in the previous unit, and if the administration of the instrument follows appropriate procedures, the data should be fairly reliable. Nevertheless, several points seem worthy of emphasis.

Recall from the previous unit that the *quality* of the questions is important. If one uses questions that are not worded well, the reliability of the test is likely to suffer. In observations, the timing of the observations as well as the recording of the data are important. Although still to be discussed (see Chapter 19), test anxiety and test wiseness may influence the reliability of the data. Educators must be constantly aware of these factors so that they can (1) obtain as reliable a set of data as possible and (2) incorporate their knowledge about the test quality when using the data.

In a previous section of this chapter, we discussed several factors that may influence reliability and that you should keep in mind when constructing tests: test length, difficulty of items, and objectivity.

---

[7]Various formulas have been developed for estimating the reliability of criterion-referenced tests. Discussion of these is beyond the scope of this book. We refer interested readers to Berk (1984), Brennan (1984), Feldt and Brennan (1989), and Subkoviak (1984, 1988).

RELIABILITY AND TEST USE

A question often asked in measurement courses is: How reliable should a test (more technically speaking, any set of scores) be in order to be useful? This question cannot be answered simply. The answer depends upon the purposes for which the scores are to be used. No major decision should be made on the basis of a single test. If the decisions the scores will help make are extremely important and/or irreversible, then the reliability of the scores is of more concern than if the decision is not quite so important and/or is tentative and reversible. If a measure is to be used to help make decisions about individuals, then the scores should be more reliable than if it is to be used to make decisions about groups. If there is very little other information on which to base a decision and a decision must be made, it may be helpful to use a test with low reliability instead of no test. (A test with low reliability may still have some validity and can therefore be useful.) On the other hand, if a good decision (or accurate prediction) can be made without any test data, it may not be worthwhile to give a test, even though it is reliable.

In standardized test selection, it is crucial for the reader of a test manual to be able to understand the reliability information reported. (This, of course, implies that reliability data are reported in the test manual.) A knowledge of the concept of reliability, different estimates of reliability, and effects on these estimates should help lead to such an understanding.

The kinds of reliability data to be reported in a test manual depend on the type of test and on how it is to be used. For general aptitude tests, the most important kind of reliability estimate would be a *stability estimate*. Because aptitude test results are used to help make long-range predictions, it is important to know how stable the aptitude results are. (If the test scores are not stable, they cannot predict themselves, much less a criterion.) For multiple aptitude tests, it is also essential to have data on the reliabilities of the subtests and the difference scores. Equivalence and internal consistency estimates are also of value for interpreting

any aptitude test, because one should have some information regarding the homogeneity of the content and the degree to which the scores are dependent upon particular questions.

For achievement tests, *equivalence reliability* estimates seem almost essential. One wants to infer from the responses to a specific set of items the degree to which a person has mastered the essential skills and/or knowledge in a much larger universe. Moreover, it would be valuable to have some indication about the homogeneity of the content. Thus, internal consistency estimates should also be provided. As with multiple aptitude tests, achievement test batteries should provide data on subtest reliabilities and on the reliabilities of difference scores. Inasmuch as most achievement tests are intentionally designed to fit the curriculum, and students learn those materials in differing amounts and rates, it is not expected that these scores will remain constant. Hence, long-range stability coefficients would be rather meaningless.

For noncognitive measures, the types of reliability information needed varies. For example, if one wishes to use an interest test to predict long-term job satisfaction, then one must assume that interests are stable, and information relevant to this assumption is needed. On the other hand, if an individual wishes to obtain a measure of a transient personality characteristic (such as temporary depression), she should not expect high-stability coefficients. Instead, she might look for internal consistency reliability.

In addition to indicating the type(s) of reliability estimates obtained, the manual must also provide other information. It is essential to know the characteristics of the sample on which the reliability estimates were computed. The sample size, its representatives, and the mean and standard deviation of sample scores should be known.

Standard errors of measurement (and how they were obtained) should be provided. Separate age and/or grade estimates should be reported. Even within an age or grade level, different S_rs should be reported (e.g., an aptitude or achievement test should report separate S_es for students performing at the high, middle, and low levels).

Critics of testing have, at times, complained about standardized tests because they lack perfect reliability. Thus, teachers are often alert to some unreliability in tests. However, they are less alert to the greater problems of reliability for such data as classroom or playground observations. Any user of any piece of data should consider the quality of the data. Reliability is one of the more important qualities.

■ SUMMARY

The principal ideas, conclusions, and implications presented in this chapter are summarized in the following statements:

1. Reliability is the degree of consistency between two measures of the same thing.
2. Some examples of sources of inconsistency, or error variance, are trait instability, sampling error, administrator error, scoring error, and errors within the person.
3. The standard error of measurement (S_e) is the estimated standard deviation of a person's observed scores about his true score. When we know a person's observed score, we can plan a confidence band of $\pm 1 S_e$ about this score and say that we are about 68 percent confident that his true score will be in that range.
4. There are many estimates of reliability. Those discussed in this chapter are categorized as measures of (a) stability, (b) equivalence, (c) stability and equivalence, and (d) internal consistency.
5. Measures of stability are obtained by administering a test to a group of individuals, readministering the same test to the same individuals at a later date, and correlating the two sets of scores. Any change in score from one time to another is treated as error.
6. Measures of equivalence are obtained by giving two forms of the test to the same group on the same day and correlating these results.

7. Measures of equivalence and stability combine the previous two procedures.
8. All measures of internal consistency require only one administration of the test.
9. The different methods of estimating reliability consider different sources of error. Which should be used depends upon how one wishes to use the results of the test.
10. In general, longer tests are more reliable.
11. Internal consistency estimates should *not* be used for speeded tests.
12. Reliability will be higher when a test is given to a heterogeneous group.
13. Difference scores are less reliable than single scores. A gain score, a special type of difference score, is particularly unreliable.
14. Traditional estimates of reliability depend on true-score variance. For criterion-referenced measures, where we are less interested in true–score variability than we are in norm-referenced measures, the traditional estimates of reliability are not completely appropriate.
15. All users of data should consider how reliable the data are prior to determining how much credence to put in the data.

■ POINTS TO PONDER

1. All measurement is subject to error. List at least eight types of errors of measurement.
2. Why should the split-half method of reliability not be used with speeded tests?
3. Which set of values shown below gives the higher reliability for difference scores?
   a. $r_{xx} = .80$, $r_{yy} = .90$, and $r_{xy} = .75$
   b. $r_{xx} = .80$, $r_{yy} = .90$, and $r_{xy} = .0$
4. A test manual reports a corrected split-half reliability of .75. What does this mean? What is the correlation between the two halves of the test?
5. Mary received a score of 75 on her spelling test. The test had a standard area of measurement of 3. What is the 95 percent confidence band for Mary's score?

Chapter 13

Validity

- ■ **Kinds of Validity Evidence**
- ■ **Methods of Expressing Validity**
- ■ **Factors Affecting Validity**
- ■ **Validity and Decision Making**
- ■ **Validity Generalization**
- ■ **Validity and Test Use**
- ■ **Validity of Criterion-Referenced Tests**

Validity can be best defined as the extent to which certain inferences can *be made accurately* from— and certain actions should be based on—test scores or other measurement. The *Standards for Educational and Psychological Testing* (AERA/APA/NCME, 1985) states that validity "refers to the appropriateness, meaningfulness, and usefulness of the specific inferences made from test scores. Test validation is the process of accumulating evidence to support such inferences" (p. 9). Messick (1989) stated that "Validity is an integrated evaluative judgment of the degree to which empirical evidence and theoretical rationales support the *adequacy* and *appropriateness* of *inferences* and *actions* based on test scores or other modes of assessment" (p. 13).

It is useful to think of validity as truthfulness: Have we made the correct inference from the test score? For an inference from a test to be valid, or

truthful, the test must first be reliable. If we cannot even get a bathroom scale to give us a consistent weight measure, we certainly cannot expect to make accurate inferences about weight from it. Note, however, that a measure might be consistent (reliable) but not accurate (valid). A scale may record weights as two pounds too heavy each time. In other words, reliability is a necessary but not a sufficient condition for validity. (Neither validity nor reliability is an either/or dichotomy; there are degrees of each.)

In discussing validity, it is useful to think of two general types of inferences: (1) making inferences about performance other than that measured; and (2) making inferences about a property (behavioral domain) of the person measured. The first is a *statistical* inference; the second is a *measurement* inference (Guion, 1983). When a score is used to infer other performance, we are, in a sense, *predicting* performance. Knowing the degree to which the prediction or inference is accurate depends on *criterion-related validity* evidence (see the following section).

When a test score is used to make an inference about a property or behavioral domain of the person measured, we can think of the test score as *representing* the property of the person. The inference to a domain is a reasonable inference to the extent that the test items do represent the behavioral domain. Tests that represent can further be differentiated as *samples* or *signs*. The distinction is based on the degree to which we can define the behavioral domain being sampled. If the items are drawn from a clearly defined universe, we speak of this as a sample. If the universe is not clearly defined, we speak of the test as a sign. Samples *describe* the domain; signs help *explain* the domain. An example of a test that *samples* a domain would be one in arithmetic computation. Not all possible arithmetic combinations and permutations would be on the test—only a sample of them. However, the inference we wish to make is typically to the total domain. An example of a test that serves as a sign would be the Rorschach inkblot test. The administrator is not interested in inferring how a person will respond to a domain of inkblots but rather to inferring personality characteristics that were not sampled. For tests to serve as samples, we need high *content-validity evidence*; to serve as signs, we need high *construct-validity evidence* (see following section).

Because a single test may be used for many different purposes, there is no single validity index for a test. A test that has some validity for one purpose may be invalid for another.

After studying this chapter, you should be able to:

1. Understand the relationship between reliability and validity.
2. Understand the basic kinds of validity evidence.
3. Interpret various expressions of validity.
4. Recognize what factors affect validity and how they affect it.

5. Recognize the relationships between test validity and decision making.

KINDS OF VALIDITY EVIDENCE

The *Standards for Educational and Psychological Testing* (AERA/APA/NCME, 1985) discuss three categories of validity evidence:

1. Content validity
2. Criterion-related validity
3. Construct validity

Although the *Standards* uses the above three labels, it goes on to say that "the use of the category labels should not be taken to imply that there are distinct types of validity . . ." (p. 9). As suggested in the introduction, different types of inferences can be made, and the justification for them frequently requires different types of validity evidence. Current authors stress that it is important to keep in mind that it is the *evidence* that can be labeled as valid or invalid. We should not really think in terms of different kinds of validity—although we, as other authors, do on occasion use the labels without adding the word "evidence" each time. We discuss each of the three kinds of validity evidence as well as two other terms you may encounter: face validity and curricular validity.

Content-Validity Evidence

As mentioned earlier, one purpose of a test (or other measurement) is to make an inference about a property or behavioral domain of a person. A test serves as a *sample* of the domain if the items are drawn from a clearly defined universe. Content validity is related to how adequately the content of—and responses to—the test samples the domain about which inferences are to be made. This has been stressed for many years. For example, more than 30 years ago, Lennon (1956, p. 294) defined validity as "the extent to which a subject's responses to the items of a test may be considered to be a representative sample of his responses to a real or hypothetical universe of situations which together constitute the area of concern to the person interpreting the test."

Content validity is particularly important for achievement tests. Typically, we wish to make an inference about a student's degree of attainment of the universe of situations and/or subject-matter domain. The test behavior serves as a sample, and the important question is whether the test items do, in fact, constitute a representative sample of behavioral stimuli. The same type of inference and, therefore, the same type of content-validity evidence is also appropriate for skill and knowledge licensure or employment tests and decisions. If a job analysis that demonstrated what skills and knowledge are required on the job has been conducted, it is important that a test adequately sample that domain (see Anastasi, 1988, p. 143).

In judging content validity, we must first define the content domain and universe of situations. In doing so, we should consider *both* the subject matter and the type of behavior or task desired from the pupils. Notice that in Lennon's (1956) definition, content validity is ascribed to the subject's responses rather than to the test questions themselves. Both content and process are important. The test user makes inferences to a behavioral universe. (For simplicity in writing from now on, we call the universe to which we wish to infer, the content domain. Remember, however, the inferences are to behavior.)

There has been some debate about how explicitly the content domain needs to be defined. In some cases, it may be desirable to define the domain as specifically as possible in terms of a complete, finite, set of behavioral objectives. This is easier for some subject-matter areas than others. For example, elementary school mathematics may be more easily defined totally than British literature. The more thoroughly defined the domain, the closer we come to being able to build a domain-referenced test (see Chapter 2). But for many subject matters (or occupations), we cannot define the total domain with complete specificity. This, of course, means we would not have perfect content validity; but it does not necessarily mean

that the content validity is inadequate. A reasonable expectation is that the test constructor specify with considerable detail the subject-matter topics and behaviors the test is designed to sample. As you may recall, we talked in Chapter 4 about test blueprints or tables of specifications for achievement tests. These are two-way grids designed to aid in constructing tests so that all appropriate topics and behaviors will be sampled in the proper proportions. If those grids are carefully constructed and carefully followed in building the test, this will do much to ensure adequate content validity.

There is no single commonly used numerical expression for content validity. Content validity is typically determined by a thorough inspection of the items. Each item is judged on whether or not it represents the total domain or the specified subdomain. Some individuals report a content-validity index as the proportion of items rated as matching the domain or subdomain, which it was originally intended to sample. Although a detailed, systematic, critical inspection of the test items is probably the single best way to determine content validity, such inspection may be a little subjective. Two persons—whether or not they have the same understanding of the content domain—may well make different judgments about the match of the items to the domain. Of course, interjudge agreements of ratings could be calculated (Tinsley & Weiss, 1975).

The task of subjectively judging content validity is made easier if the author of the test defines the universe and the sampling process. Displaying the table of specifications and the number of items from each category would greatly facilitate this judgment. The procedures followed in setting up the table of specifications as well as the methods used for classifying the items should also be described. These procedures might include using curriculum specialists as expert judges and reviewing current texts, curricular guides, and the like.

In addition to expert judgment, there are other procedures for judging content validity. One method, similar to one discussed previously in the chapter on reliability, indicates the close relationship between one type of reliability and content validity. Recall that with reliability we wished to know how confidently we could generalize from the particular score obtained to the score we might have received under different conditions. Likewise, in content validity we are interested in how adequately we can infer from a particular score to a larger domain. In either case, we wish to generalize. Thus, building two tests over the same content, giving both to the same set of pupils, and correlating the results tell us something about both equivalent-form reliability and content validity. In fact, Ebel (1975b) has suggested that instead of content validity, we might better use terms such as "content reliability" or "job sample reliability."

As Brown (1983) pointed out, in one sense content validity is a general property of a test. A test author who defines the content domain and writes items to represent the domain succeeds to some degree in attaining his or her goal. From the point of view of a test user, however, content validity is situation-specific. Does the test measure the domain to which the user wishes to infer? Is there a proper balance among the subcategories (if any) of the domain? It should be emphasized that an achievement test may have high content validity for one user and low content validity for another because they wish to infer to different domains.

For example, not all teachers (even those teaching the same course titles in the same grade) are necessarily teaching the same domain of subject matter. For that reason, they should construct their own evaluation instruments to ensure that their tests have adequate content validity for their particular courses if that is the domain to which they wish to infer. However, if they wish to make inferences to a broader domain of knowledge than that covered in a specific course, then the test should sample from that broader domain. A standardized achievement test may have good content validity for that broader inference.

Criterion-Related Validity Evidence

Criterion-related validity pertains to the empirical technique of studying the relationship between the test scores or other measures (*predictors*) and some independent external measures (*criteria*) (such as scholastic aptitude test scores and college grade point average). Some writers make a distinction between two kinds of criterion-related validity: concurrent validity and predictive validity. The only *procedural* distinction between these pertains to the time period when the criterion data are gathered. When they are collected at approximately the same time as the test data, we speak of concurrent validity. When they are gathered at a later date, we have a measure of predictive validity.

A second distinction is a logical rather than a procedural one, and is based not on time but on the purpose of testing or the inference we wish to make. In predictive validity, we are actually concerned with the usefulness of the test score in *predicting* some future performance. In concurrent validity, we are asking whether the test score can be *substituted* for some less efficient way of gathering criterion data (such as using a score from a group scholastic aptitude test instead of a more expensive-to-gather individual aptitude test score).

Although concurrent and predictive validity differ in the time period when the criterion data are gathered, they are both concerned with prediction in a *generalizability* sense of the term. In criterion-related validity, as in content validity and reliability, we wish to determine how well we can generalize from one score to other scores. In reliability, we are asking how confidently we could generalize to another measure of the same characteristic. In content validity, we wish to generalize from a sample to a total domain. In criterion-related validity, we are asking how confidently we can generalize (or predict) how well a person will do a *different task*. For example, a college admissions test may include verbal analogy items. Admissions officers are not directly interested in how well a student can perform on these items; rather they wish to measure this characteristic because it predicts a relevant criterion: college success.

The distinction between a test as *representing* versus *predicting* is not completely clear. The same test could be used for both types of inferences. A test sampling the mathematics concepts taught in grade seven could be used as a description of level of achievement in seventh-grade mathematics; it could also be used to predict success in eighth-grade mathematics.

Measuring the Criterion In studying criterion-related validity, the conceptual and operational (measurement) aspects of the criterion must be examined closely. For example, suppose we wish to determine the degree to which scores on a certain aptitude test predict "success in school." Success in school is, then, the criterion. How do we measure success in school? Traditionally, educators have used grade point average (GPA) as the operational definition of school success, but most realize that this is not a completely adequate definition. Other criterion measures, such as graduation versus withdrawal from school, are possible. Similar situations exist if we are trying to predict success on a job. In this case, supervisor ratings are often used as a criterion measure, even though they have many inadequacies. If a test score did not correlate well with the ratings, we would not know for sure whether the test did not predict on-the-job success, or whether the supervisor could not rate it accurately, or both.

One of the most difficult tasks in a study of criterion-related validity is to obtain adequate criterion data. Gathering such data is often a more troublesome measurement problem than constructing the test or predictive instrument. *Criterion measures, like all other measures, must have certain characteristics if they are to be considered adequate* (see Brown, 1983, pp. 101–102). First of all, they should be relevant. That is, the criterion measure should actually reflect the important aspects of the conceptual criterion. There is no point in obtaining a criterion measure that really does not reflect the criterion. The degree of relevance of the criterion measure is a value judgment, and not everyone will agree on any specific case. Some educators, for instance, argue that success in college should mean the amount of knowledge acquired after four years in college and that grades are a good (or at least the best available) measure of such knowledge. Others believe that amount of knowledge is a good definition of success but feel

that the grading system employed does not allow one to infer amount of knowledge from GPA. Still others may feel that success in college means marrying well, making good contacts, or something else. To these people, grades would be an irrelevant criterion measure.

A second desired characteristic of a criterion is that it be reliable. Just as test reliability affects the degree of correlation between it and the criterion, so does the reliability of the criterion affect the correlation. A general theoretical relationship is that the maximum relationship obtained between two variables is equal to the square root of the product of their respective reliabilities. Or

$$r_{xy} \leq \sqrt{(r_{xx})(r_{yy})}$$

where r_{xy} = correlation between predictor (x) and criterion (y)

r_{xx} = reliability of the test

r_{yy} = reliability of the criterion

Thus, the reliability of the criterion affects criterion-related validity every bit as much as the reliability of the predictor.

A third characteristic of the criterion measure is that it be free from bias or contamination. Criterion contamination occurs when the criterion score is influenced by the knowledge of the predictor score. Suppose that in September a ninth-grade math teacher gives and scores a test designed to predict success of her pupils in ninth-grade math. If her knowledge of these predictor scores consciously or unconsciously affects the grades (criterion scores) she assigns at the end of the year, then we have criterion contamination. The best way to avoid this problem is to make sure the rater supplying the criterion scores has no knowledge of the predictor values.

Construct-Validity Evidence

Construct validity is the degree to which one can infer certain constructs in a psychological theory from the test scores. If an instrument has construct validity, people's scores will vary as the theory underlying the construct would predict. Construct validity is important for tests purportedly measuring such characteristics (constructs) as intelligence, motivation, assertiveness, compulsiveness, paranoia, and others. A simplified example may help.

People who are interested in studying a construct such as creativity have probably hypothesized that creative people will *perform* differently from those who are not creative. It is possible to build a theory (or theories) specifying how creative people (people who possess the construct creativity) behave differently from others. Once this is done, creative people can be identified by observing the behavior of individuals and classifying them according to the theory. (They could be rated rather than classified.)

Now, suppose one wishes to build a paper-and-pencil test to measure creativity. Once built, the creativity test would be considered to have construct validity to the degree that the test scores are related to the judgments made from observing behavior identified by the psychological theory as creative. If the anticipated relationships are not found, then the construct validity of the inference that the test is measuring creativity is not supported.

A lack of a relationship could occur for several reasons. For example, the test may not really measure the construct of creativity, or the psychological theory specifying how creative people behave may be faulty. Theoretical psychologists are probably more apt to believe that the test, rather than the theory, is faulty. Even though this may be the more probable reason, psychologists should be a little more willing to reexamine their theories if empirical evidence does not support them.

Construct validity is an important concept for the educators and psychologists who are doing theoretical research on various constructs. Those with such interests surely need to delve further into the topic than we have in these few paragraphs. We suggest Cronbach and Meehl (1955), Brown (1983), Fiske (1987), and Anastasi (1988) as good references for further study.

Some authors contend that *all* validity evidence is construct-validity evidence (e.g., Cronbach, 1980). Messick (1989) has stated that "construct validity is based on an integration of *any* evidence that bears on the interpretation or meaning of the test scores" (p. 17) [italics added]. Thus, construct-related validity evidence is comprehensive—all content-validity evidence and criterion-related validity evidence can be considered as evidence for construct validity.

Some authors believe that almost always the inference one wishes to make goes beyond the simple descriptive statement strictly allowed in content validity. A very strict interpretation of content validity is that one can infer from the number of items in the test answered correctly to the number of items in the total domain that one would answer correctly. Recall that the items should sample both content and responses. Strictly speaking, one can infer from a sample of responses to multiple-choice questions to a domain of responses to multiple-choice questions. If one wishes to infer that the student *knows*, has the *ability*, or is *able* to answer a certain percentage of items correctly then, so the argument goes, one is inferring something about an underlying construct (see Linn, 1980). This is a subtle distinction that may at times be useful and at times counterproductive. The difference between performing in a certain way and having the ability (a construct) to perform in a certain way is not one we typically make in everyday language. To infer that a level of performance represents some hypothetical construct may only encourage mysticism (Ebel, 1974a). But the reminder of the *narrowness* of a content-validity inference is appropriate. If a person performs well on a test of addition of two-digit numbers horizontally arranged, we can infer that he would do well on a test with different combinations arranged in the same way. It is probably reasonable to infer that he has the "ability" to add such combinations. If a person has a low score on the test, the content-validity inference to the domain of questions asked the same way is appropriate. It would not be appropriate, however, to infer that the individual could not (or lacked the ability to) perform vertical two-digit addition problems.

The important thing to remember is that there should be some evidence—or at least good logic—for the inference we wish to make. Whether we term that evidence content or construct-validity evidence is only semantic.

Face Validity

People sometimes use the term *face validity*, but it should not be confused with content validity. Face validity is not really validity at all in the technical sense of the word. It simply refers to whether the test looks valid "on the face of it." That is, would untrained people who look at or take the test be likely to think the test is measuring what its author claims? Face validity often is a desirable feature of a test in the sense that it is useful from a public acceptance standpoint. If a test appears irrelevant, examinees may not take the test seriously, or potential users may not consider the results useful. (Occasionally, in assessment in the affective domain, one wishes to conceal the purpose of assessment in order to diminish faking. In these cases, reduced face validity could lead to increased criterion-related or construct validity.)

Curricular/Instructional Validity

The terms *curricular validity* and *instructional validity* are being used increasingly in the literature. Curricular validity relates to the degree to which the test content is covered in the curriculum materials. Instructional validity is a more restrictive term and relates to the degree to which the test content is actually taught. (At times, the terms are used interchangeably.) Instructional validity is certainly important if one wishes to make inferences about instructional effectiveness. We would surely not wish to infer from a low test score that instruction was ineffective if the content of the test did not match the instruction. We could, however, make an inference about the appropriateness of the instruction or curriculum (or the test) based on the match or lack of match of the content.

Curricular validity is considered by many to be important for any type of minimal competency test required for, as an example, high school graduation. It seems unfair to withhold a diploma from someone who did not learn something that was not covered in the curriculum. This seems true to many, even if no inference is made regarding instructional effectiveness.

The problems of obtaining evidence of curricular/instructional validity are myriad. For example, if one wishes to teach for transfer or understanding, then the students should be able to perform on tasks that depart somewhat from the specific tasks practiced in the classroom. How much the questions can differ from the instruction and still "match" is a matter of judgment; but most would agree we should not have to limit the test to questions measuring recall in order to have curricular validity.

It is much more difficult to obtain evidence on instructional validity than curricular validity. The reason is that evidence about a match between curricular materials (such as textbooks) and test questions does not necessarily mean the materials were covered in class or even assigned out of class. Some would suggest that to gather good evidence of instructional validity would require full-time, unbiased observers in the classroom. To "prove" the material in a state-mandated minimal competency test was covered would require full-time observers in every classroom in the state! Such a requirement is clearly unreasonable.

Some individuals even argue that the observers must go beyond observing what is presented since presentation is not the same as effective teaching (Hills, 1981, p. 161). We, like Hills, think such a requirement is far too stringent. Notice that we carefully used the word *covered* rather than *taught* in the previous paragraphs. One, of course, could argue that if the student has not learned, the teacher has not taught. But then, no test would have instructional validity for a person who did poorly on the test! That would be an illogical conclusion.

Fisher (1983) and Hardy (1984) describe the procedures that their two states (Florida and Alabama) used to establish that their high school graduation examinations were instructionally valid. (Other states have done similar studies.) The Florida study included an analysis of content in the curriculum by every district in the state, an audit of the district reports, a survey of all the teachers in the state, and a survey of students who were asked whether they had been taught the material. These procedures were upheld in court as providing sufficient evidence that the test had adequate curricular/instructional validity (Debra P., 1983).

The Alabama study (Hardy, 1984) asked teachers of grades seven through ten to report the proportion of students in their classes who had received instruction on each competency. (Limiting the survey to teachers of those grades was appropriate because the required competencies were considered to be skills typically taught by the ninth grade.) As of this writing, there has not been a legal challenge to the Alabama examination. As Hardy points out, "There is inadequate case law to establish precedent on what might be considered appropriate and sufficient evidence of instructional validity for a test to be used as a requirement for high school graduation" (p. 292).

Content Validity vs. Curricular Validity

Some individuals have suggested that curricular validity should be considered a subcategory of content validity. In fact, an appellate court ruling on the Debra P. case stated that "an important component of content validity is curricular validity" (1981, p. 6770). We think this is a misuse of terms and only adds to some confusion that already exists between the two. We agree with Yalow and Popham (1983), who argue that instructional/curricular validity issues are really issues regarding the adequacy of preparation for a test. As they state, "adequacy-of-preparation is not a component of content validity. Not only is it not a component of content validity, it is not a form of validity at all" (p. 12). In the Debra P. court case, for example, the concern about instructional validity had to do with the action to be taken based on a high school senior failing a basic skills test. Yalow and Popham argue that the *inference* that such a student does not possess the basic skills was not at issue: "Adequacy-of-preparation is not necessary for one to make sensible inferences about what scores signify" (p. 13).

Recall that content validity relates to the adequacy of the sampling from the domain to which one wishes to infer. Frequently, that domain does and should go far beyond the domain of materials actually taught. For example, critics of standardized achievement tests have sometimes based their criticism on the lack of a perfect match between the test and the curriculum/instruction of a particular school. They occasionally argue that because the match is not perfect, there is inappropriate content validity and the test should not be used. This is not necessarily so. It depends on the inference one wishes to make.

To suggest that a test must have curricular validity in order to have content validity would restrict us to making inferences about whether students know the specific materials on the curriculum. As Mehrens (1984a) noted: "At times we wish to infer to the specific objectives taught by a specific teacher in a specific school. More commonly we wish to infer to a general domain" (p. 9). For example, "If parents wish to infer how well their children will do in another school next year they need to infer to a general domain, not to the perhaps narrow and idiosyncratic domain of a single teacher's objectives" (p. 11). Certainly, as Cronbach (1963) observed: "In course evaluation, we need not be much concerned about making measuring instruments fit the curriculum. . . . An ideal evaluation might include measures of all the types of proficiency that might reasonably be desired in the area in question, not just the selected outcomes to which this curriculum directs substantial attention" (p. 680). As Green (1983) pointed out: "If the students have learned fundamental skills and knowledge and understand it, they will be able to answer many questions dealing with material not directly taught . . . generalized skills and understandings do develop . . . Since all the specifics can never be taught . . . this development is highly desirable and tests . . . should try to assess it. This can only be done by having items that ask about content *not* directly taught" (p. 6).

In conclusion, at times we want evidence of curricular/instructional validity; at other times we do not. It all depends on the domain to which we wish to infer.

METHODS OF EXPRESSING VALIDITY

The methods discussed below are used in expressing both criterion-related and construct evidences of validity. As mentioned before, there is no common numerical expression for content-validity evidence, and curricular-validity evidence usually involves a survey of teachers, students, and/or curricular materials. However, it should be kept in mind that one must obtain many indices before feeling justified in suggesting that any degree of construct validity has been demonstrated.

Correlation Coefficients and Related Expressions

The Pearson product moment correlation coefficient (r) is probably the most commonly used procedure in reporting validity. A fairly standard notation is to use the symbol r_{xy} for correlations representing validity coefficients. (Recall that r_{xx} is used for the reliability of measure X.) The x subscript stands for the test score (predictor); the y subscript, for the criterion measure. For example, a correlation coefficient of .60 ($r_{xy} = .60$) between Scholastic Aptitude Test scores (X) obtained in eleventh grade and college freshman GPAs (Y) may be reported. This correlation indicates a substantial relationship for this type of prediction, and, therefore, we could say that the Scholastic Aptitude Test has considerable predictive validity with regard to college freshmen grades.

The relationship between the test and the criterion is often expressed by using some modifications of the correlation coefficient. One such expression is $(r_{xy})^2$, that is, the squared correlation between the test and the criterion. A squared correlation is called a *coefficient of determination*. An often-heard expression is that $(r_{xy})^2$ indicates the proportion of criterion variance accounted for by the test variance. Thus, in the above example, where $r_{xy} = .60$, $(r_{xy})^2 = .36$. Therefore, 36 percent of the variation in college freshman GPA can be accounted for (predicted) from knowledge of the variance of the aptitude test scores.

Another statistic often reported is the *standard error of estimate* ($S_{y \cdot x}$). The symbol is read "the standard deviation of Y for a given value of X." It can be computed by

$$S_{y \cdot x} = S_y \sqrt{1 - (r_{xy})^2} \qquad (13\text{-}1)$$

where S_y = criterion standard deviation. The value $S_{y \cdot x}$ can be used to set confidence limits about an estimated criterion score, just as the standard error of measurement (S_e) is used to set confidence limits about a true score. The equation (commonly called a regression equation) used to estimate the criterion score (Y) is

$$\hat{Y} = r_{xy} \frac{S_y}{S_x} (X - \overline{X}) + \overline{Y} \qquad (13\text{-}2)$$

Of course, in order to use this equation (or compute any correlational data), we must have data for a single group of people on both the X and Y variables. If we have such data, why would we be interested in predicting Y from X? Why not just look at the Y score to see what it is? The answer is that we build the equation from one group's scores to use in predicting Y scores for other similar groups. The group we use for test-validation purposes should not be the same as the group for which we use the test in decision making. For example, suppose we wish to validate the Scholastic Aptitude Test (X) for the purpose of predicting college success (Y) (operationally defined as a college GPA). We would gather data on the Scholastic Aptitude Test for high school (e.g., twelfth-grade) students. We would follow these students through college and determine their college GPA. We would then have the X and Y data. We would use this information for assistance in predicting college GPA for future groups of high school students. If we gathered Scholastic Aptitude Test data in 1988 and college GPA data in 1992 (or more likely, GPA data in 1990 at the end of the sophomore year), then we would use these data to predict college GPAs for the 1993 high school graduating class.

Suppose we wish to predict Melinda's college GPA from knowledge of her score on the Scholastic Aptitude Test. Assume her aptitude test score (X) is 52, $\overline{X} = 50$, $r_{xy} = .60$, $S_y = 0.8$, $S_x = 10$, and $\overline{Y} = 2.4$. Melinda's predicted GPA score would be

$$\hat{Y} = .60 \frac{.8}{10} (52 - 50) + 2.4 = 2.496 = 2.5$$

It is desirable to know how much confidence can be placed in this predicted GPA. Since the standard deviation of the GPA distribution (S_y) is .8, by using Equation (13-1), we see that $S_{y \cdot x} = .8\sqrt{1 - (.60)^2} = .64$. Recall that $S_{y \cdot x}$ is the estimated standard deviation of the Y (criterion) scores for all people with a given X score. In this case, we are saying that the Y-scores' distribution for all people with an X score of 52 will have a mean of 2.5 ($\hat{Y} = 2.5$) and a standard deviation of .64 ($S_{y \cdot x} = .64$). By assuming that this distribution of Y scores is normal, we say that about 68 percent of the people with an X score of 52 will obtain a GPA (Y score) of $2.5 \pm .64$. Ninety-five percent of them will obtain a GPA between 2.5 ± 2 (.64). In setting confidence limits on Melinda's GPA, we can say that the chances are about 68 in 100 (odds of about 2 to 1) that Melinda's actual GPA will be between $2.5 \pm .64$. We can be about 95 percent confident (odds of 20 to 1) that her actual GPA will be between 2.5 ± 2 (.64). We assume that $S_{y \cdot x}$ will be the same for every value of X (this is called the assumption of homoscedasticity), so we would use the value of $S_{y \cdot x}$ found in the above example (.64) in setting confidence bands about any predicted Y score. The 68 percent confidence band is always the predicted Y score $(\hat{Y}) \pm 1 S_{y \cdot x}$; the 95 percent confidence band is always $\hat{Y} \pm 2 S_{y \cdot x}$; and the 99 percent confidence band is $\hat{Y} \pm 2.58 S_{y \cdot x}$.

Before leaving this section on expressing validity using correlational procedures, several other points should be made. Recall two points made in Chapter 10: (1) Correlation does not signify cause and effect. (2) The Pearson product moment correlation coefficient is a measure of linear relationship. If we believe that the relationship between X and Y is not linear, we should use some other measure of association.

Finally, this section and the examples in it were written as if one were predicting a person's Y score (and, therefore, making a decision about that person) on the basis of a single piece of data (X score). Such a situation should seldom, if ever, occur. We used the single-X example because it is easier to conceptualize. Typically, a test user would wish to make decisions on the basis of a variety of predictor data. Equations similar to (13-2) exist to assist us in such predictions. They are called *multiple regression equations*, indicating the use of more than one X score per person. For example, we might wish to predict college grades from *both* knowledge of high school rank (HSR) and the Scholastic Aptitude Test. Both of these variables would then be used as data in the equation. If we thought that other variables would assist in the prediction, we would use them also. Perhaps data on a scale measuring academic motivation would increase our ability to predict. Perhaps data on race or sex would assist. Any (or all) of this additional data could be used in an equation predicting college success. Further discussion of multiple regression is beyond the scope of this book. Interested readers should refer to a book such as Kerlinger and Pedhazur (1973).

At times it is appropriate to use a technique called *multiple cutoff scores* rather than multiple regression. In such a case, a decision may be made "against" an individual who falls below the cutoff score on any one of the measures. Whether to use multiple regression or multiple cutoff score techniques relates to the question of compensatory qualifications. If a deficiency on one characteristic (skill) can be compensated for by an excess on another characteristic, then it is more appropriate to use multiple regression techniques. However, for some jobs, an excess in one skill cannot compensate for a deficiency in another. In such cases, multiple cutoff scores should be used. For example, although high school math teachers should know basic mathematics and be able to relate to high school students, an excess of relating skills cannot compensate for a deficiency in math knowledge, or vice versa. In such cases, one needs to use multiple cutoff approaches.

Sometimes people get confused about the multiple cutoff approach. The data may be gathered sequentially, and the individual being tested may make the cutoff score on all but the last test. Critics will look at this final decision point and argue that the decision was inappropriately made on the basis of a single piece of data. Not so. Several pieces of data were used, but, because of the noncompensatory skills needed, a negative decision can be made if the cutoff score on one measure was not achieved. Of course, it would be permissible (and, perhaps, even wise) to give individuals several chances to pass. How many chances depends on the relative cost of false rejections and false acceptances (see pp. 279–281).

Expectancy Tables

Ordinarily, students and teachers find expectancy tables easier than correlation coefficients to interpret. A hypothetical expectancy table is given in Table 13-1. Column 1 gives the Scholastic Aptitude Test score in percentile rank form. The numbers in columns 2, 3, and 4 of the table represent the percentage of people within each of the five categories of the test who achieved college freshman GPAs of D or higher, C or higher, and B or higher, respectively. Although such a table is usually understood by high school students, two lim-

itations (or possible misinterpretations) should be noted. First, the column giving the size of the group is important. From column 5 we can see that the percentages for the last row were based on only ten people. Percentages based on such a small number of people are subject to extreme fluctuation. Second, the table should not be interpreted as if a person in the bottom fifth (0 to 19) on the Scholastic Aptitude Test has no chance of receiving a GPA of C or greater, or that a person in the middle fifth (40 to 59) has no chance of receiving a GPA of B. The table shows only that of the group sampled, no students fell in these cells of the table. Using a different sample, we would expect to find slight deviations in our predictions.

Counselors would be well advised to build expectancy tables such as Table 13-1 for their own school system. The tables can be very useful in helping students make decisions about college attendance. However, one must remember that just as there can be errors in prediction with regression equations, so there can be with expectancy tables. Like correlation data, expectancy tables do not prove cause and effect and can be built using more than one predictor variable.

Group Difference Statistics

Other methods of expressing validity employ various statistics describing the degree of difference between groups (t tests, F tests, the discriminant

TABLE 13-1 Sample Expectancy Table[a]

(1) Percentile Rank on the Scholastic Aptitude Test (National Norms)	Chances in 100 of Freshman Obtaining an Average Grade of			
	(2) D, or higher	(3) C, or higher	(4) B, or higher	(5) Size of Group (n)
80–99	99	81	32	100
60–79	95	52	12	100
40–59	80	15	—	60
20–39	50	—	—	30
0–19	30	—	—	10

[a]Expectancy table for first-year GPA, based on Scholastic Aptitude Test scores of freshman entering Central College in the fall of 1988.

function, and the percent of overlap are examples of this type of statistic). To compute these statistical values requires more information than is presented in this text. However, the test user need only understand that these procedures allow for a numerical expression of the degree to which various groups perform differently on the test. If we wish to use a test to differentiate (classify) people with various psychiatric disorders (as in the Minnesota Multiphasic Personality Inventory) or to differentiate between various occupational interest groups (as in the Strong Interest Inventory), it is important to know how successful the test is in that endeavor.

The percent of overlap is one of the more common methods used by test publishers to express the difference between groups. If two groups have a 30 percent overlap on a test, 30 percent of the total number of people in the two groups have scores higher than the lowest score in the better group and lower than the highest score in the poorer group. For example, consider two groups, A and B, each containing 200 individuals. The score range in group A is from 1 to 30 and in group B from 20 to 50. If 120 individuals (in both groups combined) score between 20 (the highest score of the poorer group) the percent overlap would be 30 percent (120/400).

Another way of expressing overlap is to determine the percent in the lower-scoring group who exceed the mean of the upper-scoring group. A much smaller percent of overlap is obtained when it is defined in that fashion. In reading studies that report an overlap statistic, one has to note carefully which definition the author is using.

FACTORS AFFECTING VALIDITY

Many factors can affect any of the validity measures previously discussed. Of course, a major factor affecting validity measures is the actual relationship between the two variables being measured. If height is actually unrelated to intelligence, then the *measures* of height and intelligence should be unrelated. However, it is possible for two variables to be highly related but for *measures* of them in a particular sample of people to indicate the contrary. This could occur for several reasons. For example, there may be an actual relationship between knowledge of eighth-grade mathematics and success in ninth-grade algebra. Yet, a test of eighth-grade mathematics may not correlate with ninth-grade success. This might be because the test is too hard or too easy, because the students did not try while taking the test, and/or because the test may simply be a poor test of knowledge of eighth-grade mathematics. These same things could all be true of the criterion measure also.

As already stated, the reliabilities of both test (predictor) and criterion measures are important. The less reliably we can measure either the test or the criterion, the lower the validity coefficient. Recall that $r_{xy} \leq \sqrt{r_{xx}r_{yy}}$. Since r_{yy} is often fairly low, r_{xy} must be fairly low. Another factor is the heterogeneity of the group with respect to both test data and criterion measures. As with reliability coefficients, other things being equal, the more heterogeneous the group, the higher the validity coefficient. Thus, it may not be reasonable, for example, to expect the Miller Analogies Test scores and grades in a doctoral program to be highly related, since the doctoral candidates are fairly homogeneous with respect to both variables. A low correlation due to homogeneity is especially likely to occur when the group on which the correlation has been obtained has already been screened (selected) on the basis of the test (or some other measure that correlates with the test score). For example, if all those who took an algebra aptitude test took algebra regardless of their test score, we would anticipate obtaining a higher correlation between test score and grade than if only those who scored in the upper half of the test could take algebra. For group-difference statistics such as percent overlap, significant differences are more likely to be found if each group is homogeneous but different from the other group(s).

The problem of interpreting validity coefficients on groups already screened or selected is particularly troublesome. Theoretically, in investigating the validity of an instrument for predicting job performance or educational success, scores from an unselected group of applicants should be used. For example, one should study the relationship between the scores on a scholastic aptitude test of all applicants for college and their later success in college. But many colleges will not allow all applicants to be admitted. (Probably no employer would hire all applicants unless there was a real shortage of workers.) Thus, the validity study must be conducted with a more homogeneous group than the group of future applicants on which decisions will be made.

A paradox exists with respect to validity. In evaluating a test to determine whether it will assist in decision making, we want the test to have high validity coefficients on unselected groups. However, if we then use the test data to help make wise selection decisions, the validity coefficient among the selected individuals may be quite small. The more successful the test is as a selection device, the smaller will be the validity coefficient within the selected group—provided that the proportion being selected is small.

If we originally evaluate the usefulness of a test using a selected group, or if for legal or other rea-

sons (see the section "Fairness of Tests to Minority Groups" in Chapter 22) we are forced after the fact (i.e., we have used it for selection purposes) to prove the test is valid, the good use of a test decreases the validity coefficient. That is, if we accurately select out those who will not succeed and select in only those who will succeed, we are decreasing the validity coefficient among the selected in-group. As Fricke (1975) points out, good personnel practices will produce low correlation coefficients among the selected individuals. Unfortunately, many users of tests do not understand this and at times incorrectly assume that low correlations among selected individuals indicate that the test was invalid for making the original selection decisions.

In addition to the decreased correlation due to the restriction of range that occurs following selection, the shape or form of the relationship between the predictor and criterion variables also plays an important role. The scattergrams in Figure 13.1 illustrate these points. Let X be the predictor and Y the criterion. Assume that the horizontal line a represents the minimum criterion score necessary to consider an individual successful. Let the vertical line b represent the predictor score necessary to be selected. The elongation

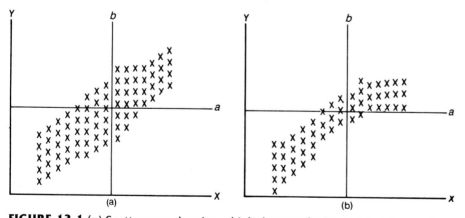

FIGURE 13.1 (a) Scattergram showing a high degree of relationship between X and Y for total range of X scores and a smaller degree of relationship for scores to the right of line b. (b) Scattergram showing a high degree of relationship for the total range of X scores and zero relationship for scores to the right of line b.

(very little scatter around a line) and general slope of the oval shapes indicate the degree of relationship between X and Y. If the pattern of scores is quite elongated and sloping, the correlation is high. If there is considerable scatter, the relationship is low. If the slope is zero, there is no relationship. In Figure 13.1a and b the overall correlation between X and Y is quite high (although for Figure 13.1b, we would not use the Pearson product moment correlation coefficient). After restricting the range through selection, we have a much lower degree of relationship in Figure 13.1a, but it is still positive. There is essentially no relationship between X and Y in Figure 13.1b after selection (for scores to the right of line b). This would be the case in situations where one needed a certain amount of characteristic X in order to be successful in endeavor Y, but "more of X" would not help a person to be more successful in Y. This might be true, for example, if X was a measure of reading comprehension and Y a job requiring that one can read well enough to comprehend instruction manuals but in which further skills in reading are irrelevant. One could validly use the reading test to select out those who could not read at a high enough level to perform their tasks. But, after the test was wisely used for that purpose, there would be no correlation between X and Y for those accepted applicants.

Thus, we see that just as the size of the reliability coefficient can be affected by so many variables, so too can the validity measures. To interpret validity data correctly, it is necessary to be aware of these various factors.

Let us take one more example to illustrate these interpretation problems. Suppose a correlation of 0.20 is found between college GPA and some measure of success as a teacher. (In this example, GPA is the predictor variable X, and success as a teacher is the criterion variable Y.) How should this fairly low correlation be interpreted? Those not aware of the factors discussed in this subsection might assume that the data indicate that knowledge of subject matter is irrelevant to teaching success. This assumption, of course, is a possibility, but there are many other possible (and more likely) reasons for the low correlation. Perhaps grades do not actually measure knowledge of subject matter. Perhaps our measure of teaching success does not actually measure what we really mean when we think of a successful teacher. Perhaps our measure of either X or Y is unreliable. Perhaps our sample is too restricted in range on either the X or the Y variable. Or perhaps a relationship exists such as that depicted in Figure 13.1b, and we have only graduated (or hired) teachers to the right of line b. (Perhaps once teachers know enough mathematics they can teach it; but to know a lot more advanced mathematics is irrelevant for teaching success.)

Before we could reasonably infer which of these "perhaps" statements is most likely, we would need information on the grading practices of the college, the reliability of the GPAs, the reliability and at least the content validity of the measure of teaching success, and the variability of the sample studied on each measure. To really know empirically the degree to which knowledge of subject matter influences teaching success, one would have to be willing to let people teach with all degrees of knowledge from none on up. Rather than do that, many of us probably would rather assume that one can logically infer that knowledge of subject matter is related to teaching success and that the low correlation cited above is due to one or more of the many factors discussed.

VALIDITY AND DECISION MAKING

Let us assume that a test manual reports a correlation coefficient of 0.50 between scores obtained on a mathematical aptitude test administered in the eighth grade and scores in a ninth-grade algebra course. Will this information have any effect on the kind(s) of educational decisions made? What if the school's policy is to have all students take ninth-grade algebra in heterogeneous classes? In this case, the benefits derived from the test score information could be used only for instructional purposes. If the school's policy is to have all students take ninth-grade algebra and if students are also grouped homogeneously, then the test score information can be used for both instructional and administrative purposes. If the school's policy is to permit students to select either ninth-grade algebra or general math, then the test score information could be used for instructional, administrative, and counseling purposes. For any of these decisions—instructional, guidance, or administrative—the important question is whether or not better decisions could be made by using test score results in addition to other data already available (e.g., teacher recommendations and previous school grades). This is an empirical question, one we would not necessarily expect the ordinary classroom teacher or counselor to answer. However, all educators should be cognizant of the following factors that are likely to make test score information useful and efficient.

1. *Availability of other data.* Tests should be used only if better decisions can be made with the data than the best decisions one would make without them. This improvement in decision making is often referred to as incremental validity. How much better the decisions would be using the data than if they were based on chance alone is not the relevant consideration. One never, or almost never, is forced to make an educational decision on the basis of no information. If fairly valid decisions can be made without test data, then the probability that the test data will improve the accuracy of the decision decreases. If the probability of making a correct decision without the test data is very low, then it may well be beneficial to give the test, even though it has only a modest correlation with the criterion.

2. *Cost of testing and faulty decisions.* Decisions are subject to two kinds of errors: (1) *false rejections,* that is, predicting failure when success would have occurred, and (2) *false acceptances,* that is, predicting success when failure is the result.[1] The value of a test is dependent upon the differ-

ence between the cost of testing (including such factors as the cost of purchasing the test, student and examiner time, and scoring) and the saving in the cost of errors that result from using the test. In the algebra example, a student could take algebra and fail or not take algebra, even though he could have passed it. The decision whether the test information is worth gathering depends upon the cost of these errors and whether the reduction in these costs by using the test is greater than the cost of gathering the data. The concepts of available data, incremental validity, and cost effectiveness often lead to *sequential* testing and decision making. In the algebra example, one may well be willing to use already available data, such as previous grades, to make decisions for a fair number of individuals. For example, in a particular school one may decide that all students with less than a B average in seventh- and eighth-grade math should not take algebra. There may be another set of students for whom the school personnel are willing to recommend ninth-grade algebra without the knowledge obtained from a mathematical aptitude test. Only those students for whom a decision could not be made would take the aptitude test. In general, in sequential testing and decision making, one uses already available data first for some initial decisions, gathers relevant data that are fairly moderate in cost for additional decision making, and uses expensive data-gathering techniques to make decisions about only a few individuals. Figure 13.2 illustrates a basic sequential decision-making strategy. As mentioned earlier, one of the misunderstandings about sequential decision making is that some people only look at the last data point in the sequence and think the decision was made on only a single piece of data. Actually, sequential decision making usually results in *more* data being collected; one can often afford to gather *more* types of data for the same cost because not all data are gathered for all individuals. (Although we have used an educational example, all of these same principles apply to employment testing also.)

Once data are gathered, the decision regarding where to set the cutoff score depends on the relative cost of the two errors. If a false rejection is

---

[1] Some authors use the terms *false positives* and *false negatives* for these two errors. The terms used here seem less confusing.

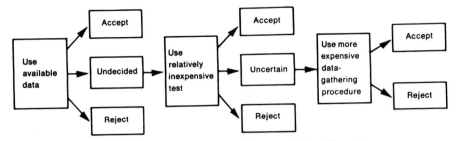

FIGURE 13.2 A Basic Sequential Decision-making Strategy.

expensive as compared to a false acceptance, then the cutoff score should be lower (i.e., the selection ratio should be higher) than if the reverse is true. Suppose, for example, we have the relationship between Y (success in college defined as GPA equal to or greater than 2.0) and X (some numerical value derived from a combination of variables such as test score information or past grades) represented by the scattergram shown in Figure 13.3a. Here, each tally above the horizontal line (defining success in college) and to the left of $X = 4$ (the minimum admission score) would represent

a false rejection. Every score below the horizontal line and to the right of the X cutoff score would be a false acceptance. The other tallies would represent correct decisions.

If the decision maker considered the costs of the two kinds of errors to be equal, then the proper approach would be to minimize the total errors and, therefore, to set the cutting score at 4, as is shown in Figure 13.3a. This would give six false rejections and five false acceptances (or 11 total errors). If, however, it was decided that false rejections are three times as costly as false accep-

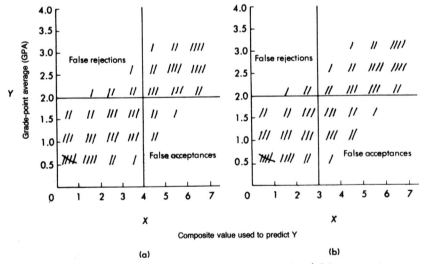

FIGURE 13.3 Scattergrams depicting (for the same data) false acceptances and false rejections for cutting scores of 4 and 3, respectively, when a GPA of 2.0 is required for success.

tances (in terms of loss to society, for example), then the cutoff score should be changed. If the cut-off score were kept at 4, we would have

6 false rejections
 at a cost of 3 units each = 18 cost units
5 false acceptances
 at a cost of 1 unit each =   5 cost units
                            23 cost units

A cutoff score of 3, as in Figure 13.3b, would produce 15 total errors but only 21 cost units, as follows:

3 false rejections
 at a cost of 3 units each = 9 cost units
12 false acceptances
 at a cost of 1 unit each = 12 cost units
                            21 cost units

This simple example illustrates again that test information does not make decisions but is used (often in conjunction with other information) to help set probability values. Many decision strategies other than the simple one illustrated here might be adopted. In some cases, for example, one might decide that false rejections are not costing anything and might simply wish to obtain the highest possible ratio of successes to failures among those selected. Or, more likely (especially in industry), one may wish to maximize some *mean level of output* and thus would not simply count a success as a success but would weight the degrees of success differentially (likewise for failures). In the latter case, the employer would decide whether the cost of testing is worthwhile by comparing the mean utility value for all those hired using the test to help make decisions versus the mean utility value of those who would be hired without the test data. If this *difference* is greater than the cost of the test, then it is cost-effective to give the test. The general point to keep in mind is that once we have set some utility values on the various outcomes of the alternatives, we can combine probabilities and utilities to arrive at better decisions. Of course, we need to keep in mind that

although from a theoretical measurement point of view we ideally obtain data such as the data presented in Figure 13.3, we often do not in practice. Typically, colleges simply do not admit, and industries do not hire, people below the cutting score. Thus, we do not know what the data to the left of the cutting-score line are really like. It is possible to mathematically make estimates of these data. One report (USES, 1983), for example, estimates that by using the General Aptitude Test Battery for maximal decision making, the U.S. Employment Service could "help improve the productivity of American industry on the order of 50 to 100 billion dollars" per year (p. v).

3. Selection ratio. In the example dealing with ninth-grade algebra, it was pointed out that if all students were required to take ninth-grade algebra, the test data would be of no value for selection purposes. If conditions are such that almost everyone is to be selected, then the data will not be so valuable in selection decisions as in cases where the selection ratio is lower.

4. Success ratio. Another factor affecting whether test data are likely to improve decision making is the success ratio (the proportion of people selected who succeed). The success ratio depends in part upon the selection ratio. Other things being equal, the smaller the selection ratio, the larger the success ratio. The success ratio, however, is also highly dependent upon base rates (Meehl & Rosen, 1955). "Base rates" refers to the proportion of people in the general population who fall in a certain category. If 99 percent of the general ninth-grade population can succeed in ninth-grade algebra, one can predict success with 99 percent accuracy simply by predicting success for everyone. It would take a very valid test to enable one to predict more accurately than that. If only 1 percent can succeed, an analogous situation exists. Base rates in clinical psychology are often so high or low (e.g., the proportion of people who commit suicide) that tests cannot improve prediction. In educational decisions, the base rates are often somewhat closer to 50 percent, the value that best enables a test score to improve the predictive accuracy.

VALIDITY GENERALIZATION

An important issue in educational and employment settings is the degree to which criterion-related evidence of validity that is obtained in one situation can be generalized (that is, transported and used) to another situation without further study of validity in the new situation. If generalization is limited, then local criterion-related evidence of validity may be necessary in most situations in which a test is used. If generalization is extensive, then situation-specific evidence of validity may not be required (AERA/APA/NCME, 1985, p. 12).

Historically, there has been a belief that the validity of an inference from a test (at least in an industrial setting) should be situation-specific. Thus, people making criterion-related validity inferences from test scores were encouraged to conduct their own local validation studies. The evidence for the belief in situational validity was that validity coefficients varied considerably across situations. More recently, that belief has been challenged. Many analysts have concluded that the reasons for the varying and usually quite modest correlations were the result of statistical artifacts, inherent in (1) sampling error due to small sample sizes, (2) criterion and test unreliability, and (3) restriction in the range of test scores.

In a 1979 conference on validity, Hunter (1980), a leading advocate of and researcher on validity generalization, began his presentation as follows: "I have come not to present theories but to verify them" (p. 119). In that paper, he made a strong argument, backed by evidence, for the belief in validity generalization. In general, the audience was receptive but felt that perhaps Hunter was overly enthusiastic. As Novick (1980) pointed out: "I think you have taken us down the right road—perhaps a bit too far" (p. 126).

Subsequent to that 1979 meeting, a fair amount of additional research has been done on validity

generalization, and many industrial psychologists currently believe that local validation is no longer *necessarily* required. Recent research results suggest that test validity is, in fact, stable across jobs and settings. A U.S. Employment Service report has provided evidence to suggest that "cognitive ability is a valid predictor of job performance for all jobs" (USES, 1983, p. 14).

While we support the notions of validity generalization, we do think it possible for local users to put too much faith in such a notion. The *Standards* seems to put the issue into a nice perspective:

> The extent to which predictive or concurrent evidence of validity generalization can be used as criterion-related evidence in new situations is in large measure a function of accumulated research. Consequently, although evidence of generalization can often be used to support a claim of validity in a new situation, the extent to which this claim is justified is constrained by the available data (AERA/APA/NCME, 1985, p. 12).

Standard 1.16 states that

> When adequate local validation evidence is not available, criterion-related evidence of validity for a specified test use may be based on validity generalization from a set of prior studies, provided that the specified test use situation can be considered to have been drawn from the same population of situations on which validity generalization was conducted (AERA/APA/NCME, 1985, p. 16).

For a local user of test data, the sensible way to go is to gather local validation data if feasible. If not feasible, assume you can generalize to your specific inference only if prior studies suggest that such generalization is appropriate. We believe that a great deal of relevant evidence exists. However, at this time, the evidence is probably greater for educational users than it is for industrial/employment uses of tests. (Actually, the evidence is almost overwhelming with respect to tests predicting success in future educational endeavors. A test that predicts success in one school almost invariably predicts success in another school.)

VALIDITY AND TEST USE

Just as people wish to know how reliable a test should be, they also wish to know how valid a test should be. The same answer must be given: It depends upon the purposes for which the test is to be used. Naturally, one should select the best test possible. Suppose, however, that no test allows us to make very valid inferences for our purposes. Does that mean we should not test? To decide, we must answer the incremental validity question raised in the preceding section: How much better a decision can we make by using the test information in addition to all other information, than we could make just from the other data alone? Once that question is answered, we must inquire whether this increase in accuracy of prediction is sufficiently greater to justify the use of the test. Theoretically, this can be answer by cost-analysis procedures if we could specify the cost of faulty decisions. It is stressed here that, in education, a test is seldom used to assist in only one decision. As Cronbach (1971) has stated: "... in educational testing the information is usually placed in the student's file and used for many later decisions: admission, choice of major, selection of courses, career planning, etc. A test with multiple uses can repay a cost that would be unreasonable if a test were to be used once and forgotten" (p. 496).

Validity is a matter of degree, and a test has many validates, each dependent upon the specific purposes for which the test is used. Eventually, the validity of any test is dependent upon how it is used in the local situation; therefore, educators and personnel directors should, where feasible, consider conducting their own validity studies (although, as mentioned, the evidence for validity generalization is impressive).

Publishers of standardized tests also have a responsibility to conduct and report research on the validity of a test. Just as for reliability, the kinds and extent of validity data that one should expect to find in a test manual depend upon the type of test and the use(s) the publishers advocate for it. As discussed previously, for achievement tests, content-validity evidence is by far the most important type of validity evidence. Depending upon their use, aptitude, interest, and personality measures should probably have evidence of criterion-related validity. If one wishes to use test data as evidence to support or refute a psychological theory, then construct-validity evidence is necessary.

In addition to reporting the type(s) of validity evidence, the manual must also provide other relevant information. The characteristics of the group(s) from which the evidence was obtained must be reported in detail. Tables of specifications and their rationale should be given in support of content-validity claims, standard errors of estimates should be reported for validity coefficients, and a large number of studies should be reported if a claim is to be made for construct validity.

Three points should be reemphasized in reference to validity and test use. First, it is extremely unlikely that any test will ever have perfect validity for any decision. Some errors are bound to occur. Our goal is to minimize errors in decision making; but one should *not* conclude that a test is invalid because it is possible to point to incorrect inferences made with the use of test data (e.g., "I scored 88 on an intelligence test and a counselor told me I couldn't succeed in college, but I now have a Ph.D; therefore, all intelligence tests are invalid."). The crucial question in validity is *not* whether errors will be made in individual cases— the answer is invariably "Yes." The crucial question is whether fewer errors will be made by using a test in addition to other data than would be made using the other data.

Second, although the examples used here have tended to be for selection decisions, remember that many decisions are for placement or classification rather than selection. It is useful for all these kinds of decisions to have some data supporting the criterion-related validity of a test. But sometimes, discriminant statistics are more relevant than correlational data.

Finally, when we gather information that will be useful in decision making, we are, in one sense of the word, using the data to make predictions. We predict what will occur if we decide on various alternative strategies. In education, we would be well advised to concentrate on how to upset negative predictions. We typically use the predictive information primarily for directing action toward desirable outcomes rather than for making a passive prediction. This goes along with what we said earlier about the difference in predictive validity before using the test and the predictive validity after using the test data for wise decision making. We should be striving to use adaptive strategies that will result in upsetting negative predictions that would have resulted under traditional treatments. But to do this we need to have the test data in order to identify which students need special attention. If we can use the data to make decisions that result in positive outcomes for those for whom we *originally* predicted negative outcomes, we should feel gratified. But we should not conclude from this that the test either was not valid or did not serve a useful function. The test did just what it was designed to do—identify individuals who needed special attention.

VALIDITY OF CRITERION-REFERENCED TESTS

The issue of the validity, like the reliability, of criterion-referenced tests has been a source of considerable disagreement among psychometricians. Since criterion-referenced tests are used primarily in the area of achievement testing, a major concern is the content validity of the test. In this respect, criterion-referenced tests should always match or exceed norm-referenced tests. Why? Because the universe of behaviors or achievement is usually more narrowly defined in criterion-referenced tests, and the rules for sampling from this universe (item-generating rules) are often more precisely defined. The content validity of crite-

rion-related tests thus constructed ought to be almost assured. Such a test would have what Mosier (1947) termed *validity by definition* or what Ebel (1961) referred to as *meaningfulness*.

However, if results of criterion-referenced tests are to be used in instructional decision making, some empirical (criterion-related) validity evidence must be provided.[2] We practically always wish to "generalize beyond the universe of content defined by the item generating rules" (Jackson, 1970, p. 13). For example, if one is using the results of a mastery test to decide whether to allow a student to proceed with the next unit of study, some evidence ought to be provided to show that people just below the cutoff score do not do so well in the subsequent material as people above the cutoff score.

If one uses correlational approaches to establish the criterion-related (predictive or concurrent) validity of criterion-referenced tests, the potentially small variability of criterion-referenced test scores (discussed earlier) will attenuate the validity coefficient just as it would the reliability coefficient. For this reason, the group difference statistical approaches are likely to be more useful. (See Hambleton & Novick, 1973; Harris et al., 1974; Millman, 1974; Swaminathan et al., 1975; and Linn, 1980, for more complete discussions of the validity of criterion-referenced tests.)

■ SUMMARY

The principal ideas, conclusions, and implications presented in this chapter are summarized in the following statements:

1. Reliability is a necessary but not sufficient condition for validity.
2. Validity can be defined as the degree to which certain inferences can be made from test

---

[2] The terms *criterion-referenced testing* and *criterion-related* can be confused. *Criterion* has a different meaning in each term. In the former, it refers to some measure of proficiency on the test itself; in the latter, it refers to a different characteristic, which is estimated from the test score.

scores (or other measurements). Since a single test may have many different purposes, there is no single validity index for a test.

3. Validity evidence is typically categorized into three kinds: content, criterion-related, and construct-validity evidence.

4. Content-validity evidence is related to how adequately the content of the test samples the domain about which inferences are to be made.

5. Criterion-related validity evidence pertains to the technique of studying the relationship between the test scores and independent, external criterion measures.

6. In order to study criterion-related validity, it is important to have a good measure of the criterion. This measure should be relevant, reliable, and free from bias.

7. Construct validity is the degree to which the test scores can be accounted for by certain explanatory constructs.

8. *Curricular validity* and *instructional validity* are terms used to express the degree to which test material has been covered in the curriculum or has actually been taught. They are not validity at all in the conventional sense of the term.

9. Various methods of expressing validity include the correlation coefficient, the coefficient of determination, the standard error of estimate, and expectancy tables.

10. Various factors affect validity—for example, reliabilities of the predictor and criterion measures, group heterogeneity, and shape of the relationship.

11. Various factors affect whether a test is valid enough to be useful in decision making—for example, availability of other data, cost of testing and faulty decisions, selection ratio, and success ratio.

12. A fair amount of evidence exists suggesting that, in many cases, one can generalize from a criterion-related validity study done in a particular setting to other settings.

13. The content validity of criterion-referenced tests should match or exceed that of norm-referenced tests.

14. The correlational approaches to determining validity are not appropriate for criterion-referenced tests to the extent that the variability of the score distribution is constricted. Therefore, discriminant statistic approaches are more likely to be useful.

■ POINTS TO PONDER

1. Is a reliable test valid? Why?
2. Which type of validity evidence would be most important for each of the following tests: an intelligence test, an art test, an achievement test, an interest inventory, an attitude inventory? Why do you think that knowledge of this type of validity is most germane?
3. You wish to use an algebra aptitude test to help decide who should take ninth-grade algebra. Two tests (A and B) are equal in every respect (cost, format, ease of scoring) except for their reliabilities and predictive validities:

	Test A	Test B
Reliability	.84	.95
Validity	.85	.80

Which test should you use?

4. Do you agree with the statement "Criterion-referenced achievement tests must demonstrate criterion-related validity?" Explain.

Unit 4

STANDARDIZED EVALUATION PROCEDURES

Chapter 14

Introduction to Standardized Tests and Inventories

- ■ **Definition and Classification of Standardized Tests**
- ■ **Functions of Standardized Tests in Schools**
- ■ **Standardized Testing Programs**

In this unit, we are going to discuss various types of standardized tests and inventories and their uses and misuses. (As you will shortly discern, there are times where *test* is the preferred term and other times where *inventory* is preferred. For ease of writing and reading we will typically use *tests* rather than *tests and inventories*.) In this chapter, we present a definition and classification of standardized tests, outline their potential functions, and discuss factors to consider when planning a testing program. After completing this chapter, you should be able to:

1. Define standardized tests.
2. Classify standardized tests.
3. Comprehend the functions of standardized tests.
4. Appreciate the necessity for cooperative planning in setting up a testing program.
5. Understand the various steps necessary in planning a testing program.

6. Use some basic information sources when selecting standardized tests.
7. Understand what factors need to be considered in selecting tests.
8. Know what questions to ask (and answers to get) when critiquing a test.
9. Understand the various steps necessary in administering a testing program.
10. Discuss who should receive information on standardized test results and how those data should be disseminated and recorded.
11. Propose and defend a standardized testing program.

DEFINITION AND CLASSIFICATION OF STANDARDIZED TESTS

Standardized tests provide methods for obtaining *samples of behavior* under *uniform procedures*. By a uniform procedure, we mean that the same *fixed set of questions* is *administered* with the *same set of directions* and timing constraints, and that the *scoring* procedure is carefully delineated and uniform. Scoring is usually *objective*, although a standardized achievement test may include an essay question, and certain unstructured personality inventories are scored in a fashion that is not completely objective. Generally, they are *commercially prepared* with the assistance of measurement experts. Usually a standardized test has been administered to a norm group (or groups) so that a person's performance can be interpreted in a norm-referenced fashion. Although some suggest that "norms" be included in the definition of "standardized," some inventories do not have norms but are ordinarily considered as standardized. And some of the diagnostic achievement tests and "criterion-referenced" tests do not have norms. Some writers seem to think of criterion-referenced tests as not being standardized. But if commercially prepared and if administered and scored under uniform conditions, they fit the definition given above, and we will consider them in this text.

The term *standardized* does *not* connote that the test necessarily measures what should be taught or what level students should be achieving. However, with the current popularity of criterion-referenced tests, commercial publishers are marketing some achievement tests that perhaps do connote at least minimal standards.

There are many ways in which standardized tests can be classified. For example, they can be classified according to administrative procedures, such as individual versus group administration, or as oral instructions versus written instructions. However, the most popular broad classification is according to *what* is measured. We will employ the following classification of tests:

1. Aptitude tests (general, multiple, and special)
2. Achievement tests (diagnostic, single-subject matter, and survey batteries)
3. Interest, personality, and attitude inventories

The first two categories are considered to contain tests of maximum performance; the third, measures of *typical* performance. Some classify aptitude and achievement tests as cognitive measures, and interest, personality, and attitude inventories as noncognitive or affective measures. Because the noncognitive measures have no factually right or wrong answers, most people prefer to refer to them as inventories rather than tests. This change in terminology may lessen the anxiety of the examinee. Whether or not these measures are referred to as tests or inventories, they do fit the definition of standardized tests given earlier. As mentioned earlier, the word *test* is frequently used in this chapter to refer to all these types of measures. This is to avoid the expression "tests and inventories." However, we would prefer that the word *test* not be used in the *titles* of noncognitive measures.

FUNCTIONS OF STANDARDIZED TESTS IN SCHOOLS

The functions of standardized tests are many and varied; however, as stated in Chapter 1 regarding all measurement devices, one can in essence sum up their functions by saying they should help in decision making. In Chapter 1 we also discussed briefly the issue of the general value of standardized tests. As mentioned there, different groups take different positions on this issue. Teachers and parents, by and large, feel standardized tests serve valuable purposes. But are there some specific functions for which standardized tests are best qualified? Yes, of course. These can be seen from Table 1–1 in Chapter 1. The functions, as listed in the table, will be explained in more detail in Chapters 15, 16, and 17 of this unit. Note that interest, personality, and attitude inventories serve fewer instructional purposes, although these measures can be very useful in the guidance functions of the school.

One of the most debatable functions of standardized achievement tests is for accountability purposes. Many states mandate the administration of tests in all school districts, publish the results, and hold educators accountable for the results.

Using tests for accountability purposes can lead to teaching too closely to the tests and may result in attenuating school improvement. Certainly, many believe that using tests for accountability purposes detracts from their usefulness as instructional aids. We will discuss this further in Chapter 21.

For all the specific functions mentioned, it should be remembered that the *ultimate* purpose of a standardized test is to help in making decisions. Some examples of the kinds of decisions that might be made more successfully by using standardized test results are as follows:

1. Do the pupils in Ms. Periwinkle's third grade need a different balance of curricular emphasis?
2. Is it advisable for Erskine to take a remedial reading course?
3. Would it be advisable for Billy to take a college-preparatory program in high school?
4. Is the phonics method of teaching reading more effective than the sight method?
5. Is Lori likely to be successful as a sales manager?

If knowledge of a test result does not enable one to make a better decision than the best decision that could be made without the use of the test, then the test serves no useful purpose and might just as well not be given. With this thought in mind, let us consider what a standardized testing program might look like.

STANDARDIZED TESTING PROGRAMS

When a local school district has full control over a testing program, it is often called an *internal* testing program. The school selects the instruments, determines the scheduling, administers the tests, and determines what to do with the results. External testing is something imposed on the district and is discussed in Chapter 21. In this section, we discuss a variety of aspects of setting up an internal testing program, including who should plan, direct, and administer the program; steps in planning the total program; how to select tests;

some administrative decisions to make and details to attend to; and the dissemination of results. We then give an example of a typical school testing program.

Who Should Be Involved?

A good school testing program should be a cooperative venture from the planning stage through the recording, interpretation, and dissemination of the results stages. Teachers, administrators, counselors, and, to some extent, parents and students, all need to understand the program and to realize that it is designed for the benefit of all groups. Without cooperative involvement, the program cannot achieve its full potential. If the original program planning is conducted by only a single individual or special-interest group, the rest of the professional staff, the parents, and the students cannot necessarily be expected to endorse and adopt the program with enthusiasm.

Cooperative planning should lead not only to more enthusiastic test use but also to a better and more complete program. Teachers, counselors, administrators, parents, and students have overlapping, yet somewhat unique, needs to be met from testing programs. The unique needs of each group may not be well known to others. For example, the instructional decisions of teachers require somewhat different data from those needed for curricular decisions made by administrators. If a member of each group does not have an opportunity to assist in the planning of a program, that program will more than likely be incomplete. Thus, a committee representing all interest groups should actively participate in the planning of a testing program.

Though it is extremely important that many subgroups be represented in the planning so that a variety of viewpoints is obtained, competent planning is of more importance than cooperative planning, and the final specific decisions should be the responsibility of the professional staff. The actual administration of the program should be made the responsibility of only a single professional person. This individual should be one who (1) is well trained in tests and measurements and is dedicated to the philosophy of measurement (i.e., that test results do aid in decision-making processes); (2) can communicate and cooperate with the various interest groups in the school; and (3) has at least a little tolerance for, and expertise in, administrative duties, since the total program from planning to ordering tests, administering tests, seeing to the scoring, analysis, recording, and appropriate distribution and interpretation of results does require administrative "know-how." This role is typically filled by a counselor who has special interest and training in testing.

Steps in Planning the Program

Several steps are necessary in planning a good testing program. The first, and probably the most important, step is that the planning committee specify as clearly as possible the purposes of the testing program for their school.

Purposes As has been repeatedly emphasized, different tests serve different purposes. Without some purposes in mind, the committee would be hard put even to designate areas the program should cover, let alone select the best instruments. Although schools will surely have some different purposes, there are many commonalities. Most schools will expect their testing programs to serve some instruction, guidance, and administrative purposes. Hopefully, all schools will also use their testing programs for research purposes, although it may be that no test would be selected solely for its research uses (except, of course, when the research has been funded by an external agency).

If specific uses are anticipated, then test selection can occur in a more sensible and systematic fashion. Quite often, one can easily decide what general kind of test is most desirable. Aptitude and achievement tests and interest, personality, and attitude inventories are not used for exactly the same specific purposes. Although all kinds of instruments can be used for occupational guidance, obviously not all serve the same *specific* purpose equally effectively. Many purposes could fall under the heading of occupational guidance, and adequate test selection demands specific preplanning. Knowing that an instrument is to be used for the purpose of comparing Jane's interests to the interests of people in various professional occupations would make the selection much easier.

Even knowing precisely the purposes for which one is testing, however, does not necessarily make selection automatic. To make a decision among mathematics achievement tests, for example, you have to decide what your specific objectives are and exactly what area of mathematics you wish to test. Although this is a problem of content validity and has been mentioned in Chapter 13, it is also a problem of determining just exactly *why* you wish to use the test. *It cannot be emphasized too strongly that the most important steps in test selection are to determine exactly why you are giving the test, what type of information you expect from it, and how you intend to use that information once you have it.*

Practical Aspects After thorough consideration has been given to what a testing program should accomplish, the committee must consider the practical aspects of the testing program. There are always unfortunate limitations such as lack of money and too few or inadequately trained personnel. Once priorities have been set, the committee is ready to make some decisions about what specific tests should be given; the when, how, and who of administration, scoring, and analysis; the system of record keeping; and the methods of distributing and interpreting results. Table 14-1 provides a sample checklist for the committee and/or administrator to follow in a testing program.

Selecting Specific Tests

Once you have determined specifically what sort of information you want to obtain from a test, how can you find out what tests will give this information, and how should you choose among them?

For school personnel to wisely select a specific test, they must be aware of various sources of in-

TABLE 14-1 A Checklist of Factors Affecting the Success of a Testing Program

	Check
1. Purposes of the program:	
Clearly defined	
Understood by parties involved	_____
2. Choice of tests:	
Valid	
Reliable	_____
Appropriate difficulty level	_____
Adequate norms	_____
Easy to administer and score	_____
Economical	_____
Best available for purpose	_____
3. Administration and scoring:	
Administrators well trained	
All necessary information provided	_____
Scorers adequately instructed	_____
Scoring carefully checked	_____
4. Physical conditions:	
Sufficient space	
Sufficient time	_____
Conveniently scheduled	_____
5. Utilization of test results:	
Definite plans for use of results	
Provision for giving teachers all necessary help in using scores	_____
Provision for systematic follow-up on use of results	_____
6. System of records:	
Necessary for purpose	
Sufficient for purpose	
Convenient form for use	_____
7. Personnel:	
Adequately trained for the purpose	_____
8. Affiliated research:	
Full advantage taken of results	
Provision for special studies, analyses, or other work	_____

Source: From R. T. Lennon, "Planning a Testing Program," Test Service Bulletin No. 55, issued by Harcourt Brace Jovanovich, Inc., New York. Reproduced by special permission of the publisher.

formation about tests, be aware of the information that publishers should make available about the tests, and be able to review and critique tests.

Sources of Information There are many sources of information that can assist in this de-cision. Some of these are Buros' *Mental Measurements Yearbooks* (1938, 1941, 1949, 1953, 1959, 1965, 1972, 1978), the *Ninth Mental Measurements Yearbook* (Mitchell, 1985), the *Tenth Mental Measurements Yearbook* (Conoley & Kramer, 1989), *Tests in Print III* (Mitchell, 1983), a six-volume series of *Test Critiques* (Keyser & Sweetland, 1985–1987), *A Counselor's Guide to Vocational Guidance Instruments* (Kapes & Mastie, 1988), *Tests: A Comprehensive Reference for Assessments in Psychology, Education, and Business, 2nd ed.* (Sweetland & Keyser, 1986), publishers' catalogs, specimen tests, professional journals, and measurement texts.

A good place to start is the *Tenth Mental Measurements Yearbook* (Conoley & Kramer, 1989). This latest edition lists information on 396 tests. This includes most of the published standardized tests that were new or revised at the time the yearbook went to press. These tests are described and evaluated by educational and psychological authorities. The MMY also contains title, acronym, subject, name, and score indexes as well as a publishers directory and index. Each school district should own the most recent copy of this book and use it extensively in the test selection process.

Tests in Print III (Mitchell, 1983) is a comprehensive test bibliography and index to the first eight books in the *Mental Measurements Yearbooks* series. A total of 2672 tests are listed. For each test mentioned in *Tests in Print III*, the following information is included:

1. Test title
2. Appropriate grade levels
3. Publication date
4. Special short comments about the test
5. Number and type of scores provided
6. Authors
7. Publisher
8. Reference to test reviews in *Mental Measurements Yearbooks*

The Buros Institute (University of Nebraska), publishers of *Tests in Print III* and the *Ninth* and *Tenth MMYs*, offers an on-line computer service through Bibliographic Retrieval Services (BRS). The database includes the test descriptions and reviews of all the tests mentioned in the *Tenth MMY*, but it is updated monthly with information and reviews on new or revised tests. The database can be accessed (under the Search Label MMYD) through any library that offers the BRS service

(see Mitchell, 1984, for a more thorough description). The Educational Testing Service also has information about new and revised tests available through the BRS services.

The *Test Critiques* volumes are sometimes seen as being in competition with the *MMY*, although others see them as supplementary rather than competitive (Harmon, 1987; Koch, 1987). The *Test Critiques* are designed for users in the field. The reviews focus on practical problems such as test administration procedures and are not nearly as technical as the MMY reviews. They are more descriptive than evaluative. Two other sources of test information are ETS's *News on Tests* and the *ETS Test Collection Catalog*. Volume 1 (1986) contains information on achievement tests and Volume 2 (1987) contains information on vocational tests.

Sources of information about unpublished or little-known instruments can be found in such references as *A Sourcebook for Mental Health Measures* (Comrey, Backer, & Glaser, 1973), *Measures for Psychological Assessment* (Chun, Cobb, & French, 1976), and a two-volume *Directory of Unpublished Experimental Mental Measures* (Goldman & Busch, 1978; Goldman & Saunders, 1974). Sources about instruments for children include two handbooks in *Tests and Measurements in Child Development: Handbooks I and II* (Johnson & Bommarito, 1971; Johnson, 1976).

Test publishers' catalogs are a particularly good source for locating new and recently revised tests. These catalogs provide basic information about the purpose and content of the test, appropriate level, working time, cost, and scoring services available. An important piece of information that is not provided in all publishers' catalogs is the copyright date (or norm date).[1]

After locating some promising tests by searching such sources as the *Mental Measurements Yearbooks*, *Test Critiques*, the *ETS Test Collections*, and the publishers' catalogs, the tests must be examined before a final selection is made and large

---

[1]Addresses of major test publishers are listed in the Appendix.

quantities are ordered. For a very nominal price, most publishers will send specimen sets of tests. These sets usually include the test booklet, answer sheet, administrator's manual, and technical manual, as well as complete information on cost and scoring services. Careful study of the set is essential in determining whether or not a given test meets the specific purposes a teacher has in mind.

For example, a seventh-grade modern math teacher may receive a brochure describing a modern math achievement test. From published reviews as well as from the descriptive literature provided, this test seems to be appropriate. But is it? Even though the professional reviewers approve the test from a technical standpoint and praise its modern content, it is still quite conceivable that this test may be inappropriate. This seventh-grade teacher may stress fundamental operations in set theory, but the test may have only two items devoted to testing this concept. The teacher may skim over binary operations, but more than 25 percent of the test may be devoted to this. The teacher may stress commutative, associative, and distributive properties without resorting to technical jargon. Although measuring these same properties, the test may assume the pupils' understanding of this mathematical language. This disparity between what the test is designed to measure and what the teacher actually teaches will not be evident except by detailed examination of the test items and the test manual.

In addition to providing the information that can be obtained from a specimen set, several publishers have regional representatives who will visit the school and answer any questions the testing committee may have about their tests. It would be wise to consider inviting such representatives to a testing committee meeting before making a final selection. These representatives typically are well qualified, often having an M.A. or a Ph.D. degree in the field of educational measurement.

Other sources of information are the test reviews found in the professional periodicals. Textbooks on measurement also typically include information on various tests.

It should be obvious that an abundance of sources of information about tests is available.

These sources should be used to a considerable extent. It makes test selection both easier and better.

Characteristics of Tests and Manuals   Several characteristics of tests and test manuals must be considered when selecting tests. Some of the data regarding these characteristics may be found in published reviews—such as in the MMY yearbooks; some may be found in publishers' catalogs; some must be obtained from the technical manuals. Unfortunately, all relevant information is just not available for some tests. The *Standards for Educational and Psychological Tests* (AERA/APA/NCME, 1985) is a guide that recommends certain uniform standards for commercially published tests as well as standards for the *use* of tests. These standards are intended to apply to most published devices for diagnosis, prognosis, and evaluation. They do not apply to devices used only for research, but rather to those that will be used as an aid in practical decision making.

The importance of the individual recommendations made in the *Standards* is indicated by two levels: primary and secondary. At different places in this text, we discuss many of the points made in the *Standards*. Nevertheless, serious developers, selectors, and users of tests should review these standards with care. Publishers should pay close attention to the standards in developing their tests and in preparing their manuals. If the publishers have good data on the norms, reliability, validity, and other characteristics of their tests, they should provide the information in the manual. If the manual does *not* have such information, it seems reasonable (but perhaps incorrect) to infer that the test developers did not do an adequate job in investigating these important qualities of the test or that the data are such that the publisher prefers not to report them.

A study by Hall (1985) on the technical characteristics of published educational achievement tests revealed that publishers do not always include all relevant information in their manuals. For example, only 54 percent of the tests in the sample studied provided information on the manner in which the test items were selected. Perhaps the reason publishers do not fully describe their tests' technical characteristics is because far too few buyers even purchase or read the manuals before purchasing the tests!

Reviewing and Critiquing a Standardized Test We have discussed some basic considerations and practical aspects of test selection. Before selecting a test, it may be helpful to use the same format for reviewing several competing tests. The following factors should be considered:

1. Purpose(s) of testing in the local school district
2. Purpose(s) and recommended use of test as stated in the manual
3. Grade level(s) of test
4. Availability of alternate forms
5. Copyright date of test
6. Format
7. Cost
8. Content appropriateness
9. Administration ease
10. Scoring ease and expense
11. Types of scores provided
12. Adequacy of the norms (including recency)
13. Test reliability
14. Test validity
15. Instructional and interpretive aids provided

Many of these factors have already been discussed. In each of Chapters 15, 16, and 17, we have thoroughly critiqued at least one test according to most of the factors listed above. After finishing the study of this unit, it is hoped that you will be able to critique tests thoroughly enough so that you are able to select the best test for your purpose among the competing existing tests. (For a proposed set of guidelines for evaluating criterion-referenced tests, see Hambleton & Eignor, 1978.)

Administrative Decisions and Details

It may seem condescending to spell out the detailed specifics in administering a testing program.

We do want to emphasize, however, that even small details are important. Many a testing session has been less than ideal because someone overlooked a detail. Sufficient tests, answer sheets, and pencils should be available. The administrator must be familiar with the test being given, and an administrator's test manual is necessary. There does need to be sufficient time for the test. Adequate seating space must be provided. A watch or clock with a second hand is frequently needed. It often is necessary to have proctors. And staff must be given directions about what to do with those little gummed labels with numbers on them that are returned from the scoring service! Two topics that deserve some additional discussion are scheduling the tests and preparing the faculty and students for the testing.

Scheduling the Tests There are many views on the question of the time at which tests should be administered. Some feel that all tests should be administered in the morning, when individuals are physically and mentally at their peaks. Some feel that tests should never be given on Mondays or Fridays.

In general, time of day and day of the week are not too important. It would probably be best not to give the test right after lunch or right before a pep rally for the homecoming game; but no valid evidence suggests that some days or times of day are particularly bad. *However, it is important in achievement testing to try to administer the test at the same time of year as when the norming was done.* Assume that the normative data for a test were gathered in October. The norm group's seventh-graders might have a mean raw score of 85; the eighth-graders, a mean raw score of 125. Can one predict from these data what a mean raw score for the norm group's seventh-graders would have been had they been tested in June (nine months after the norm group was actually tested)? Some test companies would answer affirmatively and provide interpolated norms depicting this mean to be 115 (three-fourths the distance between 85 and 125). However, in some subjects, it might well be that at the end of the year, seventh-graders perform better than beginning eighth-graders because the latter forget during the summer months. This illustrates one of the dangers of attempting to use the interpolated norms of test companies—norms that are arrived at mathematically rather than empirically (see Conklin et al., 1979). For this reason, it is best to administer achievement tests at the same time of year as the actual norm data were gathered. Another possibility is to choose a test that has norms gathered during the time of year you wish to test. (Most tests have normative data for both fall and spring.)

In fall testing, we use the results as input data or for school accountability. Spring testing is more useful for individual teacher outcome data (which will increase pressure to cheat or teach the test). We can use the data for such purposes as determining the school's standing in comparison to other schools in the district, state, or nation; in making future curriculum and instructional decisions; as *research* data in determining teaching effectiveness (but *not* to rate individual teachers); and in helping determine which students are in need of special instructional programs. All in all, the time of testing will depend, in large part, upon the uses to which the data will be put.

In addition to scheduling the time of testing, someone has to schedule the place of testing. Test administration often neglects to ensure that pupils take the test under suitable physical testing conditions.

After decisions have been made as to when and where the tests are to be given, exact schedules should be given to all professional educators in the school so that they will not plan other activities (such as field trips) for the same time. Of course, this requires two-way cooperation. The test director should not schedule tests to conflict with other scheduled activities.

Preparing Faculty and Students Each year teachers and other school personnel should have a brief in-service workshop describing various aspects of the testing program. Suggested topics for this program would include

1. Why the school gives standardized tests.
2. A brief description of each test—what it measures and its intended purpose.
3. How test results are to be interpreted and how they can assist the classroom teacher.
4. How to administer standardized tests.

The first and third topics often are inadequately covered in these workshops. Yet they are important. Teachers sometimes resent the amount of instructional time lost to standardized test administration. If the teachers could interpret the data and understand how they are instructionally useful, they might be less resentful of tests.

The last topic (how to administer standardized tests) is important because teachers, in all likelihood, will serve as test administrators. We feel that, for most group tests, the ordinary classroom teacher is capable of administering the test without any formal or specialized training beyond an in-service workshop. What must be stressed is that it is essential that if the directions in the test manual state that part one is to be given first, then test givers must administer part one first, even though they feel that it would be better to administer the test in a different order. Deviating from the directions given is likely to make the norms provided misleading. Some specific dos and don'ts follow:

DO

- Read the test manual and study the test at least two or three days before the test is administered.
- Adhere explicitly to the directions for administration printed in the test manual.
- Be sure that you are using the correct form or level of the test.
- Call the test publisher *before* the test is administered if you have any questions or note any inconsistencies in the test manual.
- Make sure that you are using the correct answer sheet if you are having the test scored by the publisher or some external agency.

DON'T

- Deviate from the printed directions—that is, do not ad lib the directions, even though you have given the test many times.

- Deviate from the specified time(s), give hints, clarify the meaning of words, and so on.
- Minimize the importance of the test, even though you may personally feel it is useless. Never make a statement such as "I'm sorry we have to waste time on this test, but the school board has ordered me to give it."

Students also need to be prepared for taking standardized tests. Individuals usually perform better at any endeavor, including test taking, if they approach that experience with a positive attitude. And yet test administrators frequently fail to establish a positive mental attitude in the individuals being tested. It is the task of the administrator to prepare the student emotionally for the test. Students should be motivated to do their best, but should not be made unduly anxious. If students are made aware of the benefits they will derive from accurate test results, this should do much toward setting the proper emotional climate.

Besides the motivating factor, there are other characteristics of students that may affect their test performance but are not related to what the test is attempting to measure. All individuals have certain personality characteristics that govern their test-taking behavior.

Students also vary in their degree of test-wiseness, or in their ability to pick up cues from the format of the test item or from the format of the test. To equate for this variable, it would be best to attempt to have all students at approximately the same level of test-taking sophistication (see Chapter 19).

Disseminating Standardized Test Results

If standardized test results are to be used effectively, they must (1) be made available (and interpreted) as quickly as possible to the users and (2) be recorded and filed in a fashion that facilitates their use. How test results are disseminated and recorded will vary from school to school because school facilities differ. However, for each test, the

school personnel must decide (1) to whom the test results should be distributed and (2) a method of disseminating information that will be efficient and yet ensure correct and adequate communication.

We take as a given that properly interpreted results should be disseminated to the pupils who have taken standardized tests and who are old enough to understand the interpretation. In this section, we will discuss who else should be told the test results.

The public correctly has two somewhat conflicting concerns regarding the dissemination of test information. They are concerned with how the schools are doing and feel that the schools should release data so that the public can judge the school's performance. Parents also want to know how their own children are doing in school and what some reasons might be for whatever performance level is reached. Thus, there is a general feeling that data should be released. On the other hand, the public correctly is concerned about schools releasing information to the wrong people. Thus, schools have to tread carefully between releasing information to those who should have it and withholding it from those who should not. Various guidelines have been written on the topic of releasing information. One of the best guidelines is by the Russell Sage Foundation (1970).

Those guidelines advocate five major principles for the collection of pupil records. First, there should be informed consent for the collection of data. Second, pupil data should be classified into categories according to potential sensitivity, and these categories should be treated differently in terms of access. Third, all data kept should be verified for accuracy. Fourth, parents and pupils should have access to the data. Fifth, no agency or persons, other than the parent or school personnel who deal directly with the child concerned, should have access to pupil data without parental or pupil permission.

A legal guideline, "Family Educational Rights and Privacy Act of 1974" (Section 438 of Public Law 93-380), specifies that parents (or students over 18) will have access to records and a right to challenge their accuracy; it also specifies a policy on the release of personal records. In general, the policy states that no personal records should be released without written parental (or student over 18) consent except to certain authorities such as school officials or state educational authorities.

Aptitude and Achievement Test Data We do not regard results of aptitude or achievement tests as private information between the test-taker and some other single individual such as the school psychologist. We take the position that the results of all achievement and aptitude tests should be disseminated to all professional staff members in the school, the individuals who were tested, and the parents of those individuals. In fact, there is precedent (Van Allen v. McCleary, 1961, Public Law 93-380, Sec 513) for the opinion that parents have a legal right to the test information contained in the official school record. (This right may not apply for students over 18, unless the student gives his or her permission to release the data to the parents.)

Goslin (1967) surveyed public school principals regarding reasons for using standardized tests. Those reasons perceived as most important involved dissemination of test-result information to pupils and parents. He also found that over 60 percent of the public secondary school students and parents of elementary school children sampled felt that intelligence-test information should be routinely reported to them. In contrast to this desire, Goslin found that approximately half the teachers in his sample had never given their pupils even a general idea of their intelligence, although nearly all teachers felt they ought to have free access to such information about their students. Goslin used this type of evidence to conclude that there is a "need for a clear statement of policy regarding the dissemination of test scores and information resulting from the test scores, both by teachers and other school personnel" (1967, p. 26). We certainly concur with that statement. Such a clear statement of policy should come from the local

school district—and not from textbook writers. The policy should be dependent upon such school characteristics as student-counselor ratio, measurement competencies of the teachers, and whether or not in-service training is available for measurement-naive teachers. The important point is that *professional* interpretation of aptitude and achievement test scores should be made to every parent and child.

Aptitude and achievement test scores should also be made available to other school systems (primary, secondary, or college) where the student intends to enroll. It is probably advisable to receive parental consent (or student's, if over 18) before such a release, but we would not deem it absolutely essential. The school should *not* release the aptitude or achievement test scores of a pupil to any other person or agency (such as a prospective employer, a physician, or psychiatrist) without written permission.

A common practice is for schools to release group achievement test results to the press. The demands for accountability data and the increased number of state-supported testing programs have served as incentives to this procedure. We have no objection to this general release of data as long as some accompanying explanatory and cautionary interpretative exposition accompanies the data. The release should *not* identify particular students' scores or the average score of any single class. See Frechtling (1989) for more details on how to report to the public.

Interest Inventory Data Interest inventory results should, in general, be made available (i.e., recorded where all would have access to it) to professional staff, students, and parents; but active dissemination and discussion of the information need only be done with the students. Naturally, interested parents should be able to receive professional interpretation of their children's interest inventory scores. Teachers should know what kind of interest inventory information is available and where it can be obtained. They should be strongly urged to avail themselves of this information and to use it, much as they would other data in the cumulative record, to aid in the full understanding of each individual child. *No interest inventory data should be released to other agencies without the written consent of the student or parent.*

Personality Inventory Data As a matter of normal routine, personality and attitude inventory results should not be made available to anyone except the student without his/her explicit permission. One way to minimize faking is to alleviate anxiety about who will have access to the test results and about how they will be used. If counselors or school psychologists wish to obtain an accurate measure from a student, they should emphasize the confidential nature of the information. If confidentiality is promised or even implied, it should not be broken. Often, however, the professional who gathered the information will deem it beneficial for the student to share the information with others, such as parents or teachers. If so, the student's permission to release the data should be obtained. It should be pointed out that whether counselors or school psychologists legally enjoy privileged communications, as do physicians or attorneys, is debatable. Public Law 93-380 specifies that parents have the right to "inspect and review any and all official records, files, and data directly related to their children . . ." (p. 89). These records could also be subpoenaed. Counselors might argue, however, that their records (including personality-test scores) are not a part of the official school records.

Recording Standardized Test Results

The recording of aptitude test, achievement test, and interest inventory results not considered private information can be accomplished by trained clerks. These results, however, are *not* in the public domain, and the clerks should be cautioned to treat the results as confidential. Test results are generally stored in pupils' cumulative folders. In the future, they will no doubt be placed in computer storage. In either case, one must somehow ensure that the information is readily available for

those who should have access to it and not available to those who should not have access to it. These two goals are hard to reach simultaneously. Test results must be kept under lock and key, but teachers should have easy access to them and be encouraged to use them. Of course, some teachers are not knowledgeable enough to use test results correctly. This places us in somewhat of an ethical dilemma when we suggest that aptitude, achievement, and interest test results be made available to all the professional staff. However, it is really the teachers' ethical responsibility to know how to use most, if not all, of the scores in the areas mentioned. If not, they should surely recognize their limitations in the area and not use the information without obtaining guidance.

All data on file should be reviewed periodically to determine their present usefulness and accuracy. Aptitude and achievement test data should probably be retained throughout secondary school for most pupils. (The achievement data may be stored even after graduation.) However, there are occasions where a test score is of doubtful validity or almost assuredly far from correct. These scores should be deleted from the record. (For example, if a student is obviously very ill while taking an exam, the test results should certainly not be made a part of the record.) Interest inventory scores are not likely to be useful for more than three or four years. There is no reason to retain such scores on a pupil's record once he has graduated (except perhaps in a very secure file for research purposes). As we have mentioned, personality inventory data should not be a regular part of the pupil's records. Anecdotal data should be reviewed annually and discarded when no longer of use.

Interpreting Test Information to Others

Just as the parent and pupil have a right to certain kinds of test information, the school has the responsibility to communicate this information so that it will be understood correctly and used appropriately. The major aspects to be communicated are (1) the type of information provided by the test score, (2) the precision of this information, and (3) how the information can be used appropriately.

Confusion often exists as to what information the test score provides. This may be due to one of two reasons: (1) the type of score (i.e., percentile, stanine, and so on) may not be understood and (2) the construct being measured may not be understood. These problems can be overcome, but the educator needs to be sufficiently aware of the possible confusion that can take place in a parent's or pupil's mind. Confusion concerning the type of score may result from mistaking percentiles for percentages, while a misunderstanding of a construct may be the result of confusing aptitude with interest. Even administrators, counselors, and teachers do this! If a professional can make such a mistake, it reinforces our belief that we must be very careful in interpreting to others what the test is measuring.

The precision of the test information is another important aspect of test interpretation. What needs to be interpreted is an accurate impression of test score precision. This, of course, varies from test to test. There has been much concern in the past about lay persons not being aware of the imprecision of tests. The attempt by some to differentiate between scores only one point apart illustrates insensitivity to the concept of errors of measurement. One should guard against this danger of overinterpretation. Although teachers or counselors cannot teach a parent or student about the theoretical concepts of reliability or standard error of measurement, they certainly can and should communicate the general idea. A good way to do this is through band interpretation.

Presenting a range of values encompassing $\pm 1 S_e$ from the observed score as indicating where the individual would probably score if he or she retook the test usually gets across the point of imprecision. The idea of band interpretation is most often accomplished using percentile bands, although raw score, z or T score bands could be used. Percentile bands are reported for the better constructed tests. If not reported, they can be easily computed for any test that reports percentiles and a standard error of measurement. One simply looks up the percentiles that correspond to $X \pm 1 S_e$. One can be about 68 percent confident that a person's true percentile will be within this range. A possible misinterpretation of percentile bands is that a person unsophisticated in this type of score may think that the percentile corresponding to a person's observed score is halfway between the two percentile band end points. (Or, as mentioned earlier, it is possible to confuse percentiles and percentages.) Because percentiles are rectangularly distributed and observed scores are typically distributed in a fairly normal fashion, this will not be the case—except when a person's observed score is equal to the mean of the distribution. Thus, if percentile bands are used, the percentile of the observed score should be given along with the two end percentiles.

Although many people overinterpret small differences in scores, it is also true that other people place too little faith in test results and underinterpret score differences. This has probably become even more true because of the criticisms of testing that have received so much space in the press. In particular, students who score poorly on tests have a tendency to discount the results. Although a teacher or counselor should not argue with a parent or student over the accuracy of a test score, the precision of a test should not be underplayed. There has been much talk about the importance of a good self-concept. This is fine, but there is no evidence to suggest that persons who have an inaccurately high self-concept will make better decisions than persons who perceive themselves accurately. A good decision, by definition, is dependent upon an accurate self-concept, not a good self-concept.

People may understand what characteristic has been measured and how accurately it has been measured without understanding how this information is useful to them. For example, the knowledge that a person is at about the 80th percentile on a test that measures creativity may not be particularly useful to that person. It is up to the test interpreter to help the individual understand how that information is related to the decisions he or she must make.

Although not ideal, it is probably acceptable to present interpretations of achievement and aptitude test results to groups of teachers. Parents and students who are somewhat less sophisticated with regard to test interpretation should receive more individualized interpretations.

Some schools routinely send home the results of standardized achievement tests accompanied by short brochures (prepared by the publishers of the tests or the local school) that describe the test and explain the meaning of the scores in terms parents can understand. We have mixed feelings about such a practice. The advantage is that it ensures broad dissemination of information. A possible disadvantage is that the information will be misunderstood. Another approach is to announce in a school paper or through direct mailings to parents that the results are available and a counselor or homeroom teacher will explain the information if the parents wish to visit the school. Another possibility is to explain routinely the scores at one of the regularly held parent-teacher conferences.[2]

The interpretation of interest inventories is best done individually, although group interpretations of some interest inventories are appropriate. If the purpose of the interest inventory is primarily to start students thinking about how their interests relate to their educational plans and the world of work, then group interpretation is appropriate. If the interest-inventory data are to be used to assist the individual in an immediate educational or vocational decision, then individual interpretation of the data in a counseling situation is necessary.

Personality inventory results should be interpreted in an individual interview by qualified personnel. Problems inherent in personality measurement lead us to recommend strongly that the results of such inventories be discussed only in general terms.

Any sharing of information between parents (or students) and teachers (or counselors) regarding test score results is subject to misinterpretation. The following guidelines should be useful in minimizing the problems (Lien, 1976, pp. 297–300).

1. Make sure that both you and the person to whom you are interpreting the rest results have a clear, immediate goal in mind that will serve as a reason for the interpretation.
2. Never discuss the implication of the scores in terms of absolute answers (e.g., "This score shows you won't get through college").
3. Try to concentrate on increasing understanding rather than posing as an expert. Use simple, nontechnical terms whenever possible.
4. Remember that understanding and acceptance are two different concepts.
5. Never compare one student with another particular student.

Much more could be said concerning specific techniques of test interpretation (see Ricks, 1959). Separate courses beyond an introductory course should be taken in counseling techniques of test interpretation. The main point to be made here is that, in any interpretation of test data, *the focus should always be on the student, not the test score*. (For a further discussion of test interpretations, see Goldman, 1971; or Mehrens & Lehmann, 1985.)

A Typical School Testing Program

As mentioned, testing programs can and should vary, depending upon such characteristics as the size of the school, the characteristics of the student body, and the number and quality of the pupil personnel workers. Nevertheless, surveys of school testing programs show a great many similarities.

One might conceptualize a typical testing program (to be routinely administered to all students) as illustrated in Table 14-2. This typical program is not necessarily the best pattern for all schools. For example, testing in the primary grades has come under attack in recent years, and some schools may choose not to test in grades K–3.

---

[2]This forcefully illustrates why classroom teachers should be knowledgeable about the interpretation of test scores.

Table 14-2   A Typical School Testing Program

Grade	Kind of Test
K	Reading readiness test
1 or 2	Reading test
2 or 3	Scholastic aptitude test
4	Achievement battery
5	Achievement battery
5	Scholastic aptitude test
6	Achievement battery
7	Achievement battery
8	Achievement battery
8 or 9	Multifactor aptitude test
10	Achievement battery
9, 10, 11, or 12	Interest inventory

Tests, other than those listed, such as individual intelligence tests, special aptitude and achievement tests, diagnostic tests, and various types of interest, value, attitude, and personality inventories should be available for use with individual students.

The specific tests chosen depend upon the characteristics and needs of each school district; but we strongly recommend that the *same* achievement battery be used at the designated grade levels to provide some continuity. Naturally, if the content validity of a specific test used at the lower grades is inappropriate in a higher grade, use of an alternate achievement battery is warranted. Also, it is helpful if schools use scholastic aptitude tests that have been normed on the same population as the achievement battery. This will permit the user to meaningfully compare scores on the two types of tests.

Because various states have different testing requirements, programs may differ from the one given. We have mixed feelings regarding these external state regulations. They do serve a useful purpose by forcing schools to maintain minimum testing programs. On the other hand, external regulations always mean a certain amount of rigidity, and there is the danger of being forced to administer tests that the schools will not use, either be-

cause they have no objectives relevant to those tests or because they are inadequately staffed to use the results correctly. It may also lead to duplication of testing. Some schools overtest.

A more recent phenomenon related to state-imposed requirements for certain standardized tests is for states actually to administer their own testing programs. We will discuss this further under external evaluation programs. One potential result of state testing programs is that some schools may feel they no longer need internal testing programs. This is not true. Many state programs are quite limited. Even if they expand considerably in future years, they are not likely to replace the need for local schools to administer those unique tests that are necessary for local decision making. Just as there can be too much overlap between local and state programs, there also can be such a concern with overlap that valuable local testing programs are overcurtailed.

If all schools would adopt the position that a test not be given unless the results are to be used, there would be less testing. *However, what is needed in most schools is probably not less testing but better use of the tests now being given.* Any unnecessary duplication of testing or administration of tests whose results remain unused should be eliminated. This is a waste of valuable time and materials, and results in a negative attitude toward testing by all involved—pupils, teachers, parents, and taxpayers.

■ SUMMARY

The major points of this chapter are summarized in the following statements:

1. Standardized tests are commercially prepared instruments for which administrative and scoring procedures are carefully delineated by the authors. Typically, norms are provided as interpretive aids.
2. Standardized tests are classified as follows: (a) aptitude tests, (b) achievement tests, and (c) interest, personality, and attitude inventories.
3. Standardized tests (like other assessment de-

vices) serve as aids in instructional, guidance, administrative, and research decisions.

4. A good school testing program should be a cooperative venture involving teachers, administrators, counselors, students, and parents.

5. In test selection, the first step is to determine the purposes for which testing is to be done.

6. *The Mental Measurements Yearbooks, Tests in Print III, Test Critiques, ETS Test Collection Catalogs,* publishers' catalogs, specimen sets, professional periodicals, and measurement textbooks are all fruitful sources of information about tests.

7. In selecting and using tests, one should consider various characteristics of tests and test manuals that are mentioned in the text.

8. Whether one should administer standardized tests in the fall or spring depends upon the uses to which the data will be put. Fall testing is more useful if one wants input data. Spring testing is more useful in providing outcome data.

9. Both faculty and students need to be prepared for the administration of standardized tests.

10. Aptitude and achievement test data should be disseminated to all professional staff members in the school, the individuals who were tested, and the parents of those individuals. They should be released to other schools where the individual intends to enroll. They should not be released to any other person or agency without written permission.

11. Interest-inventory data should be made available to professional staff, students, and parents, but active dissemination and discussion of the data need only be done with students.

12. Results from personality inventories should not be made available to anyone except the student without his explicit permission.

13. Generally, test data can be recorded by properly trained clerks if they can be trusted to keep the data confidential.

14. All data on file should be reviewed periodically to determine their present usefulness and accuracy.

15. In interpreting test information to others, we must clarify (1) what information the test score gives us, (2) the precision of this information, and (3) how the information can be used appropriately.

16. A quality school testing program will likely include aptitude and achievement tests and interest inventories.

■ POINTS TO PONDER

1. What educational decisions should be made without a consideration of standardized test data? Should any educational decisions be made in the absence of data?

2. Should public school educators be concerned with the *research* functions of standardized tests? Has too much class time been devoted to this function?

3. In determining who should be admitted to Honors Algebra, should norm-referenced or criterion-referenced measurement be considered?

4. Test administration involves many aspects. What factors must the examiner be alert to during the test administration? (*Hint:* Cheating is one such factor.)

5. You are responsible for selecting a standardized achievement survey battery for your elementary school. You have finally narrowed your selection to Test A. At the staff meeting, you announce your choice. One of your colleagues challenges your selection and states that Test B is equally good. What kinds of evidence or support should you present in defense of your choice of Test A?

Chapter 15

Standardized Aptitude Measures

- ■ **Introduction**
- ■ **Individually Administered Tests of General Intelligence (Aptitude)**
- ■ **Group Tests of General Aptitude**
- ■ **Multifactor Aptitude Tests**
- ■ **Special-Aptitude Tests**
- ■ **Using Aptitude Test Results**

This chapter is divided into six major sections. An introductory section covers (1) definitions of intelligence, (2) the structure of intelligence, (3) the etiology of intelligence, (4) the stability of intelligence, (5) the distinctions and similarities between intelligence, aptitude, and achievement, and (6) the classification of aptitude tests. In the second section, we discuss individually administered intelligence tests; the third section covers group tests of general aptitude; the fourth, multifactor aptitude tests; the fifth, special aptitude tests. The final section is devoted to a discussion of some of the uses of aptitude test results.

After studying this chapter, you should be able to:

1. Know some of the basic definitions of intelligence.
2. Understand some of the theories of the structure of intelligence.
3. Understand that both genetics and environment affect aptitude test scores.
4. Interpret the data on the stability of intelligence.
5. Compare the terms *intelligence, aptitude, ability,* and *achievement.*
6. Know a little bit about some of the more popular individual intelligence tests and recognize their advantages and limitations.
7. Recognize some of the more popular group tests of intelligence.
8. Evaluate a general aptitude test.
9. Discuss the concept of culture-fair testing.
10. Understand the desired characteristics of a multifactor aptitude test.
11. Know a little bit about some of the more popular multifactor aptitude tests.
12. Evaluate a multifactor aptitude test.
13. Recognize the existence of special aptitude

tests and the purposes they are designed to serve.

14. Recognize some instructional, guidance, administrative, and employment uses of aptitude test results.

INTRODUCTION

That society should assist each pupil "to achieve the maximum of which he is capable" is a motto often heard in educational circles. But behind that simplistic and well-meaning phrase lurk perplexing problems. How do we know what a person's capabilities are? Can we define *capacity*? Can we measure capacity? Does a person have a general capacity to acquire knowledge, or are there many different capabilities, each specific to a given type of knowledge? Is capacity constant over time? These are all relevant questions. Unfortunately, not all psychologists agree on all the answers. Nevertheless, for the past 90 years, psychologists have used various labels such as *capacity, intelligence, potential, aptitude,* and *ability* (capacity and potential are seldom used currently) to identify a construct (or set of constructs) that seems to be useful in helping to predict various kinds of behaviors. The tests designed to measure this construct (or set of constructs) vary to some extent, because test authors may not define a construct differently or indeed may be talking about different constructs.

Definitions of Intelligence

In discussing definitions of intelligence, it is useful to consider the common sense, psychological, and operational or measurement definitions of the term. Most of us use the term *intelligence* in everyday language. We think we can differentiate between highly intelligent individuals and those at the opposite extreme. We make these lay person's differentiations on the basis of the individuals' behaviors. If a person can, time after time, select an effective course of action under difficult situations, we are apt to conclude that person is intel-

ligent. Sternberg, Conway, Ketron, and Bernstein (1980) found that the views of lay persons concerning intelligence are quite well formed; that they are frequently used both in self-evaluation and in the evaluation of others; that they are closely related to existing psychological theories of intelligence; and that they are quite strongly related to intelligence as measured by an "IQ" test. The common core of peoples' beliefs about what constitutes intelligence includes problem-solving ability, verbal ability, and social competence.

A survey of 661 testing experts showed almost unanimous agreement that three attributes—abstract thinking or reasoning, the capacity to acquire knowledge, and problem-solving ability—are important elements of intelligence (Snyderman & Rothman, 1986).

Jensen (1985) suggested that the standard tests of intelligence "reflect individual differences in the speed and efficiency of basic cognitive processes more than they reflect differences in the information content to which test-takers have been exposed" (p. 557). Chi, Glaser, and Rees (1982) admitted that "more intelligent individuals have faster processing speed, longer memory span, and use more sophisticated strategies than less intelligent persons" (p. 7). However, they also argued that "a major component of intelligence is the possession of a large body of accessible and usable knowledge" (p. 8). Of course, the crucial question is whether knowledge causes, or is an effect of, the more efficient cognitive processes. Sternberg (1988), a leading theorist on intelligence, has argued against what he considers an overemphasis by Chi et al. on the importance of *domain-specific* knowledge. He pointed out that there is a distinction between domain-specific *abilities* and domain-specific *manifestations* of *general* abilities.

> Might it not be more plausible and much more parsimonious, to suggest that the ability is rather general, but that its manifestation is constrained by domain-specific knowledge (p. 64).

Most evidence would suggest that a hallmark of intelligence is the ability to generalize information from one situation to another (Campione &

Brown, 1979). Sternberg (1981) suggested that "intelligence can best be understood through the study of nonentrenched (novel) kinds of tasks. Such tasks require subjects to use concepts or form strategies that differ in kind from those to which they are accustomed"(p. 1). He and other theorists have been using a cognitive psychologist's information-processing approach to the study of intelligence.

The *operational* definitions of intelligence are those tests that claim to measure the concept. Operationally, intelligence is what an intelligence test measures. Though often scoffed at by people who do not understand the concept of operational definitions, this statement is neither meaningless nor bad. If a test measures acquired behaviors that psychologists agree can be labeled intellectual, then the test would be considered a *good* operational definition of intelligence; if it does not, it would be considered a *poor* operational definition. Although the various intelligence tests differ somewhat from each other with respect to what behaviors they measure, the correlations among the scores from such tests are typically quite high, and all such tests "measure a cluster of intellectual traits demanded in modern, technologically advanced, societies" (Anastasi, 1982, p. 182).

Cleary, Humphreys, Kendrick, and Wesman (1975, p. 19) defined intelligence as "the entire repertoire of acquired skills, knowledge, learning sets, and generalization tendencies considered intellectual in nature that are available at any one period in time." Cleary and her colleagues claimed that an intelligence test contains items that sample the components of their definition and that the definition is not circular because "there is a consensus among psychologists as to which kinds of behaviors are labeled intellectual" (p. 19). Although there is room for some debate about that last point, most psychologists would probably concur (see Snyderman & Rothman, 1986). The reason for potential debate is that intelligence is an "open" concept. That is, "the number of activities legitimately characterized as indicators has never been listed—would indeed hardly be capable of being listed" (Butcher, 1968, p. 27). Even if we could agree completely on a list of behaviors, we might

well disagree on how these are structured. In the following subsection, we discuss various theories on the *structure* of intelligence.

Recall (from Chapter 13) that tests can be either *samples* or *signs*—the former if the items are drawn from a clearly defined universe, the latter if they are not. Since intelligence is an open concept and the universe of "intellectual behaviors" is not clearly or totally defined, intelligence (aptitude) tests are *signs*, not samples. For tests to serve as signs, we need high construct validity, and the data gathered in the process of construct validation help us to understand the concept. The reading of this chapter plus the validity information in the technical manual of any intelligence test being used will aid you in the understanding of what is being measured by that particular test and how that information is likely to be useful.

To understand more fully the uses and misuses of the various instruments typically identified as intelligence or aptitude tests, it is first necessary to study briefly the various theories of the structure and development of intelligence. We will curtail this discussion drastically. Whole books have been written on the subject; many of the best known are cited in the text.

Theories of Intelligence Structure

The formal movement in testing intelligence began in the latter part of the nineteenth century with Sir Francis Galton. Galton believed that tests of sensory discrimination and reaction time were estimates of intellectual functioning, and his tests were largely of this type. James McKeen Cattell, an American psychologist, also theorized that differences in sensory keenness, reaction speed, and the like would reflect differences in intellectual functioning. Cattell (1890) first introduced the term *mental test*.

Binet and Henri (1896) began their research by measuring such characteristics as memory, attention, and comprehension. In other words, they measured complex functions rather than the unitary characteristics (such as reaction time) previously employed. Although their research involved many different kinds of tasks, they conceptualized intelligence as a very general trait, defining it as the ability to adjust effectively to one's environment. In 1905, Binet and Simon (1905) developed the first individual intelligence test (the Binet Scale) designed to be a global measure of intellectual level.

Although many other psychologists have also conceptualized intelligence as a general characteristic, several opposing theories have developed. The controversy of whether mental ability can be measured meaningfully by a single score still continues. A variety of positions have been taken in the past 60 years (see McNemar, 1964; Humphreys, 1967; Resnick, 1976). Spearman (1927) developed a two-factor theory, suggesting that intelligence is composed of a general factor (g) and many specific factors ($s_1, s_2, \ldots, s_n$). Thurstone (1933) developed a theory of multiple factors ($f_1, f_2, \ldots, f_n$), which led to his test of Primary Mental Abilities. Vernon (1961) suggested a hierarchical structure of abilities. A general factor (g) exists, but that is divided into two major group factors: verbal-educational and kinesthetic-mechanical. These major group factors are a little less general than Spearman's g but more general than Thurstone's group factors. Under each major group factor there are minor group factors; and under each of these are specific factors.

R. B. Cattell (1963, 1971) proposed a theory that suggests that intelligence is composed of both a fluid component and a crystallized component. The fluid component is the more general, and a person with a large amount of fluid intelligence would do many different tasks well. It is conceptualized as abstract, essentially nonverbal, and relatively culture-free mental efficiency. Crystallized intelligence is more closely linked to the culture or environment and represents a person's ability to achieve in more specific tasks related to the culture. It is more similar to achievement (Cattell & Horn, 1978).

Guilford (1959, 1967, 1969), in a structure-of-intellect (SOI) model, postulated many factors of intelligence. He categorized these factors under three broad dimensions according to (1) the process or operation performed, (2) the kind of prod-

uct involved, and (3) the kind of material or content involved. He then subclassified these dimensions into five operations, six types of products, and four types of content. Seeing the three main headings as faces of a cube, he ended up with 120 ($4 \times 6 \times 5$) cells within the cube, each representing a different aspect of intelligence. Guilford claimed to have demonstrated empirically that 82 of the 120 different structure-of-intellect factors exist (Guilford, 1967). He argued that each factor should be tested separately and that tests giving a single score are somewhat misleading.

Although Guilford's model received some favorable attention, most psychologists consider it to be more of theoretical interest than of practical value. Just because the model is *logical*, it does not follow that tests could be constructed to correspond to every cell of the cube. And even if such tests could be constructed, they would not necessarily be of any value. Vernon (1964) and Hunt (1961) were both very pessimistic about the predictive value of such tests. Hunt stated flatly (p. 301) that tests of these highly specific factors have no predictive value in any situation. Some educators (e.g., Meeker, 1981) have advocated using the SOI model for *diagnostic* purposes. Theoretically, examining the profile of scores for an individual would allow strengths and weaknesses in cognitive functioning to be identified in a highly specific manner. In practice, however, the tests developed from (or scored according to) the SOI model have such severe psychometric limitations that they are better reserved for research purposes than educational or clinical purposes (Clarizio & Mehrens, 1985).

Piaget (see O'Bryan & MacArthur, 1969; Pinard & Sharp, 1972; Uzziris & Hunt, 1975) believed that a child's intelligence develops in sequential stages, each stage identifiable by ways of thinking. He divided the evolution of thought into four major periods: sensorimotor (birth to age 1½ or 2 years), preoperational (from 1½ to 7), concrete operational (from 7 to 11 or 12), and formal operational (from 11 or 12 to 14 or 15).

Jensen (1968a, 1970a, 1973a, 1980) advocates a two-level theory of mental ability. Level I ability consists of rote learning and memory. It is the ability to register and retrieve information. Level II is characterized by mental manipulations, conceptualizations, reasoning, and problem solving. Level II is similar to the general factor (*g*) or Cattell's concept of fluid intelligence. Jensen (1980, 1982) and Jensen and Munro (1979) have revived Galton's earlier notion that reaction time (RT) and movement time (MT) (broadly termed "mental chronometry") are related to intelligence. They report a series of research findings showing that both RT (particularly, choice RT) and MT correlate with scores on intelligence tests. (MT is not correlated with intelligence in normal adults, but it is with children and retarded adults.) About half the total variance of *g* can be accounted for in terms of differences in RT to a few cognitive tasks (Jensen, 1984). Jensen suggested that this correlation indicates that differences in scores on intelligence tests reflect differences in fundamental cognitive and neural processes. As Jensen suggested, this study, or RT and its correlates, "brings us closer to the interface of brain and behavior—the point at which individual differences in intelligence must ultimately be understood" (1982, p. 308).

From the preceding discussion, it should be readily evident that there are many different theories concerning the structure of intelligence. Some theorists believe that intelligence is a general attribute; others think that there are many different aspects to intelligence. However disconcerting it may be, we must accept the fact that psychologists cannot totally agree on the real nature of intelligence. Although theoretical psychologists generally adopt the view that there are specific factors of intellect, most believe that there is also a general factor (*g*). Much of the most recent writing has stressed the importance of *g* (see Thorndike, 1986). As Thorndike has pointed out, although *g* received little emphasis from 1940 to 1980 "*g* refuses to die, and has a tendency to rise again like the Phoenix from the ashes" (1986, p. 6).

There are two primary reasons why many psychologists feel that the concept of general intelli-

gence cannot be abandoned. First, whenever a whole battery of current cognitive tests is given to a sample of people, a set of positively correlated scores results (see Jensen, 1986). This phenomenon of correlation among separate tasks is one of the most pervasive and stable findings of psychology and ". . . virtually forces attention to the questions of general intelligence" (Resnick, 1976, p. 7). Some individuals have suggested that we need specific ability measures that are not correlated with intelligence. Snow (1984) suggested that this is an absurd position, stating that "we simply cannot make believe that there is no such construct as intelligence reflecting variations in an organization of fairly generalized learning abilities. The concept has as much scientific status as does the concept of gravity" (p. 12). Second, a general factor of intelligence is a better predictor than specific aptitude measures of future *general* academic performance as well as job success. It is primarily for the predictive value reason that most practical psychologists are still inclined to use tests of general intelligence. For example, the *Journal of Vocational Behavior* (1986) has a whole special issue devoted to "the *g* Factor in Employment." Jensen has summarized the research as follows:

> The practical predictive validity of intelligence and aptitude tests is mainly dependent on *g*. This has been so frequently demonstrated with respect to the prediction of scholastic achievement as to not bear further reiteration. . . . The *g* factor has predictive validity for job performance in nearly all jobs, and the validity of *g* increases with job complexity (1987, pp. 99–100).

Given that *g* predicts future academic and job success, do psychologists know what it is? Partially.

> *g* reflects some property or processes of the human brain that are manifested in many forms of adaptive behavior, and in which people differ, . . . and show physiological as well as behavioral correlates, and have a hereditary component, . . . and have important educational, occupational, economic, and social correlates in all industrialized societies, and have behavioral correlates that accord with popular and com-

mon sense notions of "intelligence" (Jensen, 1986, p. 329).

Although *g* is increasingly seen as the "sine qua non of all intelligence tests" (Jensen, 1986, p. 310), one should not identify intelligence as the totality of all mental abilities. As Jensen pointed out, "besides *g* there is some indefinite number of primary or group factors independent of *g*" (pp. 310–311). This notion is compatible with Vernon's hierarchical structure mentioned earlier.

Sternberg (1986) has pointed out that intelligence is distinct from, but interrelated with, wisdom and creativity and believes that in education the instructional efforts should focus on creativity and wisdom more than they currently do.

As a result of the lack of *total* agreement about the structure of intelligence, there is a wide variety of tests that are often subsumed under the phrase *intelligence tests* (as we see later, *scholastic aptitude tests* and ability tests are often preferred terms in education). They do not all measure *exactly* the same thing (although all contain a high proportion of *g*). A rather important implication is that when selecting and interpreting an intelligence test, the user must be completely aware of the author's definition of intelligence.

Etiology of Intelligence: Heredity or Environment?

Because psychologists cannot agree on what intelligence is or how many intellectual factors there are, obviously they cannot agree on the etiology of intellectual differences. The score on any test of ability is a result of how well a person performs on that instrument at a particular time. An intelligence test measures acquired behavior. An acceptance of this statement does *not* rule out genetic influence. Being able to run the 100-yard dash in 9.2 seconds is also acquired behavior, but speed may partly be genetically based. Being able to throw a 16-pound shot 50 feet is acquired behavior, but strength may partly be genetically based. Likewise, scoring well on an intelligence test is due to acquired behavior, but intelligence may partly be genetically based.

Ignoring the possibility of chance errors for purposes of this discussion, we must ask: Why was that person able to perform as he (or she) did? Is the behavior on an aptitude test due to an individual's heredity or environment? Or does it really matter? For some purposes of testing, the preconditions affecting the test performance may be irrelevant. If the purpose of a test is to use the results simply to predict some future behavior, then the question of the usefulness of the test is an empirical one. However, educators seldom wish solely to predict. In fact, as stated before, educators are, or should be, in the business of attempting to upset negative or unfavorable predictions by changing the school environment. (This is not always easy, if at all possible.) If we are effectively to change our educational process as a result of the predictive evidence, then it may well be helpful to understand why individuals perform as they do. For this reason, some understanding of the heredity-environment controversy is necessary.

A great amount of research has been done in an attempt to resolve the heredity-environment controversy. Many of these studies compared correlations on intelligence test scores between identical or fraternal twins reared together or apart, and between other subjects hereditarily linked but in different environments. Erlenmeyer-Kimling and Jarvik (1963) reviewed 52 such studies, yielding over 30,000 correlational pairings. The average correlations of their studies are shown in Table 15-1.

Most psychologists would interpret such data as being supportive of a strong genetic base for

Table 15-1 Summary of Comparative Data on IQ Correlational Studies

Category	Median Coefficient
Foster parent–child	.20
Parent–child	.50
Siblings reared together	.49
Fraternal twins	.53
Identical twins reared apart	.75
Identical twins reared together	.87

performance on intelligence tests. Without going into detail, it may be said that by far the most popular current opinion is that there is an interaction between heredity and environment. The original question, "Which one of these factors affects an intelligence test score?" was replaced by "Which one contributes the most?" This question, in turn, has been replaced by "How do heredity and environment interact to affect test scores?" Psychologists do not yet have the complete answer to this question, and since the publication of a paper by Jensen (1968b), some have returned to the question of *how much*. Whether heredity contributes about 80 percent to the variance of scores on an intelligence test in the population, and environment 20 percent, as some suggest, is hotly debated. (These estimates are called heritability ratios.) Schoenfeldt (1968) obtained estimates of heritability as low as 0.26 and concluded that "genetic components are not as large a proportion of the total variance as previously believed" (p. 17). Vernon (1979) believed that the research converges on the estimate that roughly 60 percent of the variance is genetic, 30 percent environmental, and 10 percent an interaction between the two. Herrnstein (1982) stated that "virtually all specialists on the heritability of IQ estimate a value somewhere in the range of 50 percent to 80 percent" (p. 72). Jensen (1984) reported that research in the Soviet Union, Poland, East Germany, and other communist countries obtained heritability estimates falling between 0.60 and 0.80. Jensen finds these data "virtually indistinguishable from those of behavioral-genetic researchers in capitalist countries" (p. 462). Snyderman and Rothman (1986), in a survey of measurement experts, found that 94 percent of the 661 respondents felt there was evidence for a "significant heritable component to IQ in the American white population" (p. 89). The mean estimate of heritability was 0.60.

The debates about heritability ratios arose partly because psychologists use different mathematical formulas in computing the ratios. Although we cannot delve into those problems in this text, we can discuss briefly some pitfalls in interpreting these ratios. First, it must be emphasized that these are estimates of the proportion of

total *variance* (see Chapter 10) of a trait (e.g., intelligence) that is attributable to heredity in a *population* of people. Such a ratio tells us nothing about what proportion of a *single* individual's intelligence is due to heredity, nor can that be determined (Jensen, 1969a). Since the heritability ratios apply to populations, each applies only to a particular population at a particular point in time. As social conditions vary, so should heritability estimates. For example, if all U.S. citizens lived in environments that were *equal* (not necessarily identical) with respect to their impact on intellectual development, then none of the variance in the intellectual differences could be due to environment; all would be due to genetic differences, and the heritability ratio would be 1.0. If our environments are becoming more equal, then the heritability ratio should be getting higher. Some who wish to emphasize the environmental side have trouble accepting this mathematical fact. They would like to have environments (with respect to impact on intellectual development) become more equal but hate to think of the proportion of variability as being increasingly genetic in origin.

Some individuals like to ignore the heritability-estimates debate entirely. Since both genetics and environment contribute to our intelligence, and because they interact in this contribution, these individuals argue that it is pointless to talk about which factor contributes most. No one would suggest that the nervous system is immune from genetic influence. Likewise, no reputable writer would suggest that a person's environment does not at least partially influence his or her score on an intelligence test. Such things as severe malnutrition or extremely serious and prolonged intellectually deprived home environments, especially early in life, can inflict severe damage on intellectual growth.

One final point needs to be made. Many people seem to feel that it is better to accept the environmental side of the debate because it is more optimistic. If a person has a poor environment, we can change that and thereby increase his intelligence. If intelligence is genetically based, it is unchangeable. *Neither of the above statements is necessarily true.* Severe environmental deprivation can inflict permanent damage (see Ausubel, 1968, p. 246). And even if the damage is not necessarily permanent, it does not follow that we know enough about how to manipulate the environment to succeed in reversing the damage. Likewise, *genetic* does not mean *unchangeable*. A classic example is the low intelligence resulting from phenylketonuria (PKU), a gene-based disease. Special diets low in the amino acid phenylalanine prevent the accumulation of toxic metabolic products in the brain, and intelligence can develop to a fairly normal level. Remember, high heritability of a trait should not be automatically equated with a low level of modifiability. Nevertheless, as Scarr (1981) pointed out:

> The myth of heritability limiting malleability seems to die hard (p. 53).

Social Class, Race, and Intelligence It has long been known that relationships exist between social class and intelligence and race and intelligence. The reasons for these relationships have been much debated. The linkages conceivably could be due to genetic factors, environmental factors, test bias, or any combination of the three.

In 1968, Jensen (1968b) published "Social Class, Race, and Genetics: Implications for Education." In 1969, he published an invited paper on the same general topic (Jensen, 1969a). These papers caused more public controversy among educators and psychologists than any other two articles in recent history. The subsequent issue of the *Harvard Educational Review* carried rebuttals by other psychologists and a rejoinder by Jensen. The whole series of papers was reprinted in a paperback (*Harvard Educational Review*, 1969). Other references on this topic are Jensen (1970b, 1973a, b, 1980, 1985), Eysenck (1971, 1979, 1984), Herrnstein (1971), Gage (1972), Block and Dworkin (1974a, b), Kamin (1974), and Cronin et al. (1975). As Loehlin et al. (1975, p. 3) pointed out, when questions on social class, race, and intelligence are examined in a society riddled with unresolved tensions in these areas, "it is not sur-

prising that the result should be a massive polemic in which personal conviction and emotional commitment often have been more prominent than evidence or careful reasoning." It is difficult to discuss the controversy raised by the Jensen papers, especially in a brief space, without being misunderstood—and we certainly do not wish to be misunderstood on such an important and emotional issue. Jensen's original papers were scholarly reviews of the available evidence on causes of intellectual differences. Jensen came to the conclusion that within the white race, the heritability index (the proportion of variance on intelligence test scores due to genetic reasons) is about 0.80. This heritability index is higher than what most researchers currently believe.

Correlations between socioeconomic status (SES) and scores on intelligence tests within a race are typically around 0.3 (see Coleman et al., 1966; Jensen, 1980). This is not as high as many people seem to believe. Most psychologists believe that at least part of this correlation is due to genetics. That is, groups differing in SES would, on the average, differ in their genetic endowment of intelligence. For example, in a survey of measurement experts, 65 percent attribute the SES differences in intelligence to genes and environment, and only 14 percent think environmental variation is a complete explanation (Synderman & Rothman, 1986).

The major types of *evidence* supporting the position that differences in SES are related to genetic differences in intelligence are, of course, indirect but include such findings as (1) children who score lower on intelligence tests than their fathers go down in social class, whereas those who score higher go up in social class (Waller, 1971); and (2) childhood intelligence determines about three times more of the variance of adult educational level than the father's educational and occupational levels combined (Li, 1975).

Briefly, the rationale for the belief that SES is related to genetic differences in intelligence is as follows: If social mobility is in part a function of individual differences in ability, which in turn are in part genetically based, then status differences will tend to be associated with genetic differences.

As Loehlin et al. (1975, p. 167) pointed out, this is not (contrary to what some people think) an assertion of hereditary castes, as in an aristocracy. It is quite the opposite, since social mobility is the *key* to the genetic sorting-out process in each generation.

In general, the position on the relationship between SES and intelligence has not been attacked by psychologists (Eckland, 1967; Gottesman, 1968; Herrnstein, 1973). However, some social critics seem to feel that intelligence tests serve the (perhaps intentional) purpose of preserving social class privileges (see Bowles & Gintis, 1974). This criticism, of course, ignores evidence such as that presented by Waller and Li. Further, it ignores one of the original purposes of such tests. Originally, testing was cherished by those who hoped test use would result in birth, family, wealth, and connections counting for less and merit counting for more. Indeed, the evidence shows that is what has occurred.

The issue of the causes of the relationship between race and intelligence is much more controversial. Jensen, for example, argued as follows:

There is an increasing realization among students of the psychology of the disadvantaged that the discrepancies in their average performance cannot be completely or directly attributed to discrimination or inequalities in education. It seems not unreasonable, in view of the fact that intelligence variation has a large genetic component, to hypothesize that genetic factors may play a part in the picture. But such an hypothesis is anathema to many social scientists. The idea that the lower average intelligence and scholastic performance of Negroes could involve, not only environmental, but also genetic, factors has indeed been strongly denounced (e.g., Pettigrew, 1964). But it has been neither contradicted nor discredited by evidence.

The fact that a reasonable hypothesis has not been rigorously proved does not mean that it should be summarily dismissed ... the preponderance of the evidence is, in my opinion, less consistent with a strictly environmental hypothesis than with a genetic hypothesis, which, of course, *does not exclude the influence of environment or its interaction with genetic factors* [italics added] (1969a, p. 82).

Some people have agreed with Jensen, and some have attacked his position with vigor. Many did not see how evidence on heritability could provide a basis for social or educational policy. Cronbach stated that Jensen "does not see that, in writings for educators, it is pointless to stress heredity. The educator's job is to work on the environment; teaching him about heredity can do no more than warn him not to expect easy victories. Heritability of individual differences is not his concern" (1969, p. 197).

Jensen countered this point as follows.

I submit that the research on the inheritance of mental abilities *is* relevant to understanding educational problems and formulating educational policies. For one thing, it means that we take individual differences more seriously than regarding them as superficial, easily changed manifestations of environmental differences (1969a, p. 239).

Anastasi (1973), who leans toward the environmental position, agreed with Jensen on the *importance* of the topic. "It is only through a clear understanding of the operations of hereditary and environmental factors in behavior development that we can contribute toward effective decisions for the individual and for society" (p. 9).

Those interested in further exploring opinions on this topic should refer to Mackenzie (1984) and Loehlin et al. (1975). Several reviewers have considered the work of Loehlin and colleagues to be one of the most comprehensive and balanced reviews of the race and intelligence issue so far published. Their "final" conclusions are as follows:

1. Observed average differences in the scores of members of different U.S. racial-ethnic groups on intellectual-ability tests probably reflect in part inadequacies and biases in the tests themselves, in part differences in environmental conditions among the groups, and in part genetic differences among the groups. It should be emphasized that these factors are not necessarily independent, and may interact.

2. A rather wide range of positions concerning the relative weight to be given these three factors can reasonably be taken on the basis of current evi-

dence, and a sensible person's position might well differ for different abilities, for different groups, and for different tests.

3. Regardless of the position taken on the relative importance of these three factors, it seems clear that the differences among individuals *within* racial-ethnic (and socioeconomic) groups greatly exceed in magnitude the average differences between such groups (Loehlin et al., 1975, p. 239).

These conclusions are followed by what the authors believed to be several social and public policy implications. Two of these are as follows:

1. Given the large overlap in ability distributions, it would be both unjust and incorrect to label individual members of one group as inferior to members of another.

2. Although measured intelligence is an important variable, we must always remember that it is very far from being all-important in determining what life will be like for most persons in the United States at the present time. It is easy to make too much of these differences—whatever their origin.

In the survey of 661 testing experts mentioned earlier, "fifty-three percent believe that genes and environment are both involved in the black-white difference, compared to only 17 percent who attribute the cause entirely to the environment" (Snyderman & Rothman, 1986, p. 90). Thirty percent did not feel there was sufficient evidence to reach *any* conclusion. (The authors of this text place themselves in this last category.)

Of course, the majority opinion, even among experts, is *not* the criterion for truth. These beliefs "represent no more than subjective statements of plausibility" (Jensen, 1986, p. 314). Some will probably argue that such beliefs only prove the prevalence of racism among testing experts. And that could be true. But we doubt it. As Synderman and Rothman pointed out, experts are presumably more influenced by empirical literature than by more subjective considerations; the respondents were left-of-center politically, and demographics such as ethnicity and childhood family income were poor predictors of expert opinion.

We will close by stressing strongly that there is *no scientific proof* of genetic black-white differences in intelligence. There is very good evidence that environment affects intellectual development and that the environments of blacks and whites have been unequal. Finally, whatever the basis for group differences, there is much *incontestable* evidence that there is a considerable overlap between groups. Jensen himself argues strongly that his paper is concerned only with group differences. Every psychologist knows that we *cannot* draw *any* definite conclusions about an individual's intelligence on the basis of race or socioeconomic class. Unfortunately, some individuals, including teachers and counselors, do this; but it is hoped that readers of this book will not be among those. A wider discussion of how this problem affects testing and what steps have been taken to attempt to adjust for cultural differences is found in a later section ("Culture-Fair Tests of Intelligence") and in Chapter 22.

Stability of Intelligence

Because intelligence is now generally considered to be influenced by both heredity and environment, it logically follows that as a person's environment changes, so might his intelligence—or so at least might his score on an intelligence test, which is an operational definition of intelligence.

The extent to which intelligence is a stable or variable construct is very important. If there were no stability to intelligence test scores, then the test would be a useless instrument. On the other hand, if intelligence test scores were completely stable, then we might adopt fatalistic attitudes concerning a student's educational prognosis.

Research findings suggest that intelligence test scores are very unstable during the early years of a person's life. (See Bloom, 1964, pp. 52–94; and McCall, Appelbaum, & Hogarty, 1973, for excellent reviews of the longitudinal research.) Bayley (1949) found no relationship between intelligence measured at age 1 and age 17. Generally, preschool tests administered after the age of 2 have moderate validity in predicting subsequent intelligence test performance, but infant tests have almost none (see, e.g., McCall, Hogarty, & Hurlburt, 1972).

Certainly, the tested intelligence of very young children is quite unstable.[1] It is hard to know whether this instability is primarily caused by imprecise measuring instruments, trait instability, or both. With increased age, the stability of intelligence test performance increases rapidly. Bayley (1949) found a correlation of 0.71 between mental age at age 4 and at age 17. "This justifies our taking preschool IQ's seriously" (Cronbach, 1970, p. 231). In general, longitudinal studies have suggested that intelligence is a fairly stable characteristic after age 5. Bayley (1949) found the correlations between intelligence test scores at ages 11 and 17 to be +.92.

Most of the research on the stability of intelligence has used individual intelligence tests. Longitudinal research using group verbal and nonverbal tests shows that (1) below age 10, stability in group test scores is less than for individual tests, (2) verbal group test scores are more stable than nonverbal scores, and (3) after grade seven there is hardly any difference between the stability of individual and group verbal tests (Hopkins & Bracht, 1975).

In spite of the reasonably high stability coefficients for groups of children, individuals may show considerable growth or decline in intelligence test scores. Honzik, Macfarlane, and Allen (1948) reported that between ages 6 and 18, the scores of 59 percent of the children changed by 15 or more IQ points. Studies such as this should impress upon us the fact that, although scores on intelligence tests are reasonably stable and therefore useful as *guides* in both short- and long-term

decision making, scores can and do fluctuate, and permanent decisions (or labeling) should not be made solely on the basis of intelligence test performance.

Several books (see, e.g., Engelmann & Engelmann, 1968) and a few research studies (see Pines, 1969) have suggested that through proper intensive early stimulation, one can succeed in raising the intelligence of children. One study conducted by Hunt reported that having mothers of disadvantaged children watch the administration of intelligence tests and afterward coach their children on the test items resulted in an average gain of 30 IQ points (Pines, 1969). One must be very careful about drawing any conclusions from such data. Biehler offered the following analogy to help clarify the point.

> Assume . . . that a particular child has extremely poor vision. If you helped this child memorize the materials used in testing his vision, would you be improving his sight? With training he could pass the test with a perfect score, but would he see any better? What might happen if on the basis of the test the child was placed in a situation in which he had to have perfect vision? Would he be able to perform satisfactorily? Or would it make sense to get an *accurate* estimate of his sight and assist him to make the most of the actual vision he possessed? (Biehler, 1971, p. 447).

Besides the problem of teaching to the test, there has been some professional concern about the adequacy of the research and the inability to replicate the studies showing that early intervention produces any major changes in intelligence test scores. Also, there have been reservations expressed regarding "the ease with which tentative information may become virtual fact" (Sommer & Sommer, 1983, p. 983). For example, the Milwaukee Project, begun in the late 1960s, reported an average difference of 24 IQ points between an experimental group and a matched comparison sample of children who had not been given an enrichment program. An investigation by Sommer and Sommer showed that this research was widely discussed in textbooks, even though the original findings were never subjected to journal review and

---

[1] Data such as these have led one colleague to suggest that the best estimate we can obtain of a young child's intelligence is to take the average of the parents' intelligence. One would not have to lean heavily toward the hereditarian position to make this statement. Familial characteristics may be just as much due to environment as to heredity.

have not been replicated. Moreover, according to a review by Herrnstein (1982), the "media seem unwilling to publish anything that might challenge the certitude with which editors, politicians, judges, and others insist that we know how to increase measurable intelligence" (p. 71).

Ignoring the research where there is fairly direct teaching for the test, there is some evidence suggesting that a *marked* change in environmental conditions is needed to affect a test score greatly after the first five formative years. This is one reason why there has been so much emphasis on programs such as Project Head Start and Electric Company and why some say such projects should not cease after grades one or two.

There has also been some controversy concerning the stability of adult intelligence. Wechsler (1955), testing a cross-sectional sample of adults, found that the verbal aspects of intelligence increase until age 30 and then begin gradually to diminish. However, his method of sampling was somewhat faulty because the educational levels of the various age groups were not comparable. The younger groups had a higher educational level than the older groups, and this could have accounted for the differences he found. Bayley (1955), using longitudinal evidence, concluded that there is continued intellectual growth until 50. More recent studies (Nesselroade & Von Eye, 1985; Schaie, 1983; Schaie & Hertzog, 1986) suggest that decrements are unlikely until well past 60 but have been found by age 74 (Anastasi, 1988). A safe conclusion would be that general intellectual functioning does *not* automatically decrease with age. The environment of the adult may serve to increase or decrease his intellectual performance; but barring health problems, the 60- or 70-year-olds may well have as much intellectual ability as they had at age 25. Of course, we do not mean to deny the evidence suggesting that if one lives long enough, decrement in at least some intellectual characteristics is likely to occur. But decrement is not a necessary concomitant with aging and is not caused by aging per se (see Baltes & Schaie, 1976; Horn & Donaldson, 1976; Schaie & Hertzog, 1986).

Intelligence, Aptitude, Ability, or Achievement

The terms *aptitude*, *ability*, *intelligence*, and *achievement* are used interchangeably by some, while others suggest that subtle shades of meaning distinguish them. The first three terms are usually considered to have the most meaning in common.

The distinction between the terms *aptitude* and *intelligence* is not at all clear, but some distinctions have been made on two separate bases. One distinction that has been made is whether the measure we obtain is considered a *general* measure. If so, the test is frequently called an intelligence test. If the test measures *multiple* or *specific* factors, it is more likely termed an aptitude test. Thus, we might conceptualize different measures of intelligence (aptitude) as lying on a continuum—with global measures falling at one end and specific or multiple measures at the other. At some point along the continuum, we could arbitrarily change the label of the construct we are measuring from intelligence to aptitude. Although this scheme has been suggested by some, it certainly is not universally followed. It does present some difficulties because some tests are considered measures of a general factor, yet report subscores.

Another distinction between the meaning of the two terms has a historical basis. During the time intelligence tests were first being developed, psychologists thought of intelligence as being an innate characteristic not subject to change. This assumption is invalid. However, the term *intelligence* unfortunately still connotes complete innateness to some people. To avoid the implications of innateness, many test-makers prefer to use the term *aptitude*. Because aptitude tests are most useful in predicting future school success, some have suggested that the phrase *scholastic aptitude tests* is the most honest and descriptive. Others prefer to refer to all such tests as measures of learning ability.

Test publishers seem to generally agree with those who prefer to use the terms with a more narrow meaning. For example, the *Otis-Lennon School Ability Test* was previously referred to as the *Otis-*

Lennon Mental Ability Test. The *Cognitive Abilities Test* was previously called an intelligence test, and the *Short Form Test of Academic Aptitude* was previously called a mental maturity test (Lennon, 1980). Yet, as Lennon (1980) pointed out, "There is a certain equivocation or ambivalence on the part of their [the tests'] authors as to whether the tests continue to be intelligence or mental ability tests, or should be regarded only as measures of school learning ability" (p. 3).

Whether aptitude and achievement should be thought of as separate concepts has been the subject of much debate. Kelley defined the *jangle fallacy* as "the use of two separate words or expressions covering in fact the same basic situation, but sounding different, as though they were in truth different" (1927, p. 64). He believed that intelligence and achievement tests were examples of the jangle fallacy. Many other psychologists from his time to the present also believe that the two types of tests are quite similar. Carroll, however, notes that we must distinguish between aptitude as a *construct* and *indicants* of aptitude. He stated that

> it is difficult to see why there should be any great difficulty in distinguishing between aptitude and achievement as *concepts* . . . if aptitude for a learning task is measured prior to an individual's engaging in a task, and if achievement on the task is measured after a given amount of exposure to the learning task, the concepts of aptitude and achievement are operationally distinguishable (Carroll, 1974, p. 287).

Whether or not, or to what extent, the *measures* of aptitude and achievement differ is more debatable. There is certainly no hard-and-fast rule that allows us to distinguish an achievement test from an aptitude test by cursory examination of the test format. Further, both tests do measure behavior, and the behavior measured is acquired rather than innate. However, aptitude and achievement tests do frequently differ along several dimensions.

1. General aptitude tests typically have broader coverage than achievement tests.
2. Achievement tests are more closely tied to particular school subjects.

3. Aptitude test items are more likely to be ones that are dependent upon maturational level (such as copying a diamond) than achievement-test items.
4. Achievement tests typically measure recent learning, whereas aptitude tests sample learning from all times in the individual's past.
5. Studies generally show that aptitude tests have higher heritability indices than achievement tests.
6. Aptitude test scores are more resistant to short-term efforts to hasten their growth.
7. The purpose of aptitude tests is to predict future performance; the purpose of achievement tests is to measure the present level of knowledge or skills.

Bond (1989) illustrated some distinctions between aptitude and achievement tests by referring to the SAT. For example, the SAT quantitative section rarely requires mathematical *knowledge* that goes beyond one year of algebra and one semester of geometry. What makes it difficult is the reasoning *ability* it requires (cognitive psychologists refer to it as the procedural use of declarative knowledge). This reasoning ability is difficult to teach.

With respect to point seven above, it has often been said that the best way to predict future performance is to examine past performance. If this is true and if aptitude tests are able to predict future scholastic success, how do they differ from achievement tests? The common distinction that achievement tests measure what a pupil has learned (or past learning activities) and that aptitude tests measure ability to learn new tasks (or future performance) breaks down if past learning is the best predictor of future learning.

Thus, some people suggest that the difference is not in what the tests do but in the author's purpose and method of constructing the test. (For example, an "aptitude" test designed to predict future performance might use an external criterion in the item analysis of the items in the pilot study instead of the total test score that is likely to be used in an achievement test.) A certain achievement test may be a better predictor than a particular aptitude test for some specified purpose. If, however, the author originally constructed the test for the purpose of predicting future performance, then the test is called an aptitude test. If the purpose of the author was to measure recent learning, then the test is considered an achievement test, even though it may well be a very successful predictive instrument.

Aptitude and achievement tests are sometimes classified according to the degree to which the tasks within a test are dependent upon formal school learning. The distinction is a matter of degree. Some aptitude tests are more like achievement tests than others. As the test tasks become more and more dependent upon specific educational instruction, the test becomes more and more an achievement test. Thus, we have a continuation of the distinction between the terms *achievement* and *aptitude* on the innate-environmental continuum. Being more dependent upon specific school instruction, achievement tests are more environmentally influenced than aptitude tests.

In Chapter 11 we mentioned that publishers of some tests provide expectancy scores. These are derived scores that indicate the expected score on an achievement test based on a scholastic aptitude test score. Discrepancy scores are sometimes computed showing the difference between actual achievement and expected achievement. This information may be useful for evaluation purposes. Publishers providing such scores should be using aptitude measures that are as independent of specific instruction as possible. Further, they need to explain carefully in their manuals the differences they perceive in the two constructs and the (typically low) reliability of the discrepancy scores.

In summary, several possible distinctions have been suggested between aptitude tests and achievement tests. An author whose purpose is to develop a predictive instrument will no doubt call it an aptitude test. If the purpose is to develop an instrument to measure past performance, it will be called an achievement test. For the latter goal, the test items will be based on past school instruction;

for the former goal, that may or may not be the case. However, regardless of what an author calls a test, its uses may vary. Many achievement tests, like aptitude tests, are used to predict. This is ordinarily quite appropriate. However, aptitude tests are certainly better at predicting *general* academic performance, and, because they typically take much less time to administer, they do it more efficiently.

Classification of Aptitude Tests

Aptitude tests can be classified in a variety of ways. For purposes of discussion, aptitude tests are subdivided into four categories: (1) individually administered tests that give a general measure of intelligence[2] (or aptitude); (2) group-administered tests that give a general measure of aptitude; (3) tests that give measures of multiple aptitudes; and (4) tests that are measures of some specific kind of aptitude.

Individuals are often looking for a single measure of ability that will enable them to make a general prediction about future vocational or educational success. Tests of general intelligence best suit this purpose. For those wishing to make differential predictions, a multiple aptitude test might be better. If they wish to predict success in a specific vocation or course, a specific aptitude test may be most appropriate. The following four sections are devoted to consideration of the four categories just mentioned.

INDIVIDUALLY ADMINISTERED TESTS OF GENERAL INTELLIGENCE (APTITUDE)

For the most part, educational institutions, business, and industry make use of group tests of scho-

---

[2]The use of the term *intelligence* in no way implies that the authors of this book believe that intelligence-test scores are solely measures of an innate characteristic. We know that is not true.

lastic aptitude. However, it is occasionally more appropriate to administer an individual intelligence test. All individual tests are valuable as clinical instruments. An examiner can observe the examinees' approach to problem solving, their reaction to stress, and their general test-taking behavior patterns, thereby having the opportunity to gain valuable information. Individual administration allows the examiner not only to observe more closely but also to arrange the testing conditions so that the examinee can perform his or her best. With individual administration, examiners can better establish appropriate rapport with the examinees and instill in them the proper motivation.

The most popular individual intelligence tests are the Stanford-Binet and the various Wechsler tests. A fairly new test, the Kaufman-ABC, is being heavily promoted and shows promise of becoming quite popular. These instruments, as well as examples of some infant and preschool scales and some performance scales, are discussed in this section. However, because this book is designed to serve only as an introduction to standardized tests, these individual tests are *not* covered in any detail. For fuller coverage of individual intelligence tests, see Anastasi (1988). Proper administration of individual tests requires a great deal of training. To be adequately trained, a person needs a basic knowledge of psychology, in addition to at least one course in individual testing with much practice under supervision.

Stanford-Binet

The present Stanford-Binet test is an extensively revised outgrowth of the original Binet-Simon Scales. As previously mentioned, Binet was convinced that measures of simple sensory and motor processes were of little value as measures of intelligence. When Binet was charged with the task of identifying the mentally deficient children in the Paris schools, he collaborated with Simon to publish the 1905 scale, which consisted of 30 tasks of higher mental processes arranged in order of difficulty. This scale was revised in 1908, and the tasks were grouped into age levels. Thus, the

score of a child could be expressed as a mental age. The test was again revised in 1911.

Although several American revisions of these scales were published in the United States, the one that gained the most popularity was the Stanford revision, published in 1916 (Terman, 1916). A second Stanford revision appeared in 1937, and a third revision in 1960 (Terman & Merrill, 1937, 1960). A new set of norms was published for the third edition in 1972.

The fourth edition of the Stanford-Binet Intelligence Scale (SB4) was published in 1986 by Riverside Publishing Company. The authors of the new revision are Robert L. Thorndike, Elizabeth P. Hagen, and Jerome M. Sattler, all well-known leaders in the measurement of intelligence. The fourth edition is built on a model of intelligence that allows for an analysis of the pattern as well as the overall level of an individual's cognitive development. The theory is similar to both Vernon's (1961) and Cattell's (1963) theories discussed earlier. The test is based on a three-level hierarchical model with a general reasoning factor (g), three broad factors (crystallized abilities, fluid-analytic abilities, and short-term memory), and three more specific factors (verbal reasoning, quantitative reasoning, and visualization). There are a total of 15 tests for the fourth edition—9 have evolved from previously used item types, and 6 tests are based on new item types. Figure 15.1 depicts the theoretical model and the 15 different tests. Separate scores are available for each of the 15 tests plus a verbal reasoning score, an abstract/visual reasoning score, a quantitative reasoning score, a short-term memory score, and a complete composite score (not every subtest is available for every age).

Reviews on the SB4 are mixed. The SB4 is considered difficult to administer. While internal consistency reliabilities are high—especially for the composite score—there is insufficient information on test–retest reliabilities. Factor analyses suggest the test is primarily a measure of g, and factor structures are not constant across ages (Reynolds, Kamphaus & Rosenthal, 1988). For thorough reviews, see Anastasi (1989), Cronbach (1989), Reynolds (1987), and Walker (1987).

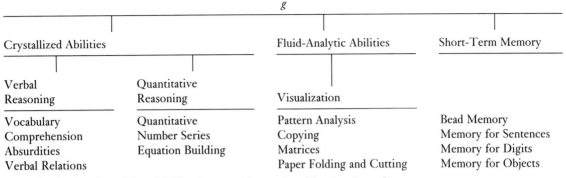

FIGURE 15.1   Cognitive Ability Factors Appraised in the Fourth Edition of the Stanford-Binet.

Wechsler Scales

The first form of the Wechsler Scales, published in 1939, was known as the Wechsler-Bellevue Intelligence Scale. This scale was specifically designed as a measure of adult intelligence. The Wechsler Intelligence Scale for Children (WISC) was first published in 1949 and was revised (WISC-R) in 1974. The original WISC was designed for ages 5 through 15; WISC-R spans the ages 6 to 16. In 1955 the Wechsler-Bellevue was revised and renamed the Wechsler Adult Intelligence Scale (WAIS). It was revised in 1981 and is currently referred to as the WAIS-R. The Wechsler Preschool and Primary Scale of Intelligence (WPPSI) was first published in 1967 and was designed for children of ages 4 to 6½. It was revised in 1989 (WPPSI-R) and now covers ages 3 to 7½.

WAIS-R

The WAIS-R (for ages 16 to 74) is composed of eleven subtests grouped into two scales: Verbal and Performance. The Verbal scale consists of six subtests: Information, Digit Span, Vocabulary, Arithmetic, Comprehension, and Similarities. The Performance scale subtests are Picture Completion, Picture Arrangement, Block Design, Object Assembly, and Digit Symbol.

The WAIS-R is considered to give a very reliable measure of adult intelligence. The separate subtests, being quite short, have lower reliabilities. Because the intent of Wechsler was to get a total or global measure of intelligence, he suggested that a profile interpretation of the scales for normal subjects would not be meaningful. There is some debate about the use of the subtest scores as clinical data. Many studies support the usefulness of the test in predicting various criteria. Unfortunately, validity data are not included in the manual.

WISC-R

The WISC-R (for ages 6 through 16) follows the same format as the WAIS-R, giving subtest scores and verbal, performance, and total IQs. The WISC-R contains 12 subtests. Two of these (Mazes and Digit Span) are used only as alternates. The 10 commonly used subtests are Information, Similarities, Arithmetic, Vocabulary, Comprehension (these comprise the verbal scale), Picture Completion, Picture Arrangement, Block Design, Object Assembly, and Coding (these make up the performance scale). Actual administration alternates Verbal and Performance subscales. The norms sample for the WISC-R was stratified on age, sex, race, geographic region, and occupation of head of household. Like the WAIS-R, no validity data are in the manual. The WISC-R performance scale has been standardized for deaf children.

WPPSI-R

The WPPSI-R (for ages 3 to 7½) contains 12 subtests, 2 of which are alternates. Nine of these are downward extensions of WISC subtests. Sentences replace Digit Span in the Verbal section, and Animal Pegs and Geometric Design replace Picture Arrangement and Coding in the Performance section.

Kaufman ABC (K-ABC)

The Kaufman Assessment Battery for Children (K-ABC), published by American Guidance Service in 1983, is an individually administered test for children from ages 2½ to 12½ years. It is somewhat different in scope, format, and process from the Stanford-Binet and Wechsler Scales. The K-ABC provides standard scores for four global areas: sequential processing, simultaneous processing, mental processing composite (sum of previous two), and achievement. The distinction the authors make between the mental processing and achievement scales is much like Cattell's (1971) distinction between fluid and crystallized abilities (see p. 308).

There are a total of 16 subtests across the various ages, but a maximum of 13 is administered to any one child. The total set of subtests is as follows:

Sequential Processing Scale
  Hand Movements, Number Recall, Word Order
Simultaneous Processing Scale
  Magic Window, Face Recognition, Gestalt Closure, Triangles, Matrix Analogies, Spatial Memory, Photo Series
Achievement Scale
  Expressive Vocabulary, Faces & Places, Arithmetic, Riddles, Reading/Decoding, Reading/Understanding

The K-ABC provides national percentile ranks and stanines, subtest age equivalent scores, arithmetic and reading grade equivalents, and sociocultural percentile ranks.

The K-ABC has met with mixed reviews. Mehrens (1984b) felt it was a good test. His review

noted some particularly noteworthy features including (1) the theoretical bases for the test, (2) the completeness of the manuals, and (3) discussions on the statistical significance and psychological significance of difference scores. Some limitations Mehrens listed had to do with (1) incomplete normative data, (2) the lack of any long-term stability reliability data, (3) lack of clarity in how to use the sociocultural norms, and (4) a lack of definition of *bias*. (The authors imply that bias is differences in means across ethnic groups.)

Hopkins and Hodge (1984) give the K-ABC a somewhat more negative review and conclude that the "K-ABC fails in its attempt to improve on current measures, and may not have done as well" (p. 107).

The fall 1984 issue of *The Journal of Special Education* is devoted to a close look at the K-ABC. This issue, as well as the reviews in the *Ninth Mental Measurement Yearbook*, should be consulted by those who have a special interest in this test.

Individual Performance Scales

An intelligence test is called a *performance* test if the tasks require a manipulation of objects, (e.g., making geometrical configurations with blocks) rather than an oral or written response. This type of test is most helpful in assessing the level of intellectual functioning for people who have language or communication difficulties. Those who speak only a foreign language, who are deaf or illiterate, or who have any type of speech or reading disability are unable to perform adequately on the instruments discussed in the preceding section. In some instances, then, performance scales must be used as replacements for other tests. It should be pointed out, however, that performance scales were originally conceived as supplements to, rather than substitutes for, the more verbally weighted tests.

Some examples of performance scales are the Pintner-Patterson Scale, the Cornell-Coxe Scale, the Arthur Point Scale of Performance Tests, the Cattell Infant Intelligence Scale, the Merrill-

Palmer Pre-School Performance Tests, and the Leiter International Performance Scale. Although a variety of tasks can be, and are, used, some of the more commonly used subtests require (1) manipulating small objects to form designs, (2) tracing and copying, (3) solving mazes or puzzles, (4) following simple directions, and (5) completing formboards.

Performance scales are most useful with young children and/or the mentally retarded, because verbal tests are not very accurate for these groups. Although scales of this kind can be very helpful in assessing the level of intellectual functioning, they are not very predictive of immediate scholastic success and are, therefore, seldom used in the schools.[3] If they are used, they should be given only by qualified personnel.

Infant and Preschool Mental Tests

As mentioned earlier, the measures of intelligence prior to age five do not correlate very well with the measures obtained at a later point in a person's life. McCall's (1980) summary suggests that scores from tests given during the first six months of life essentially are uncorrelated with later scores. The low correlations are not entirely due to imprecision of the measuring instruments. (Split-half and alternate form reliabilities of the tests used at early ages are reasonably high.) The low correlations between earlier and later testings of intelligence are also caused by the instability of the construct of intelligence from early childhood to adult and/or the nonidentity of the constructs being measured.[4] That is, the change in intelligence test scores may occur because the construct of intelligence is affected radically by environmen-

tal conditions; or the change may occur because the tasks on intelligence tests, being different at different age levels, actually measure different aspects of intelligence; or the changes may occur because of a combination of these and other factors that are continually interacting. Is, then, a change in score due to a qualitative or to a quantitative change in mental functioning? The question is a difficult one to answer, and the answer one gives depends in part upon which theory of the structure of intellect she accepts (Stott & Ball, 1965).

Doing experimental research and armchair philosophizing on the reasons for the low correlations may be enjoyable and beneficial to the experimental and theoretical psychologists. Yet practitioners have a legitimate point if they question the value of early testing. Because early intelligence testing does not allow us to do an accurate job of predicting future development, the use must be justified on the basis of measuring present developmental status. That is, these tests are really similar to achievement tests, and their use must be justified, if possible, on that basis.

Because the nonspecialist will not be involved with infant testing, these kinds of tests will not be reviewed here. However, there are many such tests. One survey lists 61 tests for infants (Katoff & Reuter, 1979). The Stanford-Binet, WPPSI-R, and Kaufman ABC are some of the most popular tests for children under 6. The McCarthy Scales of Children's Abilities is appropriate for children from ages 2½ to 8½ years. The McCarthy Screening Test, adapted from the McCarthy Scales of Children's Abilities, is specifically designed to help schools identify children between 4- and 6½-years-old who are likely to need special educational assistance. Other tests used are the Bayley Scales of Infant Development, the Boehm Test of Basic Concepts—Preschool Version, the BRIGANCE Preschool Screen, the Cattell Infant Intelligence Scale, the Columbia Mental Maturity Scale, the Gesell Developmental Schedules, the Goodenough-Harris Drawing Test, the Kaufman Infant and Preschool Scale, the Merrill-Palmer Scales, the Peabody Picture Vocabulary Test, and the Pictorial Test of Intelligence.

---

[3]Performance tests measure abilities that are somewhat different from those measured by verbal tests such as the Stanford-Binet. Correlations between verbal and performance tests range from 0.50 to 0.80.

[4]Because the constructs measured at two different ages may, indeed, be different, many people would speak of the low correlation over time as a lack of validity rather than a lack of stability reliability.

Summary of Individual Tests

The field of individual intelligence testing is dominated by five tests: The Stanford-Binet, the WAIS-R, the WISC-R, the WPPSI-R, and the K-ABC. These tests are technically sound and are useful both as predictors of future academic success and as clinical assessment devices. In comparing individual tests with the group tests to be discussed, we find that the major disadvantages are that individual tests are expensive to give and require a highly trained administrator. The major advantages are: (1) individual tests are generally more reliable; (2) they are potentially more useful in clinical settings—a qualified administrator can learn more about a person from an individual test than a score indicates; (3) they can be used with individuals who may be unable for reasons of shyness, reticence, or anxiety to perform validly on a group test; and (4) although many individual tests are highly verbal, they do require considerably less reading ability than most of the group tests to be discussed in the following section.

GROUP TESTS OF GENERAL APTITUDE

As mentioned earlier, educational institutions, businesses, and industry use group aptitude tests far more extensively than individually administered intelligence tests. Although in many schools the actual tests may be administered by a counselor or someone else with advanced training and in industry by an industrial/organizational psychologist, most group tests are designed so that any teacher with in-service training should be capable of the administrative task.

Many group tests designed to give a measure of general aptitude actually give scores on two subtests. These may be given such titles as verbal and nonverbal scales or language and performance scales. In considering the use of subscores, one must keep in mind the continuum from global to specific measures mentioned earlier. It is always hard to know just when to consider a test a measure of general aptitude and when to consider it a measure of multiple aptitudes. The classification is not solely dependent upon the number of subscores. The author's definition of aptitude or intelligence and the method of constructing the test are primarily what determines the classification.

Most authors of tests that have two subscores, such as verbal and nonverbal, are really attempting to measure the same construct (general cognitive ability or scholastic aptitude) with two separate procedures rather than attempting to obtain measures of two separate aptitudes. Tests giving a whole series of subscores are typically attempting to measure different aspects of intelligence and are referred to as multifactor aptitude tests. These are considered in the following section. In this section, we discuss the tests that are group-administered and are considered as measures of general aptitude, even though they may report more than one score.

Group tests are usually classified according to grade or age level. Some tests have different levels, each level being appropriate for certain grades. For school purposes, there are advantages to using such tests. The same construct is being measured at all levels of the tests, and norm groups are chosen to be comparable from one level to another. This permits comparison of measures obtained over a period of time.

It is impossible to list all appropriate group tests for each grade level. Because most group scholastic aptitude tests measure essentially similar skills (verbal and nonverbal), we discuss only a few of the more commonly used tests. Finally, a short subsection on culture-fair tests is included.

Primary and Elementary Level (Grades K–8) Group Aptitude (Intelligence) Tests

Although some individually administered tests attempt to measure the intelligence of very young children, group tests should ordinarily not be used for children under age 5 (preschool children). Because children of this age have difficulty following the detailed directions necessary for group-testing procedures, they need individual supervision. For five- and six-year-olds, group testing is feasible, but it is necessary to keep the number within a group as small as possible. It is suggested that no attempt be made to administer tests at the primary level to groups of more than 10 to 12 children.

Actually there is some difference of opinion on whether it is worthwhile to give aptitude tests to children in the very early grades. If only a few children are to be tested for specific reasons, individual intelligence tests are often used. Because the long-range reliability (stability) of these tests for young children leaves much to be desired, it is debatable just how useful the scores can be. Some persons argue that such measures can be helpful to the teachers in grouping their students. Others feel that any group should be very flexible and that scores on an aptitude test serve only the ill-advised purpose of making educators' decisions too rigid at this early school level. Decisions about grouping should be flexible. Using test information need not contradict this principle.

At any rate, several group tests are appropriate for these early grade levels. These tests require little or no reading or writing on the part of the student. Responses are marked directly on the test booklets, because it is difficult for young children to use separate answer sheets. Most of the items are of the type that require the student to mark the correct picture (see Figure 15.2).

Tests at the elementary level (grades 4–8) give more stable results and are, therefore, more useful than primary-level group tests. The tasks in these higher levels are generally more verbal. All tests mentioned below, except for the Boehm, also contain levels suitable for the high school grades.

We have chosen to review one of the tests mentioned in this section reasonably thoroughly to illustrate some of the important aspects to consider in test selection and use. Our choice of the Cognitive Abilities Test (CAT) is not meant to imply that we consider it the best test available. We have tried to point out previously in this book that a test must be evaluated in accordance with its intended use. No test is best for all possible uses. The Cognitive Abilities Test is considered to be technically well constructed, but so are many others. The CAT has been chosen as a representative example of those well-made tests that cover a wide age range.

Cognitive Abilities Test, Form 4 (CAT)

These tests are authored by Robert Thorndike and Elizabeth Hagen and published by the Riverside Publishing Company, 1987.

Grade Level and Content. There are two separate batteries: the Primary Battery (K–3) (Levels 1 and 2) and the Multi-Level and Separate Level Editions (grades 3–12) (Levels A–H). Because the primary tests consist of pictorial materials and oral instructions, ability to read is *not* a prerequisite for accurate assessment. There are separate scores on the Primary Battery for each of three cognitive skill areas—each score is based on two subtests—as follows: Verbal (vocabulary and verbal classification); Quantitative (relational concepts, and quantitative concepts) Nonverbal (figure classifications and matrices). The authors have attempted to include tasks that are based on content that children of this age group are likely to have experienced but to use this content in a new way. The test measures the following eight skills and competencies (Thorndike & Hagen, 1987, pp. 6–7):

1. Ability to comprehend oral English
2. Ability to follow directions
3. Ability to hold material in short-term memory
4. Possession of effective strategies for scanning pictorial and figural stimuli to obtain either specific or general information
5. Possession of a store of general information and verbal concepts
6. Ability to compare stimuli and detect similarities and differences in relative size, position, quantity, shape, and time
7. Ability to classify, categorize, or order familiar objects
8. Ability to use quantitative and spatial relationships and concepts

The Multi-Level Edition is bound into a single booklet and grouped into eight overlapping levels. The Multi-Level Edition also has three batteries

Part 1. Picture Classification items assess the ability to determine which picture in a set of five pictures does not belong with the other four.

Part 2. Picture Analogy items assess the ability to infer the relationship between two pictures and to select the picture that is related to the stimulus picture in the same way.

Part 3. Figural Classification items assess the ability to determine, in a set of five geometric figures, which figure does not belong with the others.

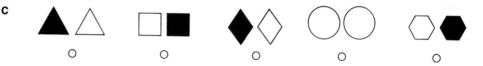

Part 4. Figural Analogy items assess the ability to infer the relationship between a pair of geometric shapes and to apply that relationship in selecting a shape that is related to the stimulus shape in the same way.

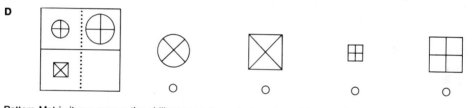

Part 5. Pattern Matrix items assess the ability to supply a missing element in a matrix composed of geometric elements.

Part 6. Series Completion items assess the ability to supply the next step in a geometric series in which each element changes according to a given rule.

FIGURE 15.2 Specimen Items from the Otis-Lennon School Ability Test. (Copyright © 1988 by Harcourt Brace Jovanovich, Inc. All rights reserved. Reproduced by permission.)

separately administered, each with three subtests: the Verbal Battery (Sentence Completion, Verbal Classification, and Verbal Analogies); the Quantitative Battery (Quantitative Relations, Number Series, and Equation Building); and the Nonverbal Battery, which is entirely pictorial or diagrammatic (Figure Analogies, Figure Classification, and Figure Analysis). For most students, the Nonverbal Battery is not quite as good a predictor of school performance as the other two batteries but is considered more useful than the Verbal Battery for students who have difficulty in reading or for whom English is not the first language (Thorndike & Hagen, *Technical Manual*, 1987, p. 11).

Types of Scores. All scores are based on two basic scales: the Universal Scale Score (USS) and the Standard Age Scale (SAS). The USS is a continuous scale across all levels. The SAS is a normalized standard score. In addition, percentile ranks by age and grade and stanines by age and grade are available.

Norming. The CAT was normed concurrently with the Iowa Tests of Basic Skills and the Tests of Achievement and Proficiency in public, Catholic, and private non-Catholic schools. For the public schools, the sample was quite large (over 160,000 students): stratified by school size (nine levels), geographical region (four regions), and socioeconomic status (five categories). The sampling procedure for this test was meticulously planned and executed. The norm group should be quite representative of the nation's schoolchildren. (Most other major publishers take similar care with their sampling plans for widely used tests.)

Reliability. Internal consistency reliability estimates computed separately for each skill area per grade for the Primary Battery are around 0.85 to 0.90. The K-R 20 reliabilities for the Multi-Level Edition cluster around 0.93 for each battery. Standard errors range from 2.4 to 3.7 raw-score points. The standard errors in SAS units range from 3.6 to 6.2 depending upon age or grade.

Stability reliability estimates over a six-month interval range from 0.72 to 0.92 for the Verbal Battery, 0.72 to 0.87 for the Quantitative Battery, and 0.64 to 0.87 for the Nonverbal Battery. Sta-

bility estimates over two- and four-year periods were in the high 0.70s to the middle 0.80s.

Reliabilities of the difference scores among the batteries were not reported in the Technical Manual—which is unfortunate, given the authors' stance that the separate battery scores provide useful intraindividual information.

Validity. Under content validity, the authors write that the test can be characterized by the following statements and that these characteristics describe behavior that it is important to measure for understanding an individual's educational and work potential:

1. The tasks deal with abstract and general concepts.
2. In most cases, the tasks require the interpretation and use of symbols.
3. In large part, it is the relationships among concepts and symbols with which the examinee must deal.
4. The tasks require the examinee to be flexible in his or her basis for organizing concepts and symbols.
5. Experience must be used in new patterns.
6. Power in working with abstract materials is emphasized, rather than speed (Thorndike & Hagen, 1987, p. 39).

Criterion-related validity evidence includes correlations with achievement tests and with school grades. The CAT Verbal Battery generally correlates (concurrently) with the various subtests of the Iowa Tests of Basic Skills (ITBS) in the high 0.70s and low 0.80s. It correlates with the ITBS composite score in the high 0.80s. The Quantitative Battery has slightly lower correlations (except with the math subtest of the ITBS). The Nonverbal Battery has even lower correlations, with the subtest correlations ranging from the low 0.40s to the high 0.60s, and the correlations with the composite in the 0.60s. Correlations between the CAT and the Tests of Achievement and Proficiency range from the high 0.60s to the low 0.80s. Predictions from grade 5 CAT scores to grade 9 ITBS scores are 0.82 for CAT Verbal with ITBS composite, 0.77 for Quantitative with composite, and 0.67 for Nonverbal with composite.

Concurrent validity correlations between CAT and grade point average range in the low 0.40s to 0.60 across grades 5, 7, and 9. The Quantitative Battery tended to correlate the highest.

Construct-validity evidence was based on a factor analysis. All subtests loaded most heavily on a general factor. The verbal subtests also loaded on the verbal factor and the nonverbal subtests on the nonverbal factor. The quantitative subtests had very low loadings except on the general factor.

Interpretation and Use. The final section of this chapter, "Using Aptitude Test Results," will deal with the interpretation and use of all the types of aptitude tests described in this chapter: general, multifactor, and specific. In discussing here the uses of the Cognitive Abilities Test, we will mention only three characteristics and explain their function, rather than outline all possible uses of the CAT. We do not mean to suggest that no other group aptitude tests would have them.

First, the continuous multilevel approach (with norms showing the comparability of levels) has two advantages: (1) it allows one to use tests of appropriate difficulty, and (2) it allows one to observe an individual's relative intellectual growth over time.

Second, the Nonverbal Battery, which uses neither words nor numbers, allows one to make an estimate of ability that is unaffected by reading skill and less susceptible to the influences of formal schooling than are the other two batteries.

Third, because both the Iowa Tests of Basic Skills and the Tests of Achievement and Proficiency are standardized on the same norm group as the CAT, a comparison between level of achievement and aptitude is possible.

This fairly thorough review of the CAT was presented as an example of what you should look for in choosing a group general aptitude test. The CAT compares well with other tests of the same type. We would classify it as one of the better measures of its kind.

Finally, some readers may wonder why this test has been classified as a general aptitude test instead of a multifactor aptitude test. After all, it does report three separate scores from three separate batteries. As we mentioned earlier, the classification of some tests is rather arbitrary. In a sense, this test is a cross between a general and a multifactor aptitude test; but the confirmatory factor analysis strongly suggests the CAT measures a general factor.

Other Examples of General Aptitude Tests

Boehm Test of Basic Concepts—Revised (Boehm-R)

Otis-Lennon School Ability Test (OLSAT)

School and College Ability Tests, Series III (SCAT III)

Test of Cognitive Skills (TCS)

High School, College, and Adult-Level Group Tests

Many tests (such as most of those reviewed above) have levels appropriate for students from primary through grade 12. Some are designed for even higher levels. When choosing a test for a certain age level, one should be careful to ensure that the ceiling on the test is adequate. If, for example, a test is to be administered to a group of above-average high school seniors, it would be best to use a test that is designed for college students as well as high school seniors so that the test has an adequate ceiling.

Two tests, not mentioned above, that are particularly useful in predicting college success at the undergraduate level are the American College Testing Program (ACT) and the College Entrance Examination Program (SAT) (they are discussed further in Chapter 21).

Culture-Fair Tests of Intelligence

Intelligence tests have often been severely criticized for their "cultural biases." This term has been defined in so many ways, however, one can never be completely sure what the criticism means. There are three common interpretations of cultural bias. To some, a test is considered culturally biased if different subgroups obtain different mean scores on the test. To others, a test is culturally biased if it measures different constructs (or achievements) for different subcultures. Still others consider the issue of cultural bias in terms of differential prediction equations and/or different selection ratios or success ratios.

Many measurement experts prefer the third definition, since it focuses on the fair *use* of tests rather than on the tests themselves. (See Chapter 22 for more information on the fair use of tests.) Nonmeasurement specialists who are critics of testing are more likely to use the first definition (e.g., tests are unfair to blacks if the mean score for blacks is lower than the mean score for whites). Measurement specialists are more likely to prefer the second definition to the first. A test is biased if it measures something different in different subcultures. Now, a test biased in the second sense will probably (but not necessarily) be biased in the first sense. The logic is much less compelling in the opposite direction. To clarify these points, let us use two examples—one of physical measurement and one of educational measurement.

If we wish to determine how fast people can run the 100-yard dash, we may measure this by timing people on this very task. If blacks obtain a faster mean time than whites (or vice versa), the measure is biased under the first definition. However, if the task is measuring the same thing for both races, it is not biased in the second sense.

If we wish to determine whether the first-grade children know the rank order of a set of numerals, we might ask a question such as "Which of the following numbers represent the least amount: 13, 17, 19, 21?" If a lower percentage of Hispanic students answer the question correctly than whites, the test is biased in the first sense. Is it biased in the second? It depends. If both the Hispanic and the white students who miss the question do so because they do not know the concept of ranking numerals, the question is *not* biased in the *second* sense. If, however, some of the Hispanic students and none of the whites miss the question because they do not know the meaning of the word

"least," the question *is* biased in the sense that it is measuring knowledge of vocabulary for (some) Hispanics and knowledge of the rank order of the numerals for whites.

Clearly, the second kind of bias is undesirable. It leads to incorrect and harmful inferences to assume that individual children (or a group of children) are inadequate in one area when in fact they have been measured (unknowingly) on something else. Test constructors try to avoid building tests that will have such biases. Research evidence (Jensen, 1976, 1980; Reynolds, 1980, 1982) tends to indicate that publishers are generally quite successful in minimizing this kind of bias. Sattler (1982, p. 360) states: "The evidence, gathered from many studies and with a variety of intelligence tests and ethnic minority groups, points to one conclusion: *Intelligence tests are not culturally biased. They have the same properties for ethnic minority children as they do for white children*" (italics in original). Nevertheless, many measurement specialists think there is at least *some* racial bias in intelligence tests (Snyderman & Rothman, 1986).

Some writers would not concur with Sattler's interpretation (see Williams, 1974; Zoref & Williams, 1980). Publishers cannot build tests that are fair in the second sense for all possible uses. If an intelligence test in the English language is given to a child who speaks only Spanish, surely the test is measuring something different from intelligence for that child. We cannot blame publishers for such a ridiculous misuse or accuse them of building a culturally biased test.

What about the unfairness of tests in the first sense—that is, of different means for different subcultures? We have already alluded to some difficulties with that definition, but it is nevertheless frequently used. Indeed, people have attempted to build tests that are "culturally fair" in that sense of the phrase. As already discussed, a person's environment (subculture) can affect his test score. People of different nations as well as people in different subcultures within the United States place different values on verbal fluency, speed, and other characteristics that influence the scores on intelligence tests. Suppose people in one subculture are less verbal than those in another subculture and that the test used requires verbal skills. Is the test fair to those of the first subculture?

In the past, psychologists have attempted to develop tests that are free from cultural influences. Failing in this—no test can be totally free from cultural influences—an attempt has recently been made to develop tests that are equally fair to members of all cultures. In the attempt to achieve this cultural fairness, these tests have included tasks that involve nonsense material, or tasks that should be equally familiar or unfamiliar to all cultures. Examples of tests of this type are the Cattell Culture-Fair Intelligence Test and the Davis-Eells Test of General Intelligence of Problem-Solving

Ability. Figure 15.3 presents examples of sample items taken from Scale 2 of the Cattell Culture-Fair Intelligence Test. Complete verbal directions are read to the subjects so that they understand the task. The items do not appear to be unfair to any culture. However, the research evidence suggests that these tests are culturally fair if by this phrase we mean that groups from one culture score as well on the tests as groups from another culture. It is very hard, if not impossible, to devise a test that will show no difference between such groups. Contrary to what many critics believed, stress on verbal skills in our current tests is not the primary cause of group differences. Flaugher (1970) has cited a number of studies showing that the greatest

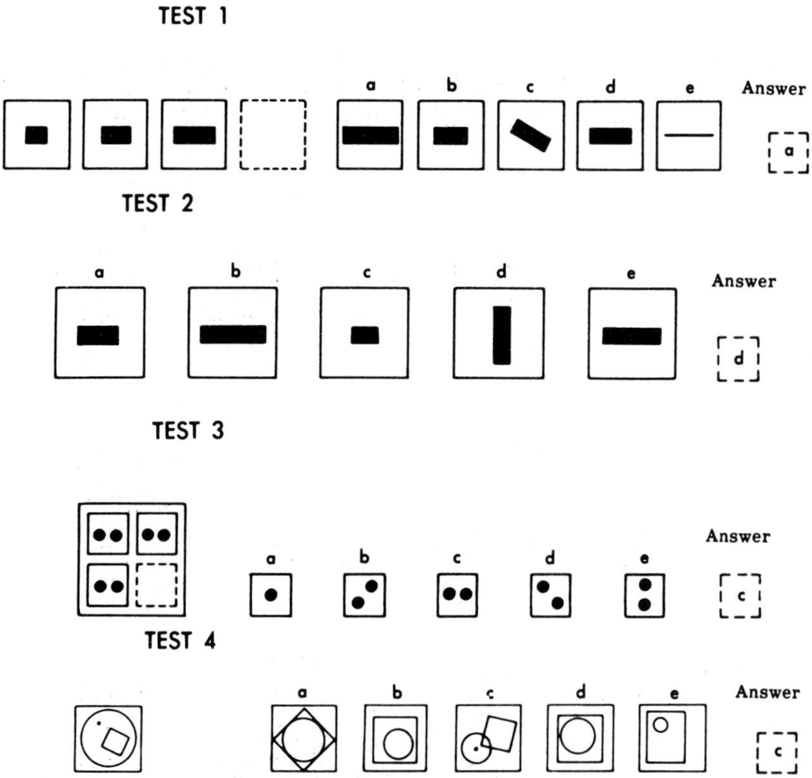

FIGURE 15.3   Sample Items from Scale 2, Form A, of the Cattell Culture-Fair Intelligence Test. (Copyright © 1949, 1960, by the Institute for Personality and Ability Testing, P.O. Box 188, Champaign, Illinois, U.S.A. 61820. All rights reserved. Reprinted with permission.)

difference in the performances of blacks and whites is on nonverbal items.

Even if we could devise a completely culture-fair test, would it be a worthwhile attainment? Some argue yes, claiming that such a measure would be relatively independent of cultural influences and therefore as nearly correlated to innate ability as possible. Others argue that to mask existing group differences by eliminating all items measuring these differences is to delimit the usefulness of the test (Tannenbaum, 1965, pp. 722–723).

A somewhat different approach to developing a culturally fair instrument is a technique known as the System of Multicultural Pluralistic Assessment (SOMPA) developed by Mercer (1977). While the approach has much in common with some of the mathematical approaches to the fair use of tests, it can be conceptualized as a new measurement technique using a battery of instruments. SOMPA is used with children 5 to 11 years old and compares a child's score not only against a national norm group but also against the scores of children from a similar social and cultural background. Information for the assessment is gathered from two sources: a test session with the child and an interview with the child's principal caregiver, usually the mother. The test sessions with the child include administering the WISC-R, the Physical Dexterity Tasks, and the Bender-Gestalt test. Information obtained from the mother includes information on the Sociocultural Modalities, which purportedly measure the distance between the culture of the home and the culture of the school, the Adaptive Behavior Inventory for Children, and a Health History Inventory. Using multiple regression equations based on the additional data, the WISC-R is "corrected." Mercer compares this correction to a golf handicap (Fiske, 1976). She feels that *uncorrected* scores should be used to determine immediate educational needs, whereas the *corrected* scores should be used to determine a child's "latent scholastic potential." Mercer wants to use the *corrected* scores to avoid labeling children as retarded and to use the *uncorrected* scores to make educational de-

cisions. This may or may not work. One danger, of course, is that users will come to regard the "corrected" scores as reflecting reality in a way that they clearly do not. Children who have not learned certain skills or capabilities, for whatever reason, remain without those skills or capabilities even after the statistical correction is made. To treat the children as if they have them or to ignore their absence on the grounds that "they're no worse than other children of similar background" does no service to the children at all.

Another danger is that many states distribute special education funds on the basis of the number of children classified as retarded. Whether the label can be removed without the loss of the additional funding available for special educational needs is as yet undetermined.

The debate as to the usefulness of a culture-fair test or one mathematically "corrected" to equate for varying cultural backgrounds depends on how we wish to use the instrument. Some people wish to get a measure of innate ability (whatever that is). Other people, who believe that innate ability can never be measured with a paper-and-pencil test, wish to use intelligence tests primarily as predictive instruments. If the environmental effects of one's culture are related to the criterion we are attempting to predict, then to eliminate these cultural differences would reduce substantially the validity of the test.

Most measurement specialists take the position that if culture-fair tests could be developed, in general they would be less useful measures than the presently existing measures that are influenced by environmental factors. We further discuss the testing of minority groups in Chapter 22.

MULTIFACTOR APTITUDE TESTS

As already mentioned, some psychologists contend that intellect is a general characteristic and that a single score can adequately represent the degree to which a person possesses intelligence. Others subscribe to a multifactor theory of intelligence but argue that the measurement of these multifactors adds little, if any, to the predictive validity of single-factor tests. The advocates of multifactor testing generally support it on both theoretical and practical bases.

Many schools and employment agencies administer multifactor aptitude tests. What are the reasons for this popularity of multifactor tests? Is the popularity justified? What are the characteristics of these tests? What are their advantages and limitations?

The development of factor-analytic techniques has certainly been the major technical development affecting the popularity of the multifactor theory.[5] Rather than simply argue whether intelligence is general, multifactor, or composed of many specific abilities, a factor analysis can be made on many different kinds of ability tests. If only one factor is obtained, then we have some support for the theory of general intelligence. If many factors are obtained, the multifactor theory is supported. If we obtain as many factors as kinds of tests, the specific aptitude theory is supported.

Some of the multifactor tests have not actually been constructed through a factor-analytic procedure; rather, they have been constructed by choosing items that have high correlations with other items in the *same* subtest but low correlations with the items (and subtest scores) in the *other* subtests. This results in a set of subtests that are internally consistent but that have low intercorrelations with each other. This should be a major characteristic of any multifactor test. Of course, the use of test construction techniques to develop a multifactor test does not enable us to argue that obtaining a set of factors proves the actual existence of the factors within a person.

Another aspect that has led to the increased popularity of multifactor aptitude tests is the vocational and educational counseling movement.

The discovery of differential abilities within a person should certainly facilitate vocational and educational counseling. But does it? Some argue that identification of differential abilities is helpful in counseling only to the extent that this knowledge allows us to differentially predict how well an individual will be able to perform in various educational curricula or vocational tasks. The degree to which multifactor tests enable us to differentially predict is an important aspect in determining their usefulness.

In general, the data indicate that multifactor aptitude tests are not very good for *differential* prediction. This is not solely because of test inadequacies in subdividing intellect into its component subparts. The problem is that the criteria (e.g., job success) are not solely dependent on specific aspects of intelligence. Thus, although we may be able to obtain measures of numerical ability and verbal ability that are distinct, there simply is not any criterion that differentially demands one aptitude and not the other. Therefore, there is little evidence of differential predictive validity. Whether this makes the test no more useful than the less expensive and less time-consuming test of general intelligence depends on the degree to which one believes that a more precise *description* is useful in counseling, regardless of whether it increases predictability. As with any belief, there are differences of opinion on this. It is not a belief easily subjected to scientific verification.

Examples of Multifactor Aptitude Tests

In a survey of secondary schools, Engen, Lamb, and Prediger (1982) reported that 66 percent of the schools administered the Armed Services Vocational Aptitude Battery (ASVAB), 34 percent used the Differential Aptitude Tests (DAT), and 24 percent used the General Aptitude Test Battery (GATB). The first two of these three widely used multifactor aptitude batteries are discussed briefly here. The Differential Aptitude Tests, published by The Psychological Corporation, is reviewed in more detail because of the wealth of material available about the test.

---

[5]Factor analysis is not covered in this book, other than noting that the correlations between the tests determine the number of factors. If the tests are all highly correlated with each other, for example, we have only a single factor. If, at the other extreme, the tests do not correlate at all with each other, then we have as many factors as tests.

Differential Aptitude Tests (DAT)

Grade Level and Content. The DAT has been designed for use in grades 8–12. The DAT has eight subsets: Verbal Reasoning (VR), Numerical Ability (NA), Abstract Reasoning (AR), Clerical Speed and Accuracy (CSA), Mechanical Reasoning (MR), Space Relations (SR), Spelling (SP), and Language Usage (LU). (The last two subtests are more appropriately considered achievement tests because they are more closely tied to the curriculum.) The authors of the test also report a ninth score, VR + NA, which is interpreted as a measure of general scholastic aptitude. Examples of some of the practice items are shown in Figure 15.4. Of course, these examples are easier than the actual items in the subtests, although they are identical in form.

Types of Scores. Percentile ranks and stanines can be obtained for the eight subtests and for the combined raw scores on the Verbal Reasoning and Numerical Ability tests.

Norming. Separate sex and grade-level (8–12) norms are provided. The testing of the normative sample was done in the fall. However, the authors also provide spring (second-semester) norms for grades 8–11. These spring norms were obtained by interpolating between the fall norms of successive grades. Because the accuracy of these interpolated norms is debatable, it is better to administer the test in the fall and to thus avoid having to use the spring norms.

Reliability. Split-half reliability coefficients computed separately for each sex and each grade are reported for both forms for all subtests except the Clerical Speed and Accuracy subtest. Because this subtest is speeded (remember that others are timed but supposedly unspeeded), an alternate form reliability is reported. The reliability coefficients for the separate subtests range from 0.87 to 0.97 for boys and from 0.83 to 0.96 for girls.

Validity. The research on the prediction of course grades is summarized according to subject areas. English grades are best predicted by VR + NA and by the LU and VR scores. Mathematics grades are best predicted by the VR + NA combination or by NA alone. Science grades can be best predicted by VR + NA, VR, NA, or LU subtests. Social studies grades can be predicted about equally well, using VR + NA, VR, NA, or LU subtests. The four major subject-matter areas can all be predicted with a fair amount of success. However, all four major subject-matter areas can be predicted successfully using the same score: VR + NA. Thus, the *differential* validity of the DAT in predicting course grades is not very well substantiated.

The prediction of achievement-test results follows essentially the same pattern as the prediction of course grades. Again, the subscores on the DAT are fairly good predictors, but they are not very adequate in differential predictions. The data showing the relationship between DAT scores and educational and occupational groups indicate the same thing.

The concurrent validity studies showing the correlation between the VR + NA score and tests of general intelligence reveal consistently high correlations. Their correlations, ranging mostly in the 0.70s and 0.80s, are as high as the correlations between most tests of general intelligence. Thus, it certainly appears that the VR + NA score serves the same purpose as general intelligence test scores, and little would be gained by administering the DAT and a test of general intelligence in the same grade.

An interesting (and perhaps surprising to many) finding is the low correlations between the subscores on the DAT and the Kuder Preference Record scores. In general, interests and aptitudes are not highly correlated and, as the DAT Manual points out, it is risky to base counseling on interest scores without having some information on a person's aptitude scores.

As mentioned in the introduction to this section on multifactor tests, one of the characteristics such tests should have if they are to be successful in differential prediction is low intercorrelations of the subtests. Although the average (across grades) intercorrelations of the DAT are reasonably low, most users would probably wish lower intercorrelations.

ABSTRACT REASONING

Each row consists of four figures called Problem Figures and five called Answer Figures. The four Problem Figures make a series. You are to find out which one of the Answer Figures would be the next (or the fifth one) in the series of Problem Figures. Here are two examples:

In Example X, note that the lines in the Problem Figures are falling down. In the first square the line stands straight up, and as you go from square to square the line falls more and more to the right. In the fifth square the line would be lying flat, so the correct answer—chosen from among the Answer Figures—is D. Therefore, the circle for D has been filled in on line X of your Answer Sheet.

CLERICAL
SPEED AND ACCURACY

This is a test to see how quickly and accurately you can compare letter and number combinations. On the following pages are groups of these combinations; each test item contains five. These same combinations appear after the number for each test item on the Answer Sheet, but they are in a different order. You will notice that in each test item one of the five is **underlined**. You are to look at the **one** combination that is underlined, find the **same** one after that item number on the Answer Sheet, and fill in the circle under it.

The following examples have been marked correctly on your Answer Sheet. Note that the combination marked on the Answer Sheet must be exactly the same as the one that is underlined in the test item.

Examples

V. <u>AB</u> AC AD AE AF   Y. Aa Ba <u>bA</u> BA bB

W. aA aB BA Ba <u>Bb</u>   Z. 3A 3B <u>33</u> B3 BB

X. A7 7A B7 <u>7B</u> AB

MECHANICAL REASONING

Find the space for Mechanical Reasoning on the Answer Sheet.

This test consists of a number of pictures and questions about those pictures. Look at the two examples below, to see just what to do.

Example X.

Which person has the heavier load? (If equal, mark C.)

SPACE RELATIONS

This test consists of 60 patterns which can be folded into figures. To the right of each pattern there are four figures. You are to decide which **one** of these figures can be made from the pattern shown. The pattern always shows the **outside** of the figure. Here is an example:

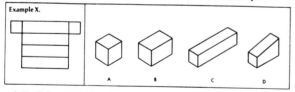

In Example X, which one of the four figures—A, B, C, D—can be made from the pattern at the left? A and B certainly cannot be made; they are not the right shape. C is correct both in shape and size. You cannot make D from this pattern. Therefore, the circle for C has been filled in on line X of your Answer Sheet.

FIGURE 15.4   Examples of Practice Items from Some of the Subtests of the Differential Aptitude Tests, Forms V and W. (Copyright © 1982, 1972 by The Psychological Corporation. All rights reserved. Reproduced by permission.)

Interpretation and Use The administration of the DAT in grades 8 or 9 can provide information that is relevant to the decisions a student must make concerning future educational plans. The general lack of differential predictive validity does not mean the test is useless. The subtests do predict a variety of criteria, and the descriptive value of the subtest scores is not to be underemphasized.

Many counselors appreciate the fact that students who would perform at a low level on a test of general intelligence may do well on some of the subtests of the DAT. Thus, the counselor can say something positive about the student's abilities, and the student leaves the counseling interview with a better self-concept than if one could only interpret the low score on a general intelligence test. The combined score (VR + NA) serves very well as a measure of general intelligence.

An optional service of potential value to counselors and students is the DAT/Career Planning Program. This program consists of a Career Planning Questionnaire and the DAT Career Planning Report, in addition to the DAT itself. The questionnaire collects data on student status, interest, and goals. A computer compares these data with the results of the DAT and prints out an interpretive report, which may confirm the appropriateness of the student's occupational choices in terms of his abilities, interests, and plans, or which may suggest alternative occupational areas. The publisher suggests that the report can be used by counselors in interviews with students and parents and/or can be given to students for further discussion and study at home.

DAT Adaptive The DAT Adaptive was published in 1986. This is a computer-administered and scored version of the DAT and, if one desires, the Career Planning Questionnaire. A computer adaptive test is one taken on a computer. It is *adaptive* because the questions each individual answers vary depending on the correctness of answers to previous questions. No individual needs to answer all the questions so there is a savings in testing time. In addition to saving time, a computer adaptive test can provide immediate results.

The DAT Adaptive is equated to the DAT and uses Form V/W norms. At the time of this writing, no technical manual was available for the DAT Adaptive. (For a discussion of computer adaptive tests in general, see Chapter 22.)

Armed Services Vocational Aptitude Battery (ASVAB) Published by the United States Military Enlistment Processing Command (USMEP-COM) in 1984, this test is designed for use both in high schools and junior colleges and for selecting and classifying all enlistees at the Armed Forces Examining and Entrance Stations. Form 14 of the test is intended for use in high schools. It has 234 items in ten subtests: General Science (GS), Arithmetic Reasoning (AR), Word Knowledge (WK), Paragraph Comprehension (PC), Numerical Operations (NO), Coding Speed (CS), Auto & Shop Information (AS), Mathematics Knowledge (MK), Mechanical Comprehension (MC), and Electronics Information (EI). The total testing time, including administrative time, is about 180 minutes.

The ASVAB-14 yields three academic composite scores and four occupational composite scores. The academic composites are Academic Ability, Verbal, and Math and indicate potential for further formal education. The Academic Ability composite was derived logically and the other two academic composites through factor analyses. The occupational composites—Mechanical & Crafts, Business & Clerical, Electronics & Electrical, and Health, Social, & Technology—indicate levels of aptitude for career areas. All occupational composites were based on regression analyses of criteria from military training programs on the ASVAB subtest scores. The composites, however, are based on weighting the relevant subtests equally.

The ASVAB norms are based on subsamples of a 1980 reference population from the Profile of American Youth study plus a sample of tenth-graders. There are norms for tenth-graders, eleventh-graders, twelfth-graders, two-year college students, and a random sample of youth between the ages of 18 and 23. The test is not currently being recommended for ninth-graders.

The alternate-form reliabilities of the composite scores are acceptably high. However, it should be pointed out that there is overlap in the subtests that constitute the various composites. For example, three of the four occupational composites have the Arithmetic Reasoning subtest as a component of the composite, and two of the composites have Electronics Information as a component of the composite. Given the overlap, the intercorrelations between the occupational composites are quite high, ranging from 0.68 to 0.93 for students in grades 11 and 12. The reliability of the difference scores between composites is, therefore, not necessarily very high.

The validity data for the ASVAB are based primarily on studies done in the military, where the criteria were performance in training programs for a variety of military occupations. Some evidence from validity generalization studies suggest the ASVAB may also be reasonably valid for civilian occupations that are counterparts to those in the military. Because of the relatively low reliability of difference scores and the pervasive problem of multifaceted criteria mentioned earlier, we should not expect much *differential* validity.

The results given to the students present total youth population percentile scores and grade/sex percentile scores. The counselors also receive opposite-sex and total grade normative information on the counselor section of the results sheet. Counselors will need to determine whether this information should be shared with the students. Probably at times it should be and at other times not, depending on the purpose of the counseling session and the ability of both the counselor and the student to understand the different norming groups and the implications of the data.

As mentioned earlier, the ASVAB is used by about twice as many schools as use the DAT. This is probably true, in part, because the test is available at no cost or obligation to the school or to the students. The widespread use of the ASVAB by schools has been somewhat controversial, however. Many points have been made to support using the ASVAB: it is free; the test provides some useful data for vocational counseling; and it is particularly helpful for those students who are considering entering the military (the largest single employer of high school graduates). Of the students that take the ASVAB in high school, approximately 15 percent enter military service. The results of the ASVAB are used by the military to assist in recruiting and to stimulate interest in the services. (This could be seen as either a positive or a negative aspect, depending upon one's point of view.)

Probably the weakest aspects of this test are the relatively sparse amount of validity evidence for predicting success in civilian jobs or training programs and the lack of reliable difference scores on the composites. (At the time of this writing, the ASVAB is undergoing extensive revisions, which should result in an improved test.)

SPECIAL-APTITUDE TESTS

A special aptitude is usually defined as a person's potential ability (or capacity to acquire proficiency) in a specified type of activity. Special-aptitude tests were developed primarily for help in making vocational and educational selection decisions as well as for counseling. Compared to multifactor aptitude tests, they are probably more useful in selection (or placement) decisions by an institution and generally less useful in personal counseling for individual decision making.

Although many kinds of special-aptitude tests could be mentioned in this section, we do not discuss any particular test because readers will not all be interested in the same areas. There are tests of Vision and Hearing, Mechanical Aptitude Tests, Clerical and Stenographic Aptitude Tests, and Musical and Artistic Aptitude Tests. Those interested in a more thorough coverage of any test or area of testing should turn to the sources of information about tests discussed in Chapter 14. We will now briefly discuss aptitude tests for specific courses and professions and tests of creativity.

Aptitude Tests for Specific Courses and Professions

Aptitude tests developed for particular school subjects such as algebra and foreign languages have been used extensively in the past to help individual pupils with their curricular choices. In recent years, however, this popular practice has diminished. Research has shown that such tests generally do not significantly increase the predictive validity over what can be obtained by a general mental ability test, the relevant subscores on multifactor aptitude tests, or achievement-test batteries. Because these latter tests are usually given in the schools, it may well be a waste of time and money to administer special-aptitude tests.

Many special-aptitude tests, such as the Law School Admission Test and the Medical College Admission Test, have also been developed for use in various graduate and professional schools. These tests are designed to be of appropriate difficulty (harder than general aptitude tests for adults) and (to at least some extent) emphasize the abilities of importance to the particular profession. Although these tests are usually slightly better predictors than general aptitude tests, their major advantage lies in their security. Many general aptitude tests could be obtained in advance by an enterprising person wishing to obtain a high score, thereby gaining admission into a professional school. The security of the professional test rules out this sort of enterprise as a factor in admission decisions.

Tests of Creativity

Some who subscribe to the general theory of intelligence suggest that creativity is an aspect of general intelligence and need not be measured separately. Others realize that, although tests of general ability are best able to predict future school

and job success, it is likely that creativity is a distinct ability. Research seems to indicate that whereas a person has to be reasonably intelligent to be creative, the converse does not hold.

We feel that more research on attempts to measure creativity and to investigate its correlates is warranted. There is now available enough evidence to suggest that creativity is something unique and not necessarily correlated with ability to perform well in an academic setting. (However, it is a misconception that creative children do poorly in schoolwork. Research shows that, as a group, creative children do quite well in school.) There are many potential benefits available if the construct of creativity can be effectively isolated and measured. Creative people are important for an advancing society. If creativity can be further understood, if the identification of creative people becomes possible, and if creativity can be taught in the schools, society is sure to benefit.

At the present time, there are few creativity tests on the market. The tests that do exist should be considered only as research instruments, and much more work is needed in the area before we can feel comfortable using the results for individual decision making. One of the better known creativity tests is the Torrance Tests of Creative Thinking. Reviews of it can be found in the *Ninth Mental Measurements Yearbook*. One study shows that the Torrance Tests are highly sensitive to changes in instruction. "A very modest induced attitude shift resulted in a shift of up to approximately a standard deviation in the creativity scores" (Lissitz & Willhoft, 1985).

USING APTITUDE TEST RESULTS

Considering all the types of aptitude tests discussed in this chapter, it can confidently be said that the average child will be given the opportunity to take (or be subjected to) at least two aptitude tests before graduating from high school. A college-bound student may easily take five or more. Government agencies, including USES, the military, and private employers also use aptitude (cognitive ability) tests. How are these tests being used? Are they helpful or harmful?

The public has been, and should be, much concerned with the uses and possible *misuses* of aptitude tests. Because tests play an allocative role in education and employment, testing is an important policy issue. However, as Snyderman and Rothman (1986) have pointed out, in the IQ controversy "the expert voice has been misinterpreted and misrepresented, and science has been perverted for political ends" (p. 81). This final section, devoted to the uses of aptitude tests, also contains warnings against potential misuses.

Table 1-1 lists some various purposes of standardized tests under four headings: instructional, guidance, administrative, and research. The use of aptitude tests under each of these categories is discussed in more detail here. We will also discuss the use of such tests in employment.

Instructional Uses

The ability level of students in a particular class should enable a teacher to evaluate the appropriateness of the class materials. A teacher should not teach the same kind of material in the same fashion to two classes—one in which the students have a mean scholastic aptitude score of 85 and the other in which the students have a mean scholastic aptitude score of 120. Neither should two students within the same class who differ widely in ability have the same assignments. Thus, knowledge of general aptitude test scores enables a teacher to make better decisions about the kind of class material presented to each student.

If educators gain more knowledge in the area of aptitude-treatment interaction (see Cronbach & Snow, 1969, 1977), scores on aptitude tests may become even more helpful in designing appropriate instructional strategies. However, it is likely that if aptitude tests are to be maximally effective in such a task, they will need to be somewhat different from those currently most popular (Chi, Glaser & Rees, 1982; Glaser, 1973). We should remember that current aptitude tests are much more useful for prognosis than for diagnosis.

An argument that has occasionally been voiced against the use of aptitude tests for instructional purposes is that teachers will use low aptitude scores as an excuse for not attempting to teach the students ("The students can't learn anyway" attitude). Unfortunately, it is probably true that some teachers have this attitude. Aptitude test scores should be used in helping teachers form *realistic* expectations of students; they should not be used to help teachers develop fatalistic expectations.

However, in agreeing that this potential danger of testing exists, we do not think it should be overemphasized. The teachers in inner-city schools who do not try their hardest because of preconceived ideas that their students cannot learn have not obtained their ideas of student deficiency primarily from aptitude test scores. Such factors as the parents' educational level, socioeconomic status, race, and occupation all contribute to teachers' opinions concerning a child's aptitude. Goslin (1967), a noted sociologist, in a comprehensive survey of teachers' opinions about tests, found that less than one-fourth of the teachers felt that abilities measured by intelligence tests are more important than other qualities for predicting school success. He also found that teachers tend to view intelligence-test results as being more influenced by environmental factors than by innate capacities. Whether or not this is true, Goslin's findings suggest that teachers are not likely to become fatalistic about a person's innate ability from intelligence-test score information.

Knowing that Denny has a low scholastic aptitude test score, that his father is an unemployed alcoholic, and that his mother entertains men to pay for the groceries, the teacher may conclude (correctly or incorrectly) that Denny will have trouble learning in school. If the teacher accepts these factors in the spirit of a challenge and does her best—fine. If the teacher adopts a fatalistic attitude toward Denny—bad. However, there is no more compelling reason to blame the test for the improper attitude of the teacher than to blame her knowledge of all the other facts.

Let us make this point clear. *Aptitude tests can help teachers develop realistic expectations for their students.* While we do not condone—in fact we condemn—teachers who develop fatalistic attitudes toward the learning abilities of their students, we do not think aptitude tests should be made the scapegoat. We admit this potential misuse of tests. There is little evidence, however, to suggest that teachers' attitudes toward the learning potential of their students are unduly influenced by test results (Teachers Opinion Poll, 1974; Airasian et al., 1977).

Research shows that a child's classroom behavior counts more than standardized tests in teacher judgments about students (Kellaghan et al., 1980; Salmon-Cox, 1981). Moreover, the teachers tend to raise, but not lower, their ratings of students' performance as a result of receiving standardized tests results. It must be remembered, however, that if we use any kind of data (including aptitude tests) to label children, we must be sure not to misuse the labels. *Labels must be treated as descriptions rather than as explanations.* Too often, a label is treated as an explanation.

Improvement in aptitude test scores should not be used as dependent variables in evaluating learning outcomes or teaching because these scores should be relatively unaffected by formal school learning. However, knowing something about the ability level of the students in a class or a school *can* help teachers determine whether the students are learning as much as is predicted from their ability level. Although some people object to the term *underachiever* (for, really, it is just an overprediction), it is nonetheless helpful to know that a person is not performing as well as could be predicted on the basis of his ability scores. If a whole class or school is performing less well (e.g., on a standardized achievement battery) than would be predicted from aptitude test scores, then this *may* be due to inadequate teaching. (See the section in Chapter 11 on "Expectancy Scores.")

As a summary of this subsection, we quote Beck:

> We do our teachers and administrators a great disservice when we pretend that ... [they] are unable to make reasoned and reasonable use of such infor-

mation [scores from scholastic aptitude tests]. Every bit of data we have, from surveys to controlled research, confirms that ... the tests are used, but not overused; valued but not revered; used to give the benefit of the doubt when they are discrepant from other information, interpreted in conjunction with other information not in isolation; and when expectancy effects exist they exist to the benefit of children (1986, p. 16).

Guidance Uses

Aptitude tests can be useful in vocational, educational, and personal counseling. These test scores are useful in counseling because the educational requirements of some vocations require considerable general ability. The correlations between general aptitude scores and success in training programs tend to run between 0.40 and 0.50 (Ghiselli, 1966). These correlations would be even higher if selections into the training programs were not based on the aptitude scores (see Chapter 13). McCall (1977) found that aptitude scores obtained on a sample of children between 3 and 18 years old predicted educational and occupational status when the sample was age 26 or older.

General aptitude tests often provide useful data for dealing with problem children. An overactive first-grader, if very bright, may be bored and need to be challenged more. Or the child may be totally incapable of doing first-grade work and, therefore, causing trouble because of frustration. If the child is of average intelligence, perhaps emotional problems are the reason for the overactivity. An individually administered intelligence test can often provide the best data available for judging which of these competing hypotheses is most tenable.

Multifactor aptitude tests are often used in counseling to give students a better idea of their differential abilities. As already discussed, the measurement of these differential abilities does not necessarily improve differential prediction, but it does lead to a fuller understanding of one's self.

For guidance, as for instructional purposes, there are some possible misuses of aptitude test scores. The problem of treating test scores as fatalistic predictors still exists. Counselors, teachers, and in fact all school personnel should remember that their job, in part, is to attempt to upset negative predictions.

A problem related to educators' becoming fatalistic is the development of a fatalistic attitude in children. A popular topic of conversation is the importance of developing a good self-concept in the students. There is no doubt that students should be self-accepting and feel that others accept them also. If a counselor interprets a low test score so that the student feels unworthy, that is indeed unfortunate. One of the advantages of a multifactor aptitude test is that a student usually performs at an acceptable level on some of the subtests, and these scores can and should serve as morale builders for the student.

As with other possible misuses of test results, we feel this problem of low aptitude scores resulting in poor self-concepts can be overemphasized. Just as test scores are not the major factors in forming teachers' opinions about the learning abilities of children, so also low aptitude test scores are probably much less influential than other factors in contributing to an undesirable (inaccurately low) self-concept. In fact, a review of relevant research by Rosenholtz and Simpson (1984) shows quite clearly that young children typically overestimate their own abilities, but their estimates begin to relate to actual classroom performance by about second grade. This shift to realism may be considered good or bad, depending on one's views. The shift is certainly not due to aptitude test results, because aptitude tests are not routinely given prior to grade 3 or 4. Children of all grade levels are found to spend considerable time determining their academic status in comparison with their classmates. Tests often seem to be blamed for educational problems that were not caused by the tests to begin with. To be sure, there is some relationship between what a person thinks he can achieve and what he will achieve. Nevertheless, it is a generally held position that counselors should help students obtain and accept an accurate self-concept, not an inaccurately high

one. Proper interpretation of aptitude tests can be helpful in this endeavor (Hodgson & Cramer, 1977). We agree totally with Carroll and Horn (1981), who state that "far from being abused by overuse, the science of human abilities is underexploited in diagnosis, counseling, and evaluation" (p. 1019).

Administrative Uses

Aptitude tests can be used in many ways by the administration. Some selection, classification, and placement decisions, such as who should be admitted to kindergarten early, who should be placed in the enriched classes, who should be placed in the remedial classes, and who should be admitted to colleges, are decisions that may be made by counselors or school psychologists who rightly may not consider themselves as administrators. Nevertheless, these are administrative decisions.

As with almost any use of aptitude tests, there are accompanying potential misuses. Some persons charge that the major misuse of tests in administrative functions is that decisions made on the basis of test scores are often treated as if they were permanent, irreversible decisions. If a child is put into a remedial class in, for example, grade 3, there is too often a tendency on the part of the administration, having once made a decision, to forget about it. The child then gets lock-stepped into a curriculum.

Now, although we do not support administrative inflexibility in the reconsideration of decisions, we should consider whether the use of test scores is really the causative factor of this inflexibility. We must admit that in some cases it is. Some people simply place far too much faith in test scores, and this results in too much faith in the correctness of decisions—so they are made and then forgotten. However, not all, or not even most, inflexibility can be charged to test score misuse. Many of the decisions made would be incorrectly treated as permanent, even if there were no test score data on the students. It is worth noting that if a decision must be made, it should be based on as much evidence as possible. Not to use valid test information in making decisions because of possible misuse is cowardly, foolish, and even unprofessional.

There are also some who argue against the use of aptitude tests for various decisions because they do not think the decision must, or should, be made at all. However, if a test is used to help implement a policy that is considered incorrect by some, there is no reason to blame the test. For example, a sizable group of educators is against ability grouping. If the policy, right or wrong, is to group on the basis of ability, it is appropriate to use an aptitude test to help decide who should be placed in what group. Some have argued that tests are unfair to different subgroups, and therefore the test results should be ignored when doing ability grouping. However, although we do *not* advocate using *only* test data, Findley (1974) reported that Kariger has shown that such a process would result in *less* separation of upper and lower SES students than if other factors in addition to test scores are used—for example, teacher grades, study habits, citizenship and industry, and social and emotional maturity. As Findley explains "stereotypes of upper and lower SES children held by school personnel result in further separation between groups than the tests alone would warrant" (1974, p. 25). We emphasize that this example is not meant to advocate ability grouping or decisions made only on test data. It does suggest that blaming *tests* for what may be considered harmful social separation is inappropriate. However, with respect to aptitude testing and grouping, we should make one important point. Some educationally deprived children are likely being inappropriately labeled as retarded and are, therefore, placed in special classes. Any time an aptitude test score is used, the user must keep in mind the environmental conditions under which the child was reared. Whether or not special classes are desirable for mentally retarded children, it certainly is not desirable to *misplace* a child into such a special class.

Let us take another example. Some people are opposed to the use of scholastic aptitude tests in college selection decisions. It is sometimes unclear whether what they oppose is the notion of selecting college students on the basis of predicted success in college or whether they oppose the use of scholastic aptitude tests in assisting in that prediction. If the former, that is a philosophical point and should be argued separately from whether tests help in predicting success. If the latter, they should read the research literature. As Samuda stated, "The evidence about college entrance tests as predictors is no longer a subject of legitimate dispute. The studies have been widespread, they number in the thousands, and the results are consistent. By and large, the higher the test scores, the more successful the students are in college" (Samuda, 1975, p. viii). In fact, there is also evidence that academic aptitude at time of college admission is significantly related to occupational level later in life (Lewis, 1975).

But don't aptitude tests serve to keep the lower SES students out of college? Were they not, in fact, designed to do that? The answer to both questions is *no*. With respect to the latter question, as Cronbach indicates in an excellent historical analysis, "Proponents of testing, from Thomas Jefferson onward, have wanted to open doors for the talented poor, in a system in which doors often are opened by parental wealth and status" (Cronbach, 1975, p. 1). With respect to the former, evidence suggests that the testing movement has accelerated the breakdown of classes by identifying able individuals from the lower strata who might otherwise have gone unnoticed (Tyler, 1976). It has been estimated that of youths in the top quarter with respect to scores on intelligence tests, 33 percent come from the working class, 42 percent come from the lower-middle class, and 25 percent come from the upper and upper-middle classes combined (see Havighurst & Neugarten, 1975). Thus, lower SES students are not kept out of college because of their aptitude test scores. Fricke (1975) demonstrated that if admission to the freshman class at the University of Michigan had been determined *entirely* by academic aptitude test scores of high school seniors, a *majority* of freshmen would have come from low SES backgrounds rather than the 10 or 15 percent that is typically the case. Using only the presumed "biased" test scores would not decrease but *increase* by a factor of four or five the number of low SES students. Again, we are not advocating the use of only test scores to make decisions. We are pointing out that it is not low test scores that are keeping low SES students (in general) out of college. At any rate, because of the proven validity of scholastic aptitude tests for predicting college success, if there is a policy, right or wrong, to limit college enrollment to those with some minimum level of scholastic aptitude, it is not incorrect to use aptitude test scores to *help* determine who should be admitted to college. Far too often, the cry of test misuse is raised because the lamenter is against the policy that the correct use of test scores helps implement, rather than because the test is not being correctly used under the existing policy.

The uses of aptitude test results for public relations and for providing information for outside agencies do have some very real potential pitfalls. Occasionally, press releases are made concerning how schools compare with each other in the average ability of their students. Although this sort of public relations may momentarily "feather the cap" of some school official, the chances that the public understands the release are dim indeed, and one is hard put to verbalize any real advantages of this sort of public release of information.

The issue of whether schools should provide an individual's aptitude test score to outside agencies is a cloudy one. The question is whether such information is to be treated as confidential. If so, then it should not be released without a student's permission. But does the consent have to be explicit, or can it be implied? For example, if a student applies for a job that requires security clearance, is the application to be interpreted as implied consent for the release of school records? This question cannot be discussed in great detail in this book. The safest procedure (both morally and legally), however, is not to release test information to any outside agency without the explicit consent of the student and/or the parents.

Another possible use of aptitude tests is for relevant supplementary information in curriculum planning and evaluation. An idea of the general ability level of the school should help educators decide, for example, how much relative emphasis to place on college preparatory curricula.

Research Uses

Aptitude test scores can be used in research in many, many ways. Ordinarily, the scores are used as independent variables (variables that influence the variable being studied) in a research design. For example, in evaluating instructional procedures, many researchers would wish to use some aptitude measure as an independent variable. Some research—such as that investigating the environmental effects on intelligence—treats the scores as dependent variables (the variables one wishes to influence). Because this book is not designed for the researcher, we preclude further discussion of this topic.

Employment Uses

As we mentioned briefly in Chapter 13, on validity, there was an earlier belief that aptitude tests seemed to predict success in some jobs and in some settings but that the validity coefficients seemed to be situation-specific. It has also been suggested by psychologists and educators that scores on aptitude tests given to children were predictive of school success but not much else. Recent research and reviews of the literature have refuted both of those positions.

With regard to the second point, Willerman writes as follows: "The results . . . clearly confirm the view that outstanding accomplishments can be predicted from IQ tests obtained in childhood, . . . if one were looking for a single childhood augury of outstanding later accomplishment, one could not do better than to obtain an intelligence test measure on the subject" (1979, p. 332). We should not infer from this that we should select job applicants based on childhood IQ scores. However, it does support both the stability and cogency of early aptitude for life success.

The validity of aptitude tests in employment situations has been studied extensively throughout the years. Current opinion is that psychologists made incorrect inferences from the early studies

Table 15-2   Mean Validities of Various Predictors for Entry-Level Jobs*

Predictor	Mean Validity	Number of Correlations	Number of Subjects
Ability composite	.53	425	32,124
Job tryout	.44	20	—
Biographical inventory	.37	12	4,429
Reference check	.26	10	5,389
Academic achievement	.21	17	6,014
Experience	.18	425	32,124
Interview	.14	10	2,694
Training and experience ratings	.13	65	—
Education	.10	425	32,124
Interest	.10	3	1,789
Age	−.01	425	32,124

*Adapted from Hunter and Hunter (1983).

showing positive but not necessarily high or statistically significant validity coefficients. It is now generally concluded that most findings of low validity were due to statistical artifacts such as small sample size, unreliable criterion data, and restriction of range. Using such techniques as meta-analysis, we currently can conclude that ability tests do, quite consistently, predict subsequent job and job training performance. Schmidt and Hunter, who have done much of the theoretical and statistical work in this area, flatly state that "professionally developed cognitive ability tests are valid predictors of performance on the job and in training for all jobs in all settings" (1981, p. 1128). While this strong statement has not been proven to everyone's satisfaction, Schmidt and Hunter do back it up with an impressive amount of evidence (see also Hunter, 1986; Schmidt, 1988).

Not only do aptitude tests predict job performance, but they do so better than any other single predictor. Hunter and Hunter (1983) summarize a set of validity studies where all the studies used supervisor ratings as the criterion. Table 15-2 shows the mean validity coefficients of various predictors for entry-level jobs where training would follow hiring; supervisor ratings were the criterion data. As can be seen, ability is, on the average, the best predictor. The findings in this table

must be taken quite seriously. They are based on a large number of correlations. Further, the criterion is one that might reasonably be influenced by interpersonal skills of the same type that might influence interview results. In spite of that, the mean validity for interviews was far down the list.

Whether or not one uses ability tests in employment decisions can have a tremendous impact on productivity. Hunter and Schmidt (1982) applied a utility model to the entire national workforce and estimated that the gain in productivity from using cognitive tests, as opposed to selecting at random, would amount to a minimum of $80 billion per year! They equate this gain as being roughly equal to total corporate profits, or 20 percent of the total federal budget. While these estimates are based on a few assumptions that are open to considerable debate, there can be no doubt but that the use of ability tests can result in more effective hiring and that effective hiring procedures can have a substantial impact on national productivity.

■ SUMMARY

The major points of this chapter are summarized in the following statements.

1. The definitions, structure, etiology, and stability of intelligence are all unsettled issues in psychology.
2. Current definitions of intelligence stress that it is a behavioral trait that is, at least in part, dependent upon past learning.
3. Theories regarding the structure of intelligence have ranged from the idea of a general factor of intelligence to the conceptualization of many specific factors. These various theories have resulted in many different kinds of tests, classified as tests of general intelligence, multifactor aptitude tests, and special-aptitude tests.
4. Both heredity and environment affect intelligence-test scores.
5. In general, intelligence measures are not very stable in early childhood, but by the age of five or so they begin to stabilize.
6. The most popular individual intelligence tests are the Stanford-Binet and the Wechsler instruments. The Kaufman-ABC is a fairly recently published test, which may well become popular. Specialized training is required to administer and interpret these tests correctly.
7. Individual tests can be better used with those who, for motivational or other reasons, do not perform accurately on group tests. Furthermore, more clinical information can be obtained from individual tests.
8. Teachers are generally qualified to administer group tests of intelligence.
9. Some attempts have been made in the past to build culture-fair intelligence tests. These results have largely failed if we define *culture fairness* as the equality of mean scores for various subcultures. Even if culture-fair tests could be devised, the usefulness of such measures is open to question.
10. Multifactor aptitude tests are used by the majority of school systems. Although designed to be differentially predictive, they have not been very successful in that respect. Nevertheless, they have remained a popular tool of the counselors to assist students in understanding themselves better and as a catalyst for career exploration.
11. Many kinds of special-aptitude tests exist. They include mechanical, clerical, musical, and art aptitude tests; tests for specific courses and professions; and creativity tests.
12. Aptitude test results can be used by teachers, counselors, administrators and employers. They can also be misused. Unfortunately, the negative attitude the public correctly displays toward test misuse has been overgeneralized and extended to the tests themselves. There can be no doubt but that the wise use of aptitude tests benefits society.

■ POINTS TO PONDER

1. Which theory of intelligence do you subscribe to? What are the advantages and limitations of accepting this theory?
2. Project Head Start implicitly makes an assumption that environment plays a significant role in intellectual development. If research shows that programs like Head Start are ineffective, must we conclude the assumption is incorrect?
3. Can you write an item that you would defend as being a measure of aptitude and *not* a measure of achievement?
4. A married couple wishes to adopt an infant. They request assurance that the infant possesses normal intelligence. What should the social worker tell this couple?
5. List five specific situations where group intelligence tests would be more appropriate than individual intelligence tests. Do the same for the reverse situation.
6. Assume that two randomly chosen groups were given the Stanford-Binet at age four. One group (group A) of students received nursery school instruction that included tasks similar to those asked on the Stanford-Binet. The other group (group B) received no such instruction. On retesting at age five, group A performs significantly better. Does this tell us anything about the stability of intelligence,

the effects of environment on intelligence, or the validity of the test?

7. Why do you think there are no multifactor aptitude tests published for the early elementary grades?

8. What are the advantages and limitations of using a multifactor aptitude test rather than a set of special-aptitude tests covering the same constructs?

9. What are the instructional advantages (if any) of being able to correctly identify highly creative children?

10. Given the question "What can books be used for?" a student responds, "To build fires." Is this a creative answer? Support your contention.

Chapter 16

Standardized Achievement Tests

- ■ Differences Between Standardized and Teacher-Made Achievement Tests
- ■ Classification of Standardized Achievement Tests
- ■ Standardized Diagnostic Achievement Tests
- ■ Criterion-Referenced Standardized Achievement Tests
- ■ Standardized Achievement Tests in Specific Subjects
- ■ Standardized Achievement-Test Survey Batteries
- ■ Individually Administered Achievement Tests
- ■ Using Achievement-Test Results
- ■ New Directions in Testing

What is an achievement test? How do standardized achievement tests differ from teacher-made achievement tests? Are there achievement tests for all subject matter areas? Will the Stanford Achievement Test be valid for my purpose? What preschool tests are available? Are they any good (valid)? What use can be made of achievement-test results? These are some of the questions that the classroom teacher, counselor, and school administrator can be expected to ask and should be able to answer. This chapter presents information that will assist the test user to answer these and other questions.

Literally hundreds of standardized tests are available to the classroom teacher, counselor,

school psychologist, and administrator. In previous chapters we have considered standardized aptitude tests and teacher-made achievement and performance tests. In Chapter 17, we will consider interest inventories and personality tests. In this chapter, we will consider standardized achievement tests that have been specifically designed for use in an educational context.

Some achievement tests are norm-referenced (NRT), while others are criterion-referenced (CRT). Some purportedly yield both norm- and criterion-referenced information. Some measure only a single subject, whereas others consist of a battery of tests measuring performance in a variety of content areas. Some are designed for only the upper grades; others are made up of an articulated series ranging from K to 12. Some provide survey-type information, while others yield diagnostic data. Most standardized achievement tests are group-administered, but some, especially those designed for the handicapped, are individually administered.

To try to cover a substantial portion of them here would be an exercise in futility. We have selected only a few of the more representative ones so that we might comment on their properties—properties that *every* user should examine when selecting a standardized test. The tests discussed here are generally of high quality. However, there are many other standardized achievement tests of equally high quality, and it should *not* be assumed that the tests discussed in this chapter are the best ones available. In the long run, the best test is the one that best measures the user's objectives most validly, reliably, efficiently, and economically.

After studying this chapter, you should be able to:

1. Understand the similarities and differences between standardized and teacher-made achievement tests.
2. Compare the three major types of standardized achievement tests—diagnostic, survey battery, and single-subject-matter—in terms of purposes, coverage, and construction.
3. Have a better conception of the newer type of standardized criterion-referenced tests and how they can be useful in the "diagnosis" of student learning problems, as well as helpful in planning for optimal instruction.
4. Recognize that most standardized achievement tests are more similar than dissimilar.
5. Critically evaluate a standardized achievement test.
6. Understand the factors to be considered in selecting a standardized achievement test.
7. Understand and discuss the various instructional, guidance, and administrative uses of standardized achievement-test data.
8. Recognize the supplemental value of standard-

ized achievement-test data to assist teachers in their decision making.

DIFFERENCES BETWEEN STANDARDIZED AND TEACHER-MADE ACHIEVEMENT TESTS

Teacher-made and commercially published standardized achievement tests are more alike than different. Where there are differences, they are more a matter of degree than intent, since the purpose of each is to measure pupil knowledge, skills, and ability.

Any test that has a representative sampling of the relevant content (i.e., possesses content validity) and that is designed to measure the extent of present knowledge and skills (from recall of factual material to the higher mental processes) is an achievement test, regardless of whether this test was constructed by the classroom teacher or by professional test-makers. The major (but not the only) distinction between the standardized achievement test and the teacher-made test is that in a standardized achievement test the systematic sampling of performance (i.e, the pupil's score) has been obtained under prescribed directions of administration. They also differ markedly in terms of their sampling of content, construction, norms, and purpose. The differences between teacher-made and standardized achievement tests are summarized in Table 16-1.

Sampling of Content

Standardized achievement tests normally cover much more material (although they need not have more items) than teacher-made tests because they are traditionally designed to assess more than one year's learning. Teacher-made achievement tests usually cover a single unit of work or that of a term. Standardized tests, in contrast to teacher-made tests, may not so readily reflect curricular changes, although test publishers attempt to "keep up with the times." This is less of a problem with

TABLE 16-1   Comparisons Between Standardized and Teacher-Made Achievement Tests

Characteristic	Teacher-Made Achievement Tests	Standardized Achievement Tests
Directions for administration and scoring	Usually no uniform directions specified	Specific instructions standardize administration and scoring procedures
Sampling of content	Both content and sampling are determined by classroom teacher	Content determined by curriculum and subject-matter experts; involves extensive investigations of existing syllabi, textbooks, and programs (i.e., contains material covered in many, if not most, classrooms); sampling of content done systematically
Construction	May be hurried and haphazard; often no test blueprints, item tryouts, item analysis, or revision; quality of test may be quite poor	Items written or at least edited by specialists. Developers use meticulous construction procedures that include constructing objectives and test blueprints, employing item tryouts, item analysis, and item revisions; only best items used
Reliability	Generally not known; can be high if test carefully made	Generally high, with reliability often over .90; small standard errors of measurement
Interpretive aids	None	Can be quite elaborate, ranging from a few suggestions to detailed remedial strategies
Norms	Only local classroom norms are available	Typically make available national and local school district and building norms
Purposes and use	Best suited for measuring particular objectives set by teacher and for intraclass comparisons	Best suited for measuring broader curriculum objectives and for interclass, school, and national comparisons

single-subject-matter tests than with survey batteries. It is easier (and often less expensive) to revise and renorm a single test than a survey battery.

Whether a person should use a commercially published standardized test or a teacher-made test depends to a large degree on the particular objectives to be measured. Norm-referenced standardized tests are constructed to measure generally accepted goals or objectives rather than unique or

particular classroom objectives. Teacher-made tests usually measure more adequately the degree to which the objectives of a particular course for a particular teacher have been met. For example, let us assume that a teacher of eleventh-grade history feels that her pupils should have an awareness of social conditions before the French Revolution. If this area is atypical of the conventional course curriculum, it should be readily evident that the teacher-made test would be more valid than the best standardized test that did not concern itself with this objective. In other words, test users must ask themselves, "How valid is this test for my objectives?" Generally, the teacher-made achievement test more closely follows a changing curriculum, as in the sciences.

Construction

Standardized achievement tests and teacher-made achievement tests differ in the relative amount of time, money, effort, and resources that are available to the commercial test constructors. It is estimated that it costs from $50,000 to $100,000 for commercial test development (APA Monitor, 1984). The following example of how a standardized achievement test is constructed by test publishers may indicate why the teacher-made test is seldom as well prepared as the standardized test.

First, the test publisher arranges a meeting of curriculum and subject matter specialists. After a thorough study and analysis of syllabi, textbooks, and programs throughout the country, a list of objectives is prepared—what information students should have, what principles they should understand, and what skills they should possess. The objectives to be sampled by the test are then reduced to a test outline or table of specifications (based on the judgments of the various experts involved in the test planning) that guides the test-maker in constructing the test. Then, with the assistance of classroom teachers and subject matter experts, a team of professional test writers prepares the items according to the specifications outlined in the grid. (Inclusion of such a grid in the publisher's test manual would be very valuable to the user in ascertaining whether the test has content validity for her. Unfortunately, few publishers include the grid.)

After careful review and editing, the tryout or experimental items are arranged in a test booklet. Then the instructions to both administrators and pupils are written, and the tryout tests are given to a sample of pupils for whom the test is designed. After the answer sheets have been scored, an item analysis is made to identify the poor items. In addition, comments from test administrators pertaining to timing and clarity of instructions for both administrator and pupils are noted. Further editing is then done on the basis of the item analysis (or more items are written if needed and the content validity is rechecked). The test is then ready to be standardized. After a representative sample of pupils has been selected, the refined test is administered and scored. Reliability and validity evidence is obtained, and norms are prepared for the standardization sample. Throughout the item-writing stage, and definitely at the item analysis stage, attention is given to preventing racial, ethnic, and gender bias. (See Diamond & Elmore, 1986, for a report of their survey on bias in standardized achievement tests.)

This brief description should demonstrate how much time, effort, and expense go into the preparation of a standardized achievement test. Without minimizing the enthusiasm, interest, and dedication of classroom teachers in constructing their own tests, teacher-made tests seldom compare in technical aspects with commercially made standardized tests. The teacher alone constructs a test; the standardized test is constructed by test specialists in cooperation with subject matter experts, curriculum specialists, and measurement experts. The teacher has a limited amount of time to devote to test construction; standardized test-makers can spend as much as two or three years on the preparation of their tests. Teachers often do not examine their items in terms of difficulty and discrimination; commercial test publishers use statistical tools in order to eliminate or to suggest ways to rewrite the poor items. Teachers, because they often are unable to try out their test beforehand, do not have the opportunity (1) to clarify ambiguous directions or (2) to alter the speededness of the test by either increasing or decreasing the number of items. The commercial test publisher tries out the items in experimental or preliminary editions and is able to ascertain how well the test and the items function. On the whole, then, it should be readily evident that commercial standardized achievement tests are superior in terms of technical features to teacher-made achievement tests. This does not imply that teacher-made achievement tests cannot be technically as sound as commercial tests. They can be, but because of the time, money, effort, and technical skill involved in preparing a good test, they normally are not.

Classroom teachers should not develop an inferiority complex because of the preceding remarks. They should recognize that they have been trained to be teachers and not test-makers.

Interpretive Aids

Another distinguishing feature between the traditional teacher-made and standardized test concerns the ancillary material accompanying the test to assist the classroom teacher in undertaking remediation of material that has not been learned by the pupils. Some standardized single-subject-matter tests have little, if any, material to aid the teacher in interpreting the pupil's performance and then undertaking corrective action. However, some standardized survey achievement batteries, such as the Metropolitan, Stanford, and Iowa Test of Basic Skills, have separate manuals devoted solely to providing suggestions to the classroom teacher for teaching/reteaching the concept(s) the pupils do not understand. Teacher-made tests have no such provision, of course.

Norms

Another feature distinguishing most standardized tests from teacher-made achievement tests is that, generally, standardized tests provide norms of one type or another: for example, sex, rural-urban, and grade. With national norms, one can make numerous comparisons of the performance of individual pupils, classes, grades, schools, and school districts with the academic progress of pupils throughout the country. Naturally, the kinds of comparisons that can be made depend on the types

of norms furnished by the test publisher. Although teacher-made tests may have norms, they are, at best, only locally based.

Purposes and Use

Standardized achievement tests, especially survey batteries, have a broad sampling of content, and may be too general in scope to meet the specific educational objectives of a particular school or teacher. Teacher-made achievement tests, on the other hand, will usually have narrow content sampling (although what is sampled may be covered thoroughly). This does not imply that the standardized achievement test is superior to the teacher-made achievement test. Because of the emphasis placed upon the various course objectives, the standardized achievement test may be superior to the teacher-made test in one instance and not in another. Both standardized and teacher-made achievement tests serve a common function: the assessment of the pupil's knowledge and skills at a particular time. It is usually agreed that the teacher-made achievement tests will assess specific classroom objectives more satisfactorily than standardized achievement tests. It should be noted, however, that all educational decisions should be based on as much empirical data as possible. Because the standardized and teacher-made achievement tests serve different purposes, school personnel should consider the supplemental value of standardized achievement-test scores to teacher-made test scores and teacher observations and judgments, rather than argue that one measurement device is better than the other.

To compare the pupils in one school with those in another school, a standardized achievement test would be appropriate. To determine whether Betty has learned her addition skills in Mr. Jones' third grade may be better accomplished by using a teacher-made test. To measure pupils' general basic skills, a standardized achievement test is the better choice. To measure pupils' knowledge in some content areas such as science, geography, and civics, a teacher-made test may be more appropriate, since the content in these areas may become outdated quickly and the locally constructed test can keep up with the times more easily. Thus, the functions or uses of the two kinds of achievement tests vary.

In addition, standardized achievement tests often have equivalent forms that allow one to measure growth without administering the same items to the examinees or to obtain a "score" on one form if an error was made on another form. Many of the newer standardized survey batteries have an articulated series of levels so that one can obtain comparable measures from K through 12. Finally, more and more survey batteries are standardized concurrently with an aptitude measure, thereby permitting one to interpret an examinee's achievement in relation to his or her ability. We consider the uses of standardized achievement tests further in the concluding section of this chapter.

CLASSIFICATION OF STANDARDIZED ACHIEVEMENT TESTS

One method of classifying tests is based on the extent of language involved—*performance* (which was discussed in Chapter 9), *verbal*, *nonverbal*, and *nonlanguage*.

As mentioned previously, *performance tests* generally involve the manipulation of objects with little, if any, use of a pencil-and-paper format.

Verbal tests require that examinees be able to comprehend written materials.

Nonverbal tests, often referred to as nonreading tests, are used for illiterates and nonreaders (regardless of age), and infant and preschool children. While no writing or reacting is required on the part of the examinees, they *must* comprehend language since the instructions are verbal. These tests are *not* suited to testing deaf or foreign language speakers.

Nonlanguage tests such as the familiar Army Beta do *not* require examinees to use either written or spoken language. Instructions are generally given in pantomime.

Other classification schemes are *diagnostic tests*, which are designed to isolate a pupil's specific strengths and weaknesses in some particular field of knowledge; *single-subject-matter achievement tests*, which are concerned with measuring the pupil's educational accomplishments in a single content area; and *survey batteries*, which consist of a group of tests in different content areas standardized on the same population so that the results of the various components may be meaningfully compared. (Some measurement texts include *prognostic tests* as a subset of achievement tests, but we prefer to discuss them under aptitude tests.)

These three types (diagnostic, single-subject-matter, and survey battery) of standardized achievement tests differ in their purposes, coverage, and construction. They differ primarily because they are designed to measure different aspects or segments of the pupil's knowledge.

Since we also discuss criterion-referenced tests (CRTs), it might be construed that there are four types of standardized achievement tests. We have purposely avoided this classification scheme, since any of the three types could be norm-referenced, criterion-referenced, or both.

Purposes and Use

Throughout this text, we have taken pain to alert test users that *no* single test should be used as the sole criterion in decision making but must be considered in concert with a variety of other information (Airasian, 1979b; Hall et al., 1985; Hall et al., 1988; Stiggins & Bridgeford, 1985; Salmon-Cox, 1981). If anything, insofar as decision making is concerned, teacher-made achievement tests are weighted more heavily than standardized tests, more so at the elementary level.

All standardized tests are designed to assess pupils' knowledge and skills at a particular point in time so that inferences about this knowledge can be made to a fairly broad, general domain. If we are interested in learning whether Alan has the prerequisite entry skills that will enable him to profit maximally from reading instruction, we will give him a reading readiness test. If we are interested in learning what Mary's specific strengths or weaknesses are in reading or spelling, we will use a diagnostic test. If we are interested in making a somewhat thorough evaluation of Mary's achievement in spelling, we should use a standardized spelling test rather than the spelling subtest of a survey battery, because the survey battery subtest will ordinarily be shorter, thereby limiting its coverage. If we are interested in learning whether Mary is a better speller than she is a reader, we should use a standardized survey battery where the total test has been standardized on the same sample. If different subject matter tests have norms based on different samples, direct comparisons cannot be made because the samples might not be equivalent.

For guidance purposes, it may be advisable to use the results of both a survey battery (which will indicate the relative strengths and weaknesses in many different subject matter fields) and a single-subject-matter test that gives more thorough information in a particular area. For example, pupils can initially be given a survey battery as a preliminary screening device. Then, certain pupils can be identified for more thorough investigation and be given a single-subject-matter and/or diagnostic test in the area of suspected weaknesses. The use of such a sequential testing (i.e., using the survey battery for an initial screening and a single survey test and/or a diagnostic test for only a few individuals) saves considerable testing.

Coverage and Construction

Standardized achievement-test batteries attempt to measure pupils' knowledge in many diverse areas; single-subject-matter tests are restricted to only a single area of knowledge such as grade 11 physics, grade 4 spelling, or grade 6 language arts. Normally, single-subject-matter tests are a little more thorough in their coverage. For example, if a spelling test requires one hour and the spelling subtests of a battery require 40 minutes, there is more opportunity for the single test to have more items and thereby to increase the content sampling.

Although the survey battery is more convenient to administer than an equal number of single tests, and although, for the most part, the survey battery is fairly valid for the average classroom teacher, some of the subtests may lack the degree of validity desired because of their more limited sampling of tasks. The general consensus, however, is that despite the more limited sampling of tasks, survey batteries are preferred over a combination of many single-subject-matter tests. This is so because the survey battery (1) gives a fairly reliable index of a pupil's relative strengths and weaknesses since it has been standardized on the same population, whereas this is seldom the case for single-subject-matter tests; (2) is more efficient timewise; (3) is usually more economical; and (4) young children generally find it easier to take the tests in a battery rather than as separate single-subject-matter tests because of the common format in the battery.

Diagnostic tests may differ markedly from the survey battery or single-subject-matter test, depending upon their use. Since diagnostic tests are designed primarily to assist the teacher in locating or attempting to isolate the genesis of some deficiency, we would expect the diagnostic test to have a thorough coverage of a limited area. For example, both a standardized achievement test of arithmetic skills and/or the arithmetic subtest of a survey battery are concerned with measuring general goals and objectives of the arithmetic curriculum. Hence, both types of arithmetic tests contain a variety of items on many different arithmetic topics. A diagnostic test, however, may be restrictive in the sense that it is concerned only with one or two aspects of arithmetic, such as addition and subtraction. Moreover, the diagnostic test is more concerned with measuring the components that are important in developing knowledge in a complex skill.

There is no appreciable difference among the various types of achievement tests in the technical and mechanical factors involved in their preparation. In many instances, it is not possible to identify the type of test solely on the basis of the item format. That is, a test item such as "9 is what percent of 36?" could conceivably be found in a survey, a single-subject-matter, or a diagnostic test. About the only way in which the various types of achievement tests may be distinguished is to make a study of the breadth or intensity of their coverage and their provisions for interpretation.

STANDARDIZED DIAGNOSTIC ACHIEVEMENT TESTS

In this and the next several sections, we present some examples of diagnostic tests, criterion-referenced achievement tests, single-subject-matter achievement tests, and standardized achievement-test survey batteries that are commonly used in the public schools. We also consider some of the factors that are relevant in determining the choice of one achievement test or battery over another.

In contrast to survey batteries (discussed in a later section), which consist of a group of subtests in different content areas standardized on the same population, there is another group of narrowly focused tests—*diagnostic*. Although some of the newer survey achievement tests—for example, the Metropolitan Achievement Tests have some diagnostic features such as the instructional level scores in reading and mathematics, and the California Achievement Tests provide error analyses and other diagnostic features—provide *limited* diagnostic information, they have *not* been specifically designed as diagnostic tests.

We must, at the outset, differentiate between medical and educational diagnosis lest misunderstanding occur. Educational diagnosis generally refers to the identification of a student's weakness or learning difficulty—for instance, Garrett is unable to do long division when regrouping is required. This differs markedly from medical diagnosis, which is concerned with the identification of the underlying cause(s) of a problem or weakness—for example, why does Garrett have a pain in his chest? Some probable causes are a heart attack, muscle contraction, or gallbladder attack. These hypotheses are further examined, in an effort to identify the probable cause(s) of the problem.

Diagnostic achievement tests are primarily concerned with measuring the skills or abilities (e.g., reading, arithmetic) that the subject-matter experts believe are essential in learning a particular subject and hence are important for diagnosis or remediation. For example, an arithmetic diagnostic test will be concerned with factors that experts in teaching arithmetic believe enter into the arithmetic process. Moreover, the items in diagnostic tests are often graded in difficulty.

Diagnostic tests have much in common with criterion-referenced tests, because (1) both attempt to obtain information about a person's performance in highly specific skills and relate this information to instructional prescriptions and (2) both have to be sharply focused. In fact, some diagnostic tests are essentially mastery tests, that is, perfect or near-perfect performance is expected by average children. For example, by the end of the first grade the average pupil is expected to demonstrate a left-right orientation in decoding, and failure to do so indicates a deficiency in that skill.

The development of a valid diagnostic test (see Webb et al., 1987) is predicated on satisfying two major assumptions: (1) the ability to analyze skills or knowledge into component subskills and (2) the ability to develop test items that will validly measure these subskills. Bejar (1984) conceptualizes the development of diagnostic tests as being either (1) an example of deficit measurement—that is, diagnosis is seen as the measurement of discrepancies from some "expected" value—or (2) an example of error analysis—that is, diagnosis involves more than collecting symptoms; examinees are categorized on the basis of the types of errors and attempts to ascribe causal relations so that appropriate remediation can be undertaken. As of now, the major work in developing standardized diagnostic tests exemplifies the error analysis approach and/or the cognitive psychology approach.

The purpose of diagnosis, and hence of a diagnostic test, is to help in selecting proper treatment. Saying that Allan, a fifth-grader, has a grade equivalent of 4.8 on the Metropolitan Mathematics Test tells us very little about Allan's strengths and weaknesses. We do know, however, that he is performing slightly below grade level in mathematics. But Allan's classroom teacher needs to know more. What kind of items did Allan fail or pass? Is there any pattern? Does Allan consistently demonstrate errors in addition or subtraction? With carrying? With multidigit items?

A good diagnostic test not only will inform the teacher that a pupil is weak or deficient in reading or arithmetic, it will also point out what areas are weak, such as word comprehension or addition with regrouping. However, it will not establish causal relationships. The teacher might learn *what* the difficulty is but *not why* the problem is there. For example, let us say that Salvador is weak in algebra. However, even the best arithmetic diagnostic test will not indicate whether this weakness may be due to his intellectual ability, poor reading skills, poor vision, psychomotor difficulties, poor study skills, emotional problems, inability to deal with polynomials, and other factors. The teacher must consider many factors to arrive at a reasonable solution to the problem. If not, the immediate problem may be remedied, but the etiological factors (having not been considered) may manifest themselves in other learning situations.

We would be remiss if we did not caution prospective users of diagnostic tests (regardless of how well they have been constructed) to be somewhat pessimistic about the value of the test's results. Diagnostic tests may point out a student's strengths and weaknesses in, say, reading or arithmetic. They may indicate, for example, that Lois has difficulty adding with regrouping but has mastered converting decimals to percentages or that Chuck is weak in reading comprehension but performs above average in his rate of reading. This does *not* mean that remedial work for Lois in addition with regrouping or special attention to Chuck will result in an improvement in their respective arithmetic and reading test scores. In fact, research has demonstrated that we do not know what constitutes effective diagnosis and remediation (Gill et al., 1979). Of what value then are diagnostic tests? We believe that they serve as hy-

pothesis generators in that they suggest possible courses of action to the teacher.

The manuals of some achievement-test batteries suggest that some of their subtests may be used for diagnostic purposes. We caution the user not to consider these subtests as diagnostic. Before a diagnostic test can be considered valid, (1) the component skills subtests should emphasize only a single type of error (such as word reversal in a reading diagnostic test) and (2) the subtest difference scores should be reliable.

A major weakness of diagnostic reading tests is the low reliabilities and high intercorrelations among the separate subtests. The low reliability is particularly significant in some of the shorter diagnostic tests, since this deficiency reduces the test's diagnostic value. The high intercorrelations suggest that the subtests are measuring *similar* skills.

Finally, before accepting a test as being diagnostic even though it may be labeled as such or claimed to be such by the publisher, ask yourself whether the subtests identify skill deficiencies that are amenable to remediation. For example, if a child does poorly on Quantitative Language (a subtest of the Metropolitan Readiness Tests), what guidance, if any, is given the teacher for remedial action? Should the pupil do more work with numbers? Should the pupil read more sentences dealing with quantitative concepts? Unless such answers are forthcoming, the test should *not* be considered as being diagnostic.

This does not mean that standardized achievement-test batteries cannot be used to diagnose *group* or *class* weaknesses. On the contrary. Curriculum evaluation would benefit greatly if achievement-test batteries were used for this purpose.

A more recent development is the inclusion of group-administered diagnostic batteries as *separate* components of survey-achievement test batteries. For example, the Stanford has the Stanford Diagnostic Reading and the Stanford Diagnostic Mathematics Tests. The Metropolitan has three separate diagnostic tests—in Reading, Mathematics, and Language.

The diagnostic batteries meet the same *rigid* quality standards as do the survey batteries. An especially noteworthy feature of each diagnostic battery was the care exercised in the delineation of current instructional objectives. Each has excellent diagnostic information provided so that optimal individualized instruction can be undertaken.

We should caution the reader regarding the use of group-administered diagnostic tests, however. Although these tests serve as excellent screening devices to identify pupils needing further attention, we concur with Anastasi (1988, p. 436) that "the diagnosis of learning disabilities and the subsequent program of remedial teaching are the proper functions of a trained specialist." The diagnosis and treatment of a severe reading (or mathematics) disability requires a team approach consisting of a clinician, pediatrician, social worker, reading specialist, and special education teacher.

It is not possible to consider in very much detail here the variety of diagnostic tests available to the classroom teacher. We have described some of the different methods used to construct diagnostic tests; we have attempted to caution users to be wary in their interpretation of diagnostic test results (because they are not elegant psychometric instruments with high validity and complete normative data); and we have taken the view that the teachers must be certain every avenue has been explored in their attempt to remedy an evident defect.[1] We now present a very brief description of two of the more popular diagnostic tests available in the elementary grades. Possibly because of the technical difficulties involved, there is a paucity of *valid* diagnostic tests.

Reading Diagnostic Tests

According to Salvia and Ysseldyke, ". . . difficulty in reading is the *most* [italics added] frequently

stated reason why students are referred for psychoeducational evaluation" (1988, p. 353).

Because reading is an integral component of the learning process and because reading skills have been identified, the majority of diagnostic tests are for reading. Diagnostic reading tests range from the conventional paper-and-pencil test, where the student reads a sentence and records the error in the sentence, to the oral procedure, where the examiner carefully notes, for example, mispronunciations, omissions, repetitions, substitutions, and reversals of letters. In the oral, or "thinking aloud," approach, the examiner is in a better position to observe and record errors as they occur and thus to see whether there is any pattern to the errors. Not only understanding the kinds of errors made but also obtaining some insight into how the pupil responds and reacts can prove invaluable for future remedial work. For example, in the oral approach, the examiner may note that the pupil is nervous, wary, concerned, and so forth. Diagnostic tests range from those that have just two or three subtests and function more like a survey battery to those that have many subtests that provide for detailed clinical analysis. Some are completely verbal; others employ equipment such as a tachistoscope for controlling the rate of exposure of printed matter; others employ elaborate photographic apparatus to record eye movements while the subject is reading.

Reading is a complex behavior consisting of many skills. Accordingly, reading diagnostic tests generally measure such factors as reading rate, comprehension (literal, inferential, listening), vocabulary, visual and auditory discrimination, word-attack skills, and motor skills. As will be evident when reading readiness tests are discussed, the skills measured by reading, reading readiness, and reading diagnostic tests are very similar, as one would expect. The major difference among them is in the range of material covered, the intensity of coverage, and the method of administration.

There appears to be some disagreement among reading experts and psychometricians regarding the value of reading diagnostic tests. Some maintain that diagnostic tests are valid and aid the class-

---

[1]Salvia and Ysseldyke (1988) mention three major problems of reading and mathematics diagnostic tests: (1) curriculum match, (2) few technically adequate tests, and (3) generalization.

room teacher immeasurably in screening out pupils who are in need of remediation. Others, like Spache (1976), are very critical of many reading diagnostic tests, claiming that, in large part, they fail to demonstrate validity. We feel that some of the newer reading diagnostic tests are beginning to overcome this deficit.

Q. Do all reading diagnostic tests measure the same thing?

A. No! Although there are more similarities than differences among most standardized reading diagnostic tests, there are nevertheless some basic differences. For example, the Durrell Analysis of Reading Difficulty and the Gates-McKillop-Horowitz Reading Diagnostic Tests are both individually administered, permitting detailed observation of the many aspects of reading, such as the visual and auditory discrimination of sounds, or listening comprehension. Both measure various factors involved in the reading process but do so in markedly different ways. In the Gates-McKillop, the subtests are analogous to power tests in that the exercises vary in their degree of difficulty. In the Durrell, this is not so. On the other hand, the Gates-McKillop-Horowitz includes tests of the child's word-attack skills, but the Durrell does not. The Durrell has eight separate subtests; the Gates-McKillup-Horowitz has fourteen tests/subtests. Although the complete Durrell is administered to the examinee, for the Gates, no set battery is administered. Rather, the examiner selects those subtests she believes necessary.

Q. How valid are the interpretations that can be made with a reading diagnostic test?

A. This depends on the test—how the items were selected (or prepared), the test's psychometric qualities, and the adequacy of the norming group. For some tests such as the Gates-McKillop-Horowitz, the training and experience of the examiner plays a vital role. The older Gates Reading Diagnostic Tests can be interpreted easily by classroom teachers. The types of interpretations that can be made are governed to a large extent by the range of material the test covers. The practical clinical value of the interpretation depends to a large extent on the check list of errors (and their validity) the publisher provides.

We must warn the user of tests in general, and definitely diagnostic prescriptive tests in particu-lar, to be on guard and to exercise extreme caution in interpreting the test results. Implementing sometimes radical prescriptive measures (remedial instruction, placement in special classes) on the basis of limited data is precarious.

Stanford Diagnostic Reading Test (SDRT) Published by Harcourt Brace Jovanovich, Inc. (1984) in two forms (G and H), the test's four overlapping levels span grades 1.6–13. It is group-administered, with six, seven, or eight scores depending on the level. Working time varies according to level, but approximately two hours are required for each level. Both timed and untimed tests are contained in each level, the number of strictly timed tests increasing as one moves from the lower to higher levels. Students can respond either on machine-scorable answer sheets or directly in the test booklet. Each of the subtest and total scores can be expressed and interpreted in terms of *both* a within-grade criterion- (content-) referenced mode (raw scores and Progress Indicators) or norm-referenced mode (percentile ranks, stanines, grade equivalents, and scaled scores). Accordingly, the SDRT is *both* norm-referenced and criterion-referenced.

Factors measured in *all* four batteries are phonetic analysis and reading comprehension, although different techniques are used to measure these factors depending upon the grade level. Factors measured in three levels are Auditory Vocabulary (grades 1, 6–8), and Structural Analysis (grades 3–13). As might be expected, at only the upper grade levels are reading rate, scanning and skimming, and reading vocabulary measured. Some examples of the types of items used in the SDRT are presented in Figure 16.1.

Criterion-related validity was studied by correlating performance on the SDRT subtests with performance on their counterparts on the Stanford Achievement Test. With the exception of the Blue level (9–13) where r's range from 0.64 to 0.74, the correlations are quite respectable, ranging from 0.67 to 0.88.

Content and criterion-related (concurrent) validity were emphasized in the test's construction. The authors caution users to interpret the test's

TEST 1: Auditory Vocabulary

SAMPLES

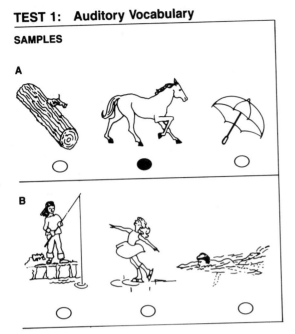

Look at the pictures in the box. The pictures are of a log, a horse, and an umbrella. (Pause.) **Now I'm going to read a question to you about these pictures. Find the picture that answers the question. Ready? Here is the question: "Which one is an *animal*?" Which picture shows an *animal*?**

Pause. Encourage replies. Then say:

Yes, it is the second picture, the picture of the horse, because a horse is an animal. The answer space under the picture of the horse has been filled in to show that it is the right answer. (Pause.) Now look at box B. (Demonstrate.) Look at the pictures in the box. (Pause.) I will read the question to you: "Which girl is fishing?" Fill in the space under the picture of the girl who is fishing. (Pause.) Which picture shows a girl fishing?

Pause for replies. Then say:

Yes, it is the first picture, the picture of the girl with the fishing pole. You should have filled in the answer space under the first picture. Are there any questions about what you are to do?

TEST 2: Auditory Discrimination

SAMPLES

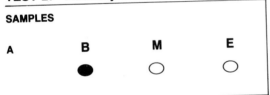

Look at row A in the shaded box marked "Samples." You see three answer spaces: one labeled "B," one labeled "M," and one labeled "E." The "B" stands for *beginning*, the "M" stands for *middle*, and the "E" stands for *end*.

Now listen to these two words: "sad" . . . "sign." Where do these two words sound the same? Do they sound the same at the beginning, in the middle, or at the end?

Pause for replies. Then say:

Yes, "sad" and "sign" sound the same at the beginning. They both begin with the sound /s/. That is why the space under "B" for "beginning" has been filled in in your booklet.

TEST 3: Phonetic Analysis (Part A)

SAMPLE

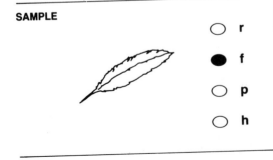

Look at the shaded box at the top of the page, where you see a picture of a feather. Think of the beginning sound of the word "feather" . . . "feather." What is the first sound in "feather"?

Pause for replies. Then say:

Yes, it is /f/ ("fuh"). "Feather" begins with the /f/ sound. Which letter in the shaded box stands for the /f/ sound?

Pause for replies. Then say:

Yes, it is "f" ("eff"); that is why the space next to the "f" has been filled in in your booklet. You will do the same with the other questions on this page.

FIGURE 16.1 Sample Items from the Stanford Diagnostic Reading Test, Third Edition. (Copyright © 1984 by Harcourt Brace Jovanovich, Inc. Reproduced by permission. All rights reserved.)

TEST 3: Phonetic Analysis (Part B)

SAMPLE

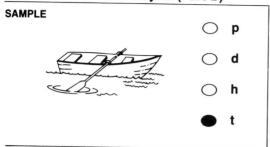

- ○ p
- ○ d
- ○ h
- ● t

Look at the shaded box at the top of the page, where you see a picture of a boat. Think of the ending sound of the word "boat" ... "boat." What is the last sound in "boat"?

Pause for replies. Then say:

Yes, it is /t/ ("tuh"). "Boat" ends with the /t/ sound. Which letter in the shaded box stands for the /t/ sound?

Pause for replies. Then say:

Yes, it is "t" ("tee"); that is why the space next to the "t" has been filled in in your booklet.

TEST 4: Word Reading

SAMPLES

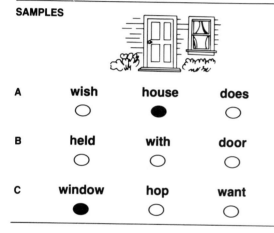

A	wish ○	house ●	does ○
B	held ○	with ○	door ○
C	window ●	hop ○	want ○

We are going to look at some pictures and then find the words that tell about each picture. Look at the shaded box at the top of the page. (Demonstrate.) You see a picture of part of a house. (Pause.) Now look at the three lines of words below the picture. In each line, there is one word that goes with the picture. You are to pick out the word in each line that goes with the picture. Look at the first line, line A. Read the words to yourself as I read them aloud: "wish . . . house . . . does." Which word goes with the picture?

TEST 5: Reading Comprehension (Part A)

SAMPLES

A **The window is broken.**

○   ●   ○

Look at the first shaded box at the top of the page. (Demonstrate.) Inside box A you see a sentence and three pictures. Read the sentence to yourself while I read it aloud: "The window is broken." One of the pictures goes with the sentence. Which picture is it?

TEST 5: Reading Comprehension (Part B)

SAMPLES

A **Fish live in the**

- ○ ground
- ○ sky
- ● water

On this page, there are some stories for you to read. Look at the story in the shaded box. Read the first sentence of the story to yourself as I read it aloud. "Fish live in the ground . . . sky . . . water." Which word best completes the sentence?

FIGURE 16.1 (concluded)

content validity in relation to the users' instructional objectives. K-R 20 reliability is reported using raw scores, and standard errors of measurement are reported for both raw and scaled scores. Alternate-form reliability was computed for the speeded subtests. All but two of the K-R 20's are above 0.80.

A variety of reports are available and, with the test manual, provide helpful information to aid in the interpretation of the pupils' or classes' performance. The authors provide a variety of instructional strategies that they feel will help ameliorate the pupils' deficiencies. Evidence as to the efficacy of these instructional strategies is missing. The manual is concisely written and is teacher-oriented, although attention is also paid to how the test scores can be used for making administrative decisions.

Users of the publisher's scoring service are given an Instructional Placement Report (IPR) that reports *level-based* rather than grade-based stanines. This type of reporting provides a profile analysis in terms of the pupils' basic instructional needs regardless of their grade placement. In addition, pupils are identified either as being in need of specific remedial instruction or as progressing satisfactorily. On each computer-generated IPR, brief instructional strategies are given. One can obtain an Individual Diagnostic Report (this contains a detailed analysis of a single pupil's performance), a Class Summary Report, a Master List Report (a listing of scores for all students in the class), a Parent Report, and a Pupil Item Analysis.

The 1984 SDRT at each level reports or classifies the test items by objective and item cluster, provides the difficulty level of each item, and designates a Progress Indicator (PI) Cut-Off Score. Progress Indicators, although not test scores per se, are cutoff scores that have been established for each SDRT Skill Domain and Item cluster to identify those pupils who have mastered or have not mastered minimum competencies in those areas deemed to be vital in the reading process development sequence. We caution users *not* to consider the PI as an absolute standard but to interpret the score in terms of their instructional objectives.

Raw scores for each subtest can be converted to norm-referenced scores—percentile ranks, scaled scores, stanines, and grade equivalents—or criterion-referenced scores—progress indicators. There are *both* fall and spring norms.

In summary, the 1984 SDRT is a well-constructed standardized test. It is attractively packaged, has clear directions, provides a rationale underlying each of the subtests, and has an excellent manual to help the teacher. The type and variety of instructional strategies provided do indeed make this a diagnostic-prescriptive test. As mentioned earlier, however, the value of the instructional strategies has not been demonstrated. Although the classroom teacher can administer, score, and interpret the test, we strongly recommend that, where feasible, an experienced reading specialist do the actual interpretation and, in conjunction with the classroom teacher, develop the appropriate corrective action.

Some Other Examples   Some other examples of diagnostic reading tests are the Woodcock Reading Mastery Tests, Durrell Analysis of Reading Difficulty, the Durrell Listening-Reading Series, the Diagnostic Reading Scales, the Gates-McKillop Reading Diagnostic Tests, the Gilmore Oral Reading Test, the Reading Recognition and Reading Comprehension subtests of the Peabody Individual Achievement Test, the Slingerland Test of Specific Language Disability, and the Word Recognition subtest of the Wide Range Achievement Test. These are all popular tests, and more information can be obtained about them and other tests by consulting the *Mental Measurements Yearbooks, Test Critiques,* and the publishers' catalogs.

Diagnostic Arithmetic Tests

With the exception of the teaching of reading, probably no subject has been more intensively studied than the teaching of arithmetic. Yet very few new arithmetic tests have been published and even fewer new diagnostic arithmetic tests.

Key Math Diagnostic Arithmetic Test
(KMDAT) Published by the American Guidance Service (1976), the test covers preschool to grade 6. It has one form. Developed originally for testing educable mentally retarded children, this individually administered test can be given, scored, and interpreted by classroom teachers who have studied the manual.

The test is divided into three major areas (content, operations, and applications) and 15 subtests, each having from 7 to 31 items. The subtests (with the number of items shown in parentheses) are as follows:

A. Content
   1. Numeration (24)
   2. Fractions (11)
   3. Geometry & Symbols (20)
B. Operations
   1. Addition (15)
   2. Subtraction (15)
   3. Multiplication (11)
   4. Division (10)
   5. Mental Computation (10), which also involves memory for digits
   6. Numerical Reasoning (12)
C. Applications
   1. Word Problems (14)
   2. Missing Elements (7)
   3. Money (15)
   4. Measurement (27)
   5. Time (19)
   6. Metric Supplement (31)

The items require almost no writing or reading ability.

With the exception of the Metric Supplement subtest, raw scores are converted to grade equivalents. These GEs can then be compared with the total score and strengths and weaknesses plotted. We caution the reader here because a change in only one or two answers can have a significant effect on the derived score and subsequent interpretation.

The validity and reliability data presented are acceptable.

The test is accompanied by an excellent manual, which provides clear directions for administration and scoring as well as behavioral objectives for each item. The test format is good, and the illustrations are exceptional in their use of color and attractiveness. A major criticism is the limited number of items in each of the subtests. This effect is the more serious since a diagnostic test should have extensive sampling of the instructional objectives.

Some other examples of arithmetic diagnostic tests are the Diagnostic Tests and Self-Helps in Arithmetic; Buswell-John Diagnostic Test for Fundamental Processes in Arithmetic; the Individual Pupil Monitoring System: Mathematics; the Individualized Mathematics Program; the Metropolitan Diagnostic Mathematics Test; the Diagnostic Mathematics Inventory: Mathematics System (DMI/MS); Diagnosis: An Instructional Aid; the Stanford Diagnostic Arithmetic Test; and the California Diagnostic Reading and Mathematics Tests.

Diagnostic Testing by Computer

Within the past few years, an active interest has been evident with respect to diagnostic testing by computer. The College Board and Educational Testing Service have developed a computerized diagnostic testing program for placing students in instructional groups. Although designed primarily for use in college and community college, the model should be adaptable to other grades (see Ward et al., 1986; Forehand, 1986, 1987).

CRITERION-REFERENCED STANDARDIZED ACHIEVEMENT TESTS

In recent years, accountability, performance contracting, formative evaluation, computer-assisted instruction, individually prescribed instruction, mastery learning, and the like have spawned an interest in and need for new kinds of tests—criterion-referenced tests (CRTs), or, as some prefer to say, content-domain or objectives-based tests?[2] Test publishers are now paying more attention to the development of CRTs, since many educators believe that norm-referenced tests (because they are concerned with making *inter*individual comparisons) are inadequate for individualized instruction decision-making purposes because they do not give specific descriptions of pupil performance.

Because instructional objectives in the basic skills of reading and arithmetic at the elementary level are more amenable to fine subdivisions, and because at this level the instructional objectives are of a hierarchial nature (i.e., the acquisition of elementary skills are a necessary prerequisite for learning the higher-order skills), CRTs are more common in the lower grades.

Today, commercially prepared standardized criterion-referenced achievement tests are generally in reading and arithmetic, although agencies are available that will produce tailor-made criterion-referenced achievement tests in a variety of subject matter fields at different grade levels (Westinghouse Learning Corporation, Instructional Objectives Exchange, CTB/McGraw-Hill, and Riverside Press).

Criterion-referenced tests vary from the single-subject-matter test to a battery of "minitests" that are designed to measure the pupils' knowledge of the various instructional objectives in detail. Moreover, test and textbook publishers are beginning to prepare complete instructional systems using a survey test, a diagnostic test(s), and a set of prescriptions (suggested instructional activities). One of the most comprehensive instructional systems has been developed by Science Research Associates in Reading and Mathematics.

The SRA package or "lab" in reading[3] consists of 34 Probes or criterion-referenced diagnostic tests measuring instructional objectives normally covered in grades 1–4; six cassettes that make for self-administration of the Probes; a Survey Test that indicates the students' strengths and weaknesses and indicates what Probes, if any, should be taken; a Prescription Guide that keys the instructional objectives measured by a particular Probe (such as, letter recognition, consonant blends, homographs) to major reading tests or supplementary activities; and a Class Progress Chart.

Prescriptive Reading Inventory (PRI) and Diagnostic Mathematics Inventory (DMI) Published by CTB/McGraw-Hill, the PRI and DMI exemplify a new approach in building criterion-referenced diagnostic tests. Both tests are designed to identify pupils with difficulties in reading and/or mathematics. Then, after appropriate remedial instruction has been given, the DMI or PRI is followed up with a criterion-referenced mastery test (Interim Evaluation Test) to ascertain the degree to which the pupil has mastered the minimal instructional objectives.[4] Although untimed, each test takes about $2\frac{3}{4}$ hours working time. In both the DMI and PRI, each test item is referenced to commonly used textbooks. In this way, the teacher is assisted in developing appropriate remedial instruction.

---

[2]As mentioned in Chapter 2, it should not be inferred that norm-referenced achievement tests (NRTs) are not based on objectives. In order for an achievement test to be valid, be it a CRT or an NRT, there must be objectives on which the test items are based.

[3]SRA also has a program (which differs from its "lab") called "Mastery: Custom Program," where users can select reading and mathematics objectives from a list of over 1,000 items. Criterion-referenced tests are then built, with three items/instructional objective.

[4]The PMI and DMI are part of an instructional management system and are sometimes referred to as PMI/MS and DMI/MS. Also included in the system are the Writing Proficiency Program (WPP) and the Writing Proficiency Program/Intermediate System (WPP/IS). We realize that the DMI and PRI, because they are diagnostic tests, could have been discussed earlier. However, because they are objectives-based in development and because of their relationship to the Interim Tests, we decided to cover the series together.

A rather novel feature of the DMI is the manner in which pupils record their answers: pupils do their work in the test booklet and write their answer in "unique, item-specific" machine-scorable answer grids.

Content validity was stressed in the construction of the DMI, PRI, and the respective Interim Evaluation Tests.

Both the DMI and PRI have a variety of reports available to pupils and teachers. The PRI has an Individual Diagnostic Map, a Class Diagnostic Map, an Individual Study Guide, a Program Reference Guide, a Class Grouping Report, and an Interpretive Handbook.

The Individual Diagnostic Map displays the student's score on each objective in the form of a "diagnostic map." The + indicates mastery of a particular instructional objective; the − indicates nonmastery; the R indicates that a review is warranted. A blank indicates that the student omitted the items related to that objective.

The Class Diagnostic Map can be used for class or group instruction. It reports average class scores on each objective.

The Individual Study Guide uses the information from the Diagnostic Map to furnish individual prescriptions for the student. For those instructional objectives not mastered, pages in the text to be studied are noted.

The Program Reference Guides direct the teacher to appropriate resource and reference materials. Guides are available for each of the reading programs keyed to the PRI.

For levels A through D, there is a Class Grouping Report that identifies (and groups) students who fail to show mastery of 60 percent of the objectives in a particular category. The teacher can then provide appropriate remediation for various groupings of student deficiencies.

The DMI has an Objective Mastery Report, a Pre-Mastery Analysis, an Individual Diagnostic Report, a Group Diagnostic Report, a Mastery Reference Guide, a Guide to Ancillary Materials, and a Learning Activities Guide. The PRI's Interpretive Handbook and the DMI's Guides contain useful suggested activities and instructional strategies that teachers can use. All test questions are keyed to the appropriate objective being measured, and most of the printouts reference the objective to a particular textbook page.

The Interim Evaluations Tests' (IET) objectives (and hence items) are organized as in the DMI or PRI with the exception that there is no IET for DMI Level C (grades 7–8). Each objective, whether in reading or in mathematics, is measured with four to six items. Guidelines for determining whether the student has mastered the objective being tested or needs to review an objective are presented in the Examiner's Manual. The test authors recommend that the IET be administered within one to seven days after appropriate remedial instruction has been given. This manual also suggests appropriate instructional activities that might be used to build mastery of the objective. A variety of output data is finished.

Use of the DMI or PRI and their respective Interim Tests permits a teacher to ascertain which students are in need of further instruction on a particular objective(s) and then to see whether, after remedial instruction, the student has mastered the objective(s). In a way, these tests can be considered part of an individualized instructional program. The rationale underlying their development is that sound and extensive work was done to identify objectives and select items. The various reports issued to the teacher and the numerous suggested instructional aids offered are excellent.

Other Tests

Other standardized CRTs are the Individual Pupil Monitoring System—Mathematics and Reading (IPMS) and Customized Objective Monitoring Service—Reading and Mathematics (COMS), and School-Curriculum Objective-Referenced Evaluation (SCORE) published by Riverside Press; the Performance Assessment in Reading (PAIR), the Assessment of Skills in Computation (ASC), the Test of Performance in Computational Skills

(TOPICS), the Writing Skills Test, the Objectives-Referenced Bank of Items and Tests (ORBIT), and the Everyday Skills Test, published by CTB/McGraw-Hill; the Basic Skills Assessment Program (BSA), published by Addison-Wesley; and the tests accompanying the Harper & Row Reading Series. The IPMS, like the SRA and CTB/McGraw-Hill tests discussed earlier, key their instructional objectives to commonly used textbooks. The COMS, like ORBIT and SCORE, tailors a test to the teachers' specifications using validated test items.

A Word of Caution About CRTs

Although we are favorably disposed to the use of criterion-referenced testing, especially in formative evaluation and in computer-assisted or individually prescribed instruction where instruction is closely integrated with testing, we must admit that we have some reservations about many CRTs, especially their reliability and validity. How valid and reliable is a test that contains one to four items per objective? What can a teacher conclude if Peter gets the right (or wrong) answer to "2 + 2"? Does this mean that Peter would answer items of this type correctly (or incorrectly)? How far can we generalize? Has the total domain of this objective been delineated? Has there been sampling from this domain? What technical data pertaining to validity and reliability evidence are presented in the manual? (Hambleton & Eignor, 1978, were somewhat perturbed about the paucity of such information in the test manuals they surveyed.) How was the "passing score" obtained? These are just some of the questions that have been raised about criterion-referenced tests. Those interested in greater coverage of the shortcomings of CRTs should consult Hambleton and Eignor (1978) and Berk (1980).

We caution test users to be very wary in accepting a test publisher's claim of providing criterion- or domain-referenced information. Relating individual test items to specific instructional objectives is *not* sufficient for establishing validity.

Until the publisher can furnish evidence regarding the generalizability of the student's performance in the skill or knowledge domains being tested, we must interpret the scores cautiously.

Summary

Criterion-referenced standardized achievement tests are primarily in reading and mathematics for the elementary grades and are designed to provide diagnostic-prescriptive information.

As discussed earlier, those responsible for constructing criterion-referenced tests still have to overcome many technical difficulties (although some success has been achieved) related to the validity and reliability of such tests—for example, having enough items to measure an objective reliably and still keep the test length manageable. In criterion-referenced tests we are faced with the problem of defining an acceptable level of performance as a criterion or standard of mastery. Doubtless a concerted effort will be made to remedy these difficulties, because the increased concern for mastery learning, basic minimal competencies, and accountability will witness a larger number of standardized, commercially published criterion-referenced achievement tests.

As we survey today's commercially prepared standardized criterion-referenced tests, we see many areas of disagreement, some sources of confusion, and very little reason for undue optimism. Research has indicated that commercially published CRTs are (1) objectives-referenced rather than domain-referenced, which means that the performance (score) on any one objective *cannot* be generalized to all the other items in that domain; (2) lacking in content validity because conventional item statistics are used to select test items, which invariably results in the very easy and very hard items being eliminated; (3) lacking with respect to acceptable reliability; in many instances, the standard error of measurement is not reported; and (4) of such poor psychometric quality that care should be taken in their use and interpretation (Hambleton & Eignor, 1978; CSE Test Evaluation Project, 1979).

STANDARDIZED ACHIEVEMENT TESTS IN SPECIFIC SUBJECTS

Standardized achievement tests are available for nearly every subject (agriculture to zoology) and for every grade level (kindergarten to professional and graduate school). There are, for example, reading readiness tests; reading tests; arithmetic, spelling, and science tests; product scales; and vocational achievement tests. For the most part, reading and arithmetic tests (as well as readiness tests in these respective subjects) are restricted to the primary grades because (1) these skills are primarily developed there and the major emphasis in the first few years of formal schooling is on reading and arithmetic and (2) the relatively uniform curriculum of the elementary school makes it possible for the survey battery to cover adequately the measurement of the important objectives of instruction. In the secondary grades, because of the nonuniform nature of the curriculum, specialized tests covering a particular course such as Latin, Spanish, or psychology are the predominant type.

As noticed earlier, the major advantages of a single-subject matter test such as algebra or science over the subtests in arithmetic or science in a survey battery are that the single-subject-matter tests may provide a more valid measure of a student's achievement in a specific content area because they (1) are usually longer and thus permit more adequate content sampling; (2) are generally more reliable; (3) may better fit the classroom teacher's instructional objectives; and (4) generally are more up-to-date vis-à-vis the changing curriculum. The major limitation of the single-subject-matter test is that since different standardization samples are used, scores on different tests are *not* comparable. For example, unless the norms groups are comparable, we cannot say that Ilene does better in English than she does in social studies.

In the next section, we will focus on reading readiness tests. Although a variety of tests have been developed to assess the child's readiness for learning—for example, the Cooperative Preschool Inventory, the Boehm Test of Basic Experiences—reading readiness tests are probably the most familiar and most frequently used in the primary grades.

Readiness Tests

The impetus to study "school readiness" evident in the 1970s and 1980s was the result of research in early cognitive development, and the fear that children growing up in impoverished educational and cultural environments would suffer when they entered school. School readiness involves what Hunt and Kirk (1974) call "entry skills," which can be assessed with readiness tests.

Readiness tests can be administered as early as infancy. The majority, however, are generally administered upon school entrance. Although some attention is paid to general information and quantitative skills, *major* emphasis is on the abilities found to be important in learning to read.

Readiness tests differ little from conventional aptitude and achievement measures. In fact, they resemble aptitude as well as diagnostic tests. A distinctive feature of a readiness test is that it is used to predict who is, or who is not, ready for instruction (an aptitude test) so that those students who do poorly might be given appropriate remedial and compensatory educational experiences or even delayed in their entry to school.

Readiness tests, to the consternation of some, are being used by many school districts as part of a mandated testing program of readiness testing before entry into kindergarten or first grade. Fromberg (1989) advanced "a new set of the 'three Rs'—readiness testing, 'red-shirting' (delayed entry) and retention." Some critics are opposed to readiness testing because they are often used as the *sole* criterion to determine kindergarten entry. We also decry this practice. The fact that a disproportionate number of children labeled as "unready" come from low-income and culturally varied groups exacerbates our concerns.

Because readiness tests are used almost exclusively by some teachers and administrators to make individual placement decisions—that is, to predict a pupil's success or failure in a particular instructional program—it is essential that readiness tests be of the highest technical quality with respect to validity, reliability, and norms. Regretfully, such instruments are extremely rare. We should not allow the fact that because a test is published and very popular, it is immune to careful scrutiny. We agree with Salvia and Ysseldyke (1988) that we shouldn't be fooled by "cash validity."

Readiness data *must* be longitudinal with respect to validity. In other words, readiness tests *must* have predictive validity. If they are unable to predict who is/is not ready for, say, reading instruction or entry into grade 1, they don't serve their purpose.

There are different kinds of readiness. A child, in order to learn, has to be ready in personal-social development and in language, motor, and intellectual development. For example, the Denver Development Screening Test is an individually administered test designed for the early identification of children with developmental and behavior problems in four areas: personal-social, language, gross motor, and fine motor. Although the psychometric quality is only fair, it is adequate if used *only* for *screening* purposes. Another test that should only be used for screening is the group-administered Boehm Test of Basic Concepts-Revised. In the main, these tests, like the Test of Basic Experiences 2 and the Preschool Inventory-Revised, are, at best, to be used for *screening* only. Some of the better readiness tests are the Metropolitan Readiness Tests and CIRCUS. Again, we refer readers to the *Mental Measurements Yearbooks*, publishers' catalogues, and *Test Critiques* for more information on these tests. Those interested in an evaluation of early childhood screening and readiness instruments published since 1980 should consult Langhorst (1989).

One of the most important areas of readiness is in reading, and it is to this area that we will pay particular attention in the next section.

Reading Readiness Tests

Usually the first type of standardized achievement test that a pupil receives is a reading readiness test. This test is administered either at or near the end of the kindergarten year or very early in the first grade. It is often considered one of the most important achievement tests that the child takes during his school years. Since efficient and adequate reading skills play a vital role in subsequent learning, anything that can be done (sectioning, placement, and remedial instruction) to provide optimal reading instruction should reap benefits insofar as future learning is concerned.

The major purposes of a reading readiness test are (1) to identify the children who are not yet ready to begin reading and (2) to identify, for grouping purposes, the children who are at essentially the same level of readiness. This grouping hopefully will assist the teacher in providing appropriate reading or prereading instruction. Reading readiness tests are *not* designed to predict reading achievement in, say, the sixth or seventh grade. They do provide valuable information insofar as predicting reading ability in the first and second grades. Reading readiness tests should not be confused with reading diagnostic tests. Although they may indicate weaknesses in certain general broad areas, such as word recognition or vocabulary, they are not designed to isolate specific reading defects. However, reading readiness and diagnostic tests contain many item *types* that are similar—visual discrimination, vocabulary, motor coordination, and the like.

There is a consensus among reading specialists that a child's readiness to participate in reading and the extent to which he will learn how to read depend upon a variety of factors: (1) intellectual ability, (2) eye-hand coordination, (3) motivation to learn how to read, (4) perceptual and visual skills, and (5) knowledge of colors, names of common things, and concepts of time and space. Although there are variations among the many reading readiness tests commercially published, all have several of the following types of items:

1. *Motor skills.* The child is required to draw lines, complete a circle, underline words, go through a finger maze.
2. *Auditory discrimination.* The child is asked either to pronounce words after they have been read to him or to select which of several similar-sounding words identify a picture.
3. *Visual discrimination.* The child is required to choose similarities or differences in words, letters, numbers, or pictures.
4. *Vocabulary.* The child's knowledge of the meaning of the words is assessed by asking him either to define a word, name various objects of the same or different class, or to select the correct word to describe a picture.
5. *Memory.* The child may be asked to reproduce a geometrical figure to which he has been exposed for a certain length of time, he may be asked to repeat a story that has been read to him, or he may be required to carry out in sequence a series of instructions that have been presented to him.
6. *Drawing/copying.* The child demonstrates his skill in copying or drawing a letter, a number, or a form.
7. *Recognition of numbers, words, and letters.* The child is required to identify numbers, words, or alphabet letters.

Although test validity and reliability are a *sine qua non* for any standardized test, the types of validity evidence vary depending upon the type of test being considered. Since readiness tests in general and reading readiness tests in particular are intended to be used for short-term predictive purposes, it is essential that they possess (and the test manual report evidence of) predictive validity.

Although reading readiness tests vary in the type and degree of coverage of these skills, all are designed to assess whether the child is ready to learn to read. It should be noted at the outset that a child requires *more* than those skills measured by

even the most valid reading readiness test before we can say with any degree of confidence that the youngster is ready for reading instruction. Factors such as the child's interest, motivation, general aptitude, and the like must also be considered. Some questions that may be raised regarding reading readiness tests are as follows:

Q. If there is a high correlation between reading test scores and intelligence test scores, why administer a reading readiness test?

A. Because intelligence tests do not survey all the skills and traits the child must have in order to learn to read. Intelligence tests, by their very nature, are not specifically designed to provide information on the child's ability to handle words, whether or not the child can use and manipulate words, whether or not the child has adequate muscular coordination, and so on; skills deemed important in the reading process. Reading readiness tests are specifically designed to assess those skills. For this reason, it is recommended that a reading readiness test be administered to kindergarten children, and the intelligence test be postponed to the first or second grade. (Research has shown that reading readiness tests given in kindergarten predict reading achievement in grade 1 *better* than aptitude tests, but that aptitude tests given in kindergarten predict reading achievement in grades 4 and 5 better than do reading readiness tests.)

Q. Do all reading readiness tests measure the same thing?

A. No! Although many of them look as if they are doing so because they contain vocabulary items, or paragraph reading, or reproduction of objects, there is usually something unique or different about each of the reading readiness tests available. For example, the Harrison-Stroud Reading Readiness Profiles has a test of auditory discrimination, but the American School Reading Readiness Test does not. The Harrison-Stroud and Gates-MacGinitie have a test on word recognition; the Lee-Clark, Metropolitan, and Murphy-Durrell do not.

Q. How are items selected for reading readiness tests?

A. Once again, there are differences among the various tests. Harrison and Stroud attempted to make a task analysis, that is, they specified the skills they believed were important in the reading process and then prepared a test on the basis of this analysis. A somewhat different procedure was employed by the constructors of the Gates and American School tests. On the basis of previously used items and those suggested by experts in the field, they assembled a preliminary pool of items, administered the items, and then selected the items that were statistically sound. Both methods are valid, and no one can say that one is better than the other.

Q. How do I know if the test is valid for my purpose?

A. You don't until you study it carefully. You must study the test manual thoroughly and determine whether the test's objectives are in agreement with your goals. Test-makers can only indicate what they think is important. It is up to the users to judge not only whether they agree with the test's purposes but also whether the manner in which the test was constructed was valid. For example, the authors of the American School Reading Readiness Test felt that auditory discrimination was not important. The Metropolitan Readiness Tests require the pupil to draw a man. The Harrison-Stroud and American School tests do not contain such an item. If the user believes that auditory discrimination is essential, she should consider a test other than the American. Similarly, if the user feels that the ability to draw a man is vital to the reading process, she is advised to consider a test other than the Harrison-Stroud or the American. The user must also make a thorough analysis of the test items and the test manual. The purpose of a test cannot be judged by only looking at the items. Do *not* judge a test by the names of the subtests. As mentioned earlier, both the Harrison-Stroud and the American School tests include items designed to measure the child's ability to follow directions. In the former, this type of item is found as a peripheral task, whereas in the latter there is a specific subtest designed to measure this skill.

Q. When should a reading readiness test be administered?

A. Research shows a readiness test can be administered before a child enters kindergarten and still have predictive validity. Rubin (1974) administered the Metropolitan Readiness Tests (MRT) to a group of pupils *prior* to kindergarten entrance and again prior to entering grade 1 and reported a one-year test–retest reliability of 0.65. Her results strongly suggest that the MRT can be validly used in the first few months prior to kindergarten entrance to predict first-grade achievement in reading, spelling, and arithmetic (although not as well as for the latter two) instead of waiting to administer them at the end of kindergarten or early in the first grade as normally is the case. The implications of these findings, if they are substantiated by further research, are that (1) pupils with school readiness deficiencies can be identified early, and consequently appropriate remedial instruction can be initiated before grade 1, and (2) pupils who are not ready to enter grade 1 can be identified.

Reading readiness tests employ a variety of procedures. Generally, all are given orally, but on one section of the Harrison-Stroud, the pupils work independently. Numerous examples or practice exercises are provided so that the children will understand what they are to do and how they are to do it. All work is done in the test booklet. The examiner should constantly check the pupils to be sure that they understand the directions. This should not be difficult, because most of the tests are untimed and should under normal circumstances be administered in small groups or individually. Some illustrative examples of reading readiness test items are shown in Figure 16.2.

Some other examples of standardized reading readiness tests are the Analysis of Readiness Skills: Reading; the Initial Survey Tests; the Macmillan Reading Readiness Tests; the PMA Readiness Level; and the School Readiness Survey.

Uses of Reading Readiness Tests The primary use of a reading readiness test is to provide the teacher with basic information about the child's *pre*reading skills so that optimal learning conditions can be provided. On the basis of a reading readiness test, classroom teachers can tailor their teaching program to best fit the needs of each pupil. For example, Paul may be deficient in his ability to recognize similarities and differences, whereas Ilene may have trouble reading numbers. After ascertaining that the deficiencies are not due to any physical factors, the teacher can institute remedial action where needed. In this illustration the test is used *both* as a prognostic device and as a criterion on which the learning materials are organized and presented by the classroom teacher.

The results of reading readiness tests may also be used by school personnel for grouping when there are two or three first-grade classes, so that the pupils who are at about the same level can be grouped together for instructional purposes. Naturally, for homogeneous grouping, the teacher should also consider other factors. But in the first grade, reading readiness may well be the most important.

We would be remiss if we did not caution the prospective user of readiness test results to be very wary of their potential *misuse*. The empirical evidence regarding the predictive validity of readiness test scores is very weak (Henderson & Long, 1970), and one should *not* use such tests for any long-range decision.

Because readiness test score results appear to play such an important role in determining teacher expectations, it is vital that *all* test users be thoroughly educated on the *limitations* of tests they are using or planning to use. They are *not* a measure of a child's overall cognitive functioning; they should *not* be used to label a child; they are influenced by the child's culture and hence must be interpreted cautiously for bilingual children; and because young children grow very quickly, readiness test results must be thought of as fairly unstable. And, as Long and Henderson (1974, p. 145) state, "If teachers are *overly* [italics added] influenced by relatively invalid tests [sic] scores, it might be better if children entering school were not tested at all."

Reading Tests

The ability to communicate by means of language is a fundamental necessity in today's society. Reading is one form of communication that must be developed in our pupils. The development of communicative skills—reading, writing, and speaking—makes up a major portion of the curriculum in the primary grades. Any survey battery will have at least one or more subtests for the assessment of a person's reading skills. The subtests may be classified in a variety of ways—reading comprehension, language arts, language skills—but regardless of the rubric used, they are essentially tests of the pupil's ability to read.

All reading tests use essentially similar procedures for measuring the pupils' reading ability. Pupils are typically required to read a series of paragraphs and answer questions about them to see whether they are facile with words and sentences. Some tests may employ prose selections only; others may use both prose and poetry to measure comprehension. Some focus on comprehension; others stress interpretation. Some of the tests are oral; others are of the silent-reading type and can be administered in a group setting. Once again, regardless of the manner of assessment, reading tests all serve a common purpose—to see how well the individual can read. As we mentioned earlier, the reading process is an extremely complex task and involves a variety of factors, some of which are continually interacting and cannot be isolated as distinct entities. No single test attempts to measure all these factors. Some of the factors, such as attitudes involved in reading or adult reading habits, are unlikely to be assessed by any test. Because opinions differ about the skills deemed important in the reading process, we see different kinds of reading tests. This is not to say that one standardized reading test is more valid than another. The evaluation of any standardized reading (actually, any achievement) test depends on the similarity of the user's and test constructor's objectives. In selecting a test, users alone must decide whether the objectives they deem important are measured by the test and how well their objectives are measured.

Recognizing that reading tests differ in the skills they measure as well as in the emphasis they place on each of the skills in the reading process, we will now look at the Gates-MacGinitie—one of the more popular reading tests in greater detail.

Gates-MacGinitie Reading Tests, Second Edition
Published by Riverside Press in 1978, it replaces the familiar Gates Reading Tests. Seven separate tests for grades 1–12. Basic R (grade 1.0–

SAY

A.   Put your finger on the little black MOON, and keep it there while I tell you what to do. Look at the BIRD with the circle under it. Look at how the circle has been filled in. Do you see it? (Point to the box with the shaded circle under it.) Now take your pencil and fill in the circle under the other BIRD in the same way. Be sure to fill in the whole circle like this.

B.   Put your finger on the little black STAR. Look at the BALL with the circle under it. Fill in the circle under the other BALL just like the first one. Remember to fill in the whole circle.

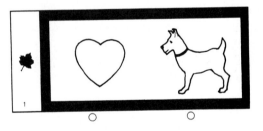

SAY

1.   Put your finger on the little black LEAF. Look at the pictures of a HEART and a DOG in the ROW. When pictures go across the page like this, we say they are in a ROW.

SAY   The HEART and DOG are in a ROW. Fill in the circle under the DOG . . . under the DOG.

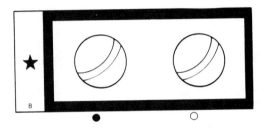

SAY   From now on, you must be sure to fill in only one circle in each row. If you fill in the wrong circle, erase it completely and then fill in the right one.

2.   Put your finger on the little black SPOON. The pictures in this row are TREE, HOUSE, THREAD. Mark the circle under the TREE . . . under the TREE.

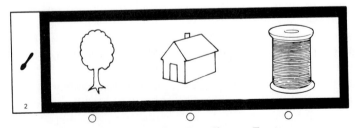

FIGURE 16.2   Types of Items Used on Reading Readiness Tests.

SAY

3.   Put your finger on the little black CAT. The pictures in the row are SCISSORS, CHAIR, HAND, FLOWER. Mark the circle under the picture of the SCISSORS . . . the circle under the SCISSORS. Remember to fill in the whole circle.

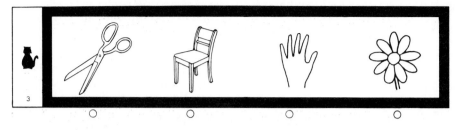

8.   Put your finger on the HAND. The pictures are SHOE, TABLE, KEY, HORSE. Mark under the picture of something that people can wear on their feet . . . the picture of something that people can wear on their feet.

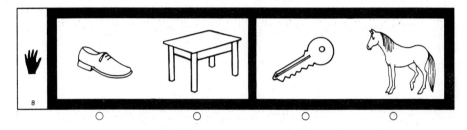

9.   Put your finger on the HAT. Look at the picture in the blue box. Now look at the other pictures in the row. The other pictures are SUN, RABBIT, AIRPLANE, and BIKE. Mark under the picture that looks just like the one in the blue box . . . the picture that looks just like the one in the blue box.

10.   Put your finger on the HEART. Listen very carefully. Look at what is in the blue box at the beginning of the row. Now look at the other pictures in the row and mark under the one that is just like something in the blue box at the beginning of the row . . . mark under the picture that is just like something in the blue box at the beginning of the row.

FIGURE 16.2 (concluded)

1.9), Level A (grade 1.5–1.9), Level B (grade 2), Level C (grade 3), Level D (grades 4–6), Level E (grades 7–9), and Level F (grades 10–12). Levels D and E have three forms each; all other levels have two forms each. With the exception of the Basic R level (designed to measure *both* general reading achievement and particular reading skills needed to read well), which yields subscores in letter-sound, vocabulary, letter recognition, and comprehension as well as a total raw score, all other levels provide scores in vocabulary and comprehension as well as a total score. The testing time for the vocabulary and comprehension subtests is 20 and 35 minutes, respectively, for Levels A–F. The Basic R test is untimed, although it is suggested that it requires about 65 minutes' testing time and that it be administered in two sittings.

The Vocabulary Test at all levels measures the child's ability to recognize or analyze isolated words. The vocabulary tests in Basic R and Levels A and B are primarily tests of decoding skills. In Basic R and Levels A and B, vocabulary is measured with pictures and words—each question consists of a picture followed by four words. The examinee has to select the word that corresponds to the picture by "sounding out" each word. Since most of the questions require that the examinee know the sound that corresponds to a specific letter or letter sequence in order to select the correct word, this can be of invaluable assistance to the teacher in helping identify specific decoding skills that the child has not yet mastered. Level C uses the same format as those of Levels A and B. However, at Level C, we have a test of the child's reading vocabulary and word knowledge rather than decoding skills. Whereas Level C asks the examinee to select the one of four words or phrases that comes closest in meaning to the "test" word, Levels D, E, and F use five words or phrases. The exercises are graduated in difficulty.

Comprehension at all levels measures the child's ability to read whole sentences and paragraphs with understanding. This is done by means of a series of reading passages that vary in length and complexity. For Basic R and Levels A and B, each passage is accompanied by four pictures from which the examinee selects the one that explains the passage or answers questions about the passage. For Levels C to F, the Comprehension Test measures the child's ability to read complete prose passages (varying in number, length, and difficulty) with understanding. The examinee is asked from two to five questions on each passage. There are both literal and inferential questions, the percentage of the latter increasing from 10 percent in Level A to 45 percent in Levels D, E, and F.

The Vocabulary and Comprehension tests at all levels except Basic R (where the easy and difficult items are interspersed throughout the test) are power tests in the sense that the tasks become increasingly difficult. On the surface, it would appear that at the higher grade levels, the Comprehension Test may also be speeded.

As is true in any test that attempts to span two or three grades, it is extremely difficult to control the difficulty of the items so that they are not too easy for the upper-level students or too difficult for the lower-level students. The Gates-MacGinitie tests are no exception, but they do show marked improvement over the older Gates Reading Tests.

Validity evidence as such is not presented. We concur with the authors that users evaluate the test in relation to their instructional objectives and curriculum, that is, content validity. Although the authors describe in a very general fashion the rationale for the tests and the manner in which the tests were constructed (e.g., they indicate what texts were surveyed to select vocabulary words), no test blueprint is provided to enable the user to judge the test's content validity. The authors state there was an initial tryout of the items, that minority group consultants were used, and that many more items were written than used. However, neither descriptive data concerning the tryout sample nor information concerning the item analyses performed is reported.

Most of the reliability coefficients are in the 0.90s. Norms were developed on a stratified random sample of about 65,000 pupils for each of the two standardization programs—beginning and end of the school year. The first and second editions of the tests were equated so that scores on alternate forms and adjacent levels could be meaningfully compared. With the exception of Basic R, where raw scores are expressed as high, average, or low (because the subtests are very short), raw scores are expressed as percentile ranks, stanines, grade equivalents, extended scale scores, and normal curve equivalents. A variety of output data is available. The tests are accompanied by a Technical Manual and a Teacher's Manual. The latter contains brief, succinct descriptions of the meanings of the various derived scores, as well as an extremely brief section on the use of the test scores. The Teacher's Manual is easy to follow.

The Gates-MacGinitie pays attention to testing in the first grade, which is as it should be, since this level is so important in the child's reading development. Another feature is a series of levels that provides for continuous measurement of reading achievement with a group of articulated tests from grades 1 to 12. The tests are attractively printed, use color appropriately, are printed in machine-scorable and hand-scorable versions, and are easy for teachers to administer and score. Unfortunately, the norms tables, the description of validity, and the standardization sample are inadequate. The Teacher's Manual is easy to follow.

Uses of Reading Tests   Reading tests, like other standardized achievement tests, are designed to measure an examinee's level of achievement. Specifically, however, reading test results can be used to help explain the reasons behind a pupil's underachievement in, say, science or mathematics. For example, Mary may be doing poorly in school not because she does not have an aptitude for learning, but because she is a poor reader. The results of reading tests can and should be used as *partial* evidence to evaluate the effectiveness of reading instruction. (Note: We did *not* say that they should be used to evaluate the teacher. In a later section we shall elaborate on the use (and misuse) of test scores for teacher evaluation.) And if Mr. Jones sees that his pupils are not doing well on his own or some standardized reading test, he can at least begin to advance some hypothesis(es)

to explain why this is so. Finally, the results of a reading test can be used to identify, albeit tentatively, those students who are having difficulty and should be given a reading diagnostic test.

Summary

The decision whether to use a single-subject-matter test, such as reading or mathematics or science, rather than the subtest of a survey battery depends upon the ultimate use of the test results. A survey test for a single-subject-matter area does not differ in principle from a battery subtest covering the same subject. *Both* are concerned with assessing the individual's present state of knowledge and contain much the same material. They do differ, however, in their degree or intensity of coverage. For example, an achievement test for arithmetic would contain more items and cover more aspects of arithmetic than would be possible in the battery's arithmetic subtests. Another advantage of a single-subject-matter test is that a particular school's objectives might be more in harmony with the objectives of a specific content test than with the subtest of a battery. There are other reasons for using single-subject-matter tests. One is to obtain more information about a pupil who has done poorly on the subtest of a battery. Another is to guide and counsel. Finally, because high schools have less of a uniform curriculum than do elementary schools, conventional test batteries will not have subtests for unique subjects such as Latin, Spanish, or psychology. Also, single-subject-matter tests normally reflect curricular changes sooner than batteries do.

STANDARDIZED ACHIEVEMENT-TEST SURVEY BATTERIES

Survey batteries are the most comprehensive way to measure educational achievement. Their major purpose is to determine examinees' *normative* performance (some of the newer batteries also are concerned with criterion-referenced performance) rather than to isolate specific strengths and

TABLE 16-2 Representative Achievement Batteries

Survey Achievement Batteries	Grade Levels Covered													
	K	1	2	3	4	5	6	7	8	9	10	11	12	13
California Achievement Tests	X	X	X	X	X	X	X	X	X	X	X	X	X	
Comprehensive Tests of Basic Skills	X	X	X	X	X	X	X	X	X	X	X	X	X	
Iowa Test of Basic Skills[a]	X	X	X	X	X	X	X	X	X	X				
Metropolitan Achievement Tests	X	X	X	X	X	X	X	X	X	X	X	X	X	
Sequential Tests of Educational Progress (STEP + CIRCUS)	X	X	X	X	X	X	X	X	X	X	X	X	X	
SRA Achievement Series	X	X	X	X	X	X	X	X	X	X	X	X	X	
SRA Survey of Basic Skills	X	X	X	X	X	X	X	X	X	X	X	X	X	
Stanford Achievement Test Series[b]	X	X	X	X	X	X	X	X	X	X	X	X	X	X
Iowa Tests of Educational Development (ITED)											X	X	X	X
Tests of Achievement and Proficiency (TAP)											X	X	X	X

[a]Coordinated with ITED and TAP to provide for assessment in grades K–12.
[b]The Stanford Early School Achievement Test (SESAT) is used in grades K–1; the Stanford Test of Academic Skills (TASK) is for grades 8–13.

weaknesses, despite the fact that some survey battery authors claim their tests can be used for diagnostic purposes and purport to give prescriptive information.

Survey batteries lend themselves best to a level where there is a common core of subjects and objectives. At one time, we found the largest number at the elementary levels. But today, many commercial test publishers may have one battery for the elementary level and another for the high school level, and they have coordinated the various levels to provide an articulated set of tests spanning grades K to 13. Table 16-2 shows the range of general achievement batteries.

When we examine the numerous survey batteries that have been published for the primary and elementary grades, we find more similarities than differences among them—no doubt because the curriculum at the primary and elementary levels tends to be similar regardless of the state, region,

or city in which schools are located. These survey batteries typically contain subtests in spelling, language, reading knowledge, vocabulary, arithmetic reasoning, arithmetic fundamentals, science, and social studies. Because of the greater flexibility high school pupils have in selecting their courses, because of the diversity of courses offered, and because of differences in the content of courses that have the same name, test publishers find it extremely difficult to develop a common core survey achievement-test battery for general high school use. Accordingly, various approaches have been used to try and develop a common core. One approach has been to build tests like the Stanford Achievement Test that measure the basic skills of reading, language, and mathematics. Another approach is to build tests like the Tests of Achievement and Proficiency (designed for grades 9–12 only) that emphasize the content stressed in high schools—mathematics, science, English, and social studies. Still another approach is to build tests such as the Sequential Tests of Educational Progress (STEP III) that are designed to measure skills and abilities that are not dependent on a particular curriculum or course of study. All these approaches have their advantages as well as limitations. For example, tests like the TAP are valid only for inferences regarding competence in a traditional curriculum. Achievement batteries like the STEP III, designed to measure general educational development and stressing critical thinking and interpretation, are more valid for inferences regarding those skills.

Survey batteries, regardless of their classification, often provide a total score as well as subscores. They often contain two or more parallel (equivalent) forms, take from two to three hours to administer (although some of the high school batteries take about five hours), and, for the younger pupils, have practice tests. Most of the batteries provide for both in-level and out-of-level testing (in out-of-level testing, a pupil in, say, the fifth grade may be given the test booklet that corresponds to, or includes, the fourth grade).

Although nearly all the survey batteries have interpretive information in either the General Manual or a Teacher's Manual, some of the batteries such as the California Achievement Tests and the Stanford Achievement Test have detailed procedures for the teacher to follow when interpreting a pupil's score and undertaking remediation. Batteries designed for the primary grades have the pupils respond directly in the test booklet; those for the upper elementary and above have answer sheets that are either hand- or machine-scorable. Standardized achievement test survey batteries often provide separate norms (sex, grade, age) to enable the user to make various comparisons. They provide for the conversion of raw scores to standard scores to assist in test interpretation.

The latest editions of the major survey batteries provide both objective-referenced and norm-referenced data. An example of a printout of an objective-referenced report from a norm-referenced test is given in Figure 16.3. From such a printout one obtains both norm-referenced information in the form of the various derived scores and the pupil's performance on each of the objectives measured by the test. The latter is expressed in terms of the level of mastery (a "+" indicates mastery, a "−" nonmastery, and a "P" partial mastery).

As mentioned earlier, because of the large number of subtests in survey batteries, the content sampling is limited. As might be expected, not all the subtests are of equal reliability, and some of the subtests may not be valid for Miss Smith's inferences while others are. The major advantage of the battery is that since all the subtests have been normed on the same sample, a pupil's performance on different subtests can be compared directly. Also, many of the survey batteries are now being normed concurrently with an aptitude test, thereby enabling the user to compare pupils' achievement with their ability.

A major trend in survey achievement test batteries over the past decade has been their emphasis on the *application* and *interpretation* of knowledge rather than on simple recall of facts.

We will now consider one of the survey batteries most frequently used in the elementary and secondary grades. Although standardized achievement survey batteries are available for college, graduate, and professional school, these will not be considered here.

Metropolitan Achievement Tests (MAT 6), 1984 Edition Published by The Psychological Corporation for grades K–12.9, these tests consist of two forms for all levels except the Primer, where there is only one form. The MAT 6 attempts to provide *both* diagnostic-prescriptive information for the instructional use of tests and general survey information in the major skill and content areas of the school curriculum. Actually then, the Metropolitan is *both* a norm-referenced and criterion-referenced battery with eight overlapping batteries spanning the Preprimer Grade (K.0–K.9) to Advanced 2 (grade 10.0–12.9). Diagnostic tests in reading, mathematics, and language that are statistically linked to the survey battery tests are available. At all levels, the MAT 6/

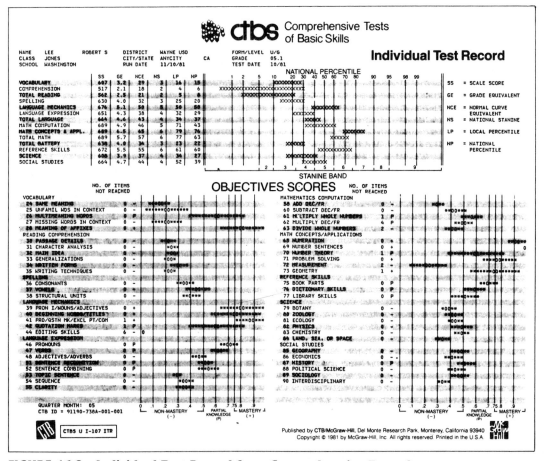

FIGURE 16.3   Individual Test Record from Comprehensive Test of Basic Skills, Form C. (Reproduced by permission of the publisher. CTB/ McGraw-Hill, Del Monte Research Park, Monterey, CA 93940. Copyright © 1981 by McGraw-Hill, Inc. All rights reserved. Printed in the U.S.A.)

Survey Battery measures reading, mathematics, and language and provides a total score in each of these areas as well as a total basic battery score. From Primary 1 through Advanced 2, tests and scores are available in social science and science. From Elementary through Advanced 2, a research skills score (this is not a test, per se, but is a score derived from items already embedded in other tests) is available. Research Skills at the Elementary Level—alphabetizing, reference, and dictionary skills—are in the Language test; graphs and statistics are in the Problem-Solving Test; and

critical analysis and inquiry skills are in *both* the Science and Social Studies tests.

Figure 16.4 illustrates some of the types of items used in the Intermediate Level battery. Although the subtests at the other levels have not been illustrated, the reader should now have a general knowledge of the types of items used. Again, we reiterate that only after examining and taking the test, and only after a careful reading of the various manuals accompanying the test, will the user be able to determine how well adapted the test will be to his or her purposes.

VOCABULARY

1 He wanted a _____ for his birthday.
   Ⓐ red   Ⓒ wagon
   Ⓑ pretty   Ⓓ again

WORD RECOGNITION SKILLS

1   **2**

green   Ⓐ belt   step   Ⓔ bet
               Ⓑ belong   Ⓕ feat
               Ⓒ bend   Ⓖ brief
               Ⓓ center   Ⓗ herb

3 Every _____ of the puzzle must be found.
   Ⓐ parted   Ⓒ parts
   Ⓑ part   Ⓓ parting

READING COMPREHENSION

> How did Bill fool Betty
> and her pet bird?

Betty has a pet bird called Tom. Tom likes cake. Her friend Bill put a peanut in Tom's cage. When Betty saw the peanut she laughed. She did not think Tom would eat the peanut.

The next day the peanut was gone. She thought she had been wrong. But Bill told her he had taken the peanut out of the cage.

1 Tom likes to eat—
   Ⓐ peanuts   Ⓒ birds
   Ⓑ cake   Ⓓ candy

2 In this story, the word saw means—
   Ⓔ a cutting tool   Ⓖ an old saying
   Ⓕ lost   Ⓗ noticed

MATHEMATICS: CONCEPTS

1 How many inches are there in one foot?
   Ⓐ 3   Ⓒ 12
   Ⓑ 10   Ⓓ 36

2 Look at the number word in the box. Which numeral is a name for this number?

> THIRTY-SIX

   Ⓔ 63   Ⓖ 306
   Ⓕ 36   Ⓗ 633

MATHEMATICS: COMPUTATION

1   Ⓐ 16
            12   Ⓑ 15
          + 3   Ⓒ 45
                               Ⓓ NG

2   Ⓔ 3
            1   Ⓕ 5
          ×4   Ⓖ 6
                               Ⓗ NG

MATHEMATICS: PROBLEM SOLVING

Teacher dictates: Alex had a box of 24 cookies. He gave 3 of them to his friend, Willie. How many cookies did he have left?

1 Ⓐ 24 − 3 = ☐   Ⓒ 24 + 3 = ☐
   Ⓑ 24 × 3 = ☐   Ⓓ 24 ÷ 3 = ☐

2 Maria has 2 green pencils and 5 red pencils. How many pencils is that in all?
   Ⓔ 5 − 2 = ☐   Ⓖ 2 + 5 = ☐
   Ⓕ 5 − ☐ = 2   Ⓗ 2 + ☐ = 5

3 There were 12 birds in the tree. Then 9 flew away. How many birds were left?
   Ⓐ 21   Ⓒ 3
   Ⓑ 4   Ⓓ 9

FIGURE 16.4   Sample Items Reproduced from the Intermediate II Battery of the Metropolitan Achievement Tests (MAT 6). (Copyright © 1985 by Harcourt Brace Jovanovich, Inc. Reproduced by permission of the publisher.)

Content cluster scores for each test domain and the components making up the domain (e.g., reading comprehension consists of literal, inferential, and critical reading scores) are available. An optional writing test is also available. Eight scores are provided—one in each content area, a research skills score, a total basic battery score, and a total survey battery score. Testing time varies from 98 to 190 minutes and from 190 to 254 minutes for the total basic and total survey battery, respectively. At the Elementary Level, for example, from 8 to 10 sittings of from 35 to 50 minutes are needed for test administration. Responses for the Preprimer, Primer, and Primary 1 levels are marked directly in the test booklet; for the other levels, a separate answer sheet is used.

Content validity was stressed in the test's development. In fact, one could say the procedures used to establish content validity should be used as an exemplar of thoroughness. Specific instructional objectives were derived from extensive analyses of textbook series, state guidelines, and school system syllabi. Test blueprints were developed to guide the item writers. The blueprints contained detailed instructional objectives within each level and subject. Items were written by curriculum and measurement specialists and were edited by persons with classroom experience. Items were reviewed by educators, including a panel of minority educators. *Both* language and illustrations were screened and edited to remove potential ethnic, cultural, regional, and class bias. In addition, normal statistical procedures were used to "flag" biased items. Extensive preliminary testing and item analyses were undertaken to select the "best" items. The authors say that criterion-related and construct validity will also be studied.

Users of the MAT 6 must decide on the curricular validity by comparing the test's instructional objectives with those of the local school or school district. The MAT 6 provides a detailed listing of all the instructional objectives for *each* test in its *Compendium of Instructional Objectives*. With this *Compendium*, users can ascertain the content validity of the tests for their own purposes.

The standardization program for MAT 6 involved over 250,000 students who also took the Otis-Lennon School Ability Test. The standardization sample was carefully chosen so as to represent the national school population in terms of geographical region, socioeconomic status (SES), ethnic background, size of school, and public versus nonpublic schools. Test reliabilities are consistent with those of other high-quality survey achievement-test batteries. For example, for the Elementary Level, the internal consistency reliabilities range from 0.90 to 0.96 for the five content areas and 0.98 for total scores on the complete battery. Although these reliabilities are for a single grade, they are *typical* rather than atypical for the other grades and other levels. The alternate-form reliabilities are in the 0.80s. Standard errors of measurement in terms of raw and scaled scores are provided for the two reliability estimates for both the fall and spring standardization.

A good feature of the MAT 6 is the provision of an Instructional Reading Level (IRL) and Instructional Mathematics Level (IML). The authors state that the IRL is "the best indicator of the specific skills that a student needs to be taught" (Prescott et al., 1986, p. 30). The IRL and IML scores are criterion-referenced and are used to select appropriate reading instructional and mathematics instructional materials, respectively, for the student. The authors are careful to point out that the IML is another way (norm- and objectives-referenced scores are also available) of interpreting a student's performance in mathematics. The IML, like the IRL, is useful in that it helps the teacher select the most appropriate level and learning materials. The students' performance in reading and mathematics is "matched" to graded basal readers and mathematics textbooks, respectively. The MAT 6 was normed concurrently with an aptitude test (the OLSAT). This permits one to predict the Metro scores based on the aptitude test scores (see Chapter 11).

Other commendable features of the 1984 Metro include (1) the cautions given and discussion of the fallibility of grade equivalents, (2) an attractive format with two-color printing and attention to such details as spacing, type size, typeface, and so on, to make the test more natural, (3) practice tests for all levels, (4) a variety of output data using the publisher's scoring service, (5) attention to minority concerns and sex bias, (6) school-based achievement "expectancy" based on SES and OLSAT data, (7) language tests at all levels from grades K–12, (8) the dictation of tests (excluding tests measuring reading) before Elementary to reduce the effects of reading ability, (9) emphasizing the instructional value of test results, (10) numerous cautions about interpreting test scores, (11) provision of a Reading Frustration and Independent Reading Level Score in addition to the IRL, (12) ease of administration, (13) emphasis on the "process" rather than factual recall in the science and social studies tests, (14) provision of a Research Skills score and a Higher Order Thinking Skills score, (15) the availability of an optional writing test where the student prepares an answer to a given prompt, (16) the involvement of parents in the testing/learning process, (17) more than one test per domain—for example, at the lower levels, MAT 6 has three reading, three mathematics, two language, one science, and one social studies test(s), (18) overlapping grades in the standardization program, (19) a "Purpose Question" preceding each reading passage to try to motivate the students, (20) diagnostic information from the spelling, mathematics, and problem-solving tests, (21) no transformational grammar, and (22) ample and clearly written interpretive materials.

As might be expected, the MAT 6 is *not* without some shortcomings. Most notable are (1) too much is expected of the teacher in reference to the interpretation of the IML and IRL, (2) the procedure used to identify those students whose predicted achievement range (PAR) suggests special attention by the teacher or counselor is questionable, and (3) more predictive validity evidence is needed to support the claims for recommended uses of the test, namely, prescriptive information. Although the content validity is well-established, it does *not* suffice for the prescriptive uses of the instructional tests.

In summary, the MAT 6 reflects the core curriculum. As with its predecessors, MAT 6 was carefully constructed, validated, and standardized.

Careful attention was paid to selecting items that were as free from bias as possible. Many of the criticisms of the previous editions appear to have been rectified (see Mehrens & Lehmann, 1969; Buros, 1965).

Some Other Survey Batteries

In addition to the tests presented in Table 16.2 (see page 372), some other examples of standardized survey achievement-test batteries are the Cooperative Primary Tests and the Tests of Basic Experiences 2 (TOBE 2). The College Board's Assessment and Placement Services Program is a survey battery containing subtests in reading, writing, mathematics, and an essay portion. This program is specifically designed to serve the community college population. The program also contains a Student Placement Inventory and can be used by the counselor to assist in recommending appropriate course selection and placement to the student.

Up to this point we have focused primarily on those achievement tests used in elementary and secondary schools. However, a significant portion of the adult population is illiterate or disadvantaged in such a way that conventional achievement tests are not valid for them. Tests are available to measure the basic skills of adults with inadequate educational backgrounds. One of these is the United States Employment Service's Basic Occupational Literacy Test (BOLT), which assesses a person's vocabulary, reading comprehension, arithmetic computation, and arithmetic reasoning skills. Other tests available for testing adults with poor educational backgrounds are SRA's Reading-Arithmetic Index and the Psychological Corporation's Adult Basic Learning Examination (ABLE).

INDIVIDUALLY ADMINISTERED ACHIEVEMENT TESTS

Although group-administered survey achievement tests and test batteries are the most frequently used, recent federal legislation on the *mainstreaming* of handicapped children into the regular classroom (the assessment of the exceptional child will be covered in detail in Chapter 18) has spawned an interest in and need for the assessment of the handicapped/exceptional child's academic performance. Generally, the pupils respond by pointing or by answering orally, although, depending on the child's condition, some writing may be required. The various individually administered survey achievement batteries provide norm-referenced, criterion-referenced, or *both* types of scores (interpretation). Some of the more popular individually administered survey achievement-test batteries are (1) the Peabody Individual Achievement Test (PIAT), which is designed for grade K to adult, (2) the Basic Achievement Skills Individual Screener (BASIS), which is designed for use in grades 1–12 and for post–high school adults, (3) the Wide Range Achievement Test (WRAT), which is designed for grade 5 to adult, (4) the Kaufman Test of Educational Achievement, which is designed for grades 1–12, and (5) the Woodcock-Johnson Psycho-Educational Battery, used for persons 3 to 80 years of age. The PIAT and WRAT are generally used only for those persons who cannot take a group test—for instance, handicapped children, very nervous children. Users of any individually administered achievement test must be very careful when interpreting the pupils' score. Since these tests tend to cover a wide age range with a limited number of items, the depth of coverage is minimal, even less so than with a group-administered survey battery. We will now consider the BASIS in more detail.

Basic Achievement Skills Individual Screener (BASIS)

Published by The Psychological Corporation (1982), BASIS is an individually administered achievement test designed for use with pupils in grades 1–12 and for post–high school adults. It is particularly useful with young children, nervous examinees, and special populations where individual educational plans (IEPs) are to be formulated and then evaluated.

BASIS provides *both* criterion-referenced and norm-referenced information. There are three required tests—reading, mathematics, and spelling—and an optional writing exercise. (The writing exercise is used in grades 3–8; the required tests in grades 1–12.) All the items for the reading, mathematics, and spelling tests are grouped in grade-referenced clusters; each cluster is designed to reflect the curriculum at a particular grade level. The test, although untimed, takes about one hour to administer (this includes the writing exercise, which takes 10 minutes).

Beginning-of-grade and interpolated end-of-grade norms are provided for grades 1–8; beginning-of-grade norms are provided for grades 9–12. Age and adult norms are also furnished. The norming sample appears to be representative of the school population enrolled in mainstreamed classes. The publishers made certain that disabled students were included in the norming sample, and they are to be commended for reporting both the incidence and the types of disabilities the students had.

K-R 20 and test–retest reliability estimates are reported, the former for each grade and age level found in the standardization sample, the latter for samples of second-, fifth-, and eighth-grade students. The K-R 20s are quite high and the manual cautions the user regarding the spuriousness of the correlations. (It is a result of the type of scoring used. BASIS scoring is similar to the basal and ceiling age approach of the Stanford-Binet, where the examinee is given credit for passing all the items below and failing all the items above a particular point.) We wonder why the publisher reported this reliability, inasmuch as most users will tend to ignore the caveat or not understand its significance.

"Logical" validity was substantiated for each of the three skills tests. Of the three tests, the mathematics test appears to be more valid than either the reading or the spelling tests, especially in terms of predicting grade-placement accurately. Very little empirical validity data, however, are reported. Although reference is made to the manner in which the validity of the writing exercise was established, too many questions remain unanswered (the number of papers rated, the number and characteristics of the raters, the number of times each paper was rated, and so forth) to permit us to comment on the findings reported.

Raw scores for each of the three skills tests (these scores are indicators of text and grade placement) can be converted to within-grade-level percentile ranks and stanines for grades 1–12 and post–high school; for ages 6–18 and post–high school, grade and age equivalents are provided. Standard scores, NCEs, and Rasch scores are also available.

BASIS has many good things going for it. A comprehensive manual contains a thorough discussion of establishing and maintaining rapport; the test booklet is reusable; the information describing the development of the test and the items is complete; and the skills tests have adequate validity to be used as part of a student's assessment and for decisions relating to the student's IEP.

Tests of Minimal Competency

Nearly every state in the nation has mandated the testing of pupils in the basic skills of reading, writing, language, and arithmetic. Many states have developed their own tests, but one commercial publisher at least—California Test Bureau/McGraw-Hill—has developed a series of tests that can be used to certify high school students as eligible for graduation. There also are some tests designed for the junior high grades to ascertain whether the pupils are making satisfactory progress in their basic and life skills. Some CTB tests are as follows:

For use in the junior high school grades:
Assessment Skills in Computation
Performance Assessment in Reading

For use in the high school:
Senior High Assessment of Reading Performance
Test of Performance in Computational Skills
Test of Everyday Writing Skill

While the majority of the minimal competency tests are designed for an in-school population, some, like ETS's *Basic Skills Assessment* (BSA), Psychological Corporation's *Adult Basic Learning Exam* (ABLE), and USES's *Basic Occupational Literacy Test* (BOLT), are appropriate for adults who have a poor educational background. Whereas the former is designed for junior high school students, the latter two are appropriate for adults with poor educational backgrounds. Research has indicated that these three programs meet high-quality psychometric standards. (See reviews by Plake and Ravitch in the *Ninth Mental Measurements Yearbook*.)

As is true for any of the areas/tests discussed in this text, the reader is encouraged to consult the test catalogs of the various test publishers (listed in the Appendix) because some areas are so rapidly changing that a test reviewed or mentioned may be revised by the time you read about it.

Summary of Standardized Achievement Tests

Achievement tests run the gamut from readiness and diagnostic tests to survey tests, from norm-referenced to criterion-referenced, and from pre-school to graduate and professional school. All are designed to give an index of what the student knows at a particular point in time.

Readiness tests are normally restricted to reading. Diagnostic tests are confined primarily to reading and arithmetic. These tests are used most frequently in the primary grades. Readiness and diagnostic tests differ from the conventional standardized achievement (subject-matter content) tests in that they are confined to very limited areas.

There are some differences, however, in standardized reading readiness tests—the differences reflecting the importance attributed to those facets deemed by the test authors to be important in beginning to learn to read.

Diagnostic tests seem to be more similar than readiness tests. Their major purpose is to help the teacher recognize the pupils' difficulties; therefore, diagnostic tests are constructed so that they permit pupils to maximize the number of errors they can make. There may be a difference of opinion whether a pupil is ready to learn to read, but there is very little disagreement as to whether he or she exhibits tendencies to reversals or omissions when reading. It is also important to remember that no single readiness or diagnostic test can assess all the skills and knowledge needed by the pupil to learn effectively.

Teachers desiring a thorough picture of the pupil's knowledge in a specific content area should select a standardized achievement test in that particular subject. Single or specific achievement tests are also valuable to the counselor.

Some survey batteries, such as the Stanford and California Achievement Tests, provide for continuous measurement from kindergarten through high school—and even of adults. Others, such as CIRCUS and the Cooperative Preschool Inventory, span the preschool/nursery to primary grades. Still others, such as the STEP III, are intended for grades 3–12. The ITBS and others span grades K–9. And still others, such as the TAP and ITED, are for only high school students. Survey batteries attempt to provide measures of achievement in the core subjects by containing tests of vocabulary, arithmetic, spelling, reading, and language. The various batteries provide separate subtest scores as well as a total score. The raw scores are transformed to some form of standard score to permit meaningful comparisons among the various subtests.

There are other differences among the various survey batteries. At the primary level (grades 1–3) the content is similar, although the format may differ from one battery to another. After the fourth or fifth grade, the contents of the various batteries differ. Some batteries measure work study skills; others do not. Some batteries may devote 15 percent of the test to measuring reading comprehension; others will devote about 30 percent. Only the Stanford has a separate test of listening comprehension. The various batteries also differ in the number of subtests. For example, at the elementary level, the Stanford yields 6 to 11 scores, whereas the ITBS gives 15 separate scores. The

ITBS and Stanford both measure the fundamental skills of reading, mathematics, and language.

The types of scores, reports, and manuals provided by the various survey batteries illustrate another point of difference. The ITBS presents percentiles, stanines, grade equivalents, age equivalents, standard scores, and normal curve equivalents. The Stanford provides only grade equivalents, percentiles, scaled scores, and stanines.

Because of the nature of their construction, survey batteries should not be used to obtain a thorough estimate of a pupil's knowledge or skills in a specific area. Although a science or language arts subscore can be obtained, this score will normally be influenced by the sample of tasks measured by that particular subtest.

Although the various batteries may differ slightly with respect to the fundamental educational goals emphasized, they all share a common purpose to help the student and teacher recognize strengths and weaknesses.

In conclusion, there are strengths and weaknesses in all standardized achievement tests. Accordingly, their limitations must be carefully considered and weighed against their virtues in test selection. In the final analysis, the good is taken with the bad, but we want to choose a test with minimum limitations and maximum advantages. We concur with Katz (1961), who states that achievement tests or test batteries that are universally recognized as "good" are not equally "good" for different school settings, situations, or circumstances.

USING ACHIEVEMENT-TEST RESULTS

The authors of many of the better standardized achievement tests and batteries suggest specific uses, and supplement their tests with valuable interpretive examples. At the same time, the ingenious classroom teacher may discover a use that is applicable only in her classroom. The remarks that follow should be thought of as only some *suggested* uses of standardized achievement tests.

The purpose of any standardized achievement test is to provide the user with information concerning an individual's knowledge or skills so that the user can make decisions—of selection and classification, for academic and vocational counseling, about the relative effectiveness of two or more methods of instruction—that are more valid than they would be if such data had not been employed to make the decision. Achievement-test results can be used to measure the outcomes of learning; to identify those pupils who are in need of remedial instruction; to identify those pupils who may lack certain fundamental skills needed before they can begin reading; to aid in the assignment of course grades; to facilitate learning by the pupils; to provide an external criterion in the evaluation of sponsored-research programs that require evidence of or information about academic performance; to provide a basis for certification and promotion decisions; and to provide a criterion in research designed to evaluate various instructional strategies. As Airasian and Madaus (1983) and Haertel and Calfee (1983) point out, achievement tests in general, but standardized tests in particular, lately have assumed greater importance in policy and curriculum decisions that have an impact on students, teachers, and other educators.

Achievement tests—be they teacher-made or standardized—are *not* designed to measure, even remotely, the affective components of our educational enterprise. They do not tell us anything about whether Allan or Ilene is interested in school, enjoys reading, or can interact effectively with peers. What achievement tests do, however—measuring the cognitive aims of instruction in an objective manner—is to accomplish more validly and reliably than is possible with teachers' subjective judgments (Levine, 1976).

Although we consider the use of standardized achievement tests under such headings as instructional uses, guidance uses, administrative uses, and research uses, the reader should be aware that this classification imposes rigidity in treatment and may result in the fallacious assumption that there is little, if any, overlap. Seldom is there a situation in which standardized achievement-test results serve only a single purpose.

Instructional Uses[5]

LeMahieu (1984) in describing the "Monitoring Achievement in Pittsburgh" project reported that the program had a profound effect on the students' achievement. Whether or not it was the monitoring aspect of the program, per se, that was the significant factor is not the issue. Rather, it was something associated with the program—the tests themselves, the instruction, the frequency of testing—that was important.

Achievement-test results can be invaluable to the classroom teacher. For example, reading readiness test scores can assist the teacher in learning which of her pupils possess the skills and knowledge needed to begin the reading program. These test scores help the teacher group the pupils (tentatively, at least) for maximum instructional benefits. Students, who on the basis of other evidence demonstrate that they should be successful in reading or arithmetic but who are experiencing difficulty or score poorly on a subject-matter test, may benefit from a diagnostic test. The diagnostic test can aid the teacher in locating the nature of the difficulty. Diagnostic tests may also be used to identify those students who might benefit from additional remedial work. Diagnostic and readiness tests may be used as an initial screening device to be followed by a more thorough investigation if needed.

---

[5]LeMahieu and Wallace (1986) present a cogent discussion regarding the distinction between tests used for diagnosis and those used for evaluation. We agree with them that "tests can be particularly well-suited to serve one or the other function, but rarely, if ever, are they appropriate for both. . . . [D]iagnostic devices do *not* [italics added] make for good evaluative tests."

Standardized diagnostic tests not only provide a more systematic approach than that of the informal method used by the classroom teacher (although we strongly favor gathering such informal data), but some of the newer diagnostic tests offer suggestions to the teacher for remediation.

Single-subject-matter tests and survey batteries help the teacher ascertain the strengths and weaknesses of her class and thereby suggest modification of her instructional method or the reteaching of certain materials. Or, the teacher can reevaluate her goals if the data suggest this. She can evaluate the effectiveness of a specific teaching method by using achievement-test results.

Standardized achievement-test results, in combination with data gathered from aptitude tests, may aid in identifying the under- and overachieving students. Be careful, though! The discrepancy between the students' performance on the different tests must be large, and these data should only be *part* of the information used in making a decision.

As will be discussed more fully in Chapter 18, Public Law 94-142, which deals with the equality of education for exceptional children, mandates that the academic progress of these children be monitored regularly. Standardized tests provide for such a systematic monitoring. In addition, exceptional children—the gifted, the mentally retarded, the physically handicapped, and the like—have unique needs and problems. Standardized achievement and aptitude tests can assist in the identification of these needs and problems.

Standardized achievement tests (excluding readiness and diagnostic tests) can also play an important role with respect to standardizing grading. Quite frequently we hear that Ms. Smith is an "easy grader" and that Ms. Jones is a "hard grader." Although standardized achievement tests should not be used to assign course grades, they can be used by teachers to evaluate their grading practices. For example, when Ms. Smith, the easy grader, compares the achievement of her pupils on standardized tests to that of other teachers' pupils and learns that her class achieves less well, she can see that the high grades she assigned may be misleading. This does not imply, however, that standardized achievement-test results should be used as the only reference point in assigning course grades. They should be used to give the individual teacher some perspective. Many other factors must be considered before Ms. Smith concludes that she is too easy in her grading. The standardized achievement test should be used as supplementary data on which to build a valid estimate of the pupil's achievement and hence his final grade.

Achievement-test results can be used to help the teacher provide optimal learning conditions for every pupil. In order to do this, the teacher should know as much as possible about every student. Standardized achievement tests will provide some of this needed information. Test results will assist in the grouping of pupils for instructional purposes. They will also be extremely valuable in assisting the teacher to fit the curriculum to each child in a class. Some children should get enriching experiences; others may require remedial work.

Cox and Sterrett (1970) present a simple model of how standardized achievement-test results can be scored so that the classroom teacher may make both criterion- and norm-referenced interpretations of the test scores. For example, Ms. Pedagogy may classify the test items in a particular standardized achievement test according to her instructional objectives. She could end up with three groups of items: one consisting of items that her pupils have studied and are expected to know; one of items that have not been studied, but which the pupils will be expected to know at a later time; and one of items that are not relevant. The test can then be administered and scored to yield three scores: Jack correctly answered 90 percent of the items he was expected to know, 45 percent of those not yet studied, and 5 percent of the remaining items. With this information for each pupil, Ms. Pedagogy can plan her instruction accordingly. (Note: If tests are to be used for grouping purposes, and if only one testing period is available, we recommend that there be an early testing so that the results will be most beneficial to both pupils and teachers.)

As mentioned earlier, commercial test publishers now provide reporting services (for a slight additional fee) that group pupils of similar abilities and offer the classroom teacher suggestions on the instructional strategy to be used with these groups, furnish item-analysis data, report the number of items answered correctly by each pupil, and the like. (See Figures 16.5 and 16.6.) These reports are generally designed to report an *individual's* performance, but some standardized achievement tests produce a "class" report. Although narrative reports may lack the precision of test norms, they do afford an excellent medium for reporting test results to unsophisticated audiences.

With education moving more and more toward individualized instruction and with the gearing of standardized achievement tests to textbooks, the results of achievement tests can aid appreciably in fitting the curriculum to the child rather than the child to the curriculum. Criterion-referenced (or scored) standardized tests, if successfully developed, should permit the teacher to prescribe individual learning experiences appropriately. These tests provide the teacher with valuable supplementary information that may be difficult or impossible to obtain with norm-referenced achievement tests, which are usually given only at the end of the year.

Conventional standardized achievement-test results should *not* be used for individual diagnosis, but they can (and should) be used effectively as a springboard for the teacher to explore areas of pupils' strengths and/or weaknesses. Once students needing remediation have been identified, their progress can be monitored using *both* standardized and teacher-made tests.

Teachers will occasionally use the results of a standardized achievement test as the major criterion in determining the status of their pupils and will then plan their instructional program accordingly. They should *never* do this! Other factors need to be strongly considered. For example, how well do the test objectives meet those of the particular teacher? How reliable is a part score in a battery or, for that matter, how reliable are, say, the four or five items used to test the pupil's

knowledge of simultaneous equations or atomic structure? Is the course structure centered on skills, on content, or on both? Because of these and other considerations, standardized achievement tests should not (1) be a major criterion in course planning or (2) be the focus of the course content to be taught by the teacher.

In closing, we would like to draw the users' attention to two important points: (1) unless there is a good "match" between the teachers' and tests' instructional objectives, the test results will be of questionable value for evaluating instructional effectiveness, and (2) the diagnostic value to be derived from the scores of group-administered diagnostic tests in general and survey battery tests in particular is highly suspect. Quite often what is *more* important than the score(s), per se, is *how* the pupil attempted to answer the test items.

Guidance and Counseling Uses

Achievement-test results, in combination with other data, can be important in vocational and educational guidance. Achievement-test results can be used to help the student plan his future educational or vocational program. It should be remembered that achievement-test data by themselves have limited meaning. They need to be augmented by other information—data about interests, aptitudes, and attitudes—to arrive at the best decision possible. An illustration may help clarify the situation.

Girder, a senior in high school, is interested in studying engineering. The school counselor has a variety of information about Girder. From both survey batteries and single-subject-matter tests given Girder at the elementary, middle, and high school levels, a pattern is readily evident that Girder's strengths are in verbal skills and that he is deficient in science and mathematics. His interest test scores suggest that he possesses interests shared by journalists. His scholastic aptitude score indicates that he is of average ability. The counselor should use all these data in helping Girder arrive at a decision concerning the appropriateness of an engineering major in college. The

MAT6 — METROPOLITAN ACHIEVEMENT TESTS — **SURVEY**

CLUSTER ANALYSIS FOR

A
TEACHER MARY FRY
SCHOOL NORTHWESTERN
SYSTEM MIDDLEBURG

B
GRADE 4
LEVEL ELEMENTARY
FORM L

AGE 9 YRS. 3 MOS.
TEST DATE 10/10
MAT6 NORMS 4.1

C SUSAN MORRIS

	Raw Score / No. Poss.	LOW	AVG	HIGH
D Skills Order of Importance For an IRL of Grade 4				
High: Vocabulary in Context				
Word Part Clues				
Some: Sight Vocabulary				
Phoneme/Grapheme: Vowels				
Rate of Comprehension				
Low: Phoneme/Grapheme: Consonants				

E F | | **G** | **H** |
A VOCABULARY	17/22		
A0-01 Subject & Predicate	5/6		
A0-02 Adj., Adv. & Preposition	5/8		
A0-03 Direct & Indirect Objects	7/8		

E **MATHEMATICS: PROBLEM SOLVING**	13/30		
E1 Problem Solving	12/25		
E1-04 Add/Subtract No Regrouping	4/5		
E1-05 Add/Subtract with Regrouping	2/10		
E1-06 Multiply/Divide Basic Facts	6/10		
Listen	7/10		
Read	5/15		
Choose	4/10		
Solve	8/15		
E2 Graphs & Statistics	1/5		

G **SPELLING**	18/21		
G1-03 Grade 3	5/5		
G1-04 Grade 4	9/10		
G1-05 Grade 5	4/6		
H **LANGUAGE**	30/42		
H2 Punctuation & Capitalization	14/21		
H2-02 Periods & Question Marks	2/3		
H2-03 Commas	5/7		
H2-05 Other Punc. & No Punc. Needed	2/4		
H2-06 Capitalization	5/7		
H3 Usage	8/9		
H4 Written Expression	5/6		
H5 Study Skills	3/6		
H5-01 Alphabetizing	2/3		
H5-03 Dictionary Skills	1/3		

I			
RESEARCH SKILLS	28/43		
H5 Reference Skills	3/6		
E2 Graphs & Statistics	1/5		
J0-005 Science Inq. & Crit. Analysis	14/16		
K0-005 Soc. St. Inq. & Crit. Analysis	10/16		

CONTENT CLUSTERS	Raw Score/No. Poss.	LOW	AVG	HIGH
B **WORD RECOGNITION SKILLS**	21/29			
B4 Phoneme/Grapheme: Consonants	6/6			
B4-01 Initial Consonants	3/3			
B4-02 Final Consonants	3/3			
B5 Phoneme/Grapheme: Vowels	10/14			
B5-01 Short Vowels	3/5			
B5-02 Long Vowels	5/5			
B5-03 Digraphs & Diphthongs	2/4			
B6 Word Part Clues	5/9			
B6-01 Affixes	3/6			
B6-02 Compound Words	2/3			
C **READING COMPREHENSION**	33/60			
C4-01 Literal (Details & Sequence)	14/17			
C4-02 Inferential	13/28			
C4-021 Inferred Meaning/Fig. Lang.	5/10			
C4-022 Cause & Effect	2/7			
C4-023 Main Idea	3/5			
C4-024 Character Analysis	3/6			
C4-03 Critical (Drawing Conclusions)	6/15			

F **MATHEMATICS COMPUTATION**	23/30			
F1 Computation: Whole Numbers	22/26			
F1-04 Add/Subtract No Regrouping	4/4			
F1-05 Add/Subtract with Regrouping	5/8			
F1-06 Multiply/Divide Basic Facts	8/8			
F1-07 Multiply/Divide Beyond Basic Facts	5/6			
F2 Computation: Decimals & Fractions	1/4			
D **MATHEMATICS: CONCEPTS**	26/35			
D1 Numeration	16/20			
D1-04 Hundreds	5/5			
D1-05 Thousands	5/5			
D1-06 Beyond Thousands	4/5			
D1-07 Decimals & Fractions	2/5			
D2 Geometry & Measurement	10/15			
D2-02 Shapes & Figures	3/3			
D2-06 Money & Time	4/6			
D2-07 Customary & Metric Measurement	3/6			

J **SCIENCE**	39/45			
J1 Physical	14/16			
J2 Earth & Space	12/14			
J3 Life	13/15			
Knowledge	9/10			
Comprehension	16/19			
Inquiry Skills	9/10			
Critical Analysis	5/6			
K **SOCIAL STUDIES**	31/45			
K1 Geography	10/11			
K2 Economics	4/9			
K3 History	4/7			
K4 Political Science	5/7			
K5 Human Behavior	8/11			
Knowledge	8/12			
Comprehension	13/17			
Inquiry Skills	7/10			
Critical Analysis	3/6			

| **J** | | | |
| 7-01 HIGHER ORDER THINKING SKILLS | 26/54 | | |

THE PSYCHOLOGICAL CORPORATION
HARCOURT BRACE JOVANOVICH, PUBLISHERS

FIGURE 16.5 Metropolitan Achievement Tests Individual Report.
(Copyright © 1985 by Harcourt Brace Jovanovich, Inc. Reproduced by permission. All rights reserved.)

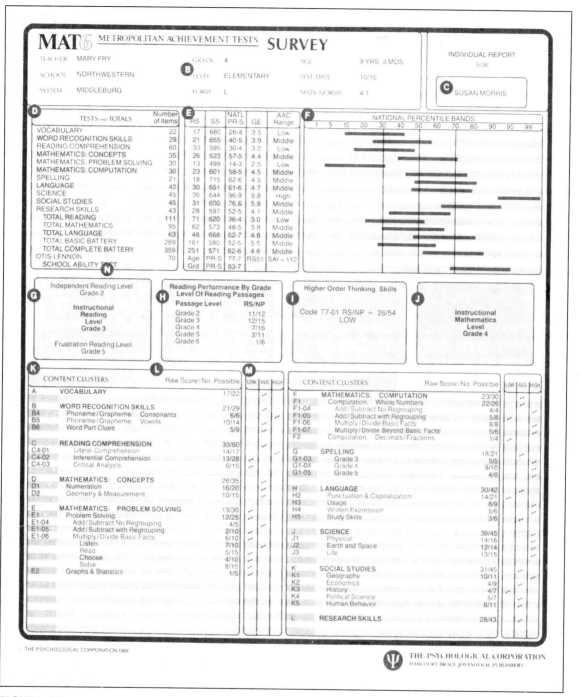

FIGURE 16.6   Metropolitan Achievement Tests Cluster Analysis.

counselor should point out to Girder that he must show marked improvement in science and mathematics in order to succeed in the engineering curriculum. Actually, what the counselor is doing here is making a tentative prediction of probable success on the basis of test data.

Achievement-test results are being used more frequently today in helping high school seniors select a college. With data from national testing programs such as the College Board's achievement tests, it is possible for high school counselors to relate (with fairly high validity) standardized achievement-test scores to college grades. In fact, some programs provide the student with an indication of his probable success at a particular college or university. If test results are used in this way, the student may be guided to an institution where, because of less competition, he will be more successful and more likely to be graduated. Remember! Test results *are fallible*. People *do* change, and future predictions can and do go awry. We should capitalize on the positive use of test results such as directing the weaker student to a less demanding college or directing the student to a more realistic vocational choice instead of saying "college is not for you."

In conclusion, it must be remembered that achievement-test results are *not* absolute measures and that success in vocational training, graduate, or professional school depends upon many factors, only one of which is prior achievement. Failure to consider these other vitally important factors will result in poor guidance and counseling.

Administrative Uses

Selection, Classification, and Placement
In many instances, achievement-test results are used to select individuals for a particular training program or for a specific vocation. In such cases, the achievement test must demonstrate high predictive validity.

Selection is more common in industry and in higher education than it is in elementary and secondary schools. For example, a life insurance company may select agents on the basis of an achievement test if the company has found that the test is a good predictor of sales volume. Likewise, a college may select its entering freshmen on the basis of a standardized achievement test if it has been found that the test is a valid predictor.

Administrators are frequently confronted with determining where the transfer student should be placed. A fourth-grader from Los Angeles should not necessarily be placed in the fourth grade in Syracuse, because the schools in each area may require different levels of achievement. The results of a standardized achievement test can be used effectively to help the administrator evaluate the transfer student's past performance. This is especially true if the same test is used in both schools. If different tests are used and no comparisons are possible, the principal should administer the test used in her school.

The data presented in Table 16-3 are for a hypothetical ten-year-old transferring from an ungraded school in San Francisco to a city school in Buffalo in January. The pupil's test scores were obtained in the fall, when he entered the "fourth" grade. The norms in both schools are based on national norms.

What do we know about this pupil? We know that (1) he is below the average fourth-grader except in spelling, (2) he is more like Buffalo third-graders than fourth-graders, (3) he is more proficient in verbal skills than in arithmetic skills, and (4) if he is placed in the fourth grade, he may experience a great deal of competition, even to the extent that he might become frustrated and develop a negative attitude toward school.

Of what help can the data in Table 16-3 be to a principal? Would she be likely to make a more valid educational decision with these data than without them? With data such as these, the principal should exercise extreme caution before automatically placing the pupil in the fourth grade because of his age.

The principal could either place the pupil in the fourth grade and recognize that the teacher will have to spend extra time with the pupil; or the principal could place the pupil in the third grade

TABLE 16-3 Hypothetical Grade Score Equivalents on the Stanford Achievement Test, Primary 3 Battery

Subtest	Transfer Student's Grade Score Equivalent	Mean Grade Score Equivalent for Buffalo Third-Graders	Mean Grade Score* Equivalent for Buffalo Fourth-Graders
Reading comprehension	3.2	3.5	4.2
Paragraph meaning	3.4	3.4	4.4
Vocabulary	3.4	3.7	4.8
Spelling	4.8	3.8	4.6
Word-study skills	3.6	3.6	4.9
Arithmetic	2.5	3.5	4.4

*Norms in both schools based on fall testing.

aware that he may be out of place physiologically and psychologically. If the pupil is placed in the fourth grade, his teacher needs to understand that he may have difficulty at first, that remedial teaching will be in order, and that additional work will be needed before the pupil will absorb the material as readily as the average fourth-grader. Regardless of the decision made, it should be obvious that the principal must consult with the student's parents, since there may be problems associated with either decision.

In this example, two kinds of decisions must be made: (1) where to place the pupil and (2) how best to assist the pupil after the decision has been made.

Another example of how standardized achievement tests can aid the user is in the classification or placement of students in special courses or programs. The kind of classification possible will depend on the type of test used and the physical facilities available in the school. For example, if a survey battery is used, much information is provided. The results may suggest that a student take algebra in an average class, English in a superior class, and social studies in a remedial class.

Comparing Test Scores Although a variety of administrative decisions concerning selection, classification, and placement can be made on the basis of standardized achievement-test results, the examples discussed above pertain to the use of the *same* test. What kinds of decisions, if any, can be made with different survey battery or single-subject-matter test results? Can comparisons be made for a pupil's scores obtained on the *same* subtest (content area) of *different* tests?

Comparing Scores on Similarly Named Subtests of Different Achievement Batteries Although it might be assumed that the Mathematics Computation subtest in the Stanford measures the *same* knowledge and skills as the Mathematics Computation test in the Metropolitan (especially since they were developed and published by the same publisher), such an assumption may be wholly unwarranted. On the surface, it might appear that the same instructional objectives (knowledge and skills) are being measured. But only a careful examination of the test manual and test blueprint will provide the information necessary to judge the comparability of the two subtests. But even this is *not* sufficient to judge the similarity of the Mathematics Computation subtests from the two survey batteries. The test items might differ in difficulty and discrimination power. The norming population may be (and often is) different. The validity and reliability of the subtests may be dissimilar. Even though it has been shown that there is a high correlation between the *total* scores obtained on the Stanford and the Metropolitan, it has also been shown that there is a low correlation between similarly named subtests in these two batteries (Goolsby, 1971). Only by carefully studying the subtests themselves as well as the respective test manuals can the user ascertain whether the subtests are similar.

Evaluation of Instruction and Teachers

One of the *mis*uses of standard achievement tests is in making educational decisions *solely* on the basis of standardized achievement-test results. We are especially concerned about this inappropriate test use because the recent flurry of federal reports and commissions on the state of American education has resulted in some drastic measures being taken to evaluate the educational enterprise—one such drastic response being the use of standardized achievement-test results for the evaluation of teachers and instruction (Berk, 1988; Rothman, 1987).

Teacher effectiveness should *not* be determined solely on the basis of test results and definitely *not* on the results of one test. The instructional objectives stressed by Mr. Jackson may be only minimally reflected in the test, but those emphasized by Miss Garcia may be highlighted in the test. Remember that even in the most valid test we only have a sampling of a teacher's instructional objectives.

Not only can a multitude of factors affect learning and hence the evaluation of instruction and teachers, but we also have statistical problems in interpreting "gain scores" since the reliability of the "gain score" is often substantially lower than the reliability of either the pre- or posttest scores.

It would be extremely difficult to compare Ms. Smith and Ms. Jones, both third-grade teachers in the same school, when we know that one classroom contains an overabundance of bright pupils and the other contains many slower pupils. Even assuming that the average ability of the two classes is comparable, how can we rate the teachers when Ms. Smith, for example, feels certain skills are more easily learned at the end of the term, whereas

Ms. Jones prefers to teach these skills at the beginning of the term, but we administer our tests in the middle of the term?

Achievement-test results, regardless of their nature, are measures that depend upon past learning. In other words, if Ms. Smith's sixth-graders are weak in certain arithmetic skills, the weakness may be due to the fact that the essential components of this skill were not developed in an earlier grade. Hence, blaming Ms. Smith because her pupils score below national norms would be utterly ridiculous. There is no doubt that teachers are instrumental in determining how well their pupils score on achievement tests. However, this is *not* analogous to the claim that *only* achievement-test results be used to rate teachers.

When achievement-test results are used to rate teachers, they frequently instill fear in the teachers. This fear conceivably may result in a reduction of teacher effectiveness and in a tendency toward "test teaching." Teaching for a test may encourage undue emphasis on a limited part of cognitive development, the end result being neglect of other areas of cognitive development and for the social, affective, psychomotor, and emotional development of pupils.

We believe that standardized achievement-test results can and should (where deemed appropriate) be used to improve the instructional program. Further, we feel that test results should be used to *help* the teacher rather than to evaluate her. Such self-help can be of marked benefit to teachers. They can see the strengths and weaknesses of their class (either as a whole or for the individual pupils) if they use a survey battery. They can, by means of an item analysis, see what skills or facts have and have not been learned. They can, using national norms, make comparisons between their students and students in the same grade nationally. They can, with local norms, compare the status of their students with other students in the same school or in the same school system. They can compare the content of their course with the content deemed appropriate by experts.

In summary, the results from standardized achievement tests should *not* be used as the *sole* criterion to evaluate teachers, since too many factors other than teaching competency can, and do, influence the test score a pupil receives. But we *do recommend* that if the tests are secure, standardized achievement-test scores be used *judiciously* as *one* of *many* variables in teacher evaluation.

Curriculum Evaluation

Achievement-test results may also be used as one of the criteria on which to evaluate the curriculum. For example, 25 years ago it was common practice to delay the teaching of a foreign language until the student reached the seventh or eighth grade. However, it has been found that elementary school children are able to master a foreign language. Findings such as these suggest that our curriculum must be flexible. Frequently, achievement-test results provide the evidence needed to instigate curriculum revision.

The preceding example of the use of achievement-test results for studying the efficacy of introducing a foreign language in the primary grades is a somewhat simple one. In some instances, however, the data on which to base curriculum revision are not so clear-cut.

The profile depicted in Figure 16.7 is for the performance of sixth-graders in a particular school, in contrast to the performance of sixth-graders in other schools in the same city. The score scale is essentially a grade equivalent with the decimals omitted (e.g., a GE of 6.3 is represented as 63). The profile is based on data collected on the Iowa Test of Basic Skills, which was administered during the first week of class. The following conclusions appear to be warranted.

1. Students in the sixth grade in the Walnut Street school have an average scaled-score performance of about 35, in contrast with a mean scaled-score performance of all other sixth-graders of about 60. Also, the Walnut Street pupils appear to be more proficient in arithmetic skills than they are in either language or work study skills.
2. The Walnut Street pupils received the highest and lowest scores on the arithmetic concepts and reading graphs and tables subtests, respec-

tively. This does not mean, however, that they are necessarily better in one than in the other. Much depends upon the variability of the pupils and the subtest intercorrelations.
3. Whether the principal should change the instructional program at the Walnut Street school is unclear. If the Walnut Street pupils come mainly from an impoverished environment, the decision made could be markedly different from that made if these pupils came from an average or above-average socioeconomic area. In the former, we would have an instance of a poor environment that may not permit pupils to experience a sufficient number of verbal and language-type activities, at least the kind that are measured by this or any other standardized achievement test. If the pupils were above average in intelligence, the principal would have to consider the adequacy of the teachers, the motivation of the pupils, the validity of the test, and other factors before making a decision.

Some modification of the curriculum might be in order for the Walnut Street school. The kind of modification (namely, having more free reading, introducing pupils to the public library, or motivating the pupils to achieve at their maximum), however, would depend upon the many factors that influence learning. It is conceivable that the curriculum may *not* have to be modified. Rather, the manner in which the curriculum is introduced may have to be altered. For example, if the test results at the end of the sixth grade showed that this discrepancy no longer exists, this would suggest that (1) the preparation of the Walnut Street pupils in the fifth grade was markedly different from that of the other sixth-graders when they were in the fifth grade or (2) the Walnut Street sixth-grade teachers either taught for the test or were able to make up any deficiencies that existed.

An interesting feature of this hypothetical profile is the strange isomorphism between the Walnut Street school sixth-graders and all sixth-graders in the city. The peaks and valleys are nearly identical. Might this indicate something about the

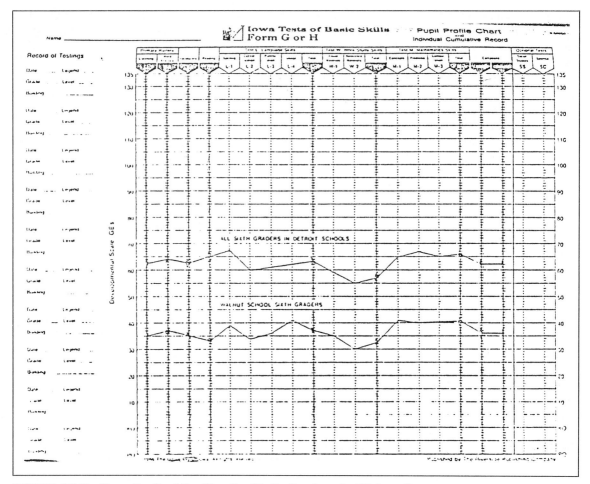

FIGURE 16.7 Hypothetical Profiles for Sixth-Graders in Walnut Street School and for Sixth-Graders in All Detroit Schools. (Copyright © 1986 by the University of Iowa. Reprinted with permission of the publisher, the Riverside Publishing Company, 8420 Bryn Mawr Avenue, Chicago, IL 60631. All rights reserved.)

curriculum in all the schools? In other words, is it reasonable to expect that more attention might have to be paid to certain work study skills? Not necessarily. From the profile, one is unable to determine the significance of the differences.

In conclusion, we must reemphasize that achievement-test scores, whether they be from standardized or teacher-made tests, must be interpreted cautiously. Test scores can and do serve as a valuable supplementary criterion on which to make more valid educational decisions. But these scores are supplementary and not absolute, and they are influenced by many factors.

Grading

In general, standardized achievement-test results should *not* be used to assign course grades. They *may* be used to assist the teacher in assigning the final course grade, provided the test reflects local objectives. As pointed out earlier, some standardized achievement tests are constructed so that they measure *broad* rather than specific outcomes of instruction. Also, the objectives of instruction may vary, not only from school to school but also from teacher to teacher. For these and other reasons, grades should typically be assigned on the basis of teacher-made tests. These tests, properly constructed, reflect the goals of the individual teacher to a much greater extent than do even the best standardized achievement tests.

Satisfying Federal Regulations

Although not directly related to the use of achievement-test results for instructional, guidance, or administrative purposes, as previously discussed, there is an area—that of securing funding from either local, state, or federal agencies—in which achievement-test results need to be obtained in order to evaluate particular programs. One such program is the Education Consolidation and Improvement Act of 1981 (it replaced the familiar "Titles" of the Elementary and Secondary Education Act), which requires the assessment and evaluation of compensatory education programs in order to receive funding. Further, this assessment and evaluation is to be realized through comprehensive testing programs in elementary and secondary schools. The administration of examinations to students and such evaluations shall include objective measurements of educational achievement. It is true that these evaluations and assessments need not be addressed solely by means of standardized achievement tests, nor should they be.

Research Uses

Standardized achievement-test results provide valuable information for researchers. For example, suppose that the Yucca Valley fifth-grade teachers want to know whether providing fifth-graders with calculators will result in their achieving higher arithmetic computation scores. At the beginning of the year, two groups of fifth-grade stu-

dents could be tested with the Arithmetic Computation subtest of the Stanford Achievement Test. One group would then be taught with the use of the calculators; the other group would be taught without calculators. At the end of the term, a parallel form of the Stanford would be given to both groups. The pre- and posttest scores would be compared, and, if the calculator group did the same as or better than the noncalculator group, we could say that further study is warranted. On the other hand, if the noncalculator group performed better than the calculator group, we would have some reservations about suggesting the purchase of calculators. This is just one example of how standardized test results can be used for educational decision making.

Conclusion

In the preceding pages we have attempted to discuss some of the more common uses of standardized achievement-test results. We have *not* treated all the possible uses. We have neglected to consider using standardized achievement test results for such purposes as (1) motivating pupils and (2) demonstrating to students what is expected of them. We have tried to emphasize that test results provide only a limited amount of information. Good teachers derive much valuable information about pupils in their daily contact with and observation of them. We hope it is evident that the use of standardized achievement tests is limited only by the resourcefulness and ingenuity of the classroom teacher and that achievement-test results should be used as a supplement to other evidence to make sound educational decisions.

NEW DIRECTIONS IN TESTING

Anrig (1986, p. v) believes that the new generation of tests will "(1) . . . serve individuals more than institutions, (2) . . . aim primarily at helping individuals learn and succeed rather than simply yielding scores for institutional decision making, (3) . . . guide instruction and self-development on a

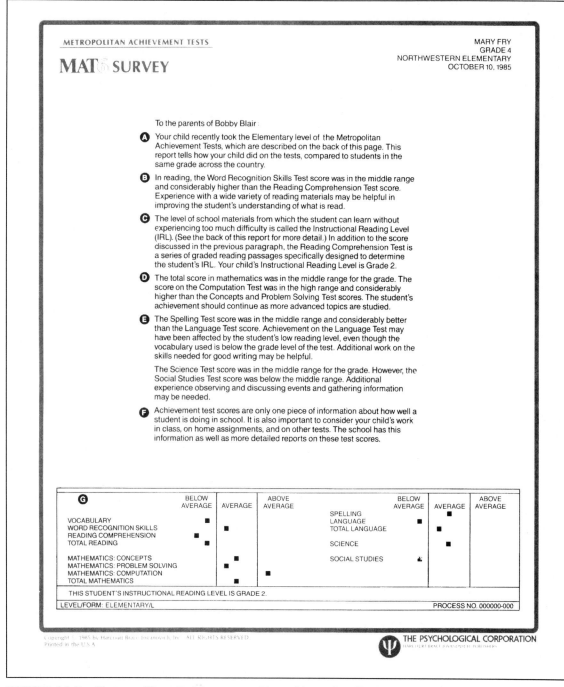

METROPOLITAN ACHIEVEMENT TESTS

MAT SURVEY

MARY FRY
GRADE 4
NORTHWESTERN ELEMENTARY
OCTOBER 10, 1985

To the parents of Bobby Blair:

A Your child recently took the Elementary level of the Metropolitan Achievement Tests, which are described on the back of this page. This report tells how your child did on the tests, compared to students in the same grade across the country.

B In reading, the Word Recognition Skills Test score was in the middle range and considerably higher than the Reading Comprehension Test score. Experience with a wide variety of reading materials may be helpful in improving the student's understanding of what is read.

C The level of school materials from which the student can learn without experiencing too much difficulty is called the Instructional Reading Level (IRL). (See the back of this report for more detail.) In addition to the score discussed in the previous paragraph, the Reading Comprehension Test is a series of graded reading passages specifically designed to determine the student's IRL. Your child's Instructional Reading Level is Grade 2.

D The total score in mathematics was in the middle range for the grade. The score on the Computation Test was in the high range and considerably higher than the Concepts and Problem Solving Test scores. The student's achievement should continue as more advanced topics are studied.

E The Spelling Test score was in the middle range and considerably better than the Language Test score. Achievement on the Language Test may have been affected by the student's low reading level, even though the vocabulary used is below the grade level of the test. Additional work on the skills needed for good writing may be helpful.

The Science Test score was in the middle range for the grade. However, the Social Studies Test score was below the middle range. Additional experience observing and discussing events and gathering information may be needed.

F Achievement test scores are only one piece of information about how well a student is doing in school. It is also important to consider your child's work in class, on home assignments, and on other tests. The school has this information as well as more detailed reports on these test scores.

G	BELOW AVERAGE	AVERAGE	ABOVE AVERAGE		BELOW AVERAGE	AVERAGE	ABOVE AVERAGE
VOCABULARY		■		SPELLING		■	
WORD RECOGNITION SKILLS		■		LANGUAGE	■		
READING COMPREHENSION	■			TOTAL LANGUAGE		■	
TOTAL READING		■					
				SCIENCE		■	
MATHEMATICS: CONCEPTS		■					
MATHEMATICS: PROBLEM SOLVING		■		SOCIAL STUDIES	■		
MATHEMATICS: COMPUTATION			■				
TOTAL MATHEMATICS		■					

THIS STUDENT'S INSTRUCTIONAL READING LEVEL IS GRADE 2.

LEVEL/FORM: ELEMENTARY/L   PROCESS NO. 000000-000

Ψ THE PSYCHOLOGICAL CORPORATION
HARCOURT BRACE JOVANOVICH, PUBLISHERS

FIGURE 16.8   Metropolitan Achievement Tests Narrative Report.
(Copyright © 1985 by Harcourt Brace Jovanovich, Inc. Reproduced by permission. All rights reserved.)

continuing basis rather than compare performance among test takers." Although Anrig writes with reference to standardized tests, his words are relevant to classroom achievement tests. Some of these sentiments are also shared by Glaser (1986).

What with technological advances, more and more schools are administering tests by computer. This therefore raises a serious question of whether or not there are differences in performance between the pencil-and-paper and computer administration of the *same* test. If so, what about the effect on the norms and the test's reliability? Although the evidence is sparse, guidelines have been issued to help users assess the comparability of scores obtained under the two types of administration (*Guidelines*, 1986; Hofer & Green, 1985).

We also feel that there will be more computer-generated report forms as depicted in Figure 16.8.

We also envision greater attention being paid to assessment techniques that are guided by "curriculum-based measurement" (see Deno & Fuchs, 1987), greater reliance on performance measures (see Stiggins, 1988), and less emphasis on multiple-choice item formats. The movement toward greater use of open-ended and free-response item formats will come about because some educators believe that traditional objective-type item formats may not be best for measuring higher-order thinking skills (Jones, 1988; see also Alexander & James, 1987, who contend that completion-type and essay items will enable one to make inferences about the thought processes used to arrive at an answer, which is not now accomplished with objective-type tests).

We would be remiss, however, if we did not say that some of the changes envisioned will come about slowly (see Embretson, 1986). We agree with Linn (1986) who said that the reason multiple-choice items are so often the basis of standardized tests despite the many critics of this format is twofold: (1) the economic viability of existing standardized tests and (2) the relatively high predictive validity. Another reason we believe the changes will be slow in coming about is that most

of our mathematical models for analyzing test results assume that the tasks or items are unidimensional, while in reality, our educational objectives and hence our test items should be multidimensional.

We believe more research will be directed to developing free-response techniques, for example, microcomputer simulation of scientific phenomena, testing hypotheses, and problem-solving tasks that measure skills not measured by multiple-choice tests.

■ SUMMARY

The principal ideas, suggestions, and recommendations made in this chapter are summarized in the following statements:

1. Standardized and teacher-made achievement tests differ markedly in terms of their purpose, method of construction, sampling of content, and availability of norms (although both have the goal of appraisal of present knowledge).
2. The trend today in standardized achievement tests is away from measuring factual knowledge and toward emphasizing application and interpretation.
3. Teacher-made and standardized achievement tests complement each other. It is futile to argue that one is more useful than the other.
4. Standardized achievement tests may be classified as diagnostic, single-subject-matter, and survey batteries and as criterion- or norm-referenced. Single-subject-matter tests may be further subdivided into readiness and prognostic tests.
5. Standardized achievement tests differ little in terms of their construction and technical features. They do differ markedly in their purpose. To determine whether a kindergarten child is ready for the first grade, a reading readiness test should be used. To obtain an indication of a pupil's strengths and weaknesses, a diagnostic test is recommended. To

learn whether a pupil is proficient in a subject-matter area such as history or physics, a single-subject-matter test should be used. To ascertain the strengths and weaknesses (actually plot a profile) of pupils in the various core subjects, a survey battery should be used.

6. Within the past few years, commercial test publishers and other firms have begun to pay more attention to producing criterion-referenced standardized achievement tests, very specific, prescriptive diagnostic tests, mastery tests, and "tailor-made" tests.

7. Standardized test publishers are paying more attention to providing teachers with prescriptive suggestions on the basis of their pupils' achievement-test performance.

8. Standardized test publishers are providing a variety of output data (for a slight additional fee) to users. Various item analyses, grouping students of similar abilities with suggestions of instructional strategies to be used with these groups, and keying items to objectives and commonly used textbooks are some of the reporting services available.

9. Various examples were given to suggest the different uses of standardized achievement-test results for instructional, guidance, administrative, and research users.

10. Many changes are on the horizon for making education more relevant to students. Accordingly, how we assess student learning must also change.

■ POINTS TO PONDER

1. Compare and contrast standardized and teacher-made achievement tests. List three specific situations where each would be preferable.

2. Of what value would it be to know the intercorrelations of the subtests in an achievement battery?

3. Which type of validity evidence is *most* important in an achievement test? Why?

4. You are an elementary school guidance coun-

selor. Your principal assigns you the task of choosing an achievement battery. How do you proceed in your task?

5. First-grade pupils are frequently grouped for instructional purposes on the basis of reading readiness tests. This grouping is not always effective. Does this suggest the elimination of reading readiness tests? Support your answer.

6. There seems to be general consensus, but not universal agreement, on the elementary curriculum. What role should standardized achievement tests play in reducing or increasing the diversity of this curriculum?

7. Mary Poppins scored at the 89th percentile (national norms) on the language subtest of the Stanford Achievement Test. However, she received only a grade of C in language arts. How can this be accounted for?

8. Discuss this statement: The California Achievement Tests subscores can be used for diagnostic purposes.

9. What problems are associated with using standardized achievement-test results to evaluate teacher effectiveness?

10. Given both aptitude and achievement-test results for a sixth-grade class, how would you select individuals for an enriched program? What other information would be desirable? What potential dangers exist in using test results for this selection procedure?

11. In what situations would you be more likely to use a criterion-referenced standardized achievement test over a norm-referenced test? Support your answer.

12. A survey battery manual states that the test can be used for diagnostic purposes. What kinds of evidence should you look for to ascertain whether it is a valid diagnostic test?

13. Your school board has jumped on the minimal competency bandwagon. What advantages and disadvantages are there in using (a) a test constructed by the school's research bureau, (b) a test constructed by the teaching staff, and (c) a commercially published standardized achievement test to determine competency?

14. In Roy Wilkin's Middle School, eighth-graders are randomly assigned to algebra sections. The superintendent of schools, studying the grade distributions, notices that there is a marked discrepancy in grades given by the different teachers. Would you use the results of a standardized algebra test to study this problem? Defend your answer.

15. Do you concur with the argument advanced by some critics of standardized achievement tests that "their continued use will result in a national or uniform curriculum"? Why do you feel this way?

Chapter 17

Interest, Personality, and Attitude Inventories

- ■ Introduction
- ■ Measuring Noncognitive Characteristics: Some Challenges
- ■ Measuring Interests
- ■ Using Interest-Inventory Results
- ■ Career Awareness and Development
- ■ Personality Assessment
- ■ Attitude and Value Assessment

Should Girder be encouraged to study engineering in college? What are Allan's interests? How can we explain why Beth, who scored at the 95th percentile on the WISC, scored only at the 45th percentile on the Stanford Achievement Test? Is Ilene really an aggressive and hostile child? Is Pearl unstrung? Are Ruth's concerns about peer acceptance atypical for an average 13-year-old? More generally, what are problem checklists? What are some of the problems when measuring affective traits? Should teachers interpret noncognitive inventories? Are there some noncognitive inventories that should be barred from the classroom? Does the information derived from interest, personality, and attitude inventories help educators make more valid decisions than could be made if such data were not used? These are some of the questions that are discussed in this chapter.

Basically, there are two ways in which we gather data about a person's characteristics: (1) by looking, that is, by the observational method (rating scales, anecdotal records, other observational techniques), and (2) by listening or asking, that is, by self-reports (standardized pencil-and-paper inventories).

In this chapter we concern ourselves only with standardized noncognitive inventories, recognizing that there are many locally constructed affective tests and inventories. Observational techniques such as rating scales and anecdotal records are useful methods, especially for adults. Although they provide much valuable data, they may not provide data as valid as those obtained from standardized inventories. Standardized noncognitive inventories are uniformly administered and, in general, objectively scored. Many of them also have valuable normative data that permit valid comparisons between a pupil in one community and pupils throughout the country. With standardized noncognitive inventories, it may be ascertained whether Ilene is abnormally aggressive or whether Ruth's concerns about peer acceptance are natural.

At this point, it may be argued that these questions could be answered by natural observation that would have an additional feature over a testing situation: People are more likely to display their true behavior in natural settings that are informal, unstructured, and nonthreatening. Teachers are able to observe their students in real life situations. But, are their observations valid? Are teachers objective? Do they know what behavior is significant and what can be overlooked? Can teachers draw correct inferences from observed behavior? As imprecise as noncognitive inventories may appear to be, they do provide valuable information about the pupil, information that the teacher cannot acquire through observation but that may be necessary to understand the pupil's behavior. Some educators argue that test scores should be used only to supplement teacher's observations. Others argue the converse. The important thing to remember is that both teachers' observations and test data provide information about the pupils' behavior, and both should be used.

After studying this chapter, you should be able to:

1. Recognize the value to teachers of information about pupil interests, attitudes, and personality.
2. Understand that noncognitive measures are not so psychometrically elegant as cognitive measures.
3. Recognize the problems involved in measur-

ing noncognitive characteristics—problems of definition, response set, faking, validity, reliability, and interpretation.
4. Recognize the three most commonly used procedures for constructing and keying noncognitive inventories—empirical, homogeneous, and logical.
5. Differentiate between attitudes and interests.
6. Discuss the major approaches used to measure interests.
7. Evaluate the more popular interest inventories in terms of their construction, grade level, content, administration, scoring, validity, reliability, and interpretability.
8. Recognize how interest-inventory results can be used for instructional and guidance purposes.
9. Appreciate the use of career awareness inventories.
10. Understand the various ways in which personality can be assessed.
11. Recognize the limitations of personality inventories.
12. Evaluate attitude scales.
13. Appreciate the value of study habits inventories.

INTRODUCTION

It is generally agreed that everyone concerned with the education of children must understand them in their totality in order that optimal learning conditions may be provided. This totality goes beyond academic skills and knowledge. The development of a healthy personality is essential to success in school. A student's mental health has direct relevance to his ability to learn, his interest in learning, and his attitudes toward the value of an education. Quite frequently, learning difficulties are related to a student's personality (Rutkowski & Domino, 1975; Calsyn & Kenny, 1977; Edwards, 1977), and any attempt to correct the difficulty is doomed to failure if the student's total strengths and weaknesses are not considered in both the cognitive and the noncognitive areas.

Whether teachers realize it or not, they are influenced by their students' attitudes, values, interests, and general makeup. If a teacher knows that her students dislike history, she could (and it is hoped, would) employ a variety of techniques—films, playacting, and humorous skits—to try to instill a positive attitude toward the value of studying history. If she knows that some students who are poor readers are interested in mechanics, she might use stories with a mechanical flavor in the reading program. Teachers can and do capitalize on the interests and attitudes of their pupils. However, before teachers can use data about their pupils' interests, attitudes, values, and general personality makeup, they must obtain these data.

The classroom teacher and counselor should at least be able to administer problem checklists, interest inventories, and general personality tests with minimal training. The counselor should be able to interpret the results of interest inventories without too much difficulty. *No one*, however, unless she has had considerable training and experience, should attempt to interpret measures designed to depict abnormality or maladjustment.

Classroom teachers, as members of a professional team vitally concerned with both cognitive and noncognitive behavior, must, in order to be effective team members, speak the language. Otherwise, they will not be able to communicate effectively with other team members—school psychologist, clinician, and counselor. In order to do so, they must know something about noncognitive inventories—what they are, what they can and cannot do, the different kinds of noncognitive inventories, and so forth—and about the behaviors they measure.

By helping establish optimal positive test-taking attitudes, teachers, through their knowledge of noncognitive assessment, can indirectly help the counselor to work with the students. Rapport is essential in any testing situation. But it may be more vital in noncognitive assessment, especially when the test is seen by the testee as threatening. Also, in noncognitive tests the pupil can fake either good or bad responses, and the teacher can aid greatly in diminishing faking by establishing rap-

port. The pupil may be more likely to trust his teacher, with whom he is in daily contact, than he is to trust the counselor or clinician, whom he sees infrequently. The classroom teacher, especially the one who is trusted and accepted by her pupils, can aid the clinician by breaking the ice and helping the child accept the clinician as someone who is trying to help him.

In summary, knowledge about pupils' interests, personalities, and attitudes is important to educators to help them understand pupils better and to help them communicate effectively with other professionals. Knowledge about noncognitive assessments (especially interest inventories) is important, because they are (1) being used in our schools, especially in the secondary grades, (2) valid in providing some information about a pupil's vocational or avocational interests, (3) more objective than the informal observational approach, and (4) frequently used in research on learning. We must reiterate that, despite their limitations, standardized noncognitive measures can play an important role in education (see Cronbach & Snow, 1977; Bloom, 1978; Messick, 1979).

MEASURING NONCOGNITIVE CHARACTERISTICS: SOME CHALLENGES[1]

There are many unresolved problems in the assessment of noncognitive traits: problems of definition, response set, faking, low validity and reliability, interpretation, and sex bias. To observe that the measurement of affect poses methodological problems not encountered in cognitive assessment is deceptively simple. Because noncognitive

---

[1] For a thorough and thought-provoking discussion of the principles to be considered in the development and use of interest inventories (many of the principles, however, are pertinent to any noncognitive inventory), see Kuder (1970). Fiske (1963), Holtzman (1964), and Anastasi (1981) discuss the measurement problems involved in assessing noncognitive characteristics. Anderson (1981) has written an excellent book on assessing affective characteristics.

assessment (or for that matter any assessment) involves the differences among individuals as well as changes in behavior over time, validity and reliability are of vital importance. It should be evident that until these problems are resolved, noncognitive assessment will be subject to much suspicion and criticism.

Problems of Definition

Noncognitive tests, even more than aptitude or achievement tests, present the problem of definition. Allport (1963) considered at least 50 definitions of personality before he advanced his own. If 100 psychologists were asked to define *personality*, they might give 100 different definitions. This fact contributes to the inconclusive and often contradictory findings in noncognitive research. Frequently, different researchers arrived at different conclusions because they were studying different variables, even though the variables studied were all labeled the same—for example, *honesty* or *aestheticism*. To some, the terms *attitudes*, *beliefs*, *values*, and *interests* are used synonymously. To others, there are definite demarcations among the terms. To still others, attitudes and values are considered one category, beliefs and opinions another, and interests still another. The concept of personality has multiple and complex meanings, the various definitions are at best crude, and the techniques for evaluation are sometimes lacking in scientific rigor. Yet we cannot give up our commitment to research or interest in the area of affective development. Grandiose and ethereal constructs such as honesty, beauty, truth, and virtue can be translated into behavioral terms. Once this is done, an attempt can be made to measure these behavioral traits.

Just as we must talk about a specific kind of validity (such as content or predictive) or reliability (stability or equivalence), so, when we discuss a personality trait such as authoritarianism, we must be specific and refer to it as, for example, the "F Scale's authoritarianism" or "Rokeach's authoritarianism." Until we are able to develop definitions for noncognitive constructs, we will be looking for a needle in a haystack without knowing what a needle looks like.

Problems of Response Set

Although response set may be present in cognitive measures, noncognitive inventories are particularly susceptible to *response set*, that is, the tendency of an individual to reply in a particular direction, almost independent of content. An individual exhibiting response set will answer questions identical in content (but presented in different formats) differently. For example, he may be predisposed to select the neutral category if a disagree-agree continuum is used, or the "true" choice in true–false items; or he may guess on all items that he is unsure of. There are many types of response sets: acquiescence, social desirability, guessing, and sacrificing accuracy for speed (or vice versa).

The response set that has been of most concern in noncognitive measurement is *social desirability* (Edwards, 1957). This is the tendency for an individual to respond favorably to the items that he feels are socially accepted, such as, "Catastrophic health insurance for the elderly should be enacted by Congress." Here, the subject may answer *not* on the basis of how he truly feels but on the basis of what he thinks is a socially acceptable or desirable answer.

Certain steps can be taken to try to control for response set. Cronbach (1950) found that response set is particularly prevalent on tests that (1) contain ambiguous items, (2) require the individual to respond on a disagree-agree continuum, and (3) lend themselves to responses in either a favorable or an unfavorable direction. Various techniques (such as the forced-choice format, randomly ordering the items, keeping the instrument relatively short, ensuring anonymity of the respondents, having an equal number of positively and negatively worded statements, or having more negative than positive statements) have been used in an attempt to control response set. These techniques have *not* eliminated the problem completely.

Those using personality, attitude, value, and interest inventories must pay particular attention to the presence of response set and must govern their conclusions and recommendations accordingly. More research is needed on response set: What kinds of people are susceptible? What kinds of items lend themselves to this? Why are some tests affected and others not? Can (or should) their influence be neutralized?

Faking

Faking can and does occur on cognitive as well as noncognitive tests, but it is more common on the latter. Although a person can fake either good or bad responses on a noncognitive inventory, he can fake only bad responses (one can fake ignorance, not knowledge) on a cognitive test. The tendency to fake is a characteristic inherent in the individual rather than a test artifact.

Although examiners expect their subjects to give valid information, they do not always receive it. Subjects come to the test and will either be truthful or lie depending upon the purpose of the test and their perception of how the test results will be used. Often, responses may be rationalizations or unconscious modifications rather than deliberate lies. A candidate for college admission might try to fake a good response if he believes the test results might affect his chances for admission. Quite frequently, a person is motivated to lie when he knows that his selection or consideration for a particular job depends upon the types of answers he gives on an interest or personality inventory. Hence, in his attempt to obtain the position, the subject will do everything possible to create the desired impression (Green, 1951). A high school senior, because of his stereotypic impression of a surgeon's life (glamor and prestige), may try to convince his guidance counselor that he likes medicine or may fake some interest inventories to indicate that he has a liking for medicine.

Although the subject will most often try to present himself in a favorable light, there are instances when subjects fake their scores so that they will appear maladjusted or abnormal. A murderer may go out of his way to exhibit tendencies of maladjustment so that he will be judged insane and unfit to stand trial.

Various procedures have been studied and are used to combat faking. One such procedure (perhaps the best) is to establish rapport with the subject and to convince him that in the long run he will be better off if he gives truthful responses. Another method is to attempt to disguise the purpose of the test. This does not always work, especially with intelligent subjects who may see through the disguise because of the nature of the test items. However, in some instances it is possible to disguise the purpose of the test. Disguising the purpose of a test, though, can result in some ethical and practical problems, can affect the image of psychologists and counselors, and can destroy future attempts at establishing rapport.

Another approach to combat faking is to use the forced-choice technique. Here, two or more equally desirable or undesirable statements are presented together, such as

A. I like to read good novels.
B. I like to watch good movies.

The subject is required to choose one answer from the set. One of the answers, however, is a better indicator of the criterion being studied than is the other(s). The forced-choice method, unfortunately, also has its defects. It requires more time to obtain an equal number of responses; it is sometimes resisted by examinees (and may result in negative attitudes toward future testing and/or the counseling interview); and it may lower the reliability because the choice is more difficult to make.

Still another approach is the construction of scales to *detect* rather than *prevent* faking. Tests such as the Minnesota Multiphasic Personality Inventory (MMPI), the Edwards Personal Preference Schedule (EPPS), and the Kuder Occupational Interest Surveys contain special subtests to detect the faker. Of the three, only the verification score of the MMPI is used to adjust the obtained score; the others use the "faking scale" to "flag" the inventory for more careful scrutiny.

In conclusion, whatever elaborate procedures are employed by the test-maker to minimize distortion—whether it be by response set or faking—we must realize that the subject will provide only the information he is able and willing to report. People interpreting both cognitive and affective tests (more so the latter) must consider this.

Reliability and Validity

The reliability of noncognitive tests tends to be much lower than that of cognitive tests of the same length. For example, in studying stability reliability, how a person behaves—that is, how he responds to an affective-type item—is governed, in part at least, by the momentary situation. For example, a person with liberal attitudes toward minorities, if interviewed a few hours after being attacked by a minority person, might respond in a bigoted fashion. Moreover, some of the more common procedures for studying reliability may be somewhat inappropriate when it comes to noncognitive tests because random, temporal fluctuations may be confused with behavioral change. Because human behavior is vacillating rather than constant, reliability coefficients derived from test–retest methods (coefficient of stability) tend to be spuriously low and misleading in judging the test's precision. Inconsistency in test responses may be either an important aspect of an individual's personality or a test artifact. The split-half, coefficient alpha, and Kuder-Richardson methods (measures of internal consistency) are most frequently used to study the reliability of noncognitive tests. When low reliabilities are found, careful attention must be paid to the interpretation of difference scores in a test profile, because only marked differences may suggest true intraindividual differences.

For noncognitive measures, we are more concerned with *construct* validity than with predictive validity. Although we are interested in predictive validity, it is difficult to obtain high predictive validity of a noncognitive measure because we infer the existence of a behavioral trait on the basis of overt test responses. In other words, we assume that an individual who says on an attitude test that he is prejudiced toward blacks will exhibit this behavior in a real situation. In some instances, making inferences of overt behavior from personality questionnaires is valid, but because of faking and response set, sometimes it is not. Also, it is difficult to ascertain the predictive validity of noncognitive measures because adequate external criterion data are often lacking.

The research conducted with noncognitive inventories has led to many attempts to improve their validity. Some of the approaches applied are (1) using correction scores rather than discarding inventories that appear to be suspect; (2) disguising the purpose of the test; (3) randomly assigning items throughout the test rather than presenting them in blocks, so that the traits being measured do not appear obvious to the examinee; (4) using verification scores to reveal test-taking attitudes; and (5) selecting test items on the basis of empirical rather than a priori grounds. Although these and other approaches are used to improve the validity of personality tests, the evidence today indicates that noncognitive tests still do not approach the criterion-related validity of intellectual measures, mainly, perhaps, because of the problem of obtaining valid external criterion data.

In conclusion, rather than conclude that noncognitive inventories do not have the desired degree of validity and reliability needed for making valid educational decisions, we should ask how much information we can get from the inventory and how it will help us. Another way to look at it is in terms of a cost analysis. In the long run, does the use of noncognitive inventories reduce the incidence of costly error?

Problems of Interpretation

Noncognitive inventories are really not tests in the sense that aptitude and achievement tests are, because there are not necessarily any right answers. Noncognitive inventories are generally interpreted in relation to the traits held by "normal" ("average") people. Hence, a Canadian exhibiting modal, normal behavior in Canada could, if behaving the same way in Peru, appear abnormal.

Another problem in the interpretation of noncognitive inventories—especially attitude scales—reflects the kinds of responses permitted. Most attitude-scale response continua provide for a neutral response. But what does a neutral response mean? Does it mean that the individual is really neutral, or does it mean that he is unwilling to commit himself? How is a neutral response interpreted? One way to circumvent the problem of neutral responses is to eliminate this type of response. But, if we do so, might we be eliminating the measurement of a *true* neutral behavioral trait and end up with untrue measurement?

An additional problem in interpreting the results from affective inventories is that there may be intervening factors that affect how an individual responds to a particular personality inventory item (Kuncel, 1973).

Perhaps one of the most serious problems in interpreting noncognitive tests is that associated with ipsative forced-choice tests. Assume one is given forced-choice items such as

A. I like to build model airplanes.
B. I like to play bridge.
C. I like to collect stamps.

and he is required to select the one statement in the triad that he likes most. Each of the three possible choices is keyed under a different subscale. Thus, if he picks A, he may receive a point on the scientific scale. If he selects B, he may receive a point on the sociability scale. If he chooses C, he may receive a point on the clerical scale. The essential characteristic of such items is that when a person makes a choice in favor of one subscale (by choosing a particular item), he is at the same time rejecting the other subscales. A test composed of forced-choice items produces an ipsative scale, and the scores are ipsative scores. Although multiple-choice cognitive tests also require the individual to make a choice, there is only one correct answer for everyone. Hence, problems associated with ipsative forced-choice tests are unique only to some noncognitive inventories.

The essential characteristic of an ipsative scale is that the total score summing across all the subscales is the same for all persons. Ipsative scores do not reflect the intensity of the subject's feeling, and yet this is something that would be of extreme value in interpreting an individual's responses. For example, three boys purchase vanilla ice cream cones. Does this imply that they all like vanilla ice cream to the same degree? Not necessarily so. Or, if each of the three boys purchased a different flavor, does this signify that the boy who wanted and chose vanilla likes vanilla more than the boy who chose chocolate? Not necessarily!

Ipsative scales permit only intraindividual comparisons. In an ipsative scale, an individual will probably have some high scores and some low scores (he could have all scores at the mean). All his scores cannot be either high or low. Some psychometrists contend that the ipsative forced-choice technique parallels real life in that a person is always forced to choose between activity A and activity B. For example, a child, when offered some ice cream, must choose, normally, among a variety of flavors. Others argue that this forced choice can sometimes induce frustration in the subject, especially when all the statement (choices) are equally desirable or undesirable.

Interpreting a forced-choice profile is very difficult. How does a person interpret to a student the profile of an ipsative interest test with ten subscales? The tester cannot say that the student's interest in outdoor activities is higher than his interest in musical activities (even though the student may have had a higher score on the outdoor scale), because the scores are not absolute. We cannot say that two persons who rank at the 90th percentile in terms of the national norm group have equal outdoor interests because the scores are ipsative.

Problems of Sex Bias

Although sex bias has been discussed in other sections, we briefly reintroduce it because much of the fervor about sex bias has been directed primarily toward interest measurement.[2] In fact, Campbell—possibly because of pressure—revised the SVIB (Strong Vocational Interest Blank) (Campbell, 1974) so that it avoided all sex stereotypes. The issue at hand is not whether a test differentiates among individuals—be it blacks versus whites, males versus females, high socioeconomic versus low socioeconomic—as long as it does so validly. In fact, the major purpose of a norm-referenced measure is one of differentiation. Just because research has shown that males tend to be more quantitative whereas females tend to be more verbal (Macoby & Jacklin, 1974; Strassberg-Rosenberg & Donlon, 1975), this is not prima facie evidence that the tests used are biased in favor of one sex over the other. Some psychologists maintain that differences in interests between males and females are the result of *basic differences* between the interests of the sexes rather than sex bias per se (Noeth et al., 1975; Shaffer, 1976) or differences in aptitude (Cegelka et al., 1974).

If the test is valid, it is supposed to point up any differences between and/or among groups or individuals. But a test is biased if the item content is in terms of sex stereotypes that affect the performance of males and females differentially or if a test is *deliberately* constructed so that male scores are separated from female scores invalidly.

Construction and Keying

Constructing and keying (scoring) noncognitive inventories also present problems. Because it is sometimes extremely difficult to distinguish between a particular technique used to construct and to key a test, both operations are considered together. Cognitive tests have only a single, accepted correct (or best) answer. Noncognitive in-

ventories, on the other hand, need not always be amenable to a "correct" answer. In a noncognitive inventory, especially one that has been empirically keyed, an item may be keyed one way as the "correct" answer for plumbers, but it may be incorrect for some other group. Three procedures are commonly used to construct and key noncognitive inventories: empirical, homogeneous, and logical.

Empirical Construction   In the empirical or criterion method, one makes no assumption about the traits or characteristics of people in different groups but attempts to develop items that will discriminate people in one group from those in another group. (Prediger, 1977, discusses the alternatives to using group membership as a criterion for validating interest inventories.) Each item is evaluated in terms of its relationship to some criterion. The criterion group, say, for a test of paranoia might be those patients in a mental institution who have been diagnosed as paranoiacs. The control group (or normals) could be those people who come to visit the paranoiacs. In a criterion-keyed interest inventory, a person's interests are compared with the interests held by people employed in various occupations (only those items that empirically differentiate among different groups are selected—the items are not selected on sheer faith, as in logical keying).

Items used in the Strong Vocational Interest Blank, the Kuder Occupational Interest Survey, the California Psychological Inventory, the Personality Inventory for Children, and the Minnesota Multiphasic Personality Inventory were empirically selected and keyed. Although the scoring is usually in terms of unitary weights, differential weights can be assigned in proportion to the difference in responses between the criterion groups.

One virtue of empirical construction (and keying) is that it is very difficult for the examinee to fake his responses. This is true because the examinee does not know how the criterion group responded to the various items.

Homogeneous Construction   The test constructor employing the homogeneous method first

---

[2]Good discussions on sex bias in interest measurement are found in AMEG (1973); Diamond (1975a, b); Tanney (1974); Tittle (1973); Hanson et al. (1977); and Tittle and Zytowski (1978). Donlon et al. (1979) discuss sex bias in standardized achievement tests. Flaugher (1978) and Gardner (1978) present general discussions of bias.

begins with a large number of items. Then, through a technique called factor analysis, clusters are identified, and the items are organized to fit the identified clusters. A psychometric characteristic of a homogeneous-keyed test is that the items of any one scale have high intracorrelations, that is, a common factor runs throughout that scale; the scale intercorrelations are relatively low (or they should be if more than one trait or cluster has been identified).

Logical Construction In the logical method the items are selected and keyed on a logical or rational basis rather than on empirical grounds. The test constructor specifies the traits or skills or knowledge needed for the task and then prepares appropriate items. She then scores the items in accordance with her perception of the underlying psychological theory. For example, let us assume that a tester prepares an interest scale and includes the following question, "I like to read blueprints." Logically, it would be expected that engineers like to read blueprints, and if logical keying was used, a $+1$ would be given on the engineering scale to those who responded affirmatively.

It is conceivable, however, that engineers do not like to read blueprints. If empirical keying had been used to key the test and if it was found that engineers do not like this activity, then a $+1$ would *not* be assigned on the engineering scale to those who responded affirmatively to this item.

MEASURING INTERESTS

As was previously mentioned, teachers must be concerned not only with what students learn but also with how and why they learn. People have a tendency to excel in or at least to devote more effort and energy to the activities they like. In order for the classroom teacher to best capitalize on the likes and dislikes of her students, it is necessary that she know something of their interests. Interest inventories assist her in gaining this knowledge. So that the counselor may aid the student in arriving at a decision in regard to his vocational

and educational plans, she also must be cognizant of interest measurement.

Teachers should certainly strive to make their objectives (whether they be cognitive skills, factual knowledge, or wholesome attitudes and values) palatable and interesting to their students. The teacher of ninth-grade social studies might explore students' interests (or at least have the students think about their interests) as they are related to various occupations when discussing the world of work. The high school teacher who knows that Bill is a poor reader may attempt to provide meaningful learning experiences by capitalizing on Bill's interests and may assign books that are related to Bill's interests. The fifth-grade teacher working on addition or subtraction skills may exploit students' interests insofar as the types of story problems used. The important thing to remember is that because the interests of students can influence how well they learn, teachers must be concerned with interest measurement.

Knowledge of an individual's interests provides a sound basis for educational and vocational guidance. Interest-inventory results may help the classroom teacher understand why a bright pupil is performing poorly academically. These results can be of assistance to the students if only to make them think more about their future.

The study of interests has received its greatest impetus from educational and vocational counseling. School and industrial psychologists share the common concern that the application of test results may permit better decisions to be made (1) by the individual selecting an occupation and (2) by the firm selecting job applicants.

Interest inventories have progressed a great deal from the initial attempts of G. Stanley Hall in 1907 to develop a questionnaire to measure children's recreational interests. In the 1920s, 1930s, and 1940s, the emphasis of researchers such as Strong and Kuder were on developing interest inventories that measured only vocational interests. But now, we have inventories that measure both vocational and avocational interests; we have inventories that measure the interests of students who are not college-bound; and we have inventories that conceptualize interests and vocational choice as an expression of an individual's personality.

We still need better theoretical foundations regarding the development of interests, more knowledge about the relationship of interests to other aspects of human behavior, such as ability, intelligence, and personality,[3] and more evidence regarding the construct of interests.

Attitudes Versus Interests

Attitudes and interests are both concerned with likes and dislikes. Both can be related to preferences for activities, social institutions, or groups. Both involve personal feelings about something. It is this "something" that distinguishes attitudes from interests. An attitude is typically conceptualized as being a feeling toward an object, a social institution, or a group. An interest, on the other hand, is conceptualized as being a feeling toward an activity.

Attitude and interest inventories share many things in common. They are both highly susceptible to faking, require frank responses from the subject, and are therefore able to assess only the characteristics that the individual is able to, or wishes to, reveal.

Types of Standardized Interest Inventories

An individual's interests (likes and dislikes, preferences and aversions) can be ascertained in a variety of ways. Super and Crites (1962, pp. 377–379) suggest four approaches that can be used to ascertain an individual's interests: (1) direct questioning, (2) direct observation, (3) tested interests, and (4) interest inventories. (Becker, 1977, discusses how expressed and inventoried interests may be discrepant because of the person's personality.) Measuring a person's interests by means of

interest inventories has proven to be the most fruitful, encouraging, and valid approach and is the only approach discussed here. Although research has shown that asking people about their vocational aspirations is as predictive as interest inventories, their joint use leads to more valid predictions (Bartling, 1979; Gottfredson, 1979). The interest inventory contains statements about various occupations and activities. These statements may be presented singly, in pairs, or in triads. The subject responds to each statement in terms of his preference for, or aversion to, the activity or occupation.

At least two dozen standardized interest inventories are commercially published, some of which are designed for vocational guidance only, others for educational guidance only, and others for both educational and vocational guidance. Some are designed for use with high school seniors, college students, and adults; others with junior high school children. Some are applicable only to students who intend to go to college; others are designed for adolescents not bound for college. Some are verbal; others, pictorial. Although research has shown the validity of biographical scales and keys for predicting vocational preferences, psychologists have shown very little interest in incorporating them in their interest inventories.

Some authors, such as Strong (1966), developed interest inventories on the assumption that interests are not a unitary trait but a complex interaction of many traits. Other authors, such as Kuder (1969), conceptualized interests as an assortment of unitary traits, and this is reflected in the homogeneity of each of Kuder's interest scales. Still other authors constructed their interest inventories on the basis of logical validity. In spite of the different construction approaches (criterion keying, homogeneous keying, and logical keying), all interest inventories share the common purpose of assessing an individual's preferences for various activities. Most interest inventories are based on some common assumptions regarding interests: (1) interests, rather than being innate, are learned as a result of the individual's being en-

---

[3]Bruch and Skovholt (1985) found Holland's congruence principle was a highly reliable predictor of marital success.

gaged in an activity; (2) interests tend to be relatively unstable for young children, but after about age 20 they tend to become stabilized, with little change occurring after age 25; (3) people in the same occupations share similar likes and dislikes regarding activities; (4) interests vary in intensity from one person to another; and (5) interests motivate the individual to action.

Because of space limitations we must restrict our discussion of interest inventories to those most frequently used in our schools. The examples of interest inventories discussed illustrate the different methods of construction and keying (that is, the different constructs of interests).

Empirically Keyed Interest Inventories

Strong Vocational Interest Blank (SVIB). The 1985 revision of the Strong is published by Stanford University Press. Intended for 14-year-olds and older, it has 6 General Occupational Themes (GOT), 23 Basic Interest Scales (BIS), and 207 Occupational Scales (OS), of which 99 are entirely new. In addition, it provides three types of Administrative Indexes and two Special Scales. It is untimed but takes from 20 to 60 minutes to complete. There is one form (Spanish and French editions are available). The Strong is suitable for older adolescents and adults considering higher-level professional or skilled occupations. The Strong contains 325 items (the *best* items from the original SVIB male and female forms), which are grouped into the following sections:

1. Occupations. Subjects respond in one of three ways—Like (L), Indifferent (I), or Dislike (D)—to each of 131 occupational titles.
2. School Subjects. Test-takers indicate their L/I/D to each of 36 school subjects.
3. Activities. Subjects indicate their L/I/D to each of 51 general occupational activities.
4. Amusements. Subjects indicate their L/I/D to each of 39 hobbies or amusements.
5. Types of People. To each of 24 kinds of people, subjects indicate their L/I/D.
6. Preference Between Activities. For each of 30 pairs of activities, subjects indicate their pref-

erence between the activity on the (R)ight, (L)eft, or (?) No Preference.
7. Your Characteristics—a quasi-personality inventory. Subjects respond Yes, No, or ? to each of 14 characteristics/traits as being *self*-descriptive.

The items are both vocational and avocational, the subject responding to most of the items (281) by means of a three-element key: like, dislike, or indifferent. Care was taken to select items that (1) were free from sex stereotypes (e.g., stewardess); (2) were balanced in terms of favoring one sex over the other (actually, there are a few more items favoring females); (3) were culture-free; (4) were neither highly popular nor unpopular; (5) were not influenced or dependent upon previous work experience but on activities that the average adolescent could be expected to know about or at least imagine; (6) covered a wide range of occupational content; (7) were easy to read and comprehend (the Strong has a reading level of about grade 7); and (8) were interesting.

Strong conceived an interest inventory as a group of items that discriminate people in specific occupations from a general group of similar-age subjects (but not in that occupation). To be included in Strong's criterion group (as a member of a specific occupation), the individual had to be between the ages of 25 and 55, employed in that occupation for at least three years, and have indicated a liking for his or her work. For each of the items, the percentage of men (or women) responding "like, dislike, indifferent" was compared with the percentage of "men (or women) in general" responding in a similar manner. (The *new* "in-general" sample, now called the General Reference Sample, or GRS, was *not* selected in as meticulous a fashion as the former reference groups.) The responses were then assigned weights ranging from $+1$ to -1. A person who receives a high score on the engineer scale, say, displays interests similar to engineers in the norming sample. This is not analogous to saying that the individual would like to be an engineer, or would be successful as a professional engineer, or should study engineering in college. Rather, the test score indicates only the similarity of interests shared by the subject and the engineers selected in the norming sample.

The General Occupational Themes (GOT) is based on Holland's typology and provides an organizing structure that aids the counselor in interpreting the Basic Interest Scales and Occupational Scales (see Figures 17.1 and 17.2). Holland (1973) has developed an occupational-classification system that postulates that people can be categorized in terms of six types—realistic, investigative, artistic, social, enterprising, or conventional —such that each person is characterized by one, or some combination, of these types (In Holland's model, people are *not* rigidly classified under the six GOTs). Now, instead of talking to counselees in terms of over 100 different occupations and/or clusters, the counselor can provide the counselees with a global picture of their occupational orientation. High scores on the GOT scales *suggest* the general kind of activities the counselees will enjoy, the type of occupational environment where they will be most comfortable, the kinds of activities they will be most willing to deal with, and the kinds of persons who will be found most appealing as co-workers. Research indicates that the themes possess adequate validity and short-term (30-day) stability.

The Basic Interest Scales (BIS), like the GOTs, aid the user in obtaining a better understanding of the Occupational Scales. Because of the heterogeneity of the occupational scales, the authors collected items into somewhat homogeneous subsets and refer to these subsets as BIS. There are 23 of them grouped under Holland's six themes, with one to five items in each theme (see Figure 17.1). Some of the BIS categories are Public Speaking, Office Practices, and Religious Activities. It was felt that the BIS would be more easily understood than the occupational scales (because one interprets a homogeneous *set* of items) and would reduce the need for endless revisions of the existing occupational scales. Since the BIS constitutes a major focus in interpreting the Strong, it is essential that more empirical evidence be presented to demonstrate the relationship between the BIS and the earlier SVIB occupational scales, as well as between the BIS and the GOT. Despite their brevity, BIS are highly reliable over short time periods.

The *Occupational Scales* (there are 207) are the *most* valid and reliable scales and have been the bulwark of the Strong since it was first published in 1927. They are now grouped under the appropriate Basic Interest Scales (see Figure 17.1). Because of societal changes, many modifications have been made. For example, 12 new occupations (24 scales) were added to the profile. Of the new scales, 17 are female scales developed to match existing male scales (e.g., chiropractor, forester), and 11 new male scales have been developed to match existing female scales (e.g., flight attendant, physical education teacher). Other changes made are as follows: The profile scores are organized into Holland's system, new In-General samples have been drawn, criteria for selecting and weighting the items for a specific occupation have been modified from the earlier rules, and new norms have been prepared. Although the ultimate goal is to have male and female samples for each criterion group, this still has not been achieved (there are still four scales normed only for males; and one only for females) because it is difficult to obtain a sufficiently large number of women in some occupations (e.g., pilot) or of men in others (e.g., secretary). Nevertheless, there are 101 matched-pair scales (based on *both* male- and female-normed groups), nearly 50 percent more than in the 1974 SCII.

Of the 325 items in the 1985 Strong, none are new. In the 1981 edition, only 2 were completely new; 180 items are common to both of the earlier booklets; 74 appeared only on the men's form; and 69 appeared only on the women's form. In the earlier editions, each sex had its own booklet and scoring keys. In the Strong, the counselor has the option of scoring the inventory on either the male scales, the female scales, or both and interpreting the scores accordingly. Campbell and Hansen (1981) contend that separately normed scales should be used if one wishes to maximize validity. The profile is organized so that scores on both

STRONG INTEREST INVENTORY OF THE
STRONG VOCATIONAL INTEREST BLANKS

PROFILE REPORT FOR: DATE TESTED:

ID: DATE SCORED:

AGE: SEX:

SPECIAL SCALES: ACADEMIC COMFORT
INTROVERSION-EXTROVERSION

TOTAL RESPONSES: INFREQUENT RESPONSES:

GOT
R
I
A
S
E
C

OCCUPATIONAL SCALES

STANDARD SCORES

		F	M	VERY DISSIMILAR	DISSIMILAR	MODERATELY DISSIMILAR	MID-RANGE	MODERATELY SIMILAR	SIMILAR	VERY SIMILAR

15 25 30 40 45 55

REALISTIC

GENERAL OCCUPATIONAL THEME - R 30 40 50 60 70 F M

BASIC INTEREST SCALES (STANDARD SCORE)

AGRICULTURE F M

NATURE F M

ADVENTURE F M

MILITARY ACTIVITIES F M

MECHANICAL ACTIVITIES F M

F	M	Occupation
(CRS)	RC	Marine Corps enlisted personnel
RC	RC	Navy enlisted personnel
RC	RC	Army officer
RI	RIC	Navy officer
R	R	Air Force officer
(C)	R	Air Force enlisted personnel
R	R	Police officer
R	R	Bus driver
R	R	Horticultural worker
RC	R	Farmer
R	RCS	Vocational agriculture teacher
RI	R	Forester
(IR)	RI	Veterinarian
RIS	(SR)	Athletic trainer
RS	R	Emergency medical technician
RI	RI	Radiologic technologist
RI	R	Carpenter
RI	R	Electrician
RIA	(ARI)	Architect
RI	RI	Engineer

15 25 30 40 45 55

INVESTIGATIVE

GENERAL OCCUPATIONAL THEME - I 30 40 50 60 70 F M

BASIC INTEREST SCALES (STANDARD SCORE)

SCIENCE F M

MATHEMATICS F M

MEDICAL SCIENCE F M

MEDICAL SERVICE F M

F	M	Occupation
IRC	IRC	Computer programmer
IRC	IRC	Systems analyst
IRC	IR	Medical technologist
IR	IR	R & D manager
IR	IR	Geologist
IR	(I)	Biologist
IR	IR	Chemist
IR	IR	Physicist
IR	(RI)	Veterinarian
IRS	IR	Science teacher
IRS	IRS	Physical therapist
IR	IRS	Respiratory therapist
IC	IR	Medical technician
IC	IE	Pharmacist
ISR	(CSE)	Dietitian
(SI)	ISR	Nurse, RN
IR	I	Chiropractor
IR	IR	Optometrist
IR	IR	Dentist
I	IA	Physician
(IR)	I	Biologist
I	I	Mathematician
IR	I	Geographer
I	I	College professor
IA	IA	Psychologist
IA	IA	Sociologist

15 25 30 40 45 55

ARTISTIC

GENERAL OCCUPATIONAL THEME - A 30 40 50 60 70 F M

BASIC INTEREST SCALES (STANDARD SCORE)

MUSIC/DRAMATICS F M

ART F M

WRITING F M

F	M	Occupation
AI	AI	Medical illustrator
A	A	Art teacher
A	A	Artist, fine
A	A	Artist, commercial
AE	A	Interior decorator
(RIA)	ARI	Architect
A	A	Photographer
A	A	Musician
AR	(EA)	Chef
(E)	AE	Beautician
AE	A	Flight attendant
A	A	Advertising executive
A	A	Broadcaster
A	A	Public relations director
A	A	Lawyer
A	AS	Public administrator
A	A	Reporter
A	A	Librarian
AS	AS	English teacher
(SA)	AS	Foreign language teacher

CONSULTING PSYCHOLOGISTS PRESS, INC.
577 COLLEGE AVENUE
PALO ALTO, CA 94306

FIGURE 17.1 Profile on the Strong Interest Inventory of the Strong Vocational Interest Blanks, Page 1. (Form reprinted with permission of the publisher.)

408

PROFILE REPORT FOR: DATE TESTED:

ID: DATE SCORED:
AGE: SEX:

OCCUPATIONAL SCALES

			STANDARD SCORES		VERY DISSIMILAR	DISSIMILAR	MODERATELY DISSIMILAR	MID-RANGE	MODERATELY SIMILAR	SIMILAR	VERY SIMILAR

SOCIAL

GENERAL OCCUPATIONAL THEME - S   30 40 50 60 70
F
M

F	M		15 25 30 40 45 55
SA	(AS)	Foreign language teacher	(AS)
SA	SA	Minister	
SA	SA	Social worker	
S	S	Guidance counselor	
S	S	Social science teacher	
S	S	Elementary teacher	
S	S	Special education teacher	
SRI	SAR	Occupational therapist	
SIA	SAI	Speech pathologist	
SI	(ISR)	Nurse, RN	(ISR)
SCI	N/A	Dental hygienist	N/A
SC	SC	Nurse, LPN	
(RIS)	SR	Athletic trainer	(RIS)
SR	SR	Physical education teacher	
SRE	SE	Recreation leader	
SE	SE	YWCA/YMCA director	
SEC	SCE	School administrator	
SCE	N/A	Home economics teacher	N/A

BASIC INTEREST SCALES (STANDARD SCORE)

TEACHING — F / M

SOCIAL SERVICE — F / M

ATHLETICS — F / M

DOMESTIC ARTS — F / M

RELIGIOUS ACTIVITIES — F / M

ENTERPRISING

GENERAL OCCUPATIONAL THEME - E   30 40 50 60 70
F
M

F	M		15 25 30 40 45 55
E	ES	Personnel director	
ES	E	Elected public official	
ES	ES	Life insurance agent	
EC	E	Chamber of Commerce executive	
EC	EC	Store manager	
N/A	ECR	Agribusiness manager	N/A
EC	EC	Purchasing agent	
EC	E	Restaurant manager	
(AR)	EA	Chef	(AR)
EC	E	Travel agent	
ECS	E	Funeral director	
(CSE)	ESC	Nursing home administrator	(CSE)
EC	ER	Optician	
E	E	Realtor	
E	(AE)	Beautician	(AE)
E	E	Florist	
EC	E	Buyer	
EI	EI	Marketing executive	
EIC	ECI	Investments manager	

BASIC INTEREST SCALES (STANDARD SCORE)

PUBLIC SPEAKING — F / M

LAW/POLITICS — F / M

MERCHANDISING — F / M

SALES — F / M

BUSINESS MANAGEMENT — F / M

CONVENTIONAL

GENERAL OCCUPATIONAL THEME - C   30 40 50 60 70
F
M

F	M		15 25 30 40 45 55
C	C	Accountant	
C	C	Banker	
CE	CE	IRS agent	
CES	CES	Credit manager	
CES	CES	Business education teacher	
(CS)	CES	Food service manager	(CS)
(ISR)	CSE	Dietitian	(ISR)
CSE	(ESC)	Nursing home administrator	(ESC)
CSE	CSE	Executive housekeeper	
CS	(CES)	Food service manager	(CES)
CS	N/A	Dental assistant	N/A
C	N/A	Secretary	N/A
C	(R)	Air Force enlisted personnel	(R)
CRS	(RC)	Marine Corps enlisted personnel	(RC)
CRS	CR	Army enlisted personnel	
CIR	CIR	Mathematics teacher	

BASIC INTEREST SCALES (STANDARD SCORE)

OFFICE PRACTICES — F / M

ADMINISTRATIVE INDEXES (RESPONSE %)

OCCUPATIONS	%	%	%
SCHOOL SUBJECTS	%	%	%
ACTIVITIES	%	%	%
LEISURE ACTIVITIES	%	%	%
TYPES OF PEOPLE	%	%	%
PREFERENCES	%	%	%
CHARACTERISTICS	%	%	%
ALL PARTS	%	%	%

FIGURE 17.1 (concluded)   Profile on the Strong Interest Inventory of the Strong Vocational Interest Blanks, Page 2. (Form reprinted with permission of the publisher.)

same-sex and opposite-sex scales can be represented. In this way, all scores are available, but at the same time normative information appropriate for each sex is presented.

In addition to the GOT, BIS, and OS previously discussed, there are two empirically derived Special (nonoccupational) scales to detect response-set problems, careless test taking, and scoring errors. These are Academic Comfort (AC) and Introversion-Extroversion (IE). Further, there are three types of Administrative Indexes (AI): Total Responses (TR), Infrequent Responses (IR), and Like Percentage, Dislike Percentage, and Indifferent Percentage (LP, DP, and IP).

The AC is a "measure of probable persistence in an academic setting" rather than a predictor of grades. The IE scale provides useful clinical information and has been shown to discriminate successfully between people-oriented and non-people-oriented occupations. The TR index indicates the total number of responses marked and suggests action only if it is less than 310. The IR index is based on responses *infrequently* selected by the GRS. The purpose of the IR index is to identify responses that may be incorrectly marked. Although a high score suggests that a problem exists, it does *not* indicate *why*. The LP, DP, and IP indices are used to detect errors that *might* be the result of incorrect scoring, a mismarked answer sheet, or misunderstood directions. On the other hand, they might indicate the subject's response style. In any event, the three AIs should be checked *before* attempting to interpret an examinee's scores on any of the other scales, since the AIs provide a preliminary check on the validity of the responses.

Reference is made in the manual to the validity and reliability of the various scales of the Strong. Since the bulk of the data are based on the SVIB, they are found in the *Handbook* (Campbell, 1971), which contains a wealth of information that should be *required* reading for every Strong user. Additional technical information is found in the SVIB/SCII manual (Campbell & Hansen, 1981;

Hansen & Campbell, 1985). On inspection, the items appear to have good face validity, and the reliability and criterion-related evidences presented are acceptable. The BIS have lower concurrent and predictive validity than the Occupational Scales, which have higher internal consistency but slightly lower consistency over time. The predictive validity of the Strong (which can be inferred from research with the SVIB) is equally good for very able black and white students. The SVIB did *not* demonstrate any racial bias (Borgen, 1972; Borgen & Harper, 1973).

Both the manual (Hansen & Campbell, 1985) and the user's guide (Hansen, 1984) contain a cornucopia of information to assist the counselor in interpreting the results and discussing alternatives with the testee.

The Strong can be scored only by computer agencies licensed by the publisher. To assist the teacher, counselor, or student in interpreting the test scores, raw scores on the BIS and OS are converted to *T* scores. A computer-generated, printed interpretive profile is also provided. In addition, the Strong profile has, for the BIS, bars printed to present the middle half or the GRS distribution; for each occupation, there is a shaded area to represent the Men-in-General sample; the open bars represent the Women-in-General sample (see Figure 17.1). These "bands" should assist in making decisions about the significance of an interest score.

Two perplexing questions are (1) Where is the evidence to support the claim made in an academic environment? (2) Where is the validity evidence for the IE scale? Despite the weaknesses noted, we believe the Strong to be the best vocational interest inventory available for those seeking managerial and professional occupations. Readers interested in a thorough critique of the Strong and its revisions should see Borgen and Bernard (1982) and Anastasi (1988).

Kuder Occupational Interest Survey (KOIS), Form DD 1985 Revision. Published by Science Research Associates, it is intended for high school students and adults. There is one form. It is untimed, but takes about 30 minutes to complete. The vocabulary level is at about the sixth grade. There are 30 core scales, 119 occupational scores—for example, bookkeeper, chemist, farmer—79 with male norms only, 40 with female norms only. Twenty occupations and 12 college majors have both male and female norm groups and are called twin scales. It covers 48 college majors—for example, nursing, architecture—divided into 29 male and 19 female groups.

In each of 100 triads of activities, the examinee selects the one most liked and least liked. The KOIS has a verification key that can assist the counselor in ascertaining how honest and careful the examinee was in responding to the inventory. Although Kuder contends that the KOIS scores are related to vocational maturity, no evidence is presented to support this (Stahmann & Matheson, 1973). The reliability is satisfactory.

It should be noted that the KOIS differs from the Strong in that it does not have a general reference group, as was done in all the Strong inventories. Rather, in the KOIS, responses were correlated with membership in occupational groups.

The KOIS has been carefully constructed and includes some features not found in other tests. It contains a well-written interpretive leaflet for the examinee. The 1979 manual, which was well written and contained some useful suggestions for the counselor, has been replaced by a report form and explanatory material about the KOIS and four different types of scales—Dependability, which replaces the (V)erification scale of earlier editions; the Vocational Interest Estimates, which provide the testee with his relative rank of preferences for 10 different kinds of activities; and Occupations and College Majors scales, which are essentially unchanged from the 1979 revision. The *improved* Survey Report Form is supplied as a counselor or testee form (the latter does not report certain technical material useful to the counselor in making interpretations).

New in the 1985 revision is an audio tape to explain the interpretation of the inventory. Regretfully, the booklet and worksheet entitled "Ex-

plaining Your Future" to help subjects explore additional occupations from their high-ranking KOIS scales has *not* been revised to reflect changes in the 1985 version.

There is no general manual for the 1985 revision. The 1985 manual supplement provides the user with a way of converting KOIS scale scores into Holland codes. There are separate norms for men and women. The discussion on the development of the test and the description of the criterion groups are clear and should be valuable to the counselor considering the use of the KOIS. A major advantage of the KOIS is that new scales are being added continuously and the manual is periodically revised. A major disadvantage of the test is that it can be scored only by the publisher.

In comparison to the Strong, the KOIS has the following advantages: (1) scoring of college-major interests, (2) a broader range of occupations (more technical and trade level), and (3) scores for females on selected men's occupational and college-major scales. The major advantages of the Strong are that it shows more evidence of predictive validity, has more reliability data, and is easier to interpret.

Homogeneous Keyed Inventories *Kuder General Interest Survey (KGIS), Form E.* Published by Science Research Associates, it was revised in 1976. It covers grades 6 through 12. There is one form. Although untimed, it takes about one hour to administer. It provides 11 scores, one of which is a verification score.

The KGIS is suitable for students in grades 6–12, and research is underway to ascertain its validity for adults. It is intended to stimulate career exploration and suggest career possibilities. The KGIS compares the examinees' interests in activities in 10 broad occupational/vocational areas with the interests of a national sample of persons in grades 6–12. Its reading level is sufficiently low to permit its use with high school students who have a limited vocabulary. The KGIS consists of 552 statements grouped into 184 triads. The subject selects the statement or activity liked "most" and the one liked "least" in each of the triads. Kuder (1966) contends that the scoring is such that the KGIS is not a purely ipsative scale, even though it is of a forced-choice format. He offers some rational arguments concerning the nonipsative nature of the KGIS, but we feel he has stretched the point in his argument. The KGIS has been constructed with younger people in mind: (1) It has a vocabulary that is at the sixth-grade level; (2) it attempts to avoid using occupational titles (the meanings associated with them are relatively unstable, especially for younger people). The KGIS differs from the Kuder Occupational Interest Survey and the Strong in that it expresses vocational choices, and this makes it better suited for younger people who either have limited experiential background or are not yet ready to focus on specific occupational exploration. There are 10 occupational scales: outdoor, mechanical, computational, scientific, persuasive, artistic, literary, musical, social service, and clerical. There is also a verification scale. The number of items assigned to a particular scale varies from 16 in the musical scale to 70 in the persuasive scale. Because the scales do not contain an equal number of items, the raw scores not only *can* vary from individual to individual but also *do* vary from one scale to another. Although this may not confuse the trained counselor, it will probably confuse the student because the KGIS can supposedly be self-administered, self-scored, and self-interpreted.

The activities referred to in the inventory are biased in favor of middle-class American values. Only a few items relate to activities that the underprivileged could be expected to experience. This strongly suggests that the KGIS not be used in poverty areas or in schools in which a major proportion of pupils come from a non-middle-class background.

The validity data for the KGIS is woefully inadequate with respect to specific occupational criterion data.

The reliability estimates provided are test–retest stability and Kuder-Richardson measures of internal consistency. The average test–retest (six-week-interval) correlations are low. This there-fore severely limits the use of the KGIS for making individual predictions. It would be of value to have data demonstrating whether over a longer period of time the highest scores tend to remain high and the lowest scores tend to remain low. Such data are especially significant in vocational and educational counseling.

There are separate sex norms (and profile sheets) for grades 6–8 and 9–12. This makes it possible for members of each sex to compare their interests with others who have similar sex-role experiences. The normative data are adequately presented in the manual. The descriptions of the sampling procedures used and the nature of the standardization sample are clear. The publishers exercised care in attempting to obtain a fairly representative sample, although some of the geographical regions are slightly under- or overrepresented.

Percentile scores can be plotted on *both* the male and female profile forms. This procedure does not eliminate the possibility that the reported score may be an inaccurate representation of the subject's interest. For example, an individual can obtain a high percentile score and still have little interest in the area, and vice versa, because of the ipsative nature of the scales.

A somewhat disturbing feature of the profile leaflet is the description of the various interest areas. Specific references are made to occupations or vocations, and these occupations are then grouped within a larger interest cluster. For example, in defining a persuasive interest, the publishers say that most salespeople, personnel managers, and buyers have high persuasive interest. Yet no empirical evidence is presented in the manual to support such a claim. For this reason we feel that the user should exercise extreme caution in interpreting the test profile. We further suggest that because of possible misinterpretation of the profile leaflet (especially by younger pupils), the counselor or teacher does the actual interpretation.

In conclusion, we are pleased that an attempt has been made to measure the interests of younger people in the Kuder General Interest Survey. Our knowledge of the development and stability of interests is not complete, but this should not dissuade us from trying to measure them. Our interest, however, in the development of such an inventory should not cause us to sacrifice quality. For the early high school years, the KGIS may be appropriate, but for older high school students who aspire to college, the new Strong appears to be superior.

Vocational Preference Inventory (VPI) 1985 Revision. Published by Consulting Psychologists Press, the inventory is in its eighth revision. There is one form. (There are three research forms.) The VPI can be used for persons 14 years of age and older. It is self-administering and untimed, but takes from 15 to 30 minutes to complete. The 1985 edition contains four new or revised occupational scales to reduce the emphasis on male occupations. The inventory yields 11 scores—6 of which (Realistic, Investigative, Social, Conventional, Enterprising, and Artistic) measure specific interests and relate them to learning environments, and 5 of which (Self-Control, Masculinity, Status, Infrequency, and Acquiescence) yield information about the subject's personality. Holland states that "its most desirable use" is as a "brief screening inventory" for high school and college students and for employed adults.

The rationale underlying Holland's VPI is that our environment can be classified into six types of combinations and that humans can also be classified into one or a combination of these six types. Holland claims that people of a particular type seek out a compatible environment of that same type, thereby giving us a person-environment match. The validity of the match between the person and his environment depends upon a variety of factors.

The subject responds to each of the 160 occupational titles presented in terms of a "Yes" (interest in that occupation) or "No" (lack of interest in that occupation) format. The highest score represents a dominant personality type; the four highest scores yield a personality interest pattern.

Although the test–retest reliabilities are moderate to high (0.62 to 0.98), they have only been computed on very small samples. Internal consistency coefficients for eight of the scales range from 0.64 to 0.89, suggesting that their content is relatively homogeneous. The other three scales—Masculinity, Status, and Infrequency—have low internal consistency estimates, which Holland claims is to be expected.

Most of the validity studies are of the construct, concurrent, and predictive type and indicate that (1) the VPI scales measure essentially similar constructs to some of those assessed by the California Psychological Inventory, the MMPI, and the Strong; (2) the VPI scores differentiate between men and women, persons in different occupations, and normal and abnormal people; (3) students' self-descriptions are consistent with their scale scores; and (4) VPI scores are correlated with such things as supervisor's ratings, choice of vocation, choice of major field, and psychiatric versus nonpsychiatric patients.

Generally, the numerous validity studies lend support to Holland's hypothesis of the relationship between occupational preferences and personality, as well as to the meaning of the scales (Cole & Hanson, 1971; Folsom, 1973). Two major limitations of the VPI are that (1) the VPI, unlike the Strong or KOIS, does *not* give subjects information on how their likes or dislikes compare with those of people in other occupations, and (2) some of the younger students might not be familiar with occupational titles such as Speculator or Financial Analyst. A former concern that there appears to be a sex bias, with many of the occupational titles not being appropriate for women, appears to have been ameliorated.

The manual is very good and outlines a clinical interpretation for each scale, presents a conceptual definition for each variable, and discusses some actual case studies. However, it does *not* contain up-to-date information on the VPI's psychometric properties—validity and reliability—and normative studies.

The VPI is quick, nonthreatening, and somewhat enjoyable to take. It is based on the hypothesis that individuals' choice of an occupation is an expression of their personality (i.e., the subjects "project" themselves into an occupational title, thereby making the VPI a structured personality inventory as well as an occupational-interest inventory); that personal stability, career satisfaction, or stable career pattern depends greatly on the "goodness of fit" between individuals' personalities and the environment in which they work; that each occupation has an environment characteristic of the people in it; and that people in a particular vocation have similar personalities. These assumptions have been tested, and the data generally support Holland's thesis.

Holland's theory (and hence the VPI) differs markedly from the conception of interests held by others such as Strong and Kuder. And, as Campbell (1974) states, "Holland's ideas have already had a substantial impact on research in the areas of vocational counseling, the measurement of interests, and occupational topology." It is our belief, however, that Holland's Self-Directed Search and VIESA (Vocational, Interest, Experience, and Skill Assessment) are much better than the Strong and the KOIS for vocational planning with younger people. (VIESA is discussed in a later section.)

Logically Keyed Interest Inventories *Ohio Vocational Interest Survey, Second Edition (OVIS II)*. Published by The Psychological Corporation, it was revised in 1981. It covers grades 7–12, college, and adult. There is one form and one level. Untimed, it usually takes about 35 to 60 minutes to administer. It has 23 scales. It is published as hand-scored, machine-scored, and microcomputer versions.

The OVIS II is a popular, well-constructed, and well-standardized vocational interest inventory for use with high school and college students, and adults. The rationale underlying the development of the OVIS was based on the *Dictionary of Occupational Titles' (DOT)*[4] cubistic model of involvement of data, people, and things. The OVIS II consists of three parts: (1) a student information questionnaire of six items—one requiring the student to indicate first and second choices from 23 job descriptions, one asking for first and second choices of school subjects liked, one on the type of high school program enrolled in (or contemplated), two questions on future plans, and one item of the student's first and second choices of 32 high school business and vocational programs; (2) a local survey information section, in which the user is given an opportunity to ask 1 to 18 questions of local concern or interest; and (3) an interest inventory. The interest inventory consists of 253 items (based on the fourth edition of the *DOT*), which are grouped into clusters of five or six items. All items are scored jointly for males and females. The 253 items used were based on refinement of the 114 homogeneous areas of the *DOT*, into 23 broad-interest categories (scales), with each scale being represented by 11 homogeneous items.[5] Of the 23 scales, 18 are common to both men and women, and 5 contain items differentiated by sex. To each item, the subject responds by means of a five-element key: would like the activity very much, would like, neutral, would dislike, and would dislike very much. The responses are weighted $+5$ to $+1$, respectively. Hence, a subject's score on any one scale may vary from 11 to 55.

Although the *DOT* model has three levels for each of data, people, and things for a total of 27 cells, the OVIS II has only 23 scales. The missing 4 scales have been purposefully omitted, since the OVIS scales are based only on the real world of work, and in the *real* world some jobs would never exist in a practical sense, although they could be portrayed theoretically.

Five of the cells are represented by two or more scales, because it was found that to describe accurately the job groups represented—a combination of data-people-things—one would have to use two (or more) scales rather than one.

Extensive and detailed planning went into the

---

[4]Published by the United States Employment Service (USES); contains descriptions of virtually all occupations.

[5]The elaborate procedure used to select items and to develop the scales is thoroughly described in the manual.

development and standardization of the original and revised OVIS. The authors are to be commended for their painstaking efforts in developing and standardizing the OVIS and OVIS II.

Although predictive and concurrent validity are of value in interest inventories, no such data are presented. Construct validity is illustrated, and a mimeographed supplement from the publisher describes the scales in detail. However, if, as the manual states, validity is to be assessed by determining the extent to which realistic plans for the student's future are developed, then evidence *must* be presented to demonstrate this.

Reliability was ascertained by means of stability and internal consistency estimates. The former range from 0.76 to 0.85; the latter are 0.83 and higher.

Normative data—including means, standard deviations, and scores at five different percentile points—are reported for each scale by sex, grade, and geographical region. Each student's raw scores, percentiles, stanines, and clarity indices (a clarity index on a given scale indicates the degree of consistency in responses to the 11 job activities on that scale) are available to the student in a personalized report folder. We question the advisability of such an approach, especially for interest inventories.

The manual and handbook are extremely well written and should prove useful to both students and school counselors. The fact that school systems can enter up to 18 custom-made local items is desirable for using these data for curriculum planning.

All in all, the OVIS II may well be one of the best interest inventories of the future, inasmuch as so much attention is placed on entering occupations as depicted by the *DOT*. The major question to which the test authors must address themselves surrounds the rationale and implementation of the data-people-things model of interests.

Comparisons Among Selected Interest Inventories

There is very little difference, if any, among the various interest inventories with respect to their general purpose. All are concerned with an assessment of one's likes and dislikes for various occupations so that the examinee, with the help of a trained counselor, can make more valid decisions regarding future educational or vocational plans than if interest inventory data were not available. There are, however, some marked differences between the various standardized interest inventories with respect to their method of construction, scoring, ease of administration, and ease of interpretation. Also, they differ in the grade level at which they can be used. We will now compare briefly the inventories previously discussed.

Method of Construction The Strong and Kuder Occupational Interest Survey (KOIS) employed criterion keying (contrasted groups). The Strong used as its criterion groups men-and-women-in-general, whereas the KOIS compared men in one occupation with those in many other occupations. The Ohio Vocational Interest Survey (OVIS) employed logical keying. The Kuder General Interest Survey (KGIS) and the Vocational Preference Inventory (VPI) used homogeneous keying.

Grade Level and Content The Strong should *not* be used below junior high school. The KOIS should *not* be used for students who are not at least juniors in high school. The VPI can be used for pupils in the ninth grade (about 15 or 16 years old). The OVIS can be used with eighth-graders. The Kuder GIS can be used for bright sixth-graders.

With respect to content, there is very little difference, if any, between the Kuder OIS, and Strong inventories. They stress activities and interests related to professional occupations and vocations. These inventories, however, differ from the OVIS II, which is concerned more with nonprofessional occupations. Because the OVIS is based on the *Dictionary of Occupational Titles (DOT)*, it may sample many activities with which the student has little knowledge or experience. The Kuder scales are the only ones that contain a verification key per se, although the Strong has six administrative indices scores to detect examinee errors in responding.

Administration and Scoring All interest inventories are untimed, but they take about 10 to 90 minutes to administer. None requires any formal training for either administration or scoring. All are group-administered. Interest inventories are, in a sense, self-administering.

The five inventories discussed here differ markedly in their ease of scoring. The KGIS is relatively easy to score and can be either hand- or machine-scored. The Strong, OVIS II, and the KOIS are complex to score and can be scored only by the publisher. The VPI is between the two extremes.

Validity and Reliability The degree of confidence that the user can place in his interpretation is directly related to both validity and stability of the instrument(s) used. The amount of evidence supporting claims for validity and reliability differs among the interest inventories. If one were to conceptualize a continuum running from most to least empirical evidence in support of reliability and validity data, the results would be as depicted in Figure 17.2. Although the Kuder GIS does not have much data to lend support to its predictive validity, it does have a little more than the VPI or OVIS.

Interpretation One may think that the less complex an inventory the easier is its interpretation. This does not hold true, at least for interest inventories. All interest inventories are difficult to interpret properly. If they are to be used for more than exploratory purposes, they should be interpreted only by a trained counselor or psychologist. Of the inventories discussed earlier, the KGIS conveys more general (rather than specific) information and hence may be frustrating to some students. It is one thing to tell a student that he exhibits the interests shared by chemists or lawyers, but it is something else when you tell him that he has scientific interests. What are scientific interests? In using the Strong or the KOIS, the counselor can be both specific (using the separate occupational scores) and general (using the cluster or area interest scores), but with the KGIS, the counselor can be only general in her evaluation of the examinee's interests. The VPI, although it gives an indication of the individual's likes and dislikes for various occupations, may be conceived as being rooted in personality theory to explain one's vocational preferences.

The Strong and KOIS are better for job orientation because the scores tell one what people in a specific vocation or profession (as well as people in broad areas such as scientific, mechanical, and business) like and dislike. Unlike the KGIS, we do not have to infer an individual's interests from a general scale such as personal-social or computational. The OVIS, because it was constructed according to the DOT, is more applicable to specific occupations than is the KGIS.

With regard to interpretation, one must keep in mind that the Kuder tests, because they are forced-choice inventories, are ipsative rather than normative scales. This means that the choice of one response automatically results in the rejection of the other(s). In other words, an ipsative scale results in a high score in one scale to be accompanied by a low score in another scale.

The VPI may be more susceptible than the other scales to responses being made in terms of stereotypes that the examinee holds rather than in terms of interests per se. The OVIS is not so applicable to higher-level professional occupations as is either the KOIS or the Strong.

Although similar labels, such as scientific, may be attached to scales in the various interest inventories, the counselor must be cautious in inferring that scales having the same designation are mea-

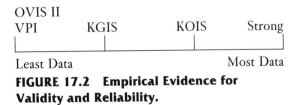

FIGURE 17.2 Empirical Evidence for Validity and Reliability.

suring exactly the same trait or characteristic. Just as one should not judge a book by its cover, the counselor should not interpret a scale by its name. The counselor must be thoroughly familiar with the test, the operational definitions of the terms used to describe the scale, and the theoretical orientation of the test constructor. All these cautions reinforce our position that, for other than exploratory information, the user be trained in terms of both formal course work and practical experience.

The KOIS and Strong are relatively unsatisfactory for people entering occupations that are below the professional-managerial level, even though there are many scales that are occupational in nature. Of the two tests, the KOIS is more suitable for persons contemplating lower-level occupations.

Other Interest Inventories

Some other interest inventories are the Interest Determination Exploration and Assessment System (IDEAS), the World of Work Inventory (WWI), and the Career Assessment Inventory (CAI). All are designed for use with younger pupils, and all are designed to assist students in exploring their vocational interests. They yield 14 to 60 scores. Of the three, the CAI is suited for students seeking careers that do not require a college degree (such as electronics technician, dental technician). Another example of an interest inventory that is a combination self-assessment/interest inventory is the Harrington-O'Shea Career Decision-Making System.

Two additional interest inventories are the Jackson Vocational Interest Survey (JVIS) and the California Occupational Preference System (COPS). The JVIS resembles the Strong in that they both use empirical and homogeneous keying/construction approaches. However, the JVIS differs markedly from the Strong in that it (1) uses construct-validity approaches in its development, (2) utilizes *broad* rather than narrow interest areas, (3) reflects a theory-based approach to test construction, and (4) employs sophisticated statistical analysis procedures. The COPS is designed to as-

sist persons (ranging from middle school students to adults) in career decision making. The COPS Professional Interest Inventory is specifically designed for adult and college populations, the COPS II and COPS-R for those with a fourth-grade and a sixth-grade reading level, respectively.

Although not considered here in any great detail, there are interest inventories for the exceptional child, such as the AAMD-Becker Reading-Free Vocational Interest Inventory for the educable mentally retarded, the Vocational Information and Evaluation Work Samples (VIEWS) for the severely mentally retarded, inventories such as the Wide-Range Interest Opinion Test for those persons who do not read English fluently, and the Jewish Employment Vocational Service Work Sample System (JEVS) for physically and mentally handicapped populations. The psychometric properties of these special inventories do not approach those of other interest inventories. They do show some promise, however, and although they should be interpreted with extreme caution, they fill a void in a vital area of assessment. Those wishing thorough but succinct reviews of these and other inventories for special populations should consult Kapes and Mastie (1988).

In addition to these interest inventories, there are some children's interest scales such as the Career Awareness Inventory and the Interest Inventory for Elementary Grades. There are also a limited number of interest inventories such as the Geist Picture Inventory for use with the culturally and educationally disadvantaged.

Significant Trends

Some significant events have already occurred, and some are looming on the horizon. Insofar as what has already occurred we have the melding of the theories of Kuder and Strong so that more and more interest inventories are providing scores on *both* homogeneous broad interest scales and specific occupational scales. Also, Holland's hexagonal model is appearing more often in new and revised interest inventories.

Also more linkages are being established between interest inventories and other data sources, for example, the SDS and Strong with large databases from the *Dictionary of Occupational Titles* (Harrington & O'Shea, 1984).

Holland (1986) raises another issue—*intervention techniques*—that goes beyond testing with interest inventories—what effect does the inventory (or for that matter any test) have on the testee?

Interest inventories over the years have, in a sense, expanded their horizons by considering more occupational levels. Initially, the emphasis was on professional careers with a few occupations requiring only a high school education. But in the new Strong, the revised Kuder Scales, the Career Directions Inventory, and the Career Assessment Inventory, there is greater concentration on skilled trades, vocational/technical occupations, semiprofessional occupations, and technical workers.

We project that within the next decade computer adaptive testing will be the rule rather than the exception insofar as the administration, scoring, and interpretation of interest inventories and psychological tests is concerned (see Brzezinski & Hiscox, 1984; Butcher, 1987; Baker, 1989). There are also some concerns and misgivings voiced (Sampson, 1983; Hofer & Green, 1985; Matarazzo, 1986). Today, we have computer revisions of the SDS, the Harrington-O'Shea Career Decision-Making System, and the Strong to name a few. We prognosticate that there will be more incorporation of interest inventories in career planning and exploration programs and in our aptitude tests. (Presently, interest data are included in the Career Planning Questionnaire of the DAT.)

Summary of Types of Interest Inventories

In summary, there are both similarities and differences among the various interest inventories. Although Kuder and Strong originally approached the measurement of interests differently, their inventories are now very similar —Strong adopting the interest clusters advocated by Kuder, and Kuder adopting the specific interest areas used by Strong. There is little difference, if any, among the various interest inventories with respect to their general purpose. All are concerned with an assessment of a person's likes and dislikes for various occupations so that examinees, with the help of a trained counselor, can make more valid decisions regarding their future educational and vocational plans than if interest-inventory data were not available. There are, however, some marked differences between the various standardized interest inventories with respect to their method of construction, scoring, ease of administration, and ease of interpretation. They differ in the types of reports produced and the ancillary materials accompanying them. They differ in grade level at which they can be used. And they differ in the validity, especially predictive validity, and the data used to support their claim to validity.

USING INTEREST-INVENTORY RESULTS

As might be expected, the greatest utility of interest-inventory results is for occupational, educational, and personal guidance and counseling. Used appropriately, the scores of these measures may help an individual crystallize his interests by encouraging him to think about his future plans or may clarify some misconceptions that he has about future occupational or vocational goals. It should be stressed here that it is not the scores per se that help achieve this self-discovery. It is the professional interpretation made of the scores. Those who interpret interest-inventory scores must be thoroughly trained and familiar with interest inventories: their uses and misuses, their fallibility, and their general value in helping make sound educational and vocational decisions.

Before considering the various instructional and guidance uses of interest-inventory results by educators, we feel that it is appropriate to summarize what research has shown regarding the nature of interests and interest inventories.

1. Interests tend to become progressively more stable with age (particularly after adolescence), but they are never permanently fixed. Although a broad area of interest, such as medicine, may not change, there can be a shift in a person's interests regarding general practice versus specialization or regarding different specialties. Using interest-inventory results to counsel students who are not yet high school juniors into making specific vocational decisions is to be discouraged, because interests are changeable at this age. This does not mean that interest-inventory results for adolescents are not reliable. On the contrary. Although the interests of adults tend to be more stable than those of adolescents, the test–retest correlations for adolescents are substantial (Kleinberg, 1976; Dolliver & Will, 1977). Interest-inventory scores can and should be used in discussions about various occupations and professions. Only the Strong has demonstrated empirically that its results are quite reliable (in terms of long-term stability) for individuals around age 25.

2. Interest inventories are susceptible to response set and faking; some more so than others. The user should therefore interpret the results of interest inventories accordingly.

3. Interest-inventory scores can be affected by the ambiguity of the questions asked. For example, two people may respond to the item "Like to play bridge" in the same way but for different reasons. One person may answer "Like" because it affords him an opportunity to meet people and establish future contacts, even though he may dislike bridge. Another person might answer "Like" for different reasons. He may like bridge because of the challenge it offers; yet this person might not like people and may avoid them whenever possible. Responses to interest-inventory items are relative rather than absolute indicators of likes and dislikes.

4. Interest inventories are verbal. The examinee must be able to comprehend what is being asked of him. Although the reading levels of the interest inventories vary, nearly all assume that the examinee can read at least at the sixth-grade level. This therefore precludes the use of such inventories as the Strong, KOIS, and KGIS for illiterates and students who have a reading deficiency.

5. There is disagreement among interest-inventory authors with respect to the kinds of items that are most valid. Kuder (1970) says that "activities" are more valid; Holland (1973) contends that "occupational titles" are more valid. Since interest-inventory authors agree that vocational interests in occupations are sex-related (Holland, 1973; Campbell, 1974), and since we seem to be so concerned with sex stereotyping and bias, the kinds of items used can be significant.

6. Interest inventories are *not* very satisfactory in predicting job success, academic success, job satisfaction, or personality adjustment. No interest test on the market will permit one to say that Maxwell should become a doctor, lawyer, or carpenter. No interest inventory will indicate whether or not Maxwell will be happy or successful in vocations or occupations in which he has obtained high scores. This does not mean that interest inventories have no predictive validity. They do, but they are not so valid as cognitive measures. There is a moderate relationship between interest-inventory scores and academic success (correlations normally are about 0.39). And there is a slight relationship between interest scores and such things as job success and personality. This, however, should not necessarily be interpreted as evidence of a relationship that is of practical significance, nor should it be construed as a cause-and-effect relationship. In predicting job satisfaction, it should be remembered that many factors must be considered, of which interests are but one factor. The relationship between interest scores and job success is vague, partly because of the problem of obtaining a

valid measure of job success. Interest-inventory scores may be related to various measures of job and/or academic success and satisfaction. However, the nature of the relationship is such that interest scores alone should never be used to predict future success or satisfaction. It is because the untrained user may make exaggerated statements about the probability or degree of success (or satisfaction) in a profession or vocation that we find interest inventories being criticized.

7. Some empirically constructed interest inventories may be more susceptible to sex bias than those constructed by the homogeneous method (Johansson & Harmon, 1972; Cole, 1973).

8. We must be very cautious in making interpretations of interest-inventory results. Research has shown that markedly different interpretations are possible depending upon the type of score used. When raw scores are used, highly divergent career suggestions are given men and women. But when same-sex standard scores are used, the career suggestions given men and women are very similar.

9. Don't confuse interest scores with ability measures. Max may want to be a surgeon like his father but may not have those abilities needed to pursue this career.

Properly used, interest-inventory results can provide valuable information for the teacher and the counselor so that they will better understand the pupils' cognitive and noncognitive behavior.

Guidance Purposes

After cognitive measures, interest-inventory results play the most important role in occupational and educational counseling. Interest-inventory results are beneficial to both the counselor and the counselee. The counselor can use the results as an introduction to the interview. The interest inventory may be used as a gambit in situations where it is difficult to establish rapport. The counselor can use the results to help open the way to discussion of other problems such as academic difficulty, personal-social relationships, and the like. The counselee, on the other hand, has an opportunity to view himself as he described himself. He can look at his present plans and with the assistance of the counselor see whether his aspirations are realistic and confirm his feelings, and then do some "reality testing." The counselee can use the test results as leads for further consideration. The counselee and the counselor can both use the inventory results to see whether the expressed interests are related or unrelated (whether they all fit into a pattern such as humanitarian or technical, or whether they are distinct), whether the program that the counselee is intending to follow is compatible with his profile of interests and abilities, and whether his vocational or avocational goal will be realized by the program he is now following.

Interest-inventory results can also be valuable in working with students who have unrealistic *academic* expectations. For example, Gregory, a pre-med student who is receiving grades of C and D in his science courses and who has a MCAT (Medical College Aptitude Test) score at the 10th percentile and still aspires to be admitted to a prestigious medical school, may be very unrealistic. Gregory may be in pre-med for a variety of reasons: (1) his parents, who are both physicians and who come from a family of physicians, want their only child to follow in their footsteps; (2) Gregory has an unrealistic picture of the glamor of a doctor's life; or (3) a combination of these and other factors. Interest-inventory results (the Strong, for instance, has a scale that reflects how compatible and comfortable one would be in various work settings) can help students like Gregory if only to make them think more realistically about their future (see Althen & Stott, 1983).

Interest-inventory results, if used cautiously, can help an individual find himself in terms of the activities he feels are important and interesting. Interest-inventory results should not be used for classroom selection purposes (though they may be useful for classification). They should not be used to tell Fred that he should enter the field of engineering. They should not be used as the major criterion in occupational and educational counseling. High scores on an interest inventory are not analogous to saying that the individual has either the aptitude or the potential for success in a particular vocation. The test scores provide only a relative index of the individual's likes and dislikes, and for some inventories it is possible to compare the student's interests with those of individuals who are successful in a vocation or profession. In actual practice, interest-inventory results should be used only for their valuable ancillary information. Other factors such as ability, aptitude, motivation, and the like must be considered. The total profile rather than just part of it must be considered so that as complete a picture as possible of the individual's interests can be obtained. Finally, we should not argue whether *expressed* vocational interests are more valid than inventoried interests. Rather, we should consider *both* when counseling students.

Instructional Purposes

Although interest-inventory results can be used for grouping students, they normally are not used for this purpose. In a somewhat indirect fashion, interest-inventory results can be used by the classroom teacher to provide optimal learning conditions. Take, for example, the junior high school student who is a poor reader. Recognizing the limitations of interest-inventory scores for junior high school students, the teacher who knows that Billy likes mechanics may attempt to motivate him to read more by suggesting books, magazines, or articles with a mechanical content. Hence, although the test score is not used as an instructional device per se, it is used to provide a learning experience that may be quite beneficial insofar as Billy's reading is concerned.

Interest inventories can be used as a learning device. For example, in the unit on "Work" in social studies, the teacher may have the students take an interest inventory. She can use this technique to get the students to think somewhat systematically about the relationships between personal interests and occupational choice. Any interest in-

ventory used in a group fashion should be used for discussion purposes only. Hopefully, divergent thinking rather than convergent thinking will ensue.

CAREER AWARENESS AND DEVELOPMENT

A person requires more than merely an interest in, and possibly an aptitude or ability for, a particular vocation in order to be counseled for that vocation. Career planning is the most sought-after service by college students (Carney et al., 1979) and is given high priority by high school students (Prediger & Sawyer, 1986). There was a void between 1958 and 1968 in the development and publication of standardized instruments to measure the various aspects of career development. Since 1968, however, at least six major career-planning programs have been initiated; numerous articles have been written; and at least eleven career-development/vocational maturity standardized tests have been published or revised—*Readiness for Vocational Planning Test*; *Cognitive Maturity Test*; *Assessment of Career Development*; *Career Development Inventory*; *Self-Directed Search*; *Planning Career Goals*; *Vocational Interest, Experience and Skills Assessment*; *Programs for Assessing Youth Employment Skills*; *Career Assessment Inventory: Enhanced Edition*; *Career Directions Inventory*; and *Career Maturity Inventory* (see Super & Crites, 1962; Super et al., 1972; Westbrook & Parry-Hill, 1973; Westbrook, 1976a, b; Peters & Hansen, 1977).

Although all these instruments are designed to measure those factors deemed important for career development, it is not surprising to find that they differ markedly in terms of the constructs measured. An analysis by Westbrook (1974) showed that the inventories differed (widely at times) in their coverage (1) of cognitive, affective, and psychomotor behaviors and (2) of specific behaviors within a given component. These findings are different from, say, an analysis of reading readiness tests, no doubt because our state of knowledge of the reading process is at a more advanced level than that for career development or vocational maturity. (Crites, 1974, discusses the methodological issues and problems in measuring career maturity.) Research has also been initiated to study the effects of computer assistance and group counseling as aids to career maturity. Any conclusions, however, still await more definitive testing.

Career-Planning Programs

Assessment batteries and programs have been developed to aid *both* the student and the counselor in vocational and educational planning.[6] This is especially significant since it has been shown that a person's vocational aspirations can be manipulated by the kind and amount of information given (Haase et al., 1978; Mallet et al., 1978). Three such programs are the Career Planning Program (CPP), sponsored by the American College Testing Program; the Career Development Program (CDP), conducted by Science Research Associates; and the Career Skills Assessment Program (CSAP), conducted by the College Board. There are many similarities among the three programs, the most striking one being that they are more than aptitude and achievement tests. They consider, in addition, such factors as interests, aspirations, career-related experiences, and work preferences. All three programs provide useful information for the student who knows his future plans, as well as for the student who is undecided. The CPP also sends information to the institution(s) selected by the student. We will now consider one of these three programs briefly. Those interested in a more comprehensive treatment of career education and development programs should see Krumboltz and Hamel (1982).

Career Planning Program (CPP) Published by the American College Testing Program (1983),

the CPP is really two programs in one: an *assessment* component (grades 8–11) and a *career-guidance* component (CPP Level 1 for grades 8–10; CPP Level 2 for grade 11–adult).[7] Both levels of the CPP are comprehensive packages of aptitude and interest inventories as well as career-related experiences in one articulated program and designed to facilitate self- and career exploration, including the exploration of self in relation to career. Besides the Vocational Interest Profile, Form A, which reports the subject's interest in six areas, and six ability scales, there is a Student Information Report (self-report measures of a variety of things such as job values, occupational preferences, certainty of occupational preferences, working-condition preferences, educational plans, and self-rated abilities). A Building and System Summary Report is also available. It provides counselors with a "comprehensive overview of students' abilities, interests, career-related experiences, and congruence of student traits." Test-retest and internal consistency reliability estimates are reported, and they appear to be respectable. Construct and criterion-related validity were studied and reported. The format is good. The directions for both administrators and student are very clear.

In 1983, a personal computer-generated report was introduced. The report not only contains the results of the ability measures but provides the counselor and counselee with a narrative report, a synthesis of the assessment results, and suggested resource materials, to name a few interpretive aids provided.

The CPP has an excellent *Handbook*, which discusses in clear fashion the development and use of the program, contains an annotated bibliography of career-guidance materials, and contains a complete lesson plan outline for a nine-unit Mini Course in Career Planning. The *Handbook* also contains a variety of norms tables.

---

[6]Although more popular with personnel researchers, Childs and Klimoski (1986) found a biographical data inventory to be a valid predictor of career success.

[7]Although our discussion centers primarily on the CPP, the material is also relevant, with minor modifications, to the CPP Level 2.

The *Student Report* is well written and should be understood by nearly all students. It gives the student step-by-step suggestions on how to interpret the information and how to go about exploring suggested career options.

An adjunct of the CPP is the Assessment of Career Development for grades 8–12. On the basis of students' responses to 42 critical questions (the user can add up to 19 locally developed questions), a school can evaluate its career-development program and modify it, if necessary, to meet students' needs.

In summary, the CPP is a well-designed instrument/program that provides measures of peoples' interests, abilities, and career-related experiences all normed on the *same* group. The test's technical qualities are acceptable, although we regret that the publisher did *not* provide empirical data to permit evaluation of the guidance component of the program. It serves both the student and the school: The former receives information that should be of assistance in career exploration and educational planning; the latter receives information on its student body that may be of value in the development or modification (as well as evaluation) of its career-guidance program. (For a review of the CPP, see Mehrens, 1982.)

Other Programs

In addition to the three programs mentioned earlier, there have also been published what might be referred to as a total career-planning program or system. Although not standardized tests, per se, career-exploration and career-development programs (and hence materials) often incorporate an interest inventory and one or more cognitive measures (such as an aptitude and/or achievement test) into a package or module that can be used effectively in a unit or course on career exploration. These prepackaged units vary from programs that use no test materials, such as SRA's *Introducing Career Concepts*, to those that use a combination of workbooks, filmstrips, and standardized interest inventories, as exemplified in CTB/McGraw-Hill's *Careers in Focus*. Although the majority of

career-exploration/development programs are designed for upper middle school and high school students, a few are intended for use in the elementary grades. On this latter point, we have some reservations. We are *not* against the use of materials or discussions about careers or employment opportunities and the like in the elementary and junior high school. In fact, we strongly endorse the inclusion of such materials as early as possible in the child's schooling. If anything, we regret that many of our syllabi and curricula, even at the high school level, pay only lip service to career-development/exploration courses. We firmly believe, however, that any career-planning program used in the elementary grades that contains an interest inventory should be interpreted with extreme caution because of the instability of interests at that age.

One approach is Houghton Mifflin's Vocational, Interest, Experience, and Skill Assessment (VIESA) program, which was published in 1977. VIESA is designed for students in grades 8–12. It is untimed, but takes about 45 minutes. There is one form. The battery consists of a standardized interest inventory with sex-balanced scales, a standardized experience inventory that assesses experiences related to interests, and a structured guide for student self-appraisal of career-related skills. Students can make interpretations related to 6 job clusters, 25 job families, and 650 occupations. Scores are represented in a graphical Job Clusters on a World-of-Work Map. Students are given suggestions of what occupations to explore, as well as references to consult. VIESA is compatible with the Career Planning Program described earlier.

More detailed information on these and other instruments and programs we have discussed can be found in the *Mental Measurement Yearbooks* and the various publishers' catalogs.

PERSONALITY ASSESSMENT

Personality characteristics are or should be of concern to classroom teachers. It is generally agreed that education must be concerned with attitudes, values, and interests to the same degree as it is concerned with the development of cognitive skills and knowledge. What value will accrue to society from individuals who can solve a quadratic equation or are able to detect the components of LSD, but who are hostile or aggressive? Education should be concerned with developing a well-rounded individual.

We will consider only the self-report inventories in this chapter. While other techniques provide valuable information, they are typically locally constructed and have been covered in Chapter 9.

Structured Self-Report Inventories

Structured self-report inventories are the most common type of personality inventories used in schools (and industry) today. They are a basic tool in the diagnosis of "illness," whether it be physical or mental. Just as the physician will ask what hurts you and where and when the pain started, the psychiatrist and clinician will ask you whether you have nightmares, a tendency to daydream, or similar questions. Over the years, the answers to these kinds of questions have been found to be more indicative of maladjustment than those to other questions that could be asked. When such questions are selected and put together in a list to be checked off by the examinee, it is a test or an inventory. Self-report inventories can be classified into either problem checklists or general adjustment inventories. They can also be classified in terms of their method of construction: criterion groups, factor analysis, or logical approach. All, however, are structured.

There are somewhat definite criteria that can be used to evaluate a standardized test—be it aptitude, achievement, or affective. However, there are fewer guidelines available for judging the validity of self-report data. Laing (1988) posits the following four principles: (1) the respondent must clearly understand what is being asked, (2) the respondent must be able to furnish the information, (3) the respondent must be willing to provide the information, and (4) the examiner must be able to interpret the information correctly.

Problem Checklists Problem checklists are the most applicable personality measure in our public schools because of their limited demand on formal training and experience for the examiner. Classroom teachers can *administer* and *score* a problem checklist. *Interpretation*, on the other hand, demands training, sophistication, and experience. It is one thing to administer a checklist and still another to interpret it.

Problem checklists can be used by classroom teachers to confirm some of their subjective impressions that were obtained by observation. Problem checklists can be used by the teacher (or counselor) to obtain a better understanding of their pupils—their problems, their behavior. Problem checklists, especially when administered to the whole class, will make pupils less self-conscious and willing to reveal their problems. This is especially true if the teacher discusses the general findings. At no time should individual responses or pupils be identified and discussed. With discussion centering on general findings, the pupil is able to see that he is not atypical, that other pupils are also bothered or concerned about a variety of things. Problem checklists also serve as excellent screening devices for the counselor. On the basis of their results and an interview, the counselor may suggest more thorough treatment if needed.

It should be remembered that problem checklists are just that—they do not make any claims to measuring personality traits. In fact, problem checklist authors caution users to avoid adopting this view. In problem checklists, the individual checks only the statements that are applicable to him (and that he wishes to check) and that he is aware of. The greatest value of problem checklists is as communication vehicles between the pupil and the counselor. The test results can help save the counselor much valuable time by indicating what the problem seems to be and can help establish rapport between the pupil and the counselor.

Problem checklists are composed of items,

which based on a review of the literature and surveys tend to be representative of problems that people face in different areas, such as family, peer relationships, finances, study skills, health, and relations with adults. Even so, they differ slightly in their format. In some, the pupil checks only the statements that he perceives as problems. In others, the pupil indicates the degree of severity: minor, moderate, severe. In still others, the pupil writes a statement about his problems. The responses to problem checklists should *not* be considered as a test or subtest score. The teacher and the counselor should use the responses as a guide for further exploration. If used in this way, problem checklists are quite helpful.

Problem checklists are primarily used to identify individuals who are concerned with social and personal relationships and may be in need of counseling or other therapy. They can also be used to help identify group problems and form a basis for group guidance.

Another type of structured self-report inventory is the adjustment inventory. This type is concerned primarily with the identification of neuroticism and pathological deviation.

General Adjustment Inventories

It is not our intent to delve too deeply into the measurement of personality by means of general adjustment inventories. However, we do feel that educators should have at least a rudimentary knowledge of the different types, as well as some awareness of their strengths and weaknesses. Moreover, as we mentioned earlier, teachers and counselors must realize that they are still able to obtain more reliable and valid information about the noncognitive characteristics of their pupils with tests than they can by other means.

General adjustment inventories are of value because they (1) help establish rapport between counselor and counselee by having some basis on which to begin an interview, (2) permit the examinee to express problems that are of relevance (or those which he *thinks* are of relevance or importance) to him, and (3) provide the counselor or

clinician with more information about the individual so that she may have a global picture of the individual. Some examples of general adjustment inventories are *The Adjustment Inventory*, *Minnesota Multiphasic Personality Inventory*, *California Psychological Inventory*, *Thurstone Temperamental Schedule*, and *The Personality Inventory*. Detailed information about the inventories can be found in Anastasi (1988) and the *Mental Measurements Yearbooks*.

Unstructured Inventories

Structured self-report inventories are not the only manner in which an individual's behavior can be measured. Another standardized approach to the assessment of personality is the one frequently used by the clinician: the unstructured or projective test. Whereas self-report structured inventories require the subject to describe himself, projective tests require the individual to interpret objects other than himself. These objects may be pictures, incomplete sentences, drawings, and the like. The difference between structured and unstructured stimuli depends on the degree of agreement regarding the stimuli. If there is consensus regarding what the stimuli represents, it is considered structured. If there is lack of agreement because of the ambiguity of the stimulus, it would be termed unstructured. The unstructured task permits the individual to project his feelings, which reflect his needs, motives, and concerns.

Anastasi (1968) classified projective techniques into five types: associative techniques (Rorschach Ink Blot Test), construction procedures (Thematic Apperception Test), completion tasks (Rotter Incomplete Sentence Test), ordering devices (Szondi Test), and expressive methods (Machover Draw-A-Person Test). In the latter, both product and processes are evaluated.

Projective tests may also be differentiated from self-report inventories in many other ways: (1) Projective tests (because they are innocuous) are more resistant to faking and the influence of response set than are self-report inventories. Even though a maladjusted person may attempt to fake his responses, it is quite conceivable that his faked responses will indicate that he is maladjusted. (2) Projective tests are interesting and novel and hence can easily be used with young children or with persons who are afraid of a formal pencil-and-paper test. (3) Projective tests can be either verbal or nonverbal, but self-report inventories are verbal and hence are not applicable to illiterates and very young children. (4) Self-report inventories, at least most of them, can be objectively scored, but projective tests are very susceptible to the subjective feelings of the scorer, even when certain guidelines are used in the scoring. (5) Projective tests are usually based on or reflect psychoanalytic theory such as that of Jung or Freud. (6) Projective tests (as do some nonprojective methods) normally utilize a global approach in the assessment of personality and often go beyond personality syndromes per se and concern themselves with creativity and critical thinking ability.

Projective tests and self-report inventories share many things in common: (1) they have relatively low validity and reliability; (2) they provide some of the information needed to obtain a better understanding of the individual; (3) scoring systems vary from elaborate multifactor systems with profiles to nonquantifiable interpretive information; (4) most have inadequate norms; and (5) they can be administered either individually or in groups. Both structured and unstructured personality tests should be interpreted only by qualified persons. Because the administration, scoring, and interpretation of projective tests are complex and because of the formal training and experience needed to work with them, we will dispense with their further evaluation.

Computer-Administered Personality Tests

The past few years has seen a proliferation of new computer-based forms of traditional pencil-and-paper psychological tests and other assessment tools. The question plaguing many is whether these formats are equivalent (Hofer & Green, 1985). Most of the research to date (Roid & Gor-

such, 1984; Lukin et al., 1985; Reardon & Loughead, 1988) has shown that the two forms of administration are *equivalent*. In addition, students seem to prefer the computer version.

Summary of Personality Inventories

In summary, personality inventories (adjustment inventories) are *not* for general use in our schools and should not be part of the test battery that is normally and routinely administered in school testing programs. Even the best of them must be used with caution and only by persons trained and experienced in the use of these techniques. With the exception of the problem checklists, we may go so far as to say that personality assessment should be withheld from the classroom teacher. This does not imply, however, that personality assessment should be barred from the public school. In order to gather empirical data (data that have been lacking for personality tests in general and projective techniques in particular), it is necessary to administer such tests to pupils. The test results, however, should be used primarily for counseling and research rather than for making instructional decisions. Until personality tests achieve the stature of our cognitive measures and of some of the interest scales, they should be handled with great caution.

ATTITUDE AND VALUE ASSESSMENT

Attitudes are learned. Because they are learned, they can be changed if deemed necessary. However, before people can alter, modify, or reinforce something, they must know the status of that "something." In fact, as early in the school year as possible, teachers should try to identify students who have positive and negative attitudes and implement appropriate strategies so as to accentuate the positive and eliminate the negative. Despite the methodological problems associated with attitude measurement, teachers should know something about attitudes and how they can be measured. The remainder of this chapter considers (1) the general characteristics of attitudes, (2) the evaluation of attitude scales, and (3) the assessment of pupil study habits inventories.

General Characteristics of Attitudes

Relevant to, and to be considered in, attitude measurement are certain traits or characteristics. These are listed below:

1. Attitudes are predispositions to respond overtly to social objects.
2. A variety of definitions have been posited for attitudes, but all share a common theme that attitudes guide and direct an individual's behavior. For this reason, it is imperative for teachers to know something about attitudes, how they are formed, how they are changed, and how they relate to the teaching-learning process.
3. Attitudes, per se, are *not* directly observable but are inferred from a person's overt behavior, both verbal and nonverbal. You cannot see prejudice but you can observe the behavior of one who is prejudiced. Thus, on the basis of observations of someone's consistent behavior pattern to a stimulus, we would conclude that the individual displays this or that attitude (Shaw, 1973). It should be noted that these observations can be either *unstructured*—the teacher makes no particular effort to observe some behavioral trait, but when the teacher does see it, the situation, event, and behavior are noted—or *structured*—the teacher is interested in learning, for example, what Mary's attitude is toward reading. The teacher then purposely contrives a situation (places some books on a table, maneuvers Mary in front of the table) and observes/records Mary's behavior. Still another approach is to measure a person's attitude(s) by means of an attitude scale.
4. Attitude scales can be constructed in a variety of ways, the most common ones being the Thurstone, Likert, Guttman, and Semantic Differential methods.
5. Attitude scales are highly susceptible to faking, and therefore any interpretation of this type of self-report behavior should be made accordingly.
6. Attitude scales, like any affective instrument, are beset with a multitude of methodological problems that make their interpretation dubious.
7. Attitudes are evaluative and can be represented on some continuum of "favorableness."
8. Attitudes vary in intensity (strength of feeling) and direction. Two persons may have the same attitude toward abortion, but they may differ in how strongly they feel about the issue. Or they may be at completely opposite ends of the "favorableness" continuum but with the *same* degree of intensity. (For example, on the abortion issue, Allan may strongly agree and Ilene may strongly disagree. Both Allan and Ilene feel strongly about their position, but they are diametrically opposed.)
9. Attitudes vary in affective saliency—that is, some attitudes (such as toward abortion) are accompanied by or connected with a person's emotions.
10. Attitudes represent varying degrees of embeddedness or interrelatedness to other attitudes. As would be expected, attitudes related to similar objects, such as integration and equality of education, are more likely to be interconnected than attitudes toward dissimilar objects, such as capital punishment and women's liberation.
11. Attitudes are relatively stable, especially in adults. This does *not* mean that they cannot be changed or modified. Rather, it is more difficult to change the attitudes of an adult than of an adolescent or young child. The fact that attitudes are relatively stable supports the belief of many social psychologists that attitude scales can provide reliable measures, although possibly less so than for tests of cognitive skills or knowledge.
12. Despite the variety of problems associated

with affective measurement, despite the fact that the validity and reliability of attitude scales are lower than for cognitive measures, and despite the reluctance of many teachers to pay appropriate attention to affective instructional/learning objectives, attitude scales can often be used effectively by the classroom teacher to obtain a better understanding of pupils. The results obtained from attitude scales can be useful in educational planning and evaluation. Acquisition of desirable attitudes is one of the major goals in our schools. Without knowledge of the prevailing attitudes of the pupil, class, or school, it would be difficult to plan accordingly.

Evaluation of Attitude Scales

The usefulness of any test or scale depends on its reliability, validity, norms, and ease of administration, scoring, and interpretation. We now briefly summarize how these factors relate to attitude scales.

Reliability. Attitude scales, by and large, have reliabilities around 0.75. This is much less than those obtained for cognitive measures, and hence the results obtained from attitude scales should be used primarily for group guidance and discussion.

Validity. In general, attitude measures have less validity data available than do other noncognitive measures. This is partly because of the problems inherent in measuring attitudes and partly because many of the measures were constructed primarily for research purposes.

The correlations obtained between the scale scores and observed behavior are typically low. Nevertheless, knowledge of the disparities between expressed attitudes and actual behavior is useful in understanding and working with the individual.

Norms. In the majority of instances, no norms accompany standardized attitude scales. The user must be careful in the interpretation of the test scores. Naturally, local norms can be prepared. Even if appropriate sampling techniques have been employed to select the standardization sample and even if the normative data are adequate, the fact that conditions affecting attitudes are so variable suggests that very recent norms be used. American attitudes toward Japan were markedly different on December 6 and December 8, 1941.

Administration, scoring, and interpretation. In contrast to the projective tests considered in the previous section, attitude scales are easy to administer and score. They require no formal training and can be handled easily by the classroom teacher. The interpretation of attitude-test scores, on the other hand, is an entirely different matter. Because of psychometric problems, the user should be cautious in her interpretations.

Assessment of Pupil Study Habits and Attitudes Toward School

As has been mentioned at various points in this text, the matter of how well a student does on an aptitude or achievement test depends upon factors other than basic ability or intelligence. Some of the factors that must be considered in assessing or appraising an individual's academic performance are (1) mental maturity, (2) motivation, (3) study habits, (4) study skills, and (5) attitudes toward the value of an education, teachers, school, and courses. The brightest student (speaking in terms of scholastic aptitude) may be performing at a somewhat mediocre level. He may be getting Cs and Ds, whereas we would predict from a valid measure of his scholastic aptitude that he should be receiving As and Bs. On the other hand, the intellectually poorer student might be getting Bs, although we would predict that he would obtain Cs. Why the discrepancy between predicted achievement and realized achievement? No doubt, how the pupil studies and his attitudes toward education play a significant role in an explanation of such discrepancies.

We now briefly consider one standardized study habits and skills inventory.

Survey of Study Habits and Attitudes (SSHA)

Published by The Psychological Corporation, 1965, the survey has two forms: H (for grades 7–

12) and C (for college students and high school seniors). It is untimed, but the majority of students complete the SSHA within 20 to 35 minutes. There are seven scores possible (based on four basic scales): Delay Avoidance (DA), Work Methods (WM), Study Habits (SH = DA + WM), Teacher Approval (TA), Educational Acceptance (EA), Study Attitudes (SA = TA + EA), and Study Orientation (SO = SH + SA or the total of the four basic scales).

The SSHA was designed (1) to identify the differences in study habits and attitudes between students who do well in their academic work and those who do poorly, (2) to assist students who might benefit from improved study habits (this improvement may result from counseling and/or instruction on how to study), and (3) to predict academic success for high school and college students. The authors recommend using it for screening, diagnosis, research and as a teaching aid.

The SSHA consists of 100 items such as the following, which attempt to assess the "motivation for study and attitudes toward academic work" syndromes rather than merely the mechanics of study.

> Daydreaming distracts my attention from my lessons while I am studying (DA).

> My teachers criticize my written work for being poorly planned or hurriedly written (WM).

> I feel that I would study harder if I were given more freedom to choose subjects that I like (EA).[8]

The authors' intent to go *beyond* measuring mechanics of study is perhaps the most differentiating factor of the SSHA from other study-habit inventories. Subjects respond to each item by means of a five-element key ranging from Rarely (0–15 percent of the time) to Almost Always (86–100 percent of the time). In an attempt to control for

response set, the "acceptable" (keyed) responses are randomly distributed at both ends of the continuum. The extreme positions are weighted twice that of the near-extreme positions. That is, if a negative item is keyed Rarely, it is given a weight of 2; a Sometimes response is given a weight of 1.

Both logical and empirical validity were stressed in the test's development. Items were chosen on the basis of interviews with students, and each item was empirically validated (correlations of the SSHA with grades, teachers' ratings, and aptitude scores) as to its applicability to the problem. For Form H (grades 7–12), student advice was obtained so that the language would be clear and meaningful to junior and senior high school students. The validity data presented in the test manual show that the SSHA is independent of scholastic achievement and that there is an increase in the predictive efficiency of grades when the SSHA is used in combination with aptitude test scores. Internal consistency (0.87–0.89) and test–retest (0.83–0.88) reliability estimates are reported for Form C. Test–retest reliabilities for Form H vary from 0.93 to 0.95. It is unfortunate that these data are based on only Texas students, especially because the correlation data reported for Form C show differences between college students in Texas and those in other parts of the country. Percentile norms are reported separately for each of the seven scores. For Form H, norms are provided for grades 7–9 combined and grades 10–12 combined. The Form H norming sample appears to be heavily weighted in favor of students from Texas and the southwestern region of the country.

To aid in test interpretation, the percentile scores can be plotted on the diagnostic profile sheet (on the reverse side of the answer sheet). The pupil's scores can then be compared with the performance of the norm group and his strengths and weaknesses identified. A separate counseling key is provided. This key enables the teacher or counselor to identify critical responses—the items that differentiate between high and low scholastic achievers. Still, the test authors recommend that the counselor and student make a detail item-by-

---

[8]Reproduced by permission. Copyright © 1953, 1965, The Psychological Corporation, New York, NY. All rights reserved.

item analysis of the responses. It would have been desirable if the test authors had presented more descriptive information on the development of this key.

In summary, the SSHA was well conceived. It is easy for the pupil to understand and complete the inventory. It is easy to administer and score. It stresses the motivational and attitudinal aspects of study more than any other study habits inventory.

Some other study habit and attitude toward school inventories are the Quality of School Life Scale, the Study Skills Test of the McGraw-Hill Basic Skills System, and some of the subtests of survey achievement batteries.

In conclusion, study habit inventories have a place in the classroom and can be administered, scored, and interpreted by the classroom teacher. Although the majority of them stress the process of locating information, the Survey of Study Habits and Attitudes stresses attitudes and motivational aspects. Study habit inventories, as with all self-report techniques, are dependent on the respondent's honesty—they are only surveys of self-report. The essential question, "Do the results of a study habit inventory in combination with previous GPA yield a higher cross-validated multiple R than do only previous GPA?" remains unanswered for most study habit inventories.

■ SUMMARY

The principal ideas, suggestions, and recommendations of this chapter are summarized in the following statements:

1. Classroom teachers need to know about their pupils' attitudes, values, interests, and personality. This not only will give them a better understanding of the pupils' behavior (both cognitive and noncognitive) but will also permit them to communicate with other professionals, such as the school diagnostician, psychologist, psychometrist, and psychiatrist.

2. With no formal training, the classroom teacher should be able to administer problem checklists, rating scales, observational schedules, and interest inventories. The classroom teacher can also interpret rating scales. Interest inventories, problem checklists, and personality tests should be interpreted to students only by specially trained personnel.

3. The major problems involved in measuring noncognitive characteristics are problems of (a) definition, (b) response set, (c) faking, (d) validity and reliability, and (e) interpretation.

4. Noncognitive assessment devices are not so psychometrically elegant as cognitive tests. Despite the limitation of noncognitive tools, they do provide useful information that cannot often be obtained by other means.

5. Three commonly used procedures for keying and constructing noncognitive inventories are empirical, homogeneous, and logical.

6. Attitudes and interests are both concerned with likes and dislikes. Whereas attitudes have groups and social situations as their referent objects, interests are related to activities.

7. Interest inventories were originally concerned with a person's vocation and were designed primarily for college-bound high school youth. Today's inventories measure avocational interests, can be used with junior high school students, and are not just "geared" to college-bound students.

8. Earlier interest inventories have focused on the subject's likes and dislikes. Today more attention is being paid to other traits—motivation and personality—as they relate to interests.

9. Although interest inventories differ in their content, their predictive validity, reliability, ease of scoring, and interpretation, they all share a common purpose of helping the user make better vocational and educational decisions. Despite the many similarities among interest inventories, there are nevertheless marked differences among them. The user must study the inventories carefully before adopting one.

10. Interests become more stable with age, but they are never permanently fixed. Thus, in-

terest-inventory results obtained in junior high school or for elementary school children should be interpreted with extreme caution.

11. Interest inventories are not designed to predict job success, academic success, job satisfaction, or personality adjustment. They are designed as a guide to the teacher or counselor in helping students make vocational and educational decisions based on the similarity of their interests with persons successful in a particular vocation or avocation.

12. Interest-inventory results can be helpful to the classroom teacher in terms of helping her develop teaching strategies that will be more relevant to her pupils' interests.

13. Much interest has been demonstrated in the study of career development and vocational maturity. Since 1968 at least six standardized tests related to these areas have been published and three large-scale career-development programs initiated. Some of the tests are concerned with the subject's value orientation, some with personality, and some with motivation.

14. Personality inventories can be classified as either structured or unstructured, as well as in terms of their method of construction.

15. Problem checklists are essentially structured self-report inventories that provide the user with information the subject feels is of concern or a cause of worry. Problem checklists have no right or wrong answers and are not intended to measure personality per se.

16. Personality inventories can assist in identifying those persons who are in need of assistance and may help in ascertaining where or what their problems are. Despite their shortcomings, if used judiciously and if proper rapport is established and maintained, these inventories do permit the user to obtain a more complete understanding of the subject. They also provide the subject an opportunity to express and discuss his feelings.

17. Computer versions of traditional pencil-and-paper personality tests yield equivalent information and are preferred by students.

18. Attitude scales are much less reliable and valid than are cognitive measures. They usually do not have norms. Although they can be administered by the classroom teacher, their interpretation may be complex. Like many other affective measures, they provide the user with a better understanding of the individual, provided the subject has been truthful. Tests of study habits and attitudes were briefly discussed.

■ POINTS TO PONDER

1. Approximately 50 percent of the variance in grades among individuals can be accounted for by aptitude and achievement tests. Using noncognitive tests in addition does not increase this percentage very much. How do you account for this?

2. Write definitions for the following terms: truthfulness, aggressiveness, rigidity, assistance, and deference. Compare your definitions with those of your classmates. Do your definitions differ? If so, does this mean you would interpret personality inventories measuring these traits differently?

3. Should response set be controlled in personality inventories? (You may wish to do a thorough review of the literature before discussing the question.)

4. How would you employ empirical keying for the Strong Vocational Interest Blank so that it might be used to differentiate the interests of "good credit risks" from those of "poor credit risks"?

5. What would be the problems in developing a predictive interest inventory for fifth-graders?

6. Consider the following interest inventories: Strong, Kuder OIS, Kuder GIS, and Career Assessment Inventory. Which one(s) would you recommend for each of the following uses? Give reasons for your choices.
   a. An inventory is needed for an eleventh-grade course exploring careers and occupational choices.

b. An inventory is required for use with eighth-grade students who desire careers that do not require a college degree.

c. An inventory to be used in a technical-vocational high school where none of the students go on to college.

d. An inventory that considers occupational choices as broad rather than specific areas.

7. Interest and general adjustment inventories have been found lacking in personnel selection uses. Why do you feel that they are of little value for this purpose?

8. If interests of adolescents are not too stable, can you in any way justify the use of interest inventories in junior or senior high school? Please explain.

9. The Kuder Scales are said to be ipsative. What significance does this have regarding their validity?

10. Is there a place for projective tests in (a) elementary school, (b) junior high school, and (c) senior high school? Defend your answer.

11. Rank the following types of standardized tests in terms of the necessity for frequent revision: achievement, aptitude, attitude, interest, problem checklists, projective, and self-adjustment inventories. Give reasons for your ranking.

12. What instructional use would you make of the results of a problem checklist?

13. As a new counselor, you find that your predecessor had been routinely administering a self-adjustment inventory as part of the school testing program. You are called to a school board meeting to explain the various tests used. Would you defend the use of the self-adjustment inventory? Why?

14. Recognizing the limitations of noncognitive instruments, what arguments can you present to support their use in the public schools?

15. Develop a 20-item scale to measure teachers' attitudes toward culturally deprived children. What type of reliability estimate should you gather? How would you validate such a scale?

Chapter 18

Assessing Exceptionality[1]

- ■ **Introduction**
- ■ **Equality of Education and the Handicapped**
- ■ **Assessing the Exceptional Child**
- ■ **Types of Special Education**
- ■ **Some Other Measures**
- ■ **The Gifted**
- ■ **Putting It All Together**

Frank, a fifth-grader, has a WISC-R IQ of 140 but has a percentile rank of 7 on the Gates-Mac-Ginitie Reading Test. Frank has had reading problems since he began school. He is also overly aggressive, constantly getting into arguments (and sometimes fisticuffs) both on and off the playground, is surly, not interested in language arts and reading but very interested in science and mathematics. Is Frank learning-disabled (LD)? The discrepancy between his IQ and reading test scores is so marked and so unusual that one must

consider the possibility that Frank is LD. But how does one validly determine whether Frank is LD? Although the authors cannot provide any cookbook diagnostic recipes, one suggestion they can make is that a variety of information must be gathered in order to obtain a comprehensive picture of Frank. Some of this information will be culled from IQ tests, some from adaptive behavior inventories, some from achievement tests, some from checklists, rating scales, and other observational tools, and so forth. And depending on the condition studied, perceptual and motor skills tests may also be used. Then, and only then, should the teacher hypothesize possible causal relations and take appropriate action.

A legitimate question that you might have raised two decades ago is "I'm not a special-education teacher, so why do I have to know anything

---

[1]Exceptionality is used in an all-inclusive sense. Although major emphasis is placed on ways to deal with children having deficiencies of one kind or another, we are aware that the gifted and talented also have special needs. Hence, the latter will also be considered in this chapter.

about tests in this area?" Such a question would not be asked today, because federal and state legislation has mandated that special-education students, where possible, be taught in the least restrictive environment, which is often the *regular* classroom (i.e., these students are *mainstreamed*). Even way back in the 1977–1978 school year, about 67 percent of handicapped children and about 37 percent of the mentally retarded received their primary educational services in regular classrooms. As we will see in later sections, early initial identification and assessment of exceptional children is often done by regular classroom teachers. Therefore, it is imperative that they be knowledgeable about and actively involved in educating and testing handicapped children. The preceding discussion should *not* be interpreted as implying that only classroom teachers need be cognizant of special-education students and issues. The counselor, school psychologist, and other educators also play a vital role, as will be seen later.

The purpose of this chapter is twofold: (1) to acquaint you with some of the legislation (Public Law 94-142 in particular) dealing with the assessment and education of handicapped children and (2) to introduce you to some of the standardized assessment tools that are used in the screening and diagnosis of exceptional children.

Although you need not become a legal scholar in order to understand federal regulations like PL 94-142 concerning the education of exceptional (e.g., handicapped) children, you should have minimal acquaintance with such legislation. Nor is it the intent of this chapter to make you a skilled clinician who is qualified to interpret some of the tests used. Rather, you should know something about the more commonly used tests so that you will be able to communicate effectively with other professionals and be able to use the test results to guide you in the development, delivery, and evaluation of an individual educational plan (IEP), which is mandated in PL 94-142.

Only within the last few decades has there been a concerted effort made to accommodate in our schools children who are handicapped because of physical, mental, or emotional deficiencies. In fact, until the early part of the twentieth century,

handicapped children were either hidden at home or were institutionalized. In any event, they were relegated to isolation, especially insofar as their educational needs were concerned.

Of the nearly nine million handicapped children in the United States today, less than one-half are receiving adequate educational services. This is indeed to be regretted in a country that has always prided itself on its educational system. Fortunately, however, with special programs and training given special-education teachers in teacher training institutions today, and because of legislation specifically aimed at improving the lot of the handicapped, the education received by these children is improving. However, in order for our special education programs to be effective, it is vital that the ordinary classroom teacher be trained to recognize and then work with handicapped children.

In this chapter, we are going to go beyond testing and will be concerned with assessment. Testing and assessment are *not* synonymous. Testing, as we have been using the term, may or may not be part of a larger process called assessment. Assessment is always an evaluative, interpretive appraisal of an individual's performance. Assessment, at least in the educational arena, is a multifaceted process that considers a variety of factors, such as current life circumstances and developmental history, when interpreting an individual's performance or behavior. Assessment considers the past as well as the present, utilizes systematic and nonsystematic observations, qualitative and quantitative data, and judgments.

After studying this chapter, you should be able to:

1. Recall the provisions of Public Law 94-142.
2. Understand the various categories of special education, as well as the various classifications within each category.
3. Discuss the various tests, scales, inventories, and other assessment tools used for special-education purposes.
4. Know what the ordinary classroom teacher should know about measurement of exceptional children in order to be able to deal effec-

tively with mainstreaming or at least be able to communicate with other professionals.

INTRODUCTION

It is assumed that you have had, or will have, a basic course in educational psychology. Accordingly, we have minimized our focus on the etiology of and classification of the various handicaps. Also, we are not concerned with the educational/instructional strategies that can be used with exceptional children (there are a variety of excellent texts dealing with this). What we are concerned with in this chapter is the screening/diagnosis and subsequent assessment of exceptional children.

Writers in the learning problems area generally agree that there are three assessment levels: (1) the *screening* or *survey* level, in which group tests play a significant role; (2) the *intermediate* level, where diagnostic tests focus on a specific skill or ability; and (3) the *case study* method, in which a detailed workup of the child is made. Some of the tests that are appropriate for the screening and intermediate levels have been considered in previous chapters and will be referred to here. Others will be discussed in more detail in the following sections.

Since the major national effort in dealing with the handicapped is an outgrowth of our concern with the equality of education for the handicapped and the resultant legislation and litigation, we will spend a few minutes discussing these areas.

EQUALITY OF EDUCATION AND THE HANDICAPPED

A movement toward equality of education for the handicapped came about through a series of landmark legal decisions that affirmed that all handicapped children, even the most severely debilitated, have the right to (1) an appropriate education, (2) due process of law, (3) nondiscriminatory testing and evaluation procedures, (4) a *free* public education, and (5) placement in the least restrictive environment. For the purpose of our discussion here, we are mainly concerned with the issue of nondiscriminatory testing and evaluation procedures, since that impinges on the role of the teacher, regardless of whether she is a regular or special-education teacher. We are also concerned in this chapter with placement insofar as it relates to using assessment results in making valid placement decisions. The other three issues, although of importance, are more relevant to the school administrator than to the classroom teacher.

Nondiscriminatory Testing and Evaluation

As previously discussed, standardized tests in general, and scholastic aptitude tests in particular, have been severely criticized and litigation has taken place in relation to the testing, identification, and placement of mentally retarded students. Two landmark California decisions were *Diana* v. *State Board of Education* (Civil Action No. C-70 37 R.F.P.N.D. Cal., Jan. 7, 1970, and June 18, 1973) and the oft-quoted *Larry P.* v. *Riles* (Civil Action No. 6-71-2270 343 F. Supp. 1036, N.D. Cal., 1972). The former case resulted in an agreement being reached whereby children were henceforth to be tested in their native language, and interpreters were to be used if bilingual examiners were not available. Also, California was directed to develop a standardized test that was valid for minority, nonwhite students. Finally, Chinese and Mexican-American children presently in classes for the educable mentally retarded were to be retested and reevaluated. In the *Larry P.* case, the judge ruled that traditional IQ tests discriminated against black students in diagnosing their mental handicaps. The judge further ruled that the San Francisco School District was *not* permitted to place black children in classes for the mentally retarded solely on the basis of IQ tests, if such placement resulted in a racial imbalance in these classes. A case similar to that of *Larry P.* was the one in Chicago (*PASE* v. *Hannon*, 1980) in which Judge Grady contradicted the decision made in the *Larry P.* case (see Chapter 22 for a fuller discussion of these cases).

Although the consequences of these legal decisions are not clear-cut, it would appear that, in California at least, factors other than a scholastic aptitude score have to be used for placing a student in a class for the mentally retarded or in some other special education program. In addition, individually administered intelligence tests have to be used; if the tests are verbal, they must be in the examinee's native language; any assessment has to include estimates of the child's adaptive behavior; the examiner has to be fluent in the examinee's native language; the tests used must be free from any racial or cultural bias; and no test that has some manipulative tasks can be used when testing the physically handicapped. The first two cases previously cited no doubt played a large part in the enactment of Public Law 94-142, with the attendant regulations that were printed in the *Federal Register* of August 23, 1977. (See Lidz, 1981, for a discussion of the educational implications of PL 94-142. For a full discussion of court rulings related to whether testing discriminates against minorities and the handicapped, see Bersoff, 1984.)

Public Law 94-142

Perhaps the most sweeping legislation since the Elementary and Secondary Education Act is Public Law 94-142, which became law in 1975. This law, also referred to as the Education for All Children Act, and the concept of **mainstreaming** has drawn all teachers—not only the special-education teachers—into the arena of evaluating and providing for the handicapped. Ordinary classroom teachers must now be, or quickly become, cognizant of and familiar with the various techniques available to identify the handicapped, the procedures available to monitor the progress of the handicapped, and the services available to help meet their educational needs.

The major provisions of PL 94-142 are as follows:

1. All handicapped children between the ages of 3 and 21 are entitled to free public education.
2. The early identification and intervention of handicapped children between the ages of 3 and 5 is encouraged by providing financial incentive grants to those that provide such children with special education.
3. A contract is drawn up so that an individually prescribed educational program is developed by a school official, the child's teacher and parents, and where possible, the child. This contract must identify the child's strengths and weaknesses, short- and long-term goals, and the services that will be used to reach those goals. Also, the contract is to indicate the amount of time the child is to spend in the regular classroom and the manner in which the child's progress is to be assessed and monitored.
4. All tests, scales, inventories, and assessment tools used to diagnose, classify, and place handicapped children must be free from racial and cultural bias. All testing is to be done in the child's native tongue.
5. Handicapped and nonhandicapped children will be taught together as long as possible. This is referred to as "mainstreaming." Handicapped children will be placed in special classes only when the type or severity of the handicap is such as to preclude them from obtaining maximally effective instruction in the regular classroom.
6. All handicapped children must be identified through preliminary screening instruments.
7. Each child is to be reevaluated regularly in the program.
8. The diagnostic assessment is to be done by a team composed of school psychologists, resource specialists, administrators, and *teachers*—with parent participation—utilizing a variety of techniques.

In order to comply with these mandates, achievement and aptitude tests must be administered to exceptional children. Most of the conventional, group-administered (and, sometimes, individually administered) aptitude and achievement tests previously discussed are invalid when dealing with many types of exceptional children. For example, can a blind child deal with the performance subtests of the WISC-R? Can a deaf child be given the verbal portion of the WISC-R or the Stanford-Binet? Would a child who is orthopedically handicapped be able to write his or her answers to any of our pencil-and-paper tests? The answer to these and similar questions is in the negative. Accordingly, special tests, or modifications of existing tests, must be used to assess the cognitive skills and abilities of many exceptional children. In the next sections, we will review some of the tests used to assess exceptional children.

PL 94-142 and the Regular Classroom Teacher Where do regular classroom teachers fit into the implementation of PL 94-142? What do they have to know about testing? According to the law, the regular classroom teacher has responsibilities in the following areas:

1. *Identification.* Is Gregory a slow learner, or is he learning-disabled? This differentiation is vital, since PL 94-142 covers the latter (and provides commensurate financial support for education) but not the former. In order to make this distinction, *both* aptitude and achievement data are needed.

2. *Individual Assessment.* The regular classroom teacher has the responsibility of gathering data about the child's competencies. This assessment will normally consider the mental, physical, language, psychomotor, adaptive, and sociological functioning of the child. Some of these data are obtained from informal classroom assessments, while other information is obtained from standardized tests. But which standardized tests? Should one use data obtained from a group or an individual test? Why? Which test(s) is (are) valid? We will answer these questions in later sections.

3. *Developing and Implementing an Individual Educational Plan.* The data gathered above determine, in large part, the child's educational objectives and the instructional strategies to be used. Generally, assessment of the degree of

accomplishment of these goals is made with informal, teacher-made tests.

In any of the activities noted above, standardized tests often play a significant role, especially in the identification, diagnosis, and learning assessment of exceptional children. Because regular classroom teachers play such an important role today in the education of the exceptional child, they must be cognizant of the measurement tools available and possess the measurement skills needed.

Before discussing the types of special education and some of the methods by which special education students can be diagnosed, we should spend a few minutes considering some of the problems involved when assessing children with special needs.

ASSESSING THE EXCEPTIONAL CHILD

Although there are problems inherent in the assessment of ordinary or "normal" children, there are even more problems when dealing with the exceptional child.[2] Fuchs et al. (1987) studied 27 norm-referenced aptitude and achievement tests and found that many of them failed to provide evidence regarding the validity of the test for handicapped students (see also Pechman, 1985; Sexton et al., 1988; Sexton, 1983.) First, most of the standardized aptitude and achievement tests have been normed using normal children, that is, the norms have been developed on the basis of performance of children who are not, for example, hyperactive, emotionally disturbed, gifted, or hard-of-hearing (Bennet, 1983; Sherman & Robinson, 1982). What is more disconcerting is the fact that there are few instances where test publishers have cautioned users regarding the validity of any interpretations, even though Standard 14.2 of the *Stan-*

---

[2]For a refreshing and unique way of looking at exceptional children from birth through old age, see Cleland and Swartz (1982).

dards (1985) suggests this be done. Hence, the norms of standardized tests when used with special-education students might not be appropriate and could raise unrealistic expectations. Second, observation is one of the most important tools that can be used to diagnose children with special needs. However, as pointed out in Chapter 9, the observational approach under ordinary circumstances (but possibly more so when used with special-education students) is fraught with many problems, particularly that of bias. Third, children with learning difficulties or behavior problems, especially the latter, may vary greatly in their behavior. Johnny may be hyperactive today and tomorrow but next week may be normal. Or Mary may be grossly uncoordinated on the playground today but behave differently tomorrow when a new game is played. Finally, remember that when dealing with the exceptional child, you are dealing with the extremes, be it of learning ability, personality, behavior, or physical coordination. This often results in measurement that is not as reliable as would be obtained if one were dealing with the average child. In dealing with the exceptional child, particularly with the learning disabled where we invariably have many scores, we must be cognizant of the unreliability of difference scores.

Another problem associated with the testing of the handicapped is the question of whether modifying the directions or the stimuli—such as using large type or Braille for the visually handicapped; oral procedures for the blind; nonverbal directions and tests for the deaf—affects the test's validity and causes differential item functioning between, for example, blind students taking a Braille edition and nonblind taking a regular edition (Bennett et al., 1989).

As of now, little empirical evidence is available to answer this question with any degree of certainty. The 1985 *Standards for Educational and Psychological Testing*, addressing the problems associated with using modified standardized tests for the handicapped, carefully points out that test publishers have a responsibility for issuing appropriate caveats in their manuals vis-à-vis test interpretation; that they should explain what modifications

have been made and how they might affect the test's validity when used with a handicapped population; that the modified test's validity and reliability are to be reported; and that special norms be available when interhandicapper comparisons are to be made. (See Laing & Farmer, 1984, for a discussion of the modifications made by the ACT Program for testing the handicapped.) We are gratified that some test publishers are addressing the problem of validating their tests for the handicapped (Bennett & Ragosta, 1985).

Despite the fact that many test publishers are negligent in their failure to issue appropriate cautions, they are only partly at fault. As we have reiterated throughout, final responsibility rests with the user. As Standard 6.3 states, "When a test is to be used for a purpose for which it has not been previously validated, or for which there is no supported claim for validity, the *user is responsible for providing evidence of validity*" (italics added) (AERA, APA, NCME, 1985, p. 42). Finally, the examiner effect, which may be operative when dealing with normal as well as handicapped persons, appears to be exacerbated when testing the handicapped. Fuchs et al. (1983, 1984, 1985a, 1985b, 1986) reported that for nonhandicapped students, there was no difference in their performance when tested with a familiar or unfamiliar examiner, but for speech and language-handicapped children, their performance was significantly higher when they knew the examiner. These researchers found a significant task complexity by response mode (gestural vs. verbal) interaction, suggesting that those tests requiring verbal responses may spuriously underestimate examinees' abilities, especially those of handicapped children. We should be aware of this, since many of our screening, diagnostic, and IQ tests, even for exceptional children, employ a verbal response mode.

There is also some concern regarding the performance of handicapped (especially the visually impaired) students on tests normed with non-handicapped students. Bennett and Ragosta's (1985) review of studies dealing with the performance of handicapped students on undergraduate admissions tests indicated that in general, students with visual and physical disabilities perform about equally with nonhandicapped students, but those with learning disabilities and hearing impairment score much lower. Regarding test validity, studies show little difference between nonhandicapped and handicapped students (Braun et al., 1986; Rock et al., 1985). Bennett et al.'s (1989) study showed that although there was very little differential performance on the SAT when item clusters were studied, there were some notable differences when the item level was considered, the most serious affecting visually impaired students taking the Braille edition. Somewhat related is the problem centering on the content validity of achievement tests designed for the normal population. How valid are these tests for handicapped children? If, say, a child is dyslexic, should we use a standardized reading test? If we are teaching reading to dyslexic children by some means other than the phonetic method, is it not somewhat ludicrous to measure the child's development in phonics for a child who will never use sounds in order to learn to read?

Strain, Sainto, and Mahan (1984) report research that suggests that current standardized tests (for reasons such as those mentioned above) may have limited value in assessing the ability and achievement of seriously handicapped persons. In fact, Gerber and Semmel (1984) contend that teachers' observations may yield more valid data than do our standardized tests. Does this mean that the seriously handicapped are untestable or that the situation is hopeless? Definitely not! It does suggest, however, that we will have to use different approaches.[3]

Ysseldyke and Thurlow (1984) contrast the norm-referenced approach (which relies almost exclusively on standardized assessment tools) and the continuous-monitoring approach (which relies heavily on more subjective data gathered from observations and parental input) for making decisions about the mildly handicapped and propose a modified norm-referenced approach that combines the two methods for making diagnoses and referral decisions.

Thus it is obvious that there are inherent problems in the assessment of exceptional children and adults. This, however, should not dissuade us in our attempts to study such individuals. Rather, it should spur professional test-makers to improve existing instrumentation and should force psychologists and educators to temper their conclusions based on test results.

Many research studies dealing with the assessment of exceptional children involve computing a correlation coefficient. Be careful! Correlation does *not* imply causation. Just because we know that children with learning disabilities often suffer from poor motor coordination, this does not mean that a pupil's dyslexia is caused by his poor motor coordination.

TYPES OF SPECIAL EDUCATION

There are different categories of students needing special education—such as the physically and visually handicapped, the speech impaired, the mentally retarded, the hard of hearing, the deaf, the gifted, the learning disabled, the emotionally disturbed, and any others needing special attention and assistance—which reflect different social, emotional, physical, and mental conditions among children. For that reason, we cannot refer to special-education students in an all-inclusive sense. Rather, we must carefully specify the type of special-education student with whom we are dealing.

In a few instances, the initial diagnosis and referral is made by a specialist rather than by the regular classroom teacher.[4] But in many, if not most, instances, the initial diagnosis and referral is

[3]Although we firmly believe that the classroom teacher, by virtue of daily contacts with students, is in the best position to make a preliminary screening and identification of the exceptional child, we agree with the courts that teacher observation, per se, is insufficient to identify learning-disabled children and should be supplemented with standardized test data (Frederick, 1977).

[4]A complete educational assessment program for the handicapped requires a team effort of classroom teacher, diagnostician, school psychologist, and medical personnel.

made by an observant teacher who notices that a pupil is not behaving normally. For example, Mary's eyes are always tearing, or Peter frequently cocks his head to the left, or Allan always appears to be tired. The tests used to diagnose children in need of special assistance can range from the highly sophisticated CAT scanner to the simple and familiar Snellen Eye Chart. Regardless of who makes the initial referral or diagnosis, the ordinary classroom teacher becomes an integral part of the treatment since she is responsible for the special-education student. The concept of "mainstreaming," which according to PL 94-142 requires that all handicapped and nonhandicapped children be educated together, places an added incentive for the regular classroom teacher to be aware of the different methods, tests, and instruments for assessing the special-education student.

The categories of special education to be considered in this chapter are as follows: *Mentally Retarded, Emotionally Disturbed, Sensory Handicapped* (visual, hearing, speech), *Physically Handicapped, Learning Disabled,* and *Gifted.* It should be noted that although we are discussing the various types of special-education students separately, it should *not* be implied that they are mutually exclusive. In fact, in many instances there is an interrelationship between one or more of the handicaps. For example, a mentally retarded child may also be emotionally disturbed.

Mentally Retarded

Four categories of mental retardation are commonly used: *slow learners, educable mentally retarded, trainable mentally retarded,* and *severely mentally retarded.* Pupils in the first three categories may be placed in special-education classes (but with present-day emphasis on mainstreaming, more and more of them are placed in regular classrooms), while the severely mentally retarded (IQ levels below 25) are generally institutionalized early in life and require constant attention.

It has been charged by critics that people have been classified as mentally retarded solely on the basis of an IQ score. In fact, it has been asserted that up until the 1970s, a standardized individual IQ test such as the Stanford-Binet or the Wechsler scales was the *sine qua non* for determining mental retardation. We deplore such action! Today, there is less rigid reliance on an IQ score than in the past and greater consideration to adaptive behavior, social and developmental history, and contemporary functioning in a variety of settings. This is evident from the latest American Association of Mental Deficiency (AAMD) definition that "mental retardation refers to significantly subaverage intellectual functioning existing concurrently with deficits in adaptive behavior and manifested during the developmental period" (Grossman, 1983, p. 11). The IQ score ranges used for the classifications are somewhat arbitrary and may vary from one school system to another. Some of the more commonly used individual intelligence tests for diagnosis and classification are the *Wechsler Intelligence Test for Children—Revised,* the *Bayley Scales of Infant Development,* and the *McCarthy Scales of Children's Abilities.* In some instances, an initial diagnosis is made by screening pupils with a group intelligence test such as the *Otis-Lennon* or *Differential Aptitudes Test.* (See various *Mental Measurements Yearbooks* for a discussion of these and other tests described in this chapter.)

Generally speaking, the slow learner and educable mentally retarded are not diagnosed before the child enters school. At that time, parents and teachers may begin noticing symptoms that will be confirmed by the child's performance on regular school tests and often by the child's behavior. In contrast, the trainable mentally retarded and definitely the severely mentally retarded are generally identified early in life. For example, hydrocephalics can be identified at birth and occasionally in the fetal stage. Children who are slow walkers or slow talkers, or generally late in their physical and mental development, can be readily identified before they enter school. Hence, the identification is made early in the child's life while at home or at birth or sometimes even before birth, with the final diagnosis being made by a specialist such as a neurologist or psychologist.

Assessment programs for the mentally retarded generally include (1) a measure of adaptive behavior in daily living situations such as the AAMD *Adaptive Behavior Scale*, the *Adaptive Behavior Inventory for Children*, *Watson's Behavior Modification Technology*, the *Vineland Adaptive Behavior Scales* (formerly the *Social Maturity Scale*), and *Balthazar's Scale of Adaptive Behavior*; (2) some measure of motor development, such as the *Bruininks-Oseretsky Test of Motor Proficiency*; and (3) some pluralistic assessment measure, such as *System of Multicultural Pluralistic Assessment* (SOMPA) (see p. 330), which includes the WISC-R (or WPPSI-R for younger children), in addition to standardized measures of the examinee's social competence in his or her environment and the examinee's physical condition (neurological and physiological); and (4) some developmental measure such as the *Bayley Scales* or the *Gesell Developmental Schedule*. (See Sexton et al., 1988, for a discussion of a promising instrument—the *Batelle Developmental Inventory*.)

Of the more than 100 adaptive behavior scales, three of the more commonly used are the *Vineland Adaptive Behavior Scale* (VABS), the *Adaptive Behavior Inventory for Children* (ABIC), and the *American Association for Mental Deficiency Adaptive Behavior Scale* (AAMD/ABS). We will now discuss the three in greater detail, paying particular attention to the Vineland.

Vineland Adaptive Behavior Scale (VABS)

Published by the American Guidance Service (1984), VABS is not only a revision but a total redevelopment of the perennial *Vineland Social Maturity Scale*. It has three forms. The Survey Form (297 items), which is most similar to the original Vineland Scale, and the Expanded Form (577 items, of which 297 are from the Survey) are designed to assess the adaptive behavior (defined by the authors as "the performance of the daily activities required for personal and social sufficiency") of persons from birth to 18 years, 11 months of age. The Classroom Form (244 items, some of which are found in the other forms) is for those students who range in age from 3 years to 12

years, 11 months. Responses are obtained by interviewing either the child's parent, primary guardian, or teacher about the child's *usual* abilities. In fact, one can collect data from each of these sources and interpret the child's behavior from each perspective.

The VABS is especially designed for the mentally retarded but can be used with other handicapped and nonhandicapped persons.

Adaptive behavior is assessed in the following four domains and subdomains:

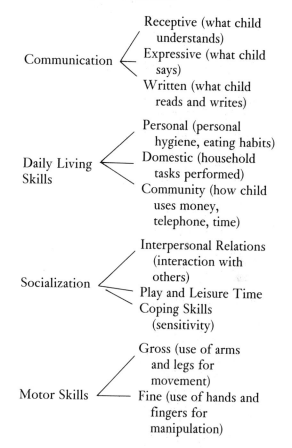

A total Adaptive Behavior Composite score is the combination of the four domains. A Maladaptive Behavior domain is included in *both* the Survey and Expanded Forms and consists of items that represent undesirable behavior.

The Survey Form is a semistructured interview of a parent or caregiver and *must* be administered by a trained interviewer. Whereas the Survey Form gives a general assessment of adaptive behavior, the Expanded Form provides for a more comprehensive assessment.

The Classroom Edition is independently completed by teachers and contains items related to basic academic functioning. However, interpretation should be done *only* by *trained clinicians*.

The Technical and Interpretive Manuals give good directions for administering, scoring, and interpreting the results and contain informative technical data. In addition, the manual and program planning report provide valuable suggestions for prescriptive educational treatment or habilitative programs.

The VABS was standardized on *stratified, representative,* national samples using 1980 census data. Supplementary norms developed with residential and nonresidential samples of emotionally disturbed, mentally retarded, visually impaired, emotionally disturbed, hearing-impaired, and hearing-handicapped children are available for the Survey and Expanded Forms. For each of the four major domain scores and total composite score, standard scores, national percentile ranks, stanines, and age equivalents are available, as is an *adaptive level* (high-, adequate-, or low-performance categorization). For the subdomains, adaptive levels and age equivalents are provided. A variety of other norms are provided in the Interpretive Manual.

Internal consistency, test–retest, and interrater reliability estimates for the Survey Form are quite respectable, ranging from the 0.70s to the 0.90s. Regretfully, they aren't as good for the Expanded Form and Classroom Edition. Validity studies are also reported.

Reports to parents are available for each form. They explain the child's derived scores in relation to his or her strengths and weaknesses. Space is also available for parental recommendations.

Six commendable features of the VABS are (1) an audiocassette that presents sample interviews; (2) substantial overlap between the standardization samples of the Survey and Expanded versions and the Classroom Edition, which allows for direct comparisons of scores; (3) substantial overlap between the standardization samples of the VABS and K-ABC; (4) a computer software program (ASSIST) that permits rapid score conversion and profiling as well as effective record keeping; (5) a Maladaptive Scale; and (6) the use of noninstitutionalized as well as institutionalized subjects for the standardization.

Adaptive Behavior Inventory for Children (ABIC) Published by The Psychological Corporation (1978), there is one form and 242 items. It is intended for ages 5 to 11. The ABIC is one of the three assessments models of SOMPA (see p. 330). Six areas of adaptive behavior are measured: Family, Peers, Community, School, Earner/Consumer, and Self-Maintenance. That is, the ABIC measures role behavior in the home, neighborhood, and community. Some of the items are as follows:

How does the child get along with the children in the neighborhood?

Does the child use a can or bottle opener?

The examiner interviews the principal guardian of the child (generally the mother). All respondents are asked the first 35 items.

The 207 items in Part II are grouped by age, and only those items appropriate for the child are asked. A 5-point scale is used. Provision is made for indicating inability to answer because of lack of knowledge. Raw and scaled scores are obtained for each of the six area scores, as is a total score.

Because the ABIC was standardized on a random sample of California children, the norms are of questionable worth, vis-à-vis generalizability to the nation's children. Split-half reliabilities for the scaled scores were computed for each age level and for each of three ethnic groups and are satisfactory.

Validity, according to Mercer (1979, p. 109), is "judged by its ability to reflect accurately the extent to which the child is meeting the expectations of the members of the social systems covered in the scales. . . ." Unfortunately, the examiner may find it difficult if not impossible to ascertain the community's expectations and therefore will be unable to ascertain validly whether the child has adapted effectively. In studying validity, various correlations were computed between the ABIC and various aptitude, achievement, and sociocultural scales. It is hoped that more empirical validity data will be forthcoming.

Adaptive Behavior Scale (ABS) The program is published by the American Association for Mental Deficiency (revised 1974). Although designed primarily for the mentally retarded, it can be used effectively with emotionally maladjusted and handicapped persons. There is one form, applicable from ages 3 to 69 years. It takes from 15 to 30 minutes to administer. Two types of competencies are assessed: *affective* and *behavioral*. Like the Vineland, the information needed is based on the observation of the examinee's everyday behavior and can be completed by anyone who has close contact with and knowledge about the examinee.

The ABS has 110 items grouped into two parts. Part I (66 items) is a developmental scale covering 10 behavioral domains concerning basic survival skills and habits deemed important to the maintenance of personal independence. For example, Independent Functioning is further categorized into eating, toilet use, care of clothing, and the like. Provision is made in scoring of questions dealing with activities the examinee has not had an opportunity to experience (e.g., eating in a restaurant). Part II (44 items) covers 14 behavior domains that focus primarily on maladaptive behavior related to personality and behavioral disorders, such as hyperactivity and withdrawal. In each of the 14 domains, a 1 is assigned to those behaviors (e.g., bites others) that occur occasionally, a 2 if occurrence is frequent.

The fact that the test was standardized on an institutionally based mentally retarded population limits the generalizability of the normative data and raises other psychometric questions. The manual does not provide any reliability data other than inter-rater reliabilities, which range from

0.71 to 0.98 for Part I and from 0.37 to 0.77 for Part II. Evidence suggests that most of the domains do not overlap. A paucity of data are furnished to demonstrate the scale's validity.

Clear administration and scoring instructions are given in the manual. In addition, the scale's authors caution the user in interpreting the scores. According to the authors, it is of paramount importance to interpret an examinee's scores relative to his or her ability to function in the environment.

The Public School Version (grades 2–6) is identical to the 1974 ABS except for the 15 items deleted to conform to public school settings. The only other marked departure from the ABS is that the rater uses a different scoring system.

Whereas Salvia and Ysseldyke (1978) are not too positive in their evaluation of either the ABS or the Public School Version, Speat (1980) is not overly critical, contending that the ABS provides valid estimates of group membership.

Other examples of adaptive behavior scales are *Watson's Behavior Modification Technology, Balthazar's Scale of Adaptive Behavior*, the *TMR Social Competency Tests*, and the *Cain-Levine Social Competency Scales*. The latter two are especially designed to assess the social competency of *trainable* mentally retarded persons.

Problems in Assessing Adaptive Behavior
It would appear that regardless of the scale used to measure adaptive behavior, there are two inherent problems: (1) the traditional adaptive behavior scales lean heavily on information gathered from "third parties," and this information may be either incorrect, biased, or both and (2) because many retarded persons have difficulty in communication, securing valid measures and information from them is very difficult, sometimes even impossible especially when other special conditions are found with the retardation.

Assessing the learning potential of the mentally retarded has been a challenging endeavor. For a variety of reasons, the contemporary scholastic aptitude measures are being replaced by *dynamic assessment* tools that are concerned with the measurement of learning and cognitive *processes* (see Feuerstein et al., 1979; Anastasi, 1988; and Switzky, 1981).

In summary, we can say that presently there are no standardized and well-normed tests of adaptive behavior covering infancy through adulthood. Unfortunately, many of the scales have been normed on an institutionalized and/or retarded population. It should be noted that there is no single, all-inclusive adaptive behavior scale that covers all areas of behavior—social, motor, and the like. Accordingly, users wishing to assess adaptive behavior must select the most valid scale. Care must also be exercised in ascertaining the relevancy of the standardization sample for a particular examinee. For example, one shouldn't use the ABS for noninstitutional examinees. Nor should the ABS even be considered if the examinee is not emotionally maladjusted or developmentally disabled.

Emotionally Disturbed

Another handicapped group worthy of special attention and consideration are those children who are classified as *emotionally disturbed*. There is disagreement as to both the definition of and the causes of emotional disturbance. Most children exhibit symptoms of emotional disturbance sometime in their lives. Have we all not fantasized or hit our head on the wall at one time? No doubt we have. But should children who on occasion exhibit such behavior be classified as emotionally disturbed? We believe not. We do believe, however, that it is necessary for the ordinary classroom teacher to be observant of what might be termed abnormal behavior. We do believe that teachers should be cognizant of the various stages of development and recognize that fighting, arguing, withdrawing, and bullying are *not* necessarily abnormal. We believe that only when such behaviors are the general pattern rather than the exception to the rule should we become concerned. In other words, the teacher's judgment is very important in the identification stage.

There are no special tests, inventories, or scales that classroom teachers can use to help in their identification of emotionally disturbed children. All we are able to say is that teachers must be observant and then, if they have any suspicions, should call in professionals.

Sensory Handicapped

Classified as *sensory handicapped* are children with vision, hearing, and speech defects.

One of the first things a teacher should do if she suspects that a pupil is experiencing either social or academic difficulty is to check the child's visual and hearing acuity. A child who has difficulty seeing or hearing or both will undoubtedly have difficulty in learning. If the student cannot see the board, he will not be able to read what is written on it and may answer a question written on the board incorrectly because he *misread* the question, not necessarily because he did not know the correct answer. And if there are many instances where the student gives an incorrect answer because of a hearing or sight problem, the student may be labeled as stupid or a smart aleck.

Visually Handicapped There are *two* categories of visually handicapped—*partially sighted* and *blind*—depending on the degree of vision expressed in terms of how well the person is able to read letters from 20 feet that a normal person can read from 20 feet. For example, a person with 20/40 vision is able to read letters at 20 feet that a normal person is able to read at 40 feet. A very simple screening test is the familiar Snellen Wall Chart.

There are three ways in which vision may be limited: (1) color vision problems, (2) field of vision (tunnel vision) limitations, and (3) visual acuity weakness. Although there are a variety of tests and instruments available for diagnostic screening for visual problems—such as the *Snellen Wall Chart*, the *Massachusetts Vision Test*, the *Fitneus Vision Tester*, the *Dvorine Pseudo-Isochromatic Plates*, and the *Ishahara Color Blind Test*—the observant teacher once again is the initial screener. Children complaining of frequent dizzy spells, with red or watery eyes, sloppy unaligned written work, tilted heads or squinting when reading, and letter reversals in reading may be suffering from vision problems.[5] An alert teacher generally is able to see the problem(s) and request additional testing by a specialist.

It should be evident that performance tests and tests that require extensive reading, such as paragraph comprehension, are *not* appropriate for assessing the aptitude or achievement level of blind examinees (although the material could be read to the examinees, they would need a phenomenal memory, especially for multiple-choice items). The most suitable procedures for testing the blind are oral examinations, although adaptations of existing tests can be used (the Binet and Wechsler have Braille editions; the SAT, the SCAT, and portions of the GRE have large-type editions). An aptitude test specifically designed for the blind is the Blind Learning Aptitude Test (BLAT). The BLAT, a tactile test, uses a bas-relief format and is designed for children between 6 and 12 years of age. Two scores are obtained: a learning-aptitude test age and a learning-aptitude test quotient. BLAT was standardized on blind children in residential and day schools. The internal consistency and test–retest reliability reported compares favorably with other special population tests. Regrettably, the validity data are woefully inadequate.

Another type of visual impairment deals with visual perception, such as eye-hand coordination, visual attention to detail, and discrimination of shapes and colors. The WISC-R in its picture completion, block design, coding, and object-assembly subtests and the *Illinois Test of Perceptual Abilities'* visual memory, visual association, visual reception, and visual closure subtests measure certain facets of visual perception. However, there are two commercially published tests that were specifically developed to assess visual-perceptual skills—the *Bender-Visual Motor Gestalt Test* and

the *Frostig Developmental Test of Visual Perception*. Although Bender and Frostig approached their tasks from different theoretical orientations, both were concerned with measuring skills deemed to be important in reading so that remediation of the defects would result in improved reading ability. Regretfully, the empirical evidence shows very little improvement in reading skill as a result of remediation in the weakness(es) shown by the tests.

Some other visual-perception tests are the *Primary Visual Motor Test*, the *Revised Visual Retention Test*, and the *Illinois Test of Psycholinguistic Abilities*.

Hearing Handicapped   There are two categories of hearing handicapped children—*hard of hearing* and *deaf* (children with a hearing loss so severe that language development does *not* occur during the prelingual period). There are some who advocate classifying deafness into two categories, depending upon when the hearing loss occurred. Furthermore, degree deafness is dependent upon frequency and intensity of sound.

Because many learning problems have as their genesis some form of auditory weakness, the early detection of hearing problems is imperative so that appropriate remediation can be initiated. Just think for a moment of what transpires in the classroom. Ms. Krone asks a question, and Charles is expected to answer the question. But regardless of how bright Charles might be, he may either not answer the question or may answer it incorrectly because he did not hear the question. Consider Mary, who appears to be very aloof, is not accepted by her peers, is a loner, and eventually becomes a behavior problem. It is quite conceivable that Mary's behavior is not the result of some personality quirk but rather the manifestation of a hearing problem. Similarly, children experiencing difficulty with speech, language, and reading and those often performing below their academic potential may well be suffering from some form of hearing problem.

Although the teacher who suspects that a child has a hearing problem might use some of the sub-

---

[5]See *Helping the Partially Sighted Child in the Classroom* (Publication T-300, National Society for the Prevention of Blindness, New York, 1965) for a list of ten behavioral signs that may be indicative of a visual problem.

tests of the WISC-R or the *Illinois Test of Psycho-linguistic Abilities*, she would better use the *Goldman-Fristoe-Woodcock Auditory Test Battery* or the *Wepman Auditory Discrimination Test*, which are specifically designed to measure auditory perception. The former consists of four major tests. The latter is very simple—the examiner says two words, and the examinee indicates whether the sounds are the same or different. Preliminary research is encouraging with respect to the Auditory Test Battery. Some other auditory perception measures are the *Auditory Memory Span Test*, the *Auditory Sequential Memory Test*, the *Flowers Test of Selective Attention* (Experimental edition), and the *Kansas State University Speech Discrimination Test*. Some of the tests can be administered by the ordinary classroom teacher. Others require a clinician. We believe that the teacher who suspects the child has a hearing problem should refer the child to a specialist for actual diagnosis and treatment.

A problem in testing the deaf is that they are generally handicapped when taking verbal exams because their language development has been negatively affected. Early performance tests such as the *Pintner-Paterson* and the *Arthur Performance Scale* were especially developed to test the deaf. Although the Wechsler Scales have been adapted for testing the deaf, the use of the norms and the tests' psychometric properties may be suspect because they have been standardized on examinees with normal hearing. To circumvent this problem, some instruments, like the *Hiskey-Nebraska Test of Learning Aptitude* (HNTLA), were developed for and standardized on the hard of hearing.

The HNTLA is an individually administered intelligence test designed for deaf and hard-of-hearing children ranging in age from 3 to 16 years. The test is administered in pantomime. Practice exercises are available. The HNTLA has 12 performance subtests. There are separate norms for the deaf and for the hard of hearing. The split-half reliabilities are in the 0.90s. Again, as with most of the tests designed for special populations, the validity evidence is sparse. Because of limited technical data, the test scores must be judiciously interpreted.

Again what is important is *not* the definition of, or the causal factors associated with, a hearing handicap. Rather, of vital importance is what, if anything, teachers can do or use to initially identify and diagnose children with hearing problems. (The final determination and treatment is left to the specialist.) Most children with mild hearing defects go undetected in classrooms because they are able to talk. But many children who are inattentive, are low achievers, or have poor listening skills may have a hearing problem rather than an emotional problem or low intelligence.

Speech Handicapped Speech is fundamental to the communication process. There are many instances where a speech defect manifests itself due to some other form of handicap. For example, a child may have a speech defect because of deficient hearing. Some speech disorders are readily observable, such as cleft palate or stuttering. Others, such as a slight huskiness, may be ignored because they are so mild. Regardless of the severity of the disorder, it is the teacher's observational skills that play a vital role. Only after an initial screening—for which no test, per se, exists—is the child referred to a specialist for further testing and diagnosis. Some of the more commonly used articulation tests are the *Templin-Darley Test of Articulation* and the *Goldman Fristoe Test of Articulation*, both of which should be administered *only* by a specialist.

Physically Handicapped

Although speech, vision, and hearing defects could conceivably be classified as types of physical handicap and have a neurological or orthopedic basis, we have purposely treated them as sensory handicaps. Accordingly, we restrict our consideration of the physically handicapped to those whose defects are *not* sensory. Also, we have selected for discussion (from the myriad of physical handicaps) the two that teachers generally will encounter: *epilepsy* and the *orthopedically handicapped*.

Epilepsy Epilepsy is characterized by the victim having a seizure. These seizures can be severe (grand mal) or of a less serious nature (petit mal). Although the seizures per se are due to electrochemical disturbances in the brain, there is the belief that the causes of epilepsy may be rooted in a variety of neurological disorders. Once again, the ordinary classroom teacher is dependent upon her skill of observation and her knowledge of some of the symptoms associated with an epileptic seizure. The final diagnosis and treatment is best left to professionals.

Orthopedically Handicapped The orthopedically handicapped, especially the severely cerebral palsied,[6] pose the greatest assessment problems.

These students generally have problems working with performance tests, since their motor coordination is severely affected; the tension that they may be working under makes the validity of their test scores suspect; and if they suffer from severe speech defects, both verbal and oral testing is nearly impossible. In addition to these problems, the examinees' susceptibility to rapid fatigue makes it imperative to have many brief testing sessions.

Most of the assessment devices developed for the orthopedically handicapped are adaptations of tests such as the *Stanford-Binet*, the *Porteous Mazes*, and the *Leiter International Performance Scale*, all of which were originally designed for testing normal people. Unfortunately, validity data for special populations are lacking.

However, tests have been developed that require the examinees only to point, to nod their heads when the correct response is read, and so on. For this reason, pictorial scales like the *Peabody Picture Vocabulary Test* and the *Columbia Mental Maturity Scale* have been found to be use-

ful and valid tests for the orthopedically handicapped (see Dunn & Dunn, 1981).

Some other types of physical disability are *cystic fibrosis, muscular dystrophy, diabetes*, and *congenital heart problems*. Unless the disability is somewhat severe, most children manifesting these illnesses are able to function well in the ordinary classroom. Granted, there may be some types of activities, such as strenuous sports or running, where such children should not be required or expected to participate as do the other class members, but these are generally exceptions to the rule.

Learning Disabled

There are many children who have no sensory or physical handicap and who are of average intelligence but have difficulty in learning one or more basic skills, generally *reading*. Such children are categorized as *learning disabled (LD)*, and they are recognized by virtue of the fact that there is a discrepancy[7] between their academic achievement and their aptitude potential, as measured by an achievement and aptitude test, respectively. In addition, LD children often have disturbances of language development, may be overly aggressive, have poor motor coordination, be hyperactive, and the like (Anastasi, 1988). As with the other categories of special education, the definition of learning disability is fraught with controversy. Some definitions specifically exclude children whose learning problem(s) may be due to mental retardation or a hearing, motor, or visual handicap. Some definitions consider sociological factors. We subscribe to the definition given by Kirk and Bateman because it offers suggestions for remediation. Their definition is as follows:

> A learning disability refers to a retardation, disorder, or delayed development in one or more of the processes of speech, language, reading, writing, arithmetic, or other school subjects resulting from a psychological handicap caused by possible cerebral

---

[6]We recognize that cerebral palsy is a neurological disorder. However, since it is restricted to disturbances of the voluntary motor system and manifests itself in uncoordinated muscular behavior, we refer to it as a type of orthopedic handicap.

---

[7]A major problem here centers on the method of computing this discrepancy (see Berk, 1984).

disfunction and/or emotional or behavioral disturbances. It is not the result of mental retardation, sensory deprivation, or cultural or instructional factors (1962, p. 263).

If one subscribes to the definition that excludes mental retardation, severe emotional disturbances, cultural or educational deprivation, and sensory loss or weakness, it should be evident that the common diagnostic instruments available will *not* readily identify the child with a learning disability.

We would be remiss if we did not at least mention that some critical measurement issues are involved in the assessment of learning disability. In addition to the definition of a "severe discrepancy between aptitude and achievement" mentioned above, there is the problem of the validity of the tests used to screen and diagnose LD persons. As of now, many of the instruments used for exceptional children are woefully inadequate with respect to their validity and reliability.

Once again, we are very dependent on the observant classroom teacher. Although parents would normally be expected to notice whether or not their child had poor motor coordination, was restless, and had a poor memory, this is seldom the case. The observant teacher, especially the kindergarten or first-grade teacher, is usually the first person to recognize the symptoms of learning disability. And if these teachers do not, surely the second- and third-grade teachers should notice children who, although of average or above-average intelligence, are having difficulty with their schoolwork and do not seem to be working up to their potential.

Generally, the assessment of children with learning disabilities is a team effort and involves a variety of tests, inventories, and other instruments. The classroom teacher will normally administer a group test, such as the *Jastak Wide Range Achievement Test* or the *Kaufman Test of Educational Achievement*, for screening purposes. She may also administer the *Slingerland Screening Test for Identifying Children with Specific Language Disability*. She will also provide the team with data gathered from the child's cumulative folder, which, if properly kept, will contain anecdotal-

type information, previous reports by other psychologists and teachers, health records, academic records, and the like. At this point, various specialists will come into play. A psychologist may then be called upon to administer and interpret an individual scholastic aptitude test to assess the child's academic potential. It may be a verbal test such as the *Stanford-Binet*, the *WISC-R*, the *WPPSI-R*, or the *McCarthy Scales of Children's Abilities* or a nonverbal test such as the *United States Employment Services Nonreading Aptitude Test* or the *Goodenough-Harris Drawing Test*. Tests such as the *WISC-R*, and *WPPSI-R*, and the *McCarthy Scales* not only provide a global index of aptitude to help one differentiate between learning disabilities and mental retardation but the subtests also provide valuable information about specific deficiencies such as memory span and visual perception.

To obtain measures of a child's academic performance, we may use teacher-made tests or standardized achievement batteries such as the *SESAT*, *CIRCUS*, the primary levels of the *Stanford Achievement Test*, or some of the tests discussed earlier. To assist the teacher in diagnosing pupil strengths and weaknesses, there are a variety of readiness and diagnostic tests available that, on close examination, show that their items closely resemble specially designed tests of learning disability such as the *Frostig Development Test of Visual Perception*, the *Visual Retention Test* (Revised), and the *Auditory Discrimination Test*.

Up to this point, our discussion of the various tests available for assessing a child's intellectual capacity has been of those that are used routinely. These, however, may be inappropriate for testing people who, for one reason or another, have difficulty responding to traditional tests. To accomplish this, three approaches have been used: (1) Adapting existing test procedures (e.g., using the large-type or Braille edition of the SCAT or not timing a timed test; unfortunately, such procedures invalidate the use of existing norms). (2) Using tests to which a handicapped person can respond (e.g., a deaf examinee can answer items on the Peabody because it uses pictures; but once again we have a problem analogous to the one before in that the test has been standardized on non-handicapped subjects). (3) Using specially designated tests. Some examples of such tests are:

a. *The Arthur Adaptation of the Leiter International Performance Scale.* Useful for deaf and speech-impaired subjects or any others who have difficulty responding verbally. Psychometric data are woefully lacking.

b. *The Pictorial Test of Intelligence.* Can be used for both normal and handicapped children. Especially suited for orthopedically handicapped children. Requires no verbal stimuli or response. Also good for children who have speech or language problems.

c. *The Columbia Mental Maturity Scale.* Originally designed for cerebral-palsied children. May be used with children who have difficulty responding verbally. The examinee makes visual-perceptual discriminations. Technically adequate. Must be interpreted cautiously since it measures only two kinds of intellectual behavior—classification and discrimination.

d. *The Illinois Test of Psycholinguistic Abilities.* Individually administered. Suitable for children 2 to 10 years of age. Uses a *channels* (auditory-vocal and visual motor) $\times$ *processes* (receptive, organizing, and expressive) $\times$ *levels* (representational and automatic) model. Heavy middle-class cultural orientation, which raises questions about validity for low SES minority children. No technical data are given.

We have purposely focused, at least in the tests of learning ability (aptitude/IQ), on individually administered tests for the following reason: Individually administered tests provide an experienced and insightful examiner with a wealth of clinical information beyond the examinee's performance or problem solving—that not only have an impact on the examinee's performance but that should be considered in the test interpretation. Some of the more commonly used individual aptitude tests are the *Wechsler Scales* (WISC-R, WAIS-R, WPPSI-R), the *Stanford-Binet-4* (SB-4), the *McCarthy Scales of Children's Abilities*, the *Slosson Intelligence Test*, and the *Peabody Picture Vocabulary Test, Re-*

vised Edition (PPVT-R). There are two other instruments that differ markedly from these. One, the *Cognitive Skills Assessment Battery* (CSAB), is criterion-referenced, whereas the others are norm-referenced. The other is the *System of Multicultural Pluralistic Assessment* (SOMPA), which bases the interpretation of the examinees' performance in the light of their cultural background.

In addition to the aptitude and achievement-test data gathered, the battery of tests used includes measures of short-term memory and perception as measured by *Benton Visual Retention Test* and *Bender-Gestalt Test,* respectively, measures of aphasia, and measures of language facility. All the data would then be collated to assist in diagnosing the nature of the learning disability. An attempt is then made to establish the causal nature of the learning disability. For example, if it is suspected that the disability is the result of a cerebral dysfunction, the child would undoubtedly be referred to a neurologist who might conceivably administer an electroencephalograph test (EEG). Or we would have to ascertain whether the problem is the result of an emotional disturbance, a behavioral disturbance, or a combination of these and other factors. Although some valuable data can be provided by the regular classroom teacher by means of careful, systematic observation, it should be readily obvious that the diagnosis and remediation of learning disability is best left to the professional clinician.

In closing, we are happy to report that new tests have been developed especially for children with learning disabilities. Those interested are referred to the *Mental Measurements Yearbooks* as well as test publisher catalogues.

We concur with Anastasi, who says

> these tests should be regarded not as psychometric instruments but as observational aids for the clinical psychologist and learning specialist (1988, p. 501).

SOME OTHER MEASURES

In addition to the individual aptitude and achievement tests discussed in Chapters 15 and 16 and the adaptive, visual, and perceptual acuity tests discussed earlier in this chapter, there are instances, especially when one is dealing with the screening/diagnosis of handicapped children, where it is desirable to obtain a measure of the child's language ability, listening ability, language performance, and psychomotor development. Although these latter measures are especially useful when dealing with the learning disabled, they are not restricted to this special population. Hence, we discuss them here rather than in the LD section.

Language Tests

In addition to the language subtests of the major survey achievement batteries, we have specific language tests such as the *Goldman-Fristoe Test of Articulation*, the *Peabody Picture Vocabulary Test, Revised Edition*, and the *Illinois Test of Psycholinguistic Abilities* which are individually administered and use either a picture stimulus completely or one as part of a total stimulus mode. Of the three, the validity and norms of the *Illinois Test of Psycholinguistic Abilities* are questionable (Salvia & Ysseldyke, 1988) and should *not* be used to select the learning disabled for remedial programs.

Listening Tests

Compared with the number of reading readiness, reading, and reading diagnostic tests available to evaluate the child's reading potential, performance, or weaknesses, there are relatively few listening skills tests. Whether this is the result of the absence of a clear definition, the problem of delineating those skills involved in listening, the difficulty in measurement, or a combination of these and other factors is a matter of conjecture. Some examples of listening tests (in addition to the general listening comprehension subtests of the *Durrell Analysis of Reading Difficulties* and the *Sequential Tests of Educational Progress II*) are the *Brown-Carlsen Listening Comprehension Test* and the *Assessment of Children's Language Comprehension*.

Assessment of Oral Language Performance

Many tests are available to measure and subsequently diagnose oral language performance. Most of the tests require the subject to respond to a stimulus (either verbal or pictorial) with a word or sentence. Some of the tests, like the Oral Vocabulary subtest of the *Gates-McKillop Reading Diagnostic Test*, use a multiple-choice and sentence-completion format. Others, like the Auditory Association subtest of the ITPA, use verbal analogies such as, "I cut with a saw, I pound with a _____." Some of the more commonly used oral language tests are the *Goldman-Fristoe Test of Articulation*, the *Auditory Discrimination Test*, and the *Denver Developmental Schedule*. Many of them are individually administered. Regrettably, the psychometric properties of most of these tests, with the possible exception of survey subtests, leave much to be desired (Sattler, 1982; Salvia & Ysseldyke, 1988).

Cutting across the various types of handicaps are those that result from some form of motor disability. We will now spend a few minutes on this topic.

Motor Development Measures

Increasingly greater attention is being paid to motor development. Whether the impetus came from Piaget's work, which emphasizes the role of sensorimotor skills in human development, or from research findings, which have shown that there is an interaction between motor development and both cognitive and affective development, is unclear at this time. In fact, if one thinks about the Stanford-Binet, the Wechsler Scales, or the McCarthy Scales, it is evident that these authors believed motor development played an important role in school readiness and intellectual development.

Once again, we are plagued with the recurring dilemma of definition or skill analysis. What do we mean by motor development? Are we talking about large or small muscle control? Are we talking about coordination, and if so, what kind of co-ordination? One of the few measures specifically designed to assess motor development is the *Bruininks-Oseretsky Test of Motor Proficiency*.

Bruininks-Oseretsky Test of Motor Proficiency   Published by the American Guidance Services (1978), it was originally issued by Oseretsky in 1923 in Russia and adapted and translated by Doll in 1946. It contains eight separate motor proficiency tests—Running Speed and Agility (1 item), Balance (8), Bilateral Coordination (8), Strength (3), Upper Limb Coordination (9), Response Speed (to a moving visual stimulus) (1), Visual Motor Control (8), and Upper Limb Speed and Dexterity (8)—which are measured with 46 items. It is designed to measure gross and fine motor functioning of children from $4\frac{1}{2}$ to $14\frac{1}{2}$ years of age and has one form. It is individually administered and takes from 45 to 60 minutes. There is a 14-item Short Form that takes from 15 to 20 minutes and yields a single index of general motor proficiency. Three scores—a Gross Motor Skills Composite (dealing with large muscles), a Fine Motor Skills Composite, and a Total Battery Score—are produced.

A stratified sample of 765 children was used as the standardization sample. For each of the three composite scores, scores can be expressed as standard scores, percentile ranks, or stanines. Age equivalents are available for each of the eight subtests. Test–retest reliabilities range from 0.86 to 0.89 for the Battery Composite and from 0.68 to 0.88 for the Fine and Gross Motor Composites. The Gross Motor Composite has somewhat higher reliabilities than the Fine Motor Composite. Standard errors of measurement range from 4.0 to 4.7. The individual subtest reliabilities are so low that the practitioner is cautioned in using them for clinical interpretation. Factor analysis and a comparison of normal with learning-disabled children were used to support the claim to validity.

Some other sensorimotor tests are the *Bender-Purdue Reflex Test*, the *Southern California Sensory Integration Tests*, and the *Motor Problems Inven-tory*. Some examples of psychomotor tests, although not motor development measures per se, are the *Stromberg Dexterity Test* and the *Crawford Small Parts Dexterity Test*. Those wishing more information about these and other tests should consult the various *Mental Measurements Yearbooks*.

Some other measures designed especially to assess the aptitude of exceptional children are as follows:

1. *The Arthur Adaptation of the Leiter International Performance Scale.* Useful for deaf and speech-impaired subjects or any others who have difficulty responding verbally. Psychometric data are woefully lacking.
2. *The Pictorial Test of Intelligence.* Can be used for both normal and handicapped children. Especially suited for orthopedically handicapped children. Requires no verbal stimuli or response. Also good for children who have speech or language problems.
3. *The Columbia Mental Maturity Scale.* Originally designed for cerebral palsied children. May be used with children who have difficulty verbally. The examinee makes visual-perceptual discriminations. Technically adequate. Must be interpreted cautiously since it measures only two kinds of intellectual behavior—classification and discrimination.

THE GIFTED

The continuum of exceptionality, or of children with special needs, can range from those who are mentally retarded and handicapped to those who are gifted with intellectual superiority. Both groups of children have special needs that must be considered by the regular classroom teacher, although treatments for the two groups differ markedly. An individually administered scholastic aptitude test is generally used to help identify the gifted. Whereas teacher observations play a vital, if not the most significant, role in identifying the mentally retarded or handicapped child, teachers do not do too well in identifying the gifted. In fact, there are some instances where the very creative child is branded as a nuisance or troublemaker because he may be bored in class.

Noppe (1980) classifies instruments for assessing creativity as follows: (1) projective tests such as the Rorschach, (2) personality scales such as the California Psychological Inventory, (3) self-report methods, (4) reports of others, (5) cognitive tests such as Torrance's Tests of Creativity, and (6) miscellaneous instruments.

As of now, there are no standardized tests of creativity that possess adequate reliability and validity to bear recommendation. There are, however, a number of experimental or research creativity tests on the market. Some of the more popular ones are *Torrance's Tests of Creative Thinking*, the *Mednick's Remote Associates Test*, the *Thinking Creatively with Sounds and Words* (research edition), and the *Make a Tree* (part of the CIRCUS test battery). In addition, a type of higher-order thinking skills (HOTS) score can be obtained by the user or the publisher generating a HOTS score from some of our more popular standardized achievement-test batteries such as the CAT, ITBS, the Metropolitan, the Stanford, and the SRA Achievement Tests.

PUTTING IT ALL TOGETHER

The most exotic spices, the finest milled wheat, the purest of ingredients, and the most advanced electronic oven will by themselves or even collectively *not* result in a cake that would win first prize or even place in a bake-off. What is important is the skill of the baker in blending everything. In the same way, the ultimate value that will accrue to those dealing with children with special needs, and hence to the children themselves, will be the manner in which all the data are collected, collated, and interpreted. At best, we should only expect our data, regardless of the manner in which they were collected, to provide teachers with the information with which to generate hypotheses.

These hypotheses can be the framework of an individualized educational plan.[8]

A Case Study: Allan

Allan is a third-grader. He is the only child from a working, lower-middle-class family. His mother and father both work, and Allan stays by himself for about two hours after returning from school. Allan's mother had a normal pregnancy and delivery. Allan's medical history indicates no unusual illnesses other than such childhood diseases as mumps and chickenpox. Other than a single case of an overdose of medication as an infant, there is nothing in Allan's medical record to be a cause for alarm. Allan is very passive in the classroom and makes little effort to enter into class discussions. This is markedly different from his behavior on the playground where Allan has a tendency to throw temper tantrums when he becomes frustrated. Allan does not seem to be interested in school, especially when reading instruction is given. Allan performs quite well in the quantitative areas such as science and mathematics. When asked a question, Allan invariably asks that it be repeated. Allan complains of frequent headaches and dizzy spells. He always appears to favor his right side.

A series of questions and, hopefully, hypotheses should be generated by the teacher. Some of these are as follows:

1. Is Allan's behavior in class and on the playground so diametrically opposed that it is indicative of abnormal behavior?
2. Is Allan basically a shy, reserved child who is introverted by nature but is seeking approval?
3. Is Allan's learning problem the result of some learning disability(ies) or physical handicap such as being hard of hearing?
4. Is Allan's lack of interest in reading a manifes-

---

[8] Two excellent sources of case histories are Mahan and Mahan (1981) and Salvia and Ysseldyke (1988).

tation of some problem(s) or weakness in reading, or is it just a lack of interest in the subject?

5. Is the fact that Allan is an only child and alone much of the time a plausible explanation for some of his problems?

6. Does Allan need remedial work in reading, and, if so, what are his verbal strengths and weaknesses? Will any remediation result in Allan becoming a better reader, for example, as shown by a higher reading test score?

7. Is Allan's performance in the quantitative areas sufficiently better than his performance in the verbal areas?

In order to obtain answers to these and other questions, a cooperative effort would have to be made by the classroom teacher, the school psychologist, and other professionals. As a starter, the teacher could administer (or have administered) a battery of tests to Allan. In addition, she could observe Allan's behavior more closely in an attempt to obtain certain kinds of information. She might even request a meeting with Allan's parents to learn more about Allan's home environment and his behavior out of school. Some of the tests that might be given Allan are as follows:

1. The WISC-R, so that both a verbal and a performance IQ score could be obtained. This will permit the teacher to obtain a measure of performance on a variety of tasks as well as obtain some global picture by means of the Kaufman (1979) factor scores (verbal comprehension, perceptual organization, and freedom from distractibility).

2. The Children's Personality Questionnaire could be used to provide information on 14 factors, such as Allan's anxiety, assertiveness, and shyness. This information could then be used to supplement that already gathered by interviews and observations.

3. The Peabody Picture Vocabulary Test could be used to check the teacher's hypothesis that Allan is weak in verbal skills. This could also be confirmed by the WISC-R and Kaufman

factor scores. If any weakness is found, diagnostic tests such as the Stanford Diagnostic Test or the Diagnostic Reading Scales could be used to identify particular strengths and weaknesses.

4. An audiometry test could be given Allan to see whether he suffers from any hearing loss.

5. The Stanford Achievement Test, which provides scores in spelling, reading, and arithmetic, and the Woodcock Reading Mastery Tests could be used to confirm the teacher's suspicion that Allan has difficulty with verbal-type materials and hence may be uninterested in language activities because he is a poor reader.

These are only some of the tests and inventories and tools that can be used when making a diagnosis. As stated earlier, it was not our intent to make you an expert in either testing or teaching children with special needs, Rather, it was to provide you with the information needed to be a more effective teacher because you understand your pupils better and to enable you to interact with other professionals such as the school psychologist and the teacher of learning-disabled children. The latter is even more important today because of our emphasis on mainstreaming.

The major functions of assessment tools and techniques as related to children with special needs is *not* to give hard-and-fast answers or to dispense prescriptions and treatments to cure the malady of pupils such as Allan. Rather, it is to provide you with sufficient information about tests so that you will be able to generate plausible, testable hypotheses when dealing with children with special needs.

In conclusion, we would like to reiterate that meeting the needs of special-education students— ranging from the handicapped to the gifted—is a matter of concern for every teacher and *not* just the specialist. We are very cognizant that the ordinary classroom teacher is *not* trained to administer many of the tests used to diagnose special needs. Nevertheless, the ordinary classroom teacher must know how to assess exceptionality as well as how to deal with such students in her classroom.

■ SUMMARY

The principal ideas, conclusions, and implications of this chapter are summarized in the following statements:

1. Assessment is a more inclusive term than testing or measurement and involves observations, data, and judgments.
2. Although ordinary classroom teachers are not trained to administer and interpret many of the tools used to diagnose special needs, they still must be knowledgeable in this area so that they can communicate intelligently with specialists and provide for optimal learning.
3. A complete educational assessment program for the handicapped requires a team effort of classroom teacher, diagnostician, school psychologist, and medical personnel.
4. The movement toward equality of education for the handicapped came about through litigation and culminated in the passage of Public Law 94-142.
5. Three landmark cases concerned with nondiscriminatory testing were the *Diana* v. *State Board of Education*, the *Larry P.* case, and the *PASE* v. *Hannon* case.
6. Public Law 94-142 has placed responsibilities on the regular classroom teacher in dealing with the handicapped student.
7. Mainstreaming legislates teaching children with special needs in the regular classroom for as long as possible.
8. There are many problems associated with assessing the exceptional child, such as using tests that have been normed on normal children; dealing with behavior that is variable, thereby making any interpretation of difference scores difficult; and dealing with extremes, which makes measurement less reliable.
9. There is a significant interaction of examiner familiarity and handicapped status. That is,

handicapped students (at least speech- and language-impaired) perform better with familiar examiners.

10. The major classifications of special education are as follows: mentally retarded, emotionally disturbed, sensory handicapped, physically handicapped, learning-disabled, and gifted.
11. A variety of tests, scales, and inventories are used to assess children with special needs. They may range from a relatively simple checklist to a complex electroencephalograph or CAT scan. Generally speaking, educational and psychological tests are less reliable than many of our physical tests.
12. There are four classifications of mentally retarded: slow learners, educable mentally retarded, trainable mentally retarded, and severely mentally retarded. Classification is made on the basis of a scholastic aptitude test.
13. Of the more than 100 adaptive behavior scales, none tests persons over 20 years of age. Also, the majority have been standardized on institutionalized samples, which makes their norms suspect when we are dealing with noninstitutionalized individuals.
14. Assessment programs for the mentally retarded generally include a measure of adaptive behavior as well as a measure of motor development.
15. Emotional disturbance cannot be identified by a test, per se. It requires a trained medical or psychological specialist.
16. The sensory handicapped child is one who has some type of vision, hearing, or speech defect. There are further classifications within the visually handicapped (partially sighted and blind) and the hearing handicapped (hard of hearing and deaf).
17. The two most common types of physical handicap that the teacher encounters are epilepsy and the orthopedically handicapped.
18. The learning-disabled child is the one who has no sensory or physical handicap and is of average or better than average intelligence, but still has difficulty in learning.
19. Some special tests such as the Hiskey-Ne-

braska Test of Learning Aptitude, the Blind Learning Aptitude Test, and the Arthur Adaptation of the Leiter International Performance Scale have been specifically developed to assess the scholastic aptitude of handicapped subjects.

20. Increased attention is being paid to motor development, since research has shown it to play an important role in cognitive development.

21. The gifted child is generally classified on the basis of a scholastic aptitude score. As of now, there are no well-validated standardized creativity tests, although there are some experimental forms, such as the Mednick Remote Associates Test, available.

22. Possibly the most important stage in assessing the exceptional child is collating the different kinds of data and putting them together into a meaningful whole.

■ POINTS TO PONDER

1. What effect, if any, has PL 94-142 had on the preparation of teachers with respect to their measurement competencies?

2. Do you think that PL 94-142 has been a boon or a bane for exceptional children? Why?

3. The assessment of the exceptional child includes a variety of tests, inventories, and scales. One of the measures prescribed by the law is an estimate of the child's adaptive behavior. What is meant by adaptive behavior? How is it measured? How valid are the tests presently being used?

4. One of the provisions of Public Law 94-142 is that the tests used must be free from racial and cultural bias. Can we meet this requirement considering our present state of the art in measurement? How would you proceed to prevent legal action being taken against you?

5. Discuss some of the major problems in assessing the exceptional child. Can any of these problems be circumvented? How?

6. Should the child with a learning disability such as dyslexia be classified as an exceptional child? Defend your position.

7. If the diagnosis of exceptionality is so technical that it should be left to specialists, what need is there for the ordinary classroom teacher to be cognizant of the various tools and techniques?

8. In what way does educational diagnosis differ from medical diagnosis? Illustrate.

9. Tim is a third-grader. He is morose, aggressive, and has a predilection to using foul language. He appears to be of average ability but does not do well in his classroom achievement tests. When you confront Tim's parents with your observations, they become very hostile and accuse you of being a racist. What would you do to support your position that Tim is in need of special help?

Chapter 19

Factors Influencing Measurements of Individuals

- ■ **Test (Evaluation) Anxiety**
- ■ **Guessing**
- ■ **Test-Wiseness**
- ■ **Coaching and Practice on Aptitude Tests**
- ■ **Coaching/ "Cheating" on Achievement Tests**
- ■ **Response Styles**
- ■ **Other Factors Affecting an Examinee's Test Performance**

Most teachers will have encountered, at one time or another, examples of students whose test performances defy nearly all of their expectations.[1] One student, for example, may appear somnolent and uncomprehending in class, may be unable to give coherent answers to the teacher's questions, and yet perform brilliantly on tests. Another, who is keen, alert, and interested in class, and who gives every appearance of understanding the material taught, encounters disaster when confronted by a test. Are the teacher's judgments wrong, and

should they be discarded in favor of the more "objective" information provided by the tests? Our answer is "No," and we would counsel teachers not to jump too quickly to conclusions in such a situation but to exercise caution in their efforts to reconcile conflicting information.

It is often difficult for teachers to accept the fact that a student can have a good understanding of what is taught and yet consistently perform poorly on tests. Our aim in this chapter is to consider some of the extraneous factors that can influence the performance of students on tests and in measurement situations generally. And what makes a factor extraneous? For a test to provide a valid measure, a person's score should be deter-

---

[1]Although we use teachers and students in many of our examples, we could easily substitute examiner and examinee or psychologist and client.

mined by his or her achievement in that particular content area (or level of the construct measured), and by nothing else. Some characteristics of the person (motivation to learn, general ability, study habits) and some characteristics of the environment (competence and dedication of the teacher, parental support and encouragement) will surely have their influence on achievement and therefore, one would hope, on test scores. But there are other factors that may affect test scores, about which we might be less happy. If a person does poorly on a test because of an inability to comprehend the test instructions, because of an inappropriate guessing strategy, because of poor apportionment of testing time, emotional disturbance, anxiety, or environmental distraction, we can only conclude that the test does not measure that student's achievement (or other construct) as accurately as it should, and therefore that the validity of the inference made from the test is lessened.

Those interpreting test scores should have some awareness of the various factors that can have detrimental effects on measurement, and be willing to take these into account if there is an indication that any of them might be seriously influencing an individual's test performance. For example, when a child's test score is at variance with the teacher's knowledge of the child, we urge the teacher not to dismiss that knowledge as "subjective, unreliable, and disproven by the test score," but instead to look more closely and to see if the disparity can be accounted for. It is in keeping with the emphasis of this book that we urge teachers to use test information to add to their previous knowledge of a child, but not to replace it.

After studying this chapter, you should be able to:

1. Identify the major extraneous factors that can detrimentally affect the measurement of individuals' achievement and ability.
2. Recognize situations where these factors could be important.
3. Take these factors into account when interpreting the performance of an individual on a test.
4. Understand the positive and negative roles played by test (evaluation) anxiety, and know how to limit and control its negative effects.
5. Evaluate the seriousness of the problems that result from guessing on objective tests.
6. Know how to apply the "correction-for-guessing" formula, the assumptions on which it is based, the research evidence concerning whether those assumptions are met, and the consequences that follow when they are not.
7. Understand and avoid the common major misconceptions about guessing on objective tests.
8. Understand the nature of test-wiseness, and know the major skills involved.
9. Be familiar with major results concerning test-wiseness, and use various methods to minimize the contribution of test-wiseness to test score variance.
10. Distinguish among the major types of programs commonly referred to as "coaching."
11. Evaluate research results on the effectiveness of coaching for standardized aptitude and achievement tests.
12. Adopt a rational and informed view with respect to public controversy over the propriety and the effectiveness of coaching on the various college and professional school entrance exams.
13. Understand the concerns regarding "cheating" (by examiners and examinees) and know what steps to take to minimize cheating.
14. Understand the different types of response styles and their effect on a person's test score.
15. Understand the role that the sex, age, personality, race, and other characteristics of the examiner can play in affecting a person's test scores.
16. Construct tests so as to minimize the effects of extraneous response styles.

TEST (EVALUATION) ANXIETY

We experience *stress* when we are placed in situations that involve demands, constraints, or opportunities (Sarason & Sarason, 1980). Exposure to these situations may cause a reaction known as *anxiety*.

Definition

Anxiety is an emotional state that includes worry, apprehension, and tension. A heavily researched specific type of anxiety has become known as *test anxiety* although it is well recognized that the anxiety is actually due to an *evaluative situation* rather than to the taking of a test. Dusek defined test anxiety as "an unpleasant feeling or emotional state that has physiological and behavioral concomitants, and that is experienced in formal testing *or other evaluative situations*" (emphasis added) (1980, p. 88). As Ebel and Frisbie have pointed out:

> Anxiety is a frequent side effect of testing, whether that testing occurs in the classroom, on the athletic field, in the art exhibit hall, in the courtroom, in the conference room where a crucial business decision is being discussed, or in the legislative chamber where a bill is being debated. Test anxiety in the classroom is not something unique. It is a part, though hopefully not too large a part, of life itself (1986, p. 205).

Test (evaluation) anxiety may not be just a personality characteristic but due in part to an inadequate knowledge of the subject matter. Any given individual will differ with respect to test (evaluation) anxiety dependent on the level of knowledge (skill) that individual has on the content over which he/she is being evaluated (Benjamin, McKeachie, Lin, & Holinger, 1981).

Theories

There are many different theories of evaluation anxiety and a variety of tests that supposedly measure it. Alpert and Haber (1960) distinguished between two kinds of response to stress, calling them "facilitating" and "debilitating" anxiety. Those who, in competitive situations, are fired up by the situation and who enthusiastically meet the challenge by performing at a maximal level have facilitating anxiety—they direct their drives to task-directed behaviors. Those who become so anxious that they are unable to perform up to their usual level suffer from debilitating anxiety—they direct their drives to task-irrelevant behaviors. Alpert and Haber found a moderate negative correlation between the two types of anxiety and suggested that the constructs are independent enough such that "persons may possess a large amount of both anxieties, or of one but not the other, or of none of either" (p. 213). However, a factor-analysis study conducted by Watson (1988) allowed her to conclude that the construct is unidimensional.

Liebert and Morris (1967) proposed that debilitating test anxiety (DTA) consists of the components of *worry* and *emotionality*. They suggested that worry is any cognitive expression of concern about one's own performance and emotionality refers to autonomic reactions to the situation such as muscle tightness, perspiration, and accelerated heartbeat. Their research suggested that worry interferes with performance but that emotionality does not.

Extensiveness

Whatever theory one may hold regarding test (evaluation) anxiety, there is reasonably common agreement that it can be fairly extensive. Kaplan and Saccuzzo (1989) suggest that test anxiety is a common problem among college students. Hill and Wigfield (1984) have estimated that "4–5 million children in elementary and secondary schools experience strong debilitating evaluation anxiety" (p. 110). It should be stressed however, that any estimates regarding the extensiveness of debilitating anxiety are just estimates. Ebel and Frisbie (1986) made the important point that what is at times claimed to be underachievement due to test anxiety may in fact be instances of overrated ability in nonevaluative situations. As they suggest: "All things considered, a teacher is well advised to take with several grains of salt any claim that a student's test performances never do justice to her/his real achievements" (p. 206).

Measures of Test Anxiety

A variety of measures of test anxiety have been developed. It is not our intent to describe them here. Interested readers should turn to a source book such as the *Mental Measurements Yearbooks* discussed earlier. Some fairly common measures are the Test Anxiety Questionnaire, the Test Anxiety Scale, and the Achievement Anxiety Test.

Correlates of Test (Evaluation) Anxiety

The major correlate of test (evaluation) anxiety is that it is negatively related to performance. That is, those who are most capable are least anxious. This is true for both aptitude and achievement tests. The relationship for standardized achievement tests appears to be fairly consistent across different subject matters (Crocker, Schmitt, & Tang, 1988). However, a meta-analysis indicated there was no relationship between test anxiety and performance for elective courses (based on four studies) (Hembree, 1988). There is some evidence to suggest that women are more test-anxious than men and that blacks are more test-anxious than whites, although test anxiety alone does not account for the differences in performance between blacks and whites (Crocker, Schmitt, & Tang, 1988). There is a reasonably strong relationship between test anxiety and self-concept of ability (the lower the self-concept, the higher the test anxiety). There is a negative correlation between test anxiety and ability to organize course material and for study skills in general (Hembree, 1988; Naveh-Benjamin, McKeachie, & Lin, 1987). It has generally been thought that there is a positive correlation between level of anxiety and level of aspiration, but a meta-analysis of eight studies brings this belief into some doubt (Hembree, 1988). There does not appear to be a relationship between test anxiety and creative thinking or level of curiosity (Hembree, 1988). Teacher anxiety correlated with students' text anxiety. Perceptions of the teacher as negative and unfriendly were moderately related to test anxiety, but perceptions of the teacher as positive and friendly were not related to the construct (Hembree, 1988).

Causes and Effects of Evaluation (Test) Anxiety

It is generally believed that evaluation anxiety emerges

> . . . during the preschool or elementary school years, when parents begin to make unrealistic demands or hold overly high expectations for their children's performance. The parents then react negatively to their children's failure to meet their expectations, and the children in turn become fearful of evaluation in achievement situations and overly concerned about adult reactions to their academic successes and failures (Hill & Wigfield, 1984, p. 106).

As Hill and Wigfield go on to point out, as children progress through school, other factors may create or enhance evaluation anxiety. Children may experience formal, frequent, and complex evaluations with which they cannot effectively cope. Further, at around grade 2, they begin comparing their performance to other children, which may increase their anxiety. Because test anxiety is greater among those of low ability and because test anxiety in turn lowers performance, there is a "never-ending loop" (Crocker, Schmitt, & Tang, 1988, p. 149) between anxiety and poor performance.

Hembree (1988) found that two conditions of testing seemed related to high test anxiety. Ego-involving high-stress conditions seemed to cause high test anxiety, and tests perceived as difficult resulted in greater test anxiety than tests perceived as easy.

As you will recall from Chapter 10, correlation does *not* imply causation. If one only had correlational data between test anxiety and performance, one would not know anything about causal implications. It could be that test anxiety causes poor performance, but the opposite implication (that poor performance causes test anxiety) is equally consistent with the data. Benjamin, Mc-Keachie, Lin, and Holinger (1981) suggested that the existing data supported the fact that poor performance and poor ability both produce anxiety. Hembree (1988) has concluded that test anxiety causes poor performance because reducing test anxiety results in increased performance.

Treatment of Test Anxiety

A meta-analysis of 137 studies (Hembree, 1988) divided the treatments into (a) *behavioral* treatments, which attend to the emotionality component, of test anxiety; (b) *cognitive* treatments, which attend to the worry; (c) *cognitive-behavioral* treatments, which attend to both; (d) *study skills* treatments; and (e) *test-wiseness* treatments. Behavioral treatments included systematic desensitization (SD), relaxation training, modeling, covert positive reinforcement, extinction, and hypnosis. *All* behavioral treatments resulted in test anxiety reduction. Hembree concluded that cognitive treatment did not appear effective in reducing test anxiety (although others might reach a different conclusion from the data). Hembree found that cognitive-behavioral treatments were about as effective as SD in reducing test anxiety. He found study skills training by itself was ineffective, but it was effective when combined with behavioral or cognitive-behavioral treatments. Hembree also found that improved test performance and GPA consistently accompanied a reduction in test anxiety and that the treatment effect does not appear to decline with the passage of time. Zimpfer (1986) concluded that the literature "strongly supports the inclusion of group counseling or study skills training along with group-based cognitive or behavioral interventions as a combined approach to the treatment of test anxiety" (p. 233).

Educational Implications

Test (evaluation) anxiety exists for a considerable number of people. It can be either facilitative or debilitating with respect to performance. Thus, one must interpret the scores of students keeping in mind the possibility that they have been negatively influenced by test anxiety. Thus, test anxiety must be confronted. Hembree suggests that researchers should investigate ways to avert the condition before it matures (1988, p. 75). Others (e.g., Ottens, Tucker, & Robbins, 1989) argue that the purpose should be not to eliminate anxiety but to provide individuals with coping skills "that can be applied when needed to attenuate anxious arousal" (p. 249). They suggest that there are six functional coping behaviors: preexam preparation, task-directed self-instructions, overt tension reduction methods, active problem solving, positive attentional focus, and normalizing self-talk. Six dysfunctional coping behaviors are compulsivity, misdirected attention, avoidance/resignation, worry, expressions of self-disgust, and impulsiveness.

Within the classroom there are many things that teachers can do. They should avoid a cold, negative attitude toward students. They should make testing (evaluation) a familiar experience. They should not give tests to "trap" students—for that is sure to increase anxiety. They should convey the message by their attitudes and actions that they have confidence that the students can do well and their purpose is to provide students with the opportunity to do well.

Teachers should recognize that students are made anxious by uncertainty. Teachers who spring tests on students without warning, teachers whose tests are so unpredictable that the students do not know what to expect, teachers who leave students in the dark as to what is expected of them, and teachers whose marking is based on whimsy all create anxiety by their measurement incompetence. While it is true that these points relate primarily to teacher-made classroom tests, nevertheless the atmosphere fostered in the classroom by teacher-made tests may permeate into the standardized test arena. Teachers who prepare students adequately for tests, and whose tests are well constructed, based on clearly expressed objectives and scored on a basis that is justifiable and well understood, should not find that their students are overly anxious about tests. The student who has not learned well and knows it should expect failure but *not* fear it. The student who has worked hard will have a justifiable fear of failure if the teacher lacks the skill to do an adequate job of test construction and test score interpretation. Increased measurement competence on the part of the teacher has many benefits; lessening students' unwarranted anxieties is just one of them. Finally, one should keep in mind the following two statements: "Perhaps the most important thing schools can do is to prepare students more thoroughly for highly evaluative achievement, aptitude, competency, and other tests" (Hill & Wigfield, 1984, p. 122); and "There is little likelihood, however, that test anxiety has any lasting influence on a pupil's mental health" (Gronlund & Linn, 1990, p. 471).

GUESSING

Many individuals believe that guessing is a major factor in determining scores on objective tests, and most of us have heard such tests (especially multiple-choice) referred to in jest as "multiple-guess." But how serious a problem is guessing, and how concerned should teachers and test developers be? Is it true that some students can increase their scores substantially by being "lucky," while other less fortunate beings are condemned to suffer "the slings and arrows of outrageous fortune"? In this section, we will give some attention to the research findings that relate to the effects of guessing, the gains made by guessing, and the means advanced as ways of counteracting guessing.

Why Do Examinees Guess?

Although the answer to this question is obvious enough, we think it needs to be asked in order to provide some perspective to the discussion that follows. Examinees "guess" because they do not have enough knowledge or ability to provide an answer about whose correctness they are certain. It follows, therefore, that there is more than one kind of guess—in particular, we would like to distinguish the "blind guess" (where an examinee chooses an answer at *random* from among the alternatives offered) from the informed guess (in which the examinee draws upon all his knowledge and abilities to choose the answer *most likely* to be correct). Those who express concern about the effects of guessing often seem to assume that what takes place in the examination setting is blind guessing. There may be situations in which this is true (as where the test is totally unsuited to the ability levels of the examinees), but such evidence as is available indicates that the amount of blind guessing that occurs in normal circumstances is very small indeed. Students who are motivated to do their best will eliminate implausible alternatives to the extent that they are able but will rarely find themselves in situations where blind guessing is all they can do. To the extent that guessing occurs on multiple-choice tests (as, of course, it does), logic and evidence suggest that it is informed guessing that predominates.

Those who dislike blind guessing (for whatever reason, be it ethical, aesthetic, or psychometric) should not allow this dislike to transfer itself to informed guessing, which is a different phenomenon altogether. Informed guessing is not morally reprehensible—if so, we, the authors, and almost everybody we know, are moral reprobates, since virtually all the decisions we make are based on informed guesses about the consequences. Nor does informed guessing detract from test validity, and there are good reasons to think that validity can be enhanced by informed guessing.

Multiple-choice tests are sometimes thought to be insensitive to "partial knowledge" because items are scored zero or one, and the student who has some knowledge, but not enough to pick the correct answer, scores zero—as does the person who has no knowledge at all. But this analysis considers only one item, not the test as a whole. If students are encouraged through test directions and scoring to use their partial knowledge in making informed guesses, where necessary, those with higher levels of partial knowledge will be correct more often than those with lower levels. Thus, although a single item appears not to reward partial knowledge, the test as a whole will reward it. It is for this reason we suppose that research has found no way of substantially improving the measurement of partial knowledge beyond that afforded by multiple-choice tests (see, e.g., Traub & Fisher, n.d.).

Those who think that examinees should answer only multiple-choice items when they know the correct answers might give some thought to the parallels that exist between multiple-choice and essay tests. On a multiple-choice item, examinees lacking complete knowledge will give either an informed guess (if they have some partial knowledge), or a blind guess, or an omit (if they have no knowledge at all). On an essay question, students lacking complete knowledge will give an incomplete or at least an imperfect answer. Students lacking any knowledge (if that is possible) will either omit the question or try to use whatever verbal skills they possess to give the best possible answer. "Bluffing," "waffling," "padding," and various less polite terms are used to describe this strategy, and it is not confined to those with little or no knowledge. All students who want to do well on an essay test can be expected to do whatever they can to make their answers convincing.

Bluffing and guessing should be seen as parallel problems, and bluffing is probably a matter that warrants greater concern. Why? There are two reasons. The first is that we suspect that there is more to be gained by bluffing on an essay test than there is by guessing on an objective test. Second, and more important, we can feel well assured that whatever advantage a student may gain from lucky guessing is only transitory—next time it will be somebody else's turn to be lucky, and, in the long run, luck of this kind evens itself out. (If it does not, then it is not luck but something else. For example, if Lois consistently "guesses" more successfully than Jim, we will soon have to accept the conclusion that Lois is not guessing—at least not blindly—and that Lois really does know something that Jim does not.) But with bluffing we have no such assurance. Those who bluff most successfully today will do so tomorrow, and the next day, and the next day, since bluffing and associated verbal skills are clearly more highly developed in some people than in others. We therefore argue that guessing, to the extent that it advantages or disadvantages anyone, has effects that are relatively minor and, in the long run, fair. Bluffing on an essay test is a greater measurement problem than guessing on an objective test.

How Much Is Gained by Guessing?

On a single multiple-choice item, there is no question that luck can play an important part—it can make the least knowledgeable score as well as the most knowledgeable. From this, does it follow that the same is true of a test, which is merely a collection of such items? Of course not. The merest knowledge concerning the operations of chance is all that is needed to see why. Consider the following example. Brian is taking a 40-item true–false test, about the content of which he knows nothing. If Brian guesses blindly on every item, we would expect him to score 20 out of 40. What is the chance that Brian will guess well enough to gain a perfect score? Almost none—1 chance in 1,099,511,627,776, or just over 1 trillion. This figure takes on more meaning if we realize that if all citizens of the United States were to write such a test every day of their lives, and guess on all items, we could expect one perfect score to be produced, on average every fifteen years. If Brian is serious about wanting a perfect score, we suggest that study would be a more advantageous strategy.

If Brian wants just a pass, not a perfect score, his task is easier. If the pass mark is set at 30 correct (which is not very stringent, since it indicates a knowledge of only 50 percent of the questions), Brian has 1 chance in 900 of passing—better odds, certainly, but still not as good as studying. And, of course, for examinations with multiple-choice items (usually four or five alternatives) and for examinations with more items, the odds against succeeding by chance alone are much greater. Replacing the true–false items by four-choice items, for example, would reduce his chance of a perfect score to approximately 1 in 1,200,000,000,000,000,000,000,000 and his chance of "passing" to 1 in 2,000,000. Lengthening the test would reduce the odds even further.

In the light of this knowledge, it is clearer that "guessing lucky" is just not an adequate explanation of any student's high score, nor is bad luck a believable excuse for a low score. Luck in guessing may raise or lower a particular student's score by a mark or two, but it will not make any notable difference unless the test is unreasonably short.

The Prevention of Guessing

Those who see guessing as a problem to be dealt with have frequently thought it desirable to discourage students from guessing, both by means of the instructions given when the test is administrated and by scoring the test in such a way as to penalize those who guess incorrectly (commonly known as *formula scoring* or, less aptly, *correcting for guessing*). Although these procedures have been sources of controversy for many years, our view is that the weight of evidence is now fairly clearly against their use. Before looking at this evidence, however, we need to look at the nature of the "correction for guessing" and at the reasons for wanting to discourage guessing.

Why Prevent Guessing?   There appear to be at least two reasons for wanting to discourage guessing. The first involves the ethical/moral belief that guessing is wrong and/or sinful because it is a form of gambling or because it reflects the intention to deceive. We do not share this view. The second major reason is that guessing can affect the psychometric properties of the test. On theoretical grounds, one could argue that guessing should, by adding a source or random variance to test scores, decrease both reliability and validity (Lord, 1963). But empirical studies into these questions have been unable to produce consistent evidence either way (Blommers & Lindquist, cited in Ebel, 1965b; Sabers & Feldt, 1968; Traub et al., 1969; Hakstian & Kansup, 1975).

There is, however, much research which indicates that instructions *not* to guess have different

effects on different students and that these differences are then reflected in their test scores. Students who have been shown to be disadvantaged by such instructions include those whose personalities have been described as "submissive" (Votaw, 1936), "characterized by introversion, rumination, anxiety, low self-esteem, and undue concern with the impression they make on others" (Sheriffs & Boomer, 1954), and unwilling to take risks (Slakter, 1968). The reason is simple; even with the application of a correction (see the next section), those who obey the "do-not guess" instructions are disadvantaged, and those who disregard the instructions profit from so doing.

Formula Scoring   Associated with "do-not-guess" instructions, there is frequently a scoring formula that is intended to nullify the effects of blind guessing. In its most common form, the formula is

$$S = R - \frac{W}{A - 1} \qquad (19\text{-}1)$$

where S = corrected score
R = number of right answers
W = number of wrong answers
A = number of alternatives per item

With four-choice items, for example, the effect of the formula is to penalize the examinee one-third of a point for every wrong answer. Justice is said to be done because an examinee who guesses blindly on four items could expect, on average, to choose one correct answer and three incorrect answers. The point gained from the one correct answer is exactly cancelled out by the point lost from the three incorrect answers, and so the examinee who guesses is no better off and no worse off than the examinee who omits. From the point of view of the examinee, the expected reward from (blind) guessing is identical to the expected reward for omitting. If this were all there was to it, the examinee could be indifferent to the choice.

But other factors come into play. As pointed out previously, the guessing that takes place on multiple-choice tests is overwhelmingly informed guessing, where the probability of success is substantially greater than chance. Even when examinees believe they can do no better than chance, the evidence is that they can do substantially better (Wood, 1973; Cross & Frary, 1977; Rowley & Traub, 1977; Bliss, 1980). In these circumstances, the expected reward from answering is greater than that from omitting, and the most honest advice to examinees would be that they should answer every question on the test, even if the test instructions tell them otherwise!

Problems arise because some examinees are more easily intimidated (by instructions, penalties, etc.) than others. We should be aware that, particularly in the case of a true–false test where the "correction" for a wrong answer is enough to cancel out a previous correct answer, the penalty can appear particularly severe. Those examinees who are most intimidated by this situation will omit questions that they could and should have answered, and their scores will suffer as a result. Slakter (1968) was correct in referring to the scoring formula as a "penalty for not guessing."

It seems that a correction formula of the form

$$S = R + O/A \qquad (19\text{-}2)$$

(where O = number of omits)

has somewhat different psychological effects (Traub et al., 1969). Examinees are, in effect, promised a chance score on any item they omit, rather than a penalty for any wrong answer. Apparently this is less inhibiting to the timid examinee. On a highly speeded test, where unrestrained guessing could be a problem, it makes it clear to the examinee that there is no advantage to randomly answering the uncompleted portion of the paper.

In general, we would counsel against the use of formula scoring. The benefits in terms of psychometric qualities are small and frequently undetectable, and the price—that the test scores will be confounded with unwanted personality factors—too high.

Misconceptions About Formula Scoring

Before leaving the subject of guessing, it seems worthwhile to give attention to some of the *misconceptions* that abound. We will discuss them only briefly.

1. Formula scores rank examinees quite differently from number-right scores. Wrong! Correlations between formula scores and number-right scores are usually above 0.95 (see, e.g., Ebel, 1972, p. 252) and will reach 1.00 if all examinees can be persuaded to answer all questions.

2. Formula scores compensate the unlucky guesser. Wrong! The penalty is determined only by the number of wrong answers, not by the examinee's belief while giving those answers. A person who is unlucky in guessing will have more wrong answers and be more heavily penalized than an equally knowledgeable examinee who guesses with greater luck.

3. If a guessing penalty is applied, examinees should omit questions if they judge that their probability of success is at chance level. Wrong! As pointed out before, examinees' probabilities of success are usually greater than they believe, and it is in their interest to attempt all items, regardless of their perceived likelihood of success.

4. The formula penalizes only guesses. Wrong again! If examinees answer a question wrongly in the genuine belief that it is correct, not only do they fail to score on that question, but they lose a fraction of a mark from somewhere else—a penalty for a "guess" they did not make!

Conclusions on Guessing

Although we must, in fairness, acknowledge that not all writers agree with us, we believe that the evidence is strong enough to justify the recommendation that the correction for guessing *not* be used and that test instructions include the recommendation that all examinees should attempt all questions, even if they do not think they know the answers. The only exceptions we see are (1) a highly speeded test, where examinees are not expected to complete all items, and (2) a diagnostic test, where the examinees' interests are best served by revealing their strengths and weakness rather than by striving to maximize their scores. Finally, we assert that guessing on multiple-choice tests is not the serious problem it has often been thought to be, and that compared to "bluffing" on essay tests, it pales into insignificance.

TEST-WISENESS

A growing body of research evidence suggests that the ability to handle testing situations is a source of test score variance over and above that which can be attributed to subject-matter competence (for comprehensive reviews of research literature on test-wiseness, see Benson, 1989, and Sarnacki, 1979).

The most widely accepted definition of test-wiseness is that proposed by Millman, Bishop, and Ebel (1965): Test-wiseness is "a subject's capacity to utilize the characteristics and formats of the test and/or the test-taking situation to receive a high score (p. 707)." The wide acceptance of this definition implies that test-wiseness is regarded as a set of cognitive skills, although few would deny that the willingness to draw upon those skills is determined largely by attitudes. While some students will call upon every resource at their command in order to "beat the examiner," there are surely others to whom the possibility would never occur.

The analysis by Millman, Bishop, and Ebel (1965) focused on two aspects of test-wise behavior: (1) those independent of test constructor or test purpose, including wise use of time, strategies for avoiding errors, sensible guessing tactics, and the use of deductive reasoning to eliminate incorrect alternatives in multiple-choice tests; and (2) those specific to particular tests or particular examiners. The latter involve recognizing test con-

struction errors and examiner idiosyncracies that can help to "give away" the answer and "reading the examiner's mind" when the intent of the question is not clear. As noted earlier, standardized tests are generally less prone to "item-error" (such as ambiguity, clues to the correct answer) than teacher-made tests. Hence, only the aspects of test-wiseness independent of the test constructor should be operative in standardized tests. Ford and Weener (1980), for example, found no effects of test-wiseness on standardized tests.

Following the work of Millman, Bishop, and Ebel, there was something of an explosion of research in the area. Measures of test-wiseness, developed by Gibb (1964), Millman (1966), Slakter, Koehler, and Hampton (1970a), and Diamond and Evans (1972), have focused on those strategies that are directed toward improving one's score on multiple-choice tests. Research has established that:

1. Test-wiseness can be effectively taught (Gibb, 1964; Slakter, Koehler, & Hampton, 1970b). But Keysor et al. (1979) found that, for a select group of college students, training appeared to have little effect.
2. The teaching of test-wiseness results in small score increases on many achievement tests (Wahlstrom & Boersma, 1968; Moore, 1971; Callenbach, 1973; Kalechstein, Kalechstein, & Docter, 1981; Scruggs, White, & Bennion, 1986; Samson, 1985).
3. Test-wiseness conveys a greater advantage when the test is multiple-choice (Rowley, 1974; Smith, 1982) and when it is poorly constructed (Bajtelsmit, 1977).
4. Test-wiseness increases with age (Slakter, Koehler, & Hampton, 1970a) and with experience in taking tests (Kreit, 1968).
5. Although logically independent of achievement, test-wiseness has moderate positive correlations with measures of achievement (Rowley, 1974) and intelligence (Diamond & Evans, 1972). Given that test-wiseness is a set of cognitive skills, this ought to be expected.

What should be done about test-wiseness? The answer seems obvious enough. It is neither possible nor desirable to take test-wiseness skills from those who already have them. It is both possible and, we believe, desirable to teach test-wiseness to those who lack it. The evidence indicates that a little instruction and experience in answering the types of questions being used can be quite effective, especially for elementary and intermediate school students. The writing of essays has long been regarded as a valuable skill that is worth teaching; the answering of other types of test questions should be seen in the same light. We concur with Ebel (1965b) who declared that "more error in measurement is likely to originate from students who have too little, rather than too much, skill in taking tests" (p. 206).

Mehrens (n.d., pp. 70–77) has offered several *general* guidelines to follow in being test-wise and several other suggestions for specific types of tests. A test-wise student will

1. know the subject matter,
2. be emotionally prepared,
3. be physically prepared,
4. use test time wisely,
5. read directions carefully,
6. read questions carefully, and
7. think through the questions.

For objective tests, a test-wise student will

8. guess when unsure,
9. use the content contained in other questions to help get the answer,
10. look for specific determiners (e.g., all, none, only, and always),
11. read *all* the options in multiple-choice questions,
12. look for grammatical clues, and
13. *not* base answers on clues alone.

For essay tests, a test-wise student will

14. know the teacher and his/her basis for scoring essays,
15. make brief notes before beginning to write,
16. organize the answers,
17. answer each question and all subparts as fully as possible,
18. answer in outline form if he or she runs out of time,
19. write *something* even if knowledge is limited,
20. write legibly, and
21. practice writing answers for essay tests.

Three other points seem worth noting. First, test-wiseness plays a greater role on a poorly constructed test than on a well-constructed test. Thus, a teacher who has developed adequate skills in test construction is part-way to solving the problem. Second, the inability to cope well with one particular test format (such as multiple-choice or essay) will not be crucial if the teacher bases her assessments upon information gleaned from many different sources (assignments, projects, quizzes, etc.). This we recommend to the extent that it can be done while remaining true to the teacher's instructional objectives. Finally, and related to an earlier point, being test-wise is *not* a substitute for knowing the material on which one is to be tested. One writer ended his book on taking tests as follows:

> If you are committed to learning test-taking, you can do it. . . . In the long run, the effort you apply to learning test-taking will pay off far more handsomely than the effort to learn most school subjects. . . . [T]ruly skilled test-takers should be able to continue to *beat the system* [italics added] (Feder, 1979, p. 156).

Now such a statement may help sell the book, but it is misleading. The first sentence of the quote is true. The second sentence could only be true if you started at an *extremely* low level of test taking skills. The last part of the quote suggests that it is possible (perhaps even clever and wise) to *substitute* test-taking skill for knowledge of the material being tested and thus *beat the system*. You would be wise *not* to believe such a statement. One would have to construct a *very* poor test indeed for such a strategy to work. While teachers are not necessarily trained or skilled in test construction, we have never seen a test so poorly constructed that test-wiseness could *replace* knowledge of the material being tested.

COACHING AND PRACTICE ON APTITUDE TESTS

Questions concerning the effects of coaching and practice on test performance cannot be neatly separated from those related to test-wiseness. Particularly for test-inexperienced students, one benefit of both coaching and practice is familiarity with the nature of the task. Taking tests is like any other activity in that one is likely to perform better when the nature of the task is familiar and well understood—that is, when one is test-wise.

We hope it would be obvious to our readers by now that lack of test-taking skills can only result in test invalidity, since it will lead the test user to a false inference—that an examinee lacks certain skills, when in fact the examinee may have had the skills but did not demonstrate them in the test situation. No test results can be valid (lead to accurate inferences) *unless* all examinees are sufficiently experienced and familiar with the testing situation to be able to demonstrate the skills that they possess. However, as Bond (1989) has pointed out, even proponents of commercial coaching schools concede that instruction on only test-wiseness does not significantly affect performance on standardized tests.

Research on the effects of coaching and practice has been difficult to interpret. There are many reasons for this, but the major difficulty comes from the wide range of meanings ascribed to both terms. *Practice* may refer to a single test-taking experience or to extensive drill on similar test items. *Coaching* can mean any of the following (Anastasi, 1981):

1. *Test-taking orientation.* Materials designed to help the student become familiar with the type of test being used and comfortable in the test-taking situation. Good examples are *Taking the*

SAT (College Entrance Examination Board, 1978) and *A Guide to Test Taking as Easy as . . . 1 2 3* (Michigan State Board of Education, undated, but released in 1981). Each is designed with the expressed aim of enabling students to perform their best on a specific test or testing program. Materials such as these are typically made as widely available as possible, and to the extent that they are effective they would have the effect of improving the quality of measurement by reducing the unwanted variance due to differences in familiarity with the test-taking task. Nearly all standardized cognitive tests, especially those designed for testing young children, have numerous practice tests and examples. Also, some test publishers are now offering films, filmstrips, and other materials to acquaint examinees with the test and the testing environment.

2. *Coaching.* Used in this context, the term generally refers to relatively short-term "cramming" sessions, sometimes commercially motivated, sometimes intended to advantage students at one or more schools compared to the bulk of examinees. Coaching courses for college admissions tests often consist of extensive practice ("drill") on sample items or on items similar to those in the test for which the coaching is designed.

3. *Instruction.* This generally refers to longer-term programs of instruction in broad cognitive skills similar to those tested. It differs from coaching in that it is intended to improve a person's performance on the whole range of abilities that the test samples. While we recognize that programs will occasionally be found that have elements of both instruction and coaching, most are fairly clear in their intentions.

Questions about coaching, practice, drill, and so on must concern us from the ethical as well as from the practical point of view. In order to clarify some of the ethical issues, we find it useful to distinguish between the domain of behavior represented by a test and the sample of behavior chosen—the items on the test. The domain may be defined very explicitly in terms of behavioral objectives, as in some criterion-referenced tests; or in terms of very broad content areas, as in many standardized achievement tests; or in terms of very broad classes of behavior (such as inferential reasoning or analogies), as on many tests designated as aptitude tests. However explicitly defined the domain may be, the distinction is clear: The domain refers to the class of behaviors about which inferences are being made; the items on the test merely sample that domain.

Test-taking orientation, as we have defined it above, will, to the extent that it is successful, remove some of the obstacles that might cause the test-taker's performance on the test to inaccurately represent his or her performance on the domain. It is in the interest of the test-takers, because it will prevent their scores from being inappropriately low. It is in the interests of the test-user, because its effect is to lessen the likelihood of false inferences about examinees, and so improve the validity of the measurement process. *Instruction*, to the extent that it is effective, will improve the examinee's performance on the domain of behaviors, with one result being improved test performance. If the test is used to predict a criterion, improved performance over the domain should result in increased performance on the criterion. *Coaching*, which attempts to increase the test score without improving domain performance, does raise ethical questions, because it is the only one of the three that aims explicitly at deception. And it may not be in the interests of the examinees if its intention is to have them admitted to a program or occupation for which the best conceivable prediction (from performance over the domain) would be that they are unsuited. We think the ethical implications should be clear to the reader.

But what of effectiveness? First, we must point out that research evidence, particularly concerning the effects of instruction and coaching, is tenuous at best. The reason for this lies in research methodology. Many studies have compared coached to uncoached groups. But since those in the group receiving the coaching are normally there because they want to be there, and those not being coached are there because they do not want to be coached, it is difficult to make any inferences from such studies. For those interested, Messick (1980, Chapter 2) has summarized research of this type. No firm conclusion can be reached. (See also Messick and Jungeblut, 1981, and Bond, 1989).

True experimental studies, in which examinees are randomly assigned to experimental and control groups, are rare (Bond, 1989, has identified four), because of the ethical and practical difficulties involved. Alderman and Powers (1980) found that special programs already in place in the eight secondary schools studied brought about an increase of around 8 points, on average, on the SAT scale of 200–800. This is very small (about one-twelfth of a standard deviation) and less than the improvement normally made on a second testing. There was a problem with this study in that the special administration of the test did not "count" in any real sense, so that students may not have been as motivated as they normally would be when taking the SAT. But the findings are consistent with the general thrust of other, less carefully designed research, which are that the best that can be hoped for from any programs of coaching, test-taking orientation, or practice is an improvement of about one-fifth of a standard deviation, and most yield less than this (Hopkins & Stanley, 1981).

In recent years there has been something of a furor over the question of the effectiveness of coaching for the SAT. Most of the attention has focused on an article by Slack and Porter (1980a), in which the authors examined literature on coaching and the SAT and concluded with a triumphant flourish that the SAT scores are "unrelated to the quality of (students') minds" (p. 172); that the SAT is coachable; and that it should therefore be replaced by standardized achievement tests (which presumably would be more coachable than the SAT).

The controversy surrounding this sweeping conclusion (see, e.g., Bond, 1989; Jackson, 1980; Messick, 1980, 1981; Slack & Porter, 1980b) has clarified several important points, and there is much of value to be learned from it.

First, we note that Slack and Porter (1980a) assume that an aptitude test measures some innate, unchanging quality of the individual that is not affected (or, as least, not appreciably affected) by that individual's experiences. This is, of course, a naive view of the nature of aptitude, which contrasts most strongly with modern thinking. Anastasi (1981) points out what should be obvious, that: "All tests reflect what he or she is able to do at the time" (p. 1086). The notion, then, that achievement tests are coachable, and that aptitude tests are not, is false. There are good reasons to hope that the former would be more responsive to instruction than the latter, but the difference is a matter of degree. For a review of the conceptual distinction between achievement and aptitude, consult Chapter 15.

The best available summaries of research on coaching, with particular reference to the SAT, are those by Bond (1989) and Messick (1980, 1981). Messick focused on the regularities that do exist among the seemingly disparate results and made many telling points. In particular, he emphasized that questions about the effectiveness of coaching are questions of degree (How much coaching? What kinds of coaching? How much improvement?) rather than yes-no questions (Does coaching work?). To this end, he has sought what he calls relational rather than categorical answers. In particular, he has shown that the score gains that can be expected increase with the time spent, that there are diminishing returns for increased coaching time, and that the verbal section (SAT-V) is less responsive to coaching than the mathematical (SAT-M). This is to be expected, given that the SAT-M is more strongly curriculum-related than the SAT-V. But Messick has also made a very cogent point about the research that has been done. Short-term coaching programs have typically been of the "cramming" kind referred to earlier, while long-term programs have concentrated more on instruction in broad cognitive skills. Summaries such as that by Slack and Porter (1980a) have confounded the two factors—

nature and *duration*—of the coaching or instruction given. Even given the diminishing returns earlier, it is not possible to conclude that a program can be made more effective by making it longer—it may be that increased effectiveness comes only with an increase in time allocation and a shift in emphasis to instruction in broad cognitive skills. And if it proves to be the case that the most effective way to improve one's SAT score is to improve one's ability across the broad repertoire of skills tapped by the SAT, who would be unhappy about that? Certainly not the Educational Testing Service, nor, we would hope, its critics.

Often mistaken for coaching—that is, a purposive treatment—is the effect of repeating a test or taking a parallel form of the test. As might be expected, those examinees who repeat the test receive higher scores on the second administration (Hutton, 1969; Nevo, 1976; Wing, 1980). Wing found that on repeating the test, examinees did slightly better on the numerical-type items than they did on the verbal-type items, although they improved slightly on both. We believe that test-users need not concern themselves too much with the effect of repeating a test, since only infrequently are examinees given the same or a parallel form of an aptitude test. When they are, users should interpret the second test score accordingly.

COACHING/ "CHEATING" ON ACHIEVEMENT TESTS

As already suggested, at some point the methods used in coaching and practice cross over an ill-defined line from a legitimate practice of teaching *to* the test to an inappropriate practice of teaching *the* test (Mehrens & Kaminski, 1989; Shepard & Kreitzer, 1987). While educators do not always agree as to where to place that line, most if not all would agree that teaching test-wiseness or test-taking skills is legitimate. Further, it is obviously appropriate to provide general instruction on a large domain of achievement, which any given test may sample. What is *generally* considered inappropriate is to focus instruction on only those objectives that happen to be assessed by the test. The reason that is considered an unacceptable practice is because the inference one typically makes from a test score is to a reasonably broad domain. If instruction is to a specific sample of objectives, any inference to a broader domain would be inappropriate and incorrect. While we admit that for some specific purposes one only wishes to infer to the particular objectives covered by a test (e.g., all 26 letters of the English alphabet), it is more common to wish to make broader inferences (e.g., ability to spell or ability to do basic arithmetic operations). It would, of course, be even more inappropriate to provide practice on a published parallel test or to provide practice on the test in advance (i.e., teach the specific test questions).

Unfortunately, the push for educational accountability and the belief that schools (or perhaps the individual teachers) are responsible for the achievement of their students will increase the pressure to teach too closely to the test. At *some* stage it becomes so blatant that, indeed, we believe it is appropriate to consider such practices as cheating.

One practice that has been widely adopted by the schools it to purchase commercially prepared achievement-test preparation programs. For example, a regional manager for Random House has estimated that their test-specific "Scoring High" materials are used in 30 to 40 percent of schools nationally (Woo, 1988). These materials are designed specifically for each of three major standardized achievement tests. As the publisher states:

> The exercises in these workbooks provide your students with the concentrated practice and review of the very skills necessary to score high on the latest edition of each test (Random House, 1987, pp. 2–3).

Mehrens and Kaminski (1989) compared the subskills in the Scoring High on the California Achievement Test (CAT) with the actual subskills tested on Level 15 of the CAT. They found that 64.5 of the 69 skills tested on the CAT were covered in the Scoring High materials—and that the Scoring High materials covered no additional skills. In *their* view, this match was so great that one could not infer to any broader set of skills from the scores on the CAT if the students had been prepared through use of the Scoring High materials. Others, of course, defend the practice as appropriate.

Of course, some people support practices such as that described above on the basis that those skills are important. We certainly tend to agree that the skills tested on standardized achievement tests are important ones. Further, if the inference were to only those skills, it would be appropriate to teach only those skills. But, as pointed out before (see also the section on content validity in Chapter 13), the inference is typically to a broader domain. Teaching to only the sample tested when the inference is to a broader domain invariably makes the inference invalid. (We should point out that the same is true of performance assessment. If we instruct on only the particular performance we evaluate, we cannot infer to a broader set of skills/performance. For example, if writing instruction is limited to writing business letters—because that is what is tested—we could not make inferences about broader writing skills.)

Of course, some methods of teaching to the test are so blatant that any reasonable person would consider them cheating. Cannell (1989) presents a whole series of letters he has received from teachers charging cheating by other teachers—and occasionally admitting to cheating themselves. In three years, 50 elementary schools have been caught cheating by officials from the California State Department of Education (McGraw & Wood, 1988). In Austin, Texas, students reported that their teacher had actually given out copies of the test for homework the week before the test! Other teachers were reported to have told special-education students to stay home on the day of the test (Ligon, 1985). Putka (1989) reported that a South Carolina teacher gave students the answers to a standardized test two days before the exam was administered. This was discovered when a student was using a crib sheet during the exam. (The teacher was fired and fined $500.00 for breaking a state test security law.) Cannell (1989) reported that the Maryland Department of Education excluded 20 percent of their total enrollment from testing and then reported that Maryland students were above the national average!

As we have mentioned, increased accountability has increased the practice of teaching to the test and cheating in more blatant ways. Unfortunately, many educators do not consider as inappropriate the same practices that most measurement specialists would. This is apparently either because they do not understand the inference to the domain issue or because they believe that the placing of inappropriate blame (or credit) on them for student achievement makes it all right to cheat. Mehrens and Kaminski (1989) have summarized some of the research on educators' attitudes toward cheating and were dismayed by the results. For example, only 37 percent of a group of teachers thought the following statement represented cheating: "If a teacher remembers specific questions and then proceeds to teach next year's students the same questions, does this constitute a form of cheating?" One more example: Cannell (1989) reported that one Los Angeles school official, when asked what he thought about having teachers teach their class the exact vocabulary words on the test, responded, "I don't see that as a significant problem. That would be evidence of growth."

What can be done about the problem of teaching too closely to the test? Obviously the problem does not exist for secure tests because teachers, principals, and other educators cannot see the exact questions in advance. Usually the public information about the content of secure tests is general enough so that it is appropriate to teach to the general content (i.e., what was considered "instruction" in the previous section on coaching and practice). Thus, one solution for other tests would be to make them secure. However, that is quite expensive. To revise all the standardized achievement tests every year and to set up the types of security arrangements that are used by SAT, ACT, and other such tests may make the standardized achievement tests as expensive as those tests. However, if nonsecure tests are used for teacher

accountability (including merit pay and career-ladder promotion), one can expect some cheating. (It should be clear that the authors of this book are opposed to using student scores on achievement tests for determining merit pay and career-ladder promotion of teachers.) Thus, one should either not use standardized tests for the purpose of accountability and restrict their use to their original purpose—evaluating students' performance to better instruct them (see Loyd, 1986)—or set up some very strict administrative/scoring conditions to minimize the opportunity for cheating to occur. Some of those methods have been spelled out by Cannell (1989).

We must stress, however, that the two things most likely to control cheating are (1) to have more reasonable accountability models and not blame (or credit) only teachers for their students' scores and (2) to educate educators about what is considered inappropriate test preparation and what their ethical obligations are to ensure that it does not occur.

RESPONSE STYLES

We will use the term *response style* to refer to a characteristic of individuals, apart from achievement or ability, that consistently affects their manner of responding to a test. On noncognitive measures the problem can be quite serious, and the term *response set* is usually preferred. For cognitive tests, we have already met several important response styles. Test-wiseness is a response style; test-wise examinees have their own repertoire of ways of dealing with test items, and if these strategies are well learned and consistently applied, they can constitute a style of response that distinguishes those examinees from others. The tendency or propensity to guess is another response style; some examinees will always guess when the opportunity arises, while others consistently pass up the opportunity, preferring to omit a question if they are unsure. Both test-wiseness and guessing can have consistent effects on examinees' test scores.

Of those we have not yet considered, perhaps the most important response style is speed of work, sometimes referred to as the "speed versus accuracy" response set. Examinees have distinct preferences regarding the speededness of tests. Some work best, and prefer to work, under highly speeded conditions, while others are favored by conditions that allow them to work slowly and deliberately through a test, without having to worry about the passage of time. Tests can, in fact, be arranged on a continuum, with "speed tests" at one end and "power tests" at the other. An example of a pure speed test would be one where no examinee finishes in the allotted time. On a pure speed test, it is assumed that the items are so easy that errors contribute at most insignificantly to score variance, and speed of response is the sole determining factor. On a power test, in comparison, sufficient time is allowed for all examinees to finish the test—in practice this might be accomplished by allowing extremely generous time limits or by having no time limits at all.

Most tests are, of course, neither pure speed tests nor pure power tests but lie somewhere between the two ends of the speed-power continuum. It is our belief that for classroom teachers, and particularly for formative evaluation, nearly all tests should be primarily power tests. The teacher's aim in classroom testing is to find out the extent to which the objectives of instruction have been achieved, and unless speed of work is an objective for which the teacher is consciously striving (e.g., in teaching typing or shorthand), this will be best achieved by allowing students sufficient time to demonstrate all that they have achieved. Administrative restraints will normally prevent the teacher from allowing unlimited time, but the experienced teacher should learn to construct tests of appropriate length so that all students, or nearly all, can complete them comfortably in the time available.

On standardized tests, the teacher does not have control over the amount of time allowed. It is advisable, however, for teachers to inspect the answer sheets to see whether the students had sufficient time to attempt all questions. If not, they should bear in mind that the test measures in part speed of work, and that low scores can result from slow work as well as from poor work.

There is a set of response styles that are particularly unique to noncognitive tests—that is, attitude, interest, and personality measures. Some of these are the examinees' predisposition to select the neutral category when an agree-disagree continuum is used, social desirability, acquiescence, and the like. These were discussed more fully in Chapter 17.

Some other examples of response set, especially operative in aptitude and achievement tests employing a multiple-choice format, are the tendency for the examinee to choose the answer in the middle or at the top or at the bottom, to select the longest (or shortest) alternative as the correct answer, and so on. It should be obvious that many of the response-set problems can be controlled by adhering to the principles of good test construction.

OTHER FACTORS AFFECTING AN EXAMINEE'S TEST PERFORMANCE

We discussed previously the effect of such administrative factors as environmental conditions, training of test administrators, test scoring, and the establishment of rapport between the examiner and the examinee on an examinee's test performance.

So far in this chapter we have discussed the impact of such factors as guessing, test anxiety, and coaching on examinees' test scores. In essence, the factors we have considered are related either to something inherent in the test, the testing conditions, or the personality of the examinee. There are, however, another set of factors—such as the *examiner's* race, sex, expectancy level, personality, and socioeconomic status—that may have an effect upon an examinee's test performance.

Examiner Effects

What do we know about examiner effects? Generally, they are more operative—that is, they have a greater effect—on individually administered tests than on group-administered tests; on younger children than on adults; on intelligence or semi-structured and projective tests than on achievement and interest tests; on emotionally disturbed and handicapped children than on normal children; when the test results are being used to make significant rather than trivial decisions; and on tests where the stimuli are ill defined and the responses scored subjectively.

We will now consider race, sex, expectancy, and other examiner effects in more detail.

Race   Contrary to popular misconception, especially among minority group members, the race of the examiner has very little impact on the examinee's test performance. The numerous studies on the effect of the examiner's race on the examinee's test performance have, for the most part, shown that it is negligible. Graziano, Varca, and Levy (1982) reviewed 29 studies to learn whether the examiner's race affected the examinees' intelligence-test performance and concluded that "these studies provide no consistent or strong evidence that examinees of different races systematically elicit different performances in black and white examinees" (p. 491). Jensen (1980), after reviewing 37 studies done between 1936 and 1977, as well as studies and reviews by Sattler (1974, 1982) and Sattler and Gwynne (1982), also concluded that the race of the examiner is not an important factor influencing an examinee's performance on mental ability tests. Although one might expect to find a significant examiner-examinee interaction for individually administered in contrast to group-administered tests (establishment and maintenance of rapport is more crucial in the former), Sattler and Gwynne (1982) found that this was not so.

One should not jump to the conclusion that the examiner's race could not influence a person's test performance because it could. However, in standardized tests, at least, the test directions are so specific that we should not expect to find a difference between a well-trained black examiner testing white children and vice versa.

Sex   Once again, one might expect that males would obtain higher test scores when examined by a male examiner and that females would do better with a female administrator. Research, however, does not corroborate this hypothesis. Although Rumenik, Capasso, and Hendrick (1977) found that when an examiner was dealing with sensitive, sexually related items, the sex of the examiner could affect the examinee's responses, they generally observed that for most personality and intelligence tests, no sex effect existed. Whereas Black and Dana (1977) noted that female examiners obtained higher WISC scores from children, Cieutat and Flick (1967) found no sex effect when the Stanford-Binet was used. Thus, the results are somewhat contradictory.

Expectancy   Another area of conflicting or uncertain evidence is the examiner's *expectancy*, or the expectancy effect.

Although Rosenthal and Jacobson (1968) claimed that teacher expectancy affected the mental ability scores that pupils received, their conclusions were disputed because of faulty methodology (Barber & Silver, 1968; Snow, 1969; Elasoff & Snow, 1971). Cronbach (1975) and Jensen (1980) among others contend that teacher expectancy has no effect on pupils' mental ability test scores.

Somewhat contradictory conclusions are voiced by Sattler (1974), Sattler, Hillix, and Neher (1970), and Sattler and Winget (1970), who found that examiners scoring WISC tests gave more favorable treatment (credit for the answer) to the responses that supposedly came from brighter pupils and gave lower scores to those they thought came from the duller pupils (the examiners did not administer the tests; they only scored them).

Thus, the expectancy effect studies yield, at best, inconsistent results. Since we really have no evidence to conclude that there is such a thing as examiner/scorer bias, we should be aware that it *may* exist and govern our interpretations of test scores accordingly.

Other Variables   An examinee's test performance may also be affected by the examiner's personality; by certain examiner characteristics such as age, training, and experience (Cohen, 1965; Dyer, 1973); and by the examiner's behavior before and during the test administration. Exner (1966) found, for example, that test-takers performed significantly better on an intelligence test when the examiners were "warm and kind" than when they were "cold and impersonal." The significant interaction between the examiner's and examinee's personalities may sometimes be quite specific—so that, for example, a particular examiner might affect Billy but not Peter primarily because the personalities "mesh" in one case but not in the other.

Summary of Examiner Effects   In conclusion, the examiner's race has a negligible influence on the examinees' test performance, whereas the data with regard to the role of the examiner's sex and expectancy are inconclusive. It is apparent, however, that examiner and other situational variables are a greater confounding factor on personality inventories, especially projective tests, than on cognitive tests. In fact, it has been found that only subtle variations in the phrasing of instructions and in examiner-examinee relationships can markedly affect examinees' performance on projective tests (Masling, 1960; Klopfer & Taulbee, 1976).

■ SUMMARY

The principal ideas, conclusions, and implications of this chapter are summarized in the following statements:

1. Some students' test performance may defy a teacher's expectations. This is sometimes due to extraneous factors that can influence the test performance.
2. In interpreting test scores, one should be aware of and take into account the various factors that may have detrimental effects on measurement.
3. There are two kinds of response to stress, facilitating and debilitating. Debilitating anxiety may result in examinees scoring lower on tests than knowledge or ability warrant.
4. Teachers can do a variety of things to minimize debilitating test anxiety. Relying on a variety of data-gathering devices (observa-

tion, teacher-made and standardized tests, rating scales) rather than on the results of just one or two tests should help decrease test anxiety.
5. Informed guessing is where students use partial knowledge to arrive at an answer. Informed guessing should be encouraged.
6. Blind guessing is not likely to have much impact on a person's score unless the test is very short.
7. Bluffing on an essay test is probably a more serious problem than guessing on an objective test.
8. In general, we recommend against using formulas to "correct" for guessing. Test instructions should encourage all students to attempt all questions.
9. Test-wiseness is the ability to utilize the characteristics and formats of the test and/or test-taking situation to receive a higher score than one would receive otherwise.
10. Test-wiseness can be effectively taught—especially to younger children; it results in small score increases on many achievement tests; it results in a bigger increase for poorly constructed tests than well-constructed tests; and it increases with age and test-taking experience.
11. Teachers should attempt to teach all of their students to be test-wise.
12. The terms *coaching* and *practice* have both been used in a variety of ways. Generally one thinks of coaching as a short-term cramming session.
13. Most measurement experts attempt to differentiate among test-taking orientation, coaching, and instruction. Test-taking orientation and instruction are good things to do. Coaching is a questionable ethical practice and may well not be in the best interests of the examinee.
14. Coaching is of some, but quite limited, usefulness in raising test scores.
15. Cheating may occur on nonsecure standardized achievement tests when results are used to punish and reward educators.
16. Response styles such as "speed versus accu-

racy," the tendency to answer true, and positional response styles can be controlled through good test construction and administrative procedures.

17. The race of the examiner has a negligible effect on the examinees' mental test performance.

18. The data concerning the influence of the examiner's sex on the examinees' mental test performance are inconclusive.

19. Studies on teacher/examiner expectancy effects yield inconclusive data.

20. A variety of factors associated with the examiner—personality, interaction with the examinee, age, training—can affect examinees' test performance.

■ POINTS TO PONDER

1. Suppose you were given a class to teach and you found that nearly all of your students were from other countries. Although their English was excellent, they were totally inexperienced in taking tests. Sketch an outline of what you would want to teach them about tests so that they could cope adequately in the United States school environment. (Choose a grade level with which you are familiar.)

2. Respond to the following students' explanations of their performance on tests:

    a. "I just guessed. If I passed, I suppose I must have guessed lucky."

    b. "I knew nothing about the third question. I passed it by bluffing."

    c. "I never do well on examinations—I get so nervous that I just go to pieces."

    d. "I think I must be born unlucky. My friends seem to be able to do well on objective tests by just guessing, but it never works for me."

    e. "I always do badly if it's multiple-choice. As soon as you put two or three alternatives in front of me, I become confused."

    f. "I was just unlucky. I knew most of the course, but on the examination we were asked only a few of the things I knew."

Unit 5

EVALUATION: ITS DISCLOSURE AND THE PUBLIC

Chapter 20

Marking and Reporting the Results of Measurement

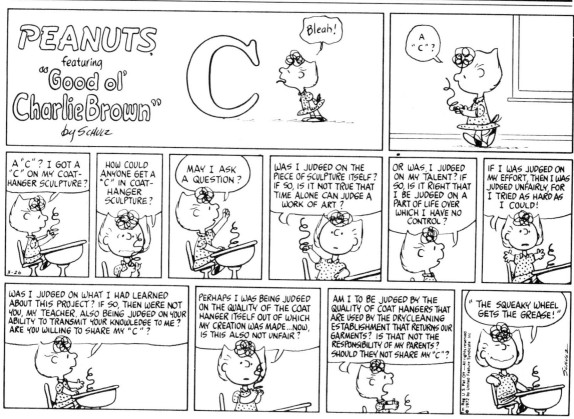

■ **Necessity for Reporting Procedures: Who Needs Them**
■ **Bases for Marking and Reporting**
■ **Marking and Reporting Procedures**
■ **Criteria for a Marking–Reporting System**

All readers of this book should be aware by now that measurement is an integral part of the teaching-learning process. Measurement and evaluation help us determine what to teach and what procedures are most effective. Few, if any, professional educators doubt the wisdom of determining what students have learned, and how well. Not to do so would mean that we could never evaluate the job schools are doing or the progress students are making. However, how to record what students have learned and in what fashion are more debatable issues. Some record keeping of student progress is necessary. Not all decisions that are dependent upon level of student achievement can be made at the time the achievement level is observed. Thus, the data should be recorded. Further, information regarding student progress needs to be systematically reported.

After completing this chapter, you should be able to:

1. Recognize the necessity for reporting schemes.
2. Understand and discuss how reports can be useful for different groups of people.
3. Know that the major basis for a report should be the degree to which a student has achieved the educational objectives of the school.
4. Understand and discuss six different systems of reporting (marks, checklists, letters, conferences, self-evaluation, and contracts) and identify the advantages and disadvantages of each.
5. Discuss factors that must be taken into account when using single summary symbols.
6. Recognize the criteria for a good marking system.

NECESSITY FOR REPORTING PROCEDURES: WHO NEEDS THEM

Many people make, or help the student make, decisions based in part upon how the student has done in school. A particular decision may depend upon highly specific information (e.g., how well the student can type) or upon much more general data (e.g., whether the student is a good writer). Thus, we obviously need a variety of reporting procedures to serve a variety of functions. Slavin (1978) categorizes the functions as incentive, feedback, and evaluation. Before discussing various reporting procedures, we should look at who needs information and how these people use it.

Students

There has been an increased emphasis in education on the importance of *feedback* to students. Of course, there are two stages to this feedback: the *measurement* of the degree to which students have reached the objectives and the *communication* of this information to them. Feedback to students serves the purpose of guidance. Research and common sense tell us that it is difficult to improve unless we know how we are presently doing. If individuals wish to become better marksmen, they should know how close their previous shots have come to the bull's-eye. Knowledge of results improves subsequent learning.

Students need information to guide them in their immediate decision making (Should I study more this weekend? Was the review session with Joe and Ted helpful enough to be repeated? Do I need to review the division of fractions?) and in their long-range plans (Should I go to medical school?). Formative evaluation (informing students of their progress during the instruction) is most helpful for the immediate decision making that students face. This kind of feedback would not require that the schools provide summary evaluations or that they keep permanent records of the achievement of the pupils. The daily interaction between teachers and students should result in the students' having fairly good knowledge of the quality of their achievements necessary for immediate decision making. Of course, this depends upon the teacher's skill in daily feedback. Effective feedback depends upon determining what students need to know to facilitate further learning, gathering accurate data, and presenting these data to the students in a fashion they will comprehend.

Although formative evaluation is perhaps most helpful to the students, summative (or terminal) evaluation of the kind provided at periodic marking periods also can assist them in their decision making—particularly in the formation of long-range plans. Pupils cannot easily combine all the daily feedback provided and obtain an overall summative picture of how they are doing. They need the insight teachers can provide. Thus, an overall summary is of value (Feldmesser, 1971).

Besides guidance, a second possible purpose of reporting to students is to enhance motivation. The motivating dimension of feedback is more debatable than the guidance dimension. (Stiggins, Frisbie, & Griswold, 1989, suggest that the purposes of communication and motivation can appear to be at odds.) It is possible for feedback to either reduce or enhance motivation, and the same reporting scheme may have different motivating impact on different students. Teachers should take this into account. Some students need friendly encouragement, some need mild chastising, others may need to be motivated through fear.

Nevertheless, many educators and students firmly believe that feedback (and recording grades) does have the effect of inducing students to apply themselves to learning things they would not otherwise learn (Katz et al., 1968; Sparks, 1969; Stallings & Lesslie, 1970). Some educators feel this is bad and that students should feel free to learn what they wish. Feldmesser addressed himself to this whole issue of motivation. He discussed whether motivation can come from feedback to the student alone or whether recording that information and using it for short-run decisions is necessary. We quote in part:

> . . . many students . . . deliberately decide, on what seems to them to be rational grounds, that the subject matter of a particular course, or particular parts of a course, are irrelevant to their needs and therefore ought not to be learned. We might say that that's their business; if they choose not to learn, they will and should bear the consequences of their decision. I think that's a cop-out; it is shirking our educational duty, if not undermining our educational pretensions. The student, after all, is young, and his very presence in a course indicates that he knows relatively little about the field. Consequently, he doesn't necessarily know what will be relevant to his needs over the long run; and in any event, his needs and his interests change. His teachers claim to have more foresight than he does, particularly with respect to what will prove relevant in their fields (if they are unwilling to make that claim, they shouldn't be his teachers). Thus, they are entitled—I would say obliged—to exert some pressure on the student to get him to learn material whose importance he is not yet in a position to perceive (Feldmesser, 1971, pp. 7, 8).

Regardless of the stand our readers may take on Feldmesser's opinion, it seems obvious that whatever the *method* of reporting, all students should receive accurate reports of how they are doing. In discussing the educational implications of self-concept theory, LaBenne and Greene (1969) stressed that teachers must be honest with their pupils. They suggest that, unfortunately, when teachers talk to students they purposely distort the evidence and provide false praise for poor performance. They stated: ". . . the student is not fooled by this sham . . . [C]onfrontation with reality in an atmosphere of warmth and acceptance is imperative for an accurate view of self" (LaBenne & Greene, 1969, pp. 28–29).

Parents

Parents also need to know how their children are doing in school, and good reporting practices should result in improved relations between school and home. Unfortunately, many schools do not do an effective enough job in this respect. Parents often do not know what the school's objectives are, let alone whether or not their children are accomplishing those objectives. Many parents would be willing to help their children in weak areas, but without knowledge of what those weak areas are, it is impossible to do so.

Since parents' opinions play a role in a child's educational and vocational planning, it behooves them to be as knowledgeable as possible in that area. Parents do not have daily contact with the school, so the quality of the formal periodic reporting scheme and the frequent informal formative reports (graded test papers, assignments, and similar evidence) is very important.

Administrators, Counselors, and Teachers

Curriculum and instructional decisions should be based primarily on the quality of student outcomes. Administrators and counselors need to make decisions with regard to the proportion of "college prep" courses they should offer, whether new curriculum innovations should be continued, whether Johnny should be placed in a special class, whether Susan should be encouraged to take trigonometry, and countless other decisions that are more rationally made with some knowledge of how the students are achieving.

Reporting also helps teachers evaluate their own strengths and weaknesses. If students are doing well in some aspects of a course, but poorly in others, a teacher should examine her instructional procedures to formulate possible hypotheses as to why that is so. Also, the task of preparing a formal report may cause a teacher to look more carefully at student achievements than she might do otherwise. If a teacher needs to submit a report, she will probably feel some obligation to develop reasonable bases for it. She will wish to be able to defend it if questioned. Thus, she will likely set up a better evaluation system, one that can provide more useful feedback to students, than if no formal report is required.

Prospective Employers

Many people may feel with some justification that how a student achieves should be private information between that student and the school. Although there is some legal basis for the nonrelease

of data without student permission, the permission is typically granted. If a student has given written permission for a transcript to be sent to an employer, the school is obligated to respond. If Don applied for a secretarial job after high school, the prospective employer may ask school personnel what secretarial courses Don took and how well he did in those courses. If Don did not agree to let the school release such data, his application might be rejected. Certainly, if Sean applies for a government job requiring security clearance, a part of that clearance will involve a search of the school records. An engineering firm considering Susan as an applicant for a position will surely want to know about her technical competencies. To not have appropriate school records or to withhold them from employers would require that these employers greatly expand their own personnel departments or make poor selection and classification decisions. Unfortunately, some evidence suggests that schools do not always respond to signed requests for transcripts. For example, an insurance company only received 93 responses from over 1200 requests (Bishop, 1989)! (One might argue that the insurance company should not have received any unless it paid for them.)

College Admissions Officers

It is generally recognized that, for most students, the best single predictor of freshman GPA is high school grades. (Contrary to beliefs of many people, there is considerable research evidence to suggest that aptitude tests are better predictors than high school grades for disadvantaged youth. See, for example, Thomas and Stanley, 1969.) Thus, practically all colleges that do not use an open admissions policy select students, in part, on their high school grade point average.

BASES FOR MARKING AND REPORTING

The phrase "bases for marking and reporting" can imply two quite different concepts: (1) what aspects or student *characteristics* we wish to report and (2) what *kinds of data* we will use as evidence in making our report. Both bases for marking interact with methods used for marking and reporting. For example, if we are going to base our marks on affective objectives, we might use a different set of symbols for reporting than we would use for reporting on cognitive objectives. And if we are going to use standardized test scores as evidence for having achieved certain objectives, we might use a different scheme for reporting than if we are going to use classroom participation. Because we seldom want to report on only one basis, this leads to the conclusion that it may well be advantageous to use different schemes for reporting. This will be dealt with further in the next section. Here, we wish to discuss briefly what aspects we may wish to report and the kinds of data we might gather for the report.

The major factor that should be reported is the degree to which the student has achieved the educational objectives of the course. This could well be accompanied by data suggestive of reasons why the student achieved at that level as opposed to some higher or lower level. But, of course, all this is not so easy as it sounds. Schools have many objectives—often too intangible and certainly too many to be reported on any reasonable report— and the task confronting educators is to choose which of those objectives are crucial and should be reported. A common fault of many traditional "report cards" is that they are so inadequate in their coverage of objectives. This relates to the problems encountered in measuring some objectives— particularly in the affective areas. But if we hold certain affective objectives to be important, we should attempt to measure them, and we should report the results of those attempts.

The data obtained through all the methods we have considered in this book are appropriate to consider in any thorough report. Informal tests, classroom observations, homework assignments, products, and standardized test results are all useful data in reporting pupil progress. Data suggestive of reasons as to the degree of objective attainment would include such things as ability level, attendance, effort, interest, and cooperation on the part of the pupil. (The last four may be objectives

in their own right, but they are also related to the achievement of other objectives.)

MARKING AND REPORTING PROCEDURES

We suggested in the preceding sections that a variety of people have good reason for desiring information about student achievement and that there are different bases for marking. Thus, the schools may need to consider different reporting procedures for communicating adequately with all interested parties. Reporting schemes may also vary, depending on the grade level of the student. For example, a single summary mark may not be desirable for the early elementary grades, whereas such a score may be almost mandatory for reporting high school students' achievements to colleges or college students' achievements to graduate schools.

The comparison of different reporting procedures should not be on an either-or basis. It is certainly possible, and usually advantageous, to use several procedures simultaneously.

In this section we discuss a variety of marking and reporting procedures and point out some advantages and disadvantages of each. We discuss marks, checklists, narrative reports, conferences, self-evaluation, and contract grading. The most important requirements of any procedure are that (1) it be understood by those persons giving and receiving the reports and (2) the reports be based on the objectives the school is striving to reach.

Marks

By marks we refer to those systems that use summary symbols of some type. These symbols may be letters such as A, B, C, D, F or O, S, U; numbers such as 9 through 1; pass-fail; or almost any other set of symbols. Because these symbols as traditionally used convey an overall impression of the student's total performance in a subject-matter area, they are more useful in summative than in formative evaluation. Whether or not marks serve any useful function depends upon how a teacher decides which symbol to give a child and whether the meaning the teacher has for the symbol is the one interpreted by the recipient of the report.

An amusing, if somewhat cynical, description of a grade is as follows:

> An inadequate report of an inaccurate judgment by a biased and variable judge of the extent to which a student has attained an undefined level of mastery of an unknown proportion of an indefinite material (Dressel, 1983, p. 12).

While we admit many teachers' "marks" may fit that description, it need not be so!

Several considerations must be taken into account when using symbols. One must decide if the grades should represent achievement or attitude. If the former, should it be achievement relative to an individual's own ability, relative to a set standard, or relative to peer performance? Should one mark on status or growth? What set of symbols should be used? How many different marks should be used? What percent of the students should fail?

Achievement or Attitude (Effort)?

Most educators believe that if only a single mark is given, it should represent achievement in the subject matter rather than attitude or effort. There are several reasons for this: (1) Achievement is easier to measure accurately; attitudes can be faked. (2) Most people interpret scores as if they indicated degree of competency rather than degree of effort. (3) Students must learn to realize that real life achievement is generally more important than effort or interest. Of course, effort affects achievement, but it is the achievement that is ultimately of more importance. (How hard surgeons or pilots try is not nearly so important as whether they do the job for which they are hired.)

Teachers are often tempted to let a single symbol represent some combination of achievement and attitude. For example, all 15 teachers interviewed in a case study approach believed that achievement of instructional objectives should be the primary basis for grades. However, 12 of them also believed strongly that effort should be considered (Stiggins, Frisbie, & Griswold, 1989). Salaganick and Epstein (1982) also found that teachers do not differentiate between achievement and effort. This is poor practice because it makes the symbol impossible to interpret. There is no way to know how much of the symbol was due to each factor or in which of the two the student was deemed better.

Teachers, however, should have the development of good attitudes as one of their objectives. It is important to evaluate the degree to which that objective is met and to report on it, in some fashion at least, to students and parents. If the student's general attitudes are to be reported via a single symbol, it should be a separate mark from the one that reports achievement level. It should be noted that there is legal precedent suggesting that it is unfair to reduce academic grades for misconduct unrelated to academic achievement (Bartlett, 1987).

Achievement Relative to a Set Standard, a Norm Group, or One's Own Ability?

Historically, marks were dependent on a set "standard" or were criterion-referenced. A student had to achieve a 94 percent for an A, an 88 percent for a B, and so forth. As we pointed out before, the percent right on a test is as dependent on test characteristics as on student characteristics. Thus, there is simply no mathematical, psychological, or educational basis for such practices as equating 94 percent or more with an A and 69 percent or less with F.

Recognizing the fallacies of such set standards, some educators have chosen a norm-referenced system of assigning marks. Thus, a student's grade is dependent upon how other students achieve. But there is considerable reaction by teachers and students *against* such norm referencing. People *mistakenly* think it means "grading on the normal curve" and therefore also means, for example, failing 5 percent and giving A's to 5 percent of every class. Marking on a normative basis does *not* necessarily mean that each class will have a normal distribution of grades or that anyone will necessarily fail. It simply means that the symbol used indicates how a student achieved relative to other students.[1]

Certainly there are dangers of using a normative basis for assigning marks if the norm group is too small. No one who knows even the rudiments of sampling would suggest that all classes should have equal distributions of grades. This is particularly true when one considers that students are rarely assigned to classes at random. Also, there is some evidence that norm-referenced marking impacts negatively on the motivation of students who regularly score toward the bottom of the class (Natriello, 1987) and discourages students from helping each other (Deutsch, 1979). Bishop (1989) suggested that a root cause of high school students' poor motivation is peer pressure against studying hard. He posited that this is due to norm referencing and that "when we set up a zero-sum competition among friends, we should not be surprised when they decide not to compete" (p. 9). He argued for a criterion-referenced system of assessment.

Nevertheless, norm referencing gives important feedback to students . . . "vital information if the student is deciding whether to apply to vocational school or medical school" (Slavin, 1978, p. 98). The belief that within-class norm referencing may harm motivation coupled with the fact that students need to have norm-referenced information to make wise educational and vocational decisions may appear to be a dilemma. However, it is easily resolved by making the norm group more inclusive than a single class. It would be better to compare students, say, against those who have taken the class the previous three years. Thus, students are not competing against their own classmates in a zero-sum game. All could be winners and achieve A's. Many measurement specialists we know use this method (see Terwilliger, 1989). Even if teachers did not use a formal system, if they would try to keep in mind the performance level of students in general and grade on a normative basis against this broader norm group, there would likely be more consistency in grading among teachers than if every teacher graded on the basis of his/her own arbitrary standards.

Actually, the debate between norms and standards is, in a sense, a false one. As Ebel (1972, p. 322) pointed out, sometimes those who argue for standards maintain that experienced teachers know what the standards should be and that inexperienced teachers can quickly learn them. But this means that "standards" are derived from observing students' performances, so they are actually norms!

If schools use mastery-learning approaches to instruction, educators should adopt criterion-referenced measurement as opposed to norm-referenced measurement so that the reporting system is based on criteria, or standards. But, as opposed to the percentage-grade procedure, the teachers using the mastery-learning approach should have the same set of standards. Thus, the "grade" a student receives might well be a statement regarding his position in the sequence of materials. (For example, if Johnny has successfully completed Unit III-A in arithmetic, his grade is III-A.) Although this grade would be standard rather than norm-based, there is nothing to prevent the report from also including some normative data. (For example, about 85 percent of the students who have been in school 3 years have finished Unit II-C, 40 percent have completed III-A, and the top 15 percent have finished Unit IV-D.)

A criticism occasionally made of marking systems based on either a norm or a set of standards is that such systems ignore individual differences. That is not true. Such systems explicitly *report* individual differences in achievement. Yet a question that often arises in education is whether one should hold different standards for students of different ability levels and let the set of symbols used in marking take on variable meaning for students of differing abilities. Of course, in one sense of the word, we should hold different standards. We should expect more from some students than from

---

[1]Interestingly enough, we once heard a parent discussing marks at a school board meeting saying that " . . my children are different, and I don't want them compared to anyone." We wondered how he knew they were different if he hadn't compared them to someone!

others. And we should report—at least in formative evaluations—whether a student is doing as well as we expect. But to give one student an A because his low achievement comes up to a level we would expect, considering his low level of ability, and to give another student a B because, although he is achieving very well, his work is not quite up to what we would expect, considering his ability level, would result in confusion. Any reporting of achievement relative to one's own ability should not be accomplished via a system that obscures information about actual level of achievement. Also, it should be pointed out that when one compares two fallible measures—level of achievement with level of aptitude—any "difference" between them is likely to be quite unreliable (see Chapter 12 on the reliability of difference scores). Thus, only reasonably large discrepancies should be noted.

Status or Growth? Some instructors and students think grades would be fairer if based on the level of improvement (growth) a student makes rather than on the final level of achievement (status). Marking on the basis of growth has similar problems to marking on effort or in comparison to aptitude:

1. Growth is hard to measure. Change scores are notably unreliable. Regression effects result in an advantage to students with initially low scores. Students soon learn to fake ignorance on pretests to present an illusion of great growth.
2. Most score interpretation is of status rather than growth.
3. In the long run, competence is more important than growth.

Of course, no teacher should ignore growth, and there should be communication of that growth (as well as it can be measured) to students and parents. This is particularly true in elementary school. But reporting growth should not be a replacement for reporting status. *Growth is more valuable in formative evaluation, while status is more important in summative reports.*

What Symbols Should Be Used? Some school officials who are antagonistic toward the A–F set of symbols that connote level of achievement have adopted a different set of symbols (such as O, S, and N for outstanding, satisfactory, and more effort needed). Such sets of symbols are usually less clear to the students and parents than the traditional A–F. While it is true that some symbols connote level of achievement (measurement) and others connote the teacher's satisfaction with that level (evaluation), it is very hard for either students or parents to interpret the latter without knowing the former. It is relatively meaningless for a teacher to communicate her value *judgment* about the student's level of achievement without first conveying some information about that level.

We know of one school that replaced the traditional letter grades with the terms *consistent progress, improvement shown,* and *improvement needed.* This supposedly allowed a teacher to "individualize" her report so that two students could receive the same "mark" even though they achieved at different levels—thus accounting for individual differences! Apart from the fact that giving the same mark for different levels of performance obscures rather than accounts for differences, the terms themselves are uninterpretable. As many teachers, parents, and students in the system pointed out, one could make consistent progress, show improvement, and need improvement simultaneously. Yet only one of the ratings was to be checked!

While we are not advocating the A–F set of symbols as opposed to other possible sets, it does seem important that the rank order of the symbols be interpretable and that they represent mutually exclusive categories. The particular symbols used are usually not that important unless they are changed—as in the case mentioned above—so as to become almost completely uninterpretable. In general, symbols should connote level of achievement, if that is what is being reported, and they should connote the teacher's affect regarding that level if that is what is to be reported.

Few Marks or Many? Many educators seem to feel that, since grades are unreliable, it is better to have only a few unique marks representing broad categories (such as honors, pass, fail) rather than using more specific categories (such as A+, A, A−, ... , D+, D, D−, F). This is a misconception. While one obviously cannot grade in finer categories than one can discriminate, it is not psychometrically advantageous to collapse reliable discriminations already made into broader categories. Dressel and Nelson (1961) noted that the five-category scheme seems the most popular. Schemes that have departed either toward more or fewer categories tend to get modified back to a five-category system.

The Pass–Fail System In spite of the higher reliability of a multicategory system of reporting, there was a considerable move toward a more restrictive two-category (pass–fail) system in the late 1960s and early 1970s (Burwen, 1971; Pinchak & Breland, 1973). There has been considerable discussion in the literature about whether this is good or bad (Warren, 1970).

The most commonly claimed justification for the P–F plan is that it encourages students to take courses they would otherwise not take because of a fear of lowering their grade-point average (GPA). Other stated purposes are that such a system reduces student anxiety, gives students greater control over the allocation of study time, and shifts students' efforts from grade-getting to learning (see, e.g., Milton, 1967; Benson, 1969; Feldmesser, 1969; Quann, 1970).

Questionnaires and empirical studies on the results of the P–F system suggest that:

1. Roughly 75 to 85 percent of the students who elect to take a course with pass–fail would have taken the course anyway (Karlins, 1969; Morishima & Micek, 1970). Warren (1975, p. 3) made an even stronger statement: "the evidence is now overwhelming that pass–fail grading does not induce students to take courses they would have avoided under a traditional grading system for fear of depressing their grade-point average."

2. Students report that they feel less anxious in P–F courses (Mellville & Stamm, 1967; Cromer, 1969; Karlins, 1969).

3. Students do use the P–F option to reduce study time in that area and concentrate on other courses (Milton, 1967; Feldmesser, 1969; Freeman, 1969; Karlins, 1969; Morishima & Micek, 1970).

4. The motivation to learn in a pass–fail course is about the same or less for 85 percent of the respondents in one study (Hales et al., 1971).

5. Students do not perform as well in P–F courses as in regular courses (Karlins, 1969; Stallings & Smock, 1971).

Whether these studies in general support or refute the advantages of a P–F system is debatable. The major goal of schooling is to induce learning, and since the evidence suggests that students neither learn nor feel as motivated to learn in P–F courses, we might consider the evidence as negative. On the other hand, we do wish to encourage students to explore different areas—and a few more probably do if we offer a P–F option. Also, if students reallocate their study time and learn less in the P–F courses, they may be learning more in their other courses.

Considering the total set of findings regarding P–F systems, some educators believe that there is more to be gained than lost in initiating a *partial* P–F system. Those schools adopting a partial P–F option may wish to consider a slight deviation of this scheme and use a Pass–No-Record grade. Using this procedure, no record at all would be entered on the transcript in the event of a no-pass. Some educators object to this because the no-pass would not count in the GPA and a student could continue going to school indefinitely until he/she finally accumulated enough credits to graduate. But this would not be necessarily bad. As Warren remarked: "The basic argument is whether students taking courses in which they can fail without penalty would constitute an inefficient use of the institution's resources. No one knows" (1970, p. 19).

To Fail or Not to Fail In considering the issue of whether or not to fail a student one needs to differentiate between two responsibilities: that to society and that to the individual students. Passing some exams or classes, or graduating with certain degrees, allows individuals to become licensed or certified to perform certain tasks in society. For example, medical doctors can practice medicine if they obtain an M.D. degree and pass an exam. Individuals can teach if they obtain the necessary standards required for teacher certification (licensure). Similar standards are required for many occupations. Indeed, one must pass a test to drive a car. In these situations the classes or tests serve as a screening device to protect society from the incompetent. We do not want incompetents operating on us, teaching us, building bridges we drive over, repairing our cars, or indeed driving on the same road we do. While it is not always easy to determine just what level of competence society should require, it should be clear that there does exist a level of competence too low to tolerate. Some people should not be allowed to operate on others, teach others, or build bridges others use. Thus, at least the potential for failure must exist if passing a course or examination carries any connotation that the person is qualified to serve society.

In some situations passing does *not* carry any connotation of being qualified to serve society. (Passing first grade would be an obvious example.) Thus, there is no reason to fail a person to protect society. In those cases we should make our decision of pass or fail based on what is best for the individual. Based on some evidence, many educators have decided that it is very seldom in the best interests of an individual to fail a grade in the public schools. This has led to social promotion and "protected adolescents from the consequences of failing to learn" (Bishop, 1989, p. 7). But it is not

at all clear that this is the best educational procedure. It may well result in graduating high school seniors who cannot read or do seventh-grade arithmetic. It is hard to know how this is in the best interest of the child.

If a child is to be retained in school, it is usually agreed that the earlier in school the more likely it will result in benefits to the child. Thus, repeating kindergarten or early primary grades is more common than repeating later grades, although most research indicates that retention should be done *exceedingly sparingly* if at all (Smith & Shepard, 1987).

Many educators believe it is reasonable to grade partially on the basis of motivation at the cut point between passing and failing (see Thomas, 1986). They argue that students who try to learn, but can't should not be punished with failure. Of course, this argument is irrelevant for normal students in the public schools. They *could* learn the minimum amount expected to pass if they so desired. (We admit there may be a few exceptions, but few teachers in American schools set anything but a very low standard for a D− or whatever other symbol represents a minimum pass.)

We believe that almost all measurement experts would agree that there should *not* be any set norm-referenced percentage of failures. Terwilliger (1989) makes the point that failure decisions should be based only upon performance on measures of minimal objectives.

Disadvantages of Marks Before listing some disadvantages and advantages of marks, we remind the reader that we are not comparing the different reporting systems on an either-or basis. The use of summary symbols in no way precludes the use of other methods.

The most often-mentioned disadvantages of using a single symbol to represent the degree to which a student has achieved certain objectives are as follows (see Anderson, 1966; Ebel, 1974b):

1. Marks are inaccurate measures of competence and are not used in a comparable way from school to school, or even teacher to teacher.

© 1973 United Feature Syndicate, Inc.

To one teacher, B may be average, while to another C− may be average. One teacher may mark on effort; another, on results. One may fail 30 percent of the class; another, none. These types of inconsistencies are very harmful and destroy the interpretability of such marking schemes.

2. Marks are not related to the important objectives of the school.
3. Marks are inadequate in communicating between the home and school.
4. Marks produce side effects detrimental to the welfare of the child. The side effects usually mentioned are:
   a. the debilitating impact of failure;
   b. the encouragement of excess competitiveness;
   c. increased cheating;
   d. a distortion of educational values, which makes marks rather than learning the important criterion of success.

These objections need not necessarily apply to marks, nor are they unique to the symbol system.

Both (1) and (2) above are sometimes relevant criticisms of existing practices, but the symbol system does not force these disadvantages. Marks should be comparable and could be made more comparable, at least within a single school district; they could and should be related to important objectives. They will always be somewhat inaccurate, but no more so than any other system of recording evaluations. Objection (3) is true. However, the implication of recognizing this is that one should supplement the marks with additional means of communication rather than eliminate marks. Every other single system is inadequate also. Most parents are in favor of marks and do not want them eliminated. Objection (4a) may be true. Certainly, many social psychologists have gathered data that they maintain support that claim. But it is really an irrelevant criticism of symbols. None of the symbols needs to represent failure in the sense of not receiving credit for the course. And failure, however defined, could be reported via any system. One does not need to use symbols to communicate inadequate performance. And if inadequate performance unduly affects self-concept, let us remember that it is the inadequate performance that is the problem, not the reporting of it. Objections (4b) through (4d) are made with little solid evidence to support them. If they are true, however, it is due to an overemphasis on reporting rather than to any inherent limitation of the *method* of reporting by symbols rather than by letters, checklists, or conferences.

Advantages of Marks Some of the advantages of marks are as follows:

1. Marks are the least time-consuming and most efficient method of reporting.
2. Symbols can be converted to numbers. Thus, GPAs (and high school ranks) can be computed. These GPAs are useful in many types of selection, placement, and classification decisions. They are the best single predictor of success in future schooling. If an organization needs to make many decisions, an actuarial approach using GPA as one of the input variables is much more efficient and results in a greater number of accurate decisions than would result if clinical decisions were made on the basis of letters of recommendation.
3. Marks relate not only to one's chances to obtain good grades in future courses; they also relate somewhat to achievements beyond school.
4. A mark serves as an overall summary index, and students want and need to know how they did on the whole—all things considered—as well as how they did on each separate subobjective. Evidence shows that students want to receive these overall summary reports (National Assessment of Educational Progress, 1970a).

Assigning Marks If single summary marks are to be recorded and reported, two other factors need to be considered: (1) How does one combine (weight) the various data to arrive at a single index, and (2) how can the meaning of the symbols be made more comparable across teachers?

Combining Data: Given data from a variety of sources such as class discussion, daily homework, major reports, quizzes, and final examinations, a teacher must combine or weight these data to end up with a single index. There is certainly no consensus as to which type of data should receive the greatest emphasis. Some educators feel that any measurement obtained for formative evaluation purposes should not be weighted in determining a final summary index. Others point out that not to use such data and to use only a final exam would result in a less reliable (and probably less valid) summary mark. Further, many teachers strongly believe that many of their students would not complete assignments if grades were not attached to them (Stiggins, Frisbie, & Griswold, 1989). The only general guideline we can offer is that weightings should reflect both the relative importance of the specific educational objectives and the reliability and validity of the data. This is certainly partly a subjective determination. Whether one feels that class discussions or final examinations measure the most relevant objectives depends on the subject matter, the objectives, the type of class discussions, and the type of final. In general, the final test score will be the most reliable single measure. Whatever subjective decision a teacher makes about weightings, the students should be informed of these weights at the beginning of the course. (This serves the same purposes as informing a student about the weights in a table of specifications. See Chapter 4.)

When finally combining data, one more point must be kept in mind—the differences in variability of the original scores affect the weights. Consider the following example. Suppose we wish the midterm to count one-fourth, the class project to count one-fourth, and the final to count one-half. Suppose Mary got the highest grade in class on the midterm and the lowest on the final, while John did just the opposite. Assume further that they both scored at the mean on the class project. Now, if the final is twice as important in determining the summary mark, it seems John should receive the highest combined score. But what if the range of raw scores on the midterm is from 25 to 58 and the range on the final is from 32 to 40? If both received a raw score of 40 on the project, they would have the following scores:

	Mary	John
Project	$1 \times 40 = 40$	$1 \times 40 = 40$
Midterm	$1 \times 58 = 58$	$1 \times 25 = 25$
Final	$2 \times 32 = \underline{64}$	$2 \times 40 = \underline{80}$
	162	145

In this example the midterm is actually more important in determining the final score than the final test, even though the final test was "weighted" twice as much! This is, of course, due to the unequal variability of the midterm and final exam score distributions. A procedure that avoids this problem is to transform all scores into standard scores (such as z or T) so as to mathematically equate the variances of the sets of scores prior to weighting and combining.

If the T scores on both the midterm and the final ranged from 35 to 65 (plus and minus 1.5 standard deviations) and the weighted T scores were combined, we would obtain the following scores:

	Mary	John
Project	$1 \times 50 = 50$	$1 \times 50 = 50$
Midterm	$1 \times 65 = 65$	$1 \times 35 = 35$
Final	$2 \times 35 = \underline{70}$	$2 \times 65 = \underline{130}$
	185	215

Using weighted T scores, we see that John obtained the higher combined score—which he should if the final is really more important than the midterm.

To combine the raw scores of tests, quizzes, homework, and so on when they are in different units is as meaningless as it is to average temperatures in Celsius and Fahrenheit! Unfortunately, most teachers do exactly that (Stiggins, Frisbie, & Griswold, 1989).

If teachers are *not* going to place data from various sources on a common scale such as a z or T score scale, they should at least attempt to assess "raw" scores so as to minimize the variance problem. In the previous example, if a teacher believes the final should count twice as much as the midterm, she should make it twice as long. If the paper and midterm are to receive equal weight, they must, at least, have the same possible *range* of points.

Making Marks Comparable: As we have mentioned, one of the limitations of marks is that they are *not* comparable from school to school or teacher to teacher. Even within a school building, where every teacher uses the same set of symbols supposedly defined the same way, we find large disparities. For example, in an A–F system some teachers will continue to use C as average, whereas others will interpret anything less than B as indicative of inadequate performance or perhaps mark so that everyone who achieves the minimum level of mastery receives an A! Such disparities are frustrating to the students and cause confusion for anyone attempting to decipher what a B really means.

There are several steps a school can take to help assure comparability. One is to make sure that teachers in the system understand both the meaning the school attaches to the symbols and the importance of the commonality of meaning across teachers. Thus, if a school is using symbols such as O, S, and U (outstanding, satisfactory, and unsatisfactory), these terms must be defined by the school. If a school is using an absolute system, it should make clear just what level of performance is necessary for an O grade. If the school is using a relative marking system, it should make clear what percentage of students can really be outstanding. Also, when using the relative system, the school will need to provide each teacher with some information about how her class compares with the total school population. This should help prevent the unfairness of an average student receiving a high grade because he is in a poor class or a good student receiving an average grade because he is in an outstanding class.

Finally, if a teacher has been given some rough guidelines as to how her grade distribution should look, these guidelines should be given very serious consideration. If a teacher simply refuses to adopt the grading system of the school, some educators believe that the school has both the moral and legal right to alter that teacher's mark. There is some legal precedence to suggest that administrators have the right to change grades and/or force teachers to conform to an official grading policy (Zirkel, 1990).

Checklists and Rating Scales

Perhaps the major limitation of a single mark is that it does not provide enough specific information to be helpful in diagnosing a student's strengths and weaknesses. The feedback to the pupil, his parents, and other teachers is just too limited for them to plan diagnostic or remedial help. One solution is to provide more detailed checklists or rating scales. These rating scales or checklists should include the major cognitive (or psychomotor) objectives for each subject-matter area. Checklists or rating scales on the affective objectives should also be developed. These affective scales may be common across all subject-matter areas (see Chapter 9 for a discussion of constructing checklists and rating scales).

If general instructional objectives have been written out for each course, these could serve as the basis for a checklist or rating scale. For example, the objectives listed at the beginning of each chapter in this book could be used for a course in measurement. The teacher could check each one according to whether the objective had been achieved, or she could rate the degree to which the objectives have been achieved on a 3- (or 5-) point scale.

A school system using a detailed report for each subject is indeed providing the reader with a great deal of information. Such a report requires that a teacher keep an accurate record of just what it is each child can do. Teachers, of course, should do this anyway, but many would not do so unless it was necessitated by such a report. One inadequately researched question is how detailed a report can be without overwhelming the reader with information overload. If a parent has three or four children in elementary school, that parent will have to devote considerable time and effort to reading the reports, let alone knowing what they mean as to how, in general, the children are doing in school.

If rating scales are to be useful, it is absolutely mandatory that they accurately reflect the school's objectives and that teachers gather sufficient data (through observations, tests, and other means) so that ratings can be completed accurately. Using rating scales in conjunction with a summary symbol that gives some relative information as to progress toward the school's objectives can provide a very meaningful report.

Narrative Reports (Letters)

Narrative reports (letters) can be used to report school progress to parents, prospective employers, and college admissions officers. They are used in a repetitive systematic fashion only with parents. An advantage of a narrative report is that it can both emphasize many different aspects of a child's school experiences yet focus on those of most significance. Physical, social, and emotional development along with subject matter achievement can be reported. A major limitation is that narrative reports are very time-consuming if done adequately. Further, although not a limitation of the method per se, some teachers do not write very well, and bad writing damages the reputation of all the teachers. Although not an inherent disadvantage of the method, most reports tend to become very monotonous, stereotyped, and minimally informative. One must keep in mind the distinction between saying something to you and telling you something. Letters often say a lot. They often don't tell you a lot!

In order to write a good report, a teacher must have not only adequate time but also a good grasp of the objectives. While we are certainly not suggesting that a teacher can assign correct symbols without having established some objectives, the lack of objectives may be less noticeable under such a system. Any vagueness in objectives will probably be noticeable in a report.

Conferences

Conferences are certainly a good idea in theory. Misunderstandings and miscommunications between home and school should be much less frequent if parents and educators meet face to face. Thus, while we support the concept of conferences, the beneficial results of actual conferences are not so great as they should be. There are several reasons for this.

1. Typically there are two conferences per year. The first is often scheduled too soon—before the teacher really knows the child. The second one is scheduled too late to do much good.
2. Teachers do not prepare well enough for conferences.
3. Parents may not take the time necessary to have a conference with all five or six of their child's teachers.
4. Some parents do not show up at all.
5. Parents and teachers are often defensive.
6. The conferences are often too short.
7. The excessive time necessary for adequate preparation and conducting of conferences may keep a teacher from performing other important tasks.

The task of holding a successful, meaningful dialogue with a parent about his or her child is not an easy one. A teacher needs considerable preparation for such a task. (A good reference is Canady and Seyfarth, 1979.) Many schools hold workshops to help teachers improve their skills in this area. Helpful guidelines to such conferences are given below (Romano, 1959):

1. Establish a friendly atmosphere free from interruption.
2. Be positive—begin and end the conference by enumerating favorable points.
3. Be truthful, yet tactful.
4. Be constructive in all suggestions to pupils and parents.
5. Help parents to achieve better understanding of their child as an individual.
6. Respect parents' and children's information as confidential.
7. Remain poised throughout the conference.
8. Be a good listener; let parents talk.
9. Observe professional ethics at all times.
10. Help parents find their own solutions to a problem.
11. Keep vocabulary simple; explain new terminology.
12. If you take notes during the conference, review them with parents.
13. Invite parents to visit and participate in school functions.
14. Base your judgments on all available facts and on actual situations.
15. Offer more than one possible solution to a problem.

Self-Evaluation

An aspect of evaluation that is being emphasized more and more is the value of student self-evaluation. Self-evaluation is obviously important if one is to be involved in self-directed learning. And self-directed learning is essential both in school and after the student leaves school. Unfortunately, research does not indicate clearly how teachers can improve students' abilities in self-evaluation (Russell, 1953; Sawin, 1969, pp. 194ff.).

Self-evaluations should *not* be used as a replacement for the marking and reporting done by the teachers. One must distinguish between self-evaluation and self-grading. Students are not always very accurate in self-evaluations or self-grading, and allowing self-grading could penalize the honest student and reward the dishonest one. However, there would be nothing wrong with allowing students to fill out self-reports, both to be sent home and filed in the school's cumulative record, regarding their perception of progress toward the educational objectives. As Geisinger (1982) reported, neither self-evaluation nor self-grading has achieved wide use.

Contract Grading

In contract grading, the student and teacher agree at the beginning of the course on the amount and quality of work necessary for a given grade. This contract may be individualized where the criteria are different for different students. The contract may involve self-evaluation of the quality on the part of the student, but that judgment is more likely to be made by the teacher. Kirschenbaum, Simon, and Napier (1971) have suggested that quantity of student work is easier to describe than the quality, and therefore the quality of work may suffer under contract grading. While student anxiety is reduced under contract grading, student reaction to it is mixed (Hassencahl, 1979). Nevertheless, the participation by the student in establishing the original contract should minimize later complaints about the unfairness of a course grade. Of course, in setting contracts, a teacher still needs to be concerned about comparability of grades. An A (if letter grades are used) should still represent outstanding achievement if that is the schoolwide meaning of an A.

CRITERIA FOR A MARKING–REPORTING SYSTEM

The following should be helpful to educators who wish to evaluate their own marking and reporting system.

1. Is the system based on a clear statement of educational objectives?

2. Is the system understood by both those making the reports and those to whom they are sent (including students)?
3. Does the system desirably affect the students' learning?
4. Is the system detailed enough to be diagnostic and yet compact enough to be operational?
5. Does the system involve *two-way* communication between home and school?
6. Does the system promote desirable public relations?
7. Is the system reasonably economical in terms of teacher time?

■ SUMMARY

The major ideas, conclusions, and implications of this chapter are summarized in the following statements:

1. Measurement and evaluation are necessary for wise educational decision making. Since all decisions are not made at the time of measurement, it is necessary to keep a record of student progress.
2. Since many people make, or help the student make, decisions based upon school achievement, we need to consider what reporting procedures can best communicate the student's achievements.
3. Students, parents, administrators, teachers, prospective employers, and college admissions officers all need information from the school to assist them in decision making.
4. Students need feedback to guide them in their decision making. They primarily should receive such information through daily interaction with their teachers, but formal periodic reports can also assist in student decision making.
5. Many educators and students believe that recording of grades motivates students to learn things they would not otherwise learn.
6. There exist a variety of reporting procedures such as marks, checklists, letters, and conferences. Each has advantages and limitations. A

school may use different schemes at different grade levels as well as use different schemes for the same grade level for reporting to different people.

7. The most important requirements of any marking-reporting procedure are that (1) those using it understand the system and (2) the reports are based on the objectives the school is striving to teach.

8. Marks refer to those systems that use summary symbols of some type.

9. If only a *single* symbol is assigned, it should represent achievement in the subject matter (not attitude) and status rather than growth.

10. In traditional classroom situations, marks should be based on a normative interpretation, but the norm group should be broader than the single class. In mastery-learning approaches to instruction, marks should be criterion-referenced.

11. Collapsing the number of categories into fewer, broader categories in a marking system will decrease the reliability of the marks.

12. The partial pass–fail system of marking is probably a beneficial educational procedure. A complete pass–fail system likely would be deleterious.

13. The major faults of grading are not inherent faults of the marking system but are due to teachers not using the system correctly.

14. Procedures should be applied that help make marks more comparable across teachers.

15. The major limitation of a single summary mark is that it does not provide enough specific information to be helpful in diagnosing a student's strengths and weaknesses.

16. Checklists or rating scales can provide more detailed information, which may help in diagnostic or remedial planning.

17. Letters are occasionally used in reporting. Their main advantage is that they can report on many different aspects of a child's school experiences. Their major limitation is that, if done correctly, they are very time-consuming.

18. If a teacher prepares properly, conferences can be a very effective method of presentation.

■ POINTS TO PONDER

1. Some educators suggest that we should not tell students when they are not doing well in school because it will hurt their self-concepts. Do you agree? State your reasons.

2. Are letters to parents more or less likely than report cards to cover the important objectives of the school? Defend your answer.

3. If you were to design the ideal report card, what would it include?

4. Under what circumstances would you be willing to fail a student in a course?

5. Should the distribution of grades be the same in a twelfth-grade calculus class as a twelfth-grade consumer math class? Why or why not?

6. Design a system of holding conferences in a middle school (grades 6–8) such that the traditional problem of parents standing in line to see teachers is minimized.

7. Should Mr. Jones, who teaches advanced math classes for the college prep students who are the most academically capable in the school, be allowed to assign more *low* grades than Mr. Smith assigns to his shop class—which happens to be composed of the academically weakest students in the school?

Chapter 21

Accountability: Testing and Evaluation Programs

- ■ **Accountability**
- ■ **External Testing Programs**

How well are our children doing in school? What are they learning? Are our schools doing a good job? Is our education better than it used to be? Will students in our state, and in our nation be able to compete successfully in the future? Americans ask questions like this everyday, but the answers to them, and to other important questions concerning adequacy of our educational system are hard to come by (Alexander & James, 1987, p. 3).

Accountability is in vogue in education! In this chapter we first discuss some political, philosophical, and measurement concerns related to accountability and some approaches to and possible consequences of accountability. Next, we discuss three kinds of external evaluation programs: college selection and placement programs, state assessment programs, and national assessment programs. The state assessment programs are outgrowths of the demand for accountability.

After studying this chapter, you should be able to:

1. Define accountability.
2. Recognize political reasons for the popularity of the accountability concept.
3. Recognize philosophical concerns related to accountability.
4. Understand measurement problems of accountability programs.
5. Judge various accountability programs with respect to their philosophical and measurement limitations.
6. Differentiate between internal and external testing programs.
7. Understand the functions of college selection and placement programs.
8. Recognize some priorities, trends, and reasons for state and national assessment programs.

ACCOUNTABILITY

Accountability means different things to different people, and it has been defined in a myriad of ways. Educational accountability had its origin in the politics and polemics surrounding education. A typical definition of accountability would include *setting* correct goals; *evaluating* their degree of achievement (we discuss program evaluation in the next section) and at what price; *presenting and interpreting* this information to the public; and *accepting responsibility* for any results that are perceived as inadequate. A few users of the term would evidently allow educators to attempt to explain why all failures may not be their fault. In the abstract, accountability is basically the process of justifying costs by presenting the positive effects derived from expenditures. Perhaps in the concrete it boils down to (1) who gets hanged when things go wrong and (2) who does the hanging? (Browder, 1971, p. 19).

Reactions to accountability among educators have been mixed. It has been said that any new idea passes through the following stages: (1) indignant rejection, (2) reasoned objection, (3) qualified opposition, (4) tentative acceptance, (5) qualified endorsement, (6) judicious modification, (7) cautious adoption, (8) impassioned espousal, (9) proud parenthood, and (10) dogmatic propagation. As Browder, Atkins, and Kaya (1973, p. vi) suggest with respect to accountability, some legislators, school boards, and commercial hucksters short-circuited the evolutionary sequence and reached a point of impassioned espousal rapidly. Others are still at the point of indignant rejection.

What does all this have to do with the contents of a textbook in measurement? Simply this: *Fair* accountability depends on good measurement and the correct uses of that measurement data. Well-meaning but measurement-naive legislators, however, may mandate the use of measurement data that result in *unfair* conclusions about school/teacher quality and impede school improvement. As accountability procedures are implemented, educators and prospective educators who are readers of this book should be alerted to the various political/philosophical and measurement aspects inherent in such programs in order to maximize their values and minimize their dangers. We, and probably most educators, are in favor of the abstract principle of accountability. But it is impossible to say in the abstract whether accountability is a blessing or burden, a miracle or mirage, a milestone or millstone, and potential problems arise when we try to move from the abstract to the specific. What are some of the political/philosophical and measurement concerns educators should be alert to, and what are some of the potential approaches to and consequences of accountability?

Political/Philosophical Concerns

Basically the political/philosophical concerns center around who is accountable and for what they are accountable. We are not suggesting that we have the answers to these questions, but we can present some different dimensions that pertain to the questions.

Who Is Accountable?   There is certainly no current agreement about who should be held accountable in education. It seems to us that the pendulum has swung too far toward holding educators accountable for lack of pupil learning in spite of any failures, deficiencies, and incompetence in the students and/or parents. Based on a 1989 poll, Elam concluded that

> Teachers tend to regard themselves as martyrs. Overwhelmingly, they believe they are unappreciated and unrewarded ... (1989, p. 785).

The definition of teaching for many educational critics has changed from an activity *intended* to induce learning to an activity that *does* induce learning. Although it seems condescending to assume that students have no responsibility for their own learning, most writers on educational accountability do not mention students' (or parents') accountability. Yet, "substituting the teacher ... for the pupil as the *only* accountable party is an example of reactionary thinking" (Campbell, 1971, p. 177). Educators *alone* cannot be held accountable for a product when they have virtually no control over their resources or raw material (Lindman, 1971).

The foregoing paragraph is not meant to let educators off the hook. Just because educators are not accountable for everything does not mean they are not accountable for anything. But we need to be somewhat moderate in any approach to accountability. Educators should be held accountable for some aspects of children's learning, but there is no easy way to discern which portions are under their control. Accountability programs must keep this in mind. The "who is accountable" question cannot at present be answered, and until (and if) it is answered, we must remember that the purpose of accountability programs should not be punitive in nature, but rather should be accepted as a means of quality control.

Accountable for What? Perhaps even more difficult than the question of whom should be held accountable is the question of "accountable for what?" A simplistic answer is that educators should be held accountable for the pupils' attainments of our educational objectives. But although there is a consensus about many desired outcomes, there still remain diverse goals or objectives held by our educational systems. Some people maintain "good citizenship" or "healthy self-concepts" are more important than reading skills. Others assert just the opposite. This difference of opinion causes considerable difficulty when it comes to instituting accountability. And since we can measure some objectives more readily than others, accountability programs may focus narrowly on these easily measured objectives. We discuss this further in the section on measurement problems related to accountability.

We are strong advocates of the position that the role of educators is to facilitate certain types of student learning. We believe that educators need to measure student outcomes in order to make wise educational decisions. But this position is not analogous to blaming teachers for any specified lack of pupil performance. Whether one wishes to say they are *accountable* for pupil outcomes depends in part on how one wants to define accountability and in part on philosophical/political considerations.

Measurement Concerns

The measurement problems in accountability are very difficult to surmount. We do not intend to discuss all these problems in detail. Rather, we wish to introduce the reader to a few key concerns. As a professional, you almost invariably will be subject to some accountability programs, and therefore you should be alert to some of the more pressing measurement problems involved.

Establishing Causal Relations The attempt to determine causal relationships is directly related to the political/philosophical issue of *whom* is to be held accountable. The abstract answer is that people should be held responsible only for those outcomes they can effect. Concrete details of how to determine that are at best incomplete. But even if we determine that a teacher can and should affect reading skills, how can we determine that a student who reads well does so because of the teacher's efforts?

Specialists in educational measurement and evaluation have historically concentrated their efforts on determining *what is*, rather than *who is responsible or accountable* for what is. Many problems still exist in the first determination, such as measurement in the affective domain. However, by comparison, we can do a fairly accurate job of measuring what is. What we cannot do very well is to establish causal relationships between these outcomes and various input and process variables. To do this requires something more than measurement; it requires a research design.

Over twenty years ago, Dyer (1970, p. 207) referred to four groups of variables that must be taken into account in any thorough accountability research design:

1. *Input variables*, or the characteristics of the *pupils* as they *enter* a particular phase of schooling—their health, level of achievement, self-concept, aspirations, and other considerations.
2. *Surrounding conditions* within which the school operates, including the home, community, and school conditions.
3. The *educational process*.

4. *Output variables*, or the characteristics of the pupils as they emerge from a particular phase of schooling.

However, it is difficult to take the first three variables into account, and many accountability programs will not be likely to do so. Thus, there is a danger that schools (and teachers) in those districts where surrounding conditions are poor will be unduly chastised for low outputs. For example, there is a general trend toward merit pay or career ladders for teachers, and some advocate basing merit pay on student outcome measures. While most, if not all, educators would deplore this as inappropriate because of a lack of an established causal relationship, it does not keep legislatures from passing bills proposing such approaches. This problem is accentuated during this period in our society when some vociferous critics of education hold the naive belief that the school can and should be held accountable for overcoming poor input and negative surrounding variables. Yet research shows quite clearly that a large proportion of the variance in performance levels is accounted for by out-of-school variables, such as pupils' socioeconomic status and home environments.

Validity   Just as the measurement problem of establishing causal relations is related to the philosophical issue of whom is to be held accountable, the measurement problem of validity is related to the "what is to be assessed" issue. Because "basic skill" areas are very important as well as the easiest areas to assess, many accountability programs focus only on these areas. Since the school's objectives are ordinarily much broader than attainment of basic skills alone, the assessment tools may have inadequate content validity. Although poor content validity is always deplorable, it is particularly troublesome when the results of an assessment device are used to hold the schools (or teachers) accountable.

Measurement and evaluation that is mandated for accountability purposes takes place in a political context. Therefore we must recognize the ever-present danger of measurement and evalua-

tion bias. Scriven (1975) has written about the problem of evaluation bias and its control. One major step in attempting to reduce bias is to use an external, independent person to gather the test data and do the evaluation.

Approaches to and Consequences of Accountability

Because educational accountability is defined in so many different ways, there are many different approaches to it. Remember that the concept of accountability usually includes setting correct goals in terms of student outcomes (often with community help), evaluating whether these goals have been achieved (through either external or internal approaches) and at what price, reporting this information to the public, and accepting responsibility for inadequacies in performance. Operationalizing a construct as complicated as this is more of a building process than simply adopting some complete and adequate accountability program.

Accountability has forced schools to do a better job of specifying and evaluating objectives. There has been an increased focus on the relationship between outcomes, input, and process variables. Schools have worked toward adopting better management techniques and fiscal controls. There have been more concerted efforts to keep the public informed of educational objectives, expenses, processes, and results. All this seems commendable.

Accountability has also lead to increased teaching "toward the test," which could be counterproductive (see Chapter 19). Such questions as whether the performances observed on an assessment instrument are indeed the school's goals or only indicants of the school's goals, and under what circumstances teaching for the test is a harmful educational practice deserve careful consideration (see Chapter 19). Whenever the performance tested is only a sample (or indicant) of our objectives, teaching directly for the test (i.e., teaching for those specific questions on the test) is inappropriate. If a test indeed covers accepted objectives, it is appropriate to teach for the general topics covered by the test. But when the objectives covered on the test are much more narrow in focus than the objectives of the school, it would be inappropriate to stress only the general objectives covered by the test, and to do so could seriously alter the overall substance of the educational product (see Mehrens, 1984a).

Various external evaluation programs are discussed in the next section of this chapter. Some of these programs were in existence long before the current use of the term *accountability*. Others have been undertaken largely in response to the accountability issue.

EXTERNAL TESTING PROGRAMS

By *external testing programs* we mean those that are administered under the control of agencies other than the school. These programs often are administered in the school by school personnel, but the school is not officially in charge. We will discuss three such types of programs: college selection and placement programs, state assessment programs, and national assessment programs.

College Selection and Placement Programs

Many colleges have limited resources and cannot admit everyone who applies. In general, admission officers have felt that their job was to admit those who have the greatest probability of success in college. The criterion for judging success has typically been grades in college. Time and time again, it has been shown that high school grades are the best single predictor of college grades, that scholastic aptitude tests are the second best predictors, and that the two predictors combined in a multiple regression equation give a significantly better prediction than either one alone. [At the professional school level, test scores are often better predictors than grades (Whitney, 1989).] The average correlation between high school performance and first-year college grades is around 0.50 to 0.55. When scholastic aptitude tests are added as a pre-

dictor, the multiple correlation is raised from .05 to .10 points (Astin, 1971; Breland, 1979; Hills, 1964). Research suggests that biographical data, interviews, references, personality variables, and work samples have seldom added any practical precision to the prediction process (Hills, 1971, p. 694). Thus, research clearly shows that if one wishes to admit students on the basis of predicted success in college, scholastic aptitude tests are useful.

In spite of overwhelming validity data, there have been some severe critics of college admission procedures. Some of these critics feel that it is the right of all high school graduates to attend college, regardless of their chances of success. They argue for an open admissions policy. The desirability of this policy is debated, but much of the debate is purely academic, since some colleges simply do not have the money to admit all who wish to attempt college and others have routinely admitted all high school graduates.

Other critics argue for admissions decisions based on a quota system. In either case, testing for college entrance would still be useful. Under an open admissions policy, one would need tests to assist in placement decisions (and, of course, the facilities to adapt treatments to student needs). (In the absence of open admission policies, placement decisions need to be made in addition to selection decisions.) Under a quota system, one would still probably want to select, within each subgroup, those who are most likely to succeed. Thus, selection tests are useful. Existing aptitude tests predict about as well within one subgroup as another (see the section in Chapter 22 on fairness of tests to minority groups for a fuller discussion of this point).

The two major organizations in this country that provide college selection and placement programs are the College Entrance Examination Board (CEEB) and the American College Testing Program (ACT). About one-third of each year's crop of high school seniors takes the CEEB Scholastic Aptitude Test (SAT), and about one-third takes the ACT test. These two tests are not taken by exactly the same third, but many students do take both batteries. The reason students may take both tests is that different colleges have different requirements, so unless students know for sure what college they will be attending, they may end up being forced to take more than one test. (Some colleges allow either test.) Because the two tests are highly correlated, and because tests are seldom if ever used as the sole criterion, it seems that some flexibility by colleges regarding which test was taken is justifiable.

College Entrance Examination Board The College Entrance Examination Board (CEEB) is "an association of schools and colleges that concerns itself primarily with the movement of students into college. The chief purpose of the College Board is to increase access to that movement and to make it more equitable and efficient" (*Report of the Commission on Tests*, 1970, p. 11). The operational phases of the CEEB are conducted by Educational Testing Service (ETS). Although the CEEB's services are not restricted to college entrance examinations, it is best known for three such exams: The Preliminary Scholastic Aptitude Test/National Merit Scholarship Qualifying Test (PSAT/NMSQT), the Scholastic Aptitude Test (SAT), and a series of achievement tests.

The PSAT/NMSQT is basically a shortened (1 hour and 40 minutes) version of the SAT. It is typically given to high school juniors, and the scores are used for college counseling and to enter into competition for scholarships awarded by the National Merit Scholarship Corporation. The PSAT/NMSQT reports two scores, verbal and mathematical. The scores range from 20 to 80. A school can receive a score report providing a summary of the answers of the students in the school. This can be compared to the national pattern of responses as well as with a set of similar schools.

The SAT is a 3-hour objective test. It is considered a test of developed ability, not of factual knowledge. Verbal, mathematics, and English scores are provided. In addition, separate scores on the reading comprehension and vocabulary subtests of the verbal test are reported. Scores range from 200 to 800. As of 1988, 84 percent of all four-year colleges used the SAT (*The College Board News*, 1988–89). The Test of Standard Written English (TSWE) is administered with the SAT and is used for placement in college English courses. Currently the College Board is considering future changes to the SAT that may include longer reading passages, open-ended mathematics questions, and a third test covering writing skills that would (once a year) include a centrally scored essay portion.

The CEEB achievement tests are a series of 1-hour tests. There currently are 14 tests in a variety of subject-matter areas such as American history and social studies, European history and world cultures, biology, chemistry, physics, English composition, literature, two levels of mathematics, and several foreign languages. Like the SAT, scores range from 200 to 800.

Some colleges require that applicants take the SAT and three of the achievement tests. Some colleges request specific achievement tests; others allow prospective students to choose among them.

Besides the admission tests already mentioned, the CEEB offers many other services. One such service is the Advanced Placement Program (APP). The APP is based on the belief that many students can complete college-level courses while still in high school. More than 8,000 high schools offer the program. The program provides outlines of college-level courses and administers and grades 3-hour exams based on these courses. As of 1988, the APP offered 27 exams, and 19.5 percent of all U.S. participants were minorities (*The College Board News*, 1988–89). College policies vary widely on the awarding of credit for passing grades. Some give credit, some give advanced placement but not credit for the basic course, and a few give neither placement or credit. Many colleges will grant sophomore standing to students presenting qualifying grades in enough Advanced Placement Examinations.

Another service is the College Level Examination Program (CLEP). CLEP is a program that allows colleges to grant credit by examination, and nearly 1,800 colleges use this service. The CLEP exams are of three types: General Examinations, which measure achievement in English composition, mathematics, natural sciences, humanities, and social sciences–history; Subject Examinations in approximately 50 undergraduate subjects; and Brief Tests, which are shorter versions of the subject exams and are used not to give individuals credit but to evaluate groups of students.

Other services that CEEB provides are the Diagnostic College Admissions Test Program (a set of diagnostic tests and study materials to prepare for the SAT), Comparative Guidance and Placement Program, the College Scholarship Service, the Student Descriptive Questionnaire, and the College Locater Service.

ACT Assessment Programs The American College Testing Program (ACT) is an independent, nonprofit corporation. The Enhanced ACT Assessment, first called the ACT Test Battery and then the ACT Assessment Program, is one of the major services of ACT. The Enhanced ACT Assessment was administered for the first time in October 1989. It replaces the ACT Assessment Program.

The Enhanced ACT Assessment instrument consists of four tests, a Student Profile Section, and an Interest Inventory. The four tests are English, Mathematics, Reading, and Sciences Reasoning. A composite score and seven subscores are also reported. The seven subscores are as follows: English: Usage/Mechanics and Rhetorical Skills; Mathematics: PreAlgebra/Elementary Algebra, Intermediate Algebra/Coordinate Geometry, and Plane Geometry/Trigonometry; Reading: Social Studies/Science and Arts/Literature. The tests

> measure as directly as possible students' readiness for college and their ability to perform the kinds of tasks they will have occasion to perform in college (American College Testing Program, 1989, p. 3).

Scores range from 1 to 36, with a mean of 18 for a nationally representative sample of self-identified, college-bound, first-semester high school seniors.

The previous ACT Assessment Program reported only four scores: English, Mathematics, Social Studies, and Natural Science. The content of the Enhanced ACT should be more current with respect to trends in high school college prep programs and expectations for college entry-level academic skills. The previous version was well developed and was of high technical quality. A technical manual for the Enhanced ACT is not available at the time of this writing.

The Student Profile Section asks for the information that a college typically requests on its application form, such as high school grades, vocational choice, and educational major. The ACT Interest Inventory (UNIACT—a component of the ACT Career Planning Program) provides six scores: Social Service, Business Contact, Business Detail, Technical, Science, and Creative Arts.

ACT also publishes the P-ACT Plus (P-ACT+) designed to help tenth-graders "initiate post-high-school planning, prepare for college admissions, and make adjustments in their high school programs that may be needed to strengthen their academic preparation" (ACT, 1989, p. 21). It is similar in content to the Enhanced ACT and reports scores for four tests, four subtests, and a composite.

In the fall of 1976 ACT launched a program called the Proficiency Examination Program (PEP). This ACT-PEP includes 47 college-level proficiency examinations in a variety of subjects. The tests are designed to certify a student's level of knowledge in specific courses and, like the CLEP exams, may be used by colleges as a basis for awarding college credit.

In addition to the Enhanced ACT Assessment, the P-ACT+, and the Proficiency Examination Program, ACT provides a Student Needs Analysis Service, an Educational Opportunity Service, a Career Planning Program, several placement programs at the post-secondary level, and the Assessment of Career Development.

State Assessment Programs

"Clearly the action in testing and assessment in 1984 is in state departments of education" (Womer, 1984, p. 3). Anderson and Pipho reported that "by the summer of 1984, 40 states were actively pursuing some form of minimum competency testing. Nineteen states are now implementing tests for some form of grade promotion" (1984, pp. 210–211). Airasian (1987) reported that 29 states required students to take tests at some grade and eight states tied grade-to-grade promotions to scores on standardized tests.

Why the push for such mandated programs? Womer (1981) identified five categories of social and educational forces for these state tests: locus of control, the strengthening of state educational agencies, educational equity, accountability, and the decline in educational attainment.

Certainly, the demand for accountability and the concern the public has shown for the quality of public school education have served as impetuses. Many recent reports on the condition of education in the country have called for, and resulted in, state legislative and board of education actions for mandated testing programs. For example, one of the recommendations from the report *A Nation at Risk* was that

> standardized tests of achievement (not to be confused with aptitude tests) should be administered at major transition points from one level of schooling to another and particularly from high school to college or work (National Commission on Excellence in Education, 1983, p. 28).

Womer stated: "Lay persons and legislators who control education see testing/assessment as a panacea for solving our concerns about excellence in education" (1984, p. 3) While we suspect that such people know indeed that it is not a cure-all, it is clear that many are hoping that testing/assessment will serve as a positive force in educational quality.

Basically, the initiative for mandated assessment programs has come about because many persons believe that the evidence suggests (1) the quality of our children's education is deteriorating and (2) mandated testing will improve the educational quality (or reverse the deteriorating process if the first point is true). Both points are debatable, and there is currently much debate around the na-

tion about whether such state-mandated programs will have positive or negative effects (Airasian, 1987). This topic is addressed at more length in Chapter 22.

National Assessment of Educational Progress (NAEP)

The National Assessment of Educational Progress (NAEP) is the most extensive assessment project ever initiated in the United States. Although NAEP testing began in 1969, the concept of a national assessment program probably began as far back as 1867 with the establishment of the United States Office of Education (USOE). One of the charges then given the commissioners was to determine the progress of education.

Because of the political climate at the time NAEP began, the original program was intentionally designed to limit its scope. Sampling did not permit state-by-state comparisons. Also, the students who were assessed were sampled by age rather than by grade, thus reducing any perceived pressure on the teachers of specific grades. Reports were purposely descriptive rather than evaluative by nature, and cause-and-effect inferences were avoided. In the current political climate, there is a demand for information that will be more useful in an accountability sense. The redesigned NAEP, for instance, samples by grade (fourth, eighth, and eleventh) as well as by age. More background questions are asked of the student; and teachers and administrators are asked to answer questions regarding curricula, teaching materials, and instructional practices.

Currently, NAEP assessments are conducted every two years, and reading is measured each time because of its importance to education. Three or four subject-matter areas are included in each assessment.

In recent years the political climate has been such that many people have advocated that the NAEP program be conducted to allow for state-by-state comparisons. For example, the Southern Regional Educational Board (1984) suggested that "a missing link in assessing student achievement in the schools is the existence of publicly accepted, nationwide measures by which states can gauge their relative progress" (p. iii). At the 1984 Education Commission of the States' Large-Scale Assessment Conference, William Pierce, director of the Council of Chief State School Officers, indicated that "the 'chiefs' have endorsed the idea of state-by-state rankings based on results from the proposed administration of National Assessment test items to samples of students in each of the 50 states" (Womer, 1984, p. 3) In the spring of 1986, eight southern states did compare the results of reading and writing tests with the NAEP results (Newsnotes, 1986). In 1988 Congress passed a law authorizing on a trial and voluntary basis the comparison of eighth-grade mathematics scores at the state level. The stated purpose is "to provide policy makers with more and better state-level information about the educational performance of their school children" (The State of Education, 1988, p. 1). Twenty-four states, three U.S. territories, and the District of Columbia participated in the 1989 Field Test, and the expectation is that about 37 states will volunteer for the 1990 assessment. Whether or not this is a good idea is clearly debatable (see Koretz, 1989; Linn, 1987).

Currently, schools (both secondary schools and colleges) are ranked either within states (secondary) or across states (college) on quality of specific athletic teams. At times, the rankings are questioned. They are not always based on sound comparative data. Some team may have "an easier schedule," and therefore its undefeated season would not mean that it was superior to some other teams who were defeated during the year but had played tougher competition. What has been the impact of the debate regarding the accuracy of the ratings? The competition during the games of ranked teams are no doubt more intense than if no rankings had been made.

Some people have argued that, whether the rankings in athletics are correct or not, they have been counterproductive because they have resulted in too much emphasis on athletics in college. Perhaps some will argue that state-by-state rankings in educational quality, whether the rankings are accurate or not, will be counterproductive because they will result in too much emphasis being placed on educational quality in the states! In our view, the ranking of states on educational quality is, *in an abstract sense*, a good thing. Whether good or ill comes from any *particular* ranking depends on whether the data are actually reflective of educational quality. If they are, and states compete to do better on the variables from which the data are gathered, that seems fine. On the other hand, if the data do not actually reflect educational quality, or reflect only a small portion of educational quality, then striving to do better may indeed be counterproductive. A good example of that is the use of average SAT scores within the states. If states wished to achieve a higher ranking on that variable, the easiest way would be to discourage all but the very brightest from taking the test. While that would raise the mean for the state, it would not result in increased quality of education. Clearly, the mean performance on NAEP data would represent better quality data than mean SAT scores, but they leave much to be desired as indicators of quality.

■ SUMMARY

The following statements summarize the major points of this chapter:

1. Accountability in education means different things to different people. However, the term usually encompasses setting correct goals, evaluating whether they have been achieved and at what price, releasing this information to the public, and accepting responsibility for any results that are perceived as inadequate.
2. Each participant in the educational process should be held responsible only for those educational outcomes that he or she can affect.
3. There is a tendency for accountability programs to focus on those objectives that are more easily measured.
4. A good accountability program would assess input variables, surrounding conditions, and the educational process, as well as the output

variables, and attempt to establish causal relations between the first three and the latter. This is an extremely difficult task.

5. There is considerable empirical evidence that college selection and placement programs assist in individual and institutional decision making.

6. The College Entrance Examination Board (CEEB) is best known for three exams: the Preliminary Scholastic Aptitude Test (PSAT), the Scholastic Aptitude Test (SAT), and a series of Achievement Tests. Both the PSAT and the SAT provide verbal and mathematical scores.

7. The CEEB also offers other services such as the Advanced Placement Program, the College Level Examination Program, the Comparative Guidance and Placement Program, the College Scholarship Service, the Student Descriptive Questionnaire, and the College Locator Service.

8. The Enhanced ACT Assessment consists of four tests and a student questionnaire. The four tests are in English, mathematics, reading, and science reasoning. ACT also offers other services such as the P-ACT+ and the Proficiency Examination Program.

9. The demands for accountability have resulted in an increased number of state competency assessment programs.

10. The usefulness of the trial voluntary state-by-state comparison of NAEP data is a debatable matter.

■ POINTS TO PONDER

1. In this chapter we have suggested that pupils, parents, and teachers all be involved in setting up the school testing program. What part should each play? What are the dangers of such a heterogeneous committee?

2. Assume you are in a financially troubled school district and are allowed to give only one aptitude test and two achievement batteries in grades K to 12. At which grade levels would you administer the tests? Why?

3. Some states have a uniform statewide testing program. Are you in favor of such programs? Explain your position.

Chapter 22

Public Concerns About and Future Trends in Evaluation

■ **Public Concerns About Measurement and Evaluation**
■ **Future Trends in Evaluation**

Many topics that could be classified as either issues or trends have already been discussed in this text. *Issues* would include such topics as

1. Should norm- or criterion-referenced tests predominate?
2. What objectives should schools hold?
3. Need objectives be stated in behavioral terms?
4. What does the regular classroom teacher have to know about test construction and interpretation?
5. What is the definition and structure of intelligence?
6. What is the etiology of intellectual differences?
7. How stable are intelligence-test scores?
8. Do we have, or should we develop, culture-fair tests?
9. Should standardized tests be used in schools?
10. What does the regular classroom teacher have

to know about measurement because of mainstreaming?
11. How should we mark and report pupil progress?
12. Is accountability a good concept, and, if so, how should we set up accountability programs?

Trends discussed have included (1) criterion-referenced tests, (2) state assessment programs, (3) testing for individualized instruction programs, and (4) testing children with special needs.

In the previous chapter we discussed some of the concerns of measurement specialists and other educators with respect to using tests for accountability purposes. One concern discussed was that the public may place too much emphasis on and confidence in what student test scores say about teacher quality.

In this final chapter we wish to discuss several public concerns about measurement and evaluation. (By public, we mean all nonmeasurement specialists. This would include teachers, counselors, and administrators as well as the lay public.) We do not mean to suggest that the public has been unconcerned about some of the previously discussed topics. They have been concerned about some issues (e.g., methods of marking) but been largely unaware of other issues. We will also briefly mention some of the more recent and predicted future trends and give some appropriate references for those who wish to read more about these topics. After studying this chapter, you should be able to:

1. Recognize several public concerns about testing.
2. Understand some of the motivating factors behind these concerns.
3. Discuss both the logic and lack of logic of the public's concerns regarding the misuse of test scores.
4. Define minimum competency testing of students and discuss reasons for its prevalence and controversial nature.
5. Discuss issues involved in testing teachers.
6. Recognize the relevant and irrelevant concerns of the invasion-of-privacy issue.
7. Discuss the concepts of fair tests and fair test use.
8. Recognize some recent and predicted future trends in measurement and evaluation.

PUBLIC CONCERNS ABOUT MEASUREMENT AND EVALUATION

Testing is an important public policy issue because tests continue to play a major allocative role in education and employment (Snyderman & Rothman, 1986, p. 81).

With an increase in testing in schools, industry, and government, it is natural and appropriate for the public to show interest in, and concern for, this enterprise. In the early 1960s, many writers criticized tests in what became a typical journal-

istic exposé fashion (Gross, 1962; Hoffmann, 1962; Black, 1963). The phrase "anti-test revolt" was often used to express public concern. By the late 1970s, much of the general public became more pro-test than anti-test, and current concern is more likely to be from special-interest groups rather than the general public. Haney (1980) discussed some of the concerns about testing. He suggested that minimum competency tests, truth in testing legislation, use of tests as gatekeepers, and bias in testing are issues that are intensely political. Lerner (1980) charged that the war on testing comes from three main groups: The National Education Association, The National Association for the Advancement of Colored People, and the Nader group. Ebel (1976, pp. 2–3) essentially agreed. He suggested that the criticism of tests and testing comes primarily from three special-interest groups.

1. Professional educators who are uneasy about the accountability associated with standardized tests and external testing in general.
2. Reformers who regard testing as part of an unsuccessful and outmoded instructional process.
3. Freelance writers whose best sellers purport to expose scandals in important human institutions.

We believe there is considerable truth to both Lerner's and Ebel's positions, although educators in *general* support tests.

The leaders of the two major teachers' unions have (until recently) taken quite different positions on standardized tests. The American Federation of Teachers (AFT) has historically strongly supported testing while the National Education Association's (NEA) leadership favored a moratorium on standardized testing. Teachers, as a group, have been much closer to the AFT position. Stetz and Beck (1981) reported that only 10 percent of a national sample of teachers supported a moratorium. A survey by Ward (1980) also found that teachers support standardized tests. There is thus considerable evidence to suggest that the opposition comes mainly from a vocal minority of professional educators.

One example of the special-interest group's opposition to testing is the publication entitled *The Fair Test Examiner* published by the National Center for Fair and Open Testing. The general tone of the articles is very much against standardized tests. In spite of their title, the organization is certainly not for more testing! Consider, for example, the following quotes:

> Standardized tests are a specialized form of fraud (Nader, 1987, p. 1).

> Standardized testing is one of the greatest self-inflicted wounds . . . ever imposed on the American people. It has had a life of about sixty years. Sixty years of idiocy is enough (Nader, 1987, p. 3).

Both quotes are from a speech Ralph Nader gave to testing reform activists at Fair Test's annual convention. He suggested that test reformers seek ways to raise the temperature of their campaigns (see *The Fair Test Examiner*, 1987, pp. 1, 3). Concerned educators should be more interested in shedding *light* on testing issues—not just creating *heat*.

Still another example of a special-interest group's attack on testing is *The Reign of ETS: The Corporation That Makes Up Minds* (Nairn et al., 1980). Published and promoted by Nader, it is commonly referred to as the Nairn/Nader report. Although it received considerable public press coverage, it is considered by professional measurement experts to be quite unscholarly and biased. (See Hargadon, 1980, and Mehrens, 1981a, for sample professional reviews of the publication. Mehrens concluded that as far as writing the truth about testing, the Nairn/Nader report represents a nadir.)

Snyderman and Rothman (1986, p. 81) suggested that "in recent years . . . critics of testing, aided by the news media, have gained the upper hand." They document the one-sided nature of the news media coverage. Herrnstein (1982) and Page (1984) also discuss the one-sided critical nature of the news media's treatment of testing.

Although the critics raise a few valid concerns, in general they also do not understand much about the field of measurement, and the result is that their criticisms are frequently invalid. As Page (1976) pointed out, measurement is a technical field, and it cannot be understood, let alone criticized intelligently, without some mastery of the content. In terms of technical competence, many of the critics are analogous to the "flat earthers" who attacked the heliocentric theory (see Snyderman & Rothman, 1986, also).

Even though the validity of the criticisms expressed in the numerous books and articles is probably inversely proportional to the public acclaim they have received, all these criticisms have been of value—if for no other reason than that of forcing psychometricians to examine the criticisms, then change practices where advisable, and to defend themselves against the sometimes unjust criticisms. Glaser and Bond suggested that "in the heat of the current controversy, it is especially necessary to be our own sternest critics" (1981, p. 997). We would concur, but add that we also must recognize and label some of the attacks for what they are ". . . *vicious, destructive, deliberately misleading,* but also *sustained, well organized,* and *well-financed*" (Anderson, 1980, p. 5). Page (1984) stated it nicely:

> Testing is struggling under attacks by many enemies, operating from many motives and conceptions, often incorrect. And testing is also under constant criticism from its friends. It is friendly criticism, of course, that most characterizes the scientific enterprise . . .
>
> We must call upon ourselves . . . to defend our field firmly against the defamations and uninformed assaults by its enemies. If we are faithful to the scientific tradition of open scientific debate and self-criticism, then testing will continue to grow and flourish (p. 34).

As professionals we have a responsibility to improve our procedures. We also have a responsibility to educate the public to the educational and social benefits of measurement and evaluation.

Since public concern encompasses so many specific yet interrelated aspects of testing, it is difficult to present the topic completely in any tightly organized fashion. Therefore, we have chosen to discuss five issues that seem of most concern to the public: (1) the use (or misuse) of test scores for making decisions about individuals, (2) minimum competency testing of students, (3) competency testing for teachers, (4) the invasion-of-privacy issue, and (5) the fairness of tests and test use to minority and majority groups. These issues are neither mutually exclusive nor exhaustive.

Use (or Misuse) of Test Scores

> Ultimately, the war over testing will be won or lost on the issue of test use (Snyderman & Rothman, 1986, p. 91).

As mentioned in Chapter 1, concern with the correct use of test scores has focused mainly on using standardized tests. We are not suggesting by this statement that data gathered from classroom evaluation procedures cannot be misused also. They can, but in general the critics are unaware or unconcerned about misuse of data from nonstandardized tests. This seems unfortunate. As Hargadon points out, the courses students take and the grades received in high school have a greater effect on educational and life chances than College Boards, there is great variation in the standards and quality of those courses and grades, and students take more teacher-made tests in a single year in high school than standardized tests in a lifetime (Hargadon, 1980). Teacher observations and the tests they give constitute the major variables on which teachers base their evaluations of student achievement (see, e.g., Stiggins & Bridgeford, 1985). Students express more anxiety about teacher-made tests and find them to be more difficult than standardized tests (Stetz & Beck, 1981).

At any rate, all types of data can be misused. The consequences of misusing tests can be quite severe and examples abound, although probably not with the frequency critics suggest. Using test scores to label or categorize a child as a nonlearner instead of to assist in understanding a person is one accusation mentioned very frequently, although research suggests teachers do not do this

to any great extent. Research has shown that a child's classroom behavior counts more than standardized tests in teacher judgments about students. Teachers tend to discount standardized test scores *below* what they would predict from classroom performance and use *higher* scores as an indication that classroom performance was perhaps an inaccurate indicator. Thus, teachers who receive standardized test information are more apt to raise their ratings of students than teachers who do not receive such information (Kellaghan et al., 1980; Salmon-Cox, 1981).

However, the important point is that misuse of tests does occur. This does not lead us to the conclusion that testing is bad; rather, it makes us aware that we must concentrate our energies toward the goal of *educating* people on the *correct* use of test results. Most of the problems regarding test misuse relate to the overgeneralizations made by users, not to the fact that the tests per se are invalid. Most standardized test constructors display integrity and professional honesty in stipulating how these tests should be used. However, educators are not being professionally honest when they use tests they are not qualified to use.

Educators' incompetence in testing is due to several factors. First, a basic measurement course is not required in many undergraduate teacher training institutions, or even in some graduate training programs. Second, pre-service teachers do not flock to the measurement courses as electives because they are often seen as harder than other courses that may be selected. There have been some attempts to have in-service (professional development) programs on measurement and evaluation, but, again, teachers do not typically select these programs if they have a choice. Furthermore, measurement and evaluation has a bit too much substance to be covered in a one- or two-hour (or even one- or two-day) in-service program.

Specialists in measurement and evaluation are aware of the educators' lack of appropriate training and have made a variety of attempts to minimize the misuse of tests by educators. For example, the *Standards for Educational and Psychological*

Testing (AERA/APA/NCME, 1985) contains many guidelines on appropriate test use. By and large, this book was written so that educators can understand at least major portions of it even though they are not highly trained in measurement. Another document designed to educate both developers and users of tests is the *Code of Fair Testing Practices in Education*. It was prepared by a Joint Committee on Testing Practices (1988) sponsored by five organizations: The American Educational Research Organization, the American Psychological Association, the National Council on Measurement in Education, the American Association for Counseling and Development/Association for Measurement and Evaluation in Counseling and Development, and the American Speech-Language-Hearing Association. This is a simply written four-page document that presents standards for developing/selecting tests, interpreting scores, striving for fairness, and informing test-takers.

Publishers of standardized tests put out a variety of materials designed to promote correct use of test data and discourage the incorrect use of test data. The National Institute of Education and the Department of Defense Dependents Schools funded a two-year research and development project to examine the relationship between assessment and instruction. "The ultimate goal of this project was to increase teachers' use of assessment data in the classroom by focusing on various methods for integrating assessment data into classroom instructional decisions" (Wanous & Mehrens, 1981, p. 3). One of the outcomes of this project was *The Data Box* (Rudman, Mehrens, & Wanous, 1983), an integrated set of materials that enable teachers to investigate the use of assessment data in a variety of instructional decision-making situations. Most large school districts have a measurement and evaluation unit that offers workshops to teachers on the correct uses of measurement data. Some of the states that have implemented a minimum competency test for teachers have a portion of the test devoted to measurement competencies. This should serve as an impetus for colleges of education in those states to teach some measurement

courses and for education students to take such courses.

Despite the various efforts we have discussed, not all educators know enough about testing to avoid misuses. In the final analysis, educators must be sufficiently professional to seek out training in areas where they need instruction and not to take on projects that are beyond their professional competence.

Many people criticize the faulty decisions made through the misuse of test information. Fewer people realize that a far more costly misuse of tests is not to use them at all. Too many critics evaluate tests against nonexistent ideal predictors. Even if only a few better decisions were made with the help of test information than would have been made without that information, the long-term benefits would likely outweigh the initial costs of testing. As Haney and Madaus (1989, p. 683) stated, "the search for alternatives [to standardized tests] is somewhat short sighted."

There is no question that tests predict imperfectly. So do all other prediction procedures. Does this make a test invalid? There is considerable misunderstanding among lay people about the concept of validity. Lay people seem more willing to argue against tests in general because of a *specific example* of misuse than they do, for example, against aspirins in general because of some specific misuse (Barclay, 1968).

Probably the concern with imperfect test validity would be less if tests were not seen as gatekeepers to better education and a better way of life. Tests are frequently designed to measure differences among individuals, and this information may help in making decisions about the allocation of limited resources or opportunities. But the limited resources are not always allocated to those who score high on tests. Compensatory education programs are obvious exceptions. Who deserves limited resources and what should be done about individual differences are *policy* questions. Tests simply provide information about what differences exist. It is not appropriate to call a test *unfair* (or invalid) because data from it are used to allocate resources in a manner that runs opposite to our personal philosophies. If it is believed that admission to a college having limited enrollment should be based on predicted academic success, if test scores increased the predictive accuracy (they do), and if the admissions offices use the test scores *correctly* in a regression equation (or set of regression equations—differentiated on ethnicity, sex, or whatever other demographic variable would increase predictive efficiency) to help predict success, then we would argue that the test was not unfair nor were the test data misused in any *measurement sense*. The correctness of the philosophy to limit enrollment based on predicted success can be debated, but *that* argument is independent of, and of a different order from, whether the test data are useful, given the philosophical stance. But the above comments are surely not to suggest that tests cannot be misused.

Another reason for misuse is that educators are frequently held accountable for *student* learning. The educators perceive many of the accountability systems to be unfair (and many are!) because they do not consider all factors when evaluating teachers. This accountability has led to some cheating on the tests—which surely is a grievous misuse (see Cannell, 1989).

Correct test use involves all aspects of testing, from selection to administration to interpretation. But we wish to stress again that if test information is used correctly, it is impossible to make (in the long run) poorer decisions by using this additional information. Thus, if the public desires accurate decision making, their concern should not be whether tests should be used, but whether tests are used properly. Users of tests have an ethical responsibility to be qualified to administer, score, and interpret tests properly. Unfortunately, many test users do not assume this responsibility. A pertinent question is *who* should stipulate users' qualifications? Is it the responsibility of the test publishers to be sure unqualified users do not obtain copies of tests? Should a professional organization such as the American Psychological Association set up standards? (Recall that the *Standards* and the *Code of Fair Testing Practices in Education* have already been published and endorsed by pro-

fessional organizations.) Should states have certification requirements? (Although many states have certification requirements for psychologists, this does not really control access to, and potential misuse of, test data.) Should a federal agency exert control? Any suggested answer to this question would probably raise as much controversy as one that decided who should assume responsibility for our safety while we ride in automobiles.

Minimum Competency Testing of Students

Minimum competency testing (MCT) is certainly one of the most controversial topics in measurement, indeed in all of education, today. In the summer of 1981, the National Institute of Education (NIE) sponsored a three-day adversary evaluation hearing on the topic (Thurstone & House, 1981). To educate the public, all testimony from both the pro and con sides was videotaped and edited for four 60-minute programs aired by the Public Broadcasting System.

What is minimum competency testing, and why has it caused so much turmoil? Many definitions of the phrase exist. We quote here the one used in the NIE hearings:

> Minimum competency testing refers to programs mandated by a state or local body which have the following characteristics: (1) All or almost all students of designated grades are required to take paper-and-pencil tests designed to measure basic academic skills, life or survival skills, or functional literacy; (2) a passing score or standard for acceptable levels of student performance has been established; and (3) test results may be used to certify students for grade promotion, graduation or diploma award; to classify students for or to place students in remedial or other special services; to allocate compensatory funds to districts; to evaluate or to certify schools or school districts; or to evaluate teachers (Thurstone & House, 1981, p. 87).

Minimum competency testing has been around for a long time. A very early minimum competency exam was when the Gilead Guards challenged the fugitives from Ephraim who tried to cross the Jordan river.

> "Are you a member of the tribe of Ephraim?" they asked. If the man replied that he was not, then they demanded, "Say Shibboleth." But if he could not pronounce the "sh" and said Sibboleth instead of Shibboleth he was dragged away and killed. As a result 42 thousand people of Ephraim died there at that time (Judges 12:5–6, *The Living Bible*).[1]

Nothing is reported concerning the debates that may have gone on among the guards regarding what competencies to measure, how to measure them, when to measure, how to set the minimum standard, or indeed what should be done with the incompetent. We do not know the ratio of false acceptances to false rejections or the relative costs of the two types of errors. We do know that a very minimum competency exam was given that 42,000 people failed—with no chance of a retake. And some people think our public school students have it bad!

But there have been other, less drastic competency exams—for example, those for certifying or licensing professionals and those for obtaining a driver's license.

If not a new concept, why so much fuss? Never before have state and local agencies been so active in setting the minimum competency standards for elementary and secondary students. For example, by 1984, 40 states were actively pursuing some form of minimum competency testing. Nineteen states were using tests for high school graduation decisions, and 5 states were using tests for grade-to-grade promotion (Anderson & Pipho, 1984). In May 1983, about 1,300 high school seniors in Florida did not receive diplomas because they failed the state's minimum competency test (Citron, 1983). Several large-city school districts—including, for example, Grand Rapids, Philadelphia, and New York—have also implemented some type of minimum competency testing program.

---

[1] This is an example of a performance test. We mention this obvious fact because some people mistakenly believe performance assessment is a new phenomenon!

General Questions About Minimum Competency Tests

Over the past several years, a multitude of questions have been raised about minimum competency testing. For example: (1) why have them at all? (2) what competencies should be measured? (3) when should we measure the competencies? (4) who should set the minimum standard? (5) how should the minimum standards be determined? and (6) what should be done with the incompetent? These questions are all related. The answer given for one has implications for the answers to the others. We will discuss briefly some aspects of these questions. Further details regarding one of the authors' views of these and other questions can be found in Mehrens (1979).

1. Why Have Standards at All? As mentioned in Chapter 1, 73 percent of the American people think that all high school students in the United States should be required to pass a standardized examination in order to get a high school diploma (Gallup & Elam, 1988).

Why the big push for minimum competency tests with specified standards? Many individuals believe the evidence suggests that the general quality of our children's education is deteriorating and that far too many children are not learning adequately the basic skills. Many believe that minimum competency testing will improve educational quality (or reverse any deterioration). Both points are debatable. We believe the first—some of you may not. The evidence is on our side. Lerner (1981) summarizes some of the relevant data and concludes that 20 percent of American 17-year-olds are illiterate and 60 percent semiliterate. On the second point, that minimum competency testing will improve our educational system, we would prefer to reserve judgment, but, as mentioned, there is some supportive evidence reported in the literature. For example, Klein (1984) stated that Wagner (1983) concluded that minimum competency has improved instruction through clearer goals, better-focused teaching, and better in-service training.

Of course there are many perceived costs as well as perceived benefits of minimum competency testing. Perkins (in Gorth & Perkins, 1979), has compiled two very complete lists. We will present five examples from each side of the debate.

Perceived Costs of Minimum Competency Testing

1. Causes less attention to be paid to difficult-to-measure learning outcomes.
2. Promotes teaching to the test.
3. Will cause "minimums" to become "maximums," thus failing to provide enough instructional challenge in school.
4. May unfairly label students and cause more of the "less able" to be retained.
5. Can be costly, especially where implementation and remediation are concerned.

Perceived Benefits of Minimum Competency Testing

1. Restores meaning to a high school diploma.
2. Certifies that students have specific minimum competencies.
3. Defines more precisely what skills must be taught and learned for students, parents, and teachers.
4. Motivates students to master basic reading, mathematics, and writing skills.
5. Provides an opportunity to remedy the effects of discrimination by identifying learning problems early in the educational process.

2. What Competencies Should Be Measured? The answer to the question of what competencies should be measured in a minimum competency program is related directly to the purposes of the test: that is, what inferences we wish to make about a person who "passes," and much less directly about the "purposes of the school." Many people apparently do not make enough of this distinction.

Although there exists a reasonable consensus about desirable adult characteristics, there is considerable diversity of opinion about their relative importance and about the role of the school in promoting those characteristics. Some people maintain that good citizenship or healthy self-concepts are more important in life than reading skills. Others assert just the opposite. And some who believe the former do not believe it is the primary purpose of the school to promote those char-

acteristics. We will never reach agreement on what characteristics we need in our society and on the role of the school in teaching, establishing, or nurturing those characteristics. But that should not deter us from determining general content for a minimum competency test. No test can be designed to assess the degree to which all the purposes of education have been achieved or even to assess whether students have achieved a level of minimal competency in all areas.

Surely no one would infer that all purposes of education have been achieved if students pass a minimum competency test. Would any reasonable citizen infer—or would we want them to infer—that a passing score means the person has "survival skills" for life? Life is very varied, and so are the skills needed to survive. We cannot believe the populace is so unrealistic or naive as to think in such grandiose terms. Schools do not and cannot teach all survival skills. Such skills cannot even be adequately enumerated (or defined), and thus they cannot be adequately measured. Since we do not want any "survival skills" inference to be drawn from a test, we should not build a test to measure such defined competencies.

The focus of most minimum competency programs is on the basic skill areas of writing, mathematics, and language arts. But if we measure only basic skills (applied to life settings), would not other areas of school suffer? Not necessarily. Remember, there is a distinction between the purposes of school and the purposes of a minimum competency test. The purpose of the latter can never be to assess all the objectives of school. We all know that. Of course, not all skills are basic, and we do not want minimums to become maximums. Few would be happy to see high school graduates who lacked maturity, self-discipline, and some understanding of their own value systems. But if we keep in mind the limitations of the inferences to be drawn from passing (or failing) a minimum competency test, such limited testing should not have deleterious effects.

We should not assume that minimum competency standards can do much to define the goals and objectives of education. They only set a lower limit of acceptable standards in certain basic skill areas. This certainly suggests that passing the minimum competency test should not be the only requirement for high school graduation. Other graduation requirements could assure breadth in other areas. In specifying the domain of basic skills, we need to keep in mind the relationship between the tested domain and what is taught in school. We should *not* be testing content that is not taught. On the other hand, we should not attempt to randomly sample *all* that is taught. The tested domain must be a *subset* of materials taught in the curriculum.

3. When Should the Competencies Be Measured? The answer to the question, "When to Measure?" (like the answer to every other question), depends on the purpose(s) of testing. Of course, the primary reason for minimum competency testing is to identify students who have not achieved the minimum. But identify for what purpose? To help the students identified by providing remediation programs? To motivate students through "fear of failure?" To make a high school diploma more meaningful?

We believe there should be periodic but *not* every-grade testing. Minimum competency programs will be more cost-effective if tests are given approximately three times during the K–12 portion of a student's schooling—for example, in grades 4, 7, and 10. Teachers, of course, gather almost continuous data. They often have already identified those students achieving inadequately. The formal tests supplement the teachers' measures and confirm or disconfirm previous judgments. This formal identification is useful. Tests help motivate students (and teachers) and help assign a minimum competency meaning to a diploma or certificate.

We are opposed to every-grade testing for *minimum competencies* because it is not cost-effective. (We are not opposed to every-grade testing with a more general achievement measure.) Only a very few students, we hope, will be identified as not achieving at a minimum level, and at any rate those identified in fourth grade would very likely overlap considerably with those in third or fifth grade.

Finally, let us stress that if minimum competency tests are used for high school certification or graduation, there must be opportunities for students who have not passed to retake the exams. Further, no test should be used for such a purpose the first year it is given. To be fair to students there should be a phase-in period.

4. Who Sets the Minimum? Obviously, the minimums must be determined by those who have the authority to do so. This will be an agency such as a state board of education or a local school board. It is more difficult to decide who should represent this agency. Of course, all constituents should be involved, but measurement experts need to play a significant leadership role—they have some useful suggestions on standard setting procedures.

5. How Should the Minimum Standard Be Determined? The actual choice of a minimum is somewhat arbitrary. Different methods of setting the minimum lead to different cutoff scores, and one cannot prove that one method (or one cutoff score) is superior to another.

While setting the standard is somewhat arbitrary, that does not necessarily mean it is capricious. Further, it is politically and economically influenced. If the standards are too high and too many students fail, then there will surely be a public outcry about the quality of the schools and the unreasonableness of the standards. Further, if one is committed to remediation, the costs of remediation could be very high. If the standards are set too low, then the program becomes meaningless, and if people become aware of the ridiculously low standards, they will again raise an outcry about the quality of the schools.

Glass raises the question of whether a criterion-referenced testing procedure entailing mastery levels is appropriate. He answers in the negative, stating that "nothing may be safer than an arbitrary something" (1978b, p. 258). Now, we certainly admire Glass, and, indeed, we might be "safer" with nothing rather than an arbitrary something. But let us take the other side.

There is no question but that we make categorical decisions in life. If some students graduate from high school and others do not, a categorical decision has been made whether or not one uses a minimum competency exam. Even if everyone graduates, it is still a categorical decision if the philosophical or practical *possibility* of failure exists. If one can *conceptualize* performance so poor that the student should not graduate, then theoretically a cutoff score exists. The proponents of minimum competency exams seem to believe, at least philosophically, that there is a level of incompetence too low to tolerate and that they ought to define that level so it is less abstract, less subjective, and perhaps a little less arbitrary than the way decisions are currently made.

The above is not an argument for using a minimum competency test alone as a graduation requirement. Nor is it an argument for using a dichotomous (as opposed to continuous) test score as one of the factors in that decision. What we are trying to make very clear is that ultimately—after combining data in some fashion—a dichotomy exists: those who receive a diploma and those who do not. No matter what type of equation is used, linear or nonlinear, no matter what variables go into the equation, no matter what coefficients precede their values, the final decision is dichotomous and arbitrary. The argument against minimum competency exams cannot be that they lead to an arbitrary decision unless one truly believes that all individuals—no matter what their level of performance—belong in the same category.

If it has been decided to set a minimum test score, how should it be done? Practically, there are many different ways that have been suggested. They are thoroughly discussed in readily available literature, and readers wishing a more thorough presentation should check Jaeger (1989) or Shepard (1984).

6. What to Do with the Incompetent? If we are going to spend money to identify the incompetent through testing, we surely ought to have a follow-up plan. The testing alone will not educate the children.

There are a variety of options for dealing with incompetents—the desirability of most somewhat debatable. Schools might:

1. Give students another chance to take the exam.

2. Encourage incompetents to drop out of school.
3. Not allow them to graduate.
4. Not allow them to receive a *regular* high school diploma.
5. Give everyone a regular diploma but give those who pass the exam a special certificate of attainment.
6. Not allow incompetents to be promoted from one grade level to the other.
7. Assign such students a less-demanding curriculum or track.
8. Provide special instructional assistance in areas of specific weaknesses.
9. Make such students attend summer school.
10. Work with parents to teach them how to help their children learn basic skills.

Now these ten are surely neither mutually exclusive nor exhaustive options. They do reasonably represent those advocated by other writers in the field. We happen to favor 1, 3, 4 or 5, 8, 9, and 10. (We are opposed to 2, 6, and 7, although they may have some merit.)

You will recall that we favor testing in about three different grades—with opportunities for retakes in between. It does not seem wise to have students who fail *repeat a whole grade*. They should receive special attention. What kind of special attention? That is a question to be answered by an instructional expert—not a measurement expert. But let us make several points.

1. A test designed to be effective in certifying competence is not an effective *diagnostic* test. Separate measures would be needed to pinpoint specific weaknesses.
2. Remediation takes time, money, trained staff, and a planned curriculum.
3. Schools should not allocate so disproportionate an amount of time, money, and staff to the less competent that the education of the vast majority of competent students is neglected.
4. Some students may never pass a minimum competency exam. For others, the costs may simply be higher than the benefits. Schools need to consider how to minimize the adverse effects of such failures.

5. If remediation is started early, there should be very few students who never achieve minimum competence.

6. The number who do not is partially dependent upon the effectiveness of remediation.

7. In the final analysis, the effectiveness of remediation is dependent on the student. As Ebel has stated, "Learning cannot be imposed. It must be pursued.... [T]he best a school or teacher can do is provide opportunities for learning and create conditions that make learning attractive" (Ebel, 1978a, p. 548).

8. To have no minimum standards in the basic skills for high school certification may well be a greater disservice to the youth of our nation than to insist on such minimum competence. As Jordan (1979) stated, "If we try to defend our right to be incompetent, we lose" (p. 27).

Future of Student Competency Testing   The minimum competency movement has received considerable public and professional educator support. Of course, opinions can change. We cannot foresee the future. In a previous edition of this book we suggested that the future of MCT was likely to be decided in the courts. However, some of the legal activity has quieted down. An important and often-quoted case is the *Debra P. v. Turlington* case in Florida. The Fifth Court of Appeals ruled that the state could impose graduation standards based on a test and that the Florida MCT was not biased. However, they did require the state to show that the MCT did accurately reflect what was taught in the classroom. This is the issue of curricular validity (discussed in Chapter 13). Further, it required the state to show that there were no lingering effects of previous school desegregation. Two years later, the federal district court upheld the Florida testing program on both issues (*Debra P. v. Turlington*, 1983). In preparing for the defense, Florida conducted a massive four-part study and collected voluminous evidence that convinced the court that the test material was taught in the Florida schools. Not all states or local districts would necessarily be able to gather such extensive data. We do not know what types of evidence of curricular validity will be deemed suffi-

cient in other cases. The future of MCT of students may depend considerably on this issue.

Finally, let us quote two fellow prognosticators with whom we agree:

> ... [T]rends in minimum competency testing ... during the past decade strongly indicate that public pressure for results and educator response to that pressure will continue and probably intensify in the 1990s (Beck, 1986, p. 132).

> Because citizens continue to demand educational accountability, it is unlikely that basic skills testing in the high schools will dissipate over the next few years. However, changes will be made in testing methodology and content. Educators and citizens will debate whether to raise minimum competency requirements as students' scores increase over time. Tests will be revised to include more than just reading, writing, and arithmetic.... High school course testing and state-by-state achievement testing will be introduced (Fisher, 1988, p. 157).

Competency Testing for Teachers

While the notion of competency testing was first revitalized for students, it has spread to teachers. As of 1986, 46 states had mandates for some sort of teacher testing (Sandefur, 1988). Twenty-five states tested prospective teachers for admission to teacher education programs, and 42 states tested teachers prior to licensure (Sandefur, 1988). The National Board for Professional Teaching Standards (1989) plans to begin voluntary testing for teacher certification (certification implies higher standards than licensure) by 1993. One motivating factor behind such teacher competency tests is that the public believes our teacher training institutions have granted diplomas to, and states have certified, teachers who are not minimally competent. They believe our colleges have failed as gatekeepers, that social promotion in colleges is as prevalent as social promotion in the public schools. Considerable evidence exists for both beliefs. For example, Feistritzer reported that "never before in the nation's history has the caliber of those entering the teaching profession been as low as it is today" (1983, p. 112). In speaking of the results of research done for the National Center for Educational Information, Feistritzer was quoted as saying:

> The certification of classroom teachers in the U.S. is a mess. There are far too many colleges where a student can show up with a high-school diploma and a checkbook and get out with a bachelor's degree in education (*U.S. News*, 1984, p. 14).

She goes on to say that one-third to one-half of the colleges operating teacher training programs "ought to be shut down."

We know of at least one state, which we will leave unidentified, in which some college graduates scored *at the chance level* on the state's teacher competency test! We suspect this finding may be fairly common across the states.

The public is dismayed at the semiliterate letters teachers send home. (Copies have made big news in various papers across the nation.) The public is dismayed that elementary school teachers have not all mastered elementary school arithmetic. The public believes teachers should be able to read, write, and do simple arithmetic. If colleges do not weed out those who cannot perform the basic functions they are supposed to teach others, state exams are their only recourse.

Gallup (1984) polls indicate that 89 percent of the public (and 63 percent of the teachers) believe that teachers "should be required to pass a state board examination to prove their knowledge in the subjects they will teach." About 75 percent of both teachers and principals also feel that new teachers should be tested on knowledge of teaching methods (*Newsnotes*, 1984). Professional education organizations also support teacher testing (Dilworth, 1986). Currently, teachers' unions do not support the testing of already certified teachers for purposes of recertification. However, a 1988 Gallup Poll indicated that 86 percent of the public believes that *experienced* teachers *should periodically* be required to pass a statewide competency test in their subject area(s) (Gallup & Elam, 1988). Teachers (57 percent) have also accepted the idea of periodic testing in their subject area (Harris & Associates, 1984).

It is easy to understand why most teachers favor such exams. Most teachers *are* qualified to teach. Most teachers *do* know the basics. Most teachers *would* pass the examinations with ease. They recognize that the examinations will provide some quality control by weeding out the incompetent. The exams should increase the public's confidence in the profession and the status of the teaching profession.

Shanker, president of the American Federation of Teachers, and Ward, its director of research, make the following points:

> We think it is perfectly appropriate and desirable to test new entrants in the teaching field to insure that they meet minimum standards.... If you do not know something, you cannot teach something.... Specifically AFT advocates a series of written examinations to test fundamental knowledge in language and computational skills, knowledge in general education and the subject area to be taught, and knowledge of pedagogy (Shanker & Ward, 1982).

Despite the popularity of teacher competency examinations, among both teachers and the public, some educators deplore this movement (Hodgkins & McKenna, 1982). They do not generally argue directly for incompetence, but they do argue against the use of measures of competence. Their main argument is that passing such a test does not guarantee one will be a good teacher. That, of course, is true but totally irrelevant. (One wonders if such an argument is not evidence for a need for a minimum competency test in logic!) The tests are not designed to be predictive among the competent or to ensure that all certified teachers will be good teachers. The tests are predicated on the notion that one cannot effectively teach what one has not learned. If one cannot read, write, or compute at a basic level, there is a strong likelihood that one cannot teach those basics. Even if one could teach knowledge and skill not personally acquired, the role model of such a person as an educator leaves much to be desired. Thus, the reasoning goes, why grant such poor risks a teaching certificate?

Another point typically raised by the opponents of teacher competency testing is that it will reduce the pool of certified black teachers. There is indeed some evidence that this is true. The competency test in Louisiana has reduced the number of certified black teachers by more than 50 percent (Kauchak, 1984). Other states also find that a disproportionate number of blacks fail to pass. There are certainly societal reasons to explain this, including the quality of colleges attended. Nevertheless, Raspberry, a black columnist who frequently speaks and writes about educational issues, wrote the following in support of such testing:

> There's a lot we don't know about educating our children, particularly disadvantaged children. That's a failure of information, which is bad enough.
>
> But we know a lot more than we are willing to act on. That is a failure of guts, which is worse. . . .
>
> We know that a lot of our teachers aren't as good as they ought to be. But we—and here I mean specifically the civil rights leadership—balk at insisting that incompetent teachers be weeded out, particularly if they are minorities. We'd rather feel sorry for them, as victims of society, than hold them to standards that would improve the quality of the schools for our children. . . .
>
> We can have well-educated children or ignorant teachers. We cannot have both (Raspberry, 1983).

All of this is surely *not* meant to argue for all tests of teacher competency. Each one must be judged against the standards discussed in this book (such as reliability and validity). Further, there are both societal benefits and potential dangers in teacher testing (see Mehrens, 1989). However, to argue against teacher tests in an abstract sense and to use illogical arguments to attack them will surely add to the public's belief that we as educators are afraid of the results. This will be likely to strengthen their belief that such tests are needed and strengthen their determination to require them.

Invasion of Privacy

Assume you are a school psychologist in a school system and are working with a disturbed youngster. You believe that additional information about the youngster will enable you to deal with him more effectively. Do you have the right to ask him to answer "true" or "false" to such questions[2] as the following?

1. I have never been in trouble because of my sexual behavior.
2. I have never indulged in any unusual sexual practices.
3. I believe there is a devil and a hell in afterlife.
4. I have had some very unusual religious experiences.
5. There is something wrong with my sex organs.

These are examples of some of the more personal questions taken from the Minnesota Multiphasic Personality Inventory (MMPI). Criticism comes from many people who are concerned that questions such as these are an invasion of privacy. Why should we tell anyone whether or not we have ever indulged in any unusual sexual practices? Some people have even suggested that the very asking of such questions is harmful to the person taking the test.

Suppose you wish to gather some data regarding a pupil's home background. Can you ask questions such as the following?

1. How much education does your father have?
2. What does your father do for a living?
3. Do you have a set of encyclopedias at home?

Questions such as these have often been asked in an attempt to gain some information about an individual's socioeconomic status. Any accountability program that wishes to take into account such variables as home conditions needs to gather such data. But, again, many people object to such questions as being an invasion of privacy.

What really is the invasion-of-privacy issue? What is the fuss all about? It varies, of course, from person to person. Some people actually find it distasteful and degrading to read personal questions. They certainly would not want their sons or

---

[2]From the Minnesota Multiphasic Personality Inventory. Reproduced by permission. Copyright 1943, renewed 1970 by the University of Minnesota. Published by The Psychological Corporation, New York, NY. All rights reserved.

daughters to read such "dirty" questions! Their objections, however, are probably not valid objections to the asking of such questions. There is no known evidence to suggest that the reading of such questions makes a person more neurotic, more psychotic, or less moral.

Other people object on different grounds. Some are concerned not about having to read or answer such questions, but rather about how the answers will be used. This gets us into such problems as scorers' qualifications, their ethics, and storage of test information. What if the answer sheets to such tests as the MMPI are kept and filed? Who, then, will have access to these files? Ethical and knowledgeable users would never reveal to a third party an answer to a specific question. Seldom would they even interpret such an answer to the client. They would, instead, look at the patterns of responses as recorded on the profile sheet. But what about others who have (or at some later date obtain) access to the files? Could not, for example, a lot of political "hay" be made by reporting a candidate's answers to the questions cited above? The merits of permanently storing data are that (1) we will have more information available to help make decisions about individual people and (2) we will be able to improve our tests and learn more about people in general by doing follow-up research. The dangers center on who does (or may in the future) have access to the stored information. Will clerks have access to the data? Can it be subpoenaed? The public concern about what information is kept on file and who has access to it are very real and important concerns, but these should be recognized as issues separate from the question of whether we have a right originally to ask personal questions.

Besides the matter of confidentiality, there is the issue of freedom versus coercion in responding to items. Some students may object to answering some questions but feel they must comply because school authorities ask them to do so. Further, school authorities may never even tell students why the data are being gathered or how it will be used. Data are often gathered from individuals in early elementary school, who may not be aware of the importance of the data. The American Psychological Association (1970, p. 266) position statement on psychological assessment and public policy asserts: "The right of an individual to decline to be assessed or to refuse to answer questions he considers improper or impertinent has never been and should not be questioned. This right should be pointed out to the examinee in the context of information about the confidentiality of the results."

An amendment to the Family Educational Rights and Privacy Act states:

> No student shall be required, as part of any applicable program, to submit to psychiatric examination, testing, or treatment, in which the primary purpose is to reveal information concerning:
>
> (1) political affiliation; (2) mental and psychological problems potentially embarrassing to the student or his family; (3) sex behavior and attitudes; (4) illegal, anti-social, self-incriminating, and demeaning behavior; (5) critical appraisals of other individuals with whom respondents have close family relationships; (6) legally recognized privileged and analogous relationships, such as those of lawyers, physicians, and ministers; or (7) income (Public Law 95-561, 1978, November 1).

Educators, in general, have not been very alert to the kinds of questions or of wording that the public will find offensive. Investigations such as those conducted by the National Assessment of Educational Progress (NAEP) (Berdie, 1971) should alert educators to potential problem areas. Questions on such topics as family finances, relationships between children and parents, religion, minority groups, and sexual practices are likely to be considered either offensive or an invasion of privacy. One state even prohibited NAEP from asking a cognitive question regarding the menstrual cycle.

Let us move briefly from the educational setting to the government and private employment setting. In making a personnel decision about a person, does an employer have a right to pry into the applicant's personality? If employers are going to invest time and money in training persons, will they not prefer stable persons with good work habits who can get along with their fellow workers?

Most psychologists would argue yes. As Hathaway (1964) has pointed out, once you decide, for example, that a Peace Corps worker should not be maladjusted, then how will you find this out? If, for reasons of privacy, investigation of personal items is prevented, is not this analogous to the prudery that would not permit medical doctors to examine the body? It is our contention that this analogy holds, and our conclusion is that qualified psychologists should have the right to ask personal questions if the questions are pertinent. (We should not have to strip before the receptionist, only before the medical doctor, and we would object to having a medical doctor examine our body if the examination were irrelevant.) The problem is that lay people have a hard time judging the relevancy of what a professional does. How do we know whether or not it is relevant for a medical doctor to check our blood pressure and perform a urinalysis? How do we know whether or not it is relevant for a psychologist to ask us if we love our mother? If tests are not relevant, they are invasions of privacy. If they are relevant, they are not invasions of privacy.

Commentators on the invasion-of-privacy topic should adhere to the important issues, that is, the relevancy of the information gathered, qualifications of the gatherer, the use to which information is put, and what is done about the storage of such information. They would thus find that they share the same concerns as professional psychologists. If we really were never allowed to find out anything about another person, then we would not even be allowed to give classroom achievement tests to find out how much students have learned.

Fairness of Tests and Test Use to Minority and Majority Groups

In Chapter 15 we discussed two topics—etiology of intellectal differences and culture-fair tests—that are related to this section; but here the discussion is more directed to the concerns of the fair use of tests with both minorities (women are considered a minority for purposes of this discussion) and with members of the "majority." It would be nice to believe that every logically thinking person in the United States is against unfairness of any sort. The question to be discussed is certainly not should we be fair but rather what is meant by fairness? What practices are and are not fair? Do tests discriminate against the disadvantaged? Are tests used in ways that discriminate against members of the majority? What is and is not discrimination? According to *Webster's* (1965), "to discriminate" is (1) "to make a distinction, to use good judgment" or (2) "to make a difference in treatment or favor on a basis other than individual merit."

Tests can and do help us make distinctions. Tests are often used to identify differences within and among individuals and within and among groups or classes of people. That is a major purpose of testing. If there were no differences in test scores (i.e., if tests did not discriminate), they would be worthless.

Can tests discriminate in an unfair sense (i.e., on the basis of the second definition of discrimination)? Suppose a company uses a selection test on which it can be shown that blacks typically do less well than whites. Is the test unfair for revealing this difference? Many would say so. The test is certainly discriminating under the first definition, but is it unfair discrimination? To be sure, we could use test results to help us unfairly discriminate. For example, we could require that blacks receive higher scores in order to be hired, or vice versa, as some advocate. Either case would constitute discrimination of the second type. These, however, would be examples of unfair use of test results rather than the use of an unfair test.

If we do not set up this kind of differential standard, is the test still unfair just because some group(s), on the average, do more poorly than others? This depends on the degree to which the test is relevant (or valid) for selecting prospective employees. If, indeed, there is a reasonable correlation between job success and test scores, it would seem to many that selection on the basis of test scores is a wise decision and is not unfair, even though members of some subcultures do better than members of other subcultures.

If, however, a test does tend to discriminate (differentiate) between races, sexes, or other subcultures, and if the differential scores are not related to what is being predicted (such as on-the-job success), then the test is unfair. This could occur. For example, the test may demand knowledge that depends upon having been raised in a certain cultural environment, whereas the criterion may not depend upon this knowledge. Thus, it can be seen that the question of test fairness is really one of test validity. A test may differentiate blacks from whites and be fair (valid) for some purposes and not for others. *Differentiation alone is not what makes a test unfair.* Cleary has offered the following definition:

> A test is biased for members of a subgroup of the population, if, in the prediction of a criterion for which the test was designed, consistent nonzero errors of prediction are made for members of the subgroup. In other words, the test is biased if the criterion score predicted from the common regression line is consistently too high or too low for members of the subgroup. With this definition of bias, there may be a connotation of "unfair," particularly if the use of the test produces a prediction that is too low (1968, p. 115).

The *Standards* (AERA/APA/NCME, 1985, p. 12) have accepted this as *the* accepted definition of predictive *bias*. Cole and Moss have defined bias as "differential validity of a given interpretation of a test score for any definable, relevant subgroup of test takers" (1989, p. 205).

Hunter and Schmidt (1976) defined three mutually incompatible ethical positions in regard to the fair and unbiased use of tests, presented five *statistical* definitions of test bias, and showed how they are related to the three ethical positions. These positions are (1) unqualified individualism, (2) qualified individualism, and (3) quotas. The *unqualified individualism* position in employment would be to give the job to the *person* best qualified to serve. Under this position it would be *unethical* not to use whatever information increases the predictive validity of performance even if such information is sex or ethnic group membership. The *unqualified individualist* interprets "discriminate" to mean *treat unfairly*, and to refuse to recognize a difference between groups would result in *unfair* treatment. The *qualified individualist* believes it is *unethical* to use information about race, sex, and so on, even if it were scientifically valid to do so. "The qualified individualist interprets the word discriminate to mean *treat differently*" (p. 1054). The *quota* position is that the ethical position is to give every well-defined group (black, white; male, female; Protestant, Catholic, Jew) its "fair share" of desirable positions. "The person who endorses quotas interprets *discriminate* to mean *select a higher proportion of persons from one group than from the other group*" (Hunter & Schmidt, 1976, p. 1054).

The Cleary definition (accepted in the *Standards*) given above is an example of unqualified individualism, and it turns out that under her definition unreliable tests are biased against whites and in favor of blacks. Thorndike (1971a) and Darlington (1971) have argued for different approaches, which Hunter and Schmidt showed to be forms of quota setting. Darlington suggested that the term *cultural fairness* be replaced with the term *cultural optimality*, which would include a subjective policy-level decision on the relative importance of two goals: maximizing test validity and minimizing test discrimination. Peterson and Novick (1976), in a detailed evaluation of the then existing models for culture-fair selection, concluded that "the concepts of culture fairness and group parity are neither useful nor tenable.... The problem, we think, should be reconceptualized as a problem in maximimizing expected utility" (see also Hunter et al., 1977). Novick and Ellis (1977, p. 307) argued that "an acceptable solution must (a) be based on statistical decision theory, which emphasizes the concept of utility rather than fairness to groups; (b) address individuals as individuals without regard to race, sex, or ethnic origin, except under narrowly delineated conditions carefully defined; (c) take direct account of individual disadvantage in providing compensation; and (d) employ more effective methods than those of group parity when race, sex, or ethnic origin are required as classifiers." Thus, since Cleary's definition first presented in 1968, there have been other definitions of bias. However, the more recent writings (e.g., AERA/APA/NCME *Standards*, 1985; Cole & Moss, 1989) have basically returned to Cleary's definition. Let us turn from the definition of bias and discuss the uses of tests in a more general fashion in employment and educational decisions.

In Employment The whole issue of the cultural fairness of tests has been raised with respect to both educational decisions and employment decisions. We will discuss first the employment aspect of cultural fairness. The Supreme Court (*Griggs* v. *Duke Power Co.*, 1971) ruled that an employer is prohibited "from requiring a high school education or passing a standardized intelligence test as a condition of employment in or transfer to jobs when (a) neither standard is shown to be significantly related to successful job performance, (b) both requirements operate to disqualify Negroes at a substantially higher rate than white applicants, and (c) the jobs in question formerly have been filled only by white employees as part of a long-standing practice of giving preference to whites."

The ruling went on to state that

> ... If an employment practice which operates to exclude Negroes cannot be shown to be related to job performance, the practice is prohibited.
> ... Nothing in the Act precludes the use of testing or measuring procedures; obviously they are useful. ... Congress has not commanded that the less qualified be preferred over the better qualified simply because of minority origins. Far from disparaging job qualifications as such, Congress has made such qualifications the controlling factor, so that race, religion, nationality, and sex become irrelevant. What Congress has commanded is that any tests used must measure the person for the job and not the person in the abstract.

Although the quotes given above are no doubt reasonable, the Court ruling did present some

problems. If "significantly related" is interpreted as statistical significance, then what should be the level of significance? If it means practical significance, how is this to be determined? The *Federal Register* (1970) contained a chapter on equal employment, with a part prescribing guidelines on employee selection procedures. Those guidelines were useful, but were just what the heading implies—guidelines. They did not spell out exact requirements. In 1973, in an attempt to improve the guidelines and the coordination across federal agencies, the Equal Employment Opportunity Coordinating Council (EEOCC) consisting of representatives of the Equal Employment Opportunity Commission, the U.S. Department of Justice, the U.S. Civil Service Commission, and the U.S. Department of Labor began work on a uniform set of guidelines. These guidelines were published in the *Federal Register* on August 25, 1978 (Federal Executive Agency, 1978).

The 1978 guidelines better represented professionally accepted standards for determining validity than the original EEOC guidelines. But, as with its predecessor, the new guidelines are just guidelines and many argue they are in need of revision. It is only through repeated, time-consuming, and costly court cases that employers will fully understand what is expected of them in terms of validity evidence. Some courts will probably be reasonable with respect to validity evidence; others, unreasonable. And how readers of this book define reasonable evidence will vary, depending upon their perceptions of the whole issue.

The entire December 1988 issue of the *Journal of Vocational Behavior* was devoted to the topic of "Fairness in Employment Testing." As Gottfredson and Sharf stated in the foreword to that issue:

> Early debates focused on relatively limited questions such as how many tests are biased against minority groups, how tests can be improved if they are biased, and what evidence is necessary for showing a test is job related and therefore permissible under *Griggs* when the test has adverse impact. Now the debate is shifting to address the question of what to do when minorities differ on tests that *meet* the earlier criteria for fairness. ... How deeply troubled should we be

over the policy question of what to do when valid tests have adverse impact? (1988, p. 226).

(It should be stressed that because most tests meet the criteria for fairness it does not mean that we should operate as if *all* do. Nevertheless, valid tests frequently do have adverse impact.)

Sharf pointed out that

"fairness" in terms of *equal* employment ... *results for groups* generally requires the *trading off* of equal employment *opportunity* for *individuals* because of group differences to date on virtually all objective standards (1988, p. 237).

The Civil Rights Act was directed to the issue of discrimination against any *individual* because of the "individual's race, color, religion, sex or national origin" (Title VII, 1964). However, as Gottfredson has stated, "Many people now distinguish between individual and group rights and accord the latter higher standing" (1988, p. 314). Ryanen argued that "preferential treatment in education and employment has been in place for so long that it has become institutionalized. Not since the days of prohibition has there been a law treated so contemptuously as Title VII of the Civil Rights Act" (1988, p. 383).

There are, of course, disagreements about whether preferential treatment based on group membership is legal or illegal and whether the ultimate impact of such treatment in our society will be positive or negative. Some argue that preferential treatment is a temporary measure that will eventually lead to full equality. Others argue that concepts of fairness "which emphasize group parity rather than individual merit, promise not to bring racial equality but to permanently consign blacks and other favored groups to second-class citizenship" (Gottfredson, 1988, p. 293); or that long-term preferential treatment will "virtually assure the continuing deterioration of relations among the races in the United States" (Ryanen, 1988, p. 385). (See Raspberry, 1987, and Sowell, 1989, for similar statements. We are certainly not suggesting these two prominent black authors

speak for all or even most blacks. There is a variety of opinions *within* ethnic groups on this issue.)

One method of reporting test scores that should assist in equal results for groups (but *not* fairness for individuals) is to use race norming. The U.S. Employment Service has used this approach with a referral system called the VG-GATB Referral System. (VG stands for validity generalization [see Chapter 13] and GATB stands for the General Aptitude Test Battery.) The GATB is a federally sponsored employment test, and the scores obtained are reported as percentile scores *within* each of three ethnic groups: black, Hispanic, and other. The use of race norming was challenged on the basis that it illegally advances the interests of one classification of people at the expense of others. On November 10, 1986, Reynolds (then Assistant Attorney General for Civil Rights) sent a letter to the U.S. Employment Service urging that race norming be ended. At the request of the Department of Labor, the National Academy of Sciences convened a committee of measurement experts to study the VG-GATB Referral System. This group of experts published their findings in a book entitled *Fairness in Employment Testing* (Hartigan & Wigdor, 1989). While the central recommendations (to be discussed shortly) are considered quite controversial, we believe the book (like the December 1988 issue of the *Journal of Vocational Behavior*) should be read by all personnel directors. The authors spend a whole chapter discussing issues in equity and law. They present their view of the philosophical foundations of social justice and civil rights policies, pointing out that economic liberalism was based on the fair competition of individuals" (1989, p. 31) and that "fairness had to do with the rules of the competition, not the distribution of wealth in society" (p. 32). The writers discuss what they refer to as "the contemporary impasse on preferential treatment," presenting arguments both for and against such action.

One of the recommendations in the report is that within-group percentiles continue to be reported but that the *corresponding norm group be identified* (not done earlier—a practice considered "deceptive"). However, it was further recommended that an expectancy score based on the *total* group be reported that is "equal to the probability that an applicant's job performance will be better than average" (p. 12). This would enable employers to determine whether "equal" within group percentiles led to similar predictions for job performance. The report is not the final word on either the *psychometric* or the *legal* issues, and the recommendations are sure to be controversial.

In Education   With respect to fairness of tests in educational uses, the major concerns seem to be in using tests either as predictors of future success (and therefore as screening devices), for certification, or for placement into special education programs. When achievement tests are used only as measures of *outcomes* of education, few people question their applicability to minority groups. In fact, results on achievement tests have been used as evidence that schools are doing a poor job of educating minority children.

As mentioned in Chapter 15, a few well-meaning psychologists have sought to devise culture-fair intelligence tests. Such tests have attempted to use only those items that do not differentiate among groups coming from different cultures. The advocates of such procedures argue that this gives them a test that is independent of environmental influences and, as close as possible, is a measure of innate ability. In general, these tests have not been well accepted by most psychologists. It is very doubtful whether we could ever devise a paper-and-pencil test to measure innate ability (whatever that is). Certainly, scores on present tests are influenced by environmental factors. There is no debate about that. But, does that make them unfair? Clifford, a black educator, has stated:

> To disparage testing programs for revealing the inequities which still exist in the social, the economic, the educational, and cultural domains of American life is as erroneous as it would be for residents of Bismarck, North Dakota, to condemn the use of thermometers as biased, when, as this is being written, the temperature of Bismarck is −11°F and in

Miami, Florida, it is 83 (Clifford & Fishman, 1963, p. 27).

It should be pointed out that Clifford's statement is based on the assumption that whoever interprets the intelligence-test scores will realize that they are *not* direct measures of genetic capacity and that they are influenced by environmental conditions. Although the test is not unfair, it would be an unfair use of a test score to interpret it as irrefutable evidence of only genetic capacity.

Most psychologists take the position that "culture-fair" tests would be less useful (valid) predictors of educational achievement than present aptitude and achievement tests. If a person's previous environment is related to school success, then using a test that masks out environmental differences will likely result in a loss of some predictive power.

Actually, considerable research has been done on the predictability (or fairness) of scholastic aptitude tests for minority students. The studies do not show that tests are biased (using Cleary's definition given earlier) against students with culturally disadvantaged backgrounds (Hills et al., 1963; Hills, 1964; Munday, 1965; Hills & Gladney, 1966; Stanley & Porter, 1967; Cleary, 1968; Kallingal, 1971; Pfeifer & Sedlacek, 1971; Temp, 1971; Wilson, 1978; Bond, 1986; Linn, 1986b). In fact, several studies suggest that the test scores overpredict the performance of blacks in college (Breland, 1978; Cleary, 1968; Kallingal, 1971; Pfeifer & Sedlacek, 1971; Silverman et al., 1976; Temp, 1971). Findley and Bryan (1971) found much the same thing in reviewing the research on different tests used in the elementary grades. This overprediction would be test bias in one sense of the word, but certainly not unfair to the minority groups. Thomas and Stanley (1969) have clearly shown that scholastic aptitude tests are better than high school grades for predicting college grades of black students. This is the reverse of findings for white students. Stanley (1971a), in a thorough review of predicting college success of the educationally disadvantaged, urged a reversal of the then current trend of waiving test scores in admitting disadvantaged applicants. He felt that the more disadvantaged an applicant, the more objective information one needs about the person.

Recently, there has been some controversy regarding whether the SAT is biased against women (see Walsh, 1989). While women get slightly higher grades than men with equal SAT scores (suggesting bias according to the accepted definition), studies that adjust the college GPA for differences in departmental grading standards show the differential prediction disappears (Strenta & Elliott, 1987; Elliott & Strenta, 1988). [To understand this, consider the following facts: (1) the ratio of men to women is higher in engineering than in education, (2) majors in engineering in general have higher SAT scores than majors in education, and (3) grading standards are more severe in engineering than in education.]

With respect to the *use* of aptitude tests, the practice of affirmative action prevails in college admissions just as it does in employment practices (see Willingham & Breland, 1982; Bunzel, 1988). However, the evidence is strong that Asians must achieve at a *higher* level than whites to have the same chance of admission (see Bunzel, 1988; Williams, 1989). As in employment testing, there are debates about whether this is fair or unfair, legal or illegal, and likely to result in improved or harmed race relations. Williams has argued that "whatever noble goals foster dual standards, one of their side effects is that of producing racial animosity and resentment" (1989, p. 38). (See also Sowell, 1989.)

The use of "intelligence" tests for placing students into programs for the mildly retarded has been the subject of much controversy. Two court cases highlighted this controversy (*Larry P. v. Riles*, 1979; and *PASE v. Hannon*, 1980). Both cases involved the overrepresentation of black students in programs for the mildly retarded and the role of intelligence testing. The rulings were on opposite sides. In *Larry P.*, Judge Peckham concluded that intelligence tests were biased against black students and that overrepresentation of blacks in such programs was illegal. In *PASE*, Judge Grady ruled that the tests were not biased

and that overrepresentation was not illegal. While the issues are multifaceted, several things seem clear to us. (1) Overrepresentation, per se, in educational programs is not unacceptable to blacks. They are certainly overrepresented in such programs as Head Start, Follow Through, and Title I programs. (2) Special education placement leads to the expenditure of substantially more, not less, money on the student's education. (3) Overrepresentation is due to academic failure and behavioral problems, not intelligence tests. Prior to being referred for testing, there must be some achievement or behavioral reason. Tests have either a neutral effect of disproportionality or tend to reduce it somewhat (Reschly, 1981). A moratorium on testing will not, in itself, reduce the disproportionate representation of blacks in such programs. (4) The concern of Judge Peckham in the *Larry P.* case was the quality of special education classes. They were referred to as "dead-end," "inferior," and so on, 27 times in the written court opinion. (5) If indeed the programs were that poor, no students, regardless of race, should have been placed in them. (See Lambert, 1981, and Reschly, 1981, for elaboration and evidence on the points noted.)

Although various test critics may have reviewed the court cases as if the tests were on trial, a more accurate appraisal—at least in the *Larry P.* case—was that special programs were on trial. We are not taking a position on the quality of special education program (although evidence suggests most are beneficial). Our expertise does not lie primarily in that area. Obviously no educator or measurement specialist would advocate using intelligence tests to place children into inferior but more expensive programs. Again, we have a prime example of the critics of testing confusing the issue of what decision should be made with the issue of what data we should use to assist in making the decision.

Reschly, Kicklighter, and McKee (1988a, b, c) present findings from several court cases showing that the court will accept the use of tests that lead to overrepresentation of minorities if evidence shows the placement is of benefit to students.

Summary of the Fairness Issue Tests should not be considered unfair just because they discriminate. That is what tests are supposed to do. Tests, however, can be invalid and therefore unfair, or people can give unfair interpretations of the results (whether the tests were valid or invalid).

Although there would be important exceptions that should be investigated, the effect of using objective measures such as test data is to make social class barriers more permeable.

Tests cannot see if a youngster is black or white, rich or poor. Making decisions on the basis of objective measures is really more fair than making them on the affective reactions (positive or negative) we have toward different subcultures.

Conclusion on Public Concern About Evaluation

It is good that people feel free to voice their concerns. Although there are many legitimate concerns about evaluation, many others are often neither logical nor relevant. If there are problems associated with test accuracy (there are), and if the misuse of tests has sometimes led to unfortunate consequences (it has), the appropriate procedure is to *correct the problems, not to stop testing*. In many instances the issues of concern to the public, such as invasion of privacy and unfair tests, are problems associated with test use rather than with the psychometric properties of the tests. Psychologists and educators are partly to blame for this misuse. They have an obligation to inform the public as to how tests should be used and as to how they are being used. However, much of the negative affect toward tests is precisely because tests are used as they should be, to help make decisions. These decisions are not always pleasant to the people involved. Since tests help make decisions, they have been attacked. Unfortunately, there are some people who assume that by doing away with tests we could *avoid making decisions*. That is not the case. Decisions must be made. Information helps us make decisions. Tests provide information. As professionals, we must ensure that valid tests are used for making appropriate decisions.

FUTURE TRENDS IN EVALUATION

We have already discussed such trends as state assessment programs, criterion-referenced tests, and testing for individualized instruction programs. Future trends are harder to discuss. It is always hard to predict. Even with tests carefully designed to help predict specific future behavior, we often cannot make accurate predictions. Yet the authors of this text—without the aid of specific test results—are audacious enough to make some tentative predictions about educational and psychological testing.

Increased Legal Involvement in Testing

Legal scrutiny of educational and psychological measurement is both a present and a future reality. Rebell (1989) has suggested that the courts have become a major public policy forum with respect to testing and that this judicial involvement "is likely to be a permanent part of the public policy landscape for the foreseeable future" (p. 137). Several issues discussed in the last section are the primary areas in measurement that are being subjected to legal involvement. Minimum competency testing and the use of tests for licensure, selection, or placement purposes in either employment or education that results in disproportionate minority representation will, no doubt, continue to be legal issues. PL 94-142 may well be a source of future litigation.

Whether all the legal scrutiny is a good or bad thing in the long run is clearly debatable. Bersoff believed the intense legal scrutiny "should be viewed as both salutary and welcome" (1981, p. 1055). However, in 1984 Bersoff suggested that a psychoanalyst might describe the relationship between the social sciences and the courts as "a highly neurotic, conflict-ridden ambivalent affair" (1984, p. 97). He added that lower-court opinions "are generally devoid of sound psychometric reasoning" (p. 98). Rebell (1989) discussed both some positive and negative attributes of court interventions. Lerner, in a discussion of minimum competency testing, argued that such issues are about educational policy choices and "should not be made by any branch of the federal government, least of all by the federal judiciary" (Lerner, 1981, 1063). Turlington, Florida, commissioner of education during the *Debra P.* case, believed that the Florida state department of education "should not have to face continued harassment from profesional litigators . . . who would seek . . . to impose their disproven philosophy upon Florida's schools and Florida's students" (Turlington, 1981, p. 204). Pullin, an attorney for the plaintiffs in the *Debra P.* case, disagreed (Pullin, 1981).

We as authors and you as readers can view all this legal scrutiny as either good or bad. But it will continue, and all users of test information should be aware of the trend. However, we should point out that to do away with testing would not in the long run cut down on legal actions. They come about primarily because the plaintiffs do not agree with the decisions being made. If other sources of data, or no sources of data, were the bases for the decisions, they too would be challenged in this era of litigation.

Computer-Aided Testing

Anyone who has read the technical manuals accompanying the better standardized tests realizes that computers already play a large role in the educational and psychological testing enterprise. Computers are used to administer tests. Computers are used in the development of tests by aiding in the processes of item writing and analysis, norming, deriving types of scores, estimating reliability and validity, and in a host of other tasks. Computers are also used in the process of scoring and the reporting of results. Recently, test publishers have greatly expanded their services in these areas and will no doubt continue improving these services. To give you some idea of the expanding interest in computers and assessment, the third edition of *Educational Measurement* (Linn,

1989) contains 2 (out of 18) chapters on the topic, whereas the previous edition (Thorndike, 1971b) had no chapters devoted to the topic.

Predictions in this rapidly growing field are certainly difficult to make. Brzezinski (1984) reported that "in 1950, the RAND Corporation predicted that because computers were so large and expensive, no more than 12 corporations in the United States would ever need or be able to afford one" (p. 7). In 1983, the Educational Testing Service predicted that by 1985 there would be anywhere from 300,000 to 650,000 microcomputers in the schools (Educational Testing Service, 1983). The December 1984 issue of *Phi Delta Kappan* reported that in the fall of 1984, the country's 50 largest school districts alone had 73,570 microcomputers, up from 36,835 the year earlier (*Newsnotes*, 1984, p. 302). Given the history of conservative predictions on computer use, we trust that our statements will be interpreted in the light of the year we wrote them (mid-1989).

Computer-Administered Tests An exciting area of research that may well have a significant and lasting impact is in using computers to administer tests (Bork, 1979; Ward, 1981). This automated approach would free professional staff time for other duties and would eliminate administrator variability as a source of error in test scores, thus improving test reliability.

Furthermore, computerized test administration will typically reduce the turn-around time for obtaining the results; it may well reduce scoring errors; and it will certainly allow flexibility in scheduling test administrations —something that would be particularly helpful in testing individual students (clients). The use of a computer in test administration should be of some benefit to individuals with various types of visual, auditory, and physical limitations (Sampson, 1983), although for some other handicapping conditions the computer might not be suitable. Finally, computer administration should allow for innovations in testing. The graphics and color capabilities, as well as the various input and output media (light pens, joysticks, touch sensitive screens, etc.), provide much more flexibility in item format. Johnson (1983) listed examples of tests in ballet that can be administered through videodiscs on which the sequences of a step may be shown. B. F. Green (1983) suggested that situations could be presented on videodiscs for firefighters' or police officers' exams so that the respondents can answer questions regarding the situation. Obviously, memory could be tested by the use of successive frames.

As we said, though, there are also potential problems connected with computer administration of tests. One of these is the counterpart of efficiency of staff time. To the extent that a professional is not supervising students while they take the test, the practitioner cannot learn from observing them. Personal observation has typically been considered a big advantage in using individual intelligence tests. Another disadvantage is that the test-takers' scores may be based in part on their ability to use the computer. Some critics have suggested that females, minorities, and those from low socioeconomic backgrounds may be somewhat less familiar with computers than white males and thus may perform less well than they would with conventional modes of presentation. There are problems connected with the confidentiality of the information. Once they are stored in a computer's memory, data may be compromised. Other drawbacks involve the norms, the equivalence of forms, and the validity of the scores from computer-administered tests. Finally, there may be some staff resistance to the use of computers.

Some attempts have been made to develop standards for computerized testing. As mentioned earlier, the revised *Standards for Educational and Psychological Testing* addresses some of the issues. Another good reference is *Guidelines for Computer-Based Tests and Interpretations* (COPS, CPTA, 1986).

A variety of computer programs for testing are also on the market. Tescor, Incorporated, for example, has a microcomputer scoring system that allows for local scoring of locally developed and standardized achievement or ability tests as well as an item bank and test development system to assist in local teacher-made tests. CTB/McGraw-Hill

has a software package called the Microcomputer Instructional Management System (MIMS), which should assist in the monitoring, diagnosis, and prescription process for individual pupils. Sampson (1984) presents a guide to microcomputer software programs in testing and assessment.

Computer-Adaptive Testing A particular type of computer-administered testing has become known as computer-adaptive testing. Computers can be programmed to present items of appropriate difficulty for an individual, as judged by that person's responses to previous items, thus providing "adaptive" tests. In an adaptive test, an examinee who answers an item correctly is administered a harder unanswered item (as judged by a difficulty index for group data). An examinee who misses an item would be administered an easier item, usually the most difficult of all the unanswered items that are easier than the one just missed. Research generally supports the notion that tailored tests are somewhat more efficient than conventional tests because one can avoid asking an individual a whole set of items that the person is almost sure to get all right (or wrong). Typically only about one-half the number of items from a conventional test are needed on an adaptive test to produce equivalent reliability estimates. Thus, testing time, boredom, and fatigue are all reduced. However, there are some potential problems with the use of adaptive testing. Because not all students take the same items, the students' scores must be accurately compared. Obviously, the items have to be scaled in some fashion. Item-response theory provides a way to do this but requires empirical information from a fairly large sample of students. Further, there is some concern, particularly among people not well versed in item-response theory, that it is not "fair" to give different individuals different questions.

Commercial test publishers as well as the military are entering into computerized adaptive testing in greater numbers. The College Board and ETS have published an adaptive computerized placement test in reading comprehension, sentence skills, arithmetic, and elementary algebra to ascertain whether prospective college students need remedial work in the basic skills. The College Board program can administer both conventional and adaptive tests and is amenable to various item formats ranging from free response to multiple choice. In addition to the computer administration and scoring features, the usual reporting services are provided as separate packages. Those desiring further information should consult ETS (see ETS developments, 1988).

Much more could be said about the exciting field of adaptive testing. For the interested reader, Green (1983), Green, Bock, Humphreys, Linn, and Reckase (1984), McBride (1980), Roid (1986), Weiss (1980), and Wood (1973) present thorough reviews of this topic.

Computer Testing and Instruction

The use of computers in the school should facilitate teaching–learning–testing cooperation. The immediate storage, analysis, and printout of a student's examination results would help the teacher plan instructional processes. Using computer facilities in conjunction with expanded item banks will allow teachers to do more instructional testing without taking an inordinate amount of their time in preparing, administering, and scoring tests. Using an interactive mode, students taking a test via computer can be told immediately whether or not an answer is correct. In some cases it may be possible to determine why an answer is wrong and to offer, through the computer, an immediate learning sequence dealing with the precise problem (Bork, 1979; McArthur & Choppin, 1984).

Computer Test Score Interpretation

The use of computers to report and interpret test scores to pupils is also receiving increasing attention. A study by Mathews (1973), comparing a traditional test report (national and local percentiles and grade equivalents for the various subsets, summary scores, and a composite score) with a locally prepared computer-generated narrative report, indicated that classroom teachers rated the narrative format superior on 15 of 18 comparisons. Some writers suggest that computer interpretations are

both more reliable and more valid (Burke & Normand, n.d.). Humans are not generally as consistent as computers, which do not have hangovers, family arguments before coming to work, and other such weaknesses. Burke and Normand summarize some research that shows that computer-generated reports are of equal or superior validity to clinical judgments. However, serious concerns have been raised about computer-based test interpretation.

> The most pressing worry of practitioners is the accuracy of computerized test interpretation. . . . Used by those with little training or awareness of test interpretation validity, computerized testing can do more harm than good. . . . Because test scores and interpretations come from a computer, they give a false impression of infallibility. And because the tests are so easy to use . . . many who are untrained will use them incorrectly for decisions involving employment, educational placement, occupational counseling, mental health diagnosis, or brain deficiency assessments (Turkington, 1984, pp. 7, 26).

Eyde and Kowal (1984) discuss both advantages and potential misuses of computer-based test interpretations. They point out that an American Psychological Association policy statement requires "professional-to-professional consultation." Thus, the interpretation obtained from the computer would be for the professional to use. It should *not* be given directly to the student (client) without professional interpretation. Further, the authors give an example of a Minnesota Multiphasic Personality Inventory (MMPI) profile as produced by four different computer software interpretation programs and by a clinician. There were some important differences. Clearly, caution must be observed in the use of computer-based test interpretations—especially with personality inventories.

Increase in Performance Assessment

We have discussed methods of assessing performance in Chapter 9. There has been an increase in performance assessment, and we expect that trend to continue. Examples include the increase of writing assessment (mandated by many states), the performance assessment of teachers, and the assessment of student behaviors (from which we might infer value acquisition).

We are in favor of quality performance assessment and are pleased to see such assessment increasing. Some variables can just not be assessed by paper-and-pencil tests—especially objectively scored tests. Further, the assessment of performance is likely to have an impact (typically positive) on instruction. Certainly writing is being taught more now that it is assessed more frequently.

However, sometimes the advocates of performance assessment overstate the case for performance assessment and make incorrect statements about the limitations of objectively scored test questions. We hope readers recognize that, for example, multiple-choice questions can test for higher-order thinking skills—we give such questions on both the midterm and final of our measurement classes.

Use of Assessment to Improve Instruction

There currently exists a strong push to design tests that will be more helpful in improving instruction. The general notion is not new (see Linn, 1989). Cook (1951) and Tyler (1951) both argued for the use of tests to facilitate learning. Tyler specifically argued that educational measurement should be considered an integral part of construction. As we pointed out in Chapter 1, Furst (1958) suggested that educational objectives, educational experiences (instruction), and evaluation procedures (testing) are all interrelated. Nitko (1989) reemphasized this theme and suggested that "designing of tests and instruction are mutually planned efforts" (p. 453).

Although linking tests and instruction is not a new concept, there is general agreement that current educational tests do a better job of describing current general levels of achievement and predicting future achievement than they do in "guiding the specifics of instruction" (Glaser, 1986, p. 45) (see also Nitko, 1989; Snow & Lohman, 1989).

The push for measurement-driven instruction (see Chapter 1) is one way to try and establish a closer link between testing and instruction, but this approach has typically not involved the *mutually* planned efforts of testing and instruction. However, two other forces at work may enhance the integration of testing and construction: computer technology and cognitive psychology. Snow and Lohman (1989) discuss "what *might* be" (p. 263, emphasis added) with respect to the contributions of cognitive psychology to educational measurement. We are cautiously optimistic that future assessment procedures will be even more closely linked to instruction than current ones.

Quality Versus Quantity

It is the authors' hope, if not our prediction, that the years ahead will bring a reduction in the number of tests designed to test the same constructs. Far too many tests of poor quality are on the market. Buros (1972) suggested that at least half the tests on the market should never have been published. We would much prefer to see fewer tests, all of higher quality. Unfortunately, with the movement toward locally developed criterion-referenced tests, this is not occurring.

Probably the only way for our hope to materialize is for educators to stop building and purchasing inadequate tests. This, of course, cannot occur unless consumers are capable of making good judgments, which leads to our last prediction.

Consumer Competence

Tests can be important and useful tools. Used correctly by competent personnel, tests will continue to play an increasingly important role in educational institutions. Tests used incorrectly by incompetent, unprofessional staffs may do more harm than good. There have been far too many instances of incorrect use of tests by school personnel. *It is our hopeful prediction that professionals' competencies in test use will increase to an acceptably high level.* If not, tests will continue to be misused.

It would be helpful if all pre-service teacher training programs included a required course in testing, measurement, and evaluation. Much use or potential misuse of test results is by classroom teachers, and, regretfully, many of them are woefully and inadequately prepared. It behooves college administrators and possibly legislators to mandate such a course as a requirement for teacher certification. The American Association of Colleges for Teacher Education, the American Federation of Teachers, the National Council on Measurement in Education, and the National Education Association (1989) have been jointly working to develop a document: *Standards for Teacher Competence in Educational Assessment of Students.* These standards, "should form a partial basis for future teacher preparation and certification programs" (p. 2).

■ SUMMARY

The major ideas, conclusions, and implications of this chapter are summarized in the following statements.

1. The public is concerned about measurement and evaluation in education. Some of these concerns are rational and relevant; others are irrational and irrelevant.
2. Tests have certainly been misused. Most of the problems related to test misuse bear on overgeneralizations made by users.
3. Many people criticize tests because their use has sometimes led to faulty decisions. What they fail to realize is that even more decisions would be faulty in the absence of test data.
4. Minimum competency testing for students is currently both very popular and very controversial. The controversy involves legal questions as well as educational questions such as what competencies should be measured, who should set the minimum standards, how should the standard be determined, and what

should be done with those not making the standard.
5. Competency testing of teachers has become very popular.
6. Whether tests invade one's privacy depends upon the relevancy of the information gathered, the qualifications of the gatherers, the use to which the information is put, and the confidentiality of the data.
7. A major purpose of tests is to differentiate (discriminate) among people. Differentiation alone does not make a test unfair.
8. There are a variety of definitions of test bias. Some are complementary, others are contradictory.
9. The major educational concern related to cultural fairness is the use of tests as screening or prediction devices. Few people suggest that achievement tests measuring the outcomes of education are unfair.
10. Culture-fair tests would probably be less valid predictors of educational achievement than present aptitude and achievement tests.
11. Research seems to show quite conclusively that, under the most common definitions of test bias, scholastic aptitude tests are *not* biased against students with culturally disadvantaged backgrounds.
12. The use of intelligence tests for placing students into special education programs has been very controversial. There have been recent court decisions on both sides.
13. Several future trends in evaluation were discussed. These include (a) increased legal involvement in testing, (b) an increased use of computers in giving tests and storing and reporting test data, (c) an increase in performance assessment, (d) increased use of assessment to improve instruction, (e) higher quality in testing, and (f) greater user competence.

■ POINTS TO PONDER

1. Some states or local districts require the passing of a minimum competency examination for

high school graduation. Are you in favor of such programs? Explain your position.

2. Should prospective teachers have to pass a basic skills test prior to being certified? Why or why not?

3. It is typical school policy to have students' cumulative records accompany them as they move from one grade to the next and from one school to another. What are the advantages and limitations of this policy? Under what conditions could it constitute an invasion of privacy?

4. Under what circumstances would it be appropriate to ask very personal questions in a standardized test?

5. Assume a test has been developed that can differentiate between pro-union and anti-union teachers. Does the school superintendent have

a right to use this instrument in helping decide whom (a) to hire and (b) to promote?

6. What would be the benefits to society of developing a test on which all subcultures perform equally well? How have you defined "subculture?"

7. A college uses test ABC for admission purposes. Research has demonstrated that the test is a reasonably valid predictor ($r = 0.58$) of college GPA. Research has also shown that some subcultures do less well on this test than others. What further evidence needs to be gathered to answer the question of whether the test discriminates unfairly?

8. If it is possible for a test to be administered by either a teacher or a computer, are two sets of norms necessary? Why?

Appendix

Selective List
of Test Publishers

Addison-Wesley Publishing Company, 2725 Sand Hill Road, Menlo Park, California, 94025

American College Testing Program, P.O. Box 168, Iowa City, Iowa, 52240

American Guidance Service, Publishers' Building, Circle Pines, Minnesota, 55014

Australian Council for Educational Research, P. O. Box 210, Hawthorn, Victoria, 3122 Australia

California Test Bureau/McGraw-Hill, Del Monte Research Park, Monterey, California, 93940

Consulting Psychologists Press, 577 College Avenue, Palo Alto, California, 94306

Educational Testing Service, Princeton, New Jersey, 08540

Guidance Centre, Ontario College of Education, University of Toronto, Toronto 289, Ontario, Canada

Houghton Mifflin Company, One Beacon Street, Boston, Massachusetts, 02107

Institute for Personality and Ability Testing, P.O. Box 188, Champaign, Illinois, 61820

The Psychological Corporation, 555 Academic Court, San Antonio, Texas, 78204-0952

Riverside Publishing Company, 8420 Bryn Mawr Avenue, Chicago, Illinois, 60631

Scholastic Testing Service, 480 Meyer Road, Bensenville, Illinois, 60106

Science Research Associates, 155 North Wacker Drive, Chicago, Illinois, 60606

Stanford University Press, Stanford, California, 94305

Western Psychological Services, 12031 Wilshire Boulevard, Los Angeles, California, 90025

References

Ackerman, T. A., & Smith, P. L. (1988). A comparison of the information provided by essay, multiple-choice, and free-response writing test, *Applied Psychological Measurement, 12,* 117–128.

AERA/APA/NCME. (1985). *Standards for educational and psychological testing.* Washington, DC: American Psychological Association.

Ahmann, J. S., & Glock, M. D. (1981). *Evaluating pupil growth* (6th ed.). Boston: Allyn and Bacon.

Aikin, W. M. (1942). *The story of the eight-year study; with conclusions and recommendations.* New York: Harper & Row.

Airasian, P. W. (1979a, April). *The effects of standardized testing and test information on teacher's perceptions and practices.* Paper presented at the annual meeting of the American Educational Research Association, San Francisco.

Airasian, P. W. (1979b). A perspective on the uses and misuses of standardized achievement tests. *NCME Measurement in Education, 10*(3), 1–12.

Airasian, P. W. (1987). State mandated testing and educational reform: Context and consequences. *American Journal of Education, 95,* 393–412.

Airasian, P. W. (1988). Measurement driven instruction: A closer look. *Educational Measurement: Issues and Practice, 7*(4), 6–11.

Airasian, P. W., Kellaghan, T., Madaus, G. F., & Pedulla, J. J. (1977). Proportion and direction of teacher rating changes of pupils' progress attributable to standardized text information. *Journal of Educational Psychology, 69*(6), 702–709.

Airasian, P. W., & Madaus, G. F. (1983, Summer). Linking testing and instruction. *Journal of Educational Measurement, 20*(2), 103–118.

Alderman, D. L., & Powers, D. E. (1980). The effects of special preparation on SAT-verbal scores. *American Educational Research Journal, 17,* 239–253.

Alexander, L., & James, H. T. (1987). *The nation's report card: Improving the assessment of student achievement.* Washington, DC: National Academy of Education.

Alker, H. A., Carlson, J. A., & Hermann, M. C. (1967, Nov.). Multiple-choice questions and student characteristics. *Educational Testing Service Research Bulletin.*

Allport, G. W. (1963). *Pattern and growth in personality.* New York: Holt, Rinehart and Winston.

Alpert, R., & Haber, R. N. (1960). Anxiety in academic achievement situations. *Journal of Abnormal and Social Psychology, 61,* 207–215.

Althen, G., & Stott, F. W. (1983, June). Advising and counseling students who have unrealistic academic objectives. *Personnel and Guidance Journal, 61,* 608–611.

AMEG. (1973). AMEG commission report on sex bias in measurement. *Measurement and Evaluation in Guidance, 6,* 171–177.

American Association of Colleges for Teacher Education, American Federation of Teachers, National Council on Measurement in Education, and National Education Association. (1989, March). Draft of the *Standards for teacher competence in educational assessment of students.* Authors.

American College Testing Program. (1989). *The Enhanced ACT Assessment.* Iowa City, IA: Author.

American Psychological Association. (1970). Psychological assessment and public policy. *American Psychologist, 25,* 264–266.

American Psychological Association. (1986). *Guidelines for computer-based tests and interpretations.* Washington, DC: Author.

Ammons, M. (1964). An empirical study of progress and product in curriculum development. *Journal of Educational Research, 27,* 451–457.

Anastasi, A. (1968). *Psychological testing* (3rd ed.). New York: Macmillan.

Anastasi, A. (1973, May). *Common fallacies about heredity, environment, and human behavior.* Research Report No. 51. Iowa City, IA: American College Testing Program.

Anastasi, A. (1981). Coaching, test sophistication, and developed abilities. *American Psychologist, 36,* 1086–1093.

Anastasi, A. (1982). *Psychological testing* (5th ed.). New York: Macmillan.

Anastasi, A. (1988). *Psychological testing* (6th ed.). New York: Macmillan.

Anastasi, A. (1989). [Review of the Stanford-Binet intelligence scale (4th ed.)]. In J. C. Conoley and J. J. Kramer (Eds.), *The tenth mental measurements yearbooks* (pp. 771–772). Lincoln, NE: Buros Institute of Mental Measurements.

Anderson, B., & Pipho, C. (1984). State-mandated testing and the fate of local control. *Phi Delta Kappan, 66,* 209–212.

Anderson, J. O. (1987, June). *Teacher practices in and attitudes towards student assessment.* Paper presented at the annual meeting of the Canadian Educational Researchers' Association, McMaster University, Hamilton, Ontario.

Anderson, L. W. (1981). *Assessing affective characteristics in the schools.* Boston: Allyn and Bacon.

Anderson, R. H. (1966). The importance and purposes of reporting. *National Elementary School Principal, 45,* 6–11.

Anderson, S. B. (1980). Going public. *Newsnotes, 15*(4), 1–5.

Angoff, W. H. (1971). Scales, norms, and equivalent scores. In R. L. Thorndike (Ed.), *Educational measurement* (2nd ed.) (pp. 508–600). Washington, DC: American Council on Education.

Angoff, W. H. (1974). The development of statistical indices for detecting cheaters. *Journal of American Statistical Association, 69,* 44–49.

Anrig, G. R. (1986). In *The redesign of testing for the 21st century* (P.V). Invitational Conference Proceedings of the Educational Testing Service. Princeton, NJ: Educational Testing Service.

Arter, J., & Salmon, J. R. (1987). *Assessing higher order thinking skills.* Portland, OR: Northwest Regional Educational Laboratory.

Astin, A. W. (1971). *Predicting academic performance in college.* New York: Free Press.

Ausubel, D. P. (1968). *Educational psychology: A cognitive view.* New York: Holt, Rinehart and Winston.

Baglin, R. F. (1981). Does "nationally" normed really mean nationally? *Journal of Educational Measurement, 18*(2), 97–107.

Bajtelsmit, J. (1977). Test wiseness and systematic desensitization programs for increasing test-taking skills. *Journal of Educational Measurement, 14,* 335–342.

Baker, F. B. (1977). Advances in item analysis. *Review of Educational Research, 47,* 151–178.

Baker, F. B. (1989). Computer technology in test construction and processing. In R. L. Linn (Ed.), *Educational measurement* (3rd ed.) (pp. 409–428). New York: Macmillan.

Baltes, P. B., & Scharie, K. W. (1976). On the plasticity of intelligence in adulthood and old age: Where Horn and Donaldson fail. *American Psychologist, 31*(10), 720–725.

Barber, T. X., & Silver M. J. (1968). Fact, fiction, and the experimenter bias effect. *Psychological Bulletin Monograph Supplement, 70,* 1–29.

Barclay, J. R. (1968). *Controversial issues in testing.* Guidance Monograph Series III. Boston: Houghton Mifflin.

Bartlett, L. (1987). Academic evaluation and student discipline don't mix: A critical review. *Journal of Law and Education, 16*(2), 155–165.

Bartling, H. C. (1979). *An eleven-year follow-up study of measured interest and inventoried choice.* Unpublished Ph.D. dissertation. Iowa City, IA: University of Iowa.

Barzun, J. (1947). *Teacher in America.* Boston: Little, Brown.

Bayley, N. (1949). Consistency and variability in the growth of intelligence from birth to eighteen years. *Journal of Genetic Psychology, 75,* 165–196.

Bayley, N. (1955). On the growth of intelligence. *American Psychologist, 10,* 805–818.

Beck, M. D. (1974). Achievement test reliability as a function of pupil-response procedures. *Journal of Educational Measurement, 11,* 109–114.

Beck, M. D. (1986). The Otis and Otis-Lennon Tests: Their contributions. *Educational Measurement: Issues and Practice, 5*(3), 12–18.

Becker, S. (1977). Personality correlates of the discrepancy between expressed and inventoried interest scores. *Measurement and Evaluation in Guidance, 10*(1), 24–30.

Bejar, I. I. (1984). Educational diagnostic assessment. *Journal of Educational Measurement, 21,* 175–189.

Benjamin, M., McKeachie, W. J., Lin, Y., & Holinger, D. P. (1981). Test anxiety: Deficits in information processing. *Journal of Educational Psychology, 73*(6), 816–824.

Bennett, R. E., & Ragosta, M. (1985). The technical characteristics of postsecondary admissions tests for handicapped examinees: A review of research. *Journal of Special Education, 19,* 255–267.

Bennett, R. E., Rock, D. A., & Noratkoski, I. (1989). Differential item functioning on the SAT-M Braille edition. *Journal of Educational Measurement, 26*(1), 67–79.

Benson, J. (1989). The psychometric and cognitive aspects of test-wiseness: A review of the literature. In M. H. Kean (Ed.), *Test-wiseness* (pp. 1–14). Center on Evaluation, Development, Research. Bloomington, IN:Phi Delta Kappa.

Benson, J., & Hocevar, D. (1985). The impact of item phrasing on the validity of attitude scales for elementary school children. *Journal of Educational Measurement, 22,* 231–240.

Benson, W. W. (1969). *Graduate grading systems.* Paper ED-036-262 presented at the Council of Graduate Schools in the United States, Washington, DC.

Benton, S. L., & Kierwa, K. A. (1986). Measuring the organizational aspects of writing ability. *Journal of Educational Measurement, 23,* 377–386.

Berdie, F. S. (1971). What test questions are likely to offend the general public? *Journal of Educational Measurement, 8,* 87–94.

Bereiter, C. E. (1963). Some persistent dilemmas in the measurement of change. In C. W. Harris (Ed.), *Problems in measuring change* (pp. 3–20). Madison: University of Wisconsin Press.

Berk, R. A. (1979). *A critical review of content domain specification/item generation strategies for criterion-referenced tests.* Paper presented at the annual meeting of the American Educational Research Association, San Francisco.

Berk, R. A. (Ed.). (1980). *Criterion-referenced measurement: The state of the art.* Baltimore: Johns Hopkins University Press.

Berk, R. A. (1984). Selecting the index of reliability. In R. A. Berk (ed.), *A guide to criterion-referenced test construction* (pp. 199–230). Baltimore: Johns Hopkins University Press.

Berk, R. A. (1986a). A consumer's guide to setting performance standards on criterion-referenced tests. *Review of Educational Research, 56*(1), 137–172.

Berk, R. A. (1986b). Minimum competency testing: Status and potential. In B. S. Plake and J. C. Witt (Eds.),

The future of testing (pp. 89–144). Hillsdale, NJ: Lawrence Erlbaum.

Berk, R. A. (1988, July). Fifty reasons why student achievement gain does not mean teacher effectiveness. *Journal of Personnel Evaluation in Education, 1*(4), 345–364.

Bersoff, D. N. (1981). Testing and the law. *American Psychologist, 36,* 1047–1056.

Bersoff, D. N. (1984). Social and legal influences on test development and usage. In B. S. Plake (Ed.), *Social and technical issues in testing* (pp. 87–110). Hillsdale, NJ: Lawrence Erlbaum.

Biehler, R. F. (1971). *Psychology applied to teaching.* Boston: Houghton Mifflin.

Bills, R. E. (1975). *A system for assessing affectivity.* University, AL: University of Alabama Press.

Binet, A., & Henri, V. (1896). Le psychologie individuell. *Année Psychologique, 2,* 411–465.

Binet, A., & Simon, T. (1905). Methodes nouvelles pour le diagnostic du niveau intellectuel des anormaux. *Année Psychologique, 11,* 191–244.

Binet, A., & Simon, T. (1916). *The development of intelligence in children.* Vineland, NJ: Training School Publication No. 11, 192.

Birenbaum, M., & Tatsuoka, K. K. (1987). Effects of "on-line" test feedback on the seriousness of subsequent errors. *Journal of Educational Measurement, 24,* 145–155.

Bishop, J. H. (1989). Why the apathy in American high schools? *Educational Researcher, 18*(1), 6–10, 42.

Black, H. (1963). *They shall not pass.* New York: Morrow.

Black, R., & Dana, R. H. (1977). Examiner sex bias and Wechsler Intelligence Scale for Children scores. *Journal of Consulting and Clinical Psychology, 45,* 500.

Bliss, L. B. (1980). A test of Lord's assumption regarding examinee guessing behavior on multiple-choice tests using elementary school children. *Journal of Educational Measurement, 17,* 147–154.

Block, J. (1972). The shifting definitions of acquiescence. *Psychological Bulletin, 78,* 10–12.

Block, N. J., & Dworkin, G. (1974a, Summer). I.Q.: Heritability and inequality—Part 1. *Philosophy and Public Affairs, 3,* 331–409.

Block, N. J., & Dworkin, G. (1974b). I.Q.: Heritability and inequality—Part 2. *Philosophy and Public Affairs, 4,* 40–99.

Bloom, B. S. (Ed.). (1956). *Taxonomy of educational objectives, handbook I: The cognitive domain.* New York: McKay.

Bloom, B. S. (1964). *Stability and change in human characteristics.* New York: Wiley.

Bloom, B. S. (1968, May). Learning for mastery. *Evaluation Comment.* UCLA. CSEIP, *1*, 2.

Bloom, B. S. (1978). New views of the learner: Implications for instruction and curriculum. *Educational Leadership, 35*, 563–576.

Bloom, B. S., Madaus, G. F., & Hastings, T. T. (1981). *Evaluation to improve learning.* New York: Mc-Graw-Hill.

Blumberg, H. H., De Soto, C. B., & Kuethe, J. L. (1966). Evaluation of rating scale formats. *Personnel Psychology, 19*, 243–260.

Board, C., & Whitney, D. R. (1972). The effect of poor item writing practices on test difficulty, reliability, and validity. *Journal of Educational Measurement, 9*, 225–233.

Bock, R. D. (1972). Estimating item parameters and latent ability when responses are scored in two or more nominal categories. *Psychometrika, 37*, 29–51.

Bond, L. (1986). Predictive contributions of tests in the admissions process. In the College Board (Eds.), *Measures in the college admissions process* (pp. 57–61). New York: College Entrance Examination Board.

Bond, L. (1989). The effects of special preparation on measures of scholastic ability. In R. L. Linn (Ed.), *Educational measurement* (3rd ed.) (pp. 429–444). New York: American Council on Education and Macmillan.

Borgen, F. H. (1972). Predicting career choices of able college men from occupational and basic interest scales of the Strong Vocational Interest Blank. *Journal of Counseling Psychology, 19*, 202–211.

Borgen, F. H., & Bernard, C. B. (1982). Review of the Strong-Campbell Interest Inventory. *Journal of Educational Measurement, 14*, 208–212.

Borgen, F. H., & Harper, G. T. (1973). Predictive validity for measured vocational interests with black and white college men. *Measurement and Evaluation in Guidance, 6*, 19–27.

Borich, G. D., & Malitz, D. (1975). Convergent and discriminant validation of three classroom observation systems: A proposed model. *Journal of Educational Psychology, 67*, 426–431.

Bork, A. (1979). Interactive learning: Millikan lecture. American Association of Physics Teachers. *American Journal of Physics, 47*(1), 5–10.

Bowles, S., & Gintis, H. (1974). IQ in the United States class structure. In A. Gartner, C. Greer, and F. Riessman (Eds.), *The new assault on equality* (pp. 7–84). New York: Harper & Row.

Bracey, G. W. (1987). Measurement-driven instruction: Catchy phrase, dangerous practice. *Phi Delta Kappan, 68*(9), 683–686.

Braun, H. I., Ragosta, M., & Kaplan, B. A. (1986). *The predictive validity of the scholastic aptitude test for disabled students.* RR-86-38. Princeton, NJ: Educational Testing Service.

Breland, H. M. (1978). *Population validity and college entrance measures.* Princeton, N.J.: Educational Testing Service.

Breland, H. M. (1979). *Population validity and college entrance measures.* Research Monograph No. 8. New York: College Entrance Examination Board.

Brennan, R. L. (1984). Estimating the dependability of the scores. In R. A. Berk (Ed.), *A guide to criterion-referenced test construction* (pp. 292–334). Baltimore: Johns Hopkins University Press.

Brennan, R. L., & Stolurow, L. M. (1971). *An elementary decision process for the formative evaluation of an instructional system.* Paper presented at the annual meeting of the American Educational Research Association. New York.

Brophy, J. E., Coulter, C. L., Crawford, W. J., Everston, C. M., & King, C. E. (1975). Classroom observation scales: Stability across time and context and relationships with student learning gains. *Journal of Educational Psychology, 67*, 873–881.

Browder, L. H., Jr. (1971). *Emerging patterns of administrative accountability.* Berkeley, CA: McCutchan.

Browder, L. H., Jr., Atkins, W. A., & Kaya, E. (1973). *Developing an educationally accountable program.* Berkeley, CA: McCutchan.

Brown, F. G. (1983). *Principles of educational and psychological testing* (3rd ed.). New York: Holt, Rinehart and Winston.

Brown, J. S., & Burton, R. R. (1978). Diagnostic models for procedural bugs in basic mathematics. *Cognitive Science, 2*, 155–192.

Brown, S. (1988). Encountering misspellings and spelling performance: Why wrong isn't right. *Journal of Educational Psychology, 80*, 488–494.

Bruch, M. A., & Skovholt, T. (1985). Congruence of Holland personality type and martial satisfaction. *Measurement and Evaluation in Counseling and Development, 18*, 100–107.

Brzezinski, E. J. (1984). Microcomputers and testing: Where are we and how did we get there? *Educational Measurement: Issues and Practice, 3*(2), 7–9.

Brzezinski, E. J., & Hiscox, M. (Eds.). (1984). Microcomputers in educational measurement. (Special Issue). *Educational Measurement: Issues and Practice, 3*, 2.

Budescu, D. V. (1980). Some measures of profile dissimilarity. *Applied Psychological Measurement, 4*(2), 261–272.

Budescu, D. V. (1988, March). On the feasibility of multiple matching tests—variations on a theme by Gulliksen. *Applied Personality Measurement, 12*(1), 5–14.

Budescu, D. V., & Nevo, B. (1985). Optimal number of options: An investigation of the assumption of proportionality. *Journal of Educational Measurement, 22*(3), 183–196.

Bunderson, C. V., Inouye, D. K., & Olsen, J. B. (1988). The four generations of computerized educational measurement. In R. L. Linn (Ed.), *Educational measurement* (pp. 367–407). New York: Macmillan.

Bunzel, J. H. (1988). Affirmative-action admissions: How it "works" at UC Berkeley. *The Public Interest, 93*, 111–129.

Burke, M. J., & Normand, J. (n.d.). *Computerized psychological testing: state of the art.* Unpublished manuscript.

Burket, G. R. (1984). Response to Hoover. *Educational Measurement: Issues and Practice, 3*(4), 15–16.

Burns, R. W. (1972). *New approaches to behavioral objectives.* Dubuque, IA: Brown.

Buros, O. K. (Ed.). (1938). *The 1938 mental measurements yearbook.* New Brunswick, NJ: Rutgers University Press.

Buros, O. K. (Ed.). (1941). *The 1940 mental measurements yearbook.* New Brunswick, NJ: Rutgers University Press.

Buros, O. K. (Ed.). (1949). *The third mental measurements yearbook.* New Brunswick, NJ: Rutgers University Press.

Buros, O. K. (Ed.). (1953). *The fourth mental measurements yearbook.* Highland Park, NJ: Gryphon Press.

Buros, O. K. (Ed.). (1959). *The fifth mental measurements yearbook.* Highland Park, NJ: Gryphon Press.

Buros, O. K. (Ed.). (1965). *The sixth mental measurements yearbook.* Highland Park, NJ: Gryphon Press.

Buros, O. K. (Ed.). (1972). *The seventh mental measurements yearbook.* Highland Park, NJ: Gryphon Press.

Buros, O. K. (Ed.). (1978). *The eighth mental measurements yearbook.* Highland Park, NJ: Gryphon Press.

Burwen, L. S. (1971). *Current practices: A national survey.* Paper presented at the annual meeting of the American Educational Research Association. New York.

Busch, J. C. (1988). Factors influencing recommended standards for essay tests. *Applied Measurement in Education, 1*, 67–78.

Butcher, H. J. (1968). *Human intelligence: Its nature and assessment.* New York: Harper & Row.

Butcher, H. J. (1987). *Computerized psychological assessment.* New York: Basic Books.

Calandra, A. (1964, Jan. 6). The barometer story. *Current Science Teacher*, 14.

Calfee, R. C., Henry, M. K., & Funderburg, J. A. (1988). A model for school change. In S. J. Samuels & P. D. Pearson, (Eds.), *Changing school reading programs* (pp. 121–141). Newark, DE: International Reading Association.

Callenbach, C. (1973). The effects of instruction and practice in content-independent test-taking techniques upon the standardized reading test scores of selected second-grade students. *Journal of Educational Measurement, 10*, 25–30.

Calsyn, R. J., & Kenny, D. A. (1977). Self-concept ability and perceived evaluation of others: Cause or effect of academic achievement? *Journal of Educational Psychology, 69*(2), 136–145.

Campbell, D. P. (1974). *Manual for the SCII.* Stanford, CA: Stanford University Press.

Campbell, D. P. (1976). Author's reaction to Johnson's review. *Measurement and Evaluation in Guidance, 9*, 45–46.

Campbell, D. P., & Hansen, J. I. C. (1981). *Manual for the SVIB-SCII* (3rd ed.). Palo Alto, CA: Stanford University Press.

Campbell, R. E. (1971). Accountability and stone soup. *Phi Delta Kappan, 53*, 176–178.

Campione, J. C., & Brown, A. L. (1979). Toward a theory of intelligence: Contributions from research with retarded children. In R. J. Sternberg & D. K. Detterman (Eds.), *Human intelligence: Perspectives on its theory and measurement* (pp. 139–164). Norwood, NJ: Ablex.

Canady, R. L., & Seyfarth, J. T. (1979). *How parent-teacher conferences build partnerships.* Bloomington, IN: Phi Delta Kappa Educational Foundation.

Cannell, J. J. (1987). *Nationally normed elementary achievement testing in America's public schools: How all fifty states are above the national average.* Daniels, WV: Friends for Education.

Cannell, J. J. (1989). *The "Lake Wobegon" report: How public educators cheat on standardized achievement tests*. Friends for Education. Albuquerque: Cottonwood Press.

Carnegie Task Force. (1986). *A nation prepared: Teachers for the 21st century*. The report of the task force on teaching as a profession. Carnegie Forum on Education and the Economy. New York: Carnegie Corporation.

Carney, C. G., Savitz, C. J., & Weiskott, G. N. (1979). Students' evaluations of a university counseling center and their intentions to use its programs. *Journal of Counseling Psychology, 26*, 242–249.

Carroll, J. B. (1974). Fitting a model of school learning to aptitude and achievement data over grade levels. In D. R. Green (Ed.), *The aptitude–achievement distinction* (pp. 53–77). Monterey, CA: CTB/McGraw-Hill.

Carroll, J. B., & Horn, J. L. (1981). On a scientific basis of ability testing. *American Psychologist, 36*(10), 1012–1020.

Carroll, L. (1916). *Alice's adventures in wonderland*. Chicago: Rand McNally.

Carter, K. (1986). Test wiseness for teachers and students. *Educational Measurement: Issues and Practice, 5*(4), 20–33.

Carver, R. P. (1974). Two dimensions of tests: Psychometric and edumetric. *American Psychologist, 29*, 512–518.

Cashen, V. M., & Ramseyer, G. C. (1969). The use of separate answer sheets by primary school children. *Journal of Educational Measurement, 6*, 155–158.

Cattell, J. McK. (1890). Mental tests and measurements. *Mind, 15*, 373–381.

Cattell, R. B. (1963). Theory of fluid and crystallized intelligence: A critical experiment. *Journal of Educational Psychology, 54*, 1–22.

Cattell, R. B. (1971). *Abilities: Their structure, growth, and action*. Boston: Houghton Mifflin.

Cattell, R. B., & Cattell, K. S. (1973). *Handbook for the individual or group culture-fair intelligence test*. Champaign, IL: Institute for Personality and Ability Testing.

Cattell, R. B., & Horn, J. L. (1978). A cross-social check on the theory of fluid and crystallized intelligence with discovery of new valid subtest designs. *Journal of Educationl Measurement, 15*(3), 139–164.

Cegelka, P. T., Omvig, C., & Larimore, D. L. (1974). Effects of attitude and sex on vocational interests. *Measurement and Evaluation in Guidance, 7*, 106–111.

Chambers, B. (1984). *Four keys to better classroom testing*. Princeton, NJ: Educational Testing Service.

Chase, C. I. (1964). Relative length of options and response set in multiple-choice items. *Journal of Educational Measurement, 1*, 38. (Abstract)

Chase, C. I. (1979). The impact of achievement expectations and handwriting quality on scoring essay tests. *Journal of Educational Measurement, 16*, 39–42.

Chase, C. I. (1983). Essay test scores and reading difficulty. *Journal of Educational Measurement, 20*(3), 293–297.

Chase, C. I. (1986). Essay test scoring: Interaction of relevant variables. *Journal of Educational Measurement, 23*(1), 33–42.

Chi, M. T. H., Glaser, R., & Rees, R. (1982). Expertise in problem solving. In R. J. Sternberg (Ed.), *Advances in the psychology of human intelligence*, Vol. 1 (pp. 7–75). Hillsdale, NJ: Lawrence Erlbaum.

Childs, A., & Klimoski, R. J. (1986, Feb.). Successfully predicting career success: An application of the biographical inventory. *Applied Psychology, 71*(1), 3–8.

Chun, K. T., Cobb, S., & French, J. R. P., Jr. (1976). *Measures for psychological assessment*. Ann Arbor: Institute for Social Research, University of Michigan.

Cieutat, V. J., & Flick, G. L. (1967). Examiner differences among Stanford-Binet items. *Psychological Reports, 21*, 613–622.

Citron, C. H. (1983). Courts provide insight on content validity requirements. *Educational Measurement: Issues and Practice, 2*(4), 6–7.

Clarizio, H. F., & Mehrens, W. A. (1985). Psychometric limitations of Guilford's structure of intellect model for identification and programming the gifted. *Gifted Child Quarterly, 29*(3), 113–120.

Claudy, J. G. (1978). A new approach to test item option weighting. *Applied Psychological Measurement, 2*, 25–30.

Claus, C. K. (1968). *Verbs and imperative sentences as a basis for stating educational objectives*. Paper given at meeting of the National Council on Measurement in Education. Chicago.

Clawson, T. W., Firment, C. K., & Trower, T. L. (1981). Test anxiety: Another origin for racial bias in standardized testing. *Measurement and Evaluation in Guidance, 13*(4), 210–215.

Cleary, T. A. (1968). Test bias: Prediction of grades of

Negro and white students in integrated colleges. *Journal of Educational Measurement, 5,* 115–124.

Cleary, T. A., Humphreys, L. G., Kendrick, A. S., & Wesman, A. (1975). Educational uses of tests with disadvantaged students. *American Psychologist, 30,* 15–41.

Cleland, C. C., & Swartz, J. D. (1982). *Exceptionalities through the lifespan.* New York: Macmillan.

Clifford, P. I., & Fishman, J. A. (1963). The impact of testing programs on college preparation and attendance. *The Impact and Improvement of School Testing Programs.* Yearbook LXII, Part II, NSSE, p. 87.

Coffman, W. E. (1971). Essay examinations. In R. L. Thorndike (Ed.), *Educational measurement* (2nd ed.) (pp. 271–302). Washington, DC: American Council on Education.

Coffman, W. E., & Kurfman, D. A. (1968). A comparison of two methods of reading essay examinations. *American Educational Research Journal, 5,* 99–107.

Cohen, A. S., & Reynolds, W. M. (1988, April). *Psychometric characteristics of university instructor developed tests.* Paper presented at the meeting of the National Council on Measurement in Education, New Orleans.

Cohen, E. (1965). Examiner differences with individual intelligence tests. *Perceptual and Motor Skills, 20,* 1324.

Cole, N. S. (1973). On measuring the vocational interests of women. *Journal of Counseling Psychology, 20,* 105–112.

Cole, N. S. (1982, March). *Grade equivalent scores: To GE or not to GE.* Vice presidential address to the meeting of the American Educational Research Association. New York.

Cole, N. S., & Hanson, G. R. (1971). An analysis of the structure of vocational interests. *Journal of Counseling Psychology, 18,* 478–487.

Cole, N. S., & Moss, P. A. (1989). Bias in test use. In R. L. Linn (Ed.), *Educational measurement* (3rd ed.) (pp. 201–220). New York: American Council on Education and Macmillan.

Coleman, J. S., et al. (1966). *Equality of educational opportunity.* Washington, DC: U.S. Department of Health, Education and Welfare, Office of Education.

The College Board News. (1981, Spring). New York experience: Fewer than five percent request SAT questions and answers, p. 1.

The College Board News. (1988–89). As program growth continues, more minorities take advantage of advanced placement examinations. *The College Board News* (p. 2). New York: The College Board.

College Entrance Examination Board. (1978). *Taking the SAT: A guide to the Scholastic Aptitude Test and the Test of Standard Written English.* New York: College Entrance Examination Board.

Commission on the Reorganization of Secondary Education. (1918). *The seven cardinal principles of secondary education.* Washington, DC: Bureau of Education, Government Printing Office.

Comrey, A. L., Backer, T. E., & Glaser, E. M. (1973). *A sourcebook for mental health measures.* Los Angeles: Human Interaction Research Institute.

Conklin, J. E., Burstein, L., & Keesling, J. W. (1979). The effects of date of testing and method of interpolation on the use of standardized test scores in the valuation of large-scale educational programs. *Journal of Educational Measurement, 16*(4), 239–246.

Conoley, J. C., & Kramer, J. J. (Eds.). (1989). *The tenth mental measurements yearbook.* Lincoln, NE: Buros Institute of Mental Measurements.

Cook, W. W. (1951). The functions of measurement in the facilitation of learning. In E. F. Lindquist (Ed.), *Educational measurement* (pp. 3–46). Washington, DC: American Council on Education.

Cooley, W. W. (1971). Techniques for considering multiple measurements. In R. L. Thorndike (Ed.), *Educational measurement* (2nd ed.) (pp. 601–622). Washington, DC: American Council on Education.

Coombs, C. H. (1964). *A theory of data.* New York: Wiley.

COPS, CPTA (Committee on Professional Standards and Committee on Psychological Tests and Assessment) (1986). *Guidelines for computer-based tests and interpretations.* Washington, DC: American Psychological Association.

Corey, S. M. (1953). *Action research to improve school practices.* New York: Teachers College, Columbia University Press.

Costa, A. L. (1989). Re-assessing assessment. *Educational Leadership, 46*(7), 2.

Costin, F. (1970). The optimum number of alternatives in multiple-choice achievement tests: Some empirical evidence for a mathematical proof. *Educational and Psychological Measurement, 30,* 353–358.

Costin, F. (1972). Three-choice versus four-choice items: Implications for reliability and validity of objective test-items. *Educational and Psychological Measurement, 32,* 1035–1038.

Cox, R. C. (1964). *An empirical investigation of the effect of item selection techniques on achievement test construction.* Unpublished doctoral dissertation. East Lansing: Michigan State University.

Cox, R. C., & Sterrett, B. G. (1970). A model for increasing the meaning of test scores. *Journal of Educational Measurement, 7,* 227–228.

Cox, R. C., & Vargas, J. S. (1966). *A comparison of item selection techniques for norm-referenced and criterion-referenced tests.* Paper presented at the annual meeting of the National Council on Measurement in Education, Chicago.

Crehan, K. D., & Haladyna, T. M. (n.d.) *The validity of two item-writing rules.* Unpublished manuscript.

Crehan, K. D., Koehler, R. A., & Slakter, M. J. (1974). Longitudinal studies of test wiseness. *Journal of Educational Measurement, 11,* 209–212.

Crites, J. O. (1974). Methodological issues in the measurement of career maturity. *Measurement and Evaluation in Guidance, 6,* 200–209.

Crocker, L. M., & Benson, J. (1980). Does answer-changing affect test quality? *Measurement and Evaluation in Guidance, 12*(4), 233–239.

Crocker, L., Schmitt, A., & Tang, L. (1988). Test anxiety and standardized achievement test performance in the middle school years. *Measurement and Evaluation in Counseling and Development, 20*(4), 149–157.

Cromer, W. (1969). *An empirical investigation of student attitudes toward the pass-fail grading system at Wellesley College.* Paper presented at a meeting of the Eastern Psychological Association, Philadelphia.

Cronbach, L. J. (1950). Further evidence on response sets and test design. *Educational and Psychological Measurement, 10,* 3–31.

Cronbach, L. J. (1951). Coefficient alpha and the internal structure of tests. *Psychometrika, 16,* 297–334.

Cronbach, L. J. (1963). Course improvement through evaluation. *Teacher's College Record, 64,* 672–683.

Cronbach, L. J. (1969). Heredity, environment, and educational policy. *Harvard Educational Review, 39,* 338–347.

Cronbach, L. J. (1970). *Essentials of psychyological testing* (3rd ed.). New York: Harper & Row.

Cronbach, L. J. (1971). Test validation. In R. L. Thorndike (Ed.), *Educational measurement* (2nd ed.) (pp. 443–507). Washington, DC: American Council on Education.

Cronbach, L. J. (1975). Five decades of public controversy over public testing. *American Psychologist, 30,* 1–14.

Cronbach, L. J. (1980). Validity on parole: How can we go straight? In W. B. Schrader (Ed.), *Measuring achievement: Progress over a decade.* In *New directions for testing and measurement* (no. 5) (pp. 99–108). San Francisco: Jossey-Bass.

Cronbach, L. J. (1989). Review of the Stanford-Binet intelligence scale (4th ed.). In J. C. Conoley and J. J. Kramer (Eds.), *The tenth mental measurements yearbook* (pp. 773–775). Lincoln, NE: Buros Mental Measurements Institute.

Cronbach, L. J. (1990). *Essentials of psycyhological testing* (5th ed.). New York: Harper & Row.

Cronbach, L. J., & Furby, L. (1970). How we should measure "change"—or should we? *Psychological Bulletin, 74*(1), 68–80.

Cronbach, L. J., Gleser, G. C., Nanda, H., & Rajaratnam, N. (1972). *The dependability of behavioral measurements: Multifacet studies of generalizability.* New York: Wiley.

Cronbach, L. J., & Meehl, P. E. (1955). Construct validity in psychological tests. *Psychological Bulletin, 52,* 281–302.

Cronbach, L. J., & Snow, R. E. (1969). *Final report: Individual differences in learning ability as a function of instructional variables.* Stanford, CA: Stanford University Press.

Cronbach, L. J., & Snow, R. E. (1977). *Aptitudes and instructional methods: A handbook for research on interaction.* New York: Irvington.

Cronbach, L. J., & Warrington, W. G. (1952). Efficiency of multiple-choice tests as a function of spread of item difficulties. *Psychometrika, 17,* 127–147.

Cronin, J., et al. (1975). Race, class, and intelligence: A critical look at the I.Q. controversy. *International Journal of Mental Health, 3*(4), 46–132.

Cross, L. H. (1984, April). *Validation study of the National Teacher Examinations for certification of entry-level teachers in the Commonwealth of Virginia.* Paper presented at the annual meeting of the American Educational Research Association and the National Council on Measurement in Education, New Orleans.

Cross, L. H., & Frary, R. B. (1977). An empirical test of Lord's theoretical results regarding formula scoring of multiple-choice tests. *Journal of Educational Measurement, 14,* 313–322.

Cross, L. H., Frary, R. B., Kelley, P. P., Small, R. C., & Impara, J. C. (1985). Esablishing minimum standard for essays: Blind versus informed review. *Journal of Educational Measurement, 22*(2), 137–146.

CSE Test Evaluation Project. (1979). *CSE criterion-referenced handbook.* Los Angeles: UCLA. Center for the Study of Evaluation.

Culler, R. E., & Hollohan, C. J. (1980). Anxiety and academic performance. *Journal of Educational Measurement, 72,* 16–20.

Cummings, O. W. (1981). Impact of response changes on objective test characteristics and outcomes for junior high school students. *Measurement and Evaluation in Guidance, 14*(1), 32–37.

D'Agostino, R. B., & Cureton, E. F. (1975). The 27 percent rule revisited. *Educational and Psychological Measurement, 35,* 47–50.

Dallis, G. T. (1970). The effect of precise objectives upon student achievement in health education. *Journal of Experimental Education, 39,* 20–23.

Daly, J. A., & Dickson-Markham, F. (1982). Contrast effects in evaluating essays. *Journal of Educational Measurement, 19,* 309–316.

Darlington, R. B. (1971). Another look at "cultural fairness." *Journal of Educational Measurement, 8,* 71–82.

Davis, F. B. (1964). *Educational measurements and their interpretation.* Belmont, CA: Wadsworth.

Dawes, R. M., & Smith, T. L. (1985). Attitude and opinion measurement. In G. Lindzey and E. Aronson (Eds.), *The handbook of social psychology* (3rd ed.) (Vol. 1) (pp. 509–566). New York: Random House.

Debra P. v. Turlington. (1981). 644 F. 2d 397, 5th cir.

Debra P. v. Turlington (1983). 564 F. Supp. 177 (M.D. Fla.).

Delahunty, R. J. (1988). Perspectives on within-group scoring. *Journal of Vocational Behavior, 33,* 463–477.

Deno, S. L., & Fuchs, L. S. (1987, April). Developing curriculum-based measurement systems for data-based special education problem solving. *Focus on Exceptional Children, 19,* 6.

Derr, R. L. (1973). *A taxonomy of social purposes of public schools.* New York: McKay.

Deutsch, M. (1979). Educational and distributive justice: Some reflections on grading systems. *American Psychologist, 34,* 379–401.

Diamond, E. E. (1975a). Guidelines for the assessment of sex bias and sex fairness. *Measurement and Evaluation in Guidance, 8,* 7–11.

Diamond, E. E. (Ed.). (1975b). *Issues of sex bias and sex fairness in career interest measurement.* Washington, DC: Government Printing Office.

Diamond, E. E., & Elmore, P. (1986). Bias in achievement testing: Follow-up report on AMECD Committee on Bias in Measurement. *Measurement in Counseling and Development, 19,* 102–112.

Diamond, J. J., & Evans, W. J. (1972). An investigation of the cognitive correlates of test wiseness. *Journal of Educational Measurement, 9,* 145–150.

Diana v. State Board of Education. Civil No. C-70, 37 RFP (N.D. CA, Jan. 7, 1970, and June 18, 1973).

Diederich P. B. (1967). Cooperative preparation and rating of essay tests. *English Journal, 56,* 573–584.

Dilworth, M. S. (1986). Teacher testing: Adjustments for schools, colleges, and departments of education. *The Journal of Negro Education, 55*(3), 368–378.

Dolliver, R. H., & Will, J. A. (1977). Ten-year follow-up of the Tyler Vocational Card Sort and the Strong Vocational Interest Blank. *Journal of Counseling Psychology, 24,* 48–54.

Donlon, T. F., Ekstrom, R. B., & Lockheed, M. E. (1979). The consequences of sex-bias in the content of major achievement test batteries. *Measurement and Evaluation in Guidance, 11,* 202–211.

Dorans, N. J., & Kulick, E. (1986). Demonstrating the utility of the standardization approach to assessing unexpected differential item performance on the Scholastic Aptitude Test. *Journal of Educational Measurement, 23,* 355–368.

Doyle, K. O., Jr. (1975). *Student evaluation of instruction.* Lexington, MA: Heath.

Dressel, P. (1983). Grades: One more tilt at the windmill. In A. W. Chickering (Ed.), *Bulletin.* Memphis: Memphis State University, Center for the Study of Higher Education.

Dressel, P. L., & Nelson, C. H. (1961). Testing and grading policies. In P. L. Dressel et al. (Eds.), *Evaluation in higher education.* Boston: Houghton Mifflin.

Dressel, P. L., & Schmidt, J. (1953). Some modifications of the multiple-choice item. *Educational and Psychological Measurement, 13,* 574–595.

DuCette, J., & Wolk, S. (1972). Test performance and the use of optional questions. *Journal of Experimental Education, 40*(3), 21–24.

Dunn, L., & Dunn L. (1981). *Peabody Picture Vocabulary Test revised: Manual for forms L and M.* Circle Pines, MN: American Guidance Services.

Dunn, T. F., & Goldstein, L. G. (1959). Test difficulty, validity, and reliability as functions of selective multiple-choice item construction principles. *Educational and Psychological Measurement, 19,* 171–179.

Dusek, T. (1980). The development of test anxiety in children. In S. G. Sarason (Ed.), *Test anxiety: Theory, research, and applications* (pp. 87–110). Hillsdale, NJ: Erlbaum.

Dyer, H. S. (1967). The discovery and development of educational goals. *Proceeding of the 1966 Invitational Conference on Testing Problems* (pp. 12–29). Princeton, NJ: Educational Testing Service.

Dyer, H. S. (1970). Toward objective criteria of professional accountability in the schools of New York City. *Phi Delta Kappan, 52,* 206–211.

Dyer, H. S. (1973). Recycling the problems in testing. *Proceedings of the 1972 Invitational Conference on Testing Problems,* (pp. 85–95). Princeton, NJ: Educational Testing Service.

Ebel, R. L. (1961). Must all tests be valid? *American Psychologist, 15,* 640–647.

Ebel, R. L. (1962). Content standard test scores. *Educational and Psychological Measurement, 22,* 15–25.

Ebel, R. L. (1965a). Confidence weighting and test reliability. *Journal of Educational Measurement, 2,* 49–57.

Ebel, R. L. (1965b). *Measuring educational achievement.* Englewood Cliffs, NJ: Prentice-Hall.

Ebel, R. L. (1969). Expected reliability as a function of choices per item. *Educational and Psychological Measurement, 29,* 565–570.

Ebel, R. L. (1970). The case for true-false items. *School Review, 78,* 373–389.

Ebel, R. L. (1972). *Essentials of educational measurement.* Englewood Cliffs, NJ: Prentice-Hall.

Ebel, R. L. (1974a). And still the dryads linger. *American Psychologist, 29,* 485–492.

Ebel, R. L. (1974b). Shall we get rid of grades? *Measurement in Education, 5(4),* 1–5.

Ebel, R. L. (1975a). Can teachers write good true-false test items? *Journal of Educational Measurement, 12,* 31–35.

Ebel, R. L. (1975b). *Prediction? Validation? Construct validity?* Mimeograph.

Ebel, R. L. (1976). The paradox of educational testing. *Measurement in Education, 7(4),* 1–8.

Ebel, R. L. (1978a). The case for minimum competency testing. *Phi Delta Kappan, 59,* 546–549.

Ebel, R. L. (1978b). The ineffectiveness of multiple true-false items. *Educational and Psychological Measurement, 38,* 37–44.

Ebel, R. L. (1979). *Essentials of educational measurement* (3rd ed.). Englewood Cliffs, NJ: Prentice-Hall.

Ebel, R. L., & Damrin, D. (1960). Tests and examinations. In C. W. Harris (Ed.), *Encyclopedia of educational research* (3rd ed.) (pp. 1502–1517). New York: Macmillan.

Ebel, R. L., & Frisbie, D. A. (1986). *Essentials of educational measurement* (4th ed.). Englewood Cliffs, NJ: Prentice-Hall.

Echternacht, G. J. (1976). Reliability and validity of item option weighting schemes. *Educational and Psychological Measurement, 36,* 301–309.

Eckland, B. K. (1967). Genetics and sociology: A reconsideration. *American Sociological Review, 32,* 173–194.

Educational Measurement: Issues and Practice. (1984). *3(2).*

Educational Measurement: Issues and Practice. (1988). *7(2).*

Educational Testing Service. (1960). *Short-cut statistics for teacher-made tests.* Princeton, NJ: Educational Testing Service.

Educational Testing Service. (1983). *Focus: Computer literacy.* Princeton, NJ: Author.

Educational Testing Service. (1986). *Test collection catalogue, Volume I: Achievement tests and measurement devices.* Phoenix: Oryx Press.

Educational Testing Service. (1987). *Test collection catalogue, Volume 2: Vocational tests and measurement devices.* Phoenix: Oryx Press.

Educational Testing Service Developments. (1988). Updated version of computerized placement tests gives colleges more control, greater flexibility. *ETS Developments, 34(2),* 2.

Edwards, A. L. (1957). *The social desirability variable in personality assessment and research.* New York: Holt, Rinehart & Winston.

Edwards, A. L. (1970). *The measurement of personality traits by scales and inventories.* New York: Holt, Rinehart & Winston.

Edwards, R. C. (1977). Personal traits and "success" in schooling and work. *Educational and Psychological Measurement, 37(1),* 125–138.

Eells, W. C. (1930). Reliability of repeated essay grading of essay type questions. *Journal of Educational Psychology, 31,* 48–52.

Eignor, D. R., & Cook, L. L. (1983). *An investigation of the feasibility of using item response theory in the preequating of aptitude tests.* Paper presented at the meeting of the American Educational Research Association, Montreal.

Eisner, E. W. (1969). Instructional and expressure educational objectives: Their formulation and use in curriculum. In W. J. Popham et al. (Ed.), *Instructional objectives* (pp. 1–18). Chicago: Rand McNally.

Ekstrom, R., & Johnson, C. (1984, Nov.). Introduction and overview. *Journal of Counseling and Development, 63*(3), 132.

Elam, S. M. (1989). The second Gallup/Phi Delta Kappa poll of teachers' attitudes toward the public schools. *Phi Delta Kappan, 70*, 785–801.

Elasoff, J., & Snow, R. E. (Eds.). (1971). *Pygmalion revisited*. Worthington, OH: C. A. Jones.

Elliott, R., & Strenta, A. C. (1988). Effects of improving the reliability of the GPA on prediction generally and on comparative predictions for gender and race particularly. *Journal of Educational Measurement, 25*, 333–348.

Ellsworth, R. A., Dunnell, P., & Duell, O. K. (1989, April). *Multiple choice items: What are text authors telling teachers and modeling for them?* Paper presented at the annual meeting of the National Council on Measurement in Education, San Francisco.

Embretson, S. E. (1986). *Test design: Developments in psychology and psychometrics*. Orlando, FL: Academic Press.

Engelhart, M. D. (1965). A comparison of several item-discrimination indices. *Journal of Educational Measurement, 2*, 69–76.

Engelmann, S., & Englemann, T. (1968). *Give your child a superior mind*. New York: Simon and Schuster.

Engen, H. B., Lamb, R. R., & Prediger, D. J. (1982). Are secondary schools still using standardized tests? *Personnel and Guidance Journal, 60*(5), 287–289.

Erlenmeyer-Kimling, L., & Jarvik, L. F. (1963, Dec.). Genetics and intelligence: A review. *Science, 142*, 1477–1479.

Exner, J. E., Jr. (1966). Variations in WISC performance as influenced by differences in pretest rapport. *Journal of General Psychology, 74*, 299–306.

Eyde, L. D., & Kowal, D. M. (1984). *Ethical and professional concerns regarding computerized test interpretation services and users*. Paper presented at the meeting of the American Psychological Association, Toronto.

Eysenck, H. J. (1971). *The IQ argument*. Freeport, NY: Library Press.

Eysenck, H. J. (1979). *The structure and measurement of intelligence*. New York: Springer-Verlag.

Eysenck, H. J. (1984). The effect of race on human abilities and mental test scores. In C. R. Reynolds and R. T. Brown (Eds.), *Perspectives on bias in mental testing*. New York: Plenum.

Fagley, N. S. (1987). Positional response bias in multiple-choice tests of learning: Its relation to testwiseness and guessing strategy. *Journal of Educational Psychology, 79*(1), 95–97.

The Fair Test Examiner. (1987). *1*(1), whole issue. National Center for Fair and Open Testing.

Falls, J. D. (1928). Research in secondary education. *Kentucky School Journal, 6*, 42–46.

Feder, B. (1979). *The complete guide to taking tests*. Englewood Cliffs, NJ: Prentice-Hall.

Federal Executive Agency. (1978, Aug. 25). Uniform guidelines on employee selection procedures. *Federal Register, 43*, 166.

Federal Register. (1970). 35, 149.

Feistritzer, C. M. (1983). *The condition of teaching*. Princeton, NJ: The Carnegie Foundation for the Advancement of Teaching.

Feldman, J. M. (1986). A note on the statistical correction of halo error. *Journal of Applied Psychology, 71*, 173–176.

Feldmesser, R. A. (1969). *The option: Analysis of an educational innovation*. Hanover, NH: Dartmouth College.

Feldmesser, R. A. (1971). *The positive function of grades*. Paper presented at the annual meeting of the American Educational Research Association, New York.

Feldt, L. A. (1967). Reliability of differences between scores. *American Educational Research Journal, 4*, 139–145.

Feldt, L. S., & Brennan, R. L. (1989). Reliability. In R. L. Linn (Ed.), *Educational measurement* (3rd ed.) (pp. 105–146). New York: American Council on Education and Macmillan.

Feuerstein, R., Rand, Y., & Hoffman, M. B. (1979). *The dynamic assessment of retarded performers: The learning potential device, theory, instruments, and techniques*. Baltimore: University Park.

Findley, W. G. (1974). Ability grouping. In G. R. Gredler (Ed.), *Ethical and legal factors in the practice of school psychology* (Chapter 3). Harrisburg: Pennsylvania State Department of Education.

Findley, W. G., & Bryan, M. M. (1971). *Ability grouping: 1970 status, impact and alternatives*. Athens: Center for Educational Improvement, University of Georgia.

Finley, C. J., & Berdie, F. S. (1970). *The national as-*

sessment approach to exercise development. Denver: National Assessment of Educational Progress.

Fisher, T. H. (1983). Implementing an instructional validity study of the Florida High School Graduation Test. *Educational Measurement: Issues and Practice*, 2(4), 8–9.

Fisher, T. H. (1988). Testing the basic skills in the high school—What's in the future? *Applied Measurement in Education*, 1(2), 157–170.

Fiske, D. W. (1963). Problems in measuring personality. In J. A. Wepman and R. W. Heine (Eds.), *Concepts of personality* (pp. 449–473). London: Aldine.

Fiske, D. W. (1987). Construct invalidity comes from method effects. *Educational and Psychological Measurement*, 47(2), 285–307.

Fiske, E. B. (1976, Feb. 18). New test developed to replace I.Q. *New York Times*, 28.

Flanagan, J. C., & Russ-Eft, D. (1975). *An empirical study to aid in formulating educational goals.* Palo Alto, CA: American Institutes for Research.

Flanagan, J. C., Shanner, W. M., & Mager, R. (1971). *Behavioral objectives: A guide for individualizing learning.* New York: Westinghouse Learning Press.

Flaugher, R. L. (1970). *Testing practices, minority groups and higher education: A review and discussion of the research* (Research Bulletin 70-41). Princeton, NJ: Educational Testing Service.

Flaugher, R. L. (1978). The many definitions of test bias. *American Psychologist*, 33, 671–679.

Fleming, M., & Chambers, B. (1983). Teacher-made tests: Windows on the classroom. In W. E. Hathaway (Ed.), *Testing in the schools, new directions in testing and measurement* (Vol. 19) (pp. 29–38). San Francisco: Jossey-Bass.

Folsom, C. H. (1973). Effects of mental abilities on obtained intercorrelations among VPI scales. *Measurement and Evaluation in Guidance*, 6, 74–81.

Ford, V. A., & Weener, P. D. (1980, April). *The influence of two test-wiseness programs upon students' test performance.* Paper presented at the annual meeting of the American Educational Research Association, Boston.

Forehand, G. A. (1986). *Computerized diagnostic testing* (ETS Res. Mem. 86-2). Princeton, NJ: Educational Testing Service.

Forehand, G. A. (1987). Development of a computerized diagnostic testing program. *Collegiate Microcomputer*, 5(1), 1–5.

Forsyth, R. A., & Spratt, K. F. (1980). Measuring problem-solving ability in mathematics with multiple-choice items: The effect of item format on selected item and test characteristics. *Journal of Educational Measurement*, 17, 31–44.

Frary, R. B. (1981). Cheating? *Teaching and Learning*, 2, 3–4.

Frary, R. B. (1989). Partial credit scoring methods for multiple-choice tests. *Applied Measurement Journal*, 2(1), 79–96.

Frechtling, J. A. (1989). Administrative uses of school testing programs. In R. L. Linn (Ed.), *Educational measurement* (3rd ed.) (pp. 475–484). New York: American Council on Education and Macmillan.

Frederick, L. T. V. (1977). *Federal Reporter* (2nd Series, 557F. 2d. 373).

Freedman, S. W. (1979). How characteristics of student essays influence teachers' evaluations. *Journal of Educational Psychology*, 71, 328–338.

Freeman, J. T. (1969). *A summary progress report on an experimental study of a pass/no report card grading system.* San Bernardino: California State College at San Bernardino.

French, J. M. (1965). Schools of thought in judging excellence of English themes. In A. Anastasi (Ed.), *Testing problems in perspective* (pp. 587–596). Washington, DC: American Council on Education.

Fricke, B. G. (1975). *Grading, testing, standards, and all that.* Ann Arbor: Evaluation and Examinations Office, University of Michigan.

Frisbie, D. A. (1971). *Comparative reliabilities and validities of true-false and multiple-choice tests.* Unpublished Ph.D. dissertation. Michigan State University.

Frisbie, D. A. (1974). The effect of item format on reliability and validity: A study of multiple-choice and true-false achievement tests. *Educational and Psychological Measurement*, 34, 885–892.

Frisbie, D. A. (1990, April). *The status of multiple true-false testing.* Paper presented at the annual meeting of the National Council on Measurement in Education, Boston.

Frisbie, D. A., & Sweeney, D. C. (1982). The relative merits of multiple true-false achievement tests. *Journal of Educational Measurement*, 19(1), 29–36.

Fuchs, D., Featherstone, N., Garwick, D. R., & Fuchs, L. S. (1984). Effects of examiner familiarity and task characteristics on speech and language-impaired children's test performance. *Measurement and Evaluation in Guidance*, 16, 198–204.

Fuchs, D., Fuchs, L. S., Benowitz, S., & Barringer, K. (1987). Norm-referenced tests: Are they valid for use with handicapped students? *Exceptional Children, 54*(3), 263–271.

Fuchs, D., Fuchs, L. S., & Blaisdell, M. L. (1986). Psychosocial characteristics of handicapped children who perform suboptimally during assessment. *Measurement and Evaluation in Counseling and Development, 18*(4), 176–184.

Fuchs, D., Fuchs, L. S., Dailey, A. M., & Power, M. H. (1983). *Effects of pretest contact with experienced and inexperienced examiners on handicapped children's performance* (Research Report No. 110). Minneapolis: University of Minnesota Institute for Research on Learning Disabilities.

Fuchs, D., Fuchs, L. S., Dailey, A. M., & Power, M. H. (1985a). *Effects of pretest contact with experienced and inexperienced examiners on handicapped children's performance* (Research Report No. 110). Minneapolis: University of Minnesota Institute for Research on Learning Disabilities.

Fuchs, D., Fuchs, L. S., Power, M. H., & Dailey, A. M. (1985b). Bias in the assessment of handicapped children. *American Educational Research Journal, 22*(2), 185–197.

Furst, E. J. (1958). *Constructing evaluation instruments.* New York: McKay.

Futcher, W. G. A. (1973). Test performance and the use of optional questions. *Journal of Experimental Education, 41*(4), 23–25.

Gaffney, R. F., & Maguire, T. O. (1971). Use of optically scored test answer sheets with young children. *Journal of Educational Measurement, 8*, 103–106.

Gage, N. L. (1972). IQ heritability, race differences, and educational research. *Phi Delta Kappan, 53*, 308–312.

Gallagher, P. D., & Gay, L. R. (1976). *The comparative effectiveness of tests versus written exercises in a competency-based research course.* Paper presented at the annual meeting of the American Educational Research Association, San Francisco.

Gallup, A. M. (1984). The Gallup Poll of teachers' attitudes toward the public schools. *Phi Delta Kappan, 66*, 97–107.

Gallup, A. M. (1986). The 18th Annual Gallup Poll of the public's attitudes toward the public schools. *Phi Delta Kappan, 68*, 43–59.

Gallup, A. M., & Elam, S. M. (1988). The 20th Annual Gallup Poll of the public's attitudes toward the public schools. *Phi Delta Kappan, 70*(1), 33–46.

Gallup, G. H. (1984). The 16th Annual Gallup Poll of the public's attitudes toward the public schools. *Phi Delta Kappan, 66*, 23–38.

Gardner, E. F. (1978). Bias. *Measurement in Education, 9*, 3.

Gaynor, J., & Millman, J. (1976). Student performance and evaluation under variant teaching and testing methods in a large lecture course. *Journal of Educational Psychology, 66*, 312–316.

Geisinger, K. F. (1982). Marking systems. In H. E. Mitzel (Ed.), *Encyclopedia of educational research* (5th ed.) (pp. 1139–1149). New York: The Free Press.

Gerber, M. M., & Semmel, M. I. (1984). Teacher as imperfect test: Reconceptualizing the referral process. *Educational Psychologist, 3*, 137–148.

Gerberich, J. R. (1956). *Specimen objective test items: A guide to achievement test construction.* New York: McKay.

Getzels, J. W., & Jackson, P. W. (1962). *Creativity and intelligence.* New York: Wiley.

Ghiselli, E. E. (1966). *The validity of occupational aptitude tests.* New York: Wiley.

Gibb, B. G. (1964). *Test wiseness as a secondary cue response.* Unpublished Ph.D. dissertation. Ann Arbor: University Microfilms, No. 64-7643, University of Michigan.

Gill, D., Vinsonhaler, J., & Sherman, G. (1979). *Defining reading diagnosis, what, when, and how* (Research Series No. 46). East Lansing: Institute for Research on Teaching, Michigan State University.

Gilman, D. A., & Ferry, P. (1972). Increasing test reliability through self-scoring procedures. *Journal of Educational Measurement, 9*, 205–207.

Glaser, R. (1963). Instructional technology and the measurement of learning outcomes. *American Psychologist, 18*, 519–521.

Glaser, R. (1973). Individuals and learning: The new aptitudes. In M. C. Wittrock (Ed.), *Changing education* (pp. 83–100). Englewood Cliffs, NJ: Prentice-Hall.

Glaser, R. (1986). The integration of testing and instruction. In *The redesign of testing for the 21st century: Proceedings of the 1985 ETS Invitational Conference.* Princeton, NJ: Educational Testing Service.

Glaser, R., & Bond, L. (1981). Testing: Concepts, policy, practice, and research. *American Psychologist, 36*(10), 997–1000.

Glaser, R., & Nitko, A. J. (1971). Measurement in learning and instruction. In R. L. Thorndike (Ed.),

Educational measurement (2nd ed.) (pp. 625–670). Washington, DC: American Council on Education.

Glass, G. V. (1975). A paradox about excellence of schools and the people in them. *Educational Researcher, 4*(3), 9–12.

Glass, G. V. (1978a). Minimum competence and incompetence in Florida. *Phi Delta Kappan, 59,* 602–605.

Glass, G. V. (1978b). Standards and criteria. *Journal of Educational Measurement, 15,* 237–261.

Godshalk, F. I., Swineford, F., & Coffman, W. (1966). *The measurement of writing ability.* New York: College Entrance Examination Board.

Goldman, B. A., & Busch, J. C. (Eds.). (1978). *Directory of unpublished experimental mental measures* (Vol. 2). New York: Human Sciences Press.

Goldman, B. A., & Saunders, J. L. (Eds.). (1974). *Directory of unpublished experimental mental measures* (Vol. 1). New York: Human Sciences Press.

Goldman, L. (1971). *Using tests in counseling* (2nd ed.). New York: Appleton.

Goolsby, T. M. (1971). Appropriateness of subtests in achievement test selection. *Educational and Psychological Measurement, 31,* 967–972.

Gorow, F. F. (1966). *Better classroom testing.* San Francisco: Chandler.

Gorth, W. P., & Perkins, M. R. (1979). *A study of minimum competency testing programs: Final program development resource document.* Amherst, MA: National Evaluation Systems.

Goslin, D. A. (1967). *Teachers and testing.* New York: Russell Sage.

Gosling, G. W. H. (1966). *Marking English compositions.* Victoria: Australian Council for Educational Research.

Gottesman, I. I. (1968). Biogenetics of race and class. In M. Deutsch, I. Katz, and A. R. Jensen (Eds.), *Social class, race, and psychological development* (pp. 11–51). New York: Holt, Rinehart and Winston.

Gottfredson, L. S. (1979). Aspiration job-match: Age trends in a large nationally representative sample of young white men. *Journal of Counseling Psychology, 26,* 319–328.

Gottfredson, L. S. (1988). Reconsidering fairness: A matter of social and ethical priorities. *Journal of Vocational Behavior, 33,* 293–321.

Gottfredson, L. S., & Sharf, J. C. (1988). Fairness in employment testing. *Journal of Vocational Behavior, 33,* 225–230.

Graziano, W. G., Varca, P. E., & Levy, J. C. (1982). Race of examiner effects and the validity of intelligence tests. *Review of Educational Research, 52*(4), 467–497.

Green, B. F. (1983). Adaptive testing by the computer. In R. B. Ekstrom (Ed.), *Measurement technology and individuality in education* (No. 17 in *New directions for testing and measurement*) (pp. 5–12). San Francisco: Jossey-Bass.

Green, B. F. (1988). Critical problems in computer-based psychological measurement. *Applied Measurement in Education, 1,* 223–231.

Green, B. F., Bock, R. D., Humphreys, L. G., Linn, R. L., & Reckase, M. D. (1984). Technical guidelines for assessing computerized adaptive tests. *Journal of Educational Measurement, 21,* 347–360.

Green, B. F., Crone, C. R., & Folk, V. G. (1989). A method for studying differential distractor functioning. *Journal of Educational Measurement, 26,* 147–160.

Green, D. R. (Ed.). (1974). *The aptitude–achievement distinction.* Monterey, CA: CTB/McGraw-Hill.

Green, D. R. (1983, April). Content validity of standardized achievement tests and test curriculum overlap. In D. Wanous (Chair), *National vs. local tests and curriculum: inferences to which domain and why.* Symposium conducted at the annual meeting of the National Council on Measurement in Education, Montreal.

Green, K. (1979). Multiple-choice and true-false: Reliability and validity compared. *Journal of Experimental Education, 48*(1), 42–44.

Green, K. E., & Stager, S. F. (1986, April). *Effects of training, grade level, and subject taught on the types of tests and test items used by teachers.* Paper presented at the annual meeting of the National Council on Measurement in Education, San Francisco.

Green, R. F. (1951). Does a selection situation induce testees to bias their answers on interest and temperament tests? *Educational and Psychological Measurement, 11,* 501–515.

Green, S. B., Halpin, G., & Halpin, G. (1989, March). *Student feedback about quality of classroom test items.* Paper presented at the annual meeting of the National Council on Measurement in Education, San Francisco.

Grier, J. B. (1975). The number of alternatives for optimum test reliability. *Journal of Educational Measurement, 12,* 109–113.

Griggs v. *Duke Power Company*. (1971). Supreme Court of the United States.

Gronlund, N. E. (1959). *Sociometry in the classroom*. New York: Harper & Row.

Gronlund, N. E. (1978). *Stating objectives for classroom instruction* (2nd ed.). New York: Macmillan.

Gronlund, N. E. (1985). *Measurement and evaluation in teaching* (5th ed.). New York: Macmillan.

Gronlund, N. E. (1988). *How to construct achievement tests* (4th ed.). Englewood Cliffs, NJ: Prentice-Hall.

Gronlund, N. E., & Linn, R. L. (1990). *Measurement and evaluation in teaching* (6th ed.). New York: Macmillan.

Gross, M. L. (1962). *The brain watchers*. New York: Random House.

Grossman, H. J. (Ed.). (1983). *Classification in mental retardation*. Washington, DC: American Association of Mental Deficiency.

Guilford, J. P. (1954). *Psychometric methods* (2nd ed.). New York: McGraw-Hill.

Guilford, J. P. (1959). Three faces of intellect. *American Psychologist, 14*, 469–479.

Guilford, J. P. (1967). *The nature of human intelligence*. New York: McGraw-Hill.

Guilford, J. P. (1969). *Intelligence, creativity and their educational implications*. San Diego: Educational and Industrial Testing Service.

Guion, R. M. (1983, Aug.). *The ambiguity of validity: The growth of my discontent*. Presidential address to the Division of Evaluation and Measurement at the meeting of the American Psychological Association, Anaheim, CA.

Gullickson, A. R. (1984). Teacher perspectives of their instructional use of tests. *Journal of Educational Research, 77*, 244–248.

Gullickson, A. R. (1986). Teacher education and teacher-perceived needs in educational measurement and evaluation. *Journal of Educational Measurement, 23*, 347–354.

Gullickson, A. R., & Ellwein, M. C. (1985). Post hoc analysis of teacher-made tests: The goodness-of-fit between prescription and practice. *Educational Measurement: Issues and Practice, 4*(3), 15–18.

Haase, R. F., Reed, C. F., Winer, J. L., & Boden, J. L. (1978). Effects of positive, negative, and mixed occupational information on cognitive and affective complexity. *Journal of Vocational Behavior, 15*, 294–302.

Haertel, E. (1986). *Choosing and using classroom tests: Teachers' perspectives on assessment*. Paper presented at the annual meeting of the American Educational Research Association, San Francisco.

Haertel, E., & Calfee, R. (1983). School achievement: Thinking about what to test. *Journal of Educational Measurement, 20*(2), 119–132.

Hakstian, A. R., & Kansup, W. (1975). A comparison of several methods of assessing partial knowledge in multiple-choice tests: II. Testing procedures. *Journal of Educational Measurement, 12*, 231–240.

Haladyna, T. M., & Downing, S. M. (1988, April). *Functional distractors: Implications for test-item writing and test design*. Paper presented at the annual meeting of the American Educational Research Association, New Orleans.

Haladyna, T. M., & Downing, S. M. (1989a). A taxonomy of multiple-choice item writing rules. *Applied Measurement in Education, 2*(1), 37–50.

Haladyna, T. M., & Downing, S. M. (1989b). Validity of a taxonomy of multiple-choice item-writing rules. *Applied Measurement in Education, 2*(1), 51–78.

Haladyna, T., & Roid, G. (1981). The role of instructional sensitivity in the empirical review of criterion-referenced test items. *Journal of Educational Measurement, 18*(1), 39–53.

Haladyna, T. M., Shindoll, M., Roby, R., & Langhammer, L. (1987, April). *Item shells: Progress and potential*. Paper presented at the annual meeting of the AERA/NCME, Washington, DC.

Hales, L. W., Bain, P. T., & Rand, L. P. (1971). *An investigation of some aspects of the pass-fail grading system*. Mimeograph.

Hales, L. W., & Tokar, E. (1975). The effect of quality of preceding responses on the grades assigned to subsequent responses to an essay question. *Journal of Educational Measurement, 12*, 115–117.

Hall, B. W. (1985). Survey of the technical characteristics of published educational achievement tests. *Educational Measurement: Issues and Practice, 4*(1), 6–14.

Hall, B. W., Caroll, D., & Comer, C. B. (1988). Test use among classroom teachers and its relationship to teaching level and teaching practices. *Applied Measurement in Education, 1*(2), 145–156.

Hall, B. W., Villeme, M. G., & Phillippy, S. W. (1985). How beginning teachers use test results in critical education decisions. *Educational Research Quarterly, 9*(3), 12–18.

Hambleton, R. K. (1984). Validating the test scores. In

R. B. Berk (Ed.), *A guide to criterion-referenced test construction* (pp. 199–230). Baltimore: Johns Hopkins University Press.

Hambleton, R. K., & Eignor, D. R. (1978). Guidelines for evaluating criterion-referenced tests and manuals. *Journal of Educational Measurement, 15,* 321–327.

Hambleton, R. K., & Eignor, D. R. (1979). Competency test development, validation, and standard setting. In R. Jaeger and C. Tittle (Eds.), *Minimum competency testing* (pp. 367–396). Berkeley, CA: McCutchan.

Hambleton, R. K., & Novick, M. (1973). Towards an integration of theory and method for criterion-referenced tests. *Journal of Educational Measurement, 10,* 159–170.

Hambleton, R. K., Swaminathan, H., Algina, J., & Coulson, D. (1978). Criterion-referenced testing and measurement: A review of technical issues and developments. *Review of Educational Research, 48,* 1–48.

Hambleton, R. K., & Traub, R. E. (1974). The effects of item order on test performance and stress. *Journal of Experimental Education, 43,* 40–46.

Haney, W. (1980, May). Trouble over testing. *Educational Leadership,* 640–650.

Haney, W., & Madaus, G. (1989). Searching for alternatives to standardized tests: Why, whats, and withers. *Phi Delta Kappan, 70*(9), 683–687.

Hanna, G. (1975). Incremental reliability and validity of multiple-choice tests with an answer-until-correct procedure. *Journal of Educational Measurement, 12,* 175–178.

Hansen, J. C. (1984). *User's guide for the SVIB-SCII.* Palo Alto, CA: Consulting Psychologists Press.

Hansen, J. C., & Campbell, D. P. (1985). *Manual for the SVIB-SCII* (4th ed). Stanford, CA: Stanford University Press.

Hanson, G. R., Prediger, D. J., & Schussel, R. H. (1977). *Development and validation of sex-balanced interest inventories* (Research Report #78). Iowa City, IA: American College Testing Program.

Hanson, R. A., Bailey, J. D., & McMorris, R. F. (1986). Differences in instructional sensitivity between item formats and between achievement test items. *Journal of Educational Measurement, 23*(1), 1–12.

Hardy, R. A. (1984). Measuring instructional validity: A report of an instructional validity study for the Alabama High School Graduation Examination. *Journal of Educational Measurement, 21*(3), 291–301.

Hargadon, F. A. (1980). Two cheers. In *Commentaries on testing.* Princeton, NJ: College Board.

Harmon, L. W. (1987). A comparison of the Ninth Mental Measurements Yearbook and Test Critiques, Volumes I-III. *Journal of Counseling and Development, 66*(3), 149–152.

Harmon, L. W. (1989). Counseling. In R. L. Linn (Ed.), *Educational measurement* (3rd ed.) (pp. 527–544). New York: American Council on Education and Macmillan.

Harrington, T. F., & O'Shea, A. J. (Eds.). (1984). *Guide for occupational exploration.* Circle Pines, MN: American Guidance Service.

Harris, C. W. (Ed.). (1963). *Problems in measuring change.* Madison: University of Wisconsin Press.

Harris, C. W., et al. (Eds.). (1974). *Problems in criterion-referenced measurement* (CSE Monograph Series in Evaluation, No. 3). Los Angeles: Center for the Study of Evaluation, University of California.

Harris, D. J., & Subkoviak, M. J. (1986). Item analysis: A short-cut statistic for mastery tests. *Educational and Psychological Measurement, 46,* 495–507.

Harris, L., & Associates. (1984). *The American teacher: The metropolitan life survey* [ED 247-230]. New York: Metropolitan Life Insurance Company.

Harris, M. L., & Stewart, D. M. (1971). *Application of classical strategies to criterion-referenced test construction: An example.* Paper presented at the annual meeting of the American Educational Research Association, New York.

Harris, W. (1977). Teachers' responses to student writing: A study of the response patterns of high school English teachers to determine the basis for teacher judgment of student writing. *Research in the Teaching of English, 11,* 175–185.

Harrow, A. J. (1972). *A taxonomy of the psychomotor domain.* New York: McKay.

Hartigan, J. A., & Wigdor, A. K. (Eds.). (1989). *Fairness in employment testing: Validity generalization, minority issues, and the general aptitude test battery.* Washington, DC: National Academy Press.

Harvard Educational Review. (1969). Environment, heredity, and intelligence (Reprint Series No. 2).

Harwell, M. R. (1983). A comparison of two item selection procedures in criterion-referenced measurement. *Dissertation Abstracts International, 45,* 125A.

Hassenchahl, F. (1979). Contract grading in the classroom. *Improving College and University Teaching, 27,* 30–33.

Hathaway, S. R. (1964). MMPI: Professional use by professional people. *American Psychologist, 19*, 204–210.

Havighurst, R. J., & Neugarten, B. C. (1975). *Society and education* (4th ed.). Boston: Allyn and Bacon.

Hays, W. A. (1988). *Statistics for psychologists* (4th ed.). New York: Holt, Rinehart, and Winston.

Hayward, P. (1967). A comparison of test performance on three answer sheet formats. *Educational and Psychological Measurement, 27*, 997–1004.

Heber, R., & Garber, H. (1975). Report no. 2: An experiment in the prevention of cultural-familial retardation. In D. A. A. Primrose (Ed.), *Proceedings of the Third Conference of the International Association for the Scientific Study of Mental Deficiency* (pp. 33–43). Warsaw: Polish Medical Publishers.

Heil, L. M., Kambly, P. E., Mainardi, M., & Weisman, L. (1946). Measurement of understanding in science. In N. B. Henry (Ed.), *The measurement of understanding*, 45th yearbook, National Society for the Study of Education, Part I (pp. 101–137). Chicago: University of Chicago Press.

Heim, A. W. & Watts, K. P. (1967). An experiment on multiple-choice versus open-ended answering in a vocabulary test. *British Journal of Educational Psychology, 37*, 339–346.

Helmstadter, G. C. (1974). *A comparison of bayesian and traditional indices of test item performance.* Paper presented at the annual meeting of the National Council on Measurement in Education, Chicago.

Hembree, R. (1988). Correlates, causes, effects, and treatment of test anxiety. *Review of Educational Research, 58*(1), 47–78.

Henderson, E. H., & Long, B. H. (1970). Predictors of success in beginning reading among Negroes and whites. In J. A. Figural (Ed.), *Reading goals for the disadvantaged* (pp. 30–42). Newark, DE: International Reading Association.

Henderson, N. B., Fay, W. H., Lindemann, S. J., & Clarkson, Q. D. (1972). Will the IQ test ban decrease the effectiveness of reading prediction? *Journal of Educational Psychology, 65*, 345–355.

Henry, N. B. (Ed.). (1946). *The measurement of understanding.* 45th yearbook, National Society for the Study of Education. Chicago: University of Chicago Press.

Henryssen, S. (1971). Gathering, analyzing, and using data on test items. In R. L. Thorndike (Ed.), *Educational measurement* (2nd ed.) (pp. 130–159). Washington, DC: American Council on Education.

Herbert, J., & Attridge, C. (1975). A guide for developers and users of observation systems and manuals. *American Educational Research Journal, 12*, 1–20.

Herman, J. L., & Dorr-Bremme, D. W. (1983). Uses of testing in the schools: A national profile. *New Directions for Testing and Measurement, 19*, 7–17.

Herman, J. L., & Dorr-Bremme, D. W. (1984). *Teachers and testing: Implications from a national study* (ERIC Document Reproduction Service No. ED 244 987). Los Angeles: Center for the Study of Evaluation, University of California.

Herrnstein, R. J. (1971, Sept.). I.Q. *Atlantic Monthly*, 43–64.

Herrnstein, R. J. (1973). *I.Q. in the meritocracy.* Boston: Little, Brown.

Herrnstein, R. J. (1982, Aug.). IQ testing and the media. *Atlantic Monthly*, 68–74.

Hiebert, E. H., & Calfee, R. C. (1989). Advancing academic literacy through teachers' assessments. *Educational Leadership, 46*(7), 50–54.

Highland, R. W. (1955). *A guide for use of performance testing in Air Force technical schools.* Lowry AFB, CO: Armament Systems Personnel Research.

Hill, K. T., & Wigfield, A. (1984). Test anxiety: A major educational problem and what can be done about it. *Elementary School Journal, 85*(1), 105–126.

Hills, J. R. (1964). Prediction of college grades for all public colleges of a state. *Journal of Educational Measurement, 1*, 155–159.

Hills, J. R. (1971). Use of measurement in selection and placement. In R. L. Thorndike (Ed.), *Educational measurement* (2nd ed.) (pp. 680–732). Washington, DC: American Council on Education.

Hills, J. R. (1981). *Measurement in evaluation in the classroom* (2nd ed.). Columbus, OH: Merrill.

Hills, J. R., & Gladney, M. B. (1966). Predicting grades from below chance test scores (Research Bulletin 3-66). Atlanta: Office of Testing and Guidance, Regents of the University System of Georgia.

Hills, J. R., Klock, J. C., & Lewis, S. (1963). *Freshman norms for the university system of Georgia, 1961–1962.* Atlanta: Office of Testing and Guidance, Regents of the University System of Georgia.

Hively, W., II., Patterson, H. L., & Page, S. H. (1968). A universe-defined system of arithmetic achievement test. *Journal of Educational Measurement, 5*, 275–290.

Hodgkins, R., & McKenna, B. (1982). Testing and teacher certification: An explosive combination. *Ed-*

ucational Measurement: Issues and Practice, 1(2), 10–16.

Hodgson, M. L. & Cramer, S. H. (1977). The relationship between selected self-estimated and measured abilities in adolescents. *Measurement and Evaluation in Guidance, 10*(2), 98–103.

Hofer, P., & Green B. (1985). The challenge of competence and creativity in computerized psychological testing. *Journal of Consulting and Clinical Psychology, 53*, 826–838.

Hoffmann, B. (1962). *The tyranny of testing.* New York: Crowell-Collier-Macmillan.

Hogan, T., & Mishler, C. (1980). Relationships between essay tests and objective tests of language skills for elementary school children. *Journal of Educational Measurement, 17*, 219–227.

Holland, J. L. (1973). *Making vocational choices: A theory of careers.* Englewood Cliffs, NJ: Prentice-Hall.

Holland, J. L. (1986). New directions for interest testing. In B. S. Plake & J. C. Witt (Eds.), *The future of testing* (pp. 245–268). Hillsdale, NJ: Lawrence Erlbaum.

Holland, J. L., Magoon, T. M., & Spokane, A. R. (1981). Counseling psychology: Career interventions, research, and theory. *Annual Review of Psychology, 32*, 279–305.

The Holmes Group. (1986). *Tomorrow's teachers: A report on The Holmes Group.* East Lansing, MI: Author.

Holtzman, W. H. (1964). Recurrent dilemmas in personality assessment. *Journal of Projective Techniques and Personality Assessment, 28*, 141–150.

Honzik, M. P., Macfarlane, J. W., & Allen, L. (1948). The stability of mental test performance between two and eighteen years. *Journal of Experimental Education, 17*, 309–324.

Hook, C. M., & Rosenshine, B. (1979). Accuracy of teacher reports of their classroom behavior. *Review of Educational Research, 49*(1), 1–12.

Hoover, H. D. (1984). The most appropriate scores for measuring educational development in the elementary schools: GE's. *Educational Measurement: Issues and Practice, 3*(4), 8–14.

Hoover, H. D. (1988). Growth expectations for low-achieving students: A reply to Yen. *Educational Measurement: Issues and Practice, 7*(4), 21–23.

Hopkins, C. J., & Antes, R. L. (1978). *Classroom measurement and evaluation.* Itasca, IL: Peacock.

Hopkins, C. J., & Antes, R. L. (1990). *Classroom measurement and evaluation.* (3rd ed.). Itasca, IL: Peacock.

Hopkins, K. D., & Bracht, G. H. (1975). Ten-year stability of verbal and nonverbal IQ scores. *American Educational Research Journal, 12*(4), 469–477.

Hopkins, K. D., & Hodge, S. E. (1984). Review of the Kaufman Assessment Battery (K-ABC) for Children. *Journal of Counseling and Development, 63*(2), 105–107.

Hopkins, K. D., & Hopkins, B. R. (1964). Intra-individual and inter-individual positional preference response styles in ability tests. *Educational and Psychological Measurement, 24*, 801–805.

Hopkins, K. D., & Stanley, J. C. (1981). *Educational and psychological measurement and evaluation* (6th ed.). Englewood Cliffs, NJ: Prentice-Hall.

Horn, J. L., & Donaldson, G. (1976). On the myth of intellectual decline in adulthood. *American Psychologist, 31*, 701–719.

Hoyt, C. J. (1941). Test reliability estimated by analysis of variance. *Psychometrika, 6*, 153–160.

Hsu, T. C., & Nitko, A. J. (1983). Microcomputer testing software teachers can use. *Educational Measurement: Issues and Practices, 2*(4), 15–18, 23–30.

Huba, G. J. (1986). Interval banded profile analysis: A quick method for matching more profiles to "soft" prototypic patterns. *Educational and Psychological Measurement, 46*, 565–570.

Huck, S. (1978). Test performance under the condition of known item difficulty. *Journal of Educational Measurement, 15*, 53–58.

Huck, S., & Bounds, W. (1972). Essay grades: An interaction between graders' handwriting clarity and neatness of examination papers. *American Educational Research Journal, 9*, 279–283.

Huck, S., & Bowers, N. D. (1972). Item difficulty level and sequence effects in multiple-choice achievement tests. *Journal of Educational Measurement, 9*, 105–111.

Huck, S. & Long, J. D. (1972, April). *The effect of behavioral objectives on student achievement.* Paper presented at the American Educational Research Association Meeting, Chicago.

Hughes, D. C., Keeling, B., & Tuck, B. F. (1980). The influence of context position and scoring method on essay scoring. *Journal of Educational Measurement, 17*, 131–135.

Hughes, D. C., Keeling, B., & Tuck, B. F. (1983). Effects of achievement expectations and handwriting quality on scoring essays. *Journal of Educational Measurement, 20*, 65–70.

Hughes, H. H., & Trimble, W. E. (1965). The use of

complex alternatives in multiple-choice items. *Educational and Psychological Measurement, 25,* 117–126.

Humphreys, L. G. (1967). Critique of Cattell, theory of fluid and crystallized intelligence—A critical experiment. *Journal of Educational Psychology, 58,* 129–136.

Hunt, J. McV. (1961). *Intelligence and experience.* New York: Ronald.

Hunt, J. McV., & Kirk, G. E. (1974). Criterion-referenced tests of school readiness: A paradigm with illustrations. *Genetic Psychology Monographs, 90,* 143–182.

Hunter, J. E. (1980). Construct validity and validity generalization. In *Construction validity in psychological measurement. Proceedings of a colloquium on theory and application in education and employment* (pp. 119–125). Princeton, NJ: U.S. Office of Personnel Management and Educational Testing Service.

Hunter, J. E. (1986). Cognitive ability, cognitive aptitudes, job knowledge, and job performance. *Journal of Vocational Behavior, 29,* 340–362.

Hunter, J. E., & Hunter, R. F. (1983). *The validity and utility of alternative predictors of job performance* (Report 83-4). Washington, DC: Office of Personnel Research and Development.

Hunter, J. E., & Schmidt, F. L. (1976). Critical analysis of the statistical and ethical implications of various definitions of test bias. *Psychological Bulletin, 83,* 1053–1071.

Hunter, J. E., & Schmidt, F. L. (1982). Fitting people to jobs: The impact of personnel selection on national productivity. In M. D. Dunnettee and E. A. Fleishman (Eds.), *Human performance and productivity: Human capability assessment.* Hillsdale, NJ: Lawrence Erlbaum.

Hunter, J. E., Schmidt, F. L., & Rauschenberger, J. M. (1977). Fairness of psychological tests: Implications of four definitions for selection utility and minority hiring. *Journal of Applied Psychology, 62,* 245–260.

Hutton, J. (1969). Practice effects on intelligence and school readiness tests for preschool children. *Training School Bulletin, 65,* 130–134.

Irwin, D. M., & Bushnell, M. M. (1980). *Observational strategies for child study.* New York: Holt, Rinehart & Winston.

Ivens, S. H. (1970). *An investigation of items analysis, reliability and validity in relation to criterion-referenced tests.* Unpublished doctoral dissertation.

Jackson, R. (1970, June). Developing criterion-referenced Tests. *ERIC Clearinghouse on Tests, Measurement, and Evaluation.*

Jackson, R. (1980). The Scholastic Aptitude Test: A response to Slack and Porter's critical appraisal. *Harvard Educational Review, 50,* 382–391.

Jaeger, R. M. (1989). Certification of student competence. In R. L. Linn (Ed.), *Educational measurement* (3rd ed.) (pp. 485–514). New York: American Council on Education and Macmillan.

Jaeger, R. M., & Freijo, T. D. (1975). Race and sex as concomitants of composite halo in teachers' evaluative rating of pupils. *Journal of Educational Psychology, 67,* 226–237.

Jaradat, D., & Sawaged, S. (1986). The subset selection technique for multiple-choice tests: An empirical inquiry. *Journal of Educational Measurement, 23*(4), 369–376.

Jenkins, J. R., & Deno, S. L. (1971). Assessing knowledge of concepts and principles. *Journal of Educational Measurement, 8,* 95–102.

Jensen, A. R. (1968a). Patterns of mental ability and socioeconomic status. *Proceedings of the National Academy of Sciences of the United States of America, 60,* 1330–1337.

Jensen, A. R. (1968b). Social class, race, and genetics: Implications for education. *American Educational Research Journal, 5,* 1–42.

Jensen, A. R. (1969a). How much can we boost IQ and scholastic achievement? *Harvard Educational Review, 39,* 1–123.

Jensen, A. R. (1969b). Reducing the heredity-environment uncertainty. Environment, heredity, and intelligence (Reprint Series No. 2). *Harvard Educational Review.*

Jensen, A. R. (1970a). Hierarchical theories of mental ability. In B. Dockrell (Ed.), *On intelligence.* Toronto: Ontario Institute for Studies in Education.

Jensen, A. R. (1970b). IQ's of identical twins reared apart. *Behavioral Genetics, 2,* 133–146.

Jensen, A. R. (1973a). *Educability and group difference.* New York: Harper & Row.

Jensen, A. R. (1973b). *Genetics and education.* New York: Harper & Row.

Jensen, A. R. (1973c). Let's understand Skodal and Skeels, finally. *Educational Psychologist, 10*(1), 30–35.

Jensen, A. R. (1975). The meaning of heritability in the behavioral sciences. *Educational Psychologist, 11*(3), 171–183.

Jensen, A. R. (1976). IQ tests are not culturally biased for blacks and whites. *Phi Delta Kappan, 57,* 676.

Jensen, A. R. (1980). *Bias in mental testing.* New York: The Free Press.

Jensen, A. R. (1982). The chronometry of intelligence. In R. J. Sternberg (Ed.), *Advances in the psychology of human intelligence* (Vol. 1) (Chap. 6). Hillsdale, NJ: Lawrence Erlbaum.

Jensen, A. R. (1984). Political ideologies and educational research. *Phi Delta Kappan, 65,* 460–462.

Jensen, A. R. (1985). Compensatory education and the theory of intelligence. *Phi Delta Kappan, 66,* 554–558.

Jensen, A. R. (1986). *g:* Artifact or reality. *Journal of Vocational Behavior, 29,* 301–331.

Jensen, A. R. (1987). The *g* beyond factor analysis. In R. R. Ronning, J. A. Glover, J. C. Conoley, and J. C. Witt (Eds.), *The influence of cognitive psychology on testing* (pp. 87–142). Hillsdale, NJ: Lawrence Erlbaum.

Jensen, A. R., & Munro, E. (1979). Reaction time, movement time, and intelligence. *Intelligence, 3,* 121–126.

Johansson, C. B., & Harmon, L. W. (1972). Strong vocational interest blank: One form or two? *Journal of Counseling Psychology, 19,* 404–410.

Johnson, J. W. (1983). Things we can measure through technology that we could not measure before. In R. Edstrom (Ed.), *Measurement, technology, and individuality in education* (No. 17 in *New directions for testing and measurement*) (pp. 13–18). San Francisco: Jossey-Bass.

Johnson, O. G. (1976). *Tests and measurement in child development: Handbook I and II.* San Francisco: Jossey-Bass.

Johnson, O. G., & Bommarito, J. W. (1971). *Tests and measurement in child development: Handbook I.* San Francisco: Jossey-Bass.

Johnston, J. A., Buescher, K. L., & Heppner, M. J. (1988, Sept.). Computerized career information and guidance systems: Caveat emptor. *Journal of Counseling and Development, 67*(1), 39–41.

Joint Committee on Testing of the American Association of School Administrators. (1962). *Testing, testing, testing.* Washington, DC: National Education Association.

Joint Committee on Testing Practices. (1988). *Code of fair testing practices in education.* Washington, DC: American Psychological Association.

Jones, L. V. (1988). Educational assessment vs. a promising area for psychometric Rasch. *Applied Measurement in Education, 1,* 233–242.

Jones, P. D., & Kaufman, G. G. (1975, Aug.). *The existence and effects of specific determiners in tests.* Paper presented at the annual meeting of the American Psychological Association, New Orleans.

Jordan, M. C. (1979). How to overcome, 1979, p. 27. *Newsweek,* Oct.

Journal of Vocational Behavior. (1986). The *g* factor in employment. Special issue, *29,* 3.

Journal of Vocational Behavior (1988). *33,* 3, whole issue.

Judges, 12:5–6. *The living Bible.*

Kalechstein, P., Kalechstein, M., & Docter, R. (1981). The effects of instruction on test taking skills in second-grade black children. *Measurement and Evaluation in Guidance, 13*(4), 198–202.

Kallingal, A. (1971). The prediction of grades for black and white students at Michigan State University. *Journal of Educational Measurement, 8,* 263–266.

Kamin, L. J. (1974). *The science and politics of IQ.* Potomac, MD: Erlbaum.

Kansup, W., & Hakstian, A. R. (1975). Comparison of several methods of assessing partial knowledge in multiple-choice tests: I. Scoring procedures. *Journal of Educational Measurement, 12,* 219–230.

Kapes, J. T., & Mastie, M. M. (1988). *A counselor's guide to career assessment instruments* (2nd ed.). Alexandria, VA: National Career Development Association.

Kaplan, R. M., & Saccuzzo, D. P. (1989). *Psychological testing: Principles, applications, and issues* (2nd ed.). Pacific Grove, CA: Brooks/Cole.

Karlins, M. (1969). Academic attitudes and performance as a function of differential grading systems: An evaluation of Princeton's pass–fail system. *Journal of Experimental Education, 37,* 38–50.

Katoff, L., & Reuter, J. (1979). A listing of infant tests. *Catalog of Selected Documents in Psychology, 9,* 56.

Katz, J., et al. (1968). *No time for youth: Growth and constraint in college students:* San Francisco: Jossey-Bass.

Katz, M. (1961). *Selecting an achievement test: Principles and procedures.* Princeton, NJ: Educational Testing Service.

Kauchak, D. (1984). Testing teachers in Louisiana: A closer look. *Phi Delta Kappan, 65*(9), 626–628.

Kaufman, A. S. (1979). WISC-R research: Implications for interpretation. *School Psychology Digest, 8,* 5–27.

Kaufman, R. A. (1971, Jan.). Accountability, a system approach and the quantitative improvement of education—An attempted integration. *Educational Technology, 11,* 21–26.

Kellaghan, T., Madaus, G. F., & Airasian, P. W. (1980). *Standardized testing in elementary schools: Effects on schools, teachers, and students.* Washington, DC: National Institute of Education, Department of Health, Education, and Welfare.

Kellaghan, T., Madaus, G. F., & Airasian, P. W. (1982). *The effects of standardized testing.* Boston: Kluwer-Nijhoff.

Kelley, T. L. (1927). *The interpretation of educational measurement.* Yonkers-on-Hudson, NY: World Book.

Kerlinger, F. N., & Pedhazur, E. J. (1973). *Multiple regression in behavioral research.* New York: Holt, Rinehart and Winston.

Keyser, D. J., & Sweetland, R. C. (Eds.). (1985–87). *Test critiques.* Kansas City, MO: Test Corporation of America.

Keysor, R. E., Williams, D. D., & VanMondrans, A. P. (1979). *The effect of "test wiseness" on professional school screening test scores.* Paper presented at the annual meeting of the National Council on Measurement in Education, San Francisco.

Kibler, R. J., Barker, L. L., & Miles, D. T. (1970). *Behavioral objectives and instruction.* Boston: Allyn and Bacon.

Kibler, R. J., Cegala, D. J., Watson, K. W., Barker, L. L., & Miles, D. T. (1981). *Objectives for instruction and evaluation* (2nd ed.). Boston: Allyn and Bacon.

Kingston, N. M., & Dorans, N. J. (1982). *The effect of a position of an item within a test on item responding behavior: An analysis based on item response theory* (GRE Board Professional Report 79-12P). Princeton, NJ: Educational Testing Service.

Kingston, N. M., & Dorans, N. J. (1984). Item location effects and their implications for IRT equating and adaptive testing. *Applied Psychological Measurement, 8,* 147–154.

Kippel, G. M. (1975). Information feedback, need achievement and retention. *Journal of Educational Research, 68,* 256–261.

Kirk, S. A., & Bateman, B. (1962). Diagnosis and remediation of learning disabilities. *Exceptional Children, 29,* 73–78.

Kirkland, M. C. (1971). The effects of tests on students and schools. *Review of Educational Research, 41,* 303–350.

Kirschenbaum, H., Simon, S. B., & Napier, R. W. (1971). *Wad-ja-get? The grading game in American education.* New York: Hart.

Klausmeier, H. J., & Goodwin, W. (1975). *Learning and human abilities: Educational psychology* (4th ed.). New York: Harper & Row.

Klein, K. (1984). Minimum competency testing: Shaping and reflecting curricula. *Phi Delta Kappan, 65*(8), 565–567.

Klein, S. P. (1971). Choosing needs for needs assessment. In S. P. Klein et al., *Procedures for needs-assessment evaluation: A symposium* (Report No. 67) (pp. 1–9). Los Angeles: Center for the Study of Evaluation, University of California.

Kleinberg, J. L. (1976). Adolescent correlates of occupational stability and change. *Journal of Vocational Behavior, 9,* 219–232.

Klockars, A. J., & Yamagishi, M. (1988). The influence of labels and position in rating scales. *Journal of Educational Measurement, 25,* 85–96.

Klopfer, W. G., & Taulbee, E. S. (1976). Projective tests. *Annual Review of Psychology, 27,* 543–568.

Knapp, T. R. (1968). *The choices study.* Unpublished report. Exploratory Committee on Assessing the Progress of Education.

Knight, S. S. (n.d.). *Systematic judgment of children's drawings.* Denver: National Assessment of Educational Progress.

Koch, W. R. (1987). The ninth mental measurements yearbook. *Journal of Educational Measurement, 24*(1), 90–94.

Kohn, S. D. (1975). The numbers game: How the testing industry operates. *The National Elementary Principal, 54*(6), 11–23.

Koretz, D. (1989). The new national assessment: What it can and cannot do. *NEA Today, 7*(6), 32–37.

Kozlowski, S. W. J., Kirsch, M. P., & Chao, G. T. (1986). Job knowledge, ratee familiarity, and halo effect: An exploration. *Journal of Applied Psychology, 71,* 45–49.

Krathwohl, D. R., Bloom, B. S., & Masia, B. B. (1964). *Taxonomy of educational objectives, handbook II: The affective domain.* New York: McKay.

Krathwohl, D. R., & Payne, D. A. (1971). Defining and assessing educational objectives. In R. L. Thorndike (Ed.), *Educational measurement* (2nd ed.) (pp. 17–45). Washington, DC: American Council on Education.

Kreit, L. H. (1968). The effects of test-taking practice on pupil test performance. *American Educational Research Journal, 5,* 616–625.

Krumboltz, J. D., & Hamel D. A. (Eds.). (1982). *Assessing career development.* Palo Alto, CA: Mayfield.

Kuder, G. F. (1966). *Kuder occupational interest survey general manual.* Chicago: Science Research Associates.

Kuder, G. F. (1969). A note on the comparability of occupational scores from different interest inventories. *Measurement and Evaluation in Guidance, 2,* 91–100.

Kuder, G. F. (1970). Some principles of interest measurement. *Educational and Psychological Measurement, 30,* 205–226.

Kulhavy, R. W. (1977). Feedback in written instruction. *Review of Educational Research, 47,* 211–232.

Kuncel, R. B. (1973). Response processes and relative location of subject and item. *Educational and Psychological Measurement, 33,* 545–563.

LaBenne, W. D., & Greene, B. I. (1969). *Educational implications of self-concept theory.* Pacific Palisades, CA: Goodyear.

Lafitte, R. G., Jr. (1984). Effects of item order on achievement test scores and students' perception of test difficulty. *Teaching of Psychology, 11,* 212–213.

Laing, J. (1988). Self-report: Can it be of value as an assessment technique? *Journal of Counseling and Development, 67*(1), 60–61.

Laing, J., & Farmer, M. (1984). *Use of the ACT assessment by examinees with disabilities* (ACT Research Report No. 94). Iowa City, IA: American College Testing Program.

Lamb, R. R., & Prediger, D. J. (1980). Construct validity of raw score and standard score reports of vocational interests. *Journal of Educational Measurement, 17,* 107–116.

Lambert, N. M. (1981). Psychological evidence in *Larry P. v. Wilson Riles*: An evaluation by a witness for the defense. *American Psychologist, 36,* 937–952.

Lange, A., Lehmann, I. J., & Mehrens, W. A. (1967). Using item analysis to improve tests. *Journal of Educational Measurement, 4,* 65–68.

Langhorst, B. H. (1989). *Assessment in early childhood education.* Portland, OR: Northwest Regional Educational Laboratory.

Larry P. v. Riles. 343 F. Supp. 130b (N.D. Cal. 1972). (preliminary injunction), affirmed, 502 F. 2d 963 (9th Cer. 1974), opinion issued No. D-71-2270 RFP (N.D. Cal. October 16, 1979).

Lehmann, I. J. (1974). Evaluating instruction. In W. Gephart and R. B. Ingle (Eds.), *Evaluation of instruction.* Bloomington, IN: Phi Delta Kappa.

LeMahieu, P. G. (1984). The effects on achievement and instructional content of a program of student monitoring through frequent testing. *Educational Evaluation and Policy Analysis, 6*(2), 175–187.

LeMahieu, P. G., & Wallace, R. C., Jr. (1986). Up against the wall: Psychometrics meets praxis. *Educational Measurement: Issues and Practice, 5*(1), 12–16.

Lennon, R. T. (1956). Assumptions underlying the use of content validity. *Educational and Psychological Measurement, 16,* 294–304.

Lennon, R. T. (1980). The anatomy of a scholastic aptitude test. *Measurement in Education, 11*(2), 1–8.

Lerner, B. (1980). The war on testing: David, Goliath and Gallup. *The Public Interest, 60,* 119–147.

Lerner, B. (1981). The minimum competence testing movement: Social scientific, and legal implications. *American Psychologist, 36,* 1057–1066.

Levine, M. (1976). The academic achievement test: Its historical context and social functions. *American Psychologist, 31,* 228–238.

Lewis, J. (1975). The relationship between academic aptitude and occupational success for a sample of university graduates. *Educational and Psychological Measurement, 35,* 465–466.

Lewis, M. & Lindaman, A. D. (1989). How do we evaluate student writing? One district's answer. *Educational Leadership, 46*(7), 70–71.

Li, C. C. (1975). *Path analysis: A primer.* Pacific Grove, CA: Boxwood Press.

Lidz, C. S. (1981). *Improving assessment of schoolchildren.* San Francisco: Jossey-Bass.

Liebert, R. N., & Morris, L. W. (1967). Cognitive and emotional components of test anxiety: A distinction and some additional data. *Psychological Reports, 20,* 975–978.

Lien, A. J. (1976). *Measurement and evaluation of learning.* Dubuque, IA: William C. Brown.

Ligon, G. (1985, April). *Opportunity knocked out: Reducing cheating by teachers on student tests.* Paper presented at the annual meeting of the American Educational Research Association, Chicago.

Lindman, E. L. (1971). The means and ends of accountability. In *Proceedings of the conference on accountability.* Princeton, NJ: Educational Testing Service.

Lindquist, E. F. (1951). Preliminary considerations in objective-test construction. In E. F. Lindquist (Ed.), *Educational measurement* (pp. 119–158). Washington, DC: American Council on Education. .

Lindvall, C. M., & Bolvin, J. O. (1967). Programmed instruction in the schools: An application of programmed principles in individually prescribed instruction. In P. Lange (Ed.), *Programmed instruction* (66th yearbook) (Part II). Chicago: National Society for the Study of Education.

Linn, R. L. (1980). Issues of validity for criterion-referenced measurement. *Applied Psychological Measurement, 4,* 547–561.

Linn, R. L. (1986a). Barriers to new test designs. In *Proceeding of the 1985 ETS invitational conference: The redesign of testing for the 21st century* (pp. 69–79). Princeton, NJ: Educational Testing Service.

Linn, R. L. (1986b). Bias in college admissions. In the College Board (Eds.), *Measures in the college admissions process* (pp. 80–85). New York: College Entrance Examination Board.

Linn, R. L. (1987). *State-by-state comparisons of student achievement: The definition of the content domain for assessment* (CSE Report No. 275). Los Angeles: Center for the Study of Evaluation, University of California.

Linn, R. L. (1989). Current perspectives and future directions. In R. L. Linn (Ed.), *Educational measurement* (3rd ed.) (pp. 1–10). New York: American Council on Education and Macmillan.

Lissitz, R. W., & Willhoft, J. L. (1985). A methodological study of the Torrance tests of creativity. *Journal of Educational Measurement, 22,* 1–12.

Livingston, S. A., & Zieky, M. J. (1982). *Passing scores: A manual for setting standards of performance on educational and occupational tests.* Princeton, NJ: Educational Testing Service.

Loehlin, J. C., et al. (1975). *Race differences in intelligence.* San Francisco: Freeman.

Long, B. H., & Henderson, E. H. (1974). Certain determinants of academic expectancies among southern and non-southern teachers. *American Educational Research Journal, 11,* 137–147.

Lord, F. M. (1952). The relationship of the reliability of multiple-choice tests to the distribution of item difficulties. *Psychometrika, 18,* 181–194.

Lord, F. M. (1963). Formula scoring and validity. *Educational and Psychological Measurement, 23,* 663–672.

Lord, F. M. (1975). Formula scoring and number-right scoring. *Journal of Educational Measurement, 12,* 7–11.

Lord, F. M. (1977). Optional number of choices per item: A comparison of four approaches. *Journal of Educational Measurement, 14,* 33–38.

Lord, F. M. (1980). *Applications of item response theory*

to practical testing problems. Hillsdale, NJ: Lawrence Erlbaum.

Loyd, B. H. (1986). Reflections on legitimate ways to prepare students for testing. In J. Hall and P. Wolmut (Eds.), *Legitimate ways to prepare students for standardized tests* (pp. 21–27). Oklahoma City OK: National Association of Test Directors, Oklahoma City Public Schools.

Loyd, B. H. (1988). Implications of item response theory for the measurement practitioner. *Applied Measurement in Education, 1*(2), 135–144.

Mackenzie, B. (1984). Explaining race differences in IQ: The logic, the methodology, and the evidence. *American Psychologist, 39,* 1211–1233.

Macoby, E. E., & Jacklin, C. N. (1974, April). *The psychology of sex differences.* Paper presented at the annual meeting of the American Educational Research Association, Chicago.

Mager, F. (1962). *Preparing objectives for programmed instruction.* Palo Alto, CA: Fearon.

Mahan, T., & Mahan, A. (1981). *Assessing children with special needs.* New York: Holt, Rinehart & Winston.

Majors, G. W., & Michael, J. J. (1975). The relationship of achievement on a teacher-made mathematics test of computational skills to two ways of recording answers and to two workspace arrangements. *Educational and Psychological Measurement, 35,* 1005–1009.

Mallet, S. D., Spokane, A. R., & Vance, F. L. (1978). Effects of vocationally relevant information on the expressed and measured interests of freshman males. *Journal of Counseling Psychology, 25,* 292–298.

Marco, L. (1988). Does the use of test assembly procedures proposed in legislation make any difference in test properties and in the test performance of black and white takers? *Applied Measurement in Education, 1*(2), 109–134.

Marshall, J. C. (1967). Composition errors and essay examination grades reexamined. *American Educational Research Journal, 4,* 375–386.

Marso, R. N. (1969). Test difficulty and student achievement. *American Educational Research Journal, 6,* 621–632.

Marso, R. N., & Pigge, F. L. (1988, April). *An analysis of teacher-made tests: Testing practices, cognitive demands, and item construction errors.* Paper presented at the annual meeting of the National Council on Measurement in Education, New Orleans.

Marso, R. N., & Pigge, F. L. (1989, April). *The status*

of classroom teachers' test construction proficiencies: Assessments by teachers, principals, and supervisors validated by analyses of actual teacher made tests. Paper presented at the annual meeting of the National Council on Measurement in Education, San Francisco.

Martin, R. B., & Srikameswaran, K. (1974). Correlation between frequent testing and student performance. *Journal of Chemical Education, 51,* 485–486.

Martin, W. H. (1976, April). *Maximizing information from free response exercises in mathematics.* Paper presented at the annual meeting of the National Council on Measurement in Education, San Francisco.

Martuza, V. (1979). *Domain definition/item generation for criterion-referenced tests: A review and directions for further research.* Paper presented at the second annual meeting of the Eastern Educational Research Association.

Masling, J. (1960). The influence of situational and interpersonal variables in projective testing. *Psychological Bulletin, 57,* 65–85.

Masters, J. R. (1974). The relationship between number of response categories and reliability of Likert-type questionnaires. *Journal of Educational Measurement, 11,* 49–55.

Matarazzo, J. (1986). Computerized clinical psychological test interpretations: Unvalidated plus all mean and no sigma. *American Psychologist, 41,* 14–24.

Mathews, W. M. (1973). Narrative format testing reports and traditional testing reports: A comparative study. *Journal of Educational Measurement, 10,* 171–178.

McArthur, D. L., & Choppin, B. H. (1984). Computerized diagnostic testing. *Journal of Educational Measurement, 21,* 391–398.

McAshan, H. H. (1974). *The goals approach to performance objectives.* Philadelphia: Saunders.

McBride, J. R. (1980). Adaptive verbal ability testing in a military setting. In D. Weiss (Ed.), *Proceedings of the 1979 computerized adaptive testing conference.* Minneapolis: Department of Psychology, University of Minnesota.

McCall, R. B. (1977). Childhood IQ's as predictors of adult educational and occupational status. *Science, 197,* 482–483.

McCall, R. B. (1980). The development of intellectual functioning in infancy and the prediction of later IQ. In. J. D. Osofsky (Ed.), *Handbook of infant development.* New York: Wiley.

McCall, R. B., Appelbaum, M. I., & Hogarty, P. S. (1973). Developmental changes in mental performance. *Monographs of the Society for Research in Child Development, 38* (3, Serial No. 150).

McCall, R. B., Hogarty, P. S., & Hurlburt, N. (1972). Transitions in infant sensorimotor development and the prediction of childhood IQ. *American Psychologist, 27,* 728–748.

McGraw, B., Wardrop, J. L., & Bunda, M. A. (1972). Classroom observation schemes: Where are the errors? *American Educational Research Journal, 9,* 13–27.

McGraw, C., & Wood, T. (1988, Sept. 18). Pressure for high scores blamed in CAP test cheating. *Los Angeles Times.*

McIntrye, R. M., Smith, D. E., & Hassett, C. E. (1984). Accuracy of performance ratings as affected by rater training and perceived purpose of rating. *Journal of Applied Psychology, 69,* 147–156.

McKee, L. E. (1967). Third grade students learn to use machine-scored answer sheets. *The School Counselor, 15,* 52–53.

McKinney, J. D., Mason, J., Peterson, K., & Clifford, M. (1975). Relationship between classroom behavior and academic achievement. *Journal of Educational Psychology, 67,* 198–203.

McMorris, R. F., De Mers, L. P., & Schwartz, S. P. (1987). Attitudes, behaviors, and reasons for changing responses following answer-changing instructions. *Journal of Educational Measurement, 24,* 131–143.

McMorris, R. F., Urbach, S. L., & Connor, M. C. (1985). Effects of incorporating humor in test items. *Journal of Educational Measurement, 22,* 147–156.

McMorris, R. F., & Weideman, A. H. (1986). Answer-changing after instruction on answer-changing. *Measurement and Evaluation in Counseling and Development 18,* 93–101.

McNemar, Q. (1964). Lost: Our intelligence? Why? *American Psychologist, 19,* 871–882.

Medley, D. M., & Mitzel, H. E. (1963). Measuring classroom behavior by systematic observation. In N. L. Gage (Ed.), *Handbook of research on teaching* (pp. 247–328). Skokie, IL: Rand McNally.

Meehl, P. E., & Rosen, A. (1955). Antecedent probability and the efficiency of psychometric signs, patterns, or cutting scores. *Psychological Bulletin, 52,* 194–216.

Meeker, M. N. (1981). *Using SOI test results: A teacher's*

guide. El Segundo, CA: Structure of Intelligence Institute.

Mehrens, W. A. (n.d.). *Educational tests: Blessing or curse?* Unpublished manuscript. East Lansing: Michigan State University.

Mehrens, W. A. (1979). The technology of competency measurement. In R. B. Ingle, M. R. Carroll, & W. J. Gephart (Eds.), *Assessment of student competence* (pp. 39–55). Bloomington, IN: Phi Delta Kappa.

Mehrens, W. A. (1981a). ETS versus Nairn/Nader: Who reigns? *Measurement and Evaluation in Guidance, 14*(2), 61–70.

Mehrens, W. A. (1981b, Feb.). *Setting standards for minimum competency tests.* Presentation given at the Michigan School Testing Conference, Ann Arbor.

Mehrens, W. A. (1982). Review of the *Career planning program.* In J. T. Kapes & M. M. Mastie (Eds.), *A counselor's guide to vocational guidance instruments* (131–135).

Mehrens, W. A. (1984a). National tests and local curriculum: Match or mismatch? *Educational Measurement: Issues and Practice, 3*(3), 9–15.

Mehrens, W. A. (1984b). A critical analysis of the psychometric properties of the K-ABC. *Journal of Special Education, 18,* 297–310.

Mehrens, W. A. (1987). Validity issues in teacher competency tests. *Journal of Personnel Evaluation in Education, 1,* 195–229.

Mehrens, W. A. (1989, March). *Social issues in teacher testing.* Paper presented at an invited address at the annual meeting of the National Council on Measurement in Education, San Francisco.

Mehrens, W. A., & Kaminski, J. (1989). Methods for improving standardized test scores: Fruitful, fruitless or fraudulent? *Educational Measurement: Issues and Practice, 8*(1), 14–22.

Mehrens, W. A., & Lehmann, I. J. (1969). *Measurement and evaluation in education and psychology.* New York: Holt, Rinehart & Winston.

Mehrens, W. A., & Lehmann, I. J. (1980). *Standardized tests in education* (3rd ed.). New York: Holt, Rinehart & Winston.

Mehrens, W. A., & Lehmann, I. J. (1985). Interpreting test scores to clients: What score should one use? *Journal of Counseling and Development, 63*(5), 317–320.

Mellville, G. L., & Stamm, E. (1967). *The pass–fail system and the change in the accounting of grades on comprehensive examination at Knox College* (Report ED-014-788). Galesburg, IL: Office of Institutional Research, Knox College.

Menges, R. J. (1973). The new reporters: Students rate instruction. In C. R. Pace (Ed.), *New directions in higher education: Evaluating learning and teaching* (pp. 59–75). San Francisco: Jossey-Bass.

Mercer, J. (1977). *SOMPA, system of multicultural pluralistic assessment.* New York: The Psychological Corporation.

Mercer, J. (1979). *System of multicultural pluralistic assessment: Technical manual.* Cleveland: The Psychological Corporation.

Messick, S. (1979). Potential uses of noncognitive measurement in education. *Journal of Educational Psychology, 71,* 281–292.

Messick, S. (1980). *The effectiveness of coaching for the SAT: Review and reanalysis of research from the fifties to the FTC.* Princeton, NJ: Educational Testing Service.

Messick, S. (1981). The controversy over coaching: Issues of effectiveness and equity. In B. F. Green (Ed.), *New directions in testing and measurement: Issues in testing, coaching, disclosure, and ethnic bias, 11* (pp. 21–54). San Francisco: Jossey-Bass.

Messick, S. (1989). Validity. In R. L. Linn (Ed.), *Educational measurement* (3rd ed.) (pp. 13–104). New York: American Council on Education and Macmillan.

Messick, S., & Jungeblut, A. (1981). Time and method in coaching for the SAT. *Psychological Bulletin, 89,* 191–216.

Michigan State Board of Education. (n.d.). *A guide to test taking as easy as . . . 1 2 3.* Michigan State Board of Education.

Mika, W. J., Jr. (1982). An NEA-VEA response. In S. B. Anderson & L. V. Coburn (Eds.), *Academic testing and the consumer* (pp. 59–62). San Francisco: Jossey-Bass.

Miller, D. C. (1983). *Handbook of research design and social measurement* (4th ed.). New York: Longman.

Miller, M. D. (1986). Patterns of time allocation and item response. *Journal of Educational Measurement, 23,* 147–156.

Miller, P. W., & Erickson, H. E. (1985). *Teacher-written student tests: A guide for planning, creating, administering, and assessing.* Washington, DC: National Educational Association.

Millman, J. (1966). *Test-wiseness in taking objective achievement and aptitude examinations: Final report.* New York: College Entrance Examination Board.

Millman, J. (1972). *Tables for determining number of items needed on domain-referenced tests and number of students to be tested* (Technical Paper No. 5). Los Angeles: Instructional Objectives Exchange.

Millman, J. (1973). Passing scores and test lengths for domain-referenced measures. *Review of Educational Research, 43,* 205–216.

Millman, J. (1974). Criterion-referenced measurement. In W. J. Popham (Ed.), *Evaluation in education: Current applications* (Chapter 6). Berkeley, CA: McCutchan,

Millman, J., & Arter, J. A. (1984). Issues in item banking. *Journal of Educational Measurement, 21,* 315–330.

Millman, J., Bishop, C. H., & Ebel, R. L. (1965). An analysis of test wiseness. *Educational and Psychological Measurement, 25,* 707–726.

Millman, J., & Westman, R. S. (1989). Computer-assisted writing of achievement test items: Toward a future technology. *Journal of Educational Measurement, 26,* 177–190.

Milton, O. (1967). *Teaching-learning issues, no. 5.* Knoxville: Learning Resources Center, University of Tennessee.

Mitchell, J. V., Jr. (Ed.). (1983). *Test in print III.* Lincoln, NE: Buros Institute of Mental Measurements, University of Nebraska.

Mitchell, J. V., Jr. (1984). What's new in testing? Serving the test user: New development from the Buros Institute. *Educational Measurement: Issues and Practice, 3*(2), 51–54.

Mitchell, J. V., Jr. (Ed.). (1985). *The ninth mental measurements yearbook.* Lincoln, NE: Buros Institute of Mental Measurements, University of Nebraska.

Monroe, W. S., & Carter, R. E. (1923). *The use of different types of thought questions in secondary schools and their relative difficulty for students* (Bulletin 20, No. 34). Urbana, IL: University of Illinois.

Moore, J. C. (1971). Test wiseness and analogy test performance. *Measurement and Evaluation in Guidance, 3,* 198–202.

Morishima, J. K., & Micek, S. S. (1970). *Pass–fail evaluation: Phase II: Questionnaire analysis.* Seattle: Office of Institutional Educational Research, University of Washington.

Morse, J. A., & Tillman, M. H. (1972, April). *Effects on achievement of possession of behavioral objectives and training concerning their use.* Paper presented at the meeting of the American Educational Research Association, Chicago.

Mosier, C. I. (1947). A critical examination of the concepts of face validity. *Educational and Psychological Measurement, 7,* 191–205.

Mosier, C. I., Myers, M. C., & Price, H. G. (1945). Suggestions for the construction of multiple-choice test items. *Educational and Psychological Measurement, 5,* 261–271.

Mueller, D. J. (1975). An assessment of the effectiveness of complex alternatives in multiple-choice achievement test items. *Educational and Psychological Measurement, 35,* 135–141.

Mueller, D. J., & Wasser, V. (1977). Implications of changing answers on objective test items. *Journal of Educational Measurement, 14,* 9–14.

Multiple choice questions: A close look. (1963). Princeton, NJ: Educational Testing Service.

Munday, L. (1965). Predicting college grades in predominantly Negro colleges. *Journal of Educational Measurement, 2,* 157–160.

Murchan, D. P. (1989, April). *Essay versus objective achievement testing in the context of large-scale assessment programs.* Paper presented at the annual meeting of the National Council of Measurement in Education, San Francisco.

Murname, R. J., & Raizen, S. A. (Eds.). (1988). *Improving indicators of the quality of science and mathematics education in grades K-12.* Washington, DC: National Academy Press.

Murphy, K. R., & Blazer, W. K. (1986). Systematic distortions in memory-based behavior ratings and performance evaluations: Consequences for rating accuracy. *Journal of Applied Psychology, 71,* 39–44.

Nader, R. (1987). Sixty years of idiocy is enough. *The Fair Test Examiner, 1*(1), 1, 3.

Nairn, A., & Associates. (1980). *The reign of ETS: The corporation that makes up minds.* Washington, DC: Author.

National Assessment of Educational Progress. (1969). *Questions and answers about national assessment of educational progress.* Ann Arbor, MI: NAEP.

National Assessment of Educational Progress. (1970a). *Citizenship: National results* (Partial Report No. 2). Denver: NAEP.

National Assessment of Educational Progress. (1970b). *Writing: National results* (Report 3, 1969–1970). Denver: NAEP.

National Board for Professional Teaching Standards. (1989). *Toward high and rigorous standards for the teaching profession.* Author.

National Commission on Excellence in Education.

(1983). *The nation at risk: The imperative for educational reform.* Washington, DC: Government Printing Office.

National Education Association. (1970). *Marking and reporting pupil progress* (Research Summary 1970-S1). Washington, DC: NEA.

National Education Association. (1980). Teachers and citizens protest the testing ripoff. *NEA Reporter, 19*(1), 3–4.

Natriello, G. (1987). The impact of evaluation processes on students. *Educational Psychologist, 22,* 155–175.

Naveh-Benjamin, M., McKeachie, W. J., & Lin, Y. (1987). Two types of text-anxious students: Support for an information processing model. *Journal of Educational Psychology, 79*(2), 131–136.

Neisser, U. (1979). The concept of intelligence. In R. J. Sternberg & D. K. Detterman (Eds), *Human intelligence: Perspectives on its theory and measurement* (pp. 179–190). Norwood, NJ: Ablex.

Nelson, C. H. (1958). *Let's build quality into our science tests.* Washington, DC: National Science Teachers Association.

Nesselroade, J. R., & Von Eye, A. (Eds.). (1985). *Individual development and social change: Exploratory analysis.* Orlando, FL: Academic Press.

Nevo, B. (1976). The effects of general practice, specific practice, and item familiarization on change in aptitude test scores. *Measurement and Evaluation in Guidance, 91,* 16–20.

Newman, D. L., Kundert, D.K, Lane, D. S., & Bull, K. S. (1988). Effect of varying item-order on multiple-choice test scores: Importance of statistical and cognitive difficulty. *Applied Measurement in Education, 1*(1), 89–97.

Newsnotes. (1984). School programs are changing in response to reform reports: ERS. *Phi Delta Kappan, 66*(4), 301.

Newsnotes. (1986). Eight southern states weigh in with student test results. *Phi Delta Kappan, 68*(4), 336.

Niedermeyer, F. C., & Sullivan, H. J. (1972). Differential effects of individual and group testing strategies in an objectives-based instructional program. *Journal of Educational Measurement, 9,* 199–204.

Nitko, A. J. (1980). Criterion-referencing schemes. In Mayo, S. T. (Ed.), *Interpreting test performance: New directions for testing and measurement* (No. 6) (pp. 35–71). San Francisco: Jossey-Bass.

Nitko, A. J. (1983). *Educational tests and measurement:* An introduction. New York: Harcourt Brace Jovanovich.

Nitko, A. J. (1989). Designing tests that are integrated with instruction. In R. L. Linn (Ed.), *Educational measurement* (3rd ed.) (pp. 447–474). New York: American Council on Education and Macmillan.

Noeth, R., Roth, J., & Prediger, D. (1975). Student career development: Where do we stand? *Vocational Guidance Quarterly, 23,* 210–219.

Noll, V. H., Scannell, D. P., & Craig, R. C. (1979). *Introduction to educational measurement* (4th ed.). Boston: Houghton Mifflin.

Noppe, L. D. (1980). Creative thinking. In R. H. Woody (Ed.), *Encyclopedia of clinical assessment* (Vol. 2). San Francisco: Jossey-Bass.

Norcini, J. (1987). The answer key as a source of error in examinations of professionals. *Journal of Educational Measurement, 24*(4), 321–331.

Norris, S. P. (1988). Controlling for background beliefs when developing multiple-choice critical thinking tests. *Educational Measurement: Issues and Practice, 7*(3), 5–11.

Novick, M. R. (1980). Discussion of Hunter's construct validity and validity generalization. In *Construct validity in psychological measurement. Proceedings of a colloquium on theory and application in education and employment* (pp. 125–129). Princeton, NJ: U.S. Office of Personnel Management and Educational Testing Service.

Novick, M. R., & Ellis, D. D., Jr. (1977). Equal opportunity in educational and employment selection. *American Psychologist, 32*(5), 306–320.

Nunnally, J. C. (1978). *Psychometric theory* (2nd ed.). New York: McGraw-Hill.

O'Bryan, K. G., & MacArthur, R. S. (1969). Reversibility, intelligence, and creativity in nine-year-old boys. *Child Development, 40,* 33–45.

On bias in selection. (1976). Special issue of the *Journal of Educational Measurement, 13,* 1.

Oosterhof, A. C. (1976). Similarity of various discrimination indices. *Journal of Educational Measurement, 13,* 145–150.

Oosterhof, A. C. (1990). *Classroom applications of educational measurement.* Columbus, OH: Merrill.

Oosterhof, A. C., & Coats, P. K. (1984). Comparison of difficulties and reliabilities of quantitative word problems in completion and multiple-choice item formats. *Applied Psychological Measurement, 8*(3), 287–294.

Oosterhof, A. C., & Glassnapp, D. R. (1974). Comparative reliabilities and difficulties of the multiple-choice and true-false formats. *Journal of Experimental Education, 42,* 62–64.

Osburn, H. G. (1968). Item sampling for achievement testing. *Educational and Psychological Measurement, 28,* 95–104.

Ottens, A. J., Tucker, K. R., & Robbins, S. B. (1989). The construction of an academic anxiety coping scale. *Journal of College Student Development, 30*(3), 249–256.

Overall, J. A., & Woodward, J. A. (1975). Unreliability of difference scores: A paradox for measurement of change. *Psychological Bulletin, 82,* 85–86.

Owens, R. E., Hanna, G. S., & Coppedge, F. L. (1970). Comparison of multiple-choice tests using different types of distracter selection techniques. *Journal of Educational Measurement, 7,* 87–90.

Page, E. B. (1966). The imminence of grading essays by computer. *Phi Delta Kappan, 47,* 238–243.

Page, E. B. (1967). Grading essays by computer: Progress report. *Proceedings of the 1966 invitational conference on testing problems* (pp. 87–100). Princeton, NJ: Educational Testing Service.

Page, E. B. (1972, April). *Progress in style and content.* Symposium presented at the annual meeting of the American Educational Research Association, Chicago.

Page, E. B. (1976). Nader vs. E. T. S. letters column. *APA Monitor, 7*(12), 2–3.

Page E. B. (1984). Struggles and possibilities: The use of tests in decision making. In B. S. Plake (Ed.), *Social and technical issues in testing* (pp. 11–38). Hillsdale, NJ: Lawrence Erlbaum.

Parents in action on special education (PASE) v. *Hannon.* No. 74-C-3586 (N.D. IL. July 16, 1980).

Parnell, D. (1973). In *Elementary and secondary education amendments of 1973: Hearings before the general subcommittee on education of the committee on education and labor, House of Representatives, Ninety-third Congress, first session.* (ON H.R. 16, H.R. 69, H.R. 5163, and H.R. 5823). Part 3 and Appendix.

Patnaik, D., & Traub, R. E. (1973). Differential weighting by judged degree of correctness. *Journal of Educational Measurement, 10,* 281–286.

Pechman, E. M. (1985). Unresolved questions pertaining to testing of handicapped students. In P. Wolmut & G. Iverson (Eds.), *National association of test directors 1985 symposium* (pp. 63–69). Portland, OR: Multnomah E.S.D.

Peddiwell, J. A. (1939). *The sabre-tooth curriculum.* New York: McGraw-Hill

Peters, H. J., & Hansen, J. C. (Eds.). (1977). *Vocational guidance and career development.* (3rd ed.). New York: Macmillan.

Peterson, N. S., Kolen, M. J., & Hoover, H. D. (1989). Scaling, norming, and equating. In R. L. Linn (Ed.), *Educational measurement* (3rd ed.) (pp. 221–262). New York: American Council on Education and Macmillan.

Peterson, N. S., & Novick, M. R. (1976). An evaluation of some models for culture-fair selection. *Journal of Educational Measurement, 13,* 3–30.

Pettie, A. A., & Oosterhof, A. C. (1976, April). *Indices of item adequacy for individually administered mastery tests.* Paper presented at the annual meeting of the National Council on Measurement in Education, San Francisco.

Pfeifer, C. M., Jr., & Sedlacek, W. E. (1971). The validity of academic predictors for black and white students at a predominantly white university. *Journal of Educational Measurement, 8,* 253–262.

Phillips, S. E., & Clarizio, H. F. (1988a). Limitations of standard scores in individual achievement testing. *Educational Measurement: Issues and Practices, 7*(1), 8–15.

Phillips, S. E., & Clarizio, H. F. (1988b). Conflicting growth expectations cannot both be real: A rejoinder to Yen. *Educational Measurement: Issues and Practice, 7*(4), 18–19.

Phillips, S. E., & Mehrens, W. A. (1988). Effects of curricular differences on achievement test data at item and objective levels. *Applied Measurement in Education, 1*(1), 33–51.

Pinard, A., & Sharp, E. (1972). IQ and point of view. *Psychology Today, 6*(1), 65–68, 90.

Pinchak, B. M., & Breland, H. M. (1973). *Grading practices in American high schools* (Research Bulletin 73-45). Princeton, NJ: Educational Testing Service.

Pines, M. (1969, July 6). Why some three-year-olds get A's—and some C's. *New York Times Magazine,* 1–17.

Pipho, C. (1988). Stateline. *Phi Delta Kappan, 70*(4), 278.

Plake, B. S., & Huntley, R. M. (1984). Can relevant grammatical clues result in invalid test items? *Educational and Psychological Measurement, 44,* 687–697.

Plake, B. S., Thompson, P. A., & Lowry, S. (1980, April). *Number right and elimination scores as a func-*

tion of item arrangement, knowledge of arrangement, and test anxiety. Paper presented at the annual meeting of the National Council on Measurement in Education, Boston.

Plake, B. S., Ansorge, C. J., Parker, C. S., & Lowry, S. R. (1982). Effects of item arrangement, knowledge of arrangement, test anxiety, and sex on test performance. *Journal of Educational Measurement, 19*(1), 49–58.

Planisek, S. L., & Planisek, R. J. (1972, April). *A description of fifteen test statistics based upon optically scanned instructor-made multiple-choice tests at Kent State University.* Paper presented at the annual meeting of the National Council on Measurement in Education, Chicago.

Popham, W. J. (1970). The instructional objectives exchange: New support for criterion-referenced instruction. *Phi Delta Kappan, 52,* 171–175.

Popham, W. J. (1972). *Criterion-referenced measurement.* Englewood Cliffs, NJ: Educational Technology Publications.

Popham, W. J. (1976). Normative data for criterion-referenced tests? *Phi Delta Kappan, 57,* 593–594.

Popham, W. J. (1978). *Criterion-referenced measurement.* Englewood Cliffs, NJ: Prentice-Hall.

Popham, W. J. (1980). Domain specification strategies. In R. A. Berk (Ed.), *Criterion-referenced measurement* (pp. 15–31). Baltimore: Johns Hopkins University Press.

Popham, W. J. (1981). *Modern educational measurement.* Englewood Cliffs, NJ: Prentice-Hall.

Popham, W. J. (1984). Specifying the domain of content or behaviors. In R. A. Berk (Ed.), *A guide to criterion-referenced test construction* (pp. 29–48). Baltimore: Johns Hopkins University Press.

Popham, W. J. (1987). The merits of measurement-driven instruction. *Phi Delta Kappan, 68*(9), 679–683.

Popham, W. J., & Husek, T. R. (1969). Implications of criterion-referenced measurement. *Journal of Educational Measurement, 6,* 1–10.

Prediger, D. J. (1971). *Converting test data to counseling information* (ACT Research Report No. 44). Iowa City, IA: American College Testing Program.

Prediger, D. J. (1977). Alternatives for validating interest inventories against group membership criteria. *Applied Psychological Measurement, 1,* 275–280.

Prediger, D. J., & Hanson, G. R. (1977). Some consequences of using raw-score reports of vocational in-terests. *Journal of Educational Measurement, 14*(4), 323–333.

Prediger, D. J., & Sawyer, R. L. (1986). Ten years of career development: A nationwide study of high school students. *Journal of Counseling and Development, 65*(1), 45–49.

Prediger, D. J., Roth, J. D., & Noeth, R. J. (1974). Career development of youth: A nationwide study. *Personnel and Guidance Journal, 53,* 97–104.

Prescott, G. A., Balow, I. H., Hogan, T. P., & Farr, R. C. (1986). *Metropolitan Achievement Tests: Survey battery manual.* New York: The Psychological Corporation.

President's Commission on Higher Education. (1947). *Higher education for American democracy* (Vol. 1). *Establishing the goals.* Washington, DC: Government Printing Office.

Public Law 93-380. (1974, Aug 21).

Public Law 95-561. (1978, Nov 1).

Pulakos, E. D. (1984). A comparison of rater training programs: Error training and accuracy training. *Journal of Applied Psychology, 69,* 581–588.

Pullin, D. (1981). Minimum competency testing and the demand for accountability. *Phi Delta Kappan, 63*(1), 20–22.

Putka, G. (1989, Nov. 2). Classroom scandal. *Wall Street Journal, 71,* 14, 1.

Pyrczak, F. (1974). Passage dependency items designed to measure the ability to identify the main ideas of paragraphs: Implications for validity. *Educational and Psychological Measurement, 34,* 343–348.

Pyrczak, F. (1976). *Context-dependence of items designed to measure the ability to derive the meanings of words from their context.* Paper presented at the annual meeting of the National Council on Measurement in Education, San Francisco.

Quann, C. J. (1970). *Pass–fail grading: What are the trends?* Paper presented at the meeting of the American Association of Collegiate Registrars and Admissions Officers, New Orleans.

Raffeld, P. (1975). The effects of Guttman weights. *Journal of Educational Measurement, 12,* 179–185.

Ragosta, M., & Kaplan, B. A. (1986). *A survey of handicapped students taking special test administrations of the SAT and GRE (RR-86-5).* Princeton, NJ: Educational Testing Service.

Ramseyer, G. C., & Cashen, V. M. (1971). The effect of practice sessions on the use of separate answer sheets by first and second graders. *Journal of Educational Measurement, 8,* 177–182.

Random House School Decision. (1987). *What makes scoring high the most widely used test preparation series* (Advertising Brochure 9972620). Westminster, MD: Author.

Raspberry, W. (1983, April 29). Teachers should pass tests, too. *Washington Post*.

Raspberry, W. (1987, Feb. 23). Affirmative action that hurts blacks. *Washington Post*, A23.

Reardon, R., & Loughead, T. (1988). A comparison of paper-and-pencil and computer versions of the self-direct search. *Journal of Counseling and Development, 67*, 249–252.

Rebell, M. A. (1986). Disparate impact of the teacher competency testing on minorities: Don't blame the test-takers—or the tests. *Yale Law & Policy Review, 4*(2), 375–403.

Rebell, M. A. (1989). Testing, public policy, and the courts. In B. R. Gifford (Ed.), *Test policy and the politics of opportunity allocation: The workplace and the law* (pp. 135–162). Boston: Kluwer Academic.

Reckase, M. D. (1984a). Scaling techniques. In G. Goldstein & M. Hersen (Eds.), *Handbook of psychological assessment* (pp. 38–53). New York: Pergamon Press.

Reckase, M. D. (1984b). Technical guidelines for assessing computerized adaptive tests. *Journal of Educational Measurement, 21*(4), 347–360.

Report of the Commission on Tests: I. Righting the balance. (1970). New York: College Entrance Examination Board.

Reschly, D. J. (1981). Psychological testing in educational classification and placement. *American Psychologist, 36*(10), 1091–1102.

Reschly, D. J., Kicklighter, R., & McKee, P. (1988a). Recent placement litigation, part I, regular education grouping: Comparison of Marshall (1984, 1985) and Hobson (1967, 1969). *School Psychology Review, 17*(1), 9–21.

Reschly, D. J., Kicklighter, R., & McKee, P. (1988b). Recent placement litigation, part II, minority EMR overrepresentation: Comparison of Larry P. (1979, 1984, 1986) with Marshall (1984, 1985) and Sil (1986). *School Psychology Review, 17*(1), 22–38.

Reschly, D. J., Kicklighter, R., & McKee, P. (1988c). Recent placement litigation, part III. Analysis of differences in Larry P., Marshall and S-1 and implications for future practices. *School Psychology Review, 17*(1), 39–50.

Resnick, L. B. (Ed.). (1976). *The nature of intelligence.* Hillsdale, NJ: Lawrence Erlbaum.

Reynolds, C. R. (1980). An examination for bias in a preschool test battery across race and sex. *Journal of Educational Measurement, 17*(2), 137–146.

Reynolds, C. R. (1982). The problem of bias in psychological assessment. In C. R. Reynolds & T. B. Gutkin (Eds.), *The Handbook of school psychology* (pp. 178–208). New York: Wiley.

Reynolds, C. R. (1987). Playing IQ roulette with the Stanford-Binet (4th ed.). *Measurement and Evaluation in Counseling and Development, 20*(3), 139–141.

Reynolds, C. R., Kamphaus, R. W., & Rosenthal, B. L. (1988). Factor analysis of the Stanford-Binet fourth edition for ages 2 years through 23 years. *Measurement and Evaluation in Counseling and Development, 21*(2), 52–63.

Ricks, J. H. (1959). *On telling parents about test results* (Test Service Bulletin No. 54). New York: The Psychological Corporation.

Roberts, D. M. (1987). Limitations of the score-difference method in detecting cheating in recognition test situations. *Journal of Educational Measurement, 24*(1), 77–81.

Rock, D. A., Bennett, R. E., & Kaplan, B. A. (1985). *The internal construct validity of the SAT across handicapped and nonhandicapped populations* (RR-85-80). Princeton, NJ: Educational Testing Service.

Rogers, B. G. (1985). Prospective teacher perceptions of how classroom teachers use evaluation methods: A qualitative research approach. *Midwestern Educational Researcher*, 613–620.

Rogosa, D. R., Brandt, D., & Zimowski, M. (1982). A growth curve approach to the measurement of change. *Psychological Bulletin, 92*, 726–748.

Rogosa, D. R., & Willet, J. B. (1983). Demonstrating the reliability of the difference score in the measurement of change. *Journal of Educational Measurement, 20*, 335–343.

Roid, G. H. (1984). Generating the test items. In R. A. Berk (Ed.), *A guide to criterion-referenced test construction* (pp. 49–77). Baltimore: Johns Hopkins University Press.

Roid, G. H. (1986). Computer technology in testing. In B. S. Plake & J. C. Witt (Eds.), *The future of testing* (pp. 29–69). Hillsdale, NJ: Lawrence Erlbaum.

Roid, G., & Gorsuch R. (1984). Development and clinical use of test interpretive programs on microcomputers. In M. D. Schwartz (Ed.), *Using computers in clinical practice* (pp. 141–149). New York: Haworth Press.

Romano, L. (1959). The parent-teacher conference. *National Education Association Journal, 48,* 21–22.

Rosenfeld, M., Thornton, R. F., & Sturnik, L. S. (1986). *Relationships between job functions and the NTE core battery* (Research Report No. 868). Princeton, NJ: Educational Testing Service.

Rosenholtz, S. J., & Simpson, C. (1984). The formation of ability conceptions: Developmental trend or social construction? *Review of Educational Research, 54*(1), 31–64.

Rosenthal, R., & Jacobson, L. (1968). *Pygmalion in the classroom.* New York: Holt, Rinehart & Winston.

Rothman, R. (1987, June 3). Using pupil scores to assess teachers criticized as unfair: Curriculum, tests do not align, new study finds. *Education Week, 6*(36).

Rowley, G. L. (1974). Which examinees are most favored by the use of multiple-choice tests? *Journal of Educational Measurement, 11,* 15–23.

Rowley, G. L. (1978). The relationship of reliability of classroom research to the amount of observation: An extension of the Spearman-Brown formula. *Journal of Educational Measurement, 15,* 165–180.

Rowley, G. L., & Traub, R. (1977). Formula scoring, number-right scoring, and test taking strategy. *Journal of Educational Measurement, 14,* 15–22.

Rubin, R. A. (1974). Preschool application of the Metropolitan Reading Tests: Validity, reliability, and preschool norms. *Educational and Psychological Measurement, 34,* 417–422.

Rudman, H. C., Mehrens, W. A., & Wanous, D. S. (1983). *The data box.* Cleveland: The Psychological Corporation.

Rulon, P. J., Tiedeman, D. V., Tatsuoka, M. M., & Langmuir, C. R. (1967). *Multivariate statistics for personnel classification.* New York: Wiley.

Rumenik, D. K., Capasso, D. R., & Hendrick, C. (1977). Experimenter sex effects in behavioral research. *Psychological Bulletin, 84,* 852–877.

Russell, D. H. (1953). What does research say about self-evaluation? *Journal of Educational Research, 46,* 561–573.

Russell Sage Foundation. (1970). *Guidelines for the collection, maintenance and dissemination of pupil records.* New York: Russell Sage.

Rutkowski, K., & Domino, G. (1975). Interrelationship of study skills and personality variables in college students. *Journal of Educational Psychology, 67,* 784–789.

Ryanen, I. A. (1988). Comments of a minor bureaucrat. *Journal of Vocational Behavior, 33*(3), 379–387.

Sabers, D. L., & Feldt, L. S. (1968). An empirical study of the effect of the correction for chance success on the reliability and validity of an aptitude test. *Journal of Educational Measurement, 5,* 251–258.

Salaganick, L. H., & Epstein, J. L. (1982, April). *The effects of effort marks on report card grades.* Paper presented at the annual meeting of the American Educational Research Association.

Salmon-Cox, L. (1981). Teachers and standardized achievement tests: What's really happening? *Phi Delta Kappan, 62*(9), 631–634.

Salvia, J., & Ysseldyke, J. E. (1978). *Assessment in special and remedial education.* Boston: Houghton Mifflin.

Salvia, J. & Ysseldyke, J. E. (1988). *Assessment in special and remedial education* (3rd ed.). Boston: Houghton Mifflin.

Samelson, F. (1972). Response style. A psychologist's fallacy? *Psychological Bulletin, 78,* 13–16.

Sampson, J. P. (1983). Computer-assisted testing and assessment: Current status and implications for the future. *Measurement and Evaluation in Guidance, 15*(4), 293–299.

Sampson, J. P. (1984). Guide to microcomputer software in testing and assessment. *AMECD Newsnotes, 19*(3), 3–9.

Sampson, J. P., Jr. (Ed.). (1986). Computer applications in testing and assessment (Special Issue). *Measurement and Evaluation in Counseling and Development, 19*(1).

Samson, E. (1985). Effective training in test-taking skills on achievement test performance: A quantitative syntheses. *Journal of Educational Research, 78,* 261–266.

Samuda, R. J. (1975). *Psychological testing of American minorities.* New York: Dodd, Mead.

Samuels, S. J., & Edwall, G. E. (1975). Measuring reading achievement: A case for criterion-referenced testing and accountability. *Measurement in Education, 6,* 2.

Sandefur, J. T. (1988, April). *Teacher competency testing: A historical perspective.* Paper presented at the annual meeting of the American Educational Research Association, New Orleans.

Sarason, H., Hill, K., & Zimbardo, P. (1964). A longitudinal study of the relation of test anxiety to performance on intelligence and achievement tests. *Monographs of the Society for Research in Child Development, 29* (7, Serial No. 98).

Sarason, I. G., & Sarason, B. R. (1980). *Abnormal psy-*

chology (3rd ed.). Englewood Cliffs, NJ: Prentice-Hall.

Sarnacki, R. E. (1979). An examination of test wiseness in the cognitive test domain. *Review of Educational Research, 49*, 252–279.

Sattler, J. M. (1974). *Assessment of children's intelligence.* Philadelphia: Saunders.

Sattler, J. M. (1982). *Assessment of children's intelligence and special abilities.* Boston: Allyn and Bacon.

Sattler, J. M. & Gwynne, J. (1982). White examiners do not generally impede test performance of black children: To debunk a myth. *Journal of Consulting and Clinical Psychology, 50*, 196–208.

Sattler, J. M., Hillix, W. A., & Neher, L. (1970). Halo effect of examiner scoring of intelligence test responses. *Journal of Consulting and Clinical Psychology, 34*, 172–176.

Sattler, J. M., & Winget, B. M. (1970). Intelligence test procedures as affected by expectancy and I.Q. *Journal of Clinical Psychology, 26*, 446–448.

Sawin, E. I. (1969). *Evaluation and the work of the teacher.* Belmont, CA: Wadsworth.

Sax, G., (1980). *Principles of educational and psychological measurement and evaluation.* Belmont, CA: Wadsworth.

Sax, G., & Cromack, T. R. (1966). The effects of various forms of item arrangements on test performance. *Journal of Educational Measurement, 3*, 309–311.

Sax, G., & Reade, M. (1964). Achievement as a function of test difficulty level. *American Educational Research Journal, 1*, 22–25.

Scannell, D. P., & Marshall, J. C. (1966). Effect of selected composition errors on grades assigned to essay examinations. *American Educational Research Journal, 3*, 125–130.

Scarr, S. (1981). Genetics and the development of intelligence. In S. Scarr (Ed.), *Race, social class, and individual differences in IQ* (pp. 3–59). Hillsdale, NJ: Lawrence Erlbaum.

Schafer, W. D., & Lissitz, R. W. (1987). Measurement training for school personnel: Recommendations and reality. *Journal of Teacher Education, 38*(3), 57–63.

Schaie, K. W. (Ed.). (1983). *Longitudinal studies of adult psychological development.* New York: Guilford Press.

Schaie, K. W., & Hertzog, C. (1986). Toward a comprehensive model of adult intellectual development. Contributions of the Seattle longitudinal study. In R. J. Sternberg (Ed.), *Advances in the psychology of human intelligence* (Vol. 3) (pp. 79–118). Hillsdale, NJ: Lawrence Erlbaum.

Scheuneman, J. D. (1987). An experimental exploratory study of causes of bias in test items. *Journal of Educational Measurement, 24*(2), 97–118.

Schittjer, C. J., & Cartledge, C. M. (1976). Item analysis programs: A comparative investigation of performance. *Educational and Psychological Measurement, 36*, 183–187.

Schmidt, F. L. (1988). The problem of group differences in ability test scores in employment selection. *Journal of Vocational Behavior, 33*(3), 272–292.

Schmidt, F. L., & Hunter, J. E. (1981). Employment testing: Old theories and new research findings. *American Psychologist, 36*(10), 1128–1137.

Schmitt, A. P., & Dorans, N. J. (1987, Aug.). *Differential item functioning for minority examinees on the SAT.* Paper presented at the annual meeting of the American Psychological Association, New York.

Schoenfeldt, L. F. (1968, Aug.). *An empirical comparison of various procedures for estimating heritability.* Paper presented at the annual meeting of the American Psychological Association.

Schrock, T. J., & Mueller, D. J. (1982). Effects of violating three multiple-choice item construction principles. *The Journal of Educational Research, 75*, 314–318.

Schwartz, J. (1955). *Pictorial test items in the ground equipment maintenance (304) career field ladder* (Evaluation Report 5515). 2200th Test Squadron, Mitchell Air Force Base, NY.

Schwenn, J. O., & Fox R. A. (Eds.). (1985). *Assessing severely and profoundly handicapped individuals* (pp. 66–84). Springfield, IL: Charles C. Thomas.

Scriven, M. (1975). *Evaluation bias and its control* (Occasional Paper No. 4). Kalamazoo: Evaluation Center, College of Education, Western Michigan University.

Scruggs, T. E., White, K. R., & Bennion, K. (1986). Teaching test-taking skills to elementary-grade students: A meta-analysis. *The Elementary School Journal, 87*, 69–82.

Secolsky, C. (1983). Using examinee judgments to detect ambiguity on teacher-made criterion-referenced tests. *Journal of Educational Measurement, 20*(1), 51–64.

Sexton, D. (1983). Developmental assessment. In A. F. Rotatori, J. O. Schwenn, & R. A. Fox (Eds.), *Assessing severely and profoundly handicapped individuals* (pp. 66–84). Springfield, IL: Charles C. Thomas.

Sexton, D., McLean, M., Boyd, R. D., Thompson, B., & McCormick, K. (1988). Criterion-related validity of a new standardized developmental measure for use with infants who are handicapped. *Measurement and Evaluation in Counseling and Development, 21*(1), 16–24.

Shaffer, M. (1976). *The use of item-favorability data as evidence of sex bias in interest inventories.* Paper presented at the annual meeting of the National Council of Measurement in Education, San Francisco.

Shanker, A. (1980, Oct. 19). The nonsense of attacking education tests. *The Washington Post.*

Shanker, A., & Ward, J. G. (1982). Teacher competency and testing: A natural affinity. *Educational Measurement: Issues and Practices, 1*(2), 6–9, 26.

Shannon, A., & Cliver, A. (1987). An application of item response theory in the comparison of four conventional item discrimination indices for criterion-referenced tests. *Journal of Educational Measurement, 24*(4), 347–356.

Shannon, G. A. (1975, April). *The construction of matching tests: An empirical statement.* Paper presented at the annual meeting of the National Council on Measurement in Education, Washington, DC.

Sharf, J. C. (1988). Litigating personnel measurement policy. *Journal of Vocational Behavior, 33*(3), 235–271.

Shaw, M. E. (1973). *A theory of attitudes.* Unpublished manuscript, University of Florida, Gainesville.

Shaw, M. E., & Wright, J. M. (1967). *Scales for the measurement of attitudes.* New York: McGraw-Hill.

Shepard, L. A. (1980). Standard setting issues and methods. *Applied Psychological Measurement, 4*(4), 447–467.

Shepard, L. A. (1984). Setting performance standards. In R. A. Berk (Ed.), *A guide to criterion-referenced test construction* (pp. 169–198). Baltimore: Johns Hopkins University Press.

Shepard, L. A., & Kreitzer, A. E. (1987). The Texas teacher test. *Educational Researcher, 16*(6), 22–31.

Sheriffs, A. C., & Boomer, D. S. (1954). Who is penalized by the penalty for guessing? *Journal of Educational Psychology, 45*, 81–90.

Sherman, S. W. (1976, April). *Multiple-choice test bias uncovered by use of an I don't know alternative.* Paper presented at the annual meeting of the American Educational Research Association, San Francisco.

Sherman, S. W., & Robinson, N. M. (Eds.). (1982). *Ability testing of handicapped people: Dilemmas for government science, and the public.* Washington, DC: National Academy Press.

Shulman, L. S. (1987). Assessment for teaching: An invitation for the profession. *Phi Delta Kappan, 69*(1), 38–44.

Silverman, B. I., Barton, F., & Lyon, M. (1976). Minority group status and bias in college admissions criteria. *Educational and Psychological Measurement, 36*(2), 401–407.

Simpson, E. J. (1966). The classification of educational objectives: Psychomotor domain. *Illinois Teacher of Home Economics, 10*(4), 110–144.

Simpson, E. J. (1972). The classification of educational objectives in the psychomotor domain. *The Psychomotor domain* (Vol. 3). Washington, DC: Gryphon House.

Sims, V. M. (1931). The objectivity, validity, and reliability of an essay examination graded by rating. *Journal of Educational Research, 24*, 216–223.

Slack, W. V., & Porter, D. (1980a). The scholastic aptitude test: A critical appraisal. *Harvard Educational Review, 50*, 154–175.

Slack, W. V., & Porter, D. (1980b). Training, validity, and the issue of aptitude: A reply to Jackson. *Harvard Educational Review, 50*, 392–401.

Slakter, M. J. (1968). The penalty for not guessing. *Journal of Educational Measurement, 5*, 141–144.

Slakter, M. J., Koehler, R. A., & Hampton, S. H. (1970a). Grade level, sex, and selected aspects of test wiseness. *Journal of Educational Measurement, 7*, 119–122.

Slakter, M. J., Koehler, R. A., & Hampton, S. H. (1970b). Learning test-wiseness by programmed texts. *Journal of Educational Measurement, 7*, 247–254.

Slavin, R. (1978). Separating incentives, feedback, and evaluation: Toward a more effective classroom system. *Educational Psychologist, 13*, 97–100.

Smith, J. K. (1982). Converging on correct answers: A peculiarity of multiple-choice items. *Journal of Educational Measurement, 19*(3), 211–220.

Smith, M. L., & Shepard, L. A. (1987). What doesn't work: Explaining policies of retention in the early grades. *Phi Delta Kappan, 69*(2), 129–134.

Smith, M., White, K. P., & Coop, R. H. (1979). The effect of item type on the consequences of changing answers on multiple-choice tests. *Journal of Educational Measurement, 16*(3), 203–208.

Smith, R. M. (1987). Assessing partial knowledge in vocabulary. *Journal of Educational Measurement, 24*(3), 217–231.

Snow, R. E. (1969). Review of Pygmalion in the classroom. *Contemporary Psychology*, *14*, 197–199.

Snow, R. E. (1984). Placing children in special education: Some comments. *Educational Researcher*, *13*(3), 12–14.

Snow, R. E., & Lohman, D. F. (1989). Implications of cognitive psychology for educational measurement. In R. L. Linn (Ed.), *Educational measurement* (3rd ed.) (pp. 263–332). New York: American Council on Education and Macmillan.

Snyderman, M., & Rothman, S. (1986). Science, politics, and the IQ controversy. *The Public Interest*, *83*, 79–97.

Sockloff, A. L., & Papacostas, A. C. (1975). Uniformity of faculty attitude. *Journal of Educational Measurement*, *12*, 281–293.

Solomon, R. J. (1965). Improving the essay test in the social studies. In H. Berg (Ed.), *Evaluation in social studies, 35th yearbook* (Chapter 7). Washington, DC: National Council for the Social Studies.

Sommer, R., & Sommer, B. A. (1983). Mystery in Milwaukee: Early intervention, IQ, and psychology textbooks. *American Psychologist*, *38*(9), 982–985.

Southern Regional Education Board. (1984). *Measuring educational progress in the South: Student achievement*. Atlanta: Author.

Sowell, T. (1989, Feb. 13). The new racism on campus. *Fortune*, 115–120.

Spache, G. D. (1976). *Diagnosing and correcting reading disabilities*. Boston: Allyn and Bacon.

Spandel, V. (1981). *Classroom applications of writing assessment: A teachers handbook*. Portland, OR: Northwest Regional Education Laboratory.

Spandel, V., & Stiggins, R. J. (1988). *Writing assessment in the classroom*. White Plains, NY: Longman.

Sparks, D. S. (1969). *Grading and student evaluation*. Paper ED-036-261. Presented at the Council of Graduate Schools in the United States, Washington, DC.

Spearman, C. (1927). *The abilities of man*. New York: Macmillan.

Speat, W. I. (1980). The adaptive behavior scale: A study of criterion validity. *American Journal of Mental Deficiency*, *85*(1), 61–68.

Stahmann, R. F., & Matheson, G. F. (1973). The Kuder as a measure of vocational maturity. *Educational and Psychological Measurement*, *33*, 477–479.

Stake, R. E., & Denny T. (1969). Needed concepts and techniques for studying more fully the potential for evaluation. In R. W. Tyler (Ed.), *Educational evaluation: New roles, new media, 68th yearbook* (pp. 370–390). National Society for the Study of Education. Chicago: University of Chicago Press.

Stallings, W. M., & Lesslie, E. K. (1970, Winter). Student attitudes toward grades and grading. *Improved College and University Teaching*, *18*, 66–68.

Stallings, W. M., & Smock, H. R. (1971). The pass-fail grading option at State University: A five semester evaluation. *Journal of Educational Measurement*, *8*, 153–160.

Stalnaker, J. M. (1938). Weighting questions in the essay type examination. *Journal of Educational Psychology*, *29*, 481–490.

Stalnaker, J. M. (1951). The essay type of examination. In E. F. Lindquist (Ed.), *Educational measurement* (pp. 495–530). Washington, DC: American Council on Education.

Stanley, J. C. (1964). *Measurement in today's schools* (4th ed.). Englewood Cliffs, NJ: Prentice-Hall.

Stanley, J. C. (1971a, Feb. 19). Predicting college success of the educationally disadvantaged. *Science*, *171*, 640–647.

Stanley, J. C. (1971b). Reliability. In R. L. Thorndike (Ed.), *Educational measurement* (2nd ed.) (pp. 356–442). Washington, DC: American Council on Education.

Stanley, J. C., & Porter, A. C. (1967). Correlation of scholastic aptitude test scores with college grades for Negroes versus whites. *Journal of Educational Measurement*, *4*, 199–218.

Stanley, J. C., & Wang, M. D. (1970). Weighting test items and test item options, an overview of the analytical and empirical literature. *Educational and Psychological Measurement*, *30*, 21–35.

Starch, D., & Elliott, E. C. (1912). Reliability of grading high school work in English. *School Review*, *20*, 442–457.

The State of Education. (1988). Congress adds new dimension of optional state assessments. *The State of Education*, *1*, 1.

Sternberg, R. J. (1981). Intelligence and nonentrenchment. *Journal of Educational Psychology*, *73*(1), 1–16.

Sternberg, R. J. (1986). Intelligence, wisdom, and creativity: Three is better than one. *Educational Psychologist*, *21*(3), 175–190.

Sternberg, R. J. (1988). GENECES: A rationale for the construct validation of theories and tests of intelligence. In H. Wainer and H. I. Braun (Eds.), *Test va-*

lidity (pp. 61–76). Hillsdale, NJ: Lawrence Erlbaum.

Sternberg, R. J., Conway, R. E., Ketron, J. L., & Bernstein, M. (1980). *People's conceptions of intelligence* (Technical Report No. 28). New Haven, CT: Yale University, Department of Psychology.

Stetz, F. P., & Beck, M. D. (1981). Attitudes toward standardized tests: Students, teachers and measurement specialists. *Measurement in Education, 12*(1), 1–11.

Stevens, S. S. (1946). On the theory of scales of measurement. *Science, 103,* 677–860.

Stiggins, R. J. (1984). *Evaluating students through classroom observation: Watching students grow.* Washington, DC: National Education Association.

Stiggins, R. J. (1988, April). *The nature and quality of teacher-developed classroom assessments.* Paper presented at the annual meeting of the National Council on Measurement in Education, New Orleans.

Stiggins, R. J., & Anderson, B. (1981). *The nature and role of performance assessment.* Portland, OR: Clearinghouse for Applied Performance Testing, Northwest Regional Educational Laboratory.

Stiggins, R. J., & Bridgeford, N. J. (1985). The ecology of classroom assessment. *Journal of Educational Measurement, 22*(4), 271–286.

Stiggins, R. J., & Conklin, N. F. (1988). *Teacher training in assessment.* Portland, OR: Northwest Regional Educational Laboratory.

Stiggins, R. J., Conklin, N. F., & Bridgeford, N. J. (1986). Classroom assessment: A key to effective education. *Educational Measurement: Issues and Practices, 5*(2), 5–17.

Stiggins, R. J., Frisbie, D. A., & Griswold, P. A. (1989). Inside high school grading practices: Building a research agenda. *Educational Measurement: Issues and Practice, 8*(2), 5–14.

Stiggins, R. J., Rubel, E., & Quellmaltz, E. (1988). *Measuring thinking skills in the classroom* (rev. ed.). Washington, DC: National Education Association.

Storey, A. G. (1966). Review of evidence for the case against the true-false item. *Journal of Educational Research, 59,* 282–285.

Stott, L. H., & Ball, R. S. (1965). Infant and preschool mental tests: Review and evaluation. *Monographs of Social Research in Child Development, 30*(3), 151.

Strain, P. S., Sainto, D. M., & Mahan, L. (1984). Toward a functional assessment of severely handicapped learners. *Educational Psychologist, 19*(3), 180–187.

Strang, H. R. (1977). The effects of technical and unfamiliar options on guessing on multiple-choice items. *Journal of Educational Measurement, 14,* 253–260.

Strassberg-Rosenberg, B., & Donlon, T. F. (1975, April). *Content influences on sex differences in performance on aptitude tests.* Paper presented at the annual meeting of the National Council on Measurement in Education, Washington, DC.

Strenta, A. C., & Elliott, R. (1987). Differential grading standards revisited. *Journal of Educational Measurement, 24,* 281–291.

Strong, E. K. (1966). *Vocational interest blank for men.* Stanford, CA: Stanford University Press.

Stroud, J. B. (1946). *Psychology in education.* New York: McKay.

Stufflebeam, D. L., et al. (1971). *Educational evaluation and decision making.* Bloomington, IN: Phi Delta Kappa.

Subkoviak, M. J. (1984). Estimating the reliability of mastery-nonmastery classifications. In R. A. Berk (Ed.), *A guide to criterion-referenced test construction* (pp. 267–291). Baltimore: Johns Hopkins University Press.

Subkoviak, M. J. (1988). A practitioner's guide to computation and interpretation of reliability indices for mastery tests. *Journal of Educational Measurement, 25*(1), 47–56.

Sullivan, H. J. (1969). Objectives, evaluation, and improved learned achievement. In W. J. Popham et al. (Eds.), *Instructional objectives* (pp. 65–90). AERA Monograph Series on Curriculum Evaluation, No. 3. Chicago: Rand McNally.

Sullivan, H. J., Smith, M., & Lopez, C. (1989, April). *Teacher bias in evaluating year-long academic progress.* Paper presented at the annual meeting of the American Educational Research Association, San Francisco.

Super, D. E., Bohn, M. J., Forrest, D. J., Jordaan, J. P., Lindeman, R. H., & Thompson, A. A. (1972). *Career development inventory.* New York: Columbia University, Teachers College Press.

Super, D. E., & Crites, J. O. (1962). *Appraising vocational fitness by means of psychological tests* (rev. ed.). New York: Harper & Row.

Supplement. (1967). *Journal of Educational Measurement, 4*(1), 1–31.

Surber, J. R., & Anderson, R. C. (1975). Delay-retention effect in natural classroom settings. *Journal of Educational Psychology, 67*, 170–173.

Swaminathan, H., Hambleton, R. K., & Algina, J. (1975). A bayesian decision-theoretic procedure for use with criterion-referenced tests. *Journal of Educational Measurement, 12*, 87–98.

Sweetland, R. C., & Keyser, D. J. (1985–87). *Test critiques: Volumes I to VI.* Kansas City, MO: Test Corporation of America.

Sweetland, R. C., & Keyser, D. J. (1986). *Tests: A comprehensive reference for assessments in psychology, education, and business* (2nd ed.). Kansas City, MO: Test Corporation of America.

Swineford, F. (1956). *Test analysis of CEEB tests of developed ability.* Princeton, NJ: Educational Testing Service.

Switzky, H. N. (1981). Review of R. Feuerstein, Y. Rand, M. B. Hoffman, and R. Miller. Instrumental enrichment. *American Journal of Mental Deficiency, 85*, 561.

Sympson, J. B. (1986, April). *Extracting information from wrong answers in computerized adaptive testing.* Paper presented at the annual meeting of the American Educational Research Association, Washington, DC.

Tannenbaum, A. J. (1965). Review of the culture-fair intelligence tests. In O. K. Buros (Ed.), *The sixth mental measurements yearbook* (pp. 721–723). Highland Park, NJ: Gryphon Press.

Tanney, M. F. (1974). *Face validity of interest measures: Sex role steryotyping.* Paper presented at the National Institute of Education Workshop on Sex Bias and Sex Fairness in Career Interest Inventories, Arlington, VA.

Tatsuoka, K. K. (1981). *Diagnosing cognitive errors: Statistical pattern classification and recognition approach* (Research Report 85-1, ONR). Urbana-Champaign, IL: University of Illinois Press.

Tchudi, S. N., & Yates, J. (1983). *Teaching writing in the content areas: Senior high school.* Washington, DC: National Educational Association.

Teachers opinion poll. (1974). *Today's Education, 63*(2), 4.

Temp, G. (1971). Validity of the SAT for blacks and whites in thirteen integrated institutions. *Journal of Educational Measurement, 8*, 245–252.

Terman, L. M. (1916). *The measurement of intelligence.* Boston: Houghton Mifflin.

Terman, L. M., & Merrill, M. A. (1937). *Measuring intelligence.* Boston: Houghton Mifflin.

Terman, L. M., & Merrill, M. A. (1960). *Stanford-Binet intelligence scale: Manual for the third revision* (Form L-M). Boston: Houghton Mifflin.

Terwilliger, J. S. (1971). *Assigning grades to students.* Glenview, IL: Scott, Foresman.

Terwilliger, J. S. (1989). Classroom standard setting and grading practices. *Educational Measurement: Issues and Practices, 8*(2), 15–19.

Thissen, D., Steinberg, L., & Fitzpatrick, A. R. (1989). Mutliple-choice models: The distractors are also part of the item. *Journal of Educational Measurement, 26*(2), 161–176.

Thomas, C. L., & Stanley, J. C. (1969). Effectiveness of high school grades for predicting college grades of black students: A review and discussion. *Journal of Educational Measurement, 6*, 203–216.

Thomas, W. C. (1986, Feb.). Grading—Why are school policies necessary? What are the issues? *NASSP Bulletin*, 23–26.

Thorndike, R. L. (1971a). Concepts of cultural fairness. *Journal of Educational Measurement, 8*, 63–70.

Thorndike, R. L. (1971b). Reproducing the test. In R. L. Thorndike (Ed.), *Educational measurement* (2nd ed.) (pp. 160–187). Washington, DC: American Council on Education.

Thorndike, R. L. (Ed.). (1971c). *Educational measurement* (2nd ed.). Washington, DC: American Council on Education.

Thorndike, R. L. (1975). Mr. Binet's test 70 years later. *Educational Researcher, 4*(5), 3–7.

Thorndike, R. L. (1986, April). *After 80 years of G is testing going to H?* NCME Invited Address. San Francisco.

Thorndike, R. L., & Hagen, E. (1977). *Measurement and evaluation in psychology and education,* (4th ed.). New York: Wiley.

Thorndike, R. L. & Hagen, E. (1987). *Cognitive abilities test.* Chicago: Riverside.

Thurstone, L. L. (1933). *The theory of multiple factors.* Privately published.

Thurstone, L. L., & Chave, L. J. (1929). *The measurement of attitude.* Chicago: University of Chicago Press.

Thurstone, P., & House, E. R. (1981). The NIE adversary hearing on minimum competency testing. *Phi Delta Kappan, 63*, 87–89.

Tinkelman, S. N. (1971). Planning the objective test. In

R. L. Thorndike (Ed.), *Educational measurement* (2nd ed.) (pp. 46–80). Washington, DC: American Council on Education.

Tinkelman, S. N. (1975). *Improving the classroom test: A manual of test construction procedures for the classroom teacher*. Albany, NY: New York State Department of Education.

Tinsley, H. E. A., & Weiss, D. J. (1975). Interrater reliability and agreement of subjective judgments. *Journal of Counseling Psychology, 22*, 358–376.

Title VII of the Civil Rights Act. (1964). Pp. 703(a), 42 U.S.C. 2000e.

Tittle, C. K. (1973). *Minimizing sex bias in interest measurement through the context of testing and interpretive materials*. Paper presented at the annual meeting of the American Personnel and Guidance Association, New Orleans.

Tittle, C. K., & Zytowski, D. G. (n.d.). *Sex-fair interest measurement: Research and implications*. Washington, DC: N.I.E.

Tittle, C. K., & Zytowski, D. G. (1978). *Sex-fair interest measurement: Research and implications*. Washington, DC: N.I.E.

Towle, N. J., & Merrill, P. F. (1975). Effects of anxiety type and item-difficulty sequencing on mathematics test performance. *Journal of Educational Measurement, 12*, 241–250.

Traub, R. E., & Fisher, C. W. (n.d.). *On the equivalence of constructed-response and multiple-choice tests*. Toronto: Ontario Institute for Studies in Education.

Traub, R. E., & Hambleton, R. K. (1972). The effect of scoring instructions and degree of speededness on the validity and reliability of multiple-choice tests. *Educational and Psychological Measurement, 32*, 737–758.

Traub, R. E., Hambleton, R. K., & Singh, B. (1969). Effects of promised reward and threatened penalty on performance on a multiple-choice vocabulary test. *Educational and Psychological Measurement, 29*, 847–861.

Trent, J. W. & Cohen, A. M. (1973). Research on teaching in higher education. In R. M. W. Travers (Ed.), *Second handbook of research on teaching* (pp. 997–1071). Skokie, IL: Rand McNally.

Trentham, L. L. (1975). The effect of distractions on sixth grade students in a testing situation. *Journal of Educational Measurement, 12*, 13–17.

Tripp, A., & Tollefson, N. (1983). Are complex multiple-choice options more difficult and discriminating than conventional multiple-choice items? *Journal of Nursing Education, 24*, 92–98.

Tucker, L. R. (1987). *Developments in classical item analysis methods* (Research Report 87-46). Princeton, NJ: Educational Testing Service.

Tuckman, B. (1979). *Measuring educational outcomes* (2nd ed.). New York: Harcourt, Brace.

Tuinman, J. J. (1974). Determining the passage dependence of comprehension questions in five major tests. *Reading Research Quarterly, 9*, 206–223.

Turkington, C. (1984, Jan.). The growing use and abuse of computer testing. *APA Monitor, 7*, 26.

Turlington, R. D. (1981). Florida's testing program: A firm foundation for improvement. *Phi Delta Kappan, 63*(3), 204.

Tuttle, F. B., Jr. (1986). *How to prepare students for writing tests*. Washington, DC: National Education Association.

Tyler, L. E. (1976). The intelligence we test. In L. B. Resnick (Ed.), *The nature of intelligence* (pp. 13–26). Hillsdale, NJ: Lawrence Erlbaum.

Tyler, R. W. (1933). Tests in biology. *School Science and Mathematics, 33*.

Tyler, R. W. (1950). *Basic principles of curriculum and instruction*. Chicago: University of Chicago Press.

Tyler, R. W. (1951). The functions of measurement in improving instruction. In E. F. Lindquist (Ed.), *Educational measurement* (pp. 47–67). Washington, DC: American Council on Education.

U.S. News and World Report. (1984, Sept.). Why many teachers don't measure up. *10*, 14.

United States Employment Service. (1983). *Overview of validity generalization for the U.S. Employment Service*. (USES Test Research Report No. 43). Washington DC: Division of Counseling and Test Development, Employment and Training Administration, Department of Labor.

Uzziris, I. C., & Hunt, J. McV. (1975). *Assessment in infancy: Ordinal scales of psychological development*. Urbana, IL: University of Illinois Press.

Vaas, C. E., & Nungester, R. J. (1982, March). *An investigation of the answer-changing behavior of adult learners*. Paper presented at the meeting of the American Educational Research Association, New York.

Vallance, T. R. (1947). Comparison of essay and objective examinations as learning experiences. *Journal of Educational Research, 41*, 279–288.

Van Allen v. *McCleary*. (1961). 27, Misc. 2d 81, 211 NYS 2d 501 (Sup. CT. Nassau, CO).

Van den Burgh, H., & Eiting, M. H. (1989). A method of estimating rater reliability. *Journal of Educational Measurement, 26*(1), 29–40.

Van Der Kamp, L. J., & Mellenbergh, G. D. (1976). Agreement between raters. *Educational and Psychological Measurement, 36*, 311–317.

Vargas, J. S. (1972). *Writing worthwhile behavioral objectives.* New York: Harper & Row.

Vernon, P. E. (1961). *The structure of human abilities* (2nd ed.). London: Methuen.

Vernon, P. E. (1964). Creativity and intelligence. *Journal of Educational Research, 6*, 163–169.

Vernon, P. E. (1979). *Intelligence: Heredity and environment.* San Francisco: W. H. Freeman.

Votaw, D. F. (1936). The effect of do-not-guess directions on the validity of true-false and multiple-choice tests. *Journal of Educational Psychology, 27*, 699–704.

Wagner, E. E., & Hoover, T. O. (1974). The effect of serial position on ranking error. *Educational and Psychological Measurement, 34*, 289–293.

Wagner, L. (1983). *Organizational heterogeneity and school policy response to proficiency assessment in California.* Unpublished doctoral dissertation. Stanford University, Stanford, CA.

Wahlstrom, M., & Boersma, F. J. (1968). The influence of test-wiseness upon achievement. *Educational and Psychological Measurement, 28*, 413–420.

Wainer, H. (1989). The future of item analysis. *Journal of Educational Measurement, 26*(2), 191–208.

Waks, L. J. (1969). Philosophy, education, and the doomsday threat. *Review of Educational Research, 39*, 607–622.

Walker, N. W. (1987). The Stanford-Binet, 4th edition: Haste does seem to make waste. *Measurement and Evaluation in Counseling and Development, 20*(3), 135–138.

Waller, J. H. (1971). Achievement and social mobility: Relationships among IQ score; education and occupation in two generations. *Social Biology, 18*, 252–259.

Walsh, M. (1989, Feb. 15). Judge finds bias in scholarships based on scores. *Education Week, 1*, 20.

Wanous, D. S., & Mehrens, W. A. (1981). Helping teachers use information. The data box approach. *Measurement in Education, 12*(4), 1–10.

Ward, B. J. (1981). Technology: Will it live up to its promise for education? *NAEP Newsletter, 14*(2), 6.

Ward, J. C. (1980). *Teachers and testing: A survey of knowledge and attitudes.* A report of the research department of the American Federation of Teachers, AFL-CIO.

Ward, W. C., Frederiksen, N., & Carlson, S. B. (1980). Construct validity of free-response and machine-scorable forms of a test. *Journal of Educational Measurement, 17*(1), 11–30.

Ward W. C., Kline, R. G., & Flaugher, J. (1986). *College board computerized placement tests: Validity of an adaptive test of basic skills* (Research Report 86-29). Princeton, NJ: Educational Testing Service.

Warren, J. R. (1970). *College grading practices: An overview.* Princeton, NJ: Educational Testing Service.

Warren, J. R. (1975). *The continuing controversy over grades* (TM Report 51, ERIC Clearinghouse on Tests, Measurement, and Evaluation). Princeton, NJ: Educational Testing Service.

Wason, P. (1961). Response to affirmative and negative binary statements. *British Journal of Psychology, 52*, 133–142.

Waters, B. K. (1976). The measurement of partial knowledge: A comparison between two empirical option-weighting methods and rights-only scoring. *Journal of Educational Research, 69*, 256–260.

Watson, J. M. (1988). Achievement anxiety test: Dimensonality and utility. *Journal of Educational Psychology, 80*(14), 585–591.

Webb, E. J., et al. (1981). *Nonreactive measures in the social sciences* (2nd ed.). Boston: Houghton Mifflin.

Webb, N. M., Herman, J. L., & Cabello, B. (1987, Summer). A domain-referenced approach to diagnostic testing using generalizability theory. *Journal of Educational Measurement, 24*(2), 119–130.

Webster's Seventh New Collegiate Dictionary. (1965). Springfield, MA: Merriam.

Wechsler, D. (1955). *Wechsler Adult Intelligence Scale, manual.* New York: The Psychological Corporation.

Weidemann, C. C. (1933, Oct.). Written examination procedures. *Phi Delta Kappan, 16.*

Weiss, D. J. (1976). *Computerized ability testing 1972–1975* (Final Report of Project NR150-343, NOO 14-67-A0113-0029). Minneapolis: University of Minnesota.

Weiss, D. J. (Ed.). (1980). *Proceedings of the 1979 computerized adaptive testing conference.* Minneapolis: Department of Psychology, University of Minnesota.

Weiss, D. J., & Davison, M. L. (1981). Test theory and methods. *Annual Review of Psychology, 32*, 629–658.

Werts, C. E., Joreskog, K. G., & Linn, R. L. (1976). Analyzing ratings with correlated intrajudge measurement errors. *Educational and Psychological Measurement, 36,* 319–328.

Wesman, A. G. (1971). Writing the test item. In R. L. Thorndike (Ed.), *Educational measurement* (2nd ed.) (pp. 81–129). Washington, DC: American Council on Education.

Westbrook, B. W. (1974). Content analysis of six career development tests. *Educational and Psychological Measurement, 7,* 172–180.

Westbrook, B. W. (1976a). Interrelationships of career choice competencies and career choice attitude of ninth-grade pupils: Testing hypotheses derived from Crites' model of career maturity. *Journal of Vocational Behavior, 8,* 1–12.

Westbrook, B. W. (1976b). Criterion related and construct validity of the career maturity inventory competence test with ninth-grade pupils. *Journal of Vocational Behavior, 9,* 377–383.

Westbrook, B. W., & Mastie, M. M. (1973). The measurement of vocational maturity: A beginning to know about. *Measurement and Evaluation in Guidance, 6,* 8–16.

Westbrook, B. W., & Parry-Hill, J. W. J. (1973). The measurement of cognitive vocational maturity. *Journal of Vocational Behavior, 3,* 3.

Westbrook, B. W., Sanford, E., Merwin, G. A., Fleenor, J., & Renzi, D. A. (1987). Reliability and construct validity of new measures of career maturity for 11th grade students. *Measurement and Evaluation in Counseling and Development, 20*(1), 18–26.

Westinghouse Learning Press. (1975a). *Learning objectives for individualized instruction: Science.* Sunnyvale, CA: Author.

Westinghouse Learning Press. (1975b). *Learning objectives for individualized instruction: Mathematics.* Sunnyvale, CA: Author.

Westinghouse Learning Press. (1975c). *Learning objectives for individualized instruction: Language arts.* Sunnyvale, CA: Author.

Westinghouse Learning Press. (1975d). *Learning objectives for individualized instruction: Social studies.* Sunnyvale, CA: Author.

Wexley, K. N., & Thornton, C. L. (1972). Effect of verbal feedback of test results upon learning. *Journal of Educational Research, 66,* 119–121.

Whalen, T. E. (1971, April). *The analysis of essays by computer: A simulation of teacher ratings.* Paper presented at the Annual Meeting of the American Educational Research Association, Chicago.

Whitney, D. R. (1989). Educational admissions and placement. In R. L. Linn (Ed.), *Educational measurement* (3rd ed.) (pp. 515–526). New York: American Council on Education and Macmillan.

Whitney, D. R., & Sabers, D. L. (1970). Improving essay examinations: Use of item analysis (Technical Bulletin #11). Iowa City, IA: University of Iowa Evaluation and Examination Service.

Wilbur, P. H. (1965). *Positional response set in the multiple-choice examination.* Unpublished Ph.D. dissertation. University of Southern California, Los Angeles.

Wilcox, R. R. (1987). Confidence intervals for true scores under an answer-until-correct scoring procedure. *Journal of Educational Measurement, 24*(3), 263–269.

Willerman, L. (1979). *The psychology of individual and group differences.* San Francisco: W. H. Freeman.

Willett, J. B. (1988). Questions and answers in the measurement of change. In E. Z. Rothkopf (Ed.), *Review of research in education* (Vol. 15) (pp. 345–422). Washington, DC: American Educational Research Association.

Williams, B. G., & Ebel, R. L. (1957). The effect of varying the number of alternatives per item on multiple-choice vocabulary test items. In E. M. Huddleston (Ed.), *Fourteenth yearbook of the National Council on Measurements Used in Education* (pp. 63–65). Princeton, NJ: NCMUE.

Williams, P. L. (1988). The time-bound nature of norms. Understandings and misunderstandings. *Educational Measurement: Issues and Practice, 7*(2), 18–21.

Williams, R. L. (1974). Stimulus/response: Scientific racism and IQ—the silent mugging of the black community. *Psychology Today, 7*(12), 32, 34, 37–38, 41, 101.

Williams, W. E. (1989, May 5). Race, scholarship, and affirmative action. *National Review,* 36–38.

Williamson, M. L., & Hopkins, K. D. (1967). The use of none of these versus homogeneous alternatives on multiple-choice tests: Experimental reliability and validity comparisons. *Journal of Educational Measurement, 4,* 53–58.

Willingham, W. W., & Breland, H. M. (1982). *Personal qualities and college admissions.* New York: College Entrance Examination Board.

Willson, V. L. (1989). Cognitive and developmental effects on item performance in intelligence and achievement tests for young children. *Journal of Educational Measurement, 26*(2), 103–119.

Wilson, K. M. (1978). *Predicting the long-term performance in college of minority and nonminority students* (Research Bulletin RB-78-b). Princeton, NJ: Educational Testing Service.

Wing, H. (1980). Practice effects with traditional mental test items. *Applied Psychological Measurement, 4,* 141–155.

Wissler, C. (1961). The correlation of mental and physical tests. In J. J. Jenkins and D. G. Paterson (Eds.), *Studies in individual differences* (pp. 32–44). New York: Appleton.

Wolf, D. P. (1989). Portfolio assessment: Sampling student work. *Educational Leadership, 46*(7), 35–39.

Womer, F. B. (1981). State-level testing: Where we have been may not tell us where we are going. In D. Carlson (Ed.), *Testing in the states: Beyond accountability* (No. 10 in *New directions for testing and measurement*) (pp. 1–12). San Francisco: Jossey-Bass.

Womer, F. B. (1984). Where's the action? *Educational Measurement: Issues and Practice, 3*(3), 3.

Woo, E. (1988, Sept 19). Teaching to the test: Dim ethical area for educators. *Los Angeles Times.*

Wood, R. (1973). Response-contingent testing. *Review of Educational Research, 43*(4), 529–544.

Yalow, E. S., & Popham, W. J. (1983). Content validity at the crossroads. *Educational Researcher, 12*(8), 10–14, 21

Yelon, S. L., & Scott, R. O. (1970). *A strategy for writing objectives.* Dubuque, IA: Kendall/Hunt.

Yen, W. M. (1988). Normative growth expectations must be realistic: A response to Phillips and Clarizio. *Educational Measurement: Issues and Practice, 7*(4), 16–17.

Ysseldyke, J. E., & Thurlow, M. L. (1984). Assessment practices in special education adequacy and appropriateness. *Educational Psychologist, 19*(3), 123–136.

Zaref, L., & Williams P. (1980). A look at content bias in IQ tests. *Journal of Educational Measurement, 17*(4), 313–322.

Zern, D. (1967). Effects of variations in question phrasing on true-false answers by grade school children. *Psychological Reports, 20,* 527–533.

Zimbardo, P., & Ebbesen, E. B. (1970). *Influencing attitudes and changing behavior.* Reading, MA: Addison-Wesley.

Zimmerman, D. W., & Williams, R. H. (1982). Gain scores in research can be highly reliable. *Journal of Educational Measurement, 19,* 149–154.

Zimpfer, D. G. (1986). Group work in the treatment of test anxiety. *Journal of Specialists in Group Work, 11*(4), 233–239.

Zirkel, P. A. (1990). Grade expectations and academic freedom. *Phi Delta Kappan, 71*(8), 643–645.

Zoref, L., & Williams, P. (1980). A look at content bias in IQ tests. *Journal of Educational Measurement, 17*(4), 313–322.

Name Index

Subject Index